I0889552

Available for the first time in English, Bogdanovich's *Russian History of the War of 1813* continues where the *History of the War of 1812* left off. In describing the events of 1813, the author strives to give an accurate portrayal of one of the most important years in European history and pays tribute to the service of the Russian army in the liberation of Germany. Russia, of course, could not defeat Napoleon alone. But the Russians, having begun the war in Prussia and the Duchy of Warsaw without the assistance of allies, managed to draw Prussia into their cause, and eventually (in Volume 2) Austria, Sweden and Britain.

This book will appeal to those interested in Napoleonic military history, as well as to wargamers, and gives a fascinating insight into the surprisingly cosmopolitan Russian army officers of that era. Although Bogdanovich had access to Russian state archives and private papers, he also makes extensive use of published German and French memoirs and histories in order to provide additional context and balance. Volume 1 covers the period from the Russian invasion of the Duchy of Warsaw up to the Armistice of June 1813, including the defection of Prussia to the Russian cause, the liberation of Berlin and Hamburg, the invasion of Saxony and the monumental battles of Lützen and Bautzen followed by the Russo-Prussian fighting retreat into Silesia. Volume 2 will cover from the resumption of hostilities in August 1813 until the Coalition advance to the Rhine by December 1813.

Born in Sumy, Ukraine, in 1805, Bogdanovich was initially educated in the Noble Regiment, being commissioned into the artillery in 1823. Bogdanovich saw combat in the Polish campaign of 1831 and upon his return in 1833, he entered the Imperial Military Academy, becoming its Director of Operations until 1839. Thereafter, he served on committees of the General Staff. He died in August, 1882 in Oranienbaum. General Bogdanovich is famed for a number of major works, making an invaluable contribution to Russian military historiography. His *History of the Patriotic War of 1812* won the Demidov Prize for History in 1861.

Peter G.A. Phillips is a veteran of 27 years in the British Army Intelligence Corps, including working as a Russian, German, and Serbo-Croat linguist, thereafter spending five years as part of a Civil Service team training British Armed Forces personnel to serve in UK diplomatic missions. He is now retired and spends his time translating Russian military histories of the Coalition Wars. His published translations include: Mikhailovsky-Danilevsky's histories of the wars of 1805 and 1806-1807; Bogdanovich's history of the war of 1812; a collaboration with renowned Napoleonic historian Dr Alexander Mikaberidze of Ilya Radozhitskii's trilogy of memoirs covering 1812-1814; and numerous articles for The Waterloo Association's website www.napoleon-series.org. Peter now lives in the Philippines with his Filipina wife of 34 years. They have two adult daughters.

The Russian History of the War of 1813 Volume 1

The War to Liberate Germany

Modest Ivanovich Bogdanovich

Translated by Peter G.A. Phillips

Helion & Company

Helion & Company Limited
Unit 8 Amherst Business Centre
Budbrooke Road
Warwick
CV34 5WE
England
Tel. 01926 499619
Email: info@helion.co.uk
Website: www.helion.co.uk
Twitter: @helionbooks
Visit our blog at http://blog.helion.co.uk/
Published by Helion & Company 2025
Designed and typeset by Mach 3 Solutions (www.mach3solutions.co.uk)
Cover designed by Paul Hewitt, Battlefield Design (www.battlefield-design.co.uk)

Original text published as *History Of The War Of 1813 For The Liberation Of Germany According To Reliable Sources. Compiled in accordance with Supreme orders.*, St Petersburg, 1863

Cover: Cossacks in Bautzen, 1813, by Bogdan Willewalde (Yekaterinburg Museum of Fine Arts)

ISBN 978-1-804516-78-2

British Library Cataloguing-in-Publication Data.
A catalogue record for this book is available from the British Library.

For details of other military history titles published by Helion & Company Limited, contact the above address, or visit our website: http://www.helion.co.uk
We always welcome receiving book proposals from prospective authors.

Contents

List of Maps

Author's Foreword

This History of the War of 1813 for the Liberation of Germany is a continuation of the History of the Patriotic War of 1812 compiled by me. The main idea behind my work was a desire to present a true picture of one of the most important eras not only in Russian but also in world history. I have no business assessing to what extent I have met the requirements of academic research in the presentation of these memorable events. I recall with gratitude both the flattering reviews and the constructive comments made on my History of 1812. I have tried to present a true image of the achievements of our compatriots without eclipsing them in the great cause of the liberation of Germany and the participation of their sons in overthrowing the yoke that weighed upon them. There was no shortage of source material, but I had the difficult task of verifying it all through mutual comparison.

From my description of the events of 1813, readers will become fully acquainted with the difficulties that Emperor Alexander I had to overcome in order to wage war so far from the borders of Russia; the part played by Prussia in the struggle against Napoleon and the sacrifices made by our Allies are also set forth by me in every detail. Having described the bloody but indecisive battles of the first campaign and their consequence – the armistice, on the basis of hitherto unknown documents, I went on to sketch a true image of the Prague conferences and the breach between Austria and Napoleon. This is followed by: a calculation of the forces on both sides; the characters of the main protagonists; a narration of operations by the huge masses: Blücher's offensive and the victory on the Katzbach; the French advance on Berlin and the battle of Großbeeren; the unsuccessful Coalition offensive into Saxony and the battles of Dresden and Kulm; the second attempt on Berlin by the French and their defeat at Dennewitz. Meanwhile, little by little, the readiness of the other nations in Germany to rise up against their oppressors is depicted: the regiments of the *Confédération du Rhin* [Confederation of the Rhine] come over to the side of the Coalition; Coalition partisans find support in lands subject to Napoleon. The Coalition armies enveloping them from several directions, strengthened from the reserves, draw closer to each other and constrain the weakened but not yet vanquished enemy. The Battle of Nations at Leipzig decides the fate of Germany; Napoleon, compelled to retreat back to France, wins once more; but this success was the final effort by the depleted hordes of the conqueror. Exhausted by forced marches, deprivation and disease, crushed by a whole series of failures, the French return across the Rhine in a most miserable condition. The *Confédération du Rhin* had been destroyed, Germany was free, and the conqueror, forced to renounce world domination, was gathering a new army for his own defence.

The participation of almost all of Europe in the war of 1813 made it of general and, one might even say, of global interest. Numerous works have appeared that set out the political and military circumstances that led to the restoration of an independent Germany, from various points of view. But not a single satisfactory work on this subject has appeared in French: the work by General Vaudoncourt (*Histoire de la guerre soutenue par les Français en Allemagne, en 1813*), for all its merits in relation to the requirements of military science, is very biased, and therefore is not true in every statement of fact; the work by Norvins (*Portefeuille de 1813*) contains many facts explaining the contemporaneous policies of the belligerent Powers, but this information is incomplete, while the military sections in Norvins are very unsatisfactory. As for Thiers (*Histoire du Consulat et de l'Empire*), there are many novelties in it, but the main element is lacking – historical authenticity, even though the author quite often claims that he used the best sources in compiling his History. German works on the war of 1813 are much more comprehensive: von Plotho's book (*Der Krieg in Deutschland und Frankreich in den Jahren 1813 und 1814*), for all the dryness of its presentation, it deserves attention for the richness of the sources it contains; Richter's work (*Geschichte des deutschen Freiheitskrieges vom Jahre 1813 bis zum Jahre 1815*) and Beitzke's (*Geschichte der deutschen Freiheitskriege in den Jahren 1813 und 1814*) contain many new facts and enlightening conclusions; in Förster's (*Geschichte der Befreiungskriege, 1813, 1814, 1815*) there are fascinating details on the events and personalities of this era; in Bernhardi's work (*Denkwürdigkeiten des Grafen von Toll*) many factors are explained that had hitherto languished in obscurity; in addition to these books, the following monographs are noteworthy: Wagner's (*Plane der Schlachten welche von der preußischen Armee in den Jahren 1813, 14 und 15 geliefert worden*), Aster's (*Schilderung der Kriegsereignisse in und vor Dresden, vom 7 März bis 28 August 1813; Die Kriegsereignisse zwischen Peterwalde, Pirna, Königstein und Priesten, im August 1813, und die Schlacht bei Kulm; Die Schlachten bei Leipzig*), Hofmann's (*Zur Geschichte des Feldzuges von 1813*), Müffling's (*Zur Kriegsgeschichte der Jahre 1813 und 1814*), Odeleben's (*Napoleons Feldzug in Sachsen*), Varnhagen von Ense's (*Biografische Denkmale*), Colomb's (*Tagebuch*), and so on. But, for all the merits of the German works, in many of them there is a desire to downplay the importance of Russian influence in the cause of the liberation of Germany. Without any doubt, Russia could not have defeated Napoleon alone, and even then, the combined efforts of Russia and Prussia were not enough. It was the accession of Austria to the Coalition against Napoleon which gave that alliance the upper hand; but it cannot be concluded from this that the honour of liberating Germany belonged chiefly to the Austrians. Emperor Alexander I had a much greater right to the gratitude of Europe, who, after the war of 1812, could have made peace with Napoleon, on terms favourable for himself, even abandoning the German Powers that had participated in the invasion of Russia. But the Russian Monarch, guided by the promptings of his innate magnanimity and far-sighted policy, acted otherwise: many years of experience had convinced him that every peace treaty with Napoleon was nothing more than a truce to be violated by the ruler of France as soon as his interests demanded it. And therefore, an impartial History must do justice to the determination of Emperor Alexander to continue the war at a time when Russia had been exhausted by the repulse of the invasion by 20 nations, and when Napoleon, having the forces of France and many neighbouring territories at his disposal, could raise a huge new army in the space of three months, while four months after this mobilisation, could produce some 400,000 soldiers. History must acknowledge that the Russian Monarch, having begun the war in Germany without the assistance of allies, was able to win over both the trust of the rulers and the devotion of the people to his side, through moderation, justice and serenity. Nobody has the right to deny that the Russians were very often the decisive element in actions in a war that, for them, was no longer existential: at Lützen, the number of Russian and Prussian troops was equal; at Bautzen – more than two-thirds consisted of Russians; on the Katzbach, there were more Russians than Prussians, and our worthy allies solemnly recognised Sacken as Blücher's fellow campaigner; at Kulm, a handful of Russians saved the Coalition Army from defeat; at Leipzig, Russian troops fought on the decisive points of the battlefield, at Wachau and Probstheida, and almost half of the total Coalition casualties were Russians. Our light detachments flew at the enemy to the rear of his main forces, competing with Prussian partisans in destroying trains, parks, raising the population to revolt against the French, and stripped the royal crown from the head of one of Napoleon's brothers. Let us pay tribute to the Coalition and to our enemies themselves; but, on their part, let us demand that, in the face of the world, the feats accomplished by our compatriots be recognised. To that end, there is no need for noisy boasting or distortions of the truth: it is enough to present events in their true form.

The sources for compiling the History of the War of 1813 have been, to a greater or lesser extent, all the most well-known books on the subject, as well as many manuscripts that had been unknown to the public. Both those and others are shown at the end of Volume II.

In order to confirm the veracity of the facts I have stated, there are footnotes, with appendices at the end of each of the chapters (more than 1,200 in total), containing: sources used; statements on the strength and composition of formations; documents not included in the text, and so on. Among the appendices are reports by the main personalities on some of the most remarkable battles.

A map of the theatre of war for 1813 in Germany is attached to the work, as well as more than 20 individual maps and battle plans. I am indebted to V.A. Poltoratsky for allowing some of the plans to be extracted from his Atlas of Battle Plans.

Translator's Foreword

Modest Ivanovich Bogdanovich was born in Sumy, Ukraine in 1805. Descended from the nobility of Kharkov Governorate, he received his initial education in the Noble Regiment, from where in June 1823 he was commissioned as an ensign into the 1st Grenadier Artillery Company of the reserve corps in the force commanded by Tsarevich Konstantin Pavlovich.

Four years later, Bogdanovich was sent to serve in the 24th Artillery Brigade, with which he took part in the Polish campaign of 1831 and was in combat at Wawer, at Grochów and Dębe Wielkie. For distinction in these battles, he was awarded the Order of St. Anna, 4th class with the inscription 'for valour' and the rank of lieutenant. In this campaign, in an action at Rogoźnica, he suffered such a severe contusion to his right leg that he was left for dead on the battlefield and was captured by the Poles, being held prisoner until August.

Upon his return to Russia in November 1833 he entered the Imperial Military Academy (later the Nikolaev Academy of the General Staff), from where, after completing a course of sciences in 1835, he was appointed to serve in the Third Department of the former office of the Quartermaster General of the General Staff, but remained in this position no more than a year and, by Supreme Command, was assigned to the Military Academy for training as an assistant professor.

Appointed shortly thereafter as Head of Chancellery of the academy, Captain Bogdanovich in September 1838 was approved as an assistant professor in the Department of Military History and Strategy and, in his spare time, taught tactics to the Noble Regiment, and also took part in the publication of the Military Journal and the Military Encyclopaedic Lexicon. He remained in the position of Director of Operations until 1839, after which in 1841, with the rank of lieutenant colonel, he was appointed as field officer supervising the officers studying at the academy and, in February 1843 he was granted the status of professor; in 1847 he was appointed a member of the military-scientific committee for the Department of the General Staff and in September 1855 he was promoted to major general.

In 1863, Bogdanovich was appointed to be at the disposal of the Minister of War and Quartermaster General of the General Staff, with the rank of honorary member of the conference of the Academy of the General Staff and Honoured Professor, and in the same year he was promoted to the rank of lieutenant general. Following that, he was co-opted as a member of the advisory committee of the General Staff, and in June 1873, on the 50th anniversary of his commissioning, he received the Order of St. Alexander Nevsky. In 1881, Bogdanovich was appointed a member of the military council. He remained in the latter position until his death in August 1882.

General Bogdanovich is known for a number of major works, which are a valuable contribution to Russian military historiography. His history of the war in 1813 follows on directly from his award-winning history of 1812. It also benefitted greatly from being published during the reign of Tsar Alexander II; a relatively liberal monarch in comparison with his predecessors, and this allowed Bogdanovich to be bolder in his assessments of Russian military performance than earlier historians, with less fear of censorship. Bogdanovich has been criticised for using so many 'foreign' sources in these works and, indeed, much of the narrative for 1813 is taken directly from German accounts, such as those by Plotho and Beitzke and there are times when the minute details of exclusively German operations does feel somewhat unnecessary in a Russian history. Nevertheless, Bogdanovich's work does much to provide a balanced account of events and the Russian contribution to that most difficult act of war – coalition operations.

I have retained the Russian weights and measures used in the original text. *Système international d'unités* and Imperial equivalents of the most common are shown here for easy reference (less common units have modern equivalents in square brackets on their first appearance in the text):

Arshin – one *arshin* equals 71.1 centimetres or 28 inches (a pace).
Sazhen – one *Sazhen* equals 2.13 metres or seven feet.
versta – one *versta* equals 1,067 metres or ⅔ statute miles (recommended maximum effective range for field artillery).
Meile – one *Meile* equals 7,467 metres or 4⅔ statute miles.
Pud – one *Pud* is around 16.4 kilogrammes or 36 pounds.
Chetvert – one (dry) *Chetvert* is around 210 litres or 5¾ bushels.

Anything that I have added to the original text, such as dates using the modern calendar, alternative spellings of place names and surnames, are in square brackets. Where places are mentioned in the text but are not marked on the accompanying maps, I have included distance and direction from a marked location for clarity. Also included from the original Russian is the practice of applying an ordinal number to namesakes in order to help distinguish them from one-another.

Peter G.A. Phillips
2024

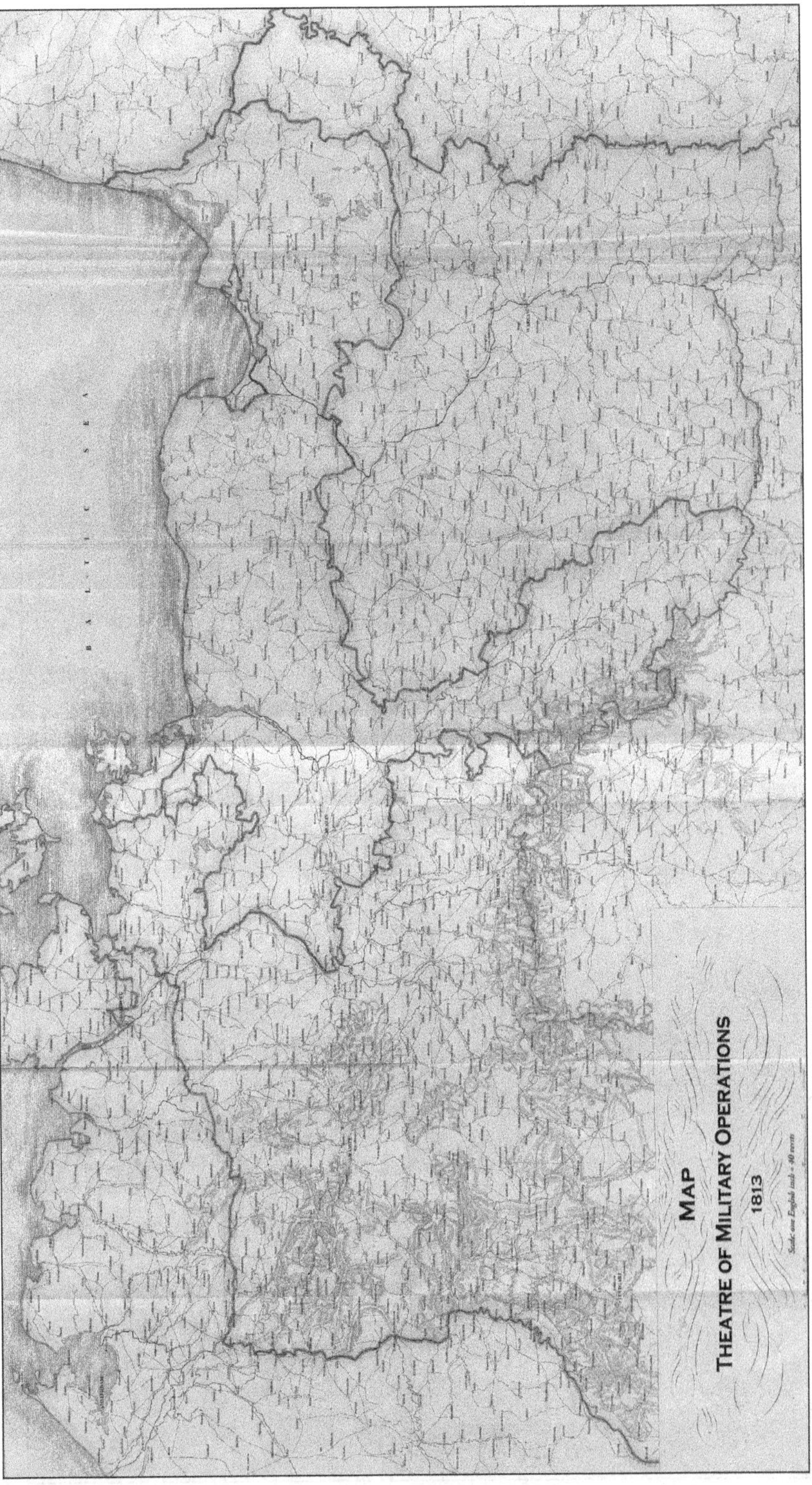

Theatre of Military Operations 1813.

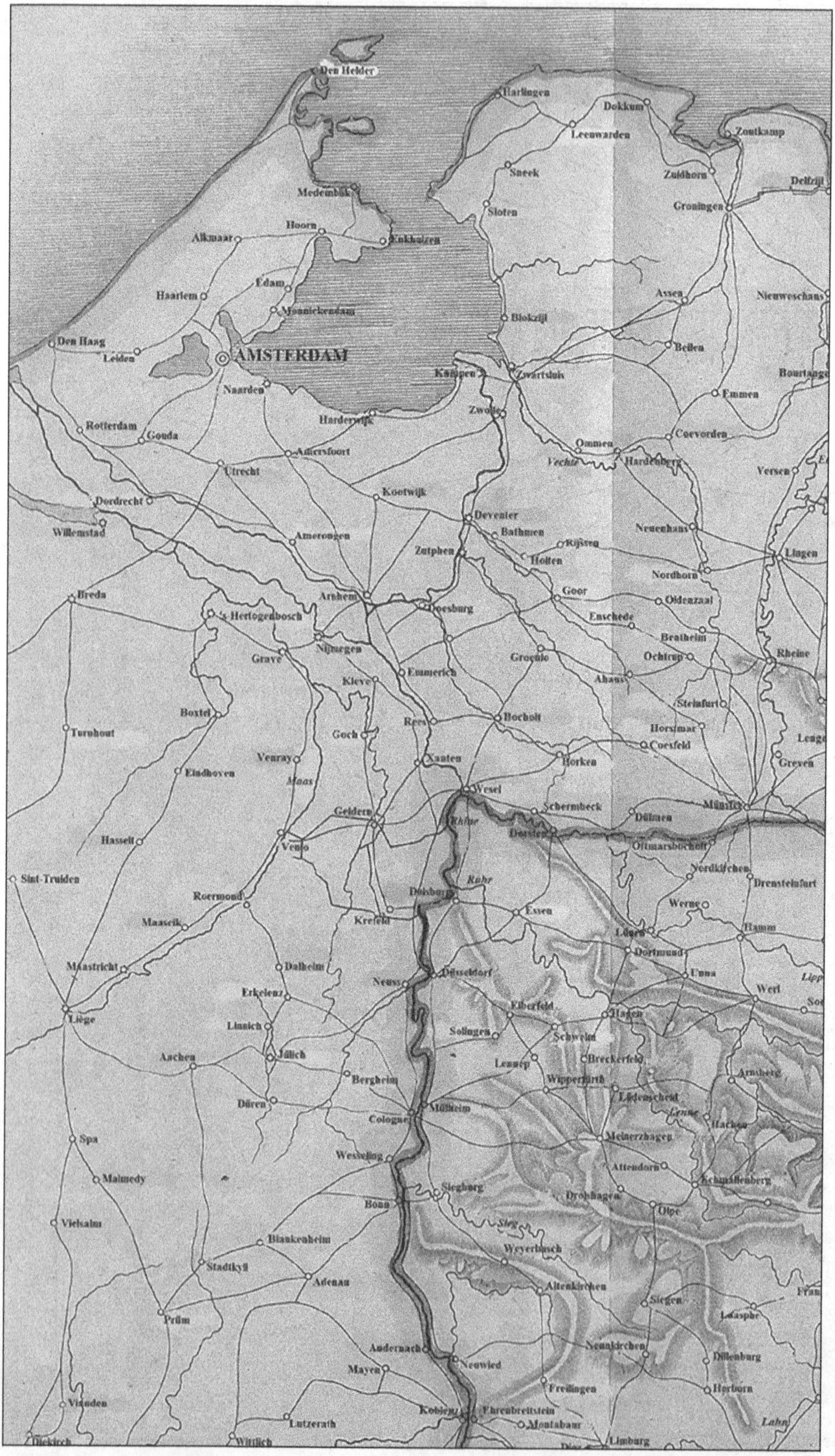
Den Helder
Harlingen
Dokkum
Leeuwarden
Zoutkamp
Sneek
Zuidhorn
Delfzijl
Medemblik
Sloten
Groningen
Hoorn
Alkmaar
Enkhuizen
Edam
Haarlem
Monnickendam
Assen
Nieuweschans
Blokzijl
Den Haag
Leiden
AMSTERDAM
Bellen
Kampen
Zwartsluis
Bourtange
Naarden
Emmen
Zwolle
Harderwijk
Rotterdam
Gouda
Coevorden
Ommen
Amersfoort
Vechte
Hardenberg
Utrecht
Versen
Kootwijk
Dordrecht
Deventer
Willemstad
Bathmen
Neuenhaus
Amerongen
Rijssen
Zutphen
Lingen
Holten
Nordhorn
Breda
Goor
Oldenzaal
Arnhem
Doesburg
's-Hertogenbosch
Enschede
Bentheim
Nijmegen
Ochtrup
Rheine
Grave
Groenlo
Emmerich
Ahaus
Kleve
Steinfurt
Boxtel
Rees
Bocholt
Turnhout
Goch
Horstmar
Coesfeld
Greven
Venray
Xanten
Borken
Eindhoven
Maas
Wesel
Schermbeck
Geldern
Münster
Dülmen
Rhine
Dorsten
Hasselt
Venlo
Ottmarsbocholt
Nordkirchen
Sint-Truiden
Ruhr
Drensteinfurt
Roermond
Duisburg
Werne
Essen
Maaseik
Krefeld
Hamm
Lünen
Dortmund
Maastricht
Dalheim
Unna
Neuss
Düsseldorf
Erkelenz
Werl
Elberfeld
Liège
Linnich
Hagen
Solingen
Schwelm
Aachen
Jülich
Breckerfeld
Lennep
Bergheim
Arnsberg
Wipperfürth
Lüdenscheid
Düren
Lenne
Cologne
Mülheim
Hachen
Meinerzhagen
Spa
Wesseling
Attendorn
Schmallenberg
Malmedy
Siegburg
Drolshagen
Bonn
Olpe
Vielsalm
Sieg
Blankenheim
Weyerbusch
Stadtkyll
Adenau
Altenkirchen
Siegen
Prüm
Laasphe
Neunkirchen
Andernach
Dillenburg
Neuwied
Mayen
Freilingen
Herborn
Vianden
Koblenz
Ehrenbreitstein
Lahn
Lutzerath
Montabaur
Diekirch
Wittlich
Limburg

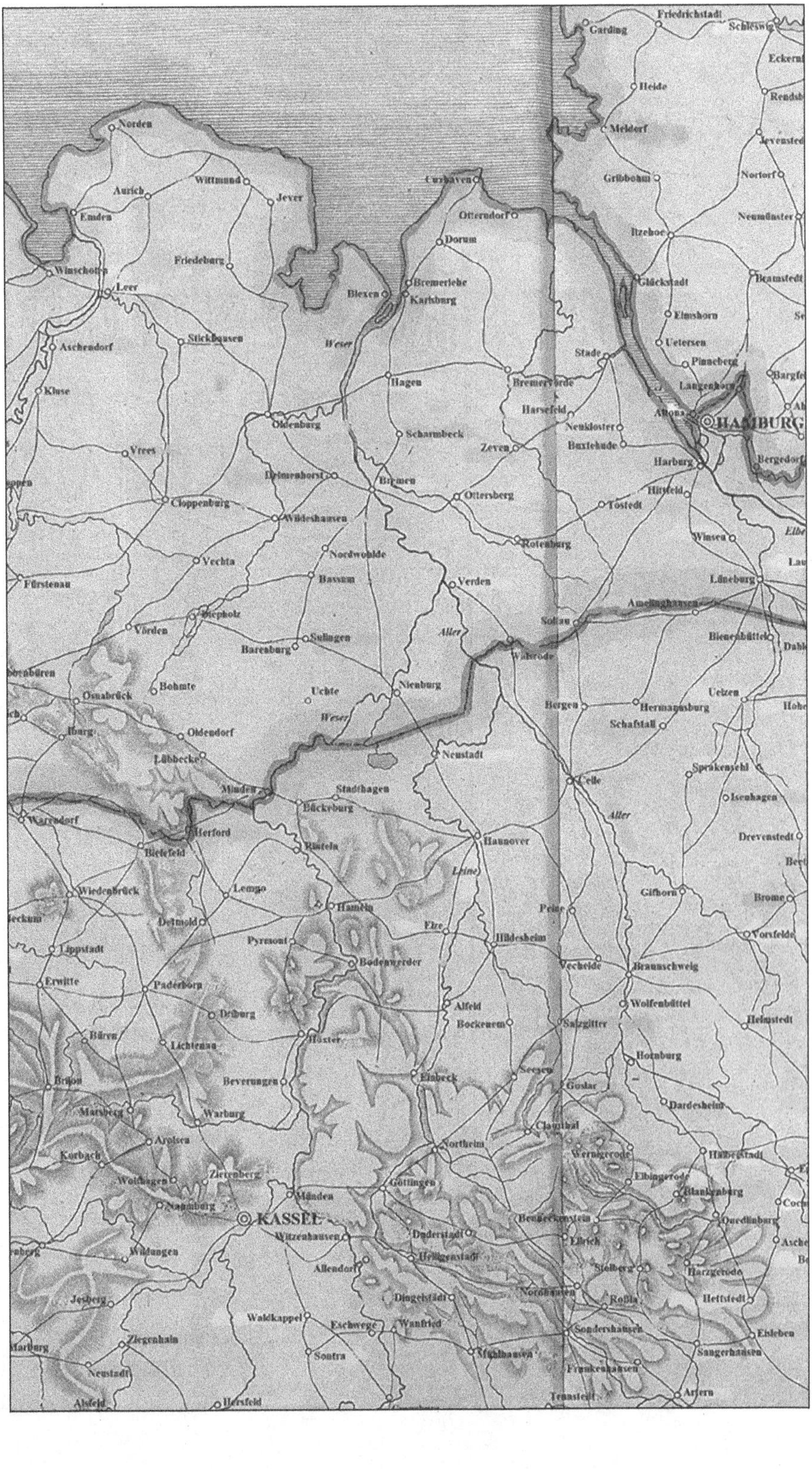
Friedrichstadt
Garding
Heide
Meldorf
Norden
Aurich
Wittmund
Jever
Emden
Cuxhaven
Otterndorf
Dorum
Itzehoe
Glückstadt
Elmshorn
Uetersen
Pinneberg
Friedeburg
Leer
Bremerlehe
Blexen
Karlsburg
Stickhausen
Aschendorf
Weser
Hagen
Bremervörde
Stade
Harsefeld
Kluse
Oldenburg
Scharmbeck
Zeven
Neukloster
Buxtehude
Altona
HAMBURG
Harburg
Bergedorf
Vrees
Delmenhorst
Bremen
Ottersberg
Tostedt
Cloppenburg
Wildeshausen
Rotenburg
Winsen
Nordwohlde
Vechta
Bassum
Verden
Lüneburg
Fürstenau
Soltau
Diepholz
Vörden
Sulingen
Barenburg
Aller
Walsrode
Bienenbüttel
Bohmte
Osnabrück
Uchte
Nienburg
Uelzen
Bergen
Hermannsburg
Schafstall
Iburg
Oldendorf
Lübbecke
Neustadt
Celle
Minden
Stadthagen
Bückeburg
Isenhagen
Herford
Bielefeld
Rinteln
Hannover
Leine
Dreyenstedt
Wiedenbrück
Lemgo
Hameln
Gifhorn
Brome
Detmold
Peine
Pyrmont
Hildesheim
Lippstadt
Bodenwerder
Vechelde
Braunschweig
Erwitte
Paderborn
Alfeld
Wolfenbüttel
Driburg
Bockenem
Salzgitter
Helmstedt
Büren
Lichtenau
Höxter
Hornburg
Beverungen
Einbeck
Seesen
Goslar
Brilon
Marsberg
Warburg
Dardesheim
Arolsen
Clausthal
Korbach
Northeim
Wernigerode
Halberstadt
Wolfhagen
Zierenberg
Elbingerode
Göttingen
Münden
Blankenburg
Naumburg
KASSEL
Witzenhausen
Quedlinburg
Duderstadt
Benneckenstein
Ellrich
Wildungen
Heiligenstadt
Stolberg
Allendorf
Harzgerode
Jesberg
Dingelstädt
Nordhausen
Roßla
Hettstedt
Waldkappel
Eschwege
Wanfried
Ziegenhain
Sondershausen
Eisleben
Marburg
Sontra
Mühlhausen
Sangerhausen
Neustadt
Frankenhausen
Alsfeld
Hersfeld
Artern

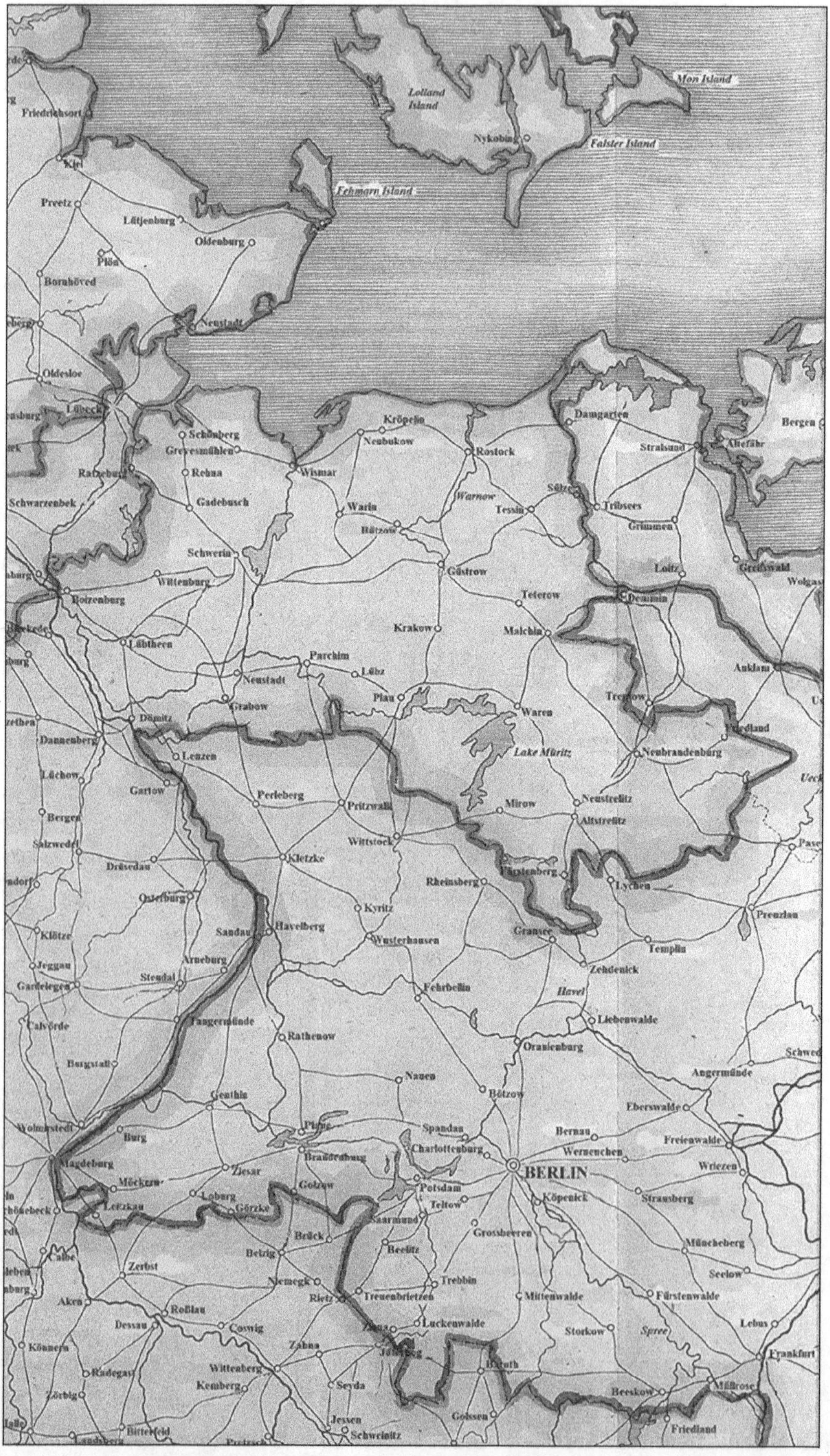
Lolland Island
Mon Island
Nykobing
Falster Island
Fehmarn Island
Friedrichsort
Kiel
Preetz
Lütjenburg
Oldenburg
Plön
Bornhöved
Neustadt
Oldesloe
Lübeck
Schönberg
Grevesmühlen
Ratzeburg
Rehna
Schwarzenbek
Gadebusch
Wismar
Kröpelin
Neubukow
Rostock
Damgarten
Bergen
Stralsund
Altefähr
Warin
Warnow
Sülze
Tribsees
Tessin
Bützow
Grimmen
Schwerin
Güstrow
Loitz
Greifswald
Wittenburg
Boizenburg
Teterow
Demmin
Krakow
Malchin
Lübtheen
Parchim
Lübz
Anklam
Neustadt
Plau
Treptow
Grabow
Waren
Friedland
Dömitz
Dannenberg
Lenzen
Lake Müritz
Neubrandenburg
Lüchow
Gartow
Perleberg
Mirow
Neustrelitz
Pritzwalk
Altstrelitz
Bergen
Salzwedel
Wittstock
Kletzke
Drüsedau
Fürstenberg
Rheinsberg
Lychen
Osterburg
Kyritz
Prenzlau
Klötze
Sandau
Havelberg
Wusterhausen
Gransee
Templin
Jeggau
Arneburg
Zehdenick
Stendal
Gardelegen
Fehrbellin
Havel
Calvörde
Tangermünde
Liebenwalde
Rathenow
Oranienburg
Burgstall
Angermünde
Nauen
Genthin
Bötzow
Eberswalde
Wolmirstedt
Spandau
Bernau
Burg
Charlottenburg
Freienwalde
Werneuchen
Magdeburg
Brandenburg
Ziesar
BERLIN
Wriezen
Möckern
Golzow
Potsdam
Loburg
Görzke
Teltow
Köpenick
Strausberg
Schönebeck
Leitzkau
Saarmund
Brück
Grossbeeren
Müncheberg
Calbe
Belzig
Beelitz
Zerbst
Niemegk
Trebbin
Seelow
Rietz
Treuenbrietzen
Mittenwalde
Fürstenwalde
Aken
Roßlau
Luckenwalde
Dessau
Coswig
Zinna
Storkow
Spree
Lebus
Könnern
Zahna
Jüterbog
Frankfurt
Radegast
Wittenberg
Baruth
Kemberg
Seyda
Beeskow
Müllrose
Zörbig
Jessen
Golssen
Schweinitz
Bitterfeld
Friedland

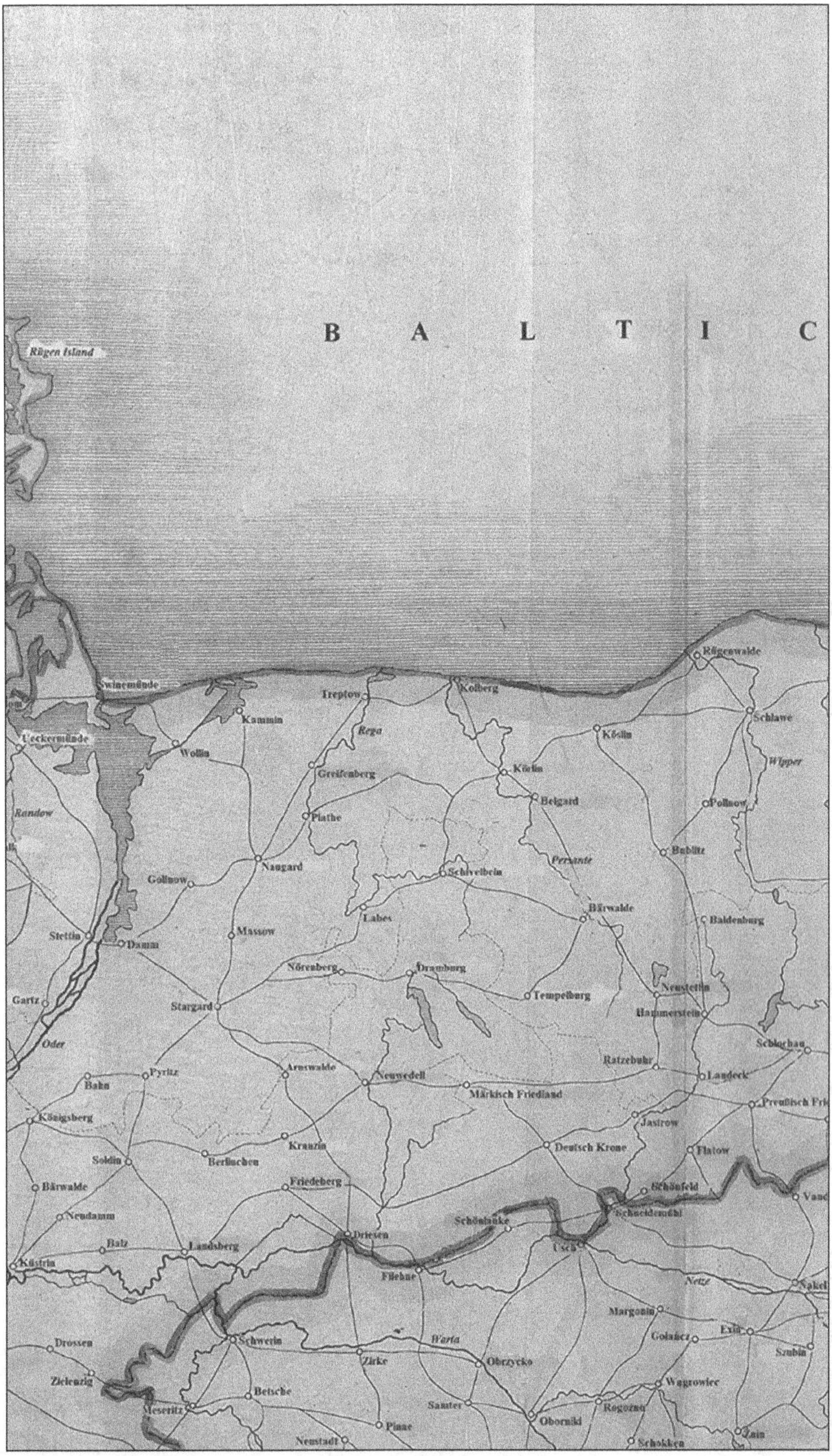
B A L T I C
Rügen Island
Swinemünde
Ueckermünde
Randow
Wollin
Kammin
Treptow
Rega
Greifenberg
Plathe
Kolberg
Köslin
Belgard
Persante
Rügenwalde
Schlawe
Wipper
Pollnow
Bublitz
Naugard
Gollnow
Stettin
Damm
Massow
Labes
Schivelbein
Bärwalde
Baldenburg
Gartz
Oder
Stargard
Nörenberg
Dramburg
Tempelburg
Neustettin
Hammerstein
Schlochau
Ratzebuhr
Landeck
Pyritz
Bahn
Arnswalde
Neuwedell
Märkisch Friedland
Königsberg
Kranzin
Berlinchen
Soldin
Deutsch Krone
Jastrow
Flatow
Friedeberg
Schönfeld
Schneidemühl
Neudamm
Schönlanke
Driesen
Balz
Landsberg
Küstrin
Usch
Filehne
Netze
Nakel
Margonin
Gołańcz
Exin
Szubin
Drossen
Schwerin
Warta
Zirke
Obrzycko
Zielenzig
Betsche
Wągrowiec
Meseritz
Samter
Rogoźno
Obornik
Pinne
Neustadt
Schokken
Znin

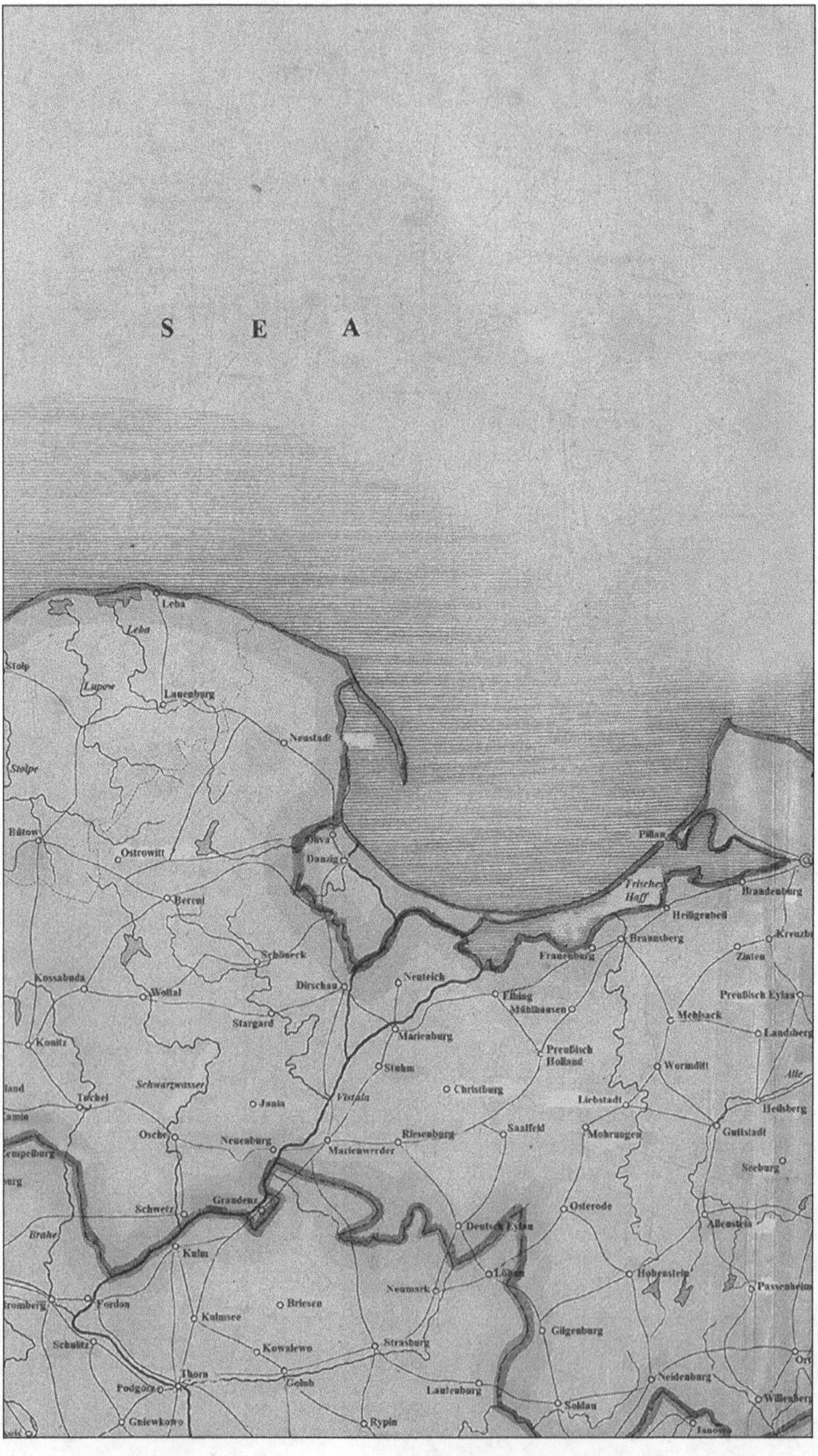
S E A
Leba
Stolp
Lupow
Lauenburg
Neustadt
Stolpe
Bütow
Ostrowitt
Oliva
Danzig
Pillau
Frisches Haff
Brandenburg
Heiligenbeil
Berent
Schöneck
Braunsberg
Frauenburg
Zinten
Kossabuda
Dirschau
Neuteich
Elbing
Mühlhausen
Preußisch Eylau
Woltal
Stargard
Mehlsack
Landsberg
Konitz
Marienburg
Preußisch Holland
Stuhm
Wormditt
Schwarzwasser
Alle
Tuchel
Janin
Christburg
Liebstadt
Heilsberg
Vistula
Osche
Neuenburg
Riesenburg
Saalfeld
Mohrungen
Guttstadt
Marienwerder
Seeburg
Graudenz
Osterode
Schwetz
Allenstein
Brahe
Deutsch Eylau
Kulm
Löbau
Hohenstein
Neumark
Passenheim
Bromberg
Fordon
Briesen
Kulmsee
Gilgenburg
Schulitz
Kowalewo
Strasburg
Thorn
Neidenburg
Podgorz
Golub
Lautenburg
Soldau
Willenberg
Gniewkowo
Rypin
Janowo

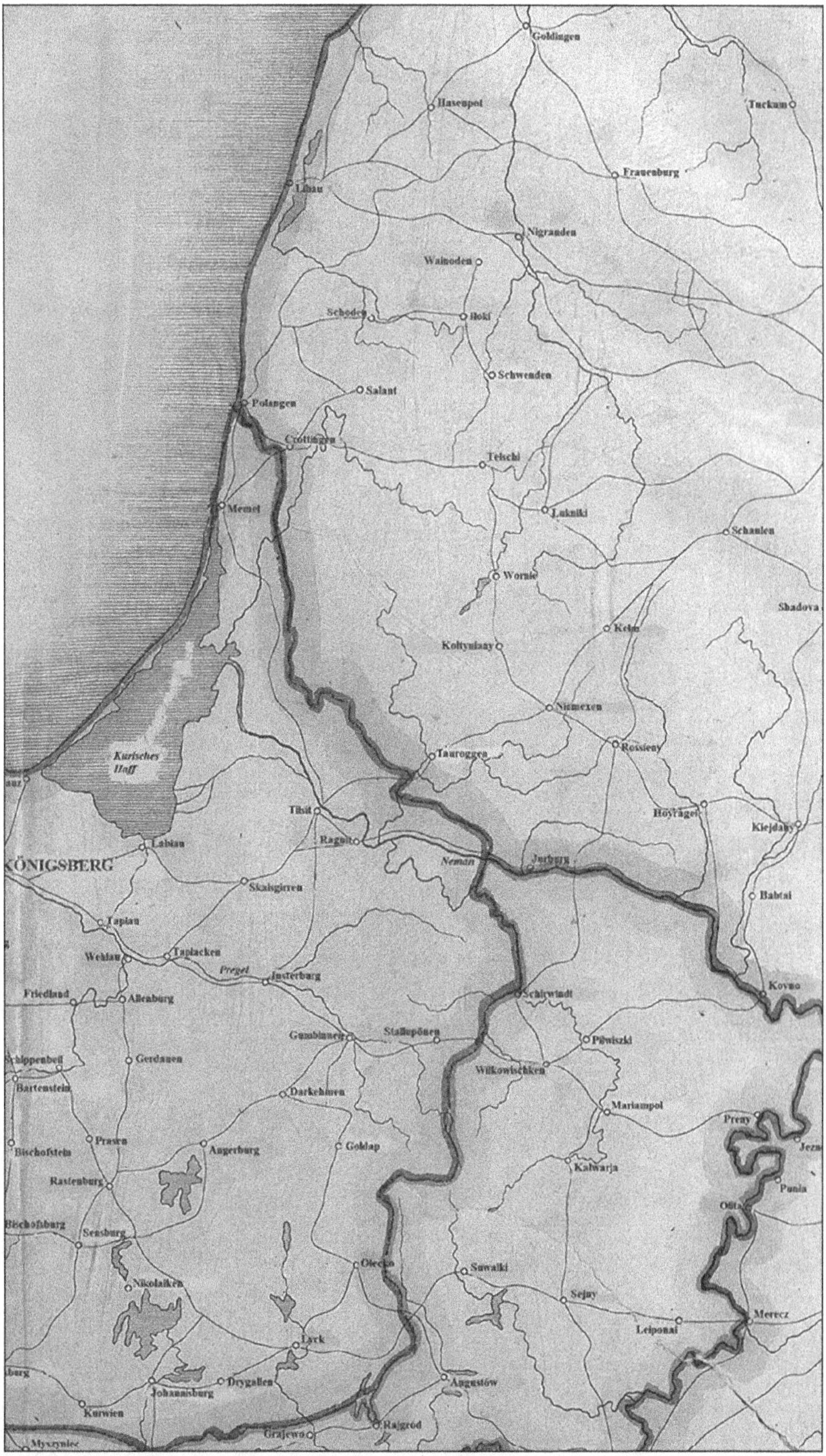
Goldingen
Hasenpot
Tuckum
Libau
Frauenburg
Nigranden
Wainoden
Schoden
Schwenden
Salant
Polangen
Crottingen
Telschi
Memel
Lukniki
Schaulen
Wornie
Shadova
Kelm
Rossieny
Tauroggen
Kurisches Haff
Tilsit
Kiejdany
Ragnit
Labiau
KÖNIGSBERG
Neman
Jurburg
Skaisgirren
Babtai
Tapiau
Wehlau
Taplacken
Pregel
Insterburg
Kovno
Friedland
Allenburg
Schirwindt
Gumbinnen
Stallupönen
Pilwiszki
Schippenbeil
Gerdauen
Wilkowischken
Bartenstein
Darkehmen
Mariampol
Preny
Bischofstein
Angerburg
Goldap
Rastenburg
Kalwarja
Punia
Olita
Bischofsburg
Sensburg
Suwalki
Nikolaiken
Sejny
Merecz
Leiponai
Lyck
Augustów
Johannisburg
Drygallen
Kurwien
Rajgród
Grajewo
Myszyniec

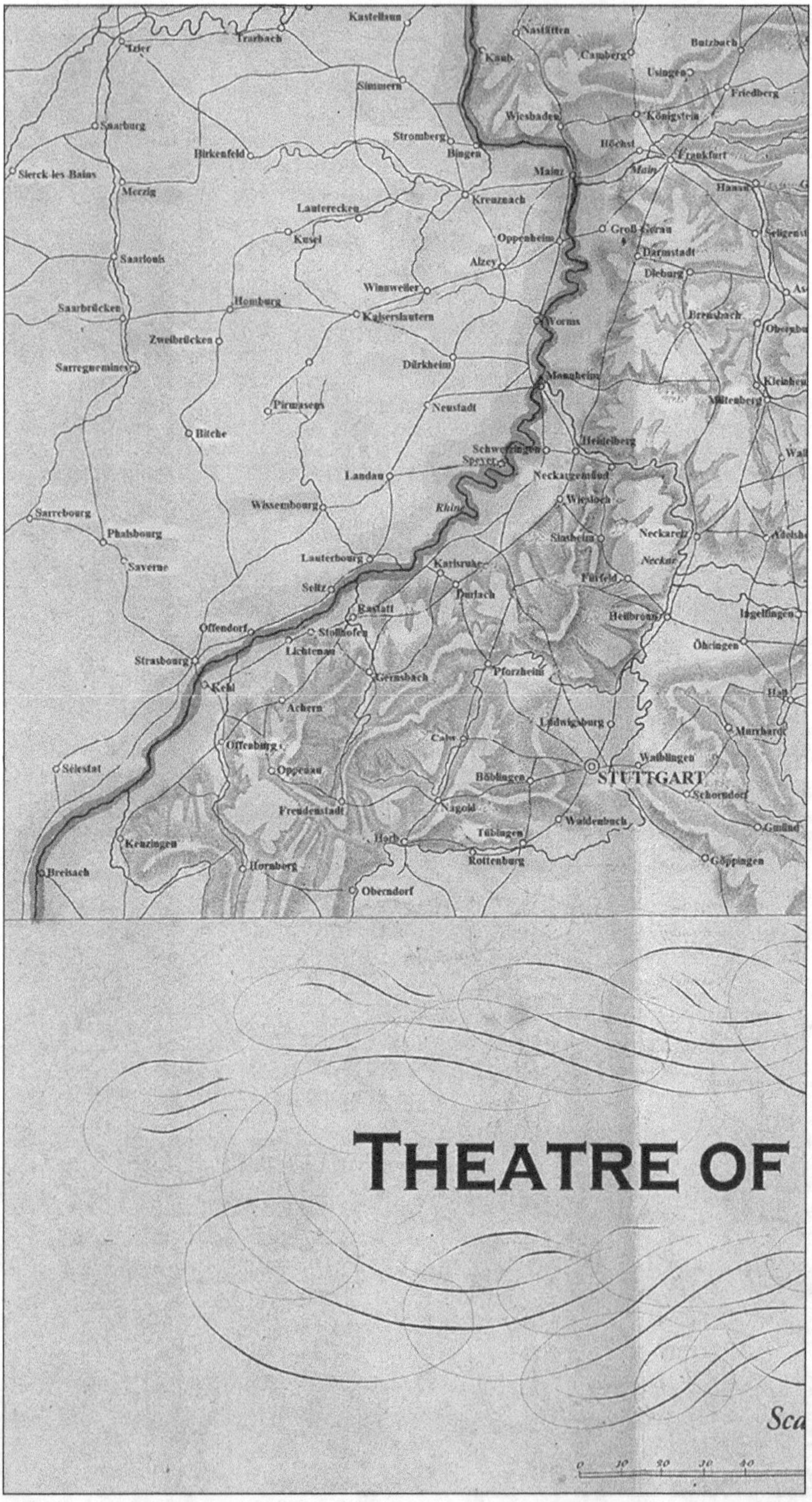
THEATRE OF
Kastellaun
Trarbach
Trier
Nastätten
Kaub
Camberg
Butzbach
Usingen
Friedberg
Simmern
Wiesbaden
Königstein
Saarburg
Stromberg
Bingen
Höchst
Frankfurt
Birkenfeld
Sierck-les-Bains
Mainz
Main
Hanau
Merzig
Kreuznach
Lauterecken
Kusel
Oppenheim
Darmstadt
Dieburg
Saarlouis
Alzey
Winnweiler
Saarbrücken
Homburg
Kaiserslautern
Worms
Zweibrücken
Sarreguemines
Dürkheim
Mannheim
Miltenberg
Pirmasens
Neustadt
Bitche
Heidelberg
Speyer
Landau
Wissembourg
Rhine
Wiesloch
Sarrebourg
Phalsbourg
Sinsheim
Neckarelz
Neckar
Saverne
Lauterbourg
Karlsruhe
Durlach
Seltz
Rastatt
Heilbronn
Offendorf
Stollhofen
Lichtenau
Öhringen
Strasbourg
Gernsbach
Pforzheim
Kehl
Achern
Ludwigsburg
Offenburg
Calw
Waiblingen
Sélestat
Oppenau
Böblingen
STUTTGART
Schorndorf
Freudenstadt
Nagold
Waldenbuch
Gmünd
Kenzingen
Horb
Tübingen
Rottenburg
Göppingen
Breisach
Hornberg
Oberndorf
Murrhardt
0 10 20 30 40

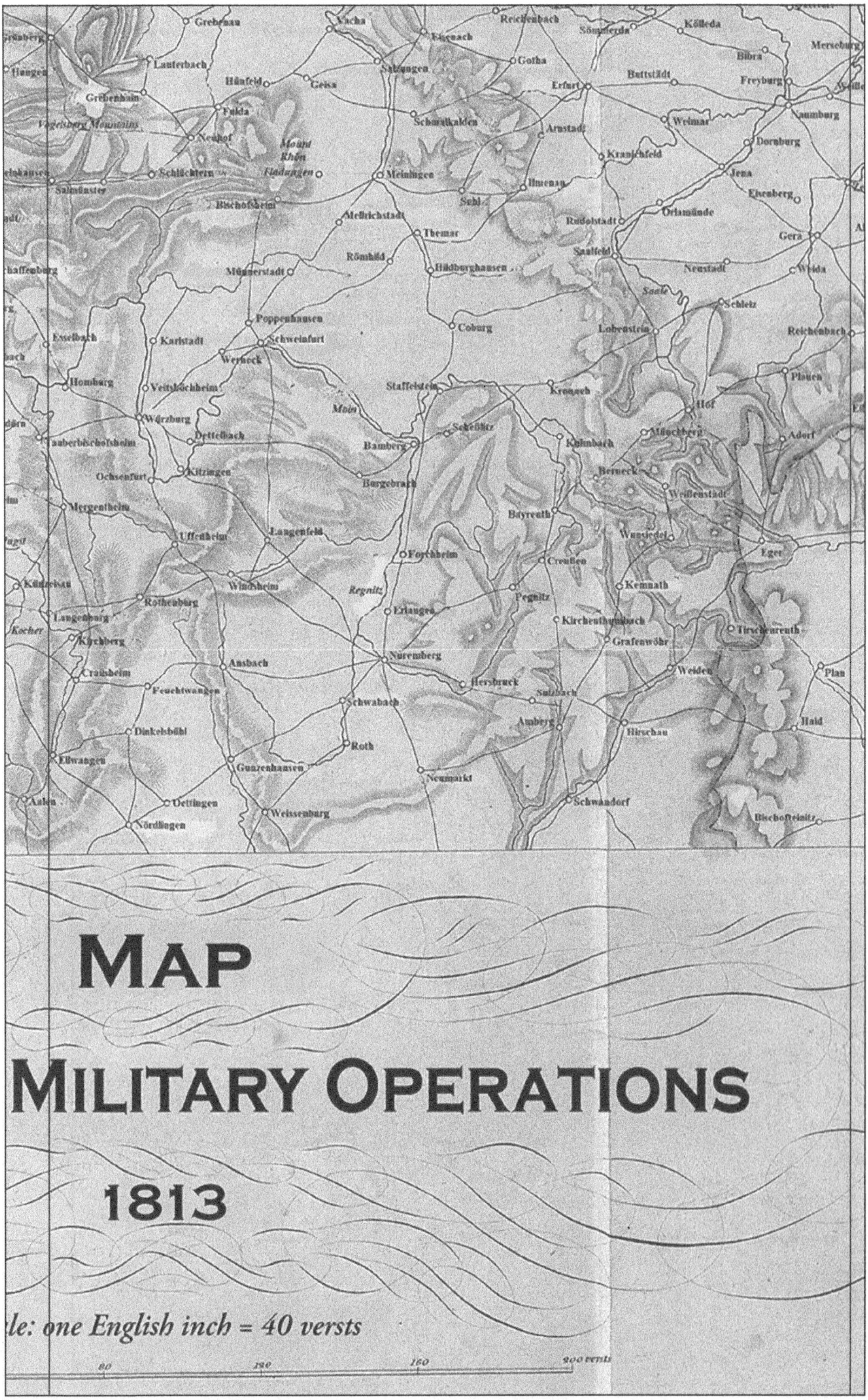
MAP
MILITARY OPERATIONS
1813
le: one English inch = 40 versts
80
120
160
200 versts
Grebenau
Vacha
Eisenach
Reichenbach
Sömmerda
Kölleda
Merseburg
Bibra
Lauterbach
Gotha
Buttstädt
Freyburg
Hünfeld
Geisa
Salzungen
Erfurt
Naumburg
Fulda
Schmalkalden
Weimar
Arnstadt
Dornburg
Neuhof
Mount Rhön
Kranichfeld
Schlüchtern
Meiningen
Jena
Salmünster
Ilmenau
Eisenberg
Bischofsheim
Suhl
Mellrichstadt
Orlamünde
Rudolstadt
Themar
Gera
Römhild
Saalfeld
Hildburghausen
Neustadt
Weida
Münnerstadt
Saale
Schleiz
Poppenhausen
Coburg
Lobenstein
Reichenbach
Esselbach
Karlstadt
Schweinfurt
Werneck
Homburg
Veitshöchheim
Staffelstein
Kronach
Plauen
Main
Hof
Würzburg
Schesslitz
Münchberg
Dettelbach
Tauberbischofsheim
Bamberg
Kulmbach
Adorf
Kitzingen
Ochsenfurt
Berneck
Burgebrach
Weißenstadt
Mergentheim
Bayreuth
Uffenheim
Langenfeld
Wunsiedel
Eger
Forchheim
Creußen
Windsheim
Regnitz
Kemnath
Pegnitz
Rothenburg
Erlangen
Kirchenthumbach
Langenburg
Kocher
Kirchberg
Grafenwöhr
Tirschenreuth
Nuremberg
Ansbach
Weiden
Crailsheim
Plan
Hersbruck
Feuchtwangen
Sulzbach
Schwabach
Amberg
Haid
Dinkelsbühl
Hirschau
Roth
Ellwangen
Gunzenhausen
Neumarkt
Aalen
Oettingen
Schwandorf
Weissenburg
Nördlingen
Bischofteinitz

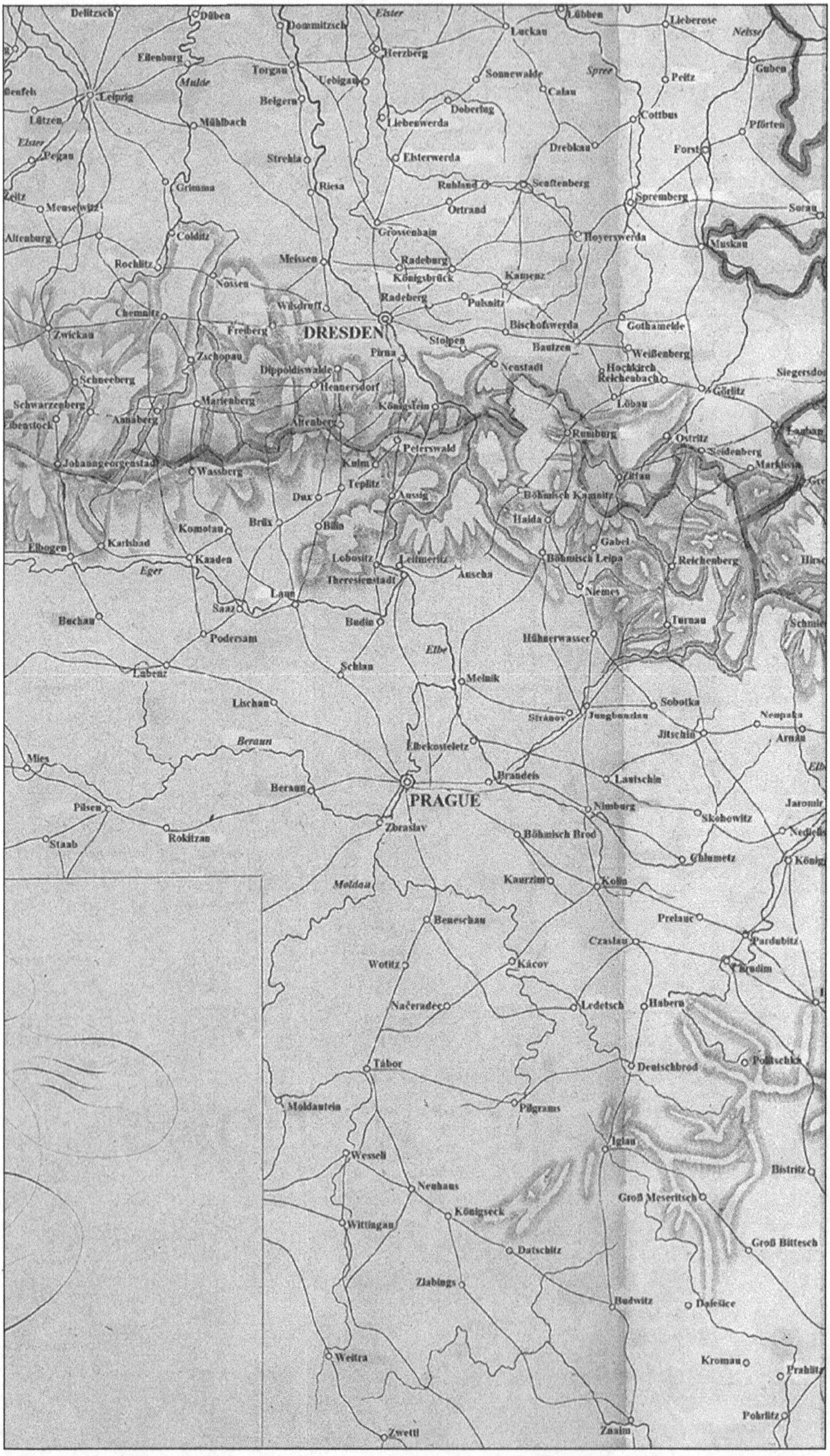
Delitzsch
Düben
Dommitzsch
Elster
Lübben
Lieberose
Neisse
Luckau
Eilenburg
Torgau
Herzberg
Sonnewalde
Spree
Peitz
Guben
Mulde
Uebigau
Calau
Leipzig
Belgern
Doberlug
Cottbus
Lützen
Mühlbach
Liebenwerda
Pförten
Elster
Drebkau
Forst
Pegau
Strehla
Elsterwerda
Riesa
Ruhland
Senftenberg
Grimma
Spremberg
Zeitz
Meuselwitz
Ortrand
Sorau
Grossenhain
Altenburg
Colditz
Hoyerswerda
Muskau
Meissen
Radeburg
Rochlitz
Königsbrück
Kamenz
Nossen
Radeberg
Wilsdruff
Pulsnitz
Chemnitz
Gothamelde
Freiberg
DRESDEN
Bischofswerda
Zwickau
Stolpen
Bautzen
Weißenberg
Zschopau
Pirna
Neustadt
Hochkirch
Dippoldiswalde
Reichenbach
Siegersdo
Schneeberg
Hennersdorf
Görlitz
Schwarzenberg
Marienberg
Löbau
Königstein
Annaberg
Altenberg
Rumburg
Ostritz
Peterswald
Seidenberg
Johanngeorgenstadt
Kulm
Zittau
Wassberg
Teplitz
Dux
Aussig
Böhmisch Kamnitz
Haida
Brüx
Bilin
Komotau
Gabel
Karlsbad
Elbogen
Lobositz
Leitmeritz
Böhmisch Leipa
Reichenberg
Kaaden
Eger
Theresienstadt
Auscha
Laun
Niemes
Saaz
Turnau
Buchau
Budin
Podersam
Hühnerwasser
Elbe
Schlan
Melnik
Lischan
Sobotka
Stránov
Jungbunzlau
Jitschin
Arnau
Beraun
Elbekosteletz
Mies
Brandeis
Lautschin
Beraun
PRAGUE
Pilsen
Nimburg
Jaromir
Skohowitz
Zbraslav
Rokitzan
Böhmisch Brod
Staab
Chlumetz
Kaurzim
Moldau
Kolin
Prelauc
Beneschau
Czaslau
Pardubitz
Wotitz
Kácov
Chrudim
Načeradec
Ledetsch
Habern
Tábor
Deutschbrod
Politschka
Moldautein
Pilgrams
Iglau
Wessell
Bistritz
Neuhaus
Groß Meseritsch
Königseck
Wittingau
Groß Bittesch
Datschitz
Zlabings
Budwitz
Dalešice
Weitra
Kromau
Prahlitz
Pohrlitz
Zwettl
Znaim

Leitersdorf
Crossen
Bober
Bomst
Züllichau
Heutschen
Tuchorza
Grätz
Buk
Stęszew
Poznań
Pudewitz
Gniezno
Trzemeszno
Kostrzyn
Kopnitz
Rakwitz
Mosina
Obra
Grünberg
Wartenberg
Kontoppe
Schlawa
Schmiegel
Kosten
Września
Powidz
Środa
Śrem
Słupca
Peisern
Freystadt
Sagan
Fraustadt
Dolzig
Książ
Żerków
Neustädtel
Lissa
Jaraczewo
Sprottau
Glogau
Reisen
Jarocin
Chocz
Rychwał
Gubrau
Poniec
Krobea
Primkenau
Polkwitz
Pleszew
Koźmin
Raudten
Köben
Görchen
Kobylin
Bunzlau
Herrnstadt
Rawicz
Jutrosin
Zduny
Krotoszyn
Raszków
Stawiszyn
Lüben
Steinau
Winzig
Sulmierzyce
Kalisz
Koźmin
Haynau
Militsch
Ostrowo
Opatówek
Löwenberg
Katzbach
Trachenberg
Liegnitz
Parchwitz
Wohlau
Goldberg
Prausnitz
Błaszki
Trebnitz
Schönau
Neumarkt
Auras
Jauer
Ostrzeszów
Grabów
Lissa
Wartenberg
Prosna
Bolkenhain
Striegau
Oels
Kempen
Breslau
Landeshut
Schweidnitz
Bernstadt
Sokolniki
Lohe
Waldenburg
Namslau
Schatzlar
Wieluń
Ohlau
Oder
Reichenbach
Konstadt
Trautenau
Nimptsch
Strehlen
Wansen
Brieg
Kreuzburg
Braunau
Neurode
Silberberg
Michelau
Schurgast
Frankenstein
Rosenberg
Skalitz
Krzepice
Wartha
Münsterberg
Grottkau
Kłobuck
Nachod
Neiße
Glatz
Oppeln
Guttentag
Habelschwerdt
Neiße
Lubliniec
Częstochowa
Neustadt
Groß Strehlitz
Mittelwalde
Koziegłowy
Geiersberg
Cosel
Tost
Peiskretscham
Leitomischl
Leobschütz
Jägerndorf
Gleiwitz
Beuthen
Zwittau
Ratibor
Trübau
Troppau
Rybnik
Mysłowice
Müglitz
Hof
Nikolai
Sohrau
Lettowitz
Littau
Sternberg
Ostrau
Chrzanów
Vistula
Pleß
Oder
Olmütz
Oder
Proßnitz
Friedeck
Skotschau
Teschen
Bielitz
Kenty
Weißkirchen
Freiberg
Brünn
Wischau
Prerau
Żywiec
Kremsier
Bistritz
Jablunkau
Austerlitz
Seelowitz
Tschadsa
Polgora

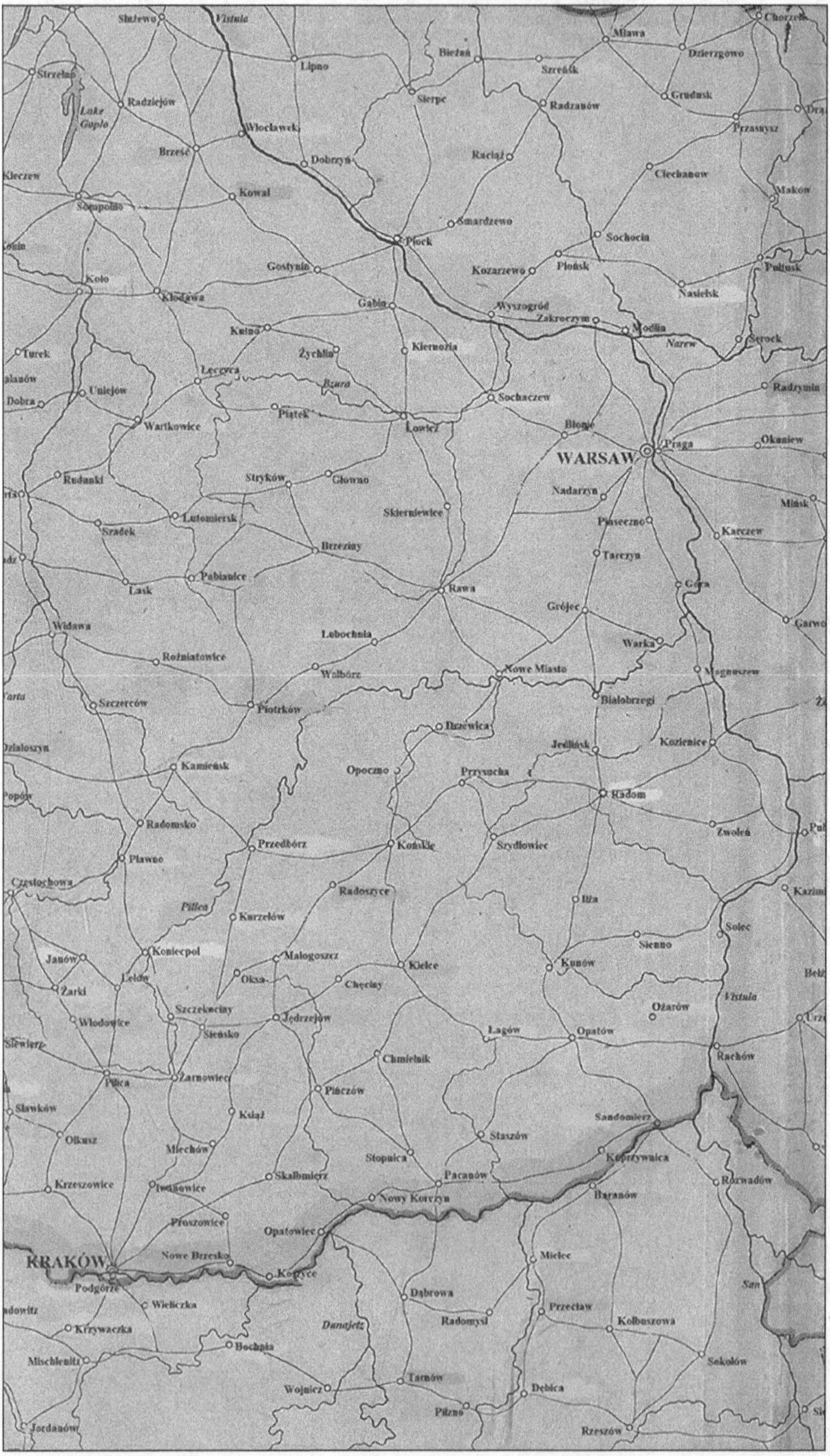
Vistula
Lipno
Bieżuń
Mława
Dzierzgowo
Szreńsk
Strzelno
Radziejów
Lake Goplo
Sierpc
Radzanów
Grudusk
Przasnysz
Włocławek
Brześć
Dobrzyń
Raciąż
Ciechanów
Kleczew
Kowal
Maków
Sompolno
Smardzewo
Płock
Sochocin
Gostynin
Kozarzewo
Płońsk
Pułtusk
Koło
Kłodawa
Nasielsk
Gąbin
Wyszogród
Zakroczym
Modlin
Kutno
Serock
Narew
Żychlin
Kiernozia
Turek
Łęczyca
Radzymin
Bzura
Uniejów
Sochaczew
Piątek
Wartkowice
Łowicz
Błonie
WARSAW
Praga
Okuniew
Rudunki
Stryków
Głowno
Nadarzyn
Mińsk
Skierniewice
Lutomiersk
Piaseczno
Karczew
Szadek
Brzeziny
Tarczyn
Pabianice
Lask
Rawa
Góra
Grójec
Widawa
Lubochnia
Warka
Rożniatowice
Wolbórz
Nowe Miasto
Magnuszew
Białobrzegi
Szczerców
Piotrków
Drzewica
Działoszyn
Jedlińsk
Kozienice
Kamieńsk
Opoczno
Przysucha
Radom
Radomsko
Zwoleń
Przedbórz
Końskie
Szydłowiec
Pławno
Częstochowa
Radoszyce
Pilica
Kurzelów
Iłża
Solec
Sienno
Koniecpol
Małogoszcz
Janów
Kunów
Kielce
Lelów
Oksa
Żarki
Chęciny
Ożarów
Vistula
Szczekociny
Jędrzejów
Włodowice
Sieńsko
Łagów
Opatów
Siewierz
Rachów
Chmielnik
Żarnowiec
Pilica
Sławków
Pińczów
Książ
Sandomierz
Staszów
Olkusz
Miechów
Koprzywnica
Stopnica
Skalbmierz
Krzeszowice
Pacanów
Rozwadów
Iwanowice
Baranów
Nowy Korczyn
Proszowice
Opatowiec
Mielec
Nowe Brzesko
KRAKÓW
Koszyce
San
Podgórze
Wieliczka
Dąbrowa
Przecław
Radomyśl
Kolbuszowa
Krzywaczka
Danajetz
Bochnia
Sokołów
Tarnów
Wojnicz
Dębica
Pilzno
Jordanów
Rzeszów

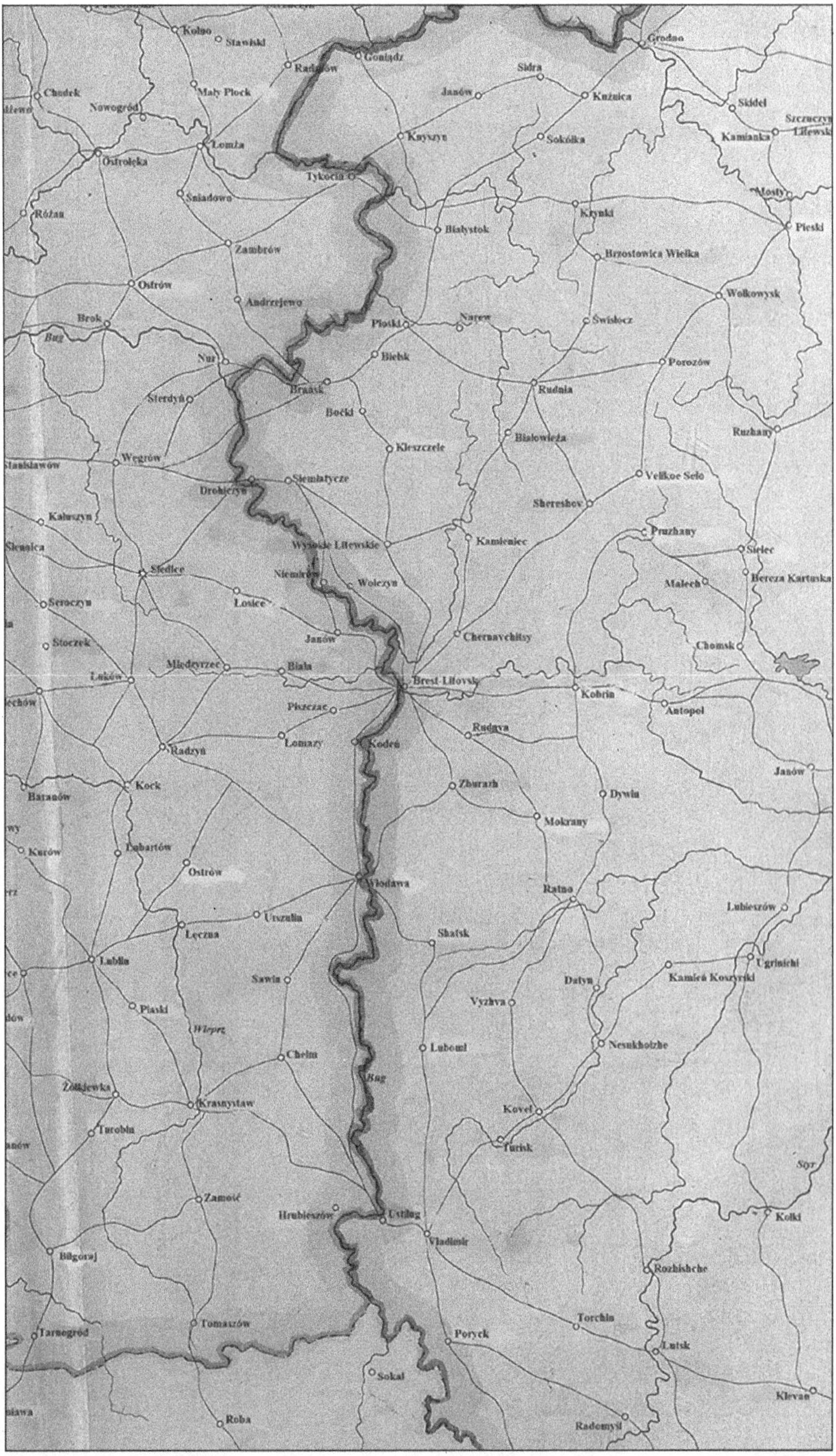
Kolno
Stawiski
Grodno
Goniądz
Sidra
Chudek
Mały Płock
Janów
Kuźnica
Skidel
Nowogród
Knyszyn
Sokółka
Kamianka
Ostrołęka
Łomża
Tykocin
Śniadowo
Mosty
Różan
Krynki
Białystok
Pieski
Zambrów
Brzostowica Wielka
Ostrów
Wołkowysk
Andrzejewo
Brok
Płoski
Narew
Świsłocz
Bug
Nur
Bielsk
Porozów
Brańsk
Rudnia
Sterdyń
Boćki
Ruzhany
Białowieża
Kleszczele
Węgrów
Velikoe Selo
Siemiatycze
Drohiczyn
Shereshov
Kałuszyn
Pruzhany
Wysokie Litewskie
Kamieniec
Sielec
Siedlce
Niemirów
Bereza Kartuska
Malech
Wołczyn
Seroczyn
Łosice
Chernavchitsy
Stoczek
Janów
Chomsk
Międzyrzec
Biała
Łuków
Brest-Litovsk
Kobrin
Antopol
Piszczac
Rudnya
Łomazy
Radzyń
Kodeń
Janów
Kock
Zhurazh
Baranów
Dywin
Mokrany
Lubartów
Kurów
Ostrów
Włodawa
Ratno
Lubieszów
Urszulin
Łęczna
Shatsk
Lublin
Ugrinichi
Datyn
Kamień Koszyrski
Sawin
Vyzhva
Piaski
Wieprz
Luboml
Chełm
Nesukhoizhe
Bug
Żółkiewka
Krasnystaw
Kovel
Turobin
Turisk
Styr
Zamość
Hrubieszów
Ustilug
Kolki
Vladimir
Biłgoraj
Rozhishche
Torchin
Tomaszów
Tarnogród
Poryck
Lutsk
Sokal
Klevan
Roba
Radomyśl

1

The situation at the beginning of 1813

The political situation in Europe; was it possible for Emperor Alexander I to avoid a continuation of the war?

The advance of the Russian forces to the Vistula. – The action at Marienwerder. – The siege of Danzig and the seizure of the fortress of Pillau. – The siege of Thorn. – The departure of Admiral Chichagov. – Murat's departure. – The Viceroy's acceptance of command over the remnants of the *Grande Armée*; the composition and disposition of his troops. – The seizure of Warsaw by Russian forces; Schwarzenberg's and Poniatowski's retreat to the Pilica, while Reynier withdrew to the Warta. – The pursuit of Reynier by Wintzingerode's detachment. – Action at Kalisz. – The advance of Russian forces from the Vistula to the Oder. – Action at Sieraków. – The Viceroy's retreat behind the Oder. – The inaction of the main body of the Russian army in anticipation of the accession of Prussia to the Coalition against Napoleon.

Few events have had such an important impact on the fate of nations as the invasion of Russia by the *Grande Armée*. This devastating war, which incinerated a wide swathe over the entire distance from the Neman to Moscow, and marked Napoleon's return path with heaps of corpses, guns, carts abandoned by the enemy; piles of ruins lay on the sites of towns and villages; the inhabitants of the devastated countryside wandered dismally, plunged into poverty and despair. Despite the efforts of the Russian government to ease the burden of evil that had fallen on these victims, the traces of the Patriotic War remained indelible for a long time. The moral influence of Napoleon's victories had been replaced by a feeling of confidence in Russia in their forces tested in practice; but the people, who had made huge sacrifices and suffered innumerable losses, felt a need for peace to heal the wounds inflicted by the war, while the Russian forces, weakened, wearied by unprecedented hardship, needed to rest. Kutuzov [Mikhail Illarionovich Golenishchev-Kutuzov], already at the end of his days himself, and many of his colleagues wished for an end to the war and considered it beneficial to open negotiations, which, in their opinion, would have crowned Russia's triumph with an honourable peace.

And indeed – the conqueror, who had intended to bend all of Europe to his will, despite the blow inflicted on his pride by the failure of the war of 1812, was ready to make peace with Emperor Alexander, on terms favourable to Russia. Subsequently, having already arrived in Erfurt with a powerful army, Napoleon expressed his inclination towards an alliance with Russia, saying: 'The swiftest and most reasonable would be – to agree directly with Emperor Alexander. I have always regarded Poland as an asset, but not as a principal concern. By satisfying Russia over Poland we have a means of humiliating Austria and reducing her to nothing. What concessions would Emperor Alexander not make if, to extricate himself from embarrassment, Poland might be ceded to him? One mission to Russian headquarters could divide the world in two.'[1]

If Napoleon, in the bosom of a large new army, was ready not only to stop the war, but also to enter into an alliance with Russia, then there is no reason to doubt his inclination towards peace at a time when the *Grande Armée* no longer existed, and when he was proposing to generate new forces. We note that at the beginning of 1813, the Russian operational forces had been extremely weakened by the winter campaign, and the reserves were still far off; the Russian state finances were depleted; the assistance of Prussia, the only one of the German domains on which Russia had any right to hope, would not be of much use, due to the exhaustion of the finances of this state, while the ambiguous position adopted by Austria, in the event of a defeat, threatened the opening of hostile operations from Galicia across the lines of communication of the Russian army. On the other hand, Napoleon's resources, despite the losses he had suffered, were huge: France, thanks to the indemnities exacted from defeated states by the right of might, had not become financially impoverished; its population could put up a huge army once again; while the fear inspired in Europe by the many years of victories of the French armed forces, compelled all of Napoleon's neighbours, except for the Spanish alone, to submit to the will of the conqueror and fight in the ranks of his armies.

Thus, almost all the material advantages were on Napoleon's side; while on Emperor Alexander I's side there was only hope for the readiness of Germany to join Him, and even then only in the event of success by Russian forces. In preparing to continue the war outside of Russia, He became the defender of all nations oppressed by French warmongering. He was fascinated by the lofty calling destined for Him by Almighty Providence. Indeed, could Emperor Alexander even rely on the solidity of treaties with Napoleon? The weakening of his power was the only guarantee of their observance, and this objective could not be achieved without another war, which was intended to put an end to French hegemony on mainland Europe.[2]

1 *'Le plus court et le plus raisonnable serait – à s'entendre directement avec l'empereur Alexandre. J'ai toujours regardé la Pologne comme un moyen, mais pas comme une affaire principale. En satisfaisant la Russie sur la Pologne nous avons un moyen, d'humilier l'Autriche et la reduire à rien. Quelle concession ne ferait pas l'empereur Alexandre, si pour se tirer d'embarras, on lui céderait la Pologne? Une mission au quartier-général russe partagerait le monde eu deux.' Lebensbilder aus dem Befreiungskriege*, III, 464.

2 *'D'après ce que Votre Majesté a daigné me confier sur le but actuel de Sa politique, Elle viserait à retablir en Europe un ordre de choses, qui en lui assurant le plus long intervalle de paix possible, donnerait également à la Russie les seules garanties solides contre de nouvelles entreprises qu'enfanterait l'ambition de Bonaparte.*

But in order to fully appreciate the determination that one had to possess in order to undertake a new struggle against a brilliant commander who had vast resources from the majority of Europe at his disposal, it is necessary to review the contemporaneous situation of the German states and to reiterate that at the beginning of 1813 Russia could not feel hopeful of their friendly assistance at all.

The Kingdom of Prussia, reduced to the status of a secondary power under the terms of the Tilsit Treaty, and, according to Napoleon, owing its continued existence solely to the intercession of Emperor Alexander I, was also completely dependent on France.[3] Prussia had been forced to pay huge war reparations, while foreign garrisons had been placed in all the most important Prussian fortresses until such time as the final settlement of these reparations to the French government. The inhabitants of Prussia were burdened with all kinds of obligations, to which there appeared to be no limit. Just as Brennus had responded to Roman criticism for his oppression with: 'woe to the vanquished' Napoleon wrote to Marshal Davout [Louis Nicolas Davout]: 'make Prussia pay, and once they have paid everything, they still owe us.'[4] It goes without saying that, acting in this way, Napoleon could not doubt the ill will of the Prussian nation towards him; his every effort was bent towards disarming the state, which, sooner or later, had to take revenge on him for all the losses and abuse. Napoleon, wishing to prevent any hostile attempt on the part of the Prussian government, obliged them to limit their army such that it would not exceed 42,000 men under any circumstances.[5] It appeared that nothing lay ahead for Prussia but slavish obedience to the whims of the conqueror, so long as it pleased him to prolong their miserable existence.

Despite the plight of Prussia after the conclusion of the Treaty of Tilsit and the general despondency and hopelessness among the people and the army, the government set about reforming many institutions that had become outdated and incompatible with current circumstances. But all these reforms were suspended due to the disagreements that had arisen between Russia and France. It was easy to foresee that Napoleon, by moving through Prussia with innumerable forces, could deal with them as with a conquered country, exhaust their resources and destroy the last vestiges of the independent existence of the monarchy. This forced Friedrich Wilhelm III to seek a favourable alliance with Napoleon and the participation of Prussia in the war against Emperor Alexander I: there is no doubt that at such a cost, the most unbearable of all, fell heavily on the heart of the King, a friend of our Tsar; but he decided to drain the cursed cup to the dregs, waiting for the dawn of the liberation of Germany. Half of the small Prussian army became part of Napoleon's

La manière la plus complette dont ce but pourrait être atteint serait sans doute que la France fut refoulée dans ses limites naturelles; que tout ce qui n'est pas situé entre le Rhin, l'Escaut, les Pyrenées et les Alpes cessat d'être soit partie integrante de l'empire français, soit même sous sa dépendance. C'est là assurement le maximum de tous les voeux que nous puissions former. Mais ils ne siauraient être réalisés sans le concours de l'Autriche et de la Prusse…' From a note submitted to Emperor Alexander I by Count Nesselrode (archive of the Foreign Ministry [A.F.M.]).

3 The Treaty of Tilsit between Russia and France, dated 7 July 1807, new style, Article 4.

4 '*faites payer la Prusse, et quand elle payera tout, elle nous devra encore.*'

5 The convention concluded in Paris on 8 September 1808 new style. Secret proviso.

horde, and measures taken to form an armed force in the event of an uprising against the common oppressor were interrupted by the flooding of the country with French troops.

The occupation of Moscow by the French had seemed a great feat that confirmed the dominance of Napoleon in the eyes of Europe. Even he, not considering a further offensive, hoped for a favourable peace and believed that the Russian government, terrified of the deep incursion by the French army, would hasten to open negotiations. Having been denied this hope, Napoleon undertook a retreat, the consequences of which were the complete destruction of the *Grande Armée* and the defection of Yorck [Johann David Ludwig von Yorck] from the French. These events jerked Prussia out of unconscious slumber but they were so unexpected that the population, oppressed by Napoleon, could hardly believe what was happening in front of their eyes, and could not suddenly become accustomed to the idea of liberation from the yoke imposed upon them. In addition, the fortresses on the Oder and the capital of Prussia itself, where the King was resident at the time, were occupied by French forces. The wounds inflicted on Prussia in the war of 1806 were still fresh, when this state had incomparably greater resources than in 1813, having lost half of its territory and paying Napoleon a huge war indemnity. And for this reason, the enthusiasm that prevailed among the people and the Prussian troops was not shared by the government, which, discussing the state of affairs dispassionately, tried to moderate the impulses of popular opinion. In obedience to the forces of circumstance, the King relieved generals Yorck and Massenbach [Eberhard Friedrich Fabian von Massenbach] of command of their forces, and ordered that the former be brought to court martial; at the same time, orders were sent to General Kleist [Friedrich Emil Ferdinand Heinrich von Kleist] to take command of the corps and be, as before, at the disposal of the *Empereur des Français* and his deputy, the king of Naples[6]. *Flügeladjutant* [equerry] Natzmer [Oldwig Anton Leopold von Natzmer], who had been sent to General Yorck's *Hauptquartier* [headquarters] bearing these orders, had been given a letter for Emperor Alexander, in which the King offered the Russian government a defensive and offensive alliance with Prussia, in the event that this state were forced to wage war against Napoleon, and asked for the unceasing advance by our forces to continue from the Vistula [Wisła] to the Oder. It was easy to predict that Natzmer would not get to the Prussian corps, stuck behind Russian lines, and therefore Yorck remained in command of the corps, as before; as for the secret mission assigned to Natzmer, he returned with an answer from Emperor Alexander, dated 1 (13) January, which included unconditional consent to all the King's proposals. This letter was delivered in Berlin by Natzmer on the night of 19 to 20 January new style, and at the same time intelligence was received that orders had been given to Marshal Augereau [Charles Pierre François Augereau] to detain the King's Person, which forced Friedrich-Wilhelm to bring forward his proposed departure to Silesia. On 10 (22) January, two days later, after the announcement of the order to dismiss Yorck in the Berlin newspapers, the King, together with the Crown Prince, set off from Potsdam for Breslau [Wrocław], where he arrived on 13 (25)

6 Murat.

January; the *Leibgarde* followed on. The leading men of Prussia gathered in Breslau: *Staatskanzler* [Prime Minister] Baron Hardenberg [Karl August von Hardenberg]; Scharnhorst [Gerhard Johann David von Scharnhorst], overtly assumed control of the *Kriegsministerium* [War Office] once more; heroes of the Prussian army, General Blücher [Gebhard Leberecht von Blücher] and General Gneisenau [August Wilhelm Anton Neidhardt von Gneisenau]. In order to dispel misunderstandings between the Prussian and French governments, Graf Hatzfeld [Franz Ludwig von Hatzfeld zu Trachenberg], who enjoyed Napoleon's special favour, was sent to Paris with a proposal to send a new auxiliary corps, as strong as the former, in order to assist the French. Following this, the King sent General Krusemarck [Friedrich Wilhelm Ludwig von Krusemarck] to Paris, asking that, in order to facilitate the proposed manning of the army, the French government should pay Prussia for supplies for Napoleon's forces, in excess of the outstanding debt, to the sum of 94,000,000 francs (about 25,000,000 silver roubles). King Friedrich Wilhelm also expressed a desire that French troops occupying Danzig [Gdańsk] and the fortresses on the Oder, Stettin [Szczecin], Küstrin [Kostrzyn nad Odrą] and Glogau [Głogów] be withdrawn from there and replaced by Prussian garrisons.[7] Had Napoleon at least partly fulfilled these requirements, then Friedrich Wilhelm, in all probability, would have returned to Berlin[8].

But how easy was it to predict that Napoleon would not agree to such proposals, the King, without waiting for a response, took measures for the rapid mobilisation of the armed forces in the greatest possible numbers. The results of the measures taken exceeded the hopes of everyone, even the King himself; but in anticipation of the assembly of the Prussian *Landwehr* [militia] and Prussia's obvious edging

7 Schoell, *Histoire abrégée des traités de paix*, III, 262. Droysen, *Das Leben des Feldmarschals Grafen York*, II, 119-120. Thiers, *Histoire du Consulat et de l'Empire, Ed. de Brux.* XV, 230. Baron Hardenberg, in a note addressed to the French ambassador, Comte Saint-Marsan, wrote: '*Il est venu au roi l'idée que rien n'avancerait plus la grande œuvre de la paix qu'une trève d'après la quelle les armées russes et françaises se retireraient à une certaine distance et établireient une ligne de démarcation en laissant un pays intermediare entre elles. L'empereur Napoléon serait-il porté à entrer dans un pareil arrangement? Consentirait-il à remettre la garde des forteresses de l'Oder et de celle de Dantzic aux troupes prussiennes conjointement avec les troupes saxonnes, et de retirer son armée jusqu'à l'Elbe, moyennant que l'empereur Alexandre retirerait toutes ses troupes derrière la Vistule.*' Note dated 15 February 1813, new style.

8 This is confirmed by the following lines from a letter to Emperor Alexander I from former Prussian Minister Stein, dated February 1813: '*L'annonce de l'arrivée de Votre Majesté Impériale à Breslau me fait supposer qu'Elle agréera avec bonté les observations suivantes sur l'esprit public et de la cour que j'ai été à même de recueillir: l'esprit général est parfait. Tous les états sont animés du desir de briser les fers, dans les quels Napoléon les tient; l'affluance des volontaires aux régiments est très grande et il ne faudrait qu'un Souverain capable lui-même d'exaltation, d'une volonté grande et forte, pour porter l'enthousiasme au plus haut dégré et lui donner la plus grande étendue. Malheureusement ce n'est point le cas: le Roi est froid; il n'a que des demi-volontés; il n'a de confiance ni en soi, ni dans son peuple; il croit que la Russie l'entraine dans un abyme et qu'en peu les armées françaises se trouveront sur la Vistule.*
Cette manière de voir est decourageante pour les gens bien pensants; elle est pernicieuse pour l'action qu'elle paralyse, elle trouve son principe dans le caractère de l'individu et dans l'atmosphère de la nullité, peut-être même de la perfidie, dont il s'est entouré...' Stein's own handwritten letter to the Tsar is held in the A.F.M.

towards an alliance against Napoleon, Russia would continue the struggle under its own resources, exhausted by the war of 1812.

Russia held out even less hope for assistance from Austria. The participation in Napoleon's invasion in 1812 by Austrian forces was involuntary: The Austrians could not forget the humiliations inflicted upon them by the conqueror, and the Viennese Cabinet, although it observed the terms of the treaty of alliance concluded with Napoleon impeccably, was constantly in communications with the Russian government. Having preserved their army, while the military forces of Russia and France were exhausted, and Prussia had not yet had time to form new forces, the Austrian government was in a very advantageous position, yet still did not dare to rebel against Napoleon, who, although he had lost a huge army in Russia, nevertheless could (as it turned out later) muster another. In addition, neither family ties, nor his sense of decency, allowed Kaiser Franz to suddenly turn from an ally into an open enemy of his son-in-law. The Austrian government preferred to act subtly, gradually moving from an alliance with Napoleon to mediation between the belligerent states, and then from mediation to an alliance with the enemies of France. In order to achieve this objective, all of Metternich's [Klemens Wenzel Lothar von Metternich] resourcefulness was needed, who at the same time informed the French ambassador in Vienna, Otto [Louis-Guillaume Otto], that Napoleon's enemies had offered Italy, Illyria and dominance in Germany to Austria, and sent the wily Lebzeltern [Ludwig von Lebzeltern] to Emperor Alexander, offering Austrian mediation. But, with the success of Napoleon's mobilisation, the views of the Austrian government in relation to Russia became more and more equivocal.[9]

In Saxony, as in every German land in general, displeasure and hatred for the French and their ruler prevailed among the people, while the Saxon troops who returned from Russia, despite respect for their commander, the French General Reynier [Jean-Louis-Ébénézer Reynier], were imbued with a sense of dread over the danger and destruction that threatened their fatherland with the impending clash of the belligerent parties.[10] The King himself abandoned his capital and went first to

9 *Mémoires tirés des papiers d'un homme d'état*, XII, 59 & 63. Count Stackelberg, who was the agent of the Russian government in Vienna, during the war of 1812, wrote in this regard to Chancellor Count Rumyantsev, on 14 (26) January 1813. Colonel Pozzo di Borgo also outlined the views of Austria in a note submitted to Emperor Alexander I dated 24 March (5 April) 1813. For the text of these latter documents, see Appendix I at the end of this chapter.

10 'Even more depressing was the prospect of the fatherland's uncertain future, whose protectors brought back not peace but war. And they were not to blame for any of this, but rather the reckless desire for conquest by the man who, in his public Bulletins, did not even consider their deeds worthy of mention, for whom they had fruitlessly sacrificed an arduous year. Bitter indignation now took the place of admiration in their hearts, and the thought that their homeland should be exposed to all the tribulations of a country in a theatre of war turned their anger into hatred for Napoleon and for everything French.' '... *Noch niederschlagender war die Aussicht auf die ungewisse Zukunft des Vaterlandes, dem seine Beschützer nicht den Frieden, sondern den Krieg mit zurückbrachten. Und von dem allen trugen nicht sie die Schuld, sondern allein die unbesonnene Eroberungsucht des Mannes, der in seinem öffentlichen Nachrichten ihre Thaten nicht einmal einer Erwähnung würdig hielt, dem sie umsonst ein mühseliges Jahr geopfert hatten. An die Stelle der Bewunderung trat in ihrer Brust nun bitterer Unwille und der Gedanke, dass ihre Heimath allen Drangsalen der*

Plauen, then to Regensburg [Ratisbon, 25 miles south of Schwandorf], and finally to Prague, where he came under the protection of Austria, in anticipation of further events. But in announcing his departure from Dresden, the King expressed the hope of returning to Saxony with the assistance of his powerful ally.[11] The other German princes, closer to France, or ruling through the grace of Napoleon, implicitly obeyed his will. The population of Germany hated the French, but encountering resistance from their rulers, and despairing that this thing that weighed on them would never be overthrown, they grumbled, but did not dare to rebel openly against the common enemy.[12]

Such was the situation in Germany at the beginning of 1813, at the time when Emperor Alexander I expressed his readiness to continue the struggle against Napoleon. German historians have ascribed all the honour of the resolve of our Sovereign – to stand up for the liberation of Germany – to their countryman, Stein [Heinrich Friedrich Karl vom und zum Stein]. Indeed, Stein rendered memorable service to his fatherland and all of Europe by arousing public opinion against Napoleon; but if Emperor Alexander had not decided to follow through on the work conceived by Stein and other enthusiasts for German independence, then all of Stein's plans would have dissipated like the dreams of Schlegel [Karl Wilhelm Friedrich Schlegel] and Dr. Jahn [Johann Friedrich Ludwig Christoph Jahn].[13]

As for Sweden, although the Stockholm Cabinet, under an agreement with Russia, from 24 March (5 April), 1812, undertook to mount a diversion on the northern coast of Germany by a 25,000 or 30,000 strong corps, but not before annexing Norway as a Swedish territory. Subsequently, this condition was cancelled, and under an agreement concluded with Britain, Sweden undertook to immediately assist the Russian forces with a corps of at least 30,000.[14] But at the opening of the campaign of 1813, Russia was unable to hope for any assistance from Sweden; Britain's participation was limited to subsidies, the agreements on which would only be concluded by June, during the armistice.[15]

Länder eines Kriegsschauplatzes ausgesetzt worden sollte, werwandelte ihren Zorn in Hass gegen Napoleon und gegen Alles was französisch war.' Erinnerungen aus dem Feldzuge in Russland im Jahr 1812 des Sächsischen Corps unter dem General Grafen Reynier, aus den Papeiren des Generallieutenants von Funck, 204-205.

11 *Mémoires tirés des papiers d'un homme d'état*, XII, 86.

12 *Mémoires tirés des papiers d'un homme d'état*, XII, 51. Colonel Pozzo di Borgo's note submitted to Emperor Alexander I dated 24 March (5 April) 1813 also mentions this. See Appendix I at the end of this chapter.

13 In Germany, as early as 1808, societies had been formed called *Tugendbund* (Society for the Practice of Public Virtues) among others, whose common goal was to liberate the fatherland from Napoleonic rule, through the transformation of Germany: some wanted the restoration of the ancient *Reich* with its districts, electors and diets; others wanted the division of Germany into two Empires: a northern (Prussian) and a southern (Austrian); finally, the third group sought to establish a German republic. The main proponent of the former system was Friedrich Schlegel, and the latter, Dr. Jahn. *Mémoires tirés des papiers d'un homme d'état*, XII, 51-53.

14 Treaty concluded in Stockholm on 3 May 1813, new style, Article 1.

15 Subsidy agreements were concluded in Reichenbach: between Britain and Prussia on 2 (14) June, and between Britain and Russia on 3 (15) June, 1813.

Let us turn to a presentation of the initial operations in 1813.

Yorck's defection from the French, the crossing of the Neman by Russian forces at the end of 1812, and their liberation of Königsberg [Kaliningrad] on 25 December (6 January 1813), marked the opening of the new campaign. The remnants of the enemy army had been ejected across our borders and the Russian Monarch, at the head of his people, having accomplished the liberation of the fatherland, was preparing to wrest Europe from many years of subjugation.

At the beginning of the year, our troops were distributed as follows;[16] Admiral Chichagov's [Pavel Vasilievich Chichagov] former Army of the Danube, Count Wittgenstein's [Pëtr Khristianovich Vitgenshtein or Ludwig Adolf Peter zu Sayn-Wittgenstein] force and Platov's [Matvey Ivanovich Platov] Cossack detachment, numbering some 55,000 men, were moving towards Elbing [Elbląg] and Thorn [Toruń], on the lower Vistula, while the remainder were heading for Płock and Warsaw, on the middle Vistula. On 31 December (12 January 1813), French forces, having evacuated Elbing, were retreating to Marienwerder [Kwidzyn]. During the night of 1 (13) January, Adjutant General Chernyshev [Alexander Ivanovich Chernyshev], marching as Platov's vanguard with ten Cossack regiments, attacked the enemy who were holding the latter town, where the Viceroy [Eugène Rose de Beauharnais], Marshal Victor [Claude-Victor Perrin] and many French generals were also located at that time. The enemy detachment fled over the ice, on the road to Poznań [Posen], abandoning 15 guns and several hundred prisoners as booty for the men of the Don. After that, Count Wittgenstein, upon crossing the Vistula at Dirschau [Tczew], assimilated 24 Cossack regiments which had been under Platov's direct command into his force (Platov had received orders to serve in the headquarters). He also detached Lieutenant General Löwis [Fëdor Fëdorovich Leviz or Friedrich von Löwis of Menar] to Danzig with 12,000 men in order to monitor this fortress. Three raiding detachments were formed from these Cossacks, under the command of Chernyshev, Benckendorff [Alexander Khristoforovich Benkendorf or Konstantin Alexander Karl Wilhelm Christoph von Benckendorff] and Tettenborn [Friedrich Karl von Tettenborn],[17] being sent forwards to operate on the left flank and rear of the Viceroy but had halted in Stargard until 1 (13) February, in anticipation of the arrival of the Western Army (formerly the Army of the Danube) on the Vistula, which, after the departure of Admiral Chichagov to St Petersburg, due to illness, came under the command of Barclay de Tolly [Mikhail Bogdanovich Barklay de Tolli or Michael Andreas Barclay de Tolly] and was subordinated to Count Wittgenstein. Meanwhile, a detachment under Major General Count Sievers 1st [Karl Karlovich Sivers or Carl Gustav von Sievers] had forced the Pillau [Baltiysk, Kaliningrad *Oblast*] fortress to surrender in capitulation.[18]

Chichagov, for his part, after granting his force a rest in winter quarters in the vicinity of Jezno [Jieznas] on the Neman, set out on 17 (29) December for Gumbinnen [Gusev, Kaliningrad *Oblast*], and onwards through Heilsberg [Lidzbark Warmiński]

16 See Map No. 1 Theatre of Military Operations 1813.
17 For details of Russian formations and detachments, see Appendix II at the end of this chapter.
18 Major General Count Sievers' report to Count Wittgenstein, dated 27 January [8 February], No. 202.

to Thorn, blockading this fortress on 16 (28) January, and having sent his vanguard, under the command of Count Vorontsov [Mikhail Semënovich Vorontsov], forwards towards Poznań, settled at Bromberg [Bydgoszcz] on 31 January (12 February) in order to cover the blockade of Thorn. Two days later, on 2 (14) February, having handed over command of his force to Barclay de Tolly, he set off for St Petersburg.

No sooner had our forces set off for the lower Vistula, where the remnants of the *Grande Armée* were then assembling, than the King of Naples (Murat [Joachim Murat]) unilaterally gave up command of the force entrusted to him by Napoleon and, handing it over to the Viceroy on 4 (16) January, left for his kingdom. The Viceroy had managed to assemble no more than 12,000 men in Poznań, among whom were several hundred Bavarian and Lithuanian cavalry. These troops were divided into three divisions: one French under Gérard [Étienne Maurice Gérard] and one Polish under Girard [Jean-Baptiste Girard] were stationed in Poznań; one Bavarian under Wrede's [Carl Philipp von Wrede] command, and then, due to his illness, under the command of Rechberg [Anton von Rechberg], at Gniezno; while the Lithuanian cavalry under Major General Prince Giedroyć [Romuald Giedroyć] were at Zirke [Sieraków] on the Warta. On 11 (23) February, two newly reformed battalions of *Jeune Garde* arrived in Poznań from Stettin, which, together with the two battalions of *Vieille Garde* co-located with the Viceroy's *quartier-général* [headquarters], made up a reserve division, numbering 2,000 men, under the command of General Roguet [François Roguet].[19] Napoleon, having received a report from the Prince de Neuchâtel (Berthier [Louis-Alexandre Berthier]) about Murat's act, announced in *Le Moniteur universel* that the King of Naples, due to illness, had been forced to give up command of the army, handing it over to the Viceroy, who was more familiar with high-level administration, and that he enjoyed the absolute confidence of the Emperor.[20]

As has already been mentioned above, with the exception of the forces under Chichagov, Wittgenstein and Platov, all other Russian formations had been directed towards the middle Vistula. The main army, being somewhat replenished by five infantry regiments under the command of Prince Urusov [Alexander Petrovich Urusov?], who had arrived in Vilna [Vilnius] on 15 (27) December,[21] was marching on Płock and Warsaw: the right column, consisting of the Grenadier Corps (III Corps), Lifeguard Corps (V Corps) and two cuirassier divisions, under the command of General-of-Cavalry Tormasov [Alexander Petrovich Tormasov],[22] numbering 17,000 men, was assigned to envelope Schwarzenberg's [Karl Philipp Fürst zu Schwarzenberg] force retreating to Warsaw from the left flank, set off from Vilna on 28 December [9 January 1813] crossed the Neman at Merecz [Merkinė], on

19 Norvins, *Portefeuille de 1813* , I, 88. Vaudoncourt, *Histoire de la guerre soutenue par les Français en Allemagne en 1813*, 20-25.

20 *'Le roi de Naples étant indisposé a dû quitter le commandement de l'armée qu'il a remis au viceroi. Ce dernier a plus l'habitude d'une grande admiistration: il a la confiance entière de l'empereur.' Moniteur du 27 fevrier 1813.*

21 War Diary, signed off by Prince Kutuzov.

22 War Diary. General Overview of Movements and Operations by Russian and Coalition Forces in the War against the French in 1812, 1813 and 1814, compiled by Lieutenant General Khatov.

1 (13) January, and having marched over the Prussian border near the town of Lyck [Ełk] on 7 (19) January, headed for Płock where this force arrived on 24 January (5 February), together with the headquarters of Emperor Alexander I and Prince Kutuzov. The Tsar was greeted with extraordinary enthusiasm in Lyck and in every other Prussian town, where he addressed the inhabitants very frequently, declaring that he had not come to them as a conqueror, but as a friend of their king and nation, and that he was convinced of the urgent need for their alliance with the Russians for the common good of both monarchies. The field marshal, shying from every expression of gratitude from the population, repeated that it was not he, but God himself who had struck Napoleon.[23]

Direct operations against Schwarzenberg had been assigned to Miloradovich [Mikhail Andreevich Miloradovich], with part of IV Corps and VII Corps, with Korff's [Fëdor Karlovich Korf or Friedrich Nikolai Georg von Korff] cavalry and Sacken's force [Fabian Vilgelmovich Osten-Saken or Fabian Gottlieb von der Osten-Sacken]. II Corps under Prinz Eugen von Württemberg [Friedrich Eugen Karl Paul Ludwig von Württemberg], Tuchkov's [Sergei Alexeevich Tuchkov] corps and several light detachments, under the overall command of Adjutant General Wintzingerode [Ferdinand Fëdorovich Vintsingerode or Ferdinand von Wintzingerode], were marching from Grodno to Chorzele and joined the vanguard of Tormasov's column directed on Płock; while upon reaching Mława, they were sent via Bieżuń and Włocławek, in order to intercept the Saxon corps under Reynier, which was retreating from Warsaw towards the Oder. Miloradovich's force followed Schwarzenberg straight towards Warsaw. Upon the occupation of this city, on 27 January (8 February), as a result of a convention concluded with the Austrian Commander-in-Chief, this force proceeded ahead of the Main Army (Tormasov's right column), towards Kalisz, with the exception of Paskevich's [Ivan Fëdorovich Paskevich] VII Corps, Bulatov's [Mikhail Leontievich Bulatov] and Count Lieven 3rd's [Ivan Andreevich Liven or Johann Georg von Lieven] corps and General Rath's [Semën Lukich Radt or Simon Rath] detachment,[24] assigned to occupy Warsaw and to blockade the fortresses of Modlin and Zamość.[25]

The entrance by Russian troops into Warsaw was the result of an agreement between Miloradovich and Schwarzenberg. A truce was concluded for an indefinite period as early as 18 (30) January, but with a condition: in the event of a resumption of hostilities, they were to warn each other 15 days in advance. Upon the arrival of the forces under Sacken and Miloradovich outside Warsaw, Schwarzenberg agreed to surrender the city, but. in order to do justice to the honour of the Austrian armed forces and to avoid any criticism from his allies, he requested:

23 Sporschill, *Die grosse Chronik*, I, 69.

24 Lieutenant General Rath's corps was formed from some of the battalions that had moved up under his command, and arrived to replenish Sacken's force, and part of Sacken's corps, which had remained on the Bug under the command of Lieutenant General Musin-Pushkin in order to monitor the border of the Duchy of Warsaw.

25 War Diary. General Overview of Movements and Operations by Russian and Coalition Forces in 1812, 1813 and 1814, compiled by Lieutenant General Khatov.

1. To not categorise sick combatants who were in Warsaw hospitals as prisoners of war, no matter what their nationality.
2. To treat them with humanitarian care.
3. To not punish residents who harboured a hostile disposition towards Russia in words or in deeds.

Miloradovich replied:

> I shall request permission from Prince Kutuzov for the first article; as for the latter two, there is no need to agree conditions on them, because the whole world knows the mercy of the Emperor: it has always served as the foundations of the behaviour of Russian troops.

On 26 January (7 February), a deputation from Warsaw visited Miloradovich in the Mokotów suburb, consisting of the prefect, sub-prefect, mayor, commander of the *Gwardia Narodowa* [national guard], two commissioners of the duchy administration and three senior members of the clergy; among these personalities there were none from the honourable noble families. The prefect greeted Miloradovich with bread and salt; the keys of the city themselves were presented by the same official who had handed them over to Suvorov [Alexander Vasilievich Suvorov] in 1794. Miloradovich, in response to the greetings of the deputies, replied that the Tsar had ordered Warsaw to be spared from military quartering. He continued: 'Moreover, you will see, not in words, but in deeds, how Russians treat the population, fulfilling the will of the most merciful of Monarchs.' Then, addressing the representatives of the clergy, he said: 'you, more than anyone else, have reason to rejoice at current events, you, who, according to your duties, should strive above all others for order and calm.'[26]

The capture of Warsaw dealt a mortal blow to the hopes of the Polish magnates, supporters of Napoleon, and freed us from the need to weaken an already small army by detaching elements to cover the left flank of our line of operations. Emperor Alexander, having received a report of this new success, granted General Miloradovich a crowned Imperial monogram to be worn on his epaulettes. Prince Kutuzov, informing Miloradovich of this award, wrote to him:

> Your great deeds have brought you so much closer to our Most-August Emperor that with this privilege bestowed by Him upon you, it has become as necessary for you to be with the Person of His Imperial Majesty, as it is for Him.

After Warsaw had been evacuated by Schwarzenberg's force, the corps under Miloradovich's command settled in the vicinity of the city in accordance with all military precautions. Officers and soldiers were released to go into Warsaw only with specific individual permission, and even then only during daylight for a few

26 Anstett's letter to Prince Kutuzov, dated 27 January [8 February], from Wilanów, archive of the M.T.D. No. 29,182.

hours; no one was allowed to leave the city at night. Subsequently, once the troops had occasion to enter Warsaw as formed units, then several weak battalions were grouped together; batteries with a strong escort were placed in the city squares and at the gates; soldiers were not placed in quarters as individuals, but were stationed in public buildings, for the most part, by battalion. The *Gwardia Narodowa* were disarmed in a dignified manner, as Kutuzov had commanded in orders to Miloradovich. Guard forces were posted at the arsenal and magazines. The strictest order was commanded to be observed, not to start quarrels with the townspeople and not to offend them, either with criticism or with curses.

Schwarzenberg's force, which consisted of some 42,000 men at the evacuation of Warsaw, retreated in various directions: Prince Poniatowski [Józef Antoni Poniatowski] went to Piotrków [Petrikau], and on to Częstochowa, with the Polish contingent, whose numbers increased along the way as officers and soldiers joined them, while Reynier went to Kalisz with the Saxon corps.

As soon as intelligence was received at our headquarters on the direction taken by Reynier's force, the detachment under General Wintzingerode was sent from Włocławek to Kalisz to intercept them. Reynier, having set out from Warsaw a few days before Poniatowski and Schwarzenberg, and not knowing about the movements of Wintzingerode's detachment, had hoped to escape from Miloradovich's force in safety, as he could no longer catch up with them, and therefore retreated rather slowly and divided the corps into several columns; Wintzingerode's force caught up with them on 27 January (8 February), at the same time as the surrender of Warsaw, and pursued them to the outskirts of Kalisz over the following days.[27] On 1 (13) February, Reynier's *Poste de commandement* arrived in Kalisz; the division under Durutte [Pierre François Joseph Durutte] held the bridges over the Prosna river, as well as part of the town and suburbs on the right bank of the river, while the division under Le Coq [Karl Christian Erdmann von Le Coq], held the villages along the roads leading to Konin, Kłodawa and Sieradz. On our side, the main body of the corps, having set out early in the morning from the overnight halt at Rychwał, linked up with Lanskoy's [Sergei Nikolaevich Lanskoy] vanguard at Stawiszyn on the Konin road at noon. At one o'clock in the afternoon, the corps set off in a single column from Stawiszyn towards Kalisz and, upon leaving Russów, made contact with the enemy lined up for battle in front of the villages of Pawłówek, Kokanin and Borków. A Saxon battery stationed at Kokanin, opened fire on the Russian force, but the cavalry quickly lined up on both sides of the main road, under the command of Major General Lanskoy, supported by a cannonade from 7th Horse Artillery Company advanced into position by Major General Nikitin [Alexei Petrovich Nikitin]. Meanwhile, enemy cavalry emerging from the direction of Borków, attempted to attack us on the left flank, but the Cossacks and Alexandria Hussars, having foiled the attack, charged the *von Polenz Chevauxleger* and six grenadier companies, scattered them and captured General Nostitz [Karl von Nostitz-Drzewiecky] and Colonel von Hann. Major General Knorring [Karl Bogdanovich Knorring] and Colonel Prince Madatov [Valerian Grigorievich Madatov] particularly distinguished themselves

27 See Map No. 2 The Kalisz Area.

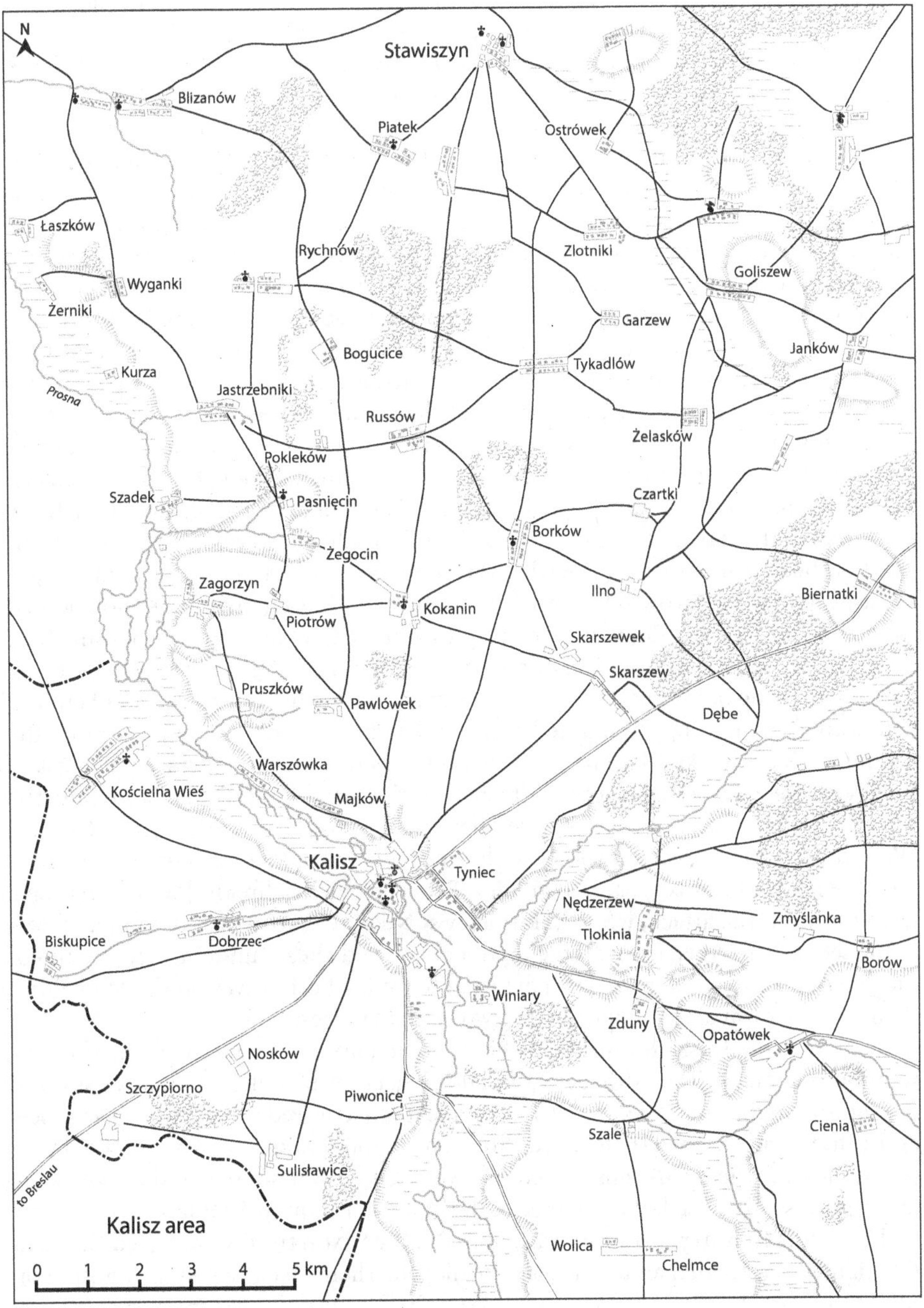

Map of the Kalisz area.

here. Whereupon General Wintzingerode, having detached the Belorussia Hussars, Livonia Mounted Jägers and Kuteynikov 4th's Cossack to the right of the main road in order to isolate the enemy defending Kokanin, ordered Major General Rennie [Robert Yegorovich Rennie] to seize this village with the 6th Jägers and 32nd Jägers. The enemy defended themselves very stubbornly, but were finally forced to yield to our troops, who captured many prisoners, two guns and a colour at this time; only three companies managed to break out and join Durutte's division at Kalisz. The detachment under Gablenz [Heinrich Adolph von Gablenz], while retreating from Skarszew towards Kalisz, were intercepted by cavalry in the defile at Winiary and separated from the Saxon force, but racing off on an alternate route, managed to escape towards Częstochowa. Meanwhile, the *Prinz Clemens Infanterie*, attacked at the very beginning of the battle by Colonel Paradovsky [Alexander Osipovich Paradovsky], with the Belorussia Hussars and Livonia Mounted Jägers, and then Major General Count Witt [Ivan Osipovich (Iosifovich) de Witt] with part of the reserve cavalry near the village of Pawłówek, held out there persistently, gaining time for the guns to get away; and after that, upon leaving the village, they formed up in two squares between which there were two guns: in this position, lashed by canister, the Saxons repelled several attacks and remained under heavy fire from our artillery for three hours; when at last their guns had fired all their projectiles, the detachment dashed to the Prosna, crossed to the other side of the river on very thin ice, or chest-deep in water, drowning several men, and abandoning their guns and rejoined the main force under Reynier retreating towards the Oder. Throughout all these actions, the brigade under *Generalmajor* von Sahr [Karl Otto Ludwig Sahrer von Sahr], consisting of four battalions with a light battery,[28] having gathered at Winiary behind the other troops, remained there under their protection, but after that the Saxons, being attacked by the cavalry under Major General Prince Trubetskoy [Vasily Sergeevich Trubetskoy], retreated to the suburb of Tyniec and into the town itself. Prinz Eugen von Württemberg, having received orders from General Wintzingerode to seize Kalisz, formed the divisions under Prince Shakhovskoy [Ivan Leontievich Shakhovskoy] and Schreider [Pëtr Petrovich Schreider] in the first wave in columns for the attack, while Bakhmetev's [Nikolai Nikolaevich Bakhmetev] was in the second. A screen from all the regiments moved ahead, under the command of Lieutenant Colonel Reibniz [Karl Pavlovich Reibniz]; both waves proceeded behind them; the first wave was supported by two large batteries.

As soon as the Russian cannonade had softened up the enemy force, the infantry went on the attack. The 4th Jägers and 20th Jägers immediately took possession of the suburb on the enemy left wing, but a wide ditch, covered with a thin sheet of ice, and a stone wall stopped them under fire from Saxon marksmen, who inflicted very painful losses. The enemy ensconced in several suburban houses on the right wing of the position held back the advance of the Tobolsk Infantry, Kremenchug Infantry and Volhynia Infantry in a similar fashion. But the Saxon troops evacuated Kalisz in the night and retreated along the road to Glogau. Their casualties in the fighting on

28 Von Sahr's brigade consisted of: von Spiegel's Grenadier Battalion, von Anger's Grenadier Battalion, von Eichelberg's Grenadier Battalion, *2. Leichte Infanterie von Sahr* and Captain Bonniot's six-pounder cannon battery. *Sachsen und seine Krieger*, 84.

1 (13) February and over the following days reached 1,500 men taken prisoner alone (including General Nostitz and 50 field officers and subalterns) and 1,500 men killed or wounded. Two colours [both from the *Prinz Anton Infanterie*] and six guns fell into the hands of the victors; on our side, 670 men were killed or wounded; among the wounded were major generals Schreider and Nikitin and Lieutenant Colonel Reibnitz.[29]

The ensuing pursuit was slow. Wintzingerode's corps, having reached Rawicz on the Silesian border, halted and sent partisan detachments under Davydov [Denis Vasilievich Davydov] and Prendel [Viktor Antonovich Prendel or Victor Anton Franz von Prendel] onto the left bank of the Oder. On 8 (20) February, Miloradovich's force moved from Warsaw towards Kalisz, where our headquarters arrived on 12 (24) February with the troops of the Main Army marching from Płock.[30]

At the same time as Wintzingerode's corps was moving towards Kalisz, the detachment under Major General Count Vorontsov from the Western Army (former Army of the Danube) was sent out from Bromberg towards Poznań, and an expedition was made from the lower Vistula to the Oder by a partisan detachment under the command of Adjutant General Chernyshev. At this time, the Viceroy was in Poznań with his main force, while Bülow [Friedrich Wilhelm von Bülow] was forming a force in Pomerania, whose mission was still unknown at that time: having been directed behind the Viceroy's lines (which exposed Chernyshev to the danger of losing communications with our other troops), it was necessary to secure himself from Bülow's direction. Captain Count Musin-Pushkin [Sergei Klavdievich Musin-Pushkin?], sent to the Prussian corps by Chernyshev for this purpose, returned with Bülow's response, stating: 'Not only will I not interfere with you, but I shall send an officer to the king to ask permission to act in concert with the Russians.' Thus, his security from Prussian forces ensured, Chernyshev moved on Schneidemühl [Piła] and Filehne [Wieleń]; there he learned about Prince Giedroyć located at Zirke with 2,000 Polish cavalry beyond the Warta. The ice on the river was barely holding, and therefore Giedroyć, considering himself completely safe from surprise attack, had stretched his detachment out from Wronki [15 miles east of Zirke] to Birnbaum [Międzychód, ten miles west of Zirke], more than 30 *verstas*. After sending out patrols, Chernyshev had no more than 500 Cossacks left, with two guns; but despite the small size of his detachment, he decided to continue moving without pause towards Zirke and, having covered a stage of about nine *Meilen* (more than 60 *verstas*) in one day, closed up to the town of Zirke on 30 January (11 February), as night was falling. As the lifting-bridge on the Warta had been raised and was guarded by a screen of skirmishers, Chernyshev sent Colonel Yefremov [Ivan Yefremovich Yefremov] onto the ice, who, having crossed the river, attacked

29 Adjutant General Wintzingerode's report to the Chief of the General Staff, Adjutant General Volkonsky, dated 4 [16] February, No. 255. Casualty returns for dead and wounded, attached to a report, dated 6 [18] February, No. 267. Communique attached to a report to Prince Kutuzov-Smolensky, dated 16 [28] February, No. 355 (Log of Incoming Documents, archive of the M.T.D. No. 29,182). Plotho, *Der Krieg in Deutschland und Frankreich*, I, 46. *Feldzüge der Sachsen in den Jahren 1812 und 1813*, 126-135. Prinz Eugen von Württemberg, *Extrait de mon journal militaire* etc. (archive of the M.T.D. No. 47,344).

30 War Diary.

the enemy from the rear, catching them by surprise, broke through to the lifting-bridge and, having lowered it, cleared the way for Chernyshev and the rest of the Cossacks together with the guns accompanying the detachment. The defeat of the enemy, taken by surprise, was total. *Général de division* Prince Giedroyć, his son (a colonel [Józef Stefan Frantisek Xavier Giedroyć]), 20 officers and 400 lower ranks were captured.[31]

From Zirke, General Chernyshev turned towards the town of Pinne [Pniewy], on the main road from Poznań to Frankfurt an der Oder, and headed for Driesen [Drezdenko], spreading alarm and confusion in the Viceroy's rear areas.[32]

At the same time as these operations were taking place, Count Vorontsov, having set out from Bromberg for Poznań, at the end of January [early February], received intelligence during the march about the location of four regiments of Polish troops and several depots in Rogoźno [Rogasen], numbering 2,000 men, attacked the enemy on 29 January (10 February), ejected them from the town and pursued them for five *verstas*. Having received reinforcements, consisting of several hundred Westphalian infantrymen, the Poles attempted to halt our detachment, but were again driven back and pursued until nightfall. The enemy lost many killed and some 200 men taken prisoner. In this action, according to Count Vorontsov, Colonel Poncet [Mikhail Ivanovich Ponset or François-Michel de Poncet] of the Quartermaster's Department (General Staff) and artillery Captain Arnoldi [Ivan Karlovich Arnoldi] particularly distinguished themselves.[33]

The offensive by Russian forces, which threatened to cut the Viceroy off from the Oder, prompted him to abandon the positions he was occupying. Having recalled the Bavarians stationed in Gniezno, on 31 January (12 February), he set out from Poznań for Frankfurt an der Oder with the French and Polish divisions while the Bavarian division withdrew towards Crossen [Krosno Odrzańskie]. By 6 (18) February, the Viceroy's force was already behind the Oder; while Reynier arrived at Glogau the following day [19 February] with the remnants of his corps.[34]

The successes gained by our troops gave us hope of holding a line along the Oder, but the cautious Field Marshal expressed his intention to proceed further only with the cooperation of the Prussian corps: Bülow's, which was concentrating in Pomerania, and Yorck's, which was stationed in East Prussia. In anticipation of their assistance, Prince Kutuzov ordered Count Wittgenstein to take Yorck's corps, 20,000 strong, under his command, as well as Bülow's, with 10,000 men, and crossing the Oder between Stettin and Küstrin, to march on Berlin, attempting to cut the enemy army off from Magdeburg.[35] The Field Marshal believed that Count Wittgenstein could concentrate 30,000 to 35,000 of his own troops, and by reinforcing with 30,000 of Yorck's and Bülow's, raise an army of 60,000; but in reality Wittgenstein had a much

31 War Diary. Adjutant General Chernyshev's reports, dated 22 January [3 February] and 2 [14] February. Count Wittgenstein's report to Prince Kutuzov-Smolensky, dated 3 [15] February, No. 41.

32 War Diary. Chernyshev's reports.

33 The Chief-of-Staff, Western Army, Lieutenant General Sabaneev's report to Prince Kutuzov-Smolensky, dated 31 January [12 February], No. 124, archive of the M.T.D. No. 29,182.

34 Vaudoncourt, 31.

35 Orders for Count Wittgenstein, dated 5 [17] February, No. 258.

smaller force, and the Prussian generals declined from assisting him in the absence of orders from their sovereign. And they could not have done otherwise: as long as Friedrich Wilhelm remained in Berlin or Potsdam, within the sphere of influence of French forces, it could be assumed that he would not start an alliance with Russia purely out of fear of being subjected to Napoleon's vengeance; but once the King had withdrawn to Breslau, then, acting independently of French influence, he could send orders to his generals for immediate cooperation with the Russian army, and therefore, not having received them, they had good reason not to unilaterally decide on an important step that exposed them to accountability.

The Field Marshal, having received reports from Count Wittgenstein that General Yorck was unwilling to go beyond Schlochau without permission from the King, and had ordered Wittgenstein to halt temporarily in the vicinity of Driesen with his force, and to put the corps into winter quarters between this town and Arnswalde [Choszczno], placing the vanguard in Landsberg [Gorzów Wielkopolski]. The Main Army was located in the vicinity of Kalisz, to where the headquarters of Emperor Alexander and Prince Kutuzov moved on 12 (24) February; the forward corps were: Wittgenstein's in Rawicz (without violating the neutrality of Silesia), and Miloradovich's in Gostyń [16 miles south-west of Jaraczewo]. Several partisan detachments were ordered to cross onto the left bank of the Oder in order to harass the enemy:[36] On the basis of this order, partisans were detached: by Count Wittgenstein, major generals Chernyshev and Benckendorff and Colonel Tettenborn; by Wintzingerode, Colonel Davydov and Lieutenant Colonel Prendel; by Miloradovich, *Flügel-Adjutant* Captain Orlov [Mikhail Fëdorovich Orlov].[37]

Such was the situation at the time of the final conclusion of the treaty of alliance between Russia and Prussia at Kalisz.

36 Orders for Count Wittgenstein, dated 9 [21] February, No. 289.
37 Orders for General-of-Infantry Miloradovich, dated 17 February [1 March], No. 326.

Appendix I

Count Stackelberg and Colonel Pozzo di Borgo's letters

Count Stackelberg's letter to Chancellor Count Rumyantsev, dated 14 (26) January 1813:

> No doubt the armistice is entirely in the interests of the auxiliary corps but His Majesty the Emperor our august Master on one occasion revealed his magnanimous intentions for Europe, that of not harming his former ally – Austria. No doubt also that this armistice fixed at three months, a time so short that, before which it is impossible to think of the concentration of a somewhat imposing French army, nevertheless it must be noted that from here until it expires the state of affairs will have settled down and we will know whether we can rely on the assistance of Germany, or if we do not find any Germans, we will have no choice but to turn back, destroying every resource of war that could be used by the enemy along the line of retreat and adopting, if necessary, a plan of campaign absolutely identical to the last...
>
> *Sans doute que l'armistice est tout dans les intérêts du corps auxiliaire, mais Sa Majesté l'Empereur notre auguste Maître a une fois mis au jour avec ses sublimes intentions pour l'Europe celle de ne point nuire à Son ancien allié – l'Autriche. Sans doute aussi que cet armistice fixé à trois mois, époque avant la quelle il n'y a pas à penser au rassemblement d'une armée française un peu imposant, se trouve avoir un terme très court, mais il faut dire que d'ici à ce qu'il soit expiré l'aspect des affaires se sera debrouillé et nous saurons à quoi nous en tenir sur le compte de l'Allemagne, ou si nous ne trouvons pas d'Allemands, il ne nous restera qu'à rebrousser chemin à temps en detruisant dans notre retraite tous les moyens de guerre pouvant être employés par l'ennemi et adoptant au besoin un plan de campagne absolument semblable au dernier...*

Colonel Pozzo di Borgo's note submitted to Emperor Alexander I, dated 24 March (5 April) 1813:

Their plan will be to risk as little as possible, to maintain their force to give weight to their intervention, and never to lose sight of the main aim of their current policy, which is, whatever they may say, to keep Napoleon on the throne and at the same time to dictate, or at least to exert a great influence on the peace.

The destruction or subjugation of the intermediate powers between Russia and France has offered, so to speak, a whole new world to Your Imperial Majesty: as Your victorious armies advance, they will find only some kind of political void, a population of about 25,000,000 men without direction, their former governments lifeless or incapable of being resuscitated, or in need of being revived under the influence of their Liberator; the situation is roughly similar from the Neman to the Rhine except for Austria which thanks to the success of Your Majesty has assumed an independent role. If it is possible for Europe to draw some benefit from past failures and calamities, it is the fortunate impotence of the secondary States and the little self-serving princes to disturb the harmony of Your Majesty's plans through their defections or petty irritations.

... Son plan sera de risquer le moins possible, de se tenir en force pour donner du poids à son intervention et de ne jamais perdre de vue le but principal de sa politique actuelle, qui est quoiqu'elle en dise de conserver Napoléon sur le trône et de commander en même tems ou du moins d'exercer une grande influence à la paix.

La destruction ou l'asservissement des puissances intermediaires entre la Russie et la France offre, pour ainsi dire, à V.M.I. un monde tout nouveau: à mesure que Ses armées victorieuses avancent, elles ne trouvent en quelque sorte qu'un vuide poitique, une population d'environ 25 millions d'hommes sans direction, les cadavres de leurs anciens gouvernements, ou incapables d'être rappelés à la vie, ou dans la necessité d'être ranimés par l'influence de leur Liberateur; excepté l'Autriche qui à la faveur des succès de V.M. assume un role indépendant, cette situation est à peu près la même depuis le Niemen jusqu'au Rhin. S'il est possible que l'Europe tire quelqu'avantage des fautes et des malheurs passés, c'est l'heureuse impuissance dans laquelle se trouvent les Etats de second ordre et les petits princes égoistes de troubler l'harmonie des plans de V.M. par leur défection ou leurs tracasseries.

Archive of the Foreign Ministry.

Appendix II

Composition of Russian formations and detachments in January 1813

General Löwis' detachment:

Kazan Dragoons (two squadrons); Yamburg Ulans; Combined Dragoons (for a total of 796 regular cavalrymen).

Ilovaisky 9th's Cossacks; Grekov 1st's Cossacks; Grekov 5th's Cossacks; Kharitonov 7th's Cossacks; Chernozubov 8th's Cossacks; Suchilin 2nd's Cossacks; Simferopol Tatars; Perekop Tatars; Yakhontov's Volunteers; Schmitt's *Freikorps*; Nirod's *Freikorps* (for a total of 2,687 irregular cavalrymen, some of whom were directed towards Berlin on 24 March [5 April]).

6th Division: Azov Infantry; Nizov Infantry; Bryansk Infantry; 3rd Jägers.

21st Division: Neva Infantry; Petrov Infantry; Lithuania Infantry; Podolsk Infantry; 44th Jägers.

25th Division: Voronezh Infantry (with a battalion of Rylsk Infantry attached); 1st Marines; 2nd Marines.

3rd Division: Reval Infantry; Koporsk Infantry; 20th Jägers; 21st Jägers (all replacement battalions).

4th Division: Volhynia Infantry; Tobolsk Infantry; Minsk Infantry; 4th Jägers; 34th Jägers (all replacement battalions).

17th Division: Ryazan Infantry; Belozersk Infantry; Brest Infantry; 30th Jägers (all replacement battalions).

25th Division: 31st Jägers; 47th Jägers (all replacement battalions).

For a total of 6,047 regular infantrymen.

Novgorod *Opolchenie* (four Groups – 370 men); St Petersburg *Opolchenie* (nine Groups – 1,000 men). For a total of 1,370 militiamen.

6th Battery Artillery Company (12 guns); 10th Light Artillery Company; 11th Light Artillery Company; 40th Light Artillery Company (35 guns); 19th Horse Artillery Company (12 guns). For a total of 900 artillerymen.

For a grand total of 11,800 men with 59 guns.

Chernyshev's, Benckendorff's and Tettenborn's detachments:

Their composition was in transition at that time, each comprised from four to six Cossack regiments with two Don artillery pieces.

Count Vorontsov's vanguard:
Eight reserve battalions from 2nd Grenadier Division; one artillery company; three Cossack regiments.

Tormasov's force (numbering 17,000 men):
III Corps (Grenadier) under Prinz Karl von Mecklenburg, with 12 battalions and four artillery companies.
V Corps (Lifeguard) under Lieutenant General Lavrov, with 13 battalions and four artillery companies.
Two cuirassier divisions; two Lifeguard horse artillery batteries; the Lifeguard Cossacks; five Cossack regiments, with 40 squadrons, two horse artillery batteries and six Cossack regiments.

Miloradovich's force:
IV Corps under Count Osterman-Tolstoy – eight battalions with three artillery companies.
VII Corps under Lieutenant General Raevsky – ten battalions with three artillery companies.
II Cavalry Corps and III Cavalry Corps, under Adjutant General Baron Korff – 32 squadrons with four horse artillery companies.
Nine Cossack regiments.
In addition, from Adjutant General Vasilchikov's detachment: two battalions of jägers and 12 squadrons from IV Cavalry Corps with one horse artillery company and three Cossack regiments.
Total for Miloradovich: 20 battalions, 44 squadrons, 11 artillery companies and 12 Cossack regiments, numbering 11,800 men.
In addition to the troops that were under Miloradovich's direct command, the following were subordinated to him: VI Corps and VIII Corps under General Dokhturov, Sacken's and Lieutenant General Prince Volkonsky 3rd's (formerly Essen 3rd's) corps, who had come from Volhynia, and Lieutenant General Rath's detachment, marching via Bialystok towards Zamość. Overall, there were some 35,000 men under Miloradovich's command.

Lieutenant General Sacken's corps:
Lieutenant General Prince Volkonsky 3rd's corps: 8th Division (eight battalions); 22nd Division (4½ battalions); Cavalry under Major General Melissino (16 squadrons); four artillery companies; four Cossack regiments.
Major General Bulatov's corps: 16th Division (six battalions); 22nd Division (ten battalions); 13th Division (three battalions); Cavalry under Major General Gamper (16 squadrons); four artillery companies; four Cossack regiments.
Major General Lieven 3rd's reserve: 10th Division (12 battalions); 22nd Division (two battalions); five cavalry squadrons; one Cossack regiment.
Total for Sacken: 45½ battalions, 37 squadrons, eight artillery companies and nine Cossack regiments, numbering 19,000 men with 96 guns.

Lieutenant General Rath's corps:

Platov's Cossacks; Turchaninov 1st's Cossacks; sub-units from Chikilev 1st's Cossacks, Vlasov 2nd's Cossacks and Panteliev 2nd's Cossacks; Pereyaslav Dragoons; Tiraspol Dragoons; Nyslott Infantry (two battalions); Okhotsk Infantry (one battalion); Penza Infantry (two battalions); 43rd Jägers (three battalions); 22nd Battery Artillery Company (12 guns); 38th Battery Artillery Company (4 guns).

For a total of 650 irregular cavalrymen, 570 regular cavalry, 3,320 regular infantry, 277 artillerymen, numbering 4,817 men with 16 guns.

(Orders for Lieutenant General Sacken, dated 8 [20] February, No. 277. Log of Outgoing Documents, 1813, archive of the Military Topographic Depot (M.T.D.) No. 29,181).

Adjutant General Wintzingerode's force:

II Corps: 3rd Division (eight battalions); 4th Division (eight battalions); One battery artillery company; two light artillery companies; one horse artillery company; two Don Cossack regiments from Miloradovich's vanguard. For a total of 2,500 infantry, 400 artillerymen.

Major General Tuchkov's corps: replacement battalions from 9th, 12th, 15th, 18th and 20th divisions (20 battalions); recruit battalions from various divisions (four battalions); 75th Ships Company; Tatar Ulans (eight squadrons); 12 replacement squadrons; six Don Cossack regiments and sub-units; 4th Reserve Artillery Brigade – 33rd Battery Artillery Company; 9th Artillery Brigade – 16th Light Artillery Company (six guns); 11th Artillery Brigade – 4th Light Artillery Company (two guns with an additional captured Austrian piece). For a total of 5,961 infantry, 1,582 regular cavalry, 1,123 Cossacks and 21 guns crewed by 315 men (Davydov shows 486 men with the artillery)

Major General Lanskoy's detachment: Alexandria Hussars (eight squadrons); Belorussia Hussars (eight squadrons); Livonia Mounted Jägers (four squadrons); 3rd Ural Cossacks; 1st Ukraine Cossacks; 3rd Ukraine Cossacks. For a total of 1,527 regular cavalry and 1,812 Cossacks.

Colonel Davydov's detachment: Popov 13th's Cossacks; 1st Bug Cossacks; hussar and newly raised Cossack sub-units, numbering 500 men.

Total for Wintzingerode: 40 battalions, 40 squadrons, six artillery companies, nine Cossack regiments and four sub-units, numbering 16,000 men with 69 guns.

This statement was extracted from the Original Log of Operations from 1812, and is in accordance with a strength return from General Wintzingerode, placed in the latest (4th) edition of the work by our famous partisan D.V. Davydov. General Khatov shows Wintzingerode as having 32 battalions, 46 squadrons, six artillery companies and eight Cossack regiments. The number of men therein is given along with the other forces under Prince Kutuzov, but from an approximate calculation it emerges that they could have contained no more than 9,000 or 10,000 men. In Plotho's work, Wintzingerode's corps is shown as having: 4,800 infantrymen, 2,400 regular cavalrymen, 1,500 Cossacks and 900 artillerymen, totalling 9,600 men.

2

The national mobilisation of Prussia

The situation in Prussia on the conclusion of the Treaty of Tilsit. – Stein and his reforms. – Transformation of the War Department. – The National Army. – Orders for the financial and administrative departments. – The situation in Prussia on the outbreak of hostilities between Russia and France in 1812, and upon the destruction of the *Grande Armée*. – Regulations on volunteers. – Mobilisation in East Prussia. – The Berlin volunteers. – Donations. – Prussian women. – Statements regarding the patriotism of Prussian subjects, by a foreigner. – Factors that delayed the conclusion of an alliance between Russia and Prussia. – Negotiations. – Treaty of Kalisz.

Mobilisation in Prussia. – Organisation of forces: the standing army; *Landwehr*; *Landsturm*; national cavalry regiments; *Freikorps* (partisan) detachments. – Overall numbers of Prussian troops. – The King's appeals to the nation and to the forces. – Declaration of war on Napoleon.

The situation of the Viceroy's force on the retreat from Poznań behind the Oder. – The indecision of the Prussian government. – The awkward situation of the Russian generals. – General Yorck's acquittal.

The crossing of Prussian partisans onto the left bank of the Oder. – Chernyshev's and Tettenborn's attempt to liberate Berlin. – The concentration of the Viceroy's forces in the Berlin area. – The state of the population of Berlin.

Simultaneously with the advance from the Vistula to the Oder by Russian forces, the inhabitants of Prussia took up arms against the French.

We shall not imitate German historians who have sought to deprive us of the glory of the liberation of Germany. Let us pay tribute to our comrades. We Russians, who had never hesitated to sacrifice our last possessions or ourselves at the time of Mother Russia's catastrophe, we fully sympathise with the great deeds of self-sacrifice by the Prussian populace. These feats were accomplished by foreigners, but they are not alien to us: they find an echo in our souls.

In order to get a clear idea of the Prussian general uprising, it is necessary to cast a glance at the contemporaneous situation in that country.

Through the treaty concluded at Tilsit, the Prussian monarchy, elevated to the status of a first-rank power by the genius of Frederick the Great [Friedrich II, der Große], had been reduced to one of the collection of territories subjugated by Napoleon. Its area, its population, and with them the resources of the kingdom, had been halved; state revenues had been soaked up within five years by war reparations imposed by Napoleon, and through the maintenance of French forces left between the Elbe and the Vistula; almost every Prussian fortress was occupied by French troops. The country had become completely impoverished; many landowners, having fallen into irredeemable debt, abandoned their birthrights and wandered the world; financiers suffered huge losses from the stagnation of business, or hid their capital. A general despondency crushed the morale of the nation: many, having lost hope of the possibility of any change for the better, settled down in disgrace and offered to exchange the chains in which the powerful hand of the conqueror held them, for a close alliance with France, in other words, total obedience to Napoleon. Finally, the army was restricted to no more than 42,000 men; and even if this restriction had not existed, then Prussia could not have had a more numerous army due to lack of resources. To all this was added the Continental System [*Blocus continental*], with all its consequences, which had a detrimental effect on Prussian trade and was the cause of their breach with Britain, Sweden, and the United States of America.

Such was the situation in Prussia: it seemed as though the last ray of hope in the souls of the population of this unfortunate country had faded irrevocably. But Almighty Providence had sent them lords who did not despair of redeeming their Fatherland to their aid, Stein and Scharnhorst. At that time, when, shortly after the conclusion of the Treaty of Tilsit, Prussia had been flooded with French troops, King Frederick William III, retreating to the farthest corner of his territories, to Memel [Klaipėda], instructed Stein to draft a reform project aimed at restoring his domains. On 5 October 1807 [new style], he was entrusted, with the appointment of minister for the management of all domestic and foreign affairs. Gifted in his maturity with the passion of a young man, Stein combined in himself a deep faith in the divine Gospel with unbending resolve in the enterprise he had conceived, the exaltation of fallen Germany to all its former greatness and glory.[1] As proud as a feudal baron, he was, at the same time, filled with love for his people and a spiritual investment in their fate. The personal appearance of this great man revealed his spiritual qualities. According to Arndt [Ernst Moritz Arndt], who knew him briefly, the distinctive features of the burly, broad-shouldered, well-built Stein were: a high forehead, an aquiline nose, small, rather quick brown eyes, and a somewhat protruding chin. He retained his youthful liveliness into his old age, was always the soul of society and never met his match in repartee and wit. Perpetually calm, immersed in deep thoughts, he was sometimes carried away by his fervent nature, and in those moments his eyes flashed like lightning and his voice resounded like thunder. On 9 October 1807, new style, just four days after Stein had been appointed

1 He was 51 years old at the time.

to his duties as a minister, the code emerged that he had long conceived, and which was later so famous, which included the chief reforms of state institutions: the law, by virtue of which only nobles alone could own estates, was repealed; small plots of peasant land were assigned to manors; serfs were granted personal freedom. Upon the arrival of the King in Königsberg on 15 January 1808, the reforms continued: the legislature was completely separated from the executive and every ministry was reformed.

The misery that had befallen Prussia and the subjugation of Germany by Napoleon instilled in their sons the idea of the closest union with each other, whose objective was to prepare the way for an uprising, in anticipation of a favourable moment. Thus the *Tugendbund* (Society for the Practice of Public Virtues) was formed, under Stein's guidance. But the reforms conceived and implemented by this great minister aroused strong opposition: people who were conservative or selfish, who had been the sole beneficiaries of privilege under the old order, became Stein's natural enemies. Among them were: *Generalfeldmarschall* Kalckreuth [Friedrich Adolf von Kalckreuth] from the military side, while from the civilian side was Senior Minister Voß [Otto Carl Friedrich von Voß]. There were some in Prussia who had been shameless enough to hand over one of Stein's letters on *Tugendbund* business to the French government: the consequences of this were Stein's dismissal from his ministerial post in November 1808, and the confiscation of his estate on Nassau territory. His administration of the ministry had lasted only a little over a year, but it constituted an era of a new order of business, and many of the wise statutes subsequently promulgated under *Staatskanzler* Hardenberg had been initiated by Stein.[2] At the opening of hostilities in 1812, having been summoned by Emperor Alexander from Prague to the headquarters of the Russian army, Stein arrived in Vilna, then went to St Petersburg and stayed there until the departure of the Tsar to the army at the end of the year.

A complete transformation of military institutions was proceeding simultaneously with the general state reforms in Prussia. The soul of this important work was General Scharnhorst. Transferring into Prussian service from Hanoverian, already 45 years old in 1801, at a time when the Prussian army was mainly in pursuit of bearing and uniformity, Scharnhorst, slouching, uncaring for sartorial elegance, explaining himself languidly and obscurely, was considered a barely competent, impractical person among his peers. One of the field officers to whom he was subordinate at that time summed him up, saying that any non-commissioned officer would be more of an asset to the service than Scharnhorst. Despite such comments, however, he was assessed as being fit for command and in 1807, was chief of staff for L'Estocq [Anton Wilhelm von L'Estocq], already in the rank of *Oberst* [colonel], and contributed to his brilliant feats in the battle of preußisch Eylau. At the conclusion of the Treaty of Tilsit, Scharnhorst, promoted to *Generalmajor*, was appointed chairman of the *Militär-Reorganisationskommission* [commission for the reorganisation of the army]; among its members were those who would later gain great renown: Gneisenau, Borstell [Karl Leopold Heinrich

2 Beitzke, *Geschichte der deutschen Freiheitskriege*, I, 53-57. *Das Leben des Ministers Freiherrn vom Stein*, G.H. Pertz, second edition, volume 2.

Ludwig von Borstell], Grolman [Karl Wilhelm Georg von Grolman] and Boyen [Ludwig Leopold Gottlieb Hermann von Boyen]. Like Stein, Scharnhorst encountered strong opposition from the unthinking champions of Fredrick the Great's system, who believed that fundamental reforms would shatter the Prussian military system to its very foundations. But no obstacles would halt the resolute, unshakable Scharnhorst; concealing his opinions in the depths of his soul and not fully revealing his intentions even to those closest to him, he brought them into execution not prematurely, but as the need for innovations arose: in this way he managed to prepare forces and resources covertly, in anticipation of the dawn of the liberation of Germany. In the era of the Treaty of Tilsit, the Prussian forces consisted of only a few thousand men; the entire materiel department of the army was in the hands of the French; the moral strength of the nation and forces was in complete decline. It was necessary to create a new army, national in nature, similar to the enemy's; to supply the troops with artillery, weapons, clothing, ammunition, horses and harness through the severely limited means of the state; introduce regulations and tactics consistent with the modern requirements of military skills; finally, to instil confidence in the men and the army in their own strength, without which all materiel resources are weak.

In order to give strength to the new regulations, it was necessary, first of all, to maintain respect for the previous ones. Even while the King was still resident in Memel, orders were issued to bring to justice those faint-hearted commandants who had surrendered their fortresses without resistance to the enemy; at the same time, every officer who had surrendered at Prenzlau was suspended from service. On 3 August 1808, new style, a new military charter was announced on crimes and punishments, on the basis of which running the gauntlet was abolished and all corporal punishment for any crime was abolished, except for dishonourable acts. Military service was made compulsory for all Prussian subjects. On the basis of an order dated 6 August 1808 new style, promotion as an officer no longer depended solely upon pedigree, but in peacetime, was conditional on education, behaviour and intelligence; in wartime, only courage and outstanding performance gave a right to promotion. At the same time, the knowledge necessary for the qualification of officers was determined, while schools were established in order to facilitate the means of acquiring this knowledge. In the course of 1810 and 1811, Scharnhorst drafted drill regulations with the assistance of several officers, which were distinguished by simplicity and practicality and are rightly regarded as exemplary.

The most important of all Scharnhorst's inspirations was the mobilisation of an armed force in the event of an uprising against Napoleon. Under the terms of a convention concluded between Prinz Wilhelm and the French government on 8 September, 1808, new style, the Prussian army was restricted to 42,000 men. But Scharnhorst found a way to prepare an incomparably larger force without enlarging the standing army. To that end, recruits, having received their tactical training, with the assistance of cadres made up of veteran soldiers, were dismissed to their homes, and in their place others were called up once more, who, in turn, were dismissed, and so on. Young soldiers who had returned to their home provinces were either placed in the reserve, or were used to build fortresses or other government work. Despite the paucity of Prussia's financial resources in this period, artillery, weapons, ammunition and war supplies were procured in large amounts and 60,000 horses were found fit for service.[3]

The payment of war reparations to Napoleon, which soaked up the income of Prussia at the time, forced the government to resort to reduced public spending. The king lived very simply during his residence in Memel and then in Königsberg; while in the spring, at the request of the queen, he moved to the village of Güben, in the vicinity of Königsberg, where he was accommodated in a few rooms with all the children. His example prompted many of those around him to moderation and donations for the common cause, but this was not enough to pay the indemnity within the fixed deadline; and in anticipation of this, it was necessary to maintain the huge French army that occupied Prussian territory at their own expense. The government, in order to satisfy the claims of Napoleon, was forced to resort to internal and foreign loans, the sale of state property and the issuance of security bonds (*Schatzscheine*). But external borrowing was hindered by ominous rumours of the abolition of the Prussian monarchy, which depended entirely upon Napoleon's whim.

On 6 June 1810, new style, Hardenberg, with his appointment as *Staatskanzler*, came to the forefront of the Prussian government; while at the end of October of the same year, the state of Prussian finances was made public and the forthcoming convocation of regional deputies in Berlin was announced (to where the King had moved back in December 1809), to explain the needs and desires of the people and to find resources in order to finally satisfy the French government. This was followed by a series of legislation, containing many reforms on indirect taxation.[4] On 23 February 1811, the meeting of the regional deputies was opened with a speech by the *Staatskanzler*, in which, trying to prove the necessity of the innovations undertaken, on behalf of the King he solemnly promised to introduce a representative form of government. On 14 September of that same year, the Regulations on the Mutual Obligations of Landlords and Peasants [*Regulierungsedikten*] were promulgated, on the basis of which the latter received their estates in full and inalienable ownership, undertaking to pay rent to the owners for the appropriation of other land, at rates determined by a commission composed of experts.[5]

By 1811, half of the war reparations had already been paid, and on the basis of the treaties, the French were to evacuate Glogau. But Napoleon violated this condition. At the commencement of hostilities between Russia and France, justifiably concerned about potential malign intentions of the *Empereur des Français*, Prussia was in need of an alliance with him, on whatever terms. Napoleon, taking

3 Beitzke, I, 58-63.

4 On 28 October 1810, taxes on food supplies and luxury goods were significantly increased; on 30 October, all monasteries were abolished, with the exception of those at which schools were located; on 2 November, trade licenses were abolished and it was permitted to freely engage as tradesmen, and, in return, a general tax was imposed on artisans [*Gewerbesteueredikt*], etcetera.

5 On the basis of this Regulation, a landowner did not have the right to evict peasants from their estate, even in the event of the latter not fulfilling their obligations. In addition, peasants received inalienable ownership of part of the land they cultivated, while for the remainder, which remained in the ownership of the landowners, they were obliged to pay rent.

advantage of his position, included a condition for the continuation of the occupation of Glogau by French troops in the treaty of alliance dated 24 February 1812, and sent his garrisons to all other Prussian fortresses, with the exception of Graudenz [Grudziądz] and Kolberg [Kołobrzeg]. Thus, in 1812, keeping 23,000 men at Glogau, Küstrin and Stettin at Prussia's expense, he increased the garrisons in Magdeburg to 12,000 and in Danzig to over 20,000 men: consequently, he could completely dominate the country, where, after the departure of the Prussian auxiliary corps to the Dvina, only 20,000 of Prussia's own troops remained under arms. Napoleon ruthlessly exploited the right of might, burdening the unfortunate inhabitants of Prussia with a huge force commitment and the delivery of food and military supplies for them.

The unsuccessful campaign of the *Grande Armée* in Russia roused the hopes of Prussia, but its population and the King himself, surrounded by French troops, were still completely dependent on Napoleon. In addition, Friedrich Wilhelm, despite the many examples of bad faith committed by Napoleon, did not dare to violate the agreements concluded with him. These were the reasons that prompted the King to remove General Yorck from command of his force. Wanting to avoid a breach with France, *Staatskanzler* Hardenberg tried to agree on the neutrality of Prussia together with Austria with Metternich; but the Viennese Cabinet were careful not to reveal their intentions. Friedrich Wilhelm was forced to wait until the French government gave him a clear pretext for rapprochement with Emperor Alexander, by refusing Prussia's just demands for withdrawing French garrisons from Prussian fortresses in exchange for writing off the amounts owed to them by Napoleon.[6] Meanwhile, wanting to be ready in the event of war, on 3 February 1813, new style, the King ordered an announcement that danger threatened the state from hostilities approaching its frontiers and required a rapid strengthening of the army, but that the government's financial resources could not cover increasing troop costs: therefore, it was decided that young men from 17 to 24 years of age, who were not obliged to enter the service, but who had the means to uniform themselves and purchase munitions at their own expense, were to form foot and mounted units of volunteer light troops (*freiwillige Jägerschaaren zu Fusse und zu Pferde*), who were intended to be attached to infantry and cavalry regiments. These volunteers were given many rights and privileges.[7] Those young men who refused to respond to the call of the fatherland were not forced into service, but could not hope for any honours or advancement,[8] for the entire duration of the war. Six days later, on 9 February, new style, all exclusions from military service were abolished.[9] Friedrich Wilhelm, apparently still hoping to induce the people to general mobilisation, on 22 February, ordered that the following announcement be made public:

6 Dr. Förster, *Geschichte der Befreiungskriege, 1813, 1814, 1815*, third edition, I, 57.

7 These Prussian volunteers were given: the choice of regiment in which they wished to serve; exclusion from service in fortress garrisons; selecting their officers from among themselves; the right to take up posts in the civil service at the end of the war.

8 For services to the state.

9 *Das Leben des Ministers Freiherrn vom Stein*, III, 298-299.

> The King, considering that, with the general laudable desire of each and every person to take part in the defence of the fatherland, it is necessary to detect and punish a few cases of cowardice or lack of passion for the common cause, has decided that:
>
> 1. Any transfer of real-estate from a father to sons not in the service shall be considered invalid if the father is less than 50 years old, and the sons have reached 24 years of age and are completely healthy.
> 2. Each of those who evade service, on some insignificant pretext, loses the rights to their estate, shall become a ward and can neither wear the Prussian cockade nor hold public office.
> 3. The head of each family or guardian who makes it difficult for his sons or young men in his care to enter military service, shall also be subject to the loss of rights of the state.[10]

It subsequently emerged that the Prussian people, enthused by feelings of duty and honour, exceeded the expectations of the King and blotted out the memory of the shameful events of 1806. Even before the promulgation of royal decrees on general mobilisation, at the general meeting of regional deputies of East Prussia, on 5 February, new style, at the suggestion of General Yorck, it was decided: to call up 13,000 reservists in order to reconstitute his corps; mobilise 20,000 *Landwehr*; establish a *Landsturm* (through universal mobilisation), from all men between 18 and 45 years of age, and form a cavalry detachment of 700 huntsmen who would undertake to equip themselves at their own expense and serve as a seed-bed for *Landwehr* officers.[11] The execution of this project was entrusted to a commission, chaired by the former *Innenminister* [Interior Minister], Graf Dohna [Friedrich Ferdinand Alexander zu Dohna-Schlobitten],[12] while *Doktor der Rechte* [Doctor of Law] Heidemann [August Wilhelm Heidemann], known for his dislike for the French, was appointed as the executive director.[13] As soon as the call to arms from the King became known in Berlin, still under French military occupation at the time, in the course of three days 9,000 young men had joined the huntsmen. A few days later, the King witnessed a significant convoy from the windows of his Breslau palace: these were some of the Berlin huntsmen who had arrived in Breslau in 80 carriages. To Scharnhorst's question of: 'My Sovereign, are you now convinced of the truth of my words?' the king responded with teary eyes, which showed the gallant minister that all former doubts had vanished. And if the national call to arms required some motivational orders from the government, then, to the eternal glory of Prussia, the sacrifice of possessions on the altar of the fatherland were brought voluntarily, at

10 *Beihefte zum Milit. Wochen-Blatt*, 1845 & 1846.

11 *Das Leben des Ministers Freiherrn vom Stein*, III, 289. Stein's letter to Emperor Alexander I, dated 25 January (6 February) 1813, from Königsberg (archive of the M.F.A.).

12 Graf Dohna, having been appointed *Innenminister* by Baron Stein in 1808, rendered important services. He left this office in 1810.

13 A monument was erected to Heidemann in Königsberg, who died in November 1813 at the age of 42, from the hard work incurred in the liberation of Germany. Beitzke, I, 143-144.

the compulsion of a general popular enthusiasm. Due to the complete devastation of Prussia by 1813, the donations by private individuals could never be equal to the huge sums offered by the [Russian] nobility and merchant classes in the Patriotic War of 1812. But even in Prussia, just as it had been in Russia, everyone offered a great deal and many sacrificed everything. Big cities and wealthy people set up foot and mounted jägers fully armed, not infrequently pledging to provide their pay throughout the war; others, who had fewer resources, donated towards the arming and equipping of the volunteers, where possible; some offered half of their salary, or pension, or donated their last pair of silver spoons; rather significant sums were sent by persons who wished to remain anonymous. Many ladies donated earrings, bracelets and even wedding rings, expressing regret that they had nothing better to give. In Breslau, where the presence of the King, who had found refuge there from the enemies of his fatherland, aroused particular delight, one young girl, wishing to participate in donations, but having nothing, went to her hairdresser and asked him to value her hair, the beauty of which astonished all who knew her. 'It may be worth ten Thaler [one Thaler had a Fine weight of 16.7 grammes of silver],' he replied.

'Well, cut it off and give me cash for it,' said the generous beauty. Struck by the unexpected offer, the stylist took up his scissors several times and finally announced to the girl that he did not dare to deprive her of such a priceless treasure. But this did not stop her, she cut her own hair and sent it to the committee established to receive donations, with the following note: 'The hairdresser, N.N. offered ten Thaler for my hair; I consider myself fortunate to be able to offer this trifling sacrifice to the fatherland.' The committee ordered bracelets and rings to be made out of the donated hair, which, in remembrance of such a wonderful deed, were sold at a high price and provided 250 Thaler to the treasury of the committee.

One Berlin jeweller received a large commission from the government for iron rings, of a distinctive shape, with the inscription: *GOLD GAB ICH FÜR EISEN, 1813.* (I donated gold for iron, 1813). Only those who had donated any kind of gold or silver items to the fatherland were entitled to receive such a ring. No sooner had this order been made public, on the very first day 150 gold wedding rings had been exchanged for iron ones; overall, approximately 160,000 gold rings, earrings, chains and other precious items were handed over. Subsequently, iron rings, inscribed: *GOLD GAB ICH FÜR EISEN*, became family heirlooms, serving as a remembrance of the sacrifices they had made.[14]

Many Prussian citizens donated all their possessions, while their wives and daughters gave up their last ornaments and precious things; others dedicated themselves to care for the sick and wounded; there were even those who, not limited to that, dressed in men's clothing, entered the ranks as soldiers, fought bravely and died for their sacred homeland: the names of 18-year-old Eleonore Prochaska [Marie Christiane Eleonore Prochaska], who joined the *Lützowsches Freikorps* [partisan] detachment under the alias August Renz, and died a glorious death in action at Göhrde, while Friederike Krüger [Sophie Dorothea Friederike Krüger, alias August Lübeck] was promoted to non-commissioned officer and received the *Eisernes Kreuz* [Iron Cross]

14 Extracted from Berlin and Breslau newspapers from 1813.

2nd class, these names deserve an honourable place in the history of the war for German independence. One young woman, originally from Stralsund, served in the cavalry, under the alias of Karl Petersen and was promoted to *Wachtmeister* [sergeant-major], suffered two wounds and, as a reward for her exploits, was decorated with the *Eisernes Kreuz* 1st class.[15]

The Spanish ambassador in Berlin, Don José Pizarro, wrote to Madrid that the population of Prussia was mobilising in the Spanish style. In one of his dispatches, he stated:

> Throughout Germany, feelings of national identity and devotion to the legitimate rulers dominate to the highest degree. But nowhere do these noble feelings manifest themselves so strongly, so similarly to the events of our glorious Spain, as in Prussian territory…
>
> … The King's sister sent all her valuable items to the state treasury, for military expenses, and within the same hour, every woman sacrificed their jewellery down to the last bauble. I say everything, not exaggerating in the least, because there were hardly any exceptions saving the poor who had nothing. Every wedding ring has been brought to the altar of the fatherland, and in their place, iron rings were distributed with the inscription: 'I gave gold for iron.' These rings, valued because of the national heroism of which they are a reminder, are distinguished by the elegance of their workmanship. If the ladies wear any other items, then they are of iron alone. Such patriotic rings cannot be bought at any price, because they are issued exclusively in exchange for donations of gold and silver items…
>
> Berlin presents a spectacle as majestic as it is moving. Every street is crowded with the wounded;[16] at every step there are the maimed, on crutches, with their arms bandaged, and so on, the only others are women, the elderly and children. Having said that, whole battalions of recruits are training on every square, cavalry platoons are engaged in sabre technique and riding school…
>
> The King is the premier soldier of his army. His facial features are adorned with placidity and import, the simplicity of his clothing, his amity, thrift, the lively interest he takes in the well-being of his subjects, make him the object of adoration and delight to Prussian citizens, who have never shown themselves to be such a great people as at the present time…[17]

This popular feeling was bound to draw the government into an open struggle against the oppressor of Germany. But the King, upon his arrival at Breslau, still vacillated in indecision, the main reason for which were the proposals by some of those close to him who feared a breach with France. The return of General Scharnhorst to the post of *Chef des Generalstabes* [Chief of the General Staff] once more, coupled with the right to be present at the Council of Ministers, strengthened the champions of

15 *Aachener Zeitung, 1844 & 1845.*
16 This letter was written in the autumn of 1813.
17 From a letter by Don José Pizarro to Antonio Cano Manuel y Ramírez de Arellano in Madrid.

an alliance with Russia, but did not give them an overwhelming advantage. There were men who assured the King that after the losses he had suffered in the past year, Napoleon had completely abandoned the idea of global hegemony, and that the essential, primary concern should be the predominance of Russia. It was believed that the *Empereur des Français*, having a pressing need for an alliance with Prussia at that time, was ready to agree to all their demands and form a large state that could serve as a barrier against Russia from this monarchy, enlarged at the expense of neighbouring domains. In addition, casting doubt on the selflessness of Emperor Alexander I's outlook, some thought that having forcibly occupied the Polish provinces that had formerly belonged to Prussia, he would take the opportunity to keep them under his control. There were rumours that many of our Sovereign's advisors had suggested that he expand the borders of Russia at Prussia's expense. In spite of all this, however, the personal relationship between King Friedrich Wilhelm and Emperor Alexander, the sympathy of the Prussian people for the Russians and the defection from the French by Yorck were destined to induce Prussia into an alliance with Russia. Upon the King's arrival in Breslau, he immediately wanted to send a confidant to negotiate with Emperor Alexander; but, at the same time, not wanting to give Napoleon a reason for distrust, he asked for his consent to send a negotiator to our headquarters; the purpose or pretext for negotiations with the Russian government was to gain recognition of the neutrality of Breslau and southern Silesia from our Sovereign. Napoleon turned this proposal down; but the King in early February new style, nevertheless sent his adjutant general, *Oberst* Knesebeck [Karl Friedrich von dem Knesebeck], to the headquarters of the Russian army incognito, under the alias of a merchant named Edeling. On 9 February new style, Knesebeck set off for our headquarters, at that time located in Kłodawa, two stages from Kalisz, and arrived there on 3 (15) February. Emperor Alexander, having received him on that same day, clearly explained His views to him: 'I wish that Prussia be restored to its former glory' said the Tsar, 'and if success should crown our efforts, to even greater splendour; the day on which the King's legitimate territories are returned to him will be the most beautiful day of my life.'

It appeared that such an opening to negotiations promised an outcome as quick as it would be successful; but things turned out differently: Knesebeck lacked the skills to discuss the reciprocal positions of Russia and Prussia, and instead of presenting a straightforward explanation to Emperor Alexander, resorted to cunning and entangled himself in the finer points of diplomacy. Believing that our government was trying to acquire East Prussia, Knesebeck did not pay attention to the true views of our Sovereign, which tended towards taking possession of the Duchy of Warsaw and to expanding the boundaries of Prussia at the expense of Saxony. Stein himself, noting that such negotiations were proving to be a waste of time and were delaying the liberation of Germany, expressed his opinion on this to Knesebeck with full frankness and wrote to Hardenberg in a similar vein. Emperor Alexander, wanting to speed matters up, broke off negotiations with the distrustful Knesebeck, and sent Stein and Anstett [Ivan Osipovich Anshtett or Johann Protasius von Anstett] to the King in Breslau, authorising them to negotiate with the Prussian government. Despite Stein suffering from a severe cold, he immediately went to Breslau, and having arrived there, on 13 (25) February, he appeared before the King and explained to him the danger of remaining in alliance with the French, because all of Prussia was opposed to it. 'It is impossible to believe Napoleon's promises' he said, 'and even if he really wanted to do something of benefit to Prussia, then he is hardly in a position to achieve his intentions; on the other hand, it would be difficult to oppose Russia, or to follow the example of Austria, which is in a completely different situation. In my opinion, Emperor Alexander has made up his mind to restore Prussia' continued Stein, 'and there is nothing left for us but to fight for the independence of Germany with the united forces of both states. In the event that the Prussian government remains in alliance with Napoleon, the Emperor will annex every province as far as the Vistula to His domains and set up Russian administrations in them.'[18]

The successful course of the negotiations was facilitated by the arrival in Breslau of the deputy for East Prussia, Major Graf Dohna [Friedrich Karl Emil zu Dohna-Schlobitten], brother of the former minister, with the news of the decision of the council of provincial officials, to call up 30,000 men for the *Landwehr* at their own expense. Although Friedrich Wilhelm did not like such unilateral decrees by the council, assembled under the auspices of the Russian authorities, nevertheless, the significant mobilisation of one of the most important provinces of Prussia should have, and in fact did have, great influence on the King, convinced in practice of the huge sacrifices the people were prepared to make in the event of a war against Napoleon. Such a general meeting of minds, on the one hand, vouched for the success of the life and death struggle for the independence of Germany, while on the other hand, it showed the inevitability of an alliance with Russia: the result of this was the conclusion of a treaty of alliance in Breslau on 15 (27) February, signed by *Staatskanzler* Hardenberg and Anstett; on the following day, 16 (28) February, this treaty was signed in Kalisz by Prince Kutuzov and General Scharnhorst, who had been sent to our headquarters at the request of the Tsar, in place of Knesebeck. From that time on, Scharnhorst was a very active and useful mediator between the forces of both Coalition powers.[19]

On the basis of the treaty between Russia and Prussia, it was decided:

1. To conclude a defensive and offensive Coalition to restore the Prussian Monarchy within such borders as were required to ensure the security of both Powers.
2. To that end, Russia undertook to field 150,000 and Prussia 80,000 men, not including fortress garrisons.
3. Both powers agreed not to conclude either a separate peace or armistice, with Napoleon.
4. To use every means to persuade Austria to take part in a coalition against France and to enter into negotiations with Britain for the supply of arms, materiel and subsidies to Prussia.

18 *Das Leben des Ministers Freiherrn vom Stein,* III, 300-302. Beitzke, I, 168-171. Friccius, I, 37.
19 *Das Leben desLeben des Ministers Freiherrn vom Stein, G.H. Pertz, second edition, volume 2. Ministers Freiherrn vom Stein,* III, 304. Beitzke, I, 171.

In accordance with the secret articles of the same treaty, Emperor Alexander I undertook not to end the war until Prussia had been restored, in statistical, geographical and financial terms, not only in accordance with the situation of the state before the war of 1806, but with the expansion of its borders into areas that would serve as a link between Old Prussia and Silesia. The Contracting Powers, foreseeing the need to cater to Britain, decided not to include Hanover among the lands that were intended to serve as compensation for Prussia.[20]

The Treaty concluded in Kalisz was not announced immediately after its signing, either to the French government or to the Prussian people. The King wanted to break off the alliance with Napoleon but not before the Prussian territories had been cleared of the French by our forces. And, meanwhile, in Prussia, the national militia honed their skills with every passing day.

The brilliant Scharnhorst was the soul of these preparations. As soon as he had taken control of the war department, orders proceeded for service call-up in Silesia (just as had already been done in Prussia and Pomerania), for all *Krümper* and soldiers on furlough;[21] at the same time, a census was taken of all recruits, as well as of horses fit for service. Graudenz was assigned as the assembly area for men in East Prussia, under the command of General Bülow, while Kolberg was selected for Neumark [Nowa Marchia], under the command of Borstell, the only fortresses in these regions that were occupied by Prussian garrisons and could serve as strongholds for the national mobilisation. From other regions occupied by French forces, volunteers made their way as best they could to assembly areas, mainly in Silesia.

In 1807, at the conclusion of the Tilsit Treaty, the infantry of the Prussian army consisted of only 11 three-battalion regiments, numbering 30,000 men (at the beginning of 1813, another line regiment was being formed, the *Brandenburgisches Infanterie-Regiment Nr. 12*). These regiments were brought up to strength with soldiers recalled from furlough, and put on war establishment of eight hundred men per battalion; while the cavalry regiments had some 150 men per squadron; the artillery and troops from the engineering department were also replenished. In addition, 52 reserve battalions were formed, also at war establishment, for a total of 41,600 men, which increased the army to 80,000. The lack of officers, very damaging in the hasty generation of forces, was eliminated by the recall of retired officers, the promotion to officer rank of sub-ensigns and the most capable non-commissioned officers, the graduation of cadets and, in particular, the promotion of young men who had served with the *Freiwillige Jäger*. Subsequently, during the armistice, reserve regiments were formed from the reserve battalions, of three-battalion composition, which were redesignated as line upon the conclusion of peace. The lack of financial resources forced the government to entrust the clothing of the newly formed troops to the population of the countryside and the transfer of all company-level horses to the cavalry and artillery. Food supply for the lower ranks was in the care of the hosts upon whom the men had been permanently billeted.

20 Treaty concluded at Breslau and Kalisz, on 15 and 16 (27 and 28) February 1813. Koch, *Histoire abrégée des traités de paix* etc. III, 263.

21 *Krümper*, trained recruits, who, having been dismissed to their homes, constituted the reserves for the army in the field.

Both infantry and cavalry regiments, on the basis of Regulations dated 3 February, were reinforced with special *Jäger-Abtheilung* formed from volunteers. The total number of men in the *Abtheilung* was equal to that laid down for companies and squadrons, namely, the infantry *Abtheilung* were 200 strong, while the cavalry *Abtheilung* were 150 strong. The formation of *freiwillige Jäger zu Fuss und zu Pferd* strengthened the army with many thousands of fighting men; but all these calculated measures were insufficient for the decisive struggle against Napoleon: the entire nation had to be mobilised, and to that end, the *Landwehr* and *Landsturm* were established.

The *Landwehr* Regulations were based on two drafts, one of which was drawn up by General Scharnhorst, back in 1808, and the other, on the *Landwehr* of East Prussia, was presented to the King by Major Graf Dohna in Breslau. This provision, which was authorised on 5 (17) March, was published in the Berlin Gazette on 11 (23) March. For calculation of the armed forces that were to be established under the name of *Landwehr*, the number of troops voluntarily proposed by the officials in East Prussia was accepted as the basis for each of the Prussian regions, and as a result it was decided to form:

In East Prussia – 20 battalions and 19 squadrons.
In Pomerania – 12 battalions and 12 squadrons.
In Neumark – 12 battalions and eight squadrons.
In Kurmark – 28 battalions and 21 squadrons.
In Silesia – 60 battalions and 40 squadrons.
For a total of 132 battalions and 100 squadrons.

Subsequently, once the land beyond the Elbe had been cleared of the enemy, and national mobilisation had been established on it, the composition of the *Landwehr* increased to 150 battalions and 124 squadrons. These troops reinforced the active army with 120,000 infantry and 20,000 cavalry, but, with the exception of the East Prussian *Landwehr*, were only formed up during the armistice.

The Regulations on the *Landsturm*, or the arming of all men capable of wielding weapons, were promulgated at the same time as the establishment of the *Landwehr*, together with the Manual, containing the principles for training the foot and mounted *Landsturm*.

In addition to all the above-mentioned mobilisation, the following were formed: *National Kavallerie Regimenter*, of which there were: one in East Prussia, consisting of five squadrons, each of 150 men and a mounted jäger detachment of 150 men; another in Pomerania, of three squadrons numbering 450 men in total; a third in Silesia, with two squadrons of hussars and a 50-man mounted jäger detachment.

Finally, the so-called *Freischaaren* were also formed, mainly from non-Prussians, which was facilitated by the general loathing for Napoleon among the population of Germany. The most important of them, the detachment under Lützow [Ludwig Adolf Wilhelm von Lützow], eventually increased to three battalions and four squadrons, with a half-battery of foot artillery and a half-battery of horse artillery. Another detachment, under *Oberstleutnant* [Lieutenant Colonel] Reiss, was made up of Westphalians, and consisted of four battalions, while a third, under *Hauptmann* [Captain] Reiche [Ludwig von Reiche], had one battalion and a jäger *Abtheilung*.

In general, the armed forces of Prussia were assembled at four locations:

1. In East Prussia, under General Yorck's command.
2. In West Prussia, at Graudenz under General Bülow's command.
3. In Pomerania and Neumark, at Kolberg, where *Generalmajor* Borstell's forces were forming up.
4. In Silesia, the bulk of the entire force was concentrating under Blücher's command.

The outcome of the national mobilisation in Prussia was the replenishment and formation of the following forces:

Line infantry – 14 regiments and 11 battalions.
Cavalry – 20 regiments and three squadrons.
For a total of 56,350 men.
Reserve battalions – 52, numbering 41,600 men.
Volunteer and jäger detachments, numbering 10,000 men.
National cavalry regiments – three, numbering 1,650 men.
Landwehr – 140,000 men.
Freikorps – 5,000 men.
Grand total: 254,000 men.[22]

Of these forces, more than 100,000 men were fielded in February and March, namely: the line regiments, some of the reserve battalions, volunteer jäger detachments and the East Prussian *Landwehr*. Subsequently, over the course of two months, Prussia completed her standing army and multiplied its strength by two and a half.

The treaty of alliance concluded in Kalisz was promulgated by the Prussian government once Berlin had been cleared of French forces; on 11 (23) March, news of the alliance with Russia,[23] appeals to the nation, to the forces and to the *Landwehr* appeared in the newspapers there. Shortly before that, on 10 March, new style, the Order of the *Eisernes Kreuz* had been established. The French ambassador

22 Prussian strength return: Line Forces: 14 infantry regiments (including two combined regiments) – 32,238 men, six grenadier battalions – 4,830 men, four jäger and sharpshooter battalions – 2,815 men, Model Battalion – 805 men, Infantry total: 40,688 men. 19 cavalry regiments – 10,356 men, Model Squadron – 150 men, *Leibgarde Uhlan* Squadron – 150 men, Cavalry total: 10,656 men. 15 foot artillery companies and ten horse artillery companies – 4,306 men, seven pioneer companies – 700 men. Line forces total: 56,350 men. Reserve Battalions: nine battalions under General Bülow in West Prussia and Neumark – 7,200 men, eight battalions under Borstell in Pomerania – 6,400 men, 26 battalions in Silesia – 20,800 men, a further nine battalions under Yorck in East Prussia etc. – 7,200 men, for a total of 41,600 men (Plotho, *Der Krieg in Deutschland und Frankreich*, I, endnote X. *Beihefte zum Militair-Wochenblatt* 1845 & 1846).

23 This article was very brief: 'Breslau, 20 March. His Majesty the King and His Majesty the Emperor of All Russia have entered into an offensive and defensive alliance.'

Saint-Marsan [Antoine Marie Philippe Asinari de Saint-Marsan] was informed of the conclusion of an alliance with Russia on 3 (15) March, on the very day that Emperor Alexander I arrived in Breslau, while a declaration of war against Napoleon was communicated in Paris, through a note from the Prussian Resident, General Krusemarck, to the French *ministre des Affaires étrangères* [Minister of Foreign Affairs], the Duc de Bassano [Hugues-Bernard Maret], on 27 March. In this note, Krusemarck asserted that Prussia could no longer remain in the precarious position in which it had been placed by Russian successes and the French retreat. Following this, he recounted all the abuses experienced by Prussia from Napoleon's autocracy, and all the actions by the French government that were in clear violation of the Treaty of Tilsit and subsequent conventions. In conclusion, the hope was expressed that the breach with France and alliance with Russia would serve to achieve Prussian independence and the return of the hereditary regions of this monarchy.[24]

In response to this note, the Duc de Bassano tried to assert to Krusemarck that the policy of the Prussian government, from the very beginning of the revolutionary wars, had never been based on unshakable principles of honour and justice, but was altered incessantly, in accordance with changes of fortune. 'Providence itself' he wrote, 'had directed the events of the past winter in order to strip the mask off treacherous friends and give assurances of the devotion of true friends; it also gave *Sa Majesté* the power to punish the former and to celebrate the latter.'[25]

Let us turn to a presentation of military operations that occurred during the negotiations in Breslau and Kalisz.

I have already mentioned that, on the occasion of the refusal by Yorck and Bülow to assist Count Wittgenstein, his offensive had been suspended and, for the time being, operations by our forces were limited to sending light detachments onto the left bank of the Oder.

On 6 (18) February, the Viceroy, with the remnants of *1er Corps*, *2e Corps*, *3e Corps*, *4e Corps* and *6e Corps* of the *Grande Armée*, numbering 9,000 men, had retreated behind the Oder, to Frankfurt (where his *quartier-général* had been moved), and to Crossen. The following day, 7 (19) February, General Reynier also withdrew behind the Oder into the fortress of Glogau with the remnants of *7e Corps*, numbering around 2,500 men. Prince Poniatowski, having learned of the outcome of the action at Kalisz, retreated from Piotrków to Częstochowa with the remnants of *5e Corps* and von Gablenz's Saxon brigade that had joined them. Shortly before the Viceroy's retreat behind the Oder, Grenier's corps [Paul Grenier], established in Italy and adopting the designation *11e Corps*, arrived in Berlin with some 20,000 men: it consisted of the divisions under Fressinet [Philibert Fressinet] and Charpentier [Henri François Marie Charpentier], the Italian *4° Reggimento Cacciatori a cavallo*, and was supplemented by two battalions and one squadron from the Würzburg contingent. Of these troops, Charpentier's division and the cavalry, some 10,000 men in all, under Grenier's personal command, joined the Viceroy's small corps at

24 For the text of the King's appeals and extracts from the text of Krusemarck's note, see Appendix III at the end of this chapter.

25 The Duc de Bassano's (Maret) response to Krusemarck's note, dated 1 April, is quoted in full in Fain, *Manuscrit de 1813*, I, 273-280.

Frankfurt an der Oder. Fressinet's division and the Würzburg infantry remained in Berlin under the command of Marshal Augereau.[26]

On our side, Count Wittgenstein, having arrived in Konitz [Chojnice] on 8 (20) February with his main body, numbering 20,000 men, halted there for several days until 11 (23) February, and meanwhile sent light detachments onto the left bank of the Oder under Adjutant General Chernyshev, Major General Benckendorff and Colonel Tettenborn. Once generals Yorck and Bülow had arrived at Konitz on 10 (22) February, Bülow had just received a letter from Knesebeck from our headquarters, in which it was suggested that both Prussian generals advance to the Oder. Bülow reported this to Yorck, who, in accordance with his views, had concluded that even before the Prussian corps had time to reach the Oder, the King would have decided to declare war on the French, and that by that time an operational plan for the Russo-Prussian army would already have been approved. The consequence of this was an offensive towards the Oder: Wittgenstein from Konitz to Driesen, where he awaited the arrival of the Prussian forces to draw level with his corps, and then to move towards Landsberg; Yorck from Elbing to Konitz and on to Soldin [Myślibórz], while Bülow was to go from Stargard to Pyritz [Pyrzyce]. All three columns were to reach the Oder by 25 February (9 March). But in anticipation of the conclusion of the alliance, both ours and the Prussian generals moved forward slowly: Count Wittgenstein considered it dangerous to go deep into enemy occupied foreign territory without the assistance of Yorck's and Bülow's corps, while the Prussian government wanted our forces to drive the French back beyond the Elbe, and did not dare to act openly against the common enemy.[27]

Count Wittgenstein, on meeting with General Yorck, was surprised at his cool reaction to the common cause, but Yorck could not do otherwise: he had to be sure that his actions would be approved by the government, especially since he had reason to doubt King Friedrich Wilhelm's favour towards him. Despite Yorck's dismissal from command of his corps, having no official notification of it, he not only continued to command the force, but, in his capacity as Governor General of East Prussia and as the Viceroy, convened the regional deputies and prompted them to arm the people. There was no response to General Yorck's report of all these activities to the King; while passing through Marienwerder, for a meeting with Count Wittgenstein in Konitz, Yorck met Major Thile [Adolf Eduard von Thile], who was on his way back from Breslau, with orders for him: 'to present a justification to a court-martial, solely in military terms, on account of the convention he had concluded.' When Yorck informed Count Wittgenstein of his forthcoming journey to Breslau, in order to justify his actions, our commander, amazed at this unexpected news, wrote to Emperor Alexander I that 'the trial of a general who has rendered such important services to the common cause may have a very unfavourable influence on public opinion.' The Tsar, in response to this report from Count Wittgenstein, ordered him to immediately reassure Yorck, with regard to his concerns, and to offer His Own

26 Vaudoncourt, *Histoire de la guerre soutenue par les Français en Allemagne, en 1813*, 31.

27 Count Wittgenstein's reports dated 3 and 11 [15 and 23] February from Konitz. Archive of the M.T.D. No. 29,182. Log of Incoming Documents, No. 220 and No. 221.

petition in his favour to him.[28] But Yorck declined this proposal, expressing his feelings of gratitude, but noting that, apparently, the whole thing had been put in train only as a formality.

It is extraordinarily remarkable how hesitantly the Prussian government set about breaking from France and allying itself with Russia. In orders to Yorck dated 8 (20) February, he was instructed:

> Advance towards the Oder in such a way as to be constantly behind Russian forces. Until further orders are issued, keep this command secret and do not commence hostilities against French troops.

Similar orders were sent to General Bülow, while Borstell was ordered to remain in Kolberg with the force he had assembled. Meanwhile, Borstell, not having received these orders in time, reported to the King that, in anticipation of further orders, he had already set out for Königsberg in der Neumark [Chojna]. He wrote: 'I beg at Your Majesty's feet: let us go.'[29] On 17 February (1 March), just after the conclusion of the Treaty of Kalisz, the King, informing Yorck, wrote:

> advance swiftly to the Oder. But do not announce the signing of the treaty of alliance yet, as continuing negotiations with France prevents this; with regard to everything else, enter into an agreement with generals Count Wittgenstein and Bülow, whom I subordinate to you until your force receives further orders; while also following orders issued by Emperor Alexander's headquarters, located there, in order to coordinate operations on a common objective (*um die Operationen zu concertiren*) with *Oberst* Knesebeck. Military operations against the French must not be opened by My forces until such time as I publicly announce that which I shall not permit you to release.

The hesitancy of the Prussian government made it very difficult for the generals forming the militia, and especially Bülow, who had arrived in Neustettin [Szczecinek] from Königsberg on 5 (17) January, with the aim of assembling his formation there before closing up to the Oder in order to protect the King and the capital. Being within the French forces' sphere of operations, Bülow came under the influence of their commanders, especially since the objective of a national mobilisation had not yet been announced. On 13 (25) January, he had received orders to send a strength return for his force and intelligence on the enemy (Russian) troops facing him, from the Viceroy's *quartier-général*, stationed in Poznań at the time. General Bülow reported that there were only eight battalions under his command, consisting of recruits who, for the next four weeks, could not be uniformed, armed or considered trained in the most essential skills; at the same time, he [the Viceroy] passed

---

28 Letter from Emperor Alexander I to Count Wittgenstein, dated 15 (27) February, from Kalisz.

29 '*Ich werde nichts weiteres unternehmen bis Ew. Maj. Befehle mir bestimmt in Königsberg in der Neumark oder früher zugegangen sein werden, bitte aber Ew. Maj. fussfällig: lassen sie uns los*). Borstell's report dated 27 February new style.

on some intelligence about Russian forces and gave notice that, in the event of an onslaught by superior forces, he should retreat towards Schwedt rather than towards Kolberg. When Bülow invoked the King's express orders to head for Kolberg, the Viceroy insisted that he retreat towards Schwedt instead. In February, Bülow was ordered to attach his force to the French *2e Corps* under Marshal Victor, stationed in Küstrin at the time. But the adamant Bülow refused to carry out this order, writing in response to the marshal that he could not decide on this before receiving orders from his sovereign. 'I leave it to you to decide' he wrote to Victor, 'whether a general, without specific orders from his own government, may submit to a commander in the service of a foreign Power.'[30]

Eventually, all misapprehensions came to an end. On 22 February (6 March), General Yorck received the following memo from Scharnhorst in Kalisz: 'I consider it my duty to inform you that His Majesty the King desires that the force under your command, if possible, move without delay to the Oder and cross this river by the tenth of this month [10 March new style].'[31]

Thus, an offensive by allied forces onto the left bank of the Oder was agreed. But Yorck's situation, threatened with punishment for his unilateral orders, was very onerous. On 15 (27) February he had sent to the King from Konitz: 'A detailed explanation of the reasons that prompted *Generalleutnant* Yorck to conclude an agreement with the Russian General Diebitsch [Ivan Ivanovich Dibich or Hans Karl Friedrich Anton von Diebitsch] at Poscherun Mill [Po˛erūnai], near Tauroggen [Tauragė].' The King entrusted the investigation of this case to a special commission, rather than to a formal court-martial. But the final verdict on this case was delayed until 12 March new style. The King's orders to Yorck, proclaimed that day, were as follows:

> Because the convention concluded by you with General Diebitsch in Imperial Russian service has been acknowledged by the commission, composed of Lieutenant General Diericke [Christoph Friedrich Otto von Diericke] and major generals Sanitz [Karl Wilhelm von Sanitz] and Schuler, no reason for any reproach is found, thus I, having given the order attached herewith, instruct you to promulgate it to all the troops entrusted to you.

In an Order of the Day, the King, announcing the total acquittal of General Yorck and not only confirmed him in command of his corps, but also, as a mark of his complete approval and unrestricted confidence, subordinated *Generalmajor* Bülow's force to him.[32]

A few days later, Emperor Alexander awarded General Yorck the Order of St Alexander Nevsky.[33]

30 Beitzke, I, 218-220.
31 Orders for General Yorck, dated 3 March new style.
32 Droysen, II, 157.
33 General Scharnhorst, who had been instructed to send the insignia of the Order of St Alexander Nevsky to Yorck, wrote to him: 'It is with indescribable pleasure that I send you the Order of Alexander; Emperor Alexander speaks of you with the greatest respect; he regards you as a man to whom we owe a great deal, and the king agrees. Therefore, I beg you most earnestly, to disregard minor inconveniences; I live only for these alone' ('*Mit*

As the above mentioned events unfolded, our partisans crossed the Oder.

Adjutant General Chernyshev, with six weak Cossack regiments, four squadrons of Izyum Hussars, two squadrons of Finland Dragoons and with two Don artillery pieces, having closed up to the Oder on 5 (17) February, 20 *verstas* downstream of Küstrin, near the town of Zellin [Czelin], found that the ice on the river was barely holding and had even parted from both banks. Having set up a scaffold bridge, Chernyshev crossed to the left bank of the Oder, while Major General Benckendorff and Colonel Tettenborn also crossed with their raiding detachments, the former near Frankfurt, while the latter crossed at Schwedt. Over the next two days, the Cossack patrols sent out by Chernyshev scattered two French detachments and captured 300 men. Thereafter, Chernyshev and Tettenborn, having linked up in Wriezen, agreed to move on Berlin as a combined force, and as a rather significant enemy formation was astride the direct route to this capital, in Werneuchen, then, by agreement of both partisan commanders, it was planned to go left-flanking around them at Altlandsberg, and head through Marzahn and Schönhausen, to Pankow, on the Stettin highway. A small unit of Cossacks was left to face the enemy at Werneuchen with orders to harass the French relentlessly, and to set large campfires in the night; the main bodies of both detachments reunited in Altlandsberg on 8 (20) February, and the following day [21 February], at four o'clock in the morning, they arrived in Pankow. Marshal Augereau was holding Berlin with at least 6,000 men with 40 guns; our partisans did not have even half this number of troops, besides which, they had no infantry whatsoever. But, having said that, the advantage of surprise was on their side, which made up for the lack of numbers.

Upon arrival at Pankow, Chernyshev and Tettenborn took up positions near this town, and sent Lieutenant Colonel Vlasov [Maxim Grigorievich Vlasov] to Charlottenburg where most of the French artillery was located, with two Cossack regiments, and placed pickets on all the roads to Berlin. It was intended to attack the enemy holding this city that night. But at around noon, the Cossacks stationed in the forward outposts reported that a small cavalry detachment was leaving the city, apparently to conduct a reconnaissance of our force. Wanting to confirm the matter, our detachment commanders went on a reconnaissance themselves. Colonel Tettenborn, seeing the enemy cavalry driving off our outposts, dashed to attack them with Kommisarov's Cossack Regiment and having driven the French back, burst into the city hot on their heels. The appearance of our partisans caused indescribable chaos in Berlin and the environs of this capital: soldiers hurried to assembly points; artillery rushed at full speed out of Charlottenburg. Meanwhile, Adjutant General Chernyshev led the remaining regiments from both detachments to the city walls, scattered the enemy who had left the Oranienburg gate to surround Tattenborn, using canister fire, and sent Colonel Yefremov's brigade through the Hamburg gate while Grekov 18th's [Timofei Dmitrievich Grekov] Cossacks went through the Königsthor. These three regiments entered the city,

unbeschreiblichem Vergnügen übersende ich Ihnen den Alexander-Orden; der Kaiser Alexander spricht von Ihnen mit der grössten Achtung; er sieht Sie an, als einen Mann, dem Wir unendlich viel zu verdanken haben, ude der König stimmt damit ein. Ich bitte sie daher inständigst, setzen sie sich über kleine Unannehmlichkeiten weg; ich lebe nur allein in diesen.'). Droysen, II, 158.

dashing through the streets under fire from enemy sub-units in the alleys and buildings, and did not stop until they reached the river Spree, over which all the wooden bridges had been dismantled, while a six-gun battery had been placed by the masonry bridge. Colonel Tettenborn also galloped along the Schönhauser Allee, but having set off for the Alexanderplatz, he was engaged by fire from an infantry square with eight guns. As the battle continued, the Berliners expressed their support for our troops with loud cheers, but were cowed into obedience to the French by the city police, who fired into the gathering crowds and dispersed them. According to Chernyshev's report:

> If the favourable attitude of the population, who tried to give us a helping hand and the women, in visible ecstasy themselves, who greeted us in every way that half-decency allows, had not been stopped by the hostile orders of the city police, and especially those of Monsieur Le Coq [Paul Ludwig Le Coq], I can assure you that the exploits of the cavalry on this day would not have been limited to the harm done to the enemy.

The impossibility of establishing a foothold in the city forced the partisan commanders to withdraw their troops into the open, where they settled in sight of the city, and the following day [22 February] they withdrew to Oranienburg. On the other hand, Colonel Vlasov had captured the town of Charlottenburg in battle along with Sysoev's Cossack regiment, taking 168 prisoners, and held the road to Potsdam. Overall, in addition to the loss of killed or wounded, the enemy lost six field officers, 12 subalterns and more than 600 lower ranks taken prisoners alone. On our side, 150 men were killed or wounded; among those killed was a Prussian subject, Captain Blumberg, who was in the detachment under Tettenborn; *Starshina* Kommisarov was severely wounded.[34]

On 7 (19) February, the Viceroy, having learned of the crossing of the Oder by our troops, decided to bring his small army closer to Berlin and arrived there on 9 (21) February with 500 *Cavalerie de la Garde*. The rest of the force, with the exception of Gérard's division, left in Frankfurt for the time being, also moved nearer Berlin in two columns, to Müncheberg and Fürstenwalde: the Italian *4° Reggimento Cacciatori a cavallo*, numbering around 1,000 men, proceeding along the former of these routes, was caught by Benckendorff's detachment on 10 (22) February, in the vicinity of Müncheberg, and was completely wiped out, with the loss of 700 men taken prisoner alone.[35] After that, General Benckendorff turned on Fürstenwalde in order to divert the Viceroy from Berlin, and attempted to capture Frankfurt, where there was still an enemy garrison at that time, but not having managed to do so,

34 Adjutant General Chernyshev's reports to General-of-Cavalry Wittgenstein, dated 8 [20] February, from Altlandsberg, No. 77, and dated 9 [21] February, from Pankow, No. 80, and Tettenborn's, dated 9 [21] February, from Pankow.

35 War Diary, signed off by Prince Kutuzov-Smolensky. Count Wittgenstein's report to Prince Kutuzov-Smolensky, dated 21 February, No. 58, with an intercepted letter from the regimental commander Hercule to General Gérard, from which it is clear that only 11 officers and 33 lower ranks escaped from the entire 4° *Reggimento Cacciatori a cavallo*. Vaudoncourt, 32. Beitzke, I, 231.

he returned to Müncheberg and, upon reaching the outskirts of Berlin, established communications with Chernyshev and Tettenborn.

The occupation of the routes leading to Berlin by our partisans forced the Viceroy to take the strictest precautions against a surprise assault: every route into the city from the right bank of the river Spree was blocked; batteries and bivouacked infantry were stationed on the left bank of the river. The cavalry were forbidden from unsaddling their horses. No one was allowed to leave the city without express permission; dead silence reigned in all the streets and squares, and even the post office was closed, because the Cossacks had completely disrupted all communications between Berlin and the surrounding countryside. The Viceroy strengthened the Berlin garrison to 15,000 men, but remained at Köpenick (ten *verstas* from Berlin) with his *quartier-général*, probably fearing an uprising by the population of the city. His force was reorganised once more: Grenier's corps together with the regiments that had arrived from Poznań, made up three divisions, under the command of generals Charpentier, Fressinet and Gérard; a reserve division, consisting of two battalions of the *Vieille Garde*, two of the *Jeune Garde* and a detachment from the Italian division, numbering 2,400 men, remained under the command of General Roguet. The cavalry consisted, in total, of 500 *Cavalerie de la Garde*, 200 horsemen from the Würzburg contingent and the remains of the Italian *4° Reggimento Cacciatori a cavallo*. Overall, the Viceroy's force in Berlin and the environs of this capital reached 26,000 men.[36] But the small size of his cavalry force allowed our raiding detachments, which did not exceed 4,000 men in total, to hold the routes into the city and keep the enemy under constant blockade.

The situation for the population in the vicinity of Berlin was very onerous. In the city itself, in addition to the troops stationed there, there were many generals, officers, support staff and sick soldiers from the former *Grande Armée*. Contagious diseases that raged in the hospitals spread from them to all neighbouring districts. The population, already made destitute, were forced to provide food not only for the French whom they hated, yet were considered allies of their Sovereign, but also for the Cossacks, viewed throughout Prussia as harbingers of deliverance. Justice must be done to the Viceroy in that he tried to lighten the burden of evil weighing on the townsfolk; the commanders of the Russian forces maintained strict discipline in their units; but the supply of fodder to our numerous cavalry and the procurement of a huge number of carts for the partisans greatly depleted the countryside. Only receipts were issued for all this, and sometimes nothing was issued at all; in particular, both the population and our troops found it difficult to communicate with one another. Quick-witted Germans, wishing to alleviate this misery, immediately compiled little dictionaries and manuals in which the meaning and pronunciation of the most essential words and whole phrases were explained in Russian and German; but there was no time to study them in this restless period. It should not be overlooked that the population of Prussia, satisfying the demands of their current allies, the French, and future allies, the Russians, willingly or otherwise, also had to fulfil the requirements of their government, to call up men from furlough, recruits,

36 Vaudoncourt, 32-33.

horses, supplies, equip the volunteers, and send them to Silesia or to Pomerania, etcetera. Such orders, often contradicting each other, spread chaos and disorder and tried the patience of even the calmest German officials. The resistance of French authorities was added to all these concerns. Both Marshal Augereau, and later the Viceroy, did everything possible to impede the military exodus to the assembly areas; but the Prussian volunteers continued to leave not only singly, but in large groups, without commanders and not infrequently without weapons. These people's *Abtheilungen* had no concept of military discipline, but their sacred love for the motherland served as a strong bond.[37]

The raid on Berlin by our partisans gave rise to Prussian Prinz Heinrich, brother of King Friedrich Wilhelm III, to write to Marshal Augereau that in the event of a second attack by the Russians, he could not guarantee good behaviour from the population, and therefore the prince asked the marshal not to defend himself within the city, rather to go out to engage our troops. Upon the departure of Augereau from Berlin, on 13 (25) February, due to illness, Saint-Cyr [Laurent de Gouvion-Saint-Cyr] took his place, and proposed to the Viceroy to attach Lauriston's corps [Jacques Jean Alexandre Bernard Law de Lauriston], located in Magdeburg, to the main force, and by concentrating more than 40,000 men on the Oder, to hold this defensive line and Berlin, which, in the opinion of the marshal, would delay the defection of Prussia from its alliance with Napoleon. But when Saint-Cyr fell ill with typhoid fever, the Viceroy abandoned any further defence of Berlin and began to prepare for a retreat behind the Elbe.[38]

Such was the state of affairs in Berlin at the time of the conclusion of the treaty of alliance in Kalisz. Let us turn now to the presentation of subsequent military operations.

37 Beitzke, I, 231-233.

38 Saint-Cyr, *Mémoires pour servir à l'histoire militaire etc. Campagne de 1813 en Saxe*, 6 & 11-13.

Appendix III

Proclamations by King Friedrich Wilhelm and extracts from General Krusemarck's note

---

Proclamations by King Friedrich Wilhelm:

> To My people. There is no need to explain the reasons for the imminent war, neither to My faithful people nor to the population of Germany. They are clear for a Europe that has emerged from its blindness.
>
> We have been languishing under the yoke of France. The peace treaty, which took half of My subjects from Me, was more disastrous for us than the war itself. Deep wounds have been inflicted upon our country. Our most important fortresses are in the hands of the enemy. Agriculture and industry, which had previously flourished, has fallen into decay. Free trade has been destroyed and all sources of national wealth and prosperity have dried up. Poverty reigns everywhere.
>
> By fulfilling the severe obligations as stipulated, I had hoped to alleviate the lot of My people and convince the *Empereur des Français* that his own interests necessitated the preservation of an independent Prussia. But all my opinions, inspired by openness, were denied in arrogance and betrayal, and now we have become completely convinced that it is even more harmful to conclude treaties with Napoleon than it is to wage war on him. The time has come to talk of our situation dispassionately.
>
> People of Brandenburg, Prussia, Silesia, Pomerania, Lithuania! You know what you have had to endure for seven years; it is also not unknown to you what awaits if we do not conclude the imminent struggle with honour. Remember the events of the past, the Great Elector, Frederick the Great. May those things won by the blood of our ancestors not be erased from our memory: religious tolerance, honour, freedom, trade, industry and science. Remember the lofty examples set by our powerful Russian allies, remember the Spanish, the Portuguese. Even small nations, in defence of these virtues, have fought against the strongest enemies and defeated them. Remember the heroes of Switzerland and the Netherlands.
>
> Great sacrifices will be required from all classes, because the task we have in mind is difficult: the enemy is powerful and has huge resources. But you would rather make sacrifices for your Fatherland and the King than for a foreign ruler who is willing to exhaust your last resource in order to achieve

an objective that is alien to you. Trusting in God, let us remain resolute and, with the assistance of powerful allies, we shall crown our valiant efforts with victory.

But whatever sacrifices each of you may make, they still cannot equal the blessings for which we are willing to fight and to die, or to win as long as we value our Fatherland.

This is the last decisive struggle for our identity, for our independence, for our well-being. Our only choice is an honourable peace, or a glorious death. Let us hope that God and our own steadfastness will crown this just cause with victory and grant us happiness, together with a glorious peace.

Breslau. 17 March 1813. Friedrich-Wilhelm.

To My troops. On more than one occasion you have expressed a desire to restore the freedom and independence of the Fatherland by force of arms. That time has come! Everyone can sense it. In all places men and youths voluntarily clamour for weapons. You who belong to the standing army, your calling is that which they do willingly. Is it even necessary to encourage you to defend the Fatherland, which every class of people have taken upon themselves?

Take a look at how many have left everything that is most precious to all in order to offer themselves up for their homeland, and feel your sacred duties redoubled. Remember this on the day of battle and on those days of labour and deprivation. Let each of your personal ambitions disappear in pursuit of the common cause. Whoever is devoted to the Fatherland forgets about himself. God Himself shall grant the victory. Make yourselves worthy of his sacred protection through obedience and the fulfilment of your duties. Be famed for your courage, patience and strict discipline. Follow the example of your ancestors; be worthy of them and may posterity have pride in you!

The inalienable rewards will be distributed for outstanding deeds; shame and severe punishment will befall those who neglect their duties!

Your King is with you; as is the Crown Prince and the other princes of his House. They and all our people shall fight together with you, while the nation that has come to help Germany, that has defended their independence with supreme feats, shall assist us. They had faith in their Sovereign, their leaders, in the justness of their cause, in their strength, and the Lord blessed their efforts. May He also bless yours! We who are also going to fight for the independence of our Fatherland.

May our response be faith in God, in courage and in patience!

Breslau, 17 March 1813. Friedrich-Wilhelm.

Extracts from General Krusemarck's note:

... The successes of the Russian forces do not permit Prussia to remain in the precarious position in which it finds itself. On the one hand, the Russian Emperor, united with the King by a bond of personal friendship, at this decisive hour, is offering Prussia the support of his might and the

> benefits of his alliance; on the other hand, His Majesty the *Empereur des Français*, as before, rejects an ally which has sacrificed itself for his cause, and contemptuously refuses to explain the reasons for his silence.

Following this, in describing the autocratic acts by Napoleon, it states:

> France has exploited odious pretexts in order to destroy the very foundations of the state and personal prosperity in Prussia. From that point on,[1] they have treated it like an annexed country… The King has suffered in sympathy with the disasters that have burdened his subjects, He hoped to quench the malice, of which he did not know the cause but felt the harmful consequences, through indulgence and every kind of sacrifice. He consoled himself with the thought of easing the lot of his subjects, fulfilling his obligations in relation to France precisely and carefully avoiding anything that might arouse distrust from Napoleon. Through extraordinary, unprecedented efforts, Prussia had paid two-thirds of the indemnity and was preparing to pay the remaining third when the disagreement arose between France and Russia; the enormous preparations by both Powers made it impossible to doubt that the flames of war threatened northern Europe. The King, constantly striving to preserve whatever remained of national independence, in assessing the future from the past, believed that he had everything to fear from France. He sacrificed these heartfelt instincts and concluded a treaty of alliance with the French government.

This treaty, on the basis of which Prussia provided the agreed corps against Russia and filled the depots of the French army with supplies, was ignominiously violated by both Napoleon and his troops.

> … While Prussia was exhausting its finite resources in order to provide the magazines with the specified amount of supplies, the French armies gorged themselves at the expense of the population. Being simultaneously obliged to fulfil the terms of the treaty and satisfy the demands of the troops. The last of the people's possessions were forcibly plundered and Prussia lost more than 70,000 horses and 20,000 wagons.

Napoleon not only forced the Prussian government, in contravention of the agreed treaty terms, to provide rations for the French garrisons of the fortresses on the Oder, but unilaterally seized the fortresses of Pillau and Spandau.

> By the end of 1812, Prussia had paid for and delivered various supplies to the French government in excess of the agreed debt of 94,000,000 francs. The King requested that even just a portion of this amount be returned to

1 From the signing of the Treaty of Tilsit.

> him until completion of a final audit of accounts, and not being responsible for the consequences in the event of a refusal.
>
> The King, seeing part of his territory occupied, and the rest threatened by foreign forces, has found it necessary to strengthen his army, and as conventional means have proved insufficient for this, all those who wish to serve under his colours have been called up. This proclamation prompted many Berliners to go to Breslau. But the Viceroy has forbidden the recruitment of troops in every Prussian region occupied by the French and tried by all possible means to prevent the assembly of volunteers and their departure to Silesia: these orders were carried out without the knowledge of the King, and thus amount to a violation of the rights of his sovereignty.
>
> Under such circumstances, the King is obliged to take decisive action. Over the course of several years, he has sacrificed everything in order to preserve his political independence; now, France exposes him to danger and refuses to defend Prussia. Russia, which could have aggravated our misfortune, has generously offered its protection. The King cannot be swayed from his intent. Staying true to his principles and duties, he is joining Emperor Alexander, changing the system but not changing his outlook. He hopes that by breaking the alliance with France and concluding one with Russia, to achieve an honourable peace, even by force of arms, the only objective of his desires: the independence of his subjects, their welfare, which should be its consequence, and the return of the heritage of their ancestors…

This note is placed in full, with Napoleon's own remarks, in the work by Fain: *Manuscrit de 1813, Deuxième édit.* I, 247-273.

3

The Liberation of Berlin

Brief description of the theatre of operations in 1813. – The primary operational objective of the Coalition, the occupation of Saxony. – The situation in the Kingdom of Saxony in political terms.

Overall operational plan of the Coalition forces. – Blücher. – Composition of the Prussian army; comparison of the composition and qualities of the Coalition armies.

The advance by the vanguard of Wittgenstein's army on Berlin. – The liberation of Berlin. – Wittgenstein's arrival in Berlin. – Offensive by the Prussian contingent of Count Wittgenstein's army: Yorck's and Bülow's corps and Borstell's brigade. – Emperor Alexander I's arrival in Breslau. – The general mobilisation of Prussia. – The involvement of each and every person in the war for the liberation of Germany. – The advance on Bunzlau by Blücher's army.

The forces under the Viceroy and their dispositions upon retreating behind the Elbe. – The deployment of the Coalition army under Wittgenstein on the liberation of Berlin. – The diverging points of view of Prince Kutuzov and Count Wittgenstein. – Colonel Tettenborn's expedition. – The liberation of Hamburg. – Vandamme in Bremen. – Morand's advance on Lüneburg. The expedition to Lüneburg by generals Chernyshev and Dörnberg. – Action at Lüneburg. – Davout's arrival on the lower Elbe. – Retreat by Chernyshev and Dörnberg to the right bank of the Elbe. – The Russian partisans are subordinated to Graf Wallmoden.

The ground which served as the theatre of the most important military operations in 1813 is bounded on the north by the Baltic Sea, on the east by the course of the Oder, on the south by the mountains separating Bohemia from Saxony, Lusatia [Lausitz] and Silesia, on the west by the course of the river Saale and the lower Elbe. Operations by significant forces outside of these boundaries, prior to the battle of Leipzig, were carried out only during the short-lived invasion through the Ore Mountains [Erzgebirge] into Bohemia by French forces. This area has previously been the stage for events that have decided the fate of nations: it was here that Widukind sought refuge from the blows of his powerful opponent Charlemagne [Karl der Große], in the same places Gustavus-Adolphus [Gustav II Adolf] defended and redeemed the political and religious independence of Germany at the cost of his own life. Like the Swedes and their courageous King, it was up to the Russians and the Blessed Alexander I to assist the nations in their sacred struggle for their homelands and restore the Crowns, shaken to their very foundations by the conqueror's lust for power.

This country had already been occupied by the French for six years, controlled as if it were their own territory. Almost all the fortresses in this area were occupied by French troops: on the Oder they possessed: Glogau, Küstrin and Stettin; on the Elbe it was the fortified city of Dresden and the fortresses of Torgau, Wittenberg and Magdeburg. The possession of these locations gave the French great advantages, strengthening their defensive lines and providing them with excellent bases in the event of switching to the offensive. In the area between the Elbe and the Rhine, hatred for them was seething among the German people, but the rulers of the *Confédération du Rhin* took the side of Napoleon, partly out of cowardice, partly out of selfish fear of incurring losses in a regime change. As for the ground between the Oder and the Neman or to the Russian border, the majority of its population, consisting of Poles, was on the side of Napoleon; almost all the fortresses there were occupied by the French and their allies. And although Napoleon's army was weakened through the maintenance of garrisons in these fortresses, nevertheless, their investment and siege weakened the Russian army even more.

Considering the general properties of this theatre of war, we find that its northern part, adjacent to the sea, presents flat terrain dotted with many lakes and swamps; the soil in this sector, for the most part, is clay, sandy, or stony, and requires intensive labour for cultivation; in contrast, the southern part of the theatre of war, from the borders of Bohemia to a line passing from Eisleben, through Altenburg, Dresden, Bautzen, and Bunzlau [Bolesławiec], to Breslau, is hilly, populous and fertile; the central sector is undulating, but quite extensive plains are found in places.

The Oder river, with the fortresses of Glogau, Küstrin and Stettin, presented the French forces with a very advantageous defensive line, which, in the opinion of Marshal Saint-Cyr, they could use to hold the Russian forces back and to keep Berlin and the whole sector between the Oder and the Elbe under their control. Indeed, if the Viceroy had succeeded in stopping our army on the Oder before the arrival of Napoleon with his newly assembled force, then the mobilisation of Prussia would have slowed down and, moreover, Napoleon, having commenced hostilities from the Oder, could have immediately broken into a sympathetic Duchy of Warsaw and could have strengthened himself with support from there.

The Elbe river, with the fortresses of Magdeburg, Wittenberg and Torgau, and with the cities of Hamburg and Dresden fortified in the second campaign of 1813, was an excellent defensive line, but due to its long length (over 400 *verstas*) it required a significant force to hold it, which compelled the Viceroy (as will be explained later) to abandon the defence of the entire sector upstream of the confluence with the Saale river and confine himself to protecting the course of the Saale and a short length of the course of the Elbe near Magdeburg. In the second campaign of 1813, after the truce, although Napoleon derived important advantages from the line he had prepared for defence along the Elbe, he was nevertheless forced to abandon it when the Coalition sent superior forces from Bohemia towards the French army's lines of communication, towards Leipzig.

In general, all the fortresses in this theatre of war had been brought into a state for a long defence by the French, which will be described in more detail when depicting these sieges.

The most important locations in this theatre of war, in military and political terms, were: Berlin, the capital of Prussia. However, with the abandonment of the line along the Oder by French forces, hanging on to Berlin was unfeasible, both due to the topographical nature of the terrain at this location, which did not present the means for an enduring defence, and due to the Berliners' dislike for Napoleon and the French; Dresden, the capital of Saxony, a kingdom whose ruler had been completely committed to Napoleon. During the second campaign of 1813, Dresden acquired a particular military importance, being fortified by the French throughout the truce and serving as their stronghold and secure crossing point. Königstein, the small Saxon fortress on the Elbe, gained strategic importance due to the crossing established there, which, in the second campaign, allowed Napoleon to operate against the lines of communication of the main Coalition army with its base in Bohemia. Hamburg, the most important of the *Hansestädte* [Hanseatic cities], the inhabitants of which, having been made involuntary subjects of the Empire of the French, hated Napoleon and were ready to take the Coalition side. Being capable of turning the defensive position, Hamburg was heavily fortified and stubbornly defended by Marshal Davout. Leipzig, an important location strategically, was the hub of many routes across north-eastern Germany, which gave the Coalition the opportunity to envelope Napoleon's deployment along the Elbe.

The main Coalition axes of operations, in the first campaign of 1813, were the routes:

1. From Landsberg through Berlin.
2. From Kalisz through Dresden.

Both routes led towards Saxony, the occupation of which was very important for both sides. The Coalition, having captured Saxony, would block enemy access to Berlin and the Duchy of Warsaw, could exploit the resources of the fertile and well-populated countryside to feed their forces, and finally, by shifting the war into Germany, they hoped to acquire allies there, or at least to contribute to a spontaneous uprising by the population. The outlook of Austria itself was very much dependent on the development of offensive operations by the Russo-Prussian army. Napoleon, for his part, could not hold out in Germany otherwise than by occupying Saxony and positioning himself along the Elbe; with the loss of this line, he would inevitably have to retreat behind the Rhine, which entailed the denial of access to the members of the *Confédération du Rhin* to him.

Based on these factors, the occupation of Saxony was the primary operational objective of the Russian army. The inhabitants of this country, like their other compatriots, were preparing to revolt against the French, and if this were to actually happen, then the subjects of the King of Westphalia [Jérôme Bonaparte or Hieronymus Napoleon] would follow the example of the Saxons and the Coalition could open hostilities on the Rhine, rather than on the Elbe: thus the liberation of Germany could have taken place sooner and would have involved infinitely less sacrifice. This would have been beneficial for Saxony in particular, which, perhaps, would not have become a theatre of war for the course of half a year and would not have lost a significant part of its territory upon the conclusion of peace.

The cause of all the catastrophes that befell Saxony was King Friedrich-August I himself. Worthy of respect in his private life, beloved by his subjects whom he had ruled for almost 45 years, the king was pious to the point of self-righteousness, conceited in everything that concerned the external appearance of his dignity, and incapable of decisiveness in important events. Napoleon and his exploits had an extraordinary influence on Friedrich-August, and the conqueror's benevolence towards him completely lulled him. Nonetheless, the Russian invasion of Prussia, the appearance of our troops in Berlin and the mobilisation of the Prussian people alarmed Friedrich-August. It was obvious that Saxony would become the theatre of military operations, and that it was imperative to adhere to one of the sides. The most dangerous thing would be to remain neutral in the midst of a clash of foreign armies; but the King not only placed himself at such a disadvantage, but withdrew from his capital, leaving the administration of the state to the *Regierungs Kommission* [governing committee]. Persuading the people to observe loyalty, peace and calm, the King expressed his intention to fulfil the duties he had assumed as a member of the *Confédération du Rhin*. On 13 (25) February, he left Dresden, accompanied by his family, some ministers and the French ambassador, Baron Serrá, taking with him 200,000 Thaler in currency, more than 4,000,000 in bonds, and most of the jewellery from the Grünes Gewölbe vaults. Two *Kürassiere* regiments and a small detachment of infantry were assigned to guard the King and his treasures. Initially, he went to Plauen towards the border with Bavaria, from where, at the end of March, he withdrew to Regensburg, thereafter, entrusting himself to the protection of Austria, he set off for Prague on 1 (13) April.

Meanwhile, Saxony had been abandoned to every happenstance of the struggle between its powerful neighbours. The King ordered all the Saxon troops to assemble in Torgau, both those who had returned from Russia and those newly formed, but instead of operating as part of the *Confédération du Rhin*, and attaching them to the army under the Viceroy, he forbade both French and Russo-Prussian forces from entering this fortress, as well as that of Königstein. Subsequently, he refused Napoleon's demand to attach the Saxon cavalry to Ney's corps [Michel Ney] several times; while equally deflected from assisting the Coalition. In doing so, he was imitating the Austrian government, but the position of Saxony did not allow for such political fence-sitting, and the King himself became convinced of this, but only once it had proven impossible to improve matters.[1]

The basic concept of the operational plan for the allied Russo-Prussian army was proposed by General Scharnhorst during his attachment to Emperor Alexander's

1 Beitzke, I, 261-264.

headquarters. According to Scharnhorst himself, initially it was agreed only that 'Wittgenstein's army should march on Magdeburg, Blücher's army on Dresden, while the Main Army was to follow Blücher's force at an interval of three stages.' Having concentrated most of the infantry and regular cavalry on the left wing of the operational front, Scharnhorst planned to fix the enemy there with stubborn resistance, and meanwhile, to envelope their left flank with light troops attached to the Coalition right wing.[2] The factors that prompted such a division of forces into two independent armies were the concerns, on the one hand, that Napoleon might repeat the flanking movement he had made in the campaign of 1806, and on the other, that by enveloping us on our right flank, he might drive the Coalition forces back to the border of neutral Bohemia. This operational plan proposed by Scharnhorst raised doubts not only in ours, but also in the Prussian *Hauptquartier*. General Knesebeck, who had gained renown as a great strategist, proposed sending the forces under Blücher and Wittgenstein to Magdeburg together, against the Viceroy and, driving him back through superior numbers, proceed with the sieges of the fortresses on the Elbe; while inciting the population of Westphalia and the former Prussian provinces to an uprising against the French by sending light troops there. But Emperor Alexander's absolute confidence in Scharnhorst caused the Coalition to prefer his proposed course of action.[3]

According to the stated Coalition plans, the Russo-Prussian forces, upon the conclusion of the Treaty of Kalisz, were to move into Saxony in two columns: the right, under the command of Count Wittgenstein, consisting of 20,000 Russian and 30,000 Prussian troops, in front of which marched Prince Repnin's vanguard [Nikolai Grigorievich Repnin-Volkonsky], directed on Berlin, while the left, under the command of Blücher, of 27,000 Prussian troops, in the vanguard of which marched 13,000 Russian troops under Adjutant General Wintzingerode,[4] was directed on Dresden. But our main army, some 30,000 men in all,[5] remained for a while partly on the Oder, partly near Kalisz, where Emperor Alexander and Prince Kutuzov had their headquarter from 12 (24) February until 27 March (8 April). The command of the Prussian forces assembled in Silesia was entrusted to the *General der Kavallerie* Blücher, due to the influence of Scharnhorst, despite the seniority and talents of *Generalfeldmarschall* Kalckreuth, and despite *Generalleutnant* Tauentzien [Bogislav Friedrich Emanuel von Tauentzien], who received the special favour of our Tsar, seeking the title of Commander-in-Chief of the force. Ardent for his advanced years, bold to the point of impertinence, Blücher was adored by the troops. *Vorwärts*! (forwards!) was the expression he uttered in battle which became his nickname. Scharnhorst, newly promoted to *Generalleutnant*, was assigned to Blücher's army as *Chef des Generalstabs* [chief of staff], while *Generalmajor* Gneisenau became his *Generalquartiermeister*.

2 Sharnhorst's letter dated 6 April new style.
3 Förster, *Geschichte der Befreiungs-kriege*, I, 180-182.
4 For details Coalition forces, see Appendix IV at the end of this chapter.
5 The Main Army consisted of: the vanguard under General Miloradovich, numbering 11,550 men with 120 guns; the main body, comprising III Corps, V Corps, VIII Corps and two cuirassier divisions, numbering 17,100 men with 200 guns (including those of VIII Corps). Plotho, I, *Beilagen*, 44-47.

The organisation of the Prussian forces, in this era, differed from the organisation of the Russian army. With our allies, the entire infantry were subordinated to brigades, each of seven battalions with detachments of jägers, altogether some 6,000 men; while the regiments, numbering 2,400 men on war establishment, each had three battalions. A brigade was commanded by a *Generalmajor* or *Oberst*; a regiment by an *Oberstleutnant*; a battalion by a major; an artillery battery had eight guns and was commanded by an *Oberleutnant or Leutnant*. In our army, in contrast, following the harsh winter campaign, in many regiments there were only 200 or 300 men per battalion. Divisions had between four and six regiments, numbering from 1,500 to 2,000 men; while corps had from 3,000 to 4,000 men. The corps, which were only slightly stronger than a Prussian regiment, were commanded by lieutenant generals; divisions and brigades were commanded by major generals; regiments, having only 200 to 600 men, were commanded by colonels; each battery had 12 guns and was commanded by a colonel or lieutenant colonel. As a result, when the forces of both armies formed combined detachments, misunderstandings sometimes arose about the relative seniority of their commanders, which was also exacerbated by mutual ignorance of the languages in which the allies had to explain themselves to one another. As for the quality of the troops, according to the opinions of independent observers, the Russian army had a decisive superiority over the Prussian: the Russian force, having not yet managed to reconstitute itself, consisted of veteran, experienced soldiers accustomed to all the rigours and hardships of military life through the campaigning of the past year. In contrast, the Prussian forces, with the exception of the Yorck's corps, had no idea of the horrors of combat and for the most part consisted of recruits who had managed to receive very basic tactical training; the cavalry in particular, formed from young soldiers, required several months for continuation training. Having said that, in regard to the morale of the troops, the Prussian warriors were not inferior, either to the Russians, their former fellow campaigners on the fields of glory, or to their enemies, the French.

The vanguard of the force under Count Wittgenstein, commanded by General Repnin, set out from Landsberg and crossed the Oder on 18 February (2 March), at Güstebiese [Gozdowice], halfway between Küstrin and Schwedt, arriving outside Berlin the following day [3 March]. The Viceroy, who had no intention of holding out in the city, concentrated his forces on the Wittenberg road on the night of 20 February (4 March), instructing General Grenier to withdraw the rearguard from Berlin. Wishing to secure the retreat of these troops, Grenier made an agreement with the Prussian government commission for the hand-over of the city gates to the national guard at midnight, who were supposed to allow our troops into Berlin in the morning. But no sooner had the protection of the city been transferred to the population than they let the nearest Cossack outposts know about the departure of the French. The detachment under Adjutant General Chernyshev entered the city first, on 20 February (4 March), at six o'clock in the morning, while the other light detachments and the vanguard followed him. Partisans and Major General Diebitsch were sent with the vanguard cavalry in order to pursue the enemy, who were retreating along the roads to Treuenbrietzen and Jüterbog towards Wittenberg; the rest of the force under Prince Repnin settled in the city.[6]

6 Count Wittgenstein's report to Prince Kutuzov-Smolensky, dated 21 February [5 March], No. 59.

On that same day, 20 February (4 March), Count Wittgenstein's main body arrived at Landsberg, and on 22 and 23 February (6 and 7 March), crossing the Oder at Güstebiese, near Zellin [Czelin], closed up to Berlin on the morning of 27 February (11 March). Their entry into the liberated capital was festive. At the Königsthor entrance, the Russian commander was met by the King's brother Prinz Heinrich, the military governor *Generalleutnant* L'Estocq, generals, officers and city deputies from among the most honourable inhabitants. Throughout the time that it took the troops to parade through the city, all the windows and even the roofs of the houses were thronged with people expressing their joy and sympathy for the Coalition with unceasing cheers of: 'long live Alexander! Long live our liberator!' Count Wittgenstein and the Russian generals dined with the Prince. In the evening, every resident willingly lit up their homes. Boxes were assigned in the theatre for the main commanders of our troops. They performed a play that resembled some kind of Russian comedy (or at least so the playwright intended). But no one paid any attention to events onstage; everyone thought only of seeing Wittgenstein and his campaign colleagues, and cheered loudly: 'long live Alexander! Long live the King!' drowning out the actors.[7]

Yorck's corps, moving in the wake of Wittgenstein's force, arrived in Arnswalde on 22 February (6 March), in Soldin the following day [7 March], and on 1 (13) March, the infantry and cavalry crossed the Oder at Güstebiese, while all the artillery crossed at Niederwutzen [Osinów Dolny, 20 miles south-west of Schwedt]. Bülow's corps, subordinated to Yorck (as already mentioned), set out on 18 February (2 March) from Neustettin, towards Stargard and Gartz, and crossed the Oder at Schwedt on 2 (14) March; one of the brigades from this corps, under the command of *Generalmajor* Thümen [Heinrich Ludwig August von Thümen], crossed there later that same day and turned towards Stettin via Penkun [20 miles south-west of Stettin] in order to invest this fortress from the left bank of the Oder until the arrival of *Generalleutnant* Tauentzien to relieve them with Pomeranian reservists; while the other brigade remained at Schwedt for the time being; Borstell's brigade initially blockaded Stettin from the right bank of the Oder, and then on 3 (15) March, crossing at Schwedt, moved via Zehdenick and Gransee, towards Rathenow. Yorck's corps went from Güstebiese directly towards Berlin and entered the capital of Prussia on 5 (17) March. Prinz Heinrich and Count Wittgenstein rode out of the city through the Königsthor with their numerous retinue, where Yorck's troops were waiting for them; innumerable crowds of people rushed there to greet their warriors. After saluting the prince, the corps ceremonially entered the city. In the evening, the inhabitants again illuminated their houses, and when General Yorck appeared in the theatre, everyone rose from their seats and greeted him three times with the customary *Hoch*!

At the same time as these celebrations, which erased entire years of oppression and disaster from the memories of the Prussian people, the inhabitants of Berlin learned of the positive intent of their government to take up arms against Napoleon: appeals had been published 'to My people' and 'to My forces;'

7 Count Wittgenstein's report to Prince Kutuzov-Smolensky, dated 1 [13] March, No. 63.

arrangements were being made for the formation of the *Landwehr.* Prussian subjects could breathe freely.[8]

The population of Breslau greeted Emperor Alexander with the same enthusiasm. Once Prussia had declared war on Napoleon, there was no longer any obstacle to a meeting between the Coalition Sovereigns. The Emperor arrived in Breslau on 3 (15) March. The King had sent *Generalleutnant* Kleist, *Oberst* Prinz von Biron von Kurland [Gustav Kalixt von Biron von Kurland] and Merkel, the president of the government commission, with the deputies of Silesia and with the senior clergy to meet Him at the Silesian border, beyond the town of Wartenberg [Syców]. Accompanying Emperor Alexander were Count Nesselrode [Karl Vasilievich Nesselrode or Karl Robert von Nesselrode-Ehreshoven], Count Arakcheev [Alexei Andreevich Arakcheev] and *Oberhofmarshal* Count Tolstoy [Nikolai Alexandrovich Tolstoy]. The King himself, accompanied by all the princes of his House, met our Tsar at Oels [Oleśnica], four *Meilen* (28 *verstas*) from Breslau. The Emperor was greeted with joyful cheers and bell ringing in every town and village. About a half *Meile* before reaching the city, both Monarchs, with their entire respective retinues, mounted horses and set off on horseback towards the royal palace, past troops lining the route and surrounded by a multitude of people, where they arrived just at dusk, about six o'clock in the evening. The ringing of bells and the thunder of artillery merged with the noisy greetings of the population and the cheering of the troops. This was how the population of Prussia greeted their liberator, and may such celebrations be remembered for life by the people, uniting the subjects of neighbouring states with inseparable ties as brothers in arms!

Overall, Prussia at that time presented the vision of a huge encampment. In every town, in the squares and streets, from magnificent halls to humble huts, the King's appeals 'to My people' and 'to My forces' were read avidly, captivating each and everyone because they expressed the general feelings of the people. Nobody felt the need to hide themselves, and they came out in full strength. The King himself, at the head of his subjects, went into the battle which was to decide the question of Prussia's existence. 'To arms!' he exclaimed, and among the intellectual sons of Germany, academe could not remain silent: philosophy and poetry became the tools of Mars. Moritz Arndt [Ernst Moritz Arndt], who had arrived in Königsberg from Russia with Stein, brought with him an essay written and published in St Petersburg by him: 'Catechism for a German soldier, explaining how a Christian soldier should behave and, with the help of God, go to battle.' This pamphlet, full of loathing for Napoleon and the French, was reprinted in Berlin and became a popular book.[9] Another work by Arndt: 'What do *Landwehr* and *Landsturm* mean?' also made a deep impression not only in Prussia, but throughout Germany. Many odes and songs appeared that roused the people to vengeance and contempt for death. Academics and the intelligentsia armed themselves to defend the fatherland. Among the volunteers was the bard of Undine, Baron Friedrich de la Motte Fouqué, and the hero Kärner. Professor of Philosophy Fichte [Johann Gottlieb Fichte], having raised the morale

8 Beitzke, I, 242-244. Plotho, I, 37-38.

9 Katechismus für den teutschen Soldaten. 1813. For an extract of the text, see Appendix V at the end of this chapter.

of his listeners with readings on the true meaning of war, equipped himself from head to toe and joined the ranks of the *Landsturm*. The director of the *Akademie der Künste* [Academy of Arts], Schadow [Johann Gottfried Schadow], assembled an entire unit from his subordinates. Even the spiritual turned to their parishioners with exhortations to fight to the last breath, instead of the Gospel of peace and love, and called the upcoming war a sacred struggle for a just cause.

The Coalition army, under the command of *General der Kavallerie* Blücher, concentrated in Breslau, set out from there in several echelons, starting from 4 to 12 (16 to 24) March, along the axis Liegnitz [Legnica] to Bunzlau, where the headquarters was moved on 10 (22) March, while the Russian corps under Wintzingerode had already seized Bautzen on the 8 (20) March. Miloradovich's corps, numbering between 13,000 and 14,000 men, had invested the fortress of Glogau, until they were relieved by Prussian troops under the command of *Generalmajor* Schuler von Senden [Ernst Julius Friedrich Schuler von Senden] on 18 (30) March, and crossed the Oder, at Miltitz. The detachment under Major General Helffreich [Bogdan Borisovich Gelfreikh or Gotthard August von Helffreich], which had been monitoring the fortress of Küstrin, was relieved by a detachment under Lieutenant General Count Vorontsov (of the former Western Army), on 5 (17) March, and joined the force under Count Wittgenstein in Berlin on 8 (20) March. The Main Army remained at Kalisz, as before, where Emperor Alexander's and Prince Kutuzov's headquarters were located, as already mentioned, until 26 March (7 April).[10]

Upon the Viceroy's retreat beyond the Elbe, his force took up the following positions: the right wing under General Reynier, from Dresden to Meissen, numbering 4,500 men; the Saxon contingent, formerly part of Reynier's *7e Corps*, were deployed in Dresden and Torgau under the supervision of the Saxon General Thielmann [Johann Adolf von Thielmann]; Marshal Davout, having arrived in Dresden from Leipzig with 3,000 men on 1 (13) March, took command of the troops assembled in the vicinity of this city; Marshal Victor, with 5,000 men recovered from Russia, occupied Wittenberg, Roßlau and Aken; Grenier was stationed at Wittenberg with *11e Corps*, 18,000 strong; General Lauriston was at Magdeburg with *5e Corps*, 16,000 strong; General Vandamme [Dominique Joseph René Vandamme] was on the lower Elbe, with Lagrange's division [Joseph Lagrange] from Lauriston's corps and with Morand's division [Joseph Morand], which had arrived from Swedish Pomerania, some 6,000 men in total; *1er Corps de Cavalerie*, under General Latour-Maubourg [Marie Victor Nicolas de Faÿ de Latour-Maubourg], numbering 1,800 men, was stationed at Magdeburg; while *2e Corps de Cavalerie*, under General Sébastiani [Horace François Bastien Sébastiani] was forming up at Braunschweig [Brunswick] with 1,000 men: consequently, some 52,000 infantry and some 3,000 cavalry had been assembled under the Viceroy on the Elbe, in addition to the *Garde* division under General Roguet, numbering 2,400 men, co-located with the Viceroy's *quartier-général* in Leipzig.[11]

10 War Diary, signed by Prince Kutuzov-Smolensky. Plotho, I, 37, 48-50 & 84.

11 Composition of the Viceroy's army following his retreat behind the Elbe: Davout's command, 7,500 men, as follows: Durutte's division – 2,500 men, Rechberg's Bavarian division – 2,000 men, *1er Corps* arriving from Leipzig – 3,000 men. Victor's *2e Corps*, made up from the cadres of the

On our side, after occupying Berlin, the partisans and the forward detachment under Major General Baron Diebitsch monitored the fortresses of Wittenberg and Magdeburg; *Generalleutnant* Kleist, was stationed at Treuenbrietzen with his vanguard; General Yorck's corps was in the Potsdam area; Berg's corps [Grigory Maximovich Berg or Gregor von Berg] was at Potsdam; Bülow's division was at Schwedt; Borstell's brigade was at Rathenow; a small Russian detachment was blockading the fortress of Spandau, until 20 March (1 April),[12] when they were relieved by the Prussian detachment under *Generalmajor* Thümen;[13] Count Wittgenstein's headquarters remained in Berlin. This was the deployment of the Coalition Army as at 14 (26) March.

The reason for the inaction of the Coalition Army after the occupation of Berlin was the disagreement between the views of Prince Kutuzov and the operational plan drawn up by General Scharnhorst. Having received a report from Count Wittgenstein about his intention to cross the Elbe, the Field Marshal reminded him of the disposition sent to both him and Blücher from headquarters the previous week: Kutuzov believed very strongly that their crossing of the Elbe, with a considerable gap between them, exposed their armies to great danger, that Count Wittgenstein should not cross in the vicinity of Magdeburg, rather, a little upstream of Meissen, simultaneously with a crossing at Dresden by Blücher, and that the Coalition armies should operate with concentrated forces towards Leipzig and Altenburg.[14] In response to the intention expressed by Count Wittgenstein to cross the Elbe as soon as the detachment under Bülow, which was monitoring Magdeburg, could be replaced by other troops, the Field Marshal noted that although the French forces assembling at Leipzig and Erfurt could be could be driven back to the Rhine by the Coalition armies, nevertheless, the reinforcements expected by the enemy must not be overlooked. And in accordance with that, Kutuzov concluded, we must wait for the arrival of our reserves, without moving beyond the Elbe for any considerable distance and restricting our operational objectives: firstly, to rousing the German population to arms against the French, and secondly, to keeping the enemy in a state of constant confusion and paralysis.[15] He wrote to General Wintzingerode in almost the same sense, explaining to him the need to refrain from rash actions that might destroy the perception of our previous successes on public opinion in Germany. The Field Marshal wrote: 'I cannot speak in such confidence with *Herr* Blücher, but it is up to Your Excellency to influence him in this direction, without making him

former *Grande Armée* – 5,000 men. Grenier's *11e Corps* – 18,000 men. Lauriston's *5e Corps* – 16,000 men. Vandamme's corps – 6,000 men. *1er Corps de Cavalerie* – 1,800 men. *2e Corps de Cavalerie* – 1,000 men. Roguet's *Garde* division – 2,400 men. Total: 55,300 men (Vaudoncourt, 49-50). Plotho gives the force under the Viceroy as 87,000 men (Plotho, I, *Beilagen*, 57).

12 The Russian blockading force at Spandau consisted of: one infantry regiment, Nezhin Mounted Jägers, Poland Ulans, 28th Battery Artillery Company, and a *Sotnia* of Cossacks.

13 General Thümen's detachment consisted of: three battalions from *Ostpreußische Infanterie Regiment Nr. 5*, two companies from *Ostpreußisches Jäger Bataillon*, the jäger sub-unit from *1es Ostpreußische Infanterie Regiment Nr. 1*, and one light artillery battery (six-pounders). Plotho, I, 44.

14 Orders for Count Wittgenstein, dated 17 [29] March. Log of Outgoing Documents, No. 515.

15 Orders for Count Wittgenstein, dated 24 March [5 April]. Log of Outgoing Documents, No. 573.

completely aware of our [lack of] means.'[16] When Count Wittgenstein reported to Prince Kutuzov on the concentration of some 50,000 men in the enemy army at Magdeburg, then the cautious commander repeated his concerns about a crossing at Roßlau and suggested that Wittgenstein move closer to Blücher as quickly as possible, attend to the establishment of a secure crossing at Meissen and destroy the bridge at Roßlau. Kutuzov wrote: 'I must repeat, if it please Your Excellency, that which you read in my previous dispatch, namely: that our rapid advance would be of no advantage to securing the main objective of the future campaign.'[17]

Throughout the duration of this correspondence, our partisans extended the sphere of their operations beyond the Elbe.

Colonel Tettenborn, sent with a detachment of four weak Cossack regiments, six squadrons and two horse artillery pieces, numbering 1,300 men, was to take Hamburg, arm the inhabitants of this city and of the countryside lying on the left bank of the lower Elbe against the French and destroy the depots and warehouses established by the enemy in northern Germany.[18] Upon his arrival in Ludwigslust [4½ miles north of Grabow], Tettenborn concluded an agreement with the Herzog zu Mecklenburg-Schwerin [Friedrich Franz I], under the terms of which the Duke undertook to call up the militia against the French. The Herzog zu Mecklenburg-Strelitz [Karl II] also came over to the Coalition side. In Lauenburg, the nearest of the Hanoverian towns that had been annexed to Napoleon's Empire, as soon as the Cossacks appeared, the inhabitants tore down the French emblems from all public buildings and armed themselves alongside the Coalition. Colonel Tettenborn received intelligence there that Hamburg was occupied by only 1,000 enemy troops and customs officers, in whose support General Morand was moving from Swedish Pomerania, via Gadebusch and Mölln [eight miles south-west of Ratzeburg] with 3,000 men and 17 guns. Meanwhile, General Carra-Saint-Cyr [Claude Carra de Saint-Cyr], commandant of Hamburg, fearing an uprising by the population, did not dare to wait for the arrival of our partisans and advanced along the left bank of the Elbe, towards Artlenburg [11 miles north of Lüneburg]. In spite of all this, Morand continued to march straight towards Hamburg, but when the Danish General Ewald [Johann Ewald], who was stationed on the Holstein border with a 3,000 man detachment, announced, at the insistence of Tettenborn, that his government would not agree to the occupation of Hamburg by French troops, Morand turned towards Zollenspieker [five miles north of Winsen] in order to cross the Elbe there. Tettenborn, having been informed of this, made a forced march towards Bergedorf and, having caught the enemy at the crossing on 5 (17) March, attacked them using dismounted Cossacks from Denisov 7th's and Grebtsov's regiments and captured six guns. After that, our detachment, on that same day, moved to Bergedorf. A deputation arrived there from Hamburg announcing the submission of the French administration located in this city. But Tettenborn announced to the deputies that Hamburg could only hope for the protection of the Coalition once it had seceded from France and restored its former government. The next day [18

16 For an extract from the text of Kutuzov's letter, see Appendix VI at the end of this chapter.

17 Orders for Count Wittgenstein, dated 25 March [6 April]. Log of Outgoing Documents, Noa. 579.

18 Disposition signed by the Chief-of-Staff, Major General Dovre.

March], a new deputation appeared in Bergedorf, proposing to equip 5,000 men to defend the city from the French, to issue 200,000 Thaler from city funds for clothing and weapons, and to open a voluntary subscription for similar items. Together with this, the deputies invited Tettenborn, on behalf of their senate and fellow subjects, to come to their city.

On 7 (19) March, our small detachment entered Hamburg. While still two *Meilen* (14 *verstas*) from the city, they were met by a cavalry detachment of civilians, then, by the national guard; while half a *Meile* from the gates, huge crowds of residents came out, welcoming the Cossacks with joyful cheers, filling the air with noisy Russian songs. Outside the gates, the keys of the city were presented to Tettenborn by senior senators Koch and Schulz, while at the entrance he was met by girls in white dresses who were waiting for him with wreaths. The tumultuous greetings of the people did not stop during the entire procession through the city by our detachment, the ringing of bells, musket and pistol shots; banners fluttered from every window. The population, lost in expressions of delight, decorated their hats with green branches and threw them high, or raised them on long poles, others scattered flowers across the route along which our soldiers marched. Friends and strangers hugged and congratulated each other; many wept tears of joy. Busts of Emperor Alexander I crowned with garlands of flowers and of laurel were displayed on every street. The whole city was illuminated that evening, until two o'clock in the morning. Upon leaving the theatre, the people unharnessed the horses from Tettenborn's carriage and drew him themselves right up to the house where quarters had been assigned to him.[19]

The liberation of Hamburg, the leading commercial city in all of Germany and the wealthiest of any city on the European mainland, produced general delight in Prussia. Berliners celebrated it like a great victory, with cannon salutes.

The very next day after the occupation of Hamburg [20 March], Colonel Tettenborn announced the restoration of free trade and communications with Britain and sent a ship to London with the news, on which the Cossack Vitichenko [Alexander Vitichenko] was sent as living proof of the success won by the Russian force. The appearance of this Cossack fired the curiosity and sympathy of the British, everyone wanted to see him, entertained him without pause, gave dinners in his honour, and this rugged son of the Don, thanks to his natural intelligence and the guidance of the official accompanying him, maintained the sympathy of the British for himself throughout his stay in London.

After the occupation of Hamburg, patrols were sent to the left bank of the Elbe, to rouse the population into an uprising against the French. In anticipation of this mobilisation, Tettenborn remained in Hamburg and proceeded to fortify the city and to form units. It was intended to form the *Hanseatische Legion*, consisting of two battalions, six squadrons and two batteries, numbering 2,800 men with 12 guns, and in addition, the *Hanseatische Bürgergarde*, for the immediate defence of the city, consisting of six battalions, each of 1,200 men. Meanwhile, Lieutenant Colonel Benckendorff, sent to Lübeck with a Cossack regiment, on 9 (21) March, was greeted by the population of this city with the same enthusiasm with which Tettenborn

19 War Diary, signed by Prince Kutuzov-Smolensky. *Hamburgischer Correspondent*, 1813.

had been greeted in Hamburg. The recruitment of volunteers into the *Hanseatische Legion* was started immediately, and in the first two days more than 500 men joined the service, at the same time, a sum of 60,000 Thaler was donated for their equipment. It was intended to form a battalion and two squadrons, numbering 1,100 men, which, together with the force in Hamburg, would have been about 4,000 men. But in reality only some 2,500 were selected; donations of cash from the *Hansestädte* were very mediocre. The delight of the wealthy Hamburg residents, who had become accustomed to the good things in life, had given way to thoughts that did not extend to full commitment. Because of this, the mobilisation they achieved was not enough to defend a vast city that could accommodate a population of some 100,000. As for external help, it was limited to the Herzog zu Mecklenburg's *Grenadier-Garde-Bataillon*, numbering 400 men, 200 Prussian infantry who had joined the Lübeck battalion, and a cadre of British troops from the King's German Legion.[20]

The inhabitants of Bremen had been preparing to follow the example of Hamburg and Lübeck, but were forced back to obedience of the French by the arrival of the detachments under Carra-Saint-Cyr and Morand and the severe measures taken by General Vandamme, the commander of *32e division militaire* of the Empire of the French. The following orders issued by him on 3 April new style may give an indication of his actions:

> The situation in which the corps entrusted to me finds itself compels me to resort to emergency measures dictated by the circumstances: I must fulfil them. From the very beginning of my military career, having experienced all kinds of upheaval, I have always known how to put myself beyond all happenstance. The position I hold imposes heavy responsibilities upon me, but with the assistance of outstanding dignitaries participating with me in the duties of faithfully serving our towering Monarch, I am firmly convinced that the enemy will pay dearly for any attempt against us. Being fortunate in all my undertakings, I have never yet experienced defeat. No one shall stand against me if I can avoid it; but having worked since my youth on the basis of the strictest principles of honour, I shall not be in breach of my duties. My only guidance will be our obligations to Sovereign and fatherland. I trust that, in accordance with my wishes, the administration and population of the *Département* entrusted to me (*Bouches du Weser*) will conduct themselves with the prudence and caution that the present circumstances demand of them. In particular, I hope for the diligence and devotion of the good city of Bremen, in which your oath serves as my guarantee of your worthy policies. No one is likely to imitate the insane acts by Hamburg. I am kind and just, by nature, character and habit, but I shall be terrifying in the performance of my duties, as a straight-forward warrior, being faithful to my duty, I shall not spare anything if the will of my Sovereign, the welfare of the fatherland or the glory of our armed forces require it.

20 War Diary, signed by Prince Kutuzov-Smolensky. Beitzke, I, 309-313.

Even before the arrival of Vandamme in Bremen from Wesel, the French generals had taken steps to keep the population of the surrounding countryside in obedience. Carra-Saint-Cyr moved northward, dispersed the *Landsturm*, and reached Bremerlehe, at the mouth of the Weser; while Morand headed for Hamburg with 2,300 men and eight guns, and on 15 (27) March was already one stage from there, at Tostedt. Here news was received about an uprising by the inhabitants of Lüneburg against the French. Indeed, as soon as Cossacks had appeared on the left bank of the Elbe, the Lüneburg townspeople had expelled French officials and customs guards, restored their former administration and formed a sharpshooter detachment. French gendarmes attempted to enter the town on the 14 (26) March, and were repulsed, taking casualties. Having gathered some 2,500 men with eight guns in Tostedt,[21] General Morand had initially intended to march on Harburg and on to Hamburg, but instead moved towards Lüneburg in order to punish the population of this town. Upon arrival there, on 20 March (1 April), the French immediately imprisoned many of the residents. Morand convened a court-martial and threatened to shoot 50 people the next day. But these unfortunates were saved by the Russian partisans who arrived suddenly outside Lüneburg.

Among them at that time was General Dörnberg [Wilhelm Caspar Ferdinand von Dörnberg], known for his attempt to capture the King of Westphalia in his own capital, Kassel in 1809. His relations with many people from Hanover was reason enough to send him beyond the Elbe with the raiding detachment under Major General Benckendorff, who was monitoring the Wittenberg fortress at the time, and had been strengthened by Prussian and Russian troops to 1,100 infantry and 2,000 cavalry with six guns.[22] On the night of 13 to 14 (25 to 26) March, General Dörnberg crossed the Elbe near Quitzöbel [eight miles downstream of Havelberg] into Werben, but on being attacked by a French detachment arriving from Magdeburg, was driven north to Neukirchen and returned to the right bank of the Elbe via Scharpenlohe [18 miles downstream of Havelberg]. Meanwhile, Chernyshev's detachment, which had been monitoring Magdeburg, closed up to Havelberg. The partisans, having gathered together, decided to recross the Elbe and operate as a combined force. On 17 (29) March, Chernyshev crossed near Behlow, just upstream of Wittenberge [eight miles south-west of Perleberg], on ferries and boats, occupied the town of Seehausen [four miles north-east of Drüsedau] and drove off the enemy who had reappeared on the Magdeburg road; while General Dörnberg moved down the right bank of the Elbe to Lenzen and also crossed to the other side of the river by boat on 19 (31) March. Thereafter, both detachments immediately moved on, in the direction of Dannenberg and Wustow [four miles south-west of Lüchow], screened

21 Morand's detachment consisted of: two battalions of Saxon *Regiment Prinz Maximillian*, one French battalion, two companies of *Douaniers*, 75 mounted men, a six-gun Saxon artillery battery and two French artillery pieces (*Beiträge zur Geschichte des Jahres 1813*). According to other sources, Morand had 3,000 infantry and 200 cavalry with 15 guns (Plotho, I, 56).

22 General Dörnberg's force consisted of: Russians – one battalion of 2nd Jägers, two squadrons of Finland Dragoons, four squadrons of Grodno Hussars, three Cossack regiments, one Bashkir regiment and two horse artillery pieces; Prussians – a *Füsilier* battalion from *1es Pommersches Infanterie Regiment Nr. 2* and four horse artillery pieces (Dörnberg's own report. *Beiträge*, I, 279).

from Magdeburg by the Cossack detachment under Colonel Vlasov, sent towards Seehausen and Arendsee [ten miles west of Drüsedau]. Having learned on the march of the danger threatening the inhabitants of Lüneburg, the partisans quickened their pace and, having covered 70 *verstas* in 24 hours, arrived at Bienenbüttel on the evening of 29 March (1 April) (about 12 *verstas* from Lüneburg), and closed up to the town early the following morning [2 April].

Lüneburg, with more than 10,000 inhabitants, lies on the left bank of the Ilmenau river. The town was surrounded by a rampart with five gates, of which two: Altenbrückertor and Lünertor, facing east, were on the river side, the Bardowick gate was to the north, the Neuentor, to the west, and Rotentor, to the south. It was intended to direct the main attack on the eastern side, and in order to divert enemy troops from there, General Chernyshev sent Colonel Pahlen [Matvey Ivanovich Palen or Carl Magnus von der Pahlen] onto the left bank of the river with two Cossack regiments, towards the Neuentor; Colonel Vlasov set off along the road to Celle with one Cossack regiment, from where Davout was expected to arrive with a significant detachment; finally, one Cossack regiment was sent along the route to Dannenberg, in order to protect the cargo vessels sent in the meantime from Lenzen to Boizenburg.

Pahlen's attack did not distract Morand, who, focusing mainly on the defence of the town from the east, held the Altenbrückertor and Lünertor in strength and sent a battalion with two cannon to the right bank of the river. This small detachment, taken by surprise by our cavalry, was scattered with the loss of 200 prisoners and both guns. After that, the Coalition artillery was positioned on high ground on the right bank of the river and opened a heavy bombardment on the enemy who occupied the town and under whose covering fire Major Essen [Gustav Ivanovich Essen] raced into the attack on the Altenbrückertor with Russian jägers, while Major Borcke [Karl August Ferdinand von Borcke] attacked the Lünertor with the Prussian battalion. For two hours a most stubborn battle ensued around both gates; eventually, the Prussian force broke into the town, captured two guns and struck the enemy defending the other entrances from behind; our infantry and the Izyum Hussars had also forced their way through the Altenbrückertor; but the fighting continued for a long time along the narrow streets of Lüneburg. The townspeople also took part in it, shooting at the enemy from windows. Morand, having lost many of his men and almost all of his artillery, managed to escape the town through the Neuentor, with just 500 men and two guns; but as soon as he reached the nearby village of Reppenstedt [2½ miles west of Lüneburg], he was engaged by Russian troops who had got ahead of him along a country lane. Struck by the fire from four guns and surrounded by numerous cavalry, Morand turned back towards the Neuentor, where he was engaged by Coalition troops who now held the town. Here the enemy, lashed by canister shot and constrained on all sides, suffered horrendous casualties. Morand himself was mortally wounded; the rest of the troops who were with him, as well as those who continued to defend themselves in the town, laid down their weapons. In this action, which lasted more than seven hours, the entire enemy detachment was destroyed. Those taken prisoner were: Morand himself (who died three days later at Boizenburg), three colonels, 80 officers and 2,200 lower ranks. Nine guns, three colours and a significant amount of transport fell into the hands of the victors. The Coalition casualties, overall, extended to 300 men: among those killed was Major Count Musin-Pushkin [Alexander Alexeevich Musin-Pushkin]; Major Essen was among those wounded.[23] In this battle, the first of the Prussian volunteers was killed, the valiant Georg Haase. The following is a letter from his parents:

> Our son Georg, at the age of 22, was struck down by a bullet in the memorable action at Lüneburg. Being among the volunteers of the *1. Pommersches Infanterie Regiment*, according to the testimony of his courageous commander, Major Borcke, he fought fearlessly and decisively and fell for the fatherland, for the independence of Germany, for the honour of our people, for our beloved King. It is a heavy loss that we have suffered; but we regret even more that we had but one son to offer up in such a grand and sacred cause.[24]

Emperor Alexander I, having received reports on the action at Lüneburg, granted Adjutant General Chernyshev the Order of St Anna, 1st class with diamonds, while General Dörnberg was awarded the Order of St George, 3rd class. Prince Kutuzov, notifying Dörnberg of this award, wrote to him: 'To show His satisfaction, His Majesty the Emperor has decorated you with the Order of St George, 3rd class. I, as an old knight of this order, pride myself on having a comrade who, on several occasions, has displayed such distinguished talents as you have brought to light.'[25] Count Wittgenstein also received the Order of St Alexander Nevsky with diamonds.[26]

The success of the uprising in northern Germany compelled the French to take more effective measures to enforce their rule there. This country, very important in terms of the wealth of the population, provided an opportunity for the British and Russians to land troops and potentially win over the Danes to their side; moreover, by leaving the coast in the hands of the Coalition, it would be impossible for the French to hold on the Elbe. Napoleon, not trusting in the loyalty of his German subjects in the least, entrusted Vandamme, infamous for his stringency, with the management of the so-called *32e division militaire* and the troops stationed there. In anticipation of their assembly, General Montbrun [Alexandre de Montbrun] (whose brother had been killed at Borodino) arrived at Lüneburg from Magdeburg the day

23 Count Wittgenstein's report to Prince Kutuzov-Smolensky, dated 24 March [5 April], No. 76. Plotho, I, 54-58. Beitzke, I, 314-319. Vaudoncourt, 55-56.

24 Förster, *Geschichte der Befreiungskriege 1813, 1814, 1815*, I, 200.

25 '*Sa Majesté l'Empereur, pour temoigner Son contentement, vous a decoré de l'ordre de St. Georges de la 3me classe. Moi, comme ancien chevalier de cet ordre, je me glorifie d'avoir un camarade qui a fait preuve d'un mêrite aussi distingué que vous avez mis au jour à plusieurs occasions.*' Prince Kutuzov's letter to General Dörnberg, dated 28 March [9 April] (Log of Outgoing Documents, No. 636).

26 Prince Kutuzov's orders to Count Wittgenstein, dated 28 March [9 April] (Log of Outgoing Documents, No. 636) state: 'His Imperial Majesty's justness could not ignore your diligence, which is directed towards your pleasure, so beneficial to the Russian armed forces, and to that end, I have been ordered to send Your Excellency the Order of St Alexander Nevsky with diamonds.'

after the liberation of this town by Coalition forces, with the vanguard of Lagrange's division, which had come under the command of Marshal Davout. He was followed by the marshal himself with the rest of the troops from this division, which was 6,000 strong. Generals Chernyshev and Dörnberg, not being able to hold back the superior strength of the enemy, retreated to Boizenburg beyond the Elbe.[27] Wishing to protect the population of Hanover from French reprisals, both of them wrote to the commanders of the enemy forces that executions of civilians would be answered for with the lives of prisoners taken by us.[28] Count Wittgenstein subsequently made a similar announcement.[29]

Meanwhile, Vandamme had managed to concentrate the divisions under Carra-Saint-Cyr, Dufour [François Marie Dufour] and Dumonceau [Jean-Baptiste Dumonceau de Bergendal] on the Weser, numbering 24,000 men. In Bremen, a court-martial was established for the inhabitants of the country involved in hostilities against the French: more than 20 people were shot; others were sentenced to hard labour or were imprisoned; significant financial penalties were imposed on many cities and towns. Despite the threats from our partisans, Vandamme was ready to punish the population of Lüneburg; but in the meantime, Marshal Davout had arrived in Celle, having been appointed commander of the *32e division militaire* once more, and under whose command all troops located on the lower Elbe now came, including also Vandamme's corps. Although the Marshal treated the population less cruelly than his predecessor, arrests, confiscations and arbitrary taxes weighed heavily on the coast of northern Germany. The Coalition Powers, having raised a revolt against Napoleon, did not properly support it: the Russo-Prussian armies were redirected towards Saxony; Britain was content with sending arms and ammunition to Hamburg; the Swedish Crown Prince [Jean-Baptiste Jules Bernadotte] did not care about assisting the German population at all; Denmark, doubting the amity of the Coalition, remained on the French side still. The wealthy *Hansestädte*, placing too much reliance on external help, had not fully developed the means for their own defence. Our partisans did not operate in unison themselves, but competed with each other. In order to centralise power over every detachment and militia in northern Germany, the Sovereign appointed the Austrian *Generalleutnant* Wallmoden [Ludwig Georg Thedel von Wallmoden-Gimborn], who transferred into our service as their commander,[30] but the forces entrusted to him were very small in number, and the militia could not be formed up quickly. This kept the Coalition inactive. Only Tettenborn's detachment remained in Hamburg until 18 (30) May. Hanover and the *Hansestädte* were destined to remain under the yoke of French rule until the final liberation of Germany.

27 Beitzke, I, 324. Vaudoncourt, 56.

28 For the text of the letter by General Dörnberg to the French generals, see Appendix VII at the end of this chapter.

29 Announcement, signed by the Chief of Staff, Major General Dovre, dated 24 April, new style.

30 Orders for Count Wittgenstein and *Generalleutnant* Wallmoden, dated 18 [30] March (Log of Outgoing Documents, No. 537 and No. 538).

Appendix IV

Composition of the Coalition Forces in February and March 1813

Chernyshev's detachment: six Cossack regiments; six squadrons of Izyum Hussars and Finland Dragoons; two Don artillery pieces, numbering some 2,000 men.

Benckendorff's detachment: five Don Cossack regiments; one Bashkir regiment; five squadrons of Combined Hussars and Finland Dragoons; two Don guns, numbering some 2,000 men.

Tettenborn's detachment: four Cossack regiments; Izyum Hussars (four squadrons); Kazan Dragoons (two squadrons), numbering around 1,500 men.

(Strength return for Count Wittgenstein's force, dated 11 [23] February, signed off by Major General Diebitsch).

Later, the detachments under Chernyshev, Benckendorff and Colonel Tettenborn consisted of: Finland Dragoons; Izyum Hussars; Combined Hussars; Kazan Dragoons (two squadrons); 14 Don Cossack regiments; one Bashkir regiment; six Don artillery pieces.

Total for Chernyshev's, Benckendorff's and Tettenborn's detachments: some 5,000 men.

Composition of Count Wittgenstein's force:
Lieutenant General Berg's corps:
Mitau Dragoons; Riga Dragoons; Perm Infantry; Sevsk Infantry; Mogilev Infantry; Kaluga Infantry; Tenginsk Infantry; Estland Infantry; Navaginsk Infantry; Tula Infantry; 23rd Jägers; 24th Jägers; 26th Jägers; six reserve battalions; 14th Battery Artillery Company; 28th Battery Artillery Company; 26th Light Artillery Company; 27th Light Artillery Company; 23rd Horse Artillery Company; one Cossack regiment; Olonets *Opolchenie*; Vologda *Opolchenie*; Captain Gerua's pioneer company.

Major General Prince Repnin's vanguard:
Grodno Hussars; all five replacement battalions from 1st Grenadier Division; four combined grenadier battalions from 5th Division and 14th Division; 2nd Jägers;

25th Jägers; 21st Battery Artillery Company; 1st Horse Artillery Company (ten guns); 5th Horse Artillery Company (two guns); seven Cossack regiments; Tver Mounted *Opolchenie.*

Total for Berg's corps and Prince Repnin's vanguard: 14,000 men.

***Generalleutnant* Yorck's corps**:
Generalmajor Hünerbein's brigade: *1. Ostpreußisches Infanterie* (three battalions); *Colbergsches Infanterie* (three battalions); *2. Ostpreußisches Infanterie* (*Füsilier* battalion); *Ostpreußisches Jäger-Bataillon* (two companies).

Oberst Horn's brigade: *Garde-Regiment zu Fuss Infanterie* (three battalions); *5. Reserve Infanterie* (three battalions); *6. Reserve Infanterie* (three battalions).

Generalmajor Corswant's cavalry brigade: *1. Westpreußisches Dragoner* (four squadrons); *2. Westpreußisches Dragoner* (four squadrons); *2. Leib-Husaren* (four squadrons); *3. Schlesisches Husaren* (four squadrons).

Oberstleutnant Schmidt's artillery: one 12-pounder foot artillery battery; three six-pounder foot artillery batteries, Nr. 1, Nr. 2 and Nr. 3; one three-pounder foot artillery battery, Nr. 6; three horse artillery batteries, Nr. 1, Nr. 2 and Nr. 3; two pioneer companies

Total for Yorck's corps: 13,452 men.

***Generalleutnant* Bülow's East Prussian and West Prussian reserve corps**:
Generalmajor Prinz Ludwig von Hessen-Homburg's brigade: *2. Ostpreußisches Grenadiere Bataillon*; *1. Ostpreußisches Infanterie* (one battalion); *2. Ostpreußisches Infanterie* (two battalions); *3. Ostpreußisches Infanterie* (four battalions); *Ostpreußisches Jäger-Bataillon* (two companies).

Generalmajor Thümen's brigade: *4. Ostpreußisches Infanterie* (three battalions); one six-pounder foot artillery battery.

Generalmajor Oppen's cavalry brigade: *1. Leib-Husaren* (four squadrons); *1. Westpreußisches Dragoner* (four squadrons).

Major Holzendorf's artillery: four 12-pounder foot artillery pieces; one six-pounder foot artillery battery; one horse artillery battery; two pioneer companies.

Total for Bülow's corps: 11,502 men

Generalmajor Borstell's Pomeranian brigade:

Pommersches Grenadiere Bataillon; *1. Pommersches Infanterie* (three battalions – the *Füsilier* battalion from this regiment, commanded by Major Borcke, was attached to General Dörnberg's detachment); *4. Ostpreußisches Infanterie* (*Füsilier battalion*); *Königin Dragoner* (four squadrons); Major Rode's artillery – one six-pounder foot artillery battery; one horse artillery battery; one pioneer company.

Total for Borstell's brigade: 5,429 men.

Extracted from the following returns:

1. Attached to the report dated 11 [23] February, No. 141 (Log of Incoming Documents, No. 269), signed by Major General Dovre, Chief-of-Staff for Count Wittgenstein's force.
2. Placed in the Appendices to Plotho's work.

Adjutant General Wintzingerode's force:
Major General Lanskoy's vanguard:
Alexandria Hussars; Belorussia Hussars; Livonia Mounted Jägers;[1] Kuteynikov 4th's Cossacks; Semenchikov's Cossacks; Grekov 9th's Cossacks; Grekov 21st's Cossacks; 3rd Ural Cossacks; 20th Jägers (one battalion); 7th Horse Artillery Company. For a total of 46 regular cavalry officers and 1,207 lower ranks; 43 Cossack officers and 1,452 lower ranks; 16 infantry officers and 458 lower ranks infantry; 6 artillery officers and 150 lower ranks.

Colonel Davydov's partisan detachment: Popov 13th's Cossacks; 1st Bug Cossacks (20 officers and 554 lower ranks); Akhtyrka Hussars and assorted Cossacks (4 officers and 100 lower ranks).

Total for the vanguard: 135 officers and 3,921 lower ranks.

Major General Prince Trubetskoy's cavalry corps:
Major General Knorring's brigade: Tatar Ulans; Sumy Hussars (two squadrons); Lithuania Ulans (two squadrons); Crimea Tatars (attached to the Tatar Ulans). For a total of 49 regular cavalry officers and 891 lower ranks; 8 irregular cavalry officers and 126 lower ranks.

Major General Witt's brigade: 1st Ukraine Cossacks; 2nd Ukraine Cossacks; Combined Dragoons; 18th Horse Artillery Company. For a total of 15 regular cavalry officers and 289 lower ranks; 54 Cossacks officers and 1,254 lower ranks; 7 artillery officers and 192 lower ranks.

Total for Prince Trubetskoy's corps: 165 officers and 3,307 lower ranks.

1 Converted from the Livonia Ulans on 17 [29] December 1812.

II Corps, under Lieutenant General Prinz Eugen von Württemberg:

3rd Division: Murom Infantry (28 officers and 502 lower ranks); Reval Infantry (32 officers and 497 lower ranks); Chernigov Infantry (31 officers and 461 lower ranks); 20th Jägers (one battalion, 38 officers and 590 lower ranks).

4th Division: Tobolsk Infantry (30 officers and 590 lower ranks); Ryazhsk Infantry (33 officers and 805 lower ranks); Volhynia Infantry (33 officers and 453 lower ranks); Kremenchug Infantry (36 officers and 560 lower ranks); 4th Jägers (40 officers and 717 lower ranks); 1st Battery Artillery Company; 6th Light Artillery Company (both from 3rd Artillery Brigade); 4th Artillery Brigade (one light artillery company); 4th Reserve Artillery Brigade (one battery artillery company). For a total of 31 artillery officers and 733 lower ranks.

Total for II Corps: 332 officers and 5,908 lower ranks.

Grand total under Wintzingerode's command: 632 officers and 13,136 men, with 72 guns (extracted from returns signed by Blücher, submitted in March 1813. Log of Incoming Documents, No. 552).

General Blücher's force:
General Röder's *Brandenburgischen Brigade*: 168 infantry officers and 7,738 lower ranks; 36 cavalry officers and 918 lower ranks; 16 artillery officers and 466 lower ranks:

Garde-Regiment zu Fuss Infanterie (three battalions); *Normal-Infanterie-Bataillon*; *Freiwillige-Jäger-Bataillon*; *Garde-Jäger-Bataillon*; *Leib-Grenadier-Bataillon*; *1. Ostpreußisches-Grenadier-Bataillon*; *Leib-Infanterie* (one battalion); *Brandenburgisches Husaren Regiment* (two squadrons); *Brandenburgisches Ulanen* (two squadrons); *1. Westpreußisches Ulanen* (four squadrons); *Garde-Batterie der Fußartillerie*; one horse artillery battery

Total for the *Brandenburgischen Brigade*: 221 officers and 9,134 men.

***Oberst* von Klüx's *Niederschlesischen Brigade*:** 107 infantry officers and 5,339 lower ranks; 17 cavalry officers and 647 lower ranks; 12 artillery officers and 455 lower ranks.

Westpreußisches Grenadier Bataillon; *1. Westpreußisches-Infanterie* (three battalions); *2. Westpreußisches Infanterie* (two battalions); *Neumarkisches Dragoner* (four squadrons); *1. Westpreußisches Dragoner* (two squadrons); one light foot artillery battery; one horse artillery battery.

Total for the *Niederschlesischen Brigade*: 136 officers and 6,441 lower ranks.

Generalmajor* von Zieten's *Oberschlesischen Brigade: 127 infantry officers and 5,969 lower ranks; 20 cavalry officers and 705 lower ranks; 13 artillery officers and 461 lower ranks.

Schlesisches Grenadier Bataillon; *1. Schlesisches Infanterie* (three battalions); *2. Schlesisches Infanterie* (two battalions); *Schlesisches Schützen Bataillon*; *1. Schlesisches Ulanen* (two squadrons); Combined *Schlesisches Husaren* (four squadrons); two light artillery batteries; one horse artillery battery.

Total for the *Oberschlesischen Brigade*: 160 officers and 7,133 lower ranks.

***Oberst* Dolffs' reserve cavalry**: 115 officers and 3,566 lower ranks.
Garde du Corps (five squadrons); *Leib Leichtes Kavallerie* (six squadrons); *Garde-Batterie Berittene Artillerie*; *Schlesisches Kürassier* (four squadrons); *Ostpreußisches Kürassier* (four squadrons); *Brandenburgisches Kürassier* (four squadrons); one horse artillery battery.

***Oberstleutnant* von Braun's reserve artillery**: 11 officers and 703 lower ranks.
One light artillery battery; one heavy artillery battery (four guns); Park; one pioneer company.

Total for Blücher's force: 643 officers and 26,977 lower ranks.

From returns signed by Blücher, submitted in March 1813 (Log of Incoming Documents, No. 552).

These returns differ somewhat from the approximate calculation of strengths found in the work by Plotho, where it shows a total strength of 26,207 men, as follows:

In the *Brandenburgischen Brigade*: 8,567 men.
In the *Niederschlesischen Brigade*: 6,157 men.
In the *Oberschlesischen Brigade*: 7,240 men.
In the cavalry reserve: 3,749 men.
In the artillery reserve: 494 men.
Plotho, I, appendices, 60-62.

Count Vorontsov's force: six combined grenadier battalions from 9th Division, 15th Division and 18th Division; 13th Jägers; 14th Jägers (under Colonel Krasovsky); 13th Horse Artillery Company; Barabanshchikov's Cossacks; Panteleev 2nd's Cossacks; Bykhalov 2nd's Cossacks.

Major General O'Rourke's detachment: Volhynia Ulans (four squadrons); Pavlograd Hussars (four squadrons); 11th Horse Artillery Company; 18th Horse Artillery Company (14 guns in total); Dyachkin's Cossacks; Melnikov 5th's Cossacks.

(Barclay de Tolly's orders, dated 17 [29] March. Log of Outgoing Documents, No. 526. Plotho, I, 43-44).

Appendix V

Extract from Katechismus für den deutschen Soldaten, 1813

To give an idea of the style and the spirit of this work, I will quote the beginning of chapter 6:

> And the abyss opened, said the Lord, and hell spat out its venom, and released the snakes that poison.
>
> And a monster was born, and a blood-stained abomination arose.
>
> And its name was Napoleon Bonaparte, a name of misery, a name of woe, a name to be cursed by widows and orphans, a name at which they will henceforth cry out when poor sinners face the place of execution.
>
> And if Satan is called the father of lies, then Bonaparte is called Satan's eldest son, etcetera.
>
> *Und der Abgrund hat sich aufgethan, spricht der Herr, und die Hölle hat ihr Gift ausgespieen, und die Schlangen losgelassen, die da gitig sind.*
>
> *Und ist ein Ungeheuer geboren und ein blutgefleckter Gräuel aufgestanden.*
>
> *Und geist sein Name Napoleon Bonaparte, ein Name des Jammers, ein Name des Weh's, ein Name des Fluchs der Wittwen und Waisen, ein Name, bei welchem sie künftig Zeter schreien werden, wann arme Sünder zum Richtplatze gegen.*
>
> *Und wenn Satan der Vater der Lüge heisst, so heisst Bonaparte Satans ältester Sohn, u.s.w.*

Appendix VI

Extract from Prince Kutuzov's letter to Adjutant General Wintzingerode, dated 24 March [5 April] from Kalisz

---

Allow me to repeat again my opinion on the speed of march of our offensive. I begin by enclosing an extract from my letter to Mr. Wittgenstein. I know that every petty individual throughout Germany is taking the liberty of complaining about our slowness. It is as though every step forward were a victory and every day lost a defeat. As for me, the duties of my appointment subject me to a reckoning, I must carefully weigh the distance from the Elbe to our reserves and enemy forces as they assemble that we might engage them at such and such a ratio. Minor victories won over small corps, which the enemy has placed to their front and which would fall back towards their main force, would swell it like a snowball as they retreated. I must balance our progressive weakening through a rapid offensive march against our progressive separation from our resources, and this imposes a duty upon me to inspire a similar caution in the generals commanding large corps, and persuade them that a check inflicted on one of our Corps by the enemy would destroy the perception of prestige which we have in our favour in Germany. I cannot speak in such confidence with Mr. Blücher, but it is up to Your Excellency to influence him in this direction, without making him completely aware of our means.

Permettez moi de répéter encore mon opinion sur la rapidité de nos marches en avant. Je commence par vous joindre un extrait de ma lettre à Mr Witgenstein. Je sais que dans toute l'Allemagne chaque petit individu se permet de crier contre notre lenteur. On croit que chaque marche en avant équivaut à une victoire et chaque journée perdue est une défaite. Moi, qui par les devoirs de ma place suis assujettis à des calculs, je dois bien peser les distances de l'Elbe à nos reserves et les forces de l'ennemi dans tout son rassemblement que nous pouvons rencontrer à telle ou telle hauteur. Des petites victoires remportées sur de petits corps, que l'ennemi a en avaut et qui se retireraient sur leur gros, le grossiraient comme un ballon de neige à mesure de leur retraite. Je dois confronter notre affaiblissement progressif dans une marche rapide en avant avec notre éloignement progressif de nos ressources, et ceci m'impose le devoir d'inspirer la même défiance aux généraux qui commandent des grands Corps, et soyez persuadé qu'un echec porté par l'ennemi à un de nos Corps detruirait le prestige de l'opinion que nous avons en notre faveur dans l'Allemagne. Je ne peux pas parler avec toute cette confiance à Mr. Blücher, mais c'est à Votre Excellence de l'influencer dans ce sens, sans lui faire une parfaite confidence sur nos moyens.

Log of Outgoing Documents, No. 574.

Appendix VII

General Dörnberg's letter to the French generals

I have learned through the correspondence of Generals Morand and Carra-Saint-Cyr that it has been proposed to take strict measures in relation to the population of Hanover, who, having been liberated by the victorious armed forces of His Majesty the Russian Emperor, having received orders in His Name to identify themselves as subjects of their legitimate sovereign, and to whom the commander of Russian forces gave emphatic orders to arm themselves in defence of their persons and their country.

It has been their duty to carry out these orders. Had they departed from their duty, they would have incurred a just and severe punishment. And through this it is obvious that it is impossible to treat any of the Hanoverians as rebels without violating peoples' rights recognised by all civilised nations. I do not believe, gentlemen generals, that you would act so cruelly. Nevertheless, as a precaution, I declare that I have decided to resort to retribution, and that every prisoner I have taken, as well as all those who might be captured in the future, from the foremost to the lowest, shall be answerable for the lives of those who, having armed themselves according to binding orders from the commanders of Russian forces, have performed their duties to their sovereign and fatherland.

Boizenburg, 5 April 1813.

4

The Coalition capture of Dresden and the fall of Częstochowa

The advance of the left column of the Coalition force. – Dispositions of Reynier and Davout at Dresden. – Davydov in Dresden-Neustadt. – The departure of the Viceroy's troops from Dresden and the occupation of the city by Russian forces. – Wintzingerode's further advance. – Blücher's advance through Dresden towards Altenburg.

The situation of the Viceroy's army behind the river Saale. – His thoughts. – Wittgenstein's advance on Magdeburg. – His plans. – The Viceroy's troop dispositions forwards of Magdeburg. – The offensive against him by Coalition forces under Count Wittgenstein. – The actions at Dannigkow, Vehlitz and Zeddenick. – The Viceroy's retreat behind the Elbe. – The factors that prevented Count Wittgenstein from exploiting the victory. – His crossing of the Elbe. – His attempt to seize Wittenberg. – Situation of Coalition forces in Saxony before the appearance of Napoleon's newly formed army in the theatre of war.

The situation in the rear of the Coalition armies. – The situation in Poland. – Dispositions in the Duchy of Warsaw. – Sacken's operations. – Capture of Częstochowa. – The removal of Poniatowski's corps.

Formation of the *Zentral Verwaltungs Rat* for the administration of German territory occupied by the Coalition armies. – The arrival of the King of Prussia in Kalisz and the review of Russian troops. – The departure of the Russian Main Army for Silesia. – Prince Kutuzov's illness. – The arrival of the Coalition sovereigns in Dresden. – The forces of both sides on the river Saale. – Kutuzov's final orders. – His demise.

The advance of the left column of the Coalition force from Silesia into Saxony was completed in three main echelons: Wintzingerode's corps leading; behind them came Blücher's corps; further back was Miloradovich's corps. The Main Army, with whom were co-located the headquarters of Emperor Alexander and Prince Kutuzov, remained in Kalisz.

The partisans under Davydov, Prendel and Prince Madatov, and behind them the vanguard of Wintzingerode's corps, commanded by Major General Lanskoy, were streaming towards the Elbe in front of the left Coalition column. Davydov and Prince Madatov had gained widespread and well-deserved renown during the Patriotic War: Davydov, had been the pioneer of partisan operations; Madatov, a horseman by vocation, the idol of the dashing Alexandria Hussar Regiment, had become famous throughout the army for his courage and resourcefulness in the actions at Borisov and Kalisz. With regard to Prendel, his comrades-in-arms, contemporaries, unvarnished judges and connoisseurs of valour, say completely otherwise. According to their evidence, Prendel tried to inspire fear of himself through his appearance: his eyes flashed like lightning; his long moustache, the rattling of weapons and loud threats terrified civilians, yet in the course of his whole combat career, he not only did nothing remarkable, but was rarely exposed to any obvious danger. His entire partisan activity was limited to capturing isolated, wandering enemy and compiling very detailed reports from their interrogations.[1]

On 8 (20) March, Wintzingerode seized Bautzen with his main body, sending General Lanskoy and the partisans towards the Elbe, where the detachment under *Flügel-Adjutant* Captain Orlov, detached by Miloradovich to Hoyerswerda, had also been sent.

General Reynier was in command of the troops that had managed to assemble in Dresden over several days, some 3,500 men, occupied the city and especially its eastern part on the right bank of the Elbe (Neustadt), started building fortifications there and announced to the population that, in the event of an enemy attack, he had been ordered to blow up one of the piers of the stone bridge. After that, the French began to install demolition charges under the bridge; but they were faced with strong opposition from the residents, roused to resistance by the general hatred of the Germans for Napoleon and the desire to preserve one of the finest monuments of national architecture. It came to the point that the people, having gathered in a noisy crowd at the Brühlsche Palais, occupied by General Reynier, smashed several panes of glass in the windows of his apartments with stones and rioted late into the night. But soon after, on 1 (13) March, Davout arrived at Dresden with reinforcements eventually strengthening the garrison to 12,000 men. Having received orders from the Viceroy: to hold the enemy on the Elbe, but not to be drawn into a decisive battle with superior forces under Blücher, rather, upon the arrival of the Coalition army at Dresden, to evacuate this city, as well as Meissen, occupied by the Bavarian detachment under Count Rechberg, and to destroy both bridges, the marshal actively continued the demolition preparations. Thirty miners sent from Freiberg worked in shifts day and night to dig five pits around the fourth pier, eight to ten feet deep. Communications with the right bank of the river were forbidden and the inhabitants of Dresden were ordered to stay in their homes continuously as soon as the first cannon shot was heard across the river, and to treat violators of this order as if they were spies; the garrison were ordered to shoot at the populace if they gathered in crowds, and so on.[2]

1 Denkwürdigkeiten eines Livländers, II, 5.
2 Norvins, *Portefeuille de 1813*, I, 131-132. *Tagebuch der Begebenheiten in Dresden vom 13 bis 27 März 1813*, 4-13.

On 7 (19) March, Davout, having learned about the leading elements of the Coalition Army approaching Dresden, transferred the troops and transport from Neustadt to the left bank of the river, except for several Saxon companies left there, under the command of Major Eschka, and ordered that part of the bridge under which the charges had been laid be blown up. The effect of the charges, calculated with precision by skilful French engineers, was limited to the demolition of one pier and the two arches either side of it. No other buildings were damaged, no window glass was shattered, and only a few of the inhabitants even heard the dull crack of the charges detonating.[3] On that same day [19 March], Davout departed from Dresden, entrusting command over the remnants of the former *7e Corps* to Durutte, following the illness of General Reynier: the force entrusted to him consisted of his own division and the Saxon division under Le Coq, some 3,000 men in total. Meanwhile, Colonel Davydov, having learned of the destruction of the Dresden bridge from the inhabitants of the surrounding countryside and realising that half of the city, lying on the right bank of the Elbe, had either been completely abandoned by the enemy, or was weakly held by them, approached the city on the evening of 8 (20) March. Having deployed his small detachment in a wide arc on the high ground near Dresden and having ordered the Cossacks to make huge camp fires, Davydov sent a *parlementaire* Staff Captain Löwenstern [Vladimir Ivanovich Levenshtern or Woldemar Hermann von Löwenstern] to Neustadt the next morning [21 March], demanding the surrender of the city, threatening an assault in the event of a refusal. General Durutte, who was stationed in the Altstadt, expressed the wish to meet with a field officer authorised to negotiate by the commander of the Russian detachment. The outcome from this was the departure to Dresden of Lieutenant Colonel Khrapovitsky [Iason (Yason) Semënovich Khrapovitsky] of the Volhynia Ulan Regiment. Durutte, estimating that Davydov's detachment was incomparably stronger than it was in reality, and having received intelligence during the day of the appearance of Coalition forces and their attempts to cross the Elbe upstream and downstream of Dresden, at nine o'clock in the evening approved an agreement signed by representatives of both parties. It was determined that Russian forces would occupied the Neustadt at noon on 10 (22) March, and that hostilities were to be suspended in the city and to a distance of one *Meile* upstream and downstream of it; each of the contracting parties undertook to announce the resumption of hostilities to the enemy 48 hours before their commencement; finally, Durutte also agreed that Saxon troops occupying the Neustadt were to salute the Russians before departing from there; but demanded only that this article not be included in the capitulation.[4] Thus, Davydov now held the closest part of Dresden, but had aroused the displeasure of General Wintzingerode in the process, who, having relieved him of command of his detachment, ordered him to hand over the force to Prendel and return to headquarters. The reason for this, according to Wintzingerode, was that: 'negotiations with the enemy, which have been strictly prohibited since the invasion

3 Tagebuch, 10-11. Vaudoncourt, 52. Davydov wrote erroneously that the Dresden bridge was blown up on 8 (20) March.

4 A copy of the capitulation is attached to Adjutant General Wintzingerode's report to Prince Kutuzov, dated 13 [25] March, No. 501 (Log of Incoming Documents No. 488).

of Russia, and the conclusion of a truce being a crime against the state, deserved exemplary punishment.'[5]

On the following day, 10 (22) March, after the enemy had evacuated the Neustadt, the Saxon detachment under Le Coq set off from Dresden for Torgau to rejoin Thielmann's force stationed there; while several hundred Bavarian infantry arrived to replace them. All in all Durutte had some 2,000 men with 18 guns; whereupon the French from the Dresden garrison set off in several small groups from the city, and only the Bavarians remained to defend it, meanwhile, intelligence had been received about a Russian crossing at Riesa, Durutte, not daring to hold on in Dresden any longer, retreated in the direction of the Saale river during the night of 14 to 15 (26 to 27) March. Indeed, the crossing of the Elbe by a partisan detachment under *Flügel-Adjutant* Orlov at Debelsdorf downstream of Meissen and several Cossack patrols between Dresden and the Bohemian border made the enemy concerned for their line of retreat and evacuate the Saxon capital. Seizing this opportunity, Wintzingerode sent part of his force onto the left bank of the river, occupied Dresden Altstadt on 15 (27) March, ordered General Nikitin to build a floating bridge and crossed the Elbe on 19 (31) March with the rest of the vanguard. Three days later, on 22 March (3 April), Wintzingerode settled in Leipzig, while on 29 March (10 April), the masonry bridge at Dresden was reopened to traffic.[6] Blücher's Prussian corps was proceeding directly behind the vanguard and passed through Dresden between 18 and 22 March (30 March and 3 April). The flower of the population of Prussia was under this military leader, with grey hair but vigorous and strong in body and soul; accompanying him were: the king's brother Prinz Wilhelm [Friedrich Wilhelm Karl], the Prussian princes August and Friedrich and the queen's brother, Herzog Karl zu Mecklenburg-Strelitz; while the Prussian *Kronprinz* arrived the next day.

Hoping for the support of the population of Saxony for the common cause of Germany, as he was crossing the Silesian border, Blücher announced in an appeal to his troops that they should deal with the Saxons as with future allies.[7] But instead of support, the Coalition encountered distrust of themselves in Saxony and indifference to the common cause.[8] Requisitions of essential goods were delivered with an extreme lack of urgency. The absence of King Friedrich-August and the hesitation of the government commission, not knowing whether they should follow the old policy, or act in favour of the Coalition, forced Blücher to appeal to the people and to appease public opinion; to that end, he allowed press freedom and ordered the release of the Dresden residents imprisoned in Fort Königstein for shattering the windows of the Brühlsche Palais. But all of this did not induce the Saxons to take part in the Coalition against Napoleon in the least.

5 Memoirs by D.I. Davydov, 4th edition. General Wintzingerode's report to Prince Kutuzov, dated 13 [25] March, No. 501.

6 General Wintzingerode's report to Prince Kutuzov-Smolensky, dated 15 [27] March, No. 520. Beitzke, I, 348. Vaudoncourt, 52-53. Plotho, I, 48-49.

7 Förster, I, 224-225. Richter, *Geschichte des deutschen Freiheitskrieges*, I, 108-110.

8 One of the main reasons for Saxon hostility towards the Coalition was Blücher's proclamation to the inhabitants of *Kreis* Cottbus, in which, in the name of his Sovereign, he announced the annexation of this territory to Prussia, taken away by Napoleon in accordance with the Treaty of Tilsit, in favour of Saxony. Richter, *Geschichte des deutschen Freiheitskrieges*, I, 110-111.

On 22 March (3 April), Blücher set out from Dresden for Altenburg with the tail-end group of his corps, where his *Hauptquartier* arrived on 2 (14) April; his troops were placed in quarters between Borna [20 miles south of Leipzig] and Zwickau; the Prussian corps remained in these positions for two whole weeks, until 16 (28) April.[9]

Friedrich-August's actions at this time, were perceived as leaning in favour of the Coalition. According to Scharnhorst, he had sent a representative to Breslau, who was instructed to assure the King of Prussia of the willingness of the Saxon government to contribute to the common cause, noting, however, that this was dependent on circumstances that would allow decisive action. The Coalition proposed that Friedrich-August's Saxon forces gathered in Torgau join their army and to announce his decision to mobilise in defence of Germany, promising, for their part, a guarantee of the inviolability of his territory, with the exception of *Kreis* [county] Cottbus and Westphalian land, and payment, or remuneration for all goods supplied to Coalition forces. But, for two months, the King not only gave no inkling of a definitive answer to these proposals, but left both the government commission and General Thielmann, in command of Saxon forces, completely in the dark with regard to his views.[10]

The situation in Saxony, with regard to the Coalition, was articulated by Stein as follows:

> Most of the population are devoted to their sovereign and wished for his return. However, one should not assume that feeble yet eloquent people who are attached to their possessions most of all are capable of rebellion. It is repulsive to see that subjugation and all the disasters of their fatherland are less offensive to them than the hardships associated with the war, the absence of their king and the destruction of the Dresden bridge…
>
> … In the event that the king stubbornly remains on Napoleon's side, it is possible to entrust the administration to the committee of state and use the resources of the country for the common cause. Such a situation would be better than the presence of a proud, weak, stubborn king, who would hinder the running of matters in every way…[11]

Following the evacuation of Dresden, the Viceroy's army retreated behind the river Saale. General Lauriston's *5e Corps* was located on the Elbe, downstream from Magdeburg to Werben [seven miles north of Sandau]; General Grenier's *11e Corps* held Magdeburg; several battalions from Marshal Victor's *2e Corps* were stationed at Calbe and Bernburg; Durutte's division and Rechberg's Bavarian contingent were in the Harz mountains, near Stolberg. The occupation of a defensive line along the river Saale and the lower Elbe, allowed the Viceroy to concentrate a significant part of his forces in the vicinity of Magdeburg, and facilitated his offensive operations

9 General Wintzingerode's letter to Prince Kutuzov, dated 15 [27] April (Log of Incoming Documents No. 522). Beitzke, I, 349-351. Plotho, I, 37.

10 *Leben des Ministers Freiherrn vom Stein*, III, 328. Beitzke, I, 353-354.

11 Extracted from Stein's letter to Nesselrode, dated 11 April new style, from Dresden (archive of the Ministry of Foreign Affairs (M.F.A.)).

Legend to Map:

French Forces		Coalition Forces	
A.A.	Grenier's corps	G.	Bülow's column
B.B.	Maison's division	H.	Borstell's column
C.C.	Puthod's division	I.	Berg's [Russian] column
D.D.	Rochambeau's division	K.	Yorck's column
E.E.	Garde impériale		
F.F.	Outposts		

against Count Wittgenstein. By threatening to march on Berlin, the Viceroy hoped to keep our commander from crossing in the vicinity of Wittenberg and from moving towards Leipzig, which would not only allow coordinated operations by both Coalition armies, but also exposed the Viceroy to loss of communications with Napoleon's forces assembling on the Main and Rhine. Thus, Prince Eugène was concerned that the army under Count Wittgenstein might move beyond the Elbe in the direction indicated by Prince Kutuzov.[12] Count Wittgenstein, for his part, decided to close up to the Elbe having been reinforced by Bülow's corps that had arrived from Stettin. His force, departing from the Berlin area on 15 (27) March, were deployed as follows by 21 March (2 April): General Borstell's brigade was at Vehlitz, 1½ *Meilen* (ten *verstas*) east of Magdeburg; the *Hauptquartier* and Yorck's corps were at Zerbst; Berg's corps was at Lietzo [7½ miles north of Zerbst]; Bülow's corps was at Ziesar. The disadvantages of such a deployment of army elements, at an interval of one to two stages between each other, were increased by the poor quality of the roads along which they had to march towards the Elbe.[13]

In mid (late) March, the Viceroy concentrated the infantry corps under Lauriston and Grenier, the *1er corps de cavalerie*, *2e corps de cavalerie* and the *Garde*, numbering about 40,000 men, in Magdeburg and in front of this fortress, on the right bank of the Elbe.[14] Count Wittgenstein, whose forces, following the dispatch of detachments into the rear of the army, reached some 35,000 men,[15] decided to attack the enemy despite their superiority in troop strength, with the aim of securing Berlin from the Viceroy's attempts, and to open communications with the corps under Wintzingerode and Blücher by crossing the Elbe upstream of Magdeburg. Based on these considerations, Count Wittgenstein and Scharnhorst drew up a general disposition for Coalition operations.[16] General Borstell was ordered to engage the enemy,

12 Vaudoncourt, 54 & 57.
13 Beitzke, I, 333-334. Plotho, I, 61-63. Förster, I, 202. The factors that influenced Count Wittgenstein are set out in an account by the Chief of Staff of his army, General Dovre, to Prince Volkonsky. For details, see Appendix VIII at the end of this chapter.
14 Norvins, I, 135. According to him, the Viceroy had 60,000, but this number, in all probability, shows all the other troops then stationed on the Saale and the lower Elbe; Vaudoncourt, 49-50.
15 These troop numbers are from Count Wittgenstein's report to Prince Kutuzov-Smolensky, dated 14 [26] March, No. 24 (Log of Incoming Documents, No. 482). Plotho (I, 64) and Richter (I, 94) both show Count Wittgenstein with a total of 27,000 men.
16 Count Wittgenstein's report to Prince Kutuzov-Smolensky, dated 23 March [4 April], No. 27, with the disposition attached (Log of Incoming Documents, No. 561).

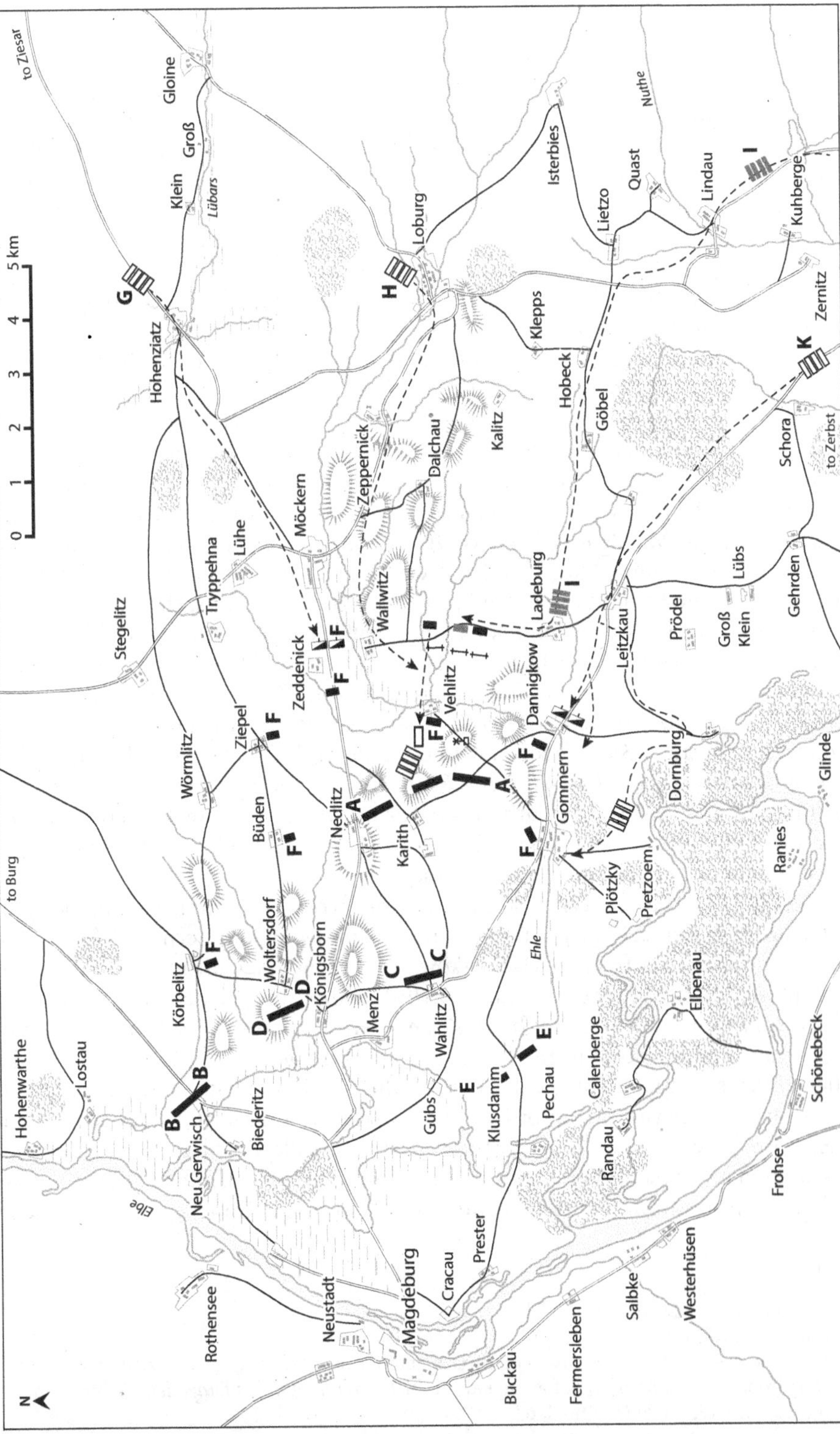

Map of the Magdeburg Area.

but not to be drawn into a decisive battle, to try to lure the Viceroy from the advantageous position he occupied in front of Magdeburg and draw him as far as possible from this fortress; meanwhile, it was intended to envelope the enemy corps on their right flank using the forces under Yorck and Berg and to sever their line of retreat. On 21 and 22 March (2 and 3 April), Borstell, under attack from superior numbers, retreated in perfect order towards Gloine.[17] But the Viceroy had guessed his adversary's intention and remained in his positions: Grenier's corps was deployed in the centre on the Nedlitz plateau, shielded by the boggy Ehle stream; the right wing was near the village of Gommern, adjacent to the aforementioned stream, while the left was on the road to Burg, near the village of Neu Gerwisch, also protected by swamps and was held by the troops under Lauriston. The *Garde* were stationed in reserve by the Klusdamm causeway, a very important defile through extensive swamps on the road from Gommern to Magdeburg.[18]

As the Viceroy could not be drawn out, Count Wittgenstein gave orders to attack the enemy positions and allocated 25 March (6 April) as the day for this; meanwhile, the construction of bridges at Roßlau was actively continued. However, when a report came in from the forward outposts on 24 March (5 April) that the enemy force was pulling back into Magdeburg, then Wittgenstein, not wanting to lose the opportunity to deliver his intended blow, decided to attack the Viceroy immediately. The Coalition marched from their assembly areas in three columns: the left, consisting of Yorck's corps, with *Generalmajor* Hünerbein's detachment [Friedrich Heinrich Karl Georg von Hünerbein] in the lead,[19] advancing on Gommern via Leitzkau; the centre comprised Borstell's force marching from Zeppernick towards Vehlitz, where they were to link up with Berg's Russian corps, moving up from Lietzo; the right was made up of Bülow's force, with *Generalmajor* Oppen [Adolf Friedrich von Oppen] leading with *1. Leib-Husaren Regiment*, advancing from Ziesar along the Berlin highway toward the village of Möckern. Overall, the attacks were delivered over a frontage of a German *Meile* (seven *verstas*), which did not allow the proper coordination of operations to be maintained.

General Hünerbein, having waited for the arrival of Yorck's main body at Leitzkau from Zerbst, moved along the road towards Gommern and forced the enemy outposts to retreat to Dannigkow. Two French squadrons were stationed in front of this village; the Prussian *2. Leib-Husaren* immediately drove them off, but on approaching the nearest houses, they were engaged by fire from a screen of skirmishers and forced to retreat. Prussian jägers dashed up to the entrance to the village, but were repulsed by the detachment that was holding it as well as a battalion sent from Gommern, on the orders of the Viceroy himself. General Hünerbein opened fire with four guns and sent the jägers to attack the village once more; but this attempt also failed. As the enemy was reinforcing the defenders of Dannigkow with fresh troops from Gommern, Hünerbein, wanting to impede their movement,

17 See Map No. 3: Map of the Magdeburg Area.
18 Vaudoncourt, 57-58.
19 Hünerbein's detachment consisted of: three battalions of *1. Ostpreußisches Infanterie*, two squadrons of *2. Leib-Husaren*, four squadrons of *1. Westpreußisches Dragoner*, 12 guns and one Cossack regiment (Plotho, I, 63).

sent *Leutnant* Hansel's horse artillery battery to the left of the village under attack, escorted by dragoons, which opened enfilade fire on the enemy; at the same time, Major Lobenthal [Karl Friedrich Ludwig von Lobenthal] attacked them frontally with two battalions of *1. Ostpreußisches Infanterie*, while skirmishers, crossing the Ehle stream via a ford, got into the rear of the force defending the bridge, which forced the enemy to evacuate the village and retreat to Gommern. In the meantime, Major Cramon, who had been sent via Dornburg towards Gommern with a *Füsilier* battalion, reached this location, but, being engaged by superior enemy numbers, withdrew and positioned himself in line with Lobenthal's force. At five o'clock in the afternoon Count Wittgenstein and General Yorck arrived at Dunningkow with six battalions, *Oberst* Jürgaß's dragoons [Georg Ludwig Alexander von Wahlen-Jürgaß], and three artillery batteries. The arrival of fresh troops helped Hünerbein to hang on to Dannigkow, but the fighting was now limited to a cannonade that continued until nightfall. The casualties in the left column of killed and wounded overall, reached 140 men, including three officers.[20]

At four o'clock in the afternoon, at the same time as the fighting at Dannigkow was in full swing, General Borstell, having heard the powerful cannonade thundering at that location, set out from Zeppernick with his dragoons and a horse artillery battery towards Wallwitz and Vehlitz, and ordered his infantry and foot artillery to proceed there as quickly as possible. The village of Vehlitz was defended by two battalions; four guns fired at the bridge and the long causeway on the Ehle stream; the infantry were stationed behind the village in several squares. Upon arrival at the enemy position, Borstell found Berg's corps already there, forming up on the near side of the stream, and started a fairly strong cannonade; this artillery was joined by Borstell's horse artillery battery; while his foot artillery battery joined once it had arrived. Thus, 24 guns were active at this point on the Coalition side. At five o'clock orders were received from General Yorck to seize Vehlitz. In accordance with Berg's agreement with Borstell, the Coalition force attacked the village in three columns: both wings were made up of Prussian troops,[21] while the centre consisted of the Russian 26th Jägers and soldiers from the Olonets *Opolchenie* and Vologda *Opolchenie*, under General Roth's command [Loggin Osipovich Roth]. The swampy stream was crossed by fording, waist-deep in water. Marksmen, scattered in front of the left column, attacked the battery stationed at the entrance to the village and captured two guns. Several enemy squadrons raced to the rescue of the lost artillery and recaptured them, but the Prussian *Füsilier*s had managed to render these guns unserviceable by sticking bayonets into the touch-holes and breaking off the tips. To the right of the causeway, the lead battalion had crossed the stream in line and was preparing to reform into column for the assault; at that very moment several French squadrons appeared on his right flank; but the Prussian infantry had managed to wheel into square and, having engaged the enemy cavalry with volleys at a range of 50 paces, scattered them and drove them off in disorder, some towards Vehlitz,

20 Plotho, I, 64-65. Förster, I, 204-206.

21 The right hand column consisted of two battalions of *1. Pommersches Infanterie*, while the left had the *Füsilier* battalion of *4. Ostpreußisches Infanterie* and the *Pommersches Grenadier Bataillon* (Plotho, I, 66).

some across the stream towards Leitzkau. The Prussian *Königin Dragoner* and the Grodno Hussars pursued the fleeing enemy and completed their destruction. After that, the one battalion of *Pommersches Infanterie* captured Vehlitz in combat, while the grenadier battalion, the other battalion of *Pommersches Infanterie* and Roth's force attacked the French on the Windmühlenberg, captured a gun and drove the enemy back towards Nedlitz. The casualties in Borstell's brigade reached some 250 men, including six officers. Overall, the Russians lost some 50 men.[22]

Generalmajor Oppen, marching as the vanguard of Bülow's corps with the *1. Leib-Husaren*, which had set out from Ziesar in the morning, encountered the enemy at Zeddenick. In front of this village, behind a deep ditch, stood cavalry from seven different regiments, numbering about 1,000 men, with an horse artillery battery; infantry stood behind them in three small squares. General Oppen, after waiting for the arrival of four more squadrons of dragoons (*Litthauisches Dragoner* and *1. Westpreußisches Dragoner*), with *Hauptmann* Steinwehr's horse artillery battery, leaving one squadron of hussars to escort the artillery, while he led the remaining seven to attack the enemy cavalry. The French opened fire with carbines at the hussars, who, having reached the ditch, halted. At this very moment, Bülow, having just arrived on the battlefield, sent Major Platen [Gottlieb Wilhelm Christian von Platen] into the attack with the *Litthauisches Dragoner*, numbering 200 men. *Der tolle* [the great] Platen, as they used to call him, dashed forwards, crossed the ditch with an Hurrah! drove off the incomparably stronger enemy and captured 150 men. The French infantry, covering the retreat of the cavalry under fire from the Prussian horse artillery battery, was forced to retreat to Nedlitz. The losses to the Prussian cavalry in the action at Zeddenick reached some 140 men; overall, in all three actions on 24 March (5 April), nine officers and about 600 lower ranks were killed or wounded on the Coalition side. On the French side, the loss of prisoners alone reached some 20 officers and about 1,000 lower ranks; the number of dead and wounded was also very significant; generals Grenier and Grundler [Louis Sébastien Grundler] were wounded.[23]

After dark, the enemy retreated into Magdeburg, destroying the bridges on the Klusdamm, and even their floating bridges on the Elbe. It was obvious that the Viceroy had completely abandoned his attempt to advance on Berlin, and this was confirmed the next day by the movement of French forces along the left bank of the Elbe towards the lower Saale.[24]

The actions on 24 March (5 April) not only secured Berlin and enabled Count Wittgenstein to start crossing the Elbe, but instilled the Prussian troops with confidence in themselves and their commanders. Unfortunately, Count Wittgenstein could take no further advantage of this victory. Magdeburg, Wittenberg and Torgau demanded observation detachments; the fortress of Spandau was being blockaded: thus, the Coalition were compelled to weaken the already insignificant forces

22 Plotho, I, 66-67. Beitzke, I, 335-338. Vaudoncourt claimed (page 59) that the Coalition force did not cross the Ehle stream until late at night.

23 Plotho, I, 67-68. Beitzke, I, 338-339. Förster, I, 207-208. According to him, the French lost 1,200 killed or wounded. Vaudoncourt, 59.

24 Plotho, I, 69.

with which they were preparing for operations beyond the Elbe. The forces under Bülow and Borstell were left near Magdeburg; *Generalleutnant* Kleist, with a Russo-Prussian detachment, numbering 7,000 men, with 40 guns,[25] was near Wittenberg; Count Wittgenstein crossed the Elbe near Roßlau on 29 March (10 April) with the remainder of the units from the corps under Yorck and Berg, and positioned them at Dessau and Köthen [8½ miles north of Radegast].[26]

Count Wittgenstein, wishing to have a more secure crossing on the Elbe, opened communications with Saxon General Thielmann, whose troops held Torgau; but Thielmann, although he showed sympathy for the common cause of Germany, nevertheless could not surrender the fortress entrusted to him to the Coalition, having orders from King Friedrich-August not to give access either to the French or to their opponents. Meanwhile, having received intelligence from Thielmann about the possibility of capturing Wittenberg with a minimum of effort, Wittgenstein decided to storm this fortress and assigned 5 (17) April as the day. Indeed, the fortifications of Wittenberg were rather weak and its garrison consisted of only 1,500 Polish troops under General Dąbrowski [Jan Henryk Dąbrowski] and 1,000 Frenchmen. But the commandant of this fortress, General La Poype [Jean François de La Poype], a veteran of revolutionary wars, through the stubborn defence of Wittenberg proved the well-known axiom that the main strength of any fortress lies not in its walls, but in the courage of the garrison and in the spirit of resolve of the force commander.[27]

The French and Poles, who made up the garrison of Wittenberg, occupied the fortress, which, as is well known, lies on the right bank of the Elbe, as well as a bridgehead on the opposite bank. Count Wittgenstein, having linked up with Kleist's force on the eve of the day assigned for the attack on the enemy, was present on 5 (17) April, during the assault and capture of the suburbs. Thereafter, the Coalition bombarded the town for two days, while General Kazachkovsky [Kirill Fëdorovich Kazachkovsky] attempted to seize the bridgehead. But every attempt proved unsuccessful. Casualties on both sides reached some 300 men.[28]

On 7 (19) April, having received intelligence of Napoleon's advance, which was aimed at reuniting his army with the force under the Viceroy and dividing the Coalition corps, Wittgenstein decided to leave only the most essential detachments on the right bank of the Elbe, and concentrate all other forces on the left bank of this river for joint operations with Blücher. To that end, Yorck's corps were to move from Köthen, followed by Major General Helffreich, with the Tenginsk Infantry and Estland Infantry regiments, to Zörbig and on to Düben; Berg's corps were also to move from Dessau to Düben; having left an observation detachment near

25 Kleist's detachment comprised: 23rd Jägers, 24th Jägers, 14th Battery Artillery Company, 21st Battery Artillery Company and a Cossack regiment, from the Russian forces; *2. Ostpreußisches Infanterie, Colbergsches Infanterie, Brandenburgsches Husaren* and *Hauptmann* Ziegler's six-pounder foot artillery battery, from the Prussian corps under Yorck and Bülow. In total, 2,000 Russians and 5,000 Prussians, with 24 Russian guns and 16 Prussian guns (Plotho, I, 73).

26 Beitzke, I, 340.

27 Norvins, I, 134-135. Plotho, I, 72.

28 Vaudoncourt, 62. Plotho, I, 73-77.

Wittenberg,[29] and another detachment to guard the bridgehead at Roßlau,[30] General Kleist set off with the rest of his force for Halle via Dessau. The arrival of the Russian detachments under Count Vorontsov and General Harpe [Vasily Ivanovich Garpe or Otto Wilhelm Harpe] on the Elbe, the former from Küstrin via Frankfurt to Magdeburg, and the latter from Pillau to Wittenberg, allowed Count Wittgenstein to transfer Bülow's corps and the force left by Kleist near Wittenberg onto the left bank of the Elbe.[31] Following the capture of Spandau, Thümen's brigade moved to the Elbe to join Bülow's corps. Thus, by mid (late) April, the Coalition force under Count Wittgenstein's command, which consisted of some 30,000 men, having established communications with Blücher's force, was deployed as follows: Count Wittgenstein's headquarters, together with Berg's corps, were at Leipzig; Yorck's corps was in the vicinity of Schkeuditz [eight miles north-west of Leipzig]; Kleist's detachment was in Halle, Bülow's was in Köthen, with the exception of Thümen's brigade which remained on the right bank of the Elbe.

Let us turn to a presentation of events to the rear of the Coalition Army deployed in Saxony.

At the same time as Blücher and Count Wittgenstein were crossing the Elbe, many locations in the countryside they had covered were still occupied by enemy troops: Zamość on the right bank of the Vistula; Danzig, Thorn and Modlin, on the Vistula; Stettin, Küstrin and Glogau, on the Oder; Magdeburg, Wittenberg and Torgau on the Elbe. Warsaw was occupied by a detachment under Count Pahlen [Pëtr Petrovich Palen or Peter Johann Christoph von der Pahlen]; a significant siege corps under Herzog Alexander von Württemberg [Alexander Friedrich Karl von Württemberg] had assembled near Danzig; the fortress of Thorn was under siege by Barclay de Tolly; Modlin and Zamość were also under blockade. Postponing the description of the sieges until the capture of the fortresses by Coalition Forces, I shall confine myself to a presentation of military and political events in Poland.

The situation in this country was very precarious. For a long time past, many Poles had been convinced of the inevitability of the union of Poland with Russia. Emperor Alexander I appealed to their hearts. Putting aside the age-old enmity that divided

29 The following remained at Wittenberg under Prussian Major Siegholm's command: two battalions of *2. Ostpreußisches Infanterie*, one squadron of hussars, *Leutnant* Fischer's *3. Reitende Artillerie Batterie* and a Cossack regiment (Plotho, I, 80).

30 The following Russian troops remained at Roßlau: 23rd Jägers, 24th Jägers and 21st Battery Artillery Company (Plotho, I, 80).

31 Count Vorontsov at Magdeburg: Colonel Krasovsky's brigade: 13th Jägers, 14th Jägers. Six combined battalions from 9th Division, 15th Division and 18th Division and one battalion from the Sevsk Infantry Regiment. Major General O'Rourke's brigade: Pavlograd Hussars, Volhynia Ulans. 11th Horse Artillery Company, 13th Horse Artillery Company, 26th Light Artillery Company. Six Cossack regiments. Numbering: 5,500 men (Log of Outgoing Documents, No. 526. Plotho, I, *Beilagen*, 97). General Harpe at Wittenberg: Navaginsk Infantry, Tula Infantry. 21st Battery Artillery Company (detached from the force at Roßlau). Two Cossack regiments. Numbering some 2,000 men (Plotho, I, *Beilagen*, 96). General Thümen at the fortress of Spandau: three battalions of *4. Ostpreußisches Infanterie*, two companies of jägers and a volunteer unit, *Hauptmann* Lüdwig's six-pounder foot artillery battery, Nezhin Mounted Jägers, Poland Ulans, Lieutenant Colonel Salzmann's light artillery company, one *Sotnia* of Cossacks, numbering some 2,300 men (Plotho, I, *Beilagen*, 84-85).

peoples of the same tribe, the noblest sons of Poland wished to unite under the power of the younger brother of the Russian Tsar. Prince Adam Czartoryski [Adam Jerzy Czartoryski], former Russian Minister of Foreign Affairs and later a member of the Council of State, returning to Poland at the opening of the war of 1812, and being, as before, awarded the authority of Emperor Alexander I, tried to convince his compatriots of the magnanimity of the Russian Monarch's vision, but the party of Prince Poniatowski, supported by the influence of the Catholic clergy, destroyed every peaceful attempt by Russia and Prussia. The occupation of Danzig and Modlin by French troops in 1813 kept the dreams of the Poles afloat, who still considered Napoleon their liberator, despite many examples of his duplicity and indifference to the fate of Poland. In Poznań, in Bialystok, in the Duchy of Warsaw, the arrival of the conqueror with a new army was awaited and preparations were made for a general uprising. It was intended, on that same day, to drive out the Germans, Russians and Jews from the entire duchy. There were rumours that Napoleon, having received news of the mobilisation by Prussia, had said: 'The House of Hohenzollern is unworthy of a crown; the Prussian monarchy is to be dissolved: East and West Prussia shall go to Poland, Silesia shall be returned to Austria, the other regions shall join the Kingdom of Westphalia.' Catholic priests inflamed their parishioners' hatred of the Russians and Prussians instead of preaching the Gospel of Peace. The uprising was intended to break out on Good Friday.[32]

Under these circumstances, it was vital to organise the administration of the Duchy of Warsaw, to subdue the Polish fortresses still occupied by the enemy, and to expel Poniatowski's corps from the southwestern part of the duchy, to where he had retreated from Warsaw. In order to manage the civil administration of Poland, a Supreme Council was established in Warsaw, chaired by the Active Privy Councillor Lanskoy [Vasily Sergeevich Lanskoy]. In order to concentrate control of military matters, General of Infantry Dokhturov [Dmitry Sergeevich Dokhturov] was entrusted with overall command of all forces stationed in the duchy, namely: Lieutenant General Pahlen's force in the Warsaw area; Major General Paskevich, near Modlin, and Major General Rath, near Zamość. The 27th Division under Major General Neverovsky [Dmitry Petrovich Neverovsky], on the march from Vilna to Wyszogród, was also subordinated to General Dokhturov, as were all troops that were intended to enter Poland throughout the entire sector from Płock to Lublin.[33]

In order to clear the southwestern part of the duchy of enemy troops, an independent detachment entrusted to Lieutenant General Sacken was formed from some of the forces stationed in the vicinity of Warsaw under the command of Lieutenant General Count Pahlen.[34] Having departed from Warsaw on 25 February (9 March),

32 Droysen, *Das Leben des Ministers Freiherrn vom Stein, Feldmarschalls Grafen Yorck*, II, 162-163.

33 Prince Kutuzov's orders for General-of-Infantry Dokhturov, dated 17 [29] March (Log of Outgoing Documents, No. 524).

34 Prince Kutuzov's orders for General Sacken, dated 8 [20] February, No. 314. Composition of Sacken's detachment: Yaroslavl Infantry, Crimea Infantry, 8th Jägers, 39th Jägers, Serpukhov Ulans, 4th Ukraine Cossacks, Yezhov's Don Cossacks, 10th Battery Artillery Company, 18th Horse Artillery Company. Later, the following arrived: Okhotsk Infantry, Kamchatka Infantry, 29th Jägers, Smolensk Dragoons, Vladimir Ulans, Lukovkin's Don Cossacks, Chernozubov's Don Cossacks, 2nd Mounted Bashkirs, 2nd Mounted Kalmyks, 38th Battery Artillery

Sacken approached the fortress of Częstochowa on 20 (22) March and had invested it by 13 (25) March. Over the course of several days, four batteries were erected, under the direction of Lieutenant Colonel Rochouart of the Quartermaster's Department (General Staff). On 23 March (4 April), a bombardment by 28 guns was opened across the fortress, from which three large buildings caught fire; but General Sacken ordered a halt to the bombardment: 'in order to preserve the monument of the Eastern Church, the church of the Most Holy Theotokos and its miraculous image [Matka Boska Częstochowska].' On 25 March (6 April), the garrison surrendered as prisoners of war, including 56 field officers and subalterns, and 1,026 lower ranks, but the Tsar, on Sacken's request, deigned to dismiss the captured Poles to their homes, obliging them to sign a pledge not to serve against Russia, with the condition that if any of them later broke their promise, then they would be shot as a criminal.[35] 24 guns and a fairly significant amount of military stores and provisions were found in the fortress. Among the prisoners was *Porucznik* Żubr [Maciej Żubr], whose wife [Joanna Żubr, née Pasławska] had served in her husband's company for seven years and was in combat and assaults 17 times.[36] General Sacken received the Order of St Alexander Nevsky for the capture of Częstochowa.

Throughout the duration of this siege, the Polish force under Prince Poniatowski, separated from our blockade corps by a cordon of Austrian outposts, tried to relieve Częstochowa, but were kept inactive by the Austrians, who, covering the Poles from our troops and keeping their allies from determined attempts, had warned General Sacken of their intentions.[37]

These actions by the commander of the Austrian auxiliary corps, General Frimont [Johann Maria Philipp Frimont von Palota], were a consequence of the negotiations in Kalisz. During Emperor Alexander I's stay in this town, Herr Lebzeltern arrived there from Vienna with a letter from Prinz Metternich, which expressed the willingness of the Austrian government to mediate between the belligerent Powers. This proposal was declined:

> There has not yet been a precedent of a state offering its mediation while still participating in a war. Nevertheless, without being insistent on this observation, the Russian government has formally announced that the Austrian proposal could be accepted only with the consent of the Powers allied with them: Britain, Prussia and Sweden.[38]

Company, 24th Light Artillery Company. A Prussian detachment under Oberstleutnant Kanitz, numbering 2,000 men. Overall, there were some 9,000 Russians in Sacken's detachment, while the addition of the Prussians brought the total to some 11,000 men.

35 Prince Kutuzov's orders to General Sacken, dated 27 March [8 April], No. 619. These orders conclude with the words: 'My correspondence with Your Excellency is all the easier because I find it unnecessary to give you instructions constantly.'

36 General Sacken's reports to Prince Kutuzov-Smolensky, dated 25 March [6 April], No. 51 and dated 29 March [10 April], No. 55 (archive of the M.T.D. No. 16,644).

37 Lieutenant General Sacken's dispatches to Adjutant General Prince Volkonsky, dated 20 March [1 April], No. 46 (archive of the M.T.D. No. 16,644).

38 Schoell, *Histoire abrégée des traités de paix*, III, 276.

Yet a very important consequence of Lebzeltern's mission was the conclusion of a convention, according to the terms of which, upon concluding the truce with the Austrians it was necessary for Russian forces to move around the flanks of Frimont's Corps, which was ordered to retreat gradually parallel to our demonstrations to behind the right bank of the upper Vistula, maintaining outposts on the left bank in Kraków, Opatowiec and Sandomierz. The retreat by the Austrian force was intended to induce Prince Poniatowski to disband the Polish corps, which General Frimont was obliged to cooperate with, declaring that Poles crossing from the Duchy of Warsaw into Galicia would only be allowed as small, disarmed units. General Sacken was instructed to execute these measures, which, in all likelihood, would induce most of the Poles to return to areas occupied by Russian forces.[39]

After the capture of Częstochowa, having left a small garrison there, Sacken marched to Sławków on 29 March (10 April), where he assimilated 2,000 Prussian troops into his corps, under the command of *Oberst* Kanitz. As they advanced, the Austrian corps retreated behind the right bank of the Vistula, in accordance with the armistice agreement signed by Generals Sacken and Frimont.[40] General Sacken, having closed up to Kraków, personally agreed on the expulsion of Polish troops to Bohemia via Galicia and Silesia with General Frimont on 22 April (4 May). It was intended that they would depart from the Podgórze area in five groups, between 25 and 29 April (7 and 11 May). As the French resident Bignon [Édouard Bignon] and members of the former Polish government did not want to leave Kraków, General Frimont suggested that Sacken occupy this city with our forces. As soon as news arrived in Kraków of the imminent arrival of Cossacks, Kalmyks and Bashkirs, who were with the Russian corps, Bignon and the Polish ministers fled to Galicia. The president of the Kraków administration presented the keys of the city to General Sacken, who would not accept them, expressing to the delegation that met him that it would be most pleasing to him to see them in the hands of the good residents of Kraków. This act placed not only the population but also the Austrians in our favour.[41]

Thus, about 10,000 Polish and Saxon troops, who had made the final subjugation of the Duchy of Warsaw difficult, were removed from the theatre of operations and went to Bohemia in small groups and disarmed (their weapons were transported behind them on carts, at an interval of several stages). Sacken's corps was ordered to join the main body of the Russian army via Silesia.[42]

In the meantime, the great cause of the liberation of Germany had been approved in Breslau through an agreement between the Russian and Prussian governments.

Based on the convention for the administration of countries liberated during the war, signed by the plenipotentiaries Stein and Count Nesselrode, on behalf of Russia, and Hardenberg and Scharnhorst on behalf of Prussia, it was decided:

39 Active Councillor of State Anstett's letter to General Sacken, dated 17 (29) March, from Kalisz (archive of the M.F.A.).

40 Convention concluded in Kraków, dated 18 (30) April.

41 General Sacken's dispatches to Prince Volkonsky: dated 12 [24] April, No. 72; 23 April [5 May], No. 79; 30 April [12 May], No. 90; 2 [14] May, No. 91; 6 [18] May, No. 92 and 12 [24] May No. 94 (archive of the M.T.D. No. 16,644).

42 War Diary of Lieutenant General Sacken's Corps (archive of the M.T.D., No. 16,643).

1. To issue a proclamation, in the name of the two Coalition Powers, expressing their proposed objective of freeing Germany from French influence and inviting all the princes and peoples subject to them to assist in the liberation of their fatherland. Each German ruler who refuses to participate in support of the common cause before a given date is to suffer losses to his territories.
2. To establish a *Zentral Verwaltungs Rat* [Central Governing Council], with unrestricted powers, composed of members appointed by the Coalition Powers, one from each. German rulers who have joined the Coalition have the right to appoint one member to the Council, by common consent.
3. The main agenda for Council meetings shall be: the administration of occupied countries and the use of their resources for the benefit of the common cause.
4. Revenue from lands occupied by Coalition forces is to be divided equally between Russia and Prussia. The Hanoverian administration is also to receive a share in proportion to the number of troops it has fielded.
5. All occupied territory from Saxony to the borders of Holland, excepting former Prussian and Hanoverian provinces, is to be divided into five regions, as follows:
   a) Saxony together with its duchies.
   b) The Kingdom of Westphalia, with the exception of Hanover and provinces formerly held by Prussia.
   c) The duchies of Berg and Nassau.
   d) Departement der Lippe [*Département de la Lippe*].
   e) Departement der Elbe Mündung [*Département des Bouches-de-l'Elbe*] and territories of Mecklenburg.
6. Two governors are to be appointed to each of these regions, one civil and the other military. The former is in the gift of the *Zentral Verwaltungs Rat*, while the latter, of the Commander in Chief. A territorial regional council is to be appointed by the civil governor.
7. The *Zentral Verwaltungs Rat* shall be responsible for all matters relating to the recruitment of troops, requisitions and stores for the army in the field, as well as mobilisation in the occupied areas.
8. Mobilisation is to be: firstly, regular forces; secondly, *Landwehr*; thirdly, *Landsturm*. Upon the formation of these forces, it is to be announced that in no event are they to serve except for the defence of Germany against France. Their formation must be secured by one of the corps of the Coalition Army.
9. The *Zentral Verwaltungs Rat* has the right to appoint to governorate and other positions persons known for their abilities and who have earned the respect of their fellow citizens to governorate and other positions.
10. The proposed regulations must be communicated without delay to the Austrian and British governments.[43]

43 Convention concluded at Breslau, dated 7 (19) March.

The proclamation regarding the war aims undertaken by Russia and Prussia against France was made public a few days after the conclusion of the aforementioned convention. In this proclamation, drafted under Stein's influence, the intention of the Coalition to restore the political independence of the rulers and peoples of Germany was announced; at the same time, a just punishment was to befall each of the German princes who might treacherously betray the common cause.[44]

The appeal by the Coalition sovereigns aroused general sympathy for their cause among the peoples of Germany, but the rulers of the *Confédération du Rhin*, who cherished the patronage of Napoleon, kept their subjects subdued. The King of Saxony, exalted by the *Empereur des Français* at the expense of Prussia, by standing up for the independence of Germany was more likely to lose than gain. The King of Bavaria [Maximilian I. Joseph], who owed the extension of his territory and his elevation to royal rank to Napoleon, had familial ties with him, through the marriage of the Viceroy of Italy to the Bavarian prinzessin Auguste [née Auguste Amalia Ludovika von Bayern]. The King of Württemberg [Friedrich Wilhelm Karl von Württemberg], the father-in-law of King Jérôme of Westphalia, was indebted to Napoleon for permission to remain autocratic and arbitrary in his territory. The Duke of Baden [Karl Ludwig Friedrich von Baden], husband of the French princess Stéphanie Beauharnais [Stéphanie Louise Adrienne de Beauharnais or Stéphanie Napoléon], who had expanded his territory through the grace of Napoleon, was a neighbour of France and would not dare to think of an uprising against the conqueror. Finally, the French rulers of Westphalia, Berg and Frankfurt were completely loyal to Napoleon.

Thus the dissolution of the *Confédération du Rhin*, held together by the vested interests of its members, proved more difficult than the powers that had taken up arms in defence of Germany believed. In order to enforce the convention of 7 (19) March, the *Zentral Verwaltungs Rat* was established on 23 March (4 April), to which Emperor Alexander appointed Count Kochubey [Viktor Pavlovich Kochubey] and Baron Stein as members; while the King of Prussia appointed *Geheimrat* [Privy Councillor] Schön [Heinrich Theodor von Schön] and *Staatsrat* Rödiger; the Russian Interior Minister Kozodavlev [Osip Petrovich Kozodavlev] was ordered to be chairman of the Council, and, in his absence, Stein, who, two days later, on 25 March (6 April), left Kalisz for Dresden, where the seat of the *Zentral Verwaltungs Rat* had been assigned.[45]

Meanwhile, our Main Army had set out for Silesia. The King of Prussia had just arrived in Kalisz on 21 March (2 April). Emperor Alexander I was waiting for him on the last stage to Kalisz, and upon approaching this town, the Allied Monarchs were greeted by Kutuzov in front of the corps of the Main Army assembled there. The commander, weakened by his terminal illness, could not mount a horse and remained on foot near the Sovereigns at the beginning of the parade by the troops, and soon, completely drained, left for Kalisz. On review were: V Corps (Lifeguard),

44 Proclamation dated 13 (25) March, signed in Kalisz, in the names of His Majesty the Emperor of All Russia and His Majesty the King of Prussia, by Prince Kutuzov-Smolensky. *Vossische Zeitung*, 3 April, 1813.

45 *Das Leben des Ministers Freiherrn vom Stein*, III, 323 & 326.

III Corps (grenadiers), the two cuirassier divisions, the Lifeguard Light Cavalry Division and four artillery companies, 17,800 men in total, with 48 guns. The troops were in brilliant condition, but the King was struck by the small size of the so-called Main Army.[46] On the evening of the same day, he visited the sick Field Marshal, granted him the *Schwarzer Adlerorden* [Order of the Black Eagle] and a snuff-box studded with diamonds, and sent Chancellor Hardenberg to him the following day [3 April], who announced to Kutuzov that should the war end successfully, then the King would grant him an estate in Prussia. The Field Marshal declined this offer, saying: 'My Tsar shall not neglect me or my children.'[47]

The King stayed in Kalisz for two days. Upon his departure, the Main Army, together with Emperor Alexander's and Prince Kutuzov's headquarters, set off for Silesia on 26 March (7 April). Their advance was a truly festive procession. In every city and town, at the entrances, triumphal gates had been erected, with inscriptions: *Der Deutsche dem Russen* (from the Germans to the Russians) and *Gott mit Dir* (God be with you), or *des Allmächtigen Hand schütze Dich* (may the hand of the Almighty protect you), and so on. The people came out to meet the Russian troops and accompanied them with joyful cheers. At the entrance to the gates stood young girls in white dresses, with garlands and laurel wreaths. Ringing bells were heard whenever the Tsar appeared, merging with loud cheering and greetings. In the evenings, translucent paintings shone in the windows, illuminated by multi-coloured lights, with various images and inscriptions in honour of Emperor Alexander.

Upon the arrival of the headquarters in Bunzlau on 6 (18) April, Prince Kutuzov's illness, aggravated by a cold, forced him to halt. Here, amid the celebrations inflamed by the advance of the Coalition forces, he was destined to end his glorious life. Emperor Alexander and the King of Prussia remained in Bunzlau until 9 (21) April and visited the old commander every day, who, already on his deathbed, had the consolation of handing the Sovereign the keys to Thorn, the final trophy of the army entrusted to him! Upon departing for Dresden, Emperor Alexander left his most important colleagues, Prince Volkonsky [Nikita Grigorievich Volkonsky] and Toll [Karl Wilhelm von Toll], with the Field Marshal.

In Saxony, despite the devotion of King Friedrich-August to Napoleon, the Coalition Monarchs were greeted as liberators. On 12 (24) April, on the eve of Easter Sunday, Emperor Alexander and the King of Prussia, who had rejoined the army on 2 (14) April in the town of Steinau [Ścinawa], ceremonially entered Dresden. The weather was most beautiful, the sun, shining in all its splendour, gilding nature on the blooming banks of the Elbe. Russian and Prussian troops lined both sides of the road leading to the city, to which the Saxon guard joined. People came out to meet the Coalition Sovereigns three *verstas* from the gates. During their journey on horseback along the lines of troops, music thundered and joyful cheering by the inhabitants were heard. Upon entering the city, the Monarchs stopped in the square, where all the troops paraded past them, and then the King escorted our Tsar to the Brühlsche Palais and went to the house assigned to him, in the Neustadt. Soon after, Emperor Alexander, having dismissed all the Saxon officials who had gathered at

46 Bernhardi, II, 421-422.
47 Emperor Alexander and his Contemporaries, Vol. III.

the palace and our residents who had arrived from various German cities, set off on foot to cross the river to the King. As soon as the Tsar left his apartments, the people surrounded and escorted him across the bridge and back, with incessant cheers of Hurrah![48]

Thus, on 12 (24) April, the Coalition forces under Count Wittgenstein, Blücher, Miloradovich and the Main Army, numbering more than 90,000 men, were in the sector between the middle Elbe and the Saale, pushing forward detachments up to the latter river. At the same time, the newly formed French army, numbering more than 120,000 men, was concentrated in the vicinity of Erfurt, to where Napoleon's *quartier-général* had moved; while the force under the Viceroy, numbering 45,000, was stationed partly on the lower Saale, partly holding positions on the left bank of the river, covered the advance by Napoleon's main army. In addition, Davout was on the lower Elbe with 10,000 men, while Reynier was reforming *7e Corps*, which, in anticipation of assimilating the Saxon troops, counted about 5,000 men in its ranks: consequently, more than 180,000 men were assembling with Napoleon on the Saale and the lower Elbe.[49]

The Field Marshal, on the verge of terminal illness, concerned about the concentration of forces of the Coalition Army, wrote to Count Wittgenstein: 'once Marshal Ney moves towards Dresden from Franconia,[50] then, without any doubt, the corps concentrated near Magdeburg will make a diversion towards Berlin. In this case, pay no attention to this movement, if you please, think only of uniting with Blücher and with our Main Army. Do not detach yourself from Dresden, or weaken our forces in this place such that the enemy would be able to break out across the Elbe and reopen communications with the Duchy of Warsaw. Leave Berlin a little and in the air, maintain our main line of operations. The Prussian Court itself can see the need for this.'[51]

These were the Field Marshal's final orders. The King of Prussia sent the renowned physician Hufeland [Christoph Wilhelm Hufeland] to attend him. But Kutuzov's days were already numbered. On 16 (28) April, he passed. Escorted into eternity by the blessings of his contemporaries, he must live in the memory of his descendants as an instrument of Almighty Providence, which struck the conqueror as unexpectedly as mighty Goliath was struck by the hand of slight David. As a commander, we shall not compare Kutuzov with his brilliant opponent, to whom he himself gave precedence; but let us say that he was the leader of the Russians in the great war that shattered the predominance of Napoleon, that, in fulfilling the orders of the Blessed Monarch, he sacrificed his final days to the great cause of the liberation of Germany. History shall not forget these deeds. It would allow onto its pages, neither exclamations of flattery, nor hissing of envy, equally offensive to the sacred memory of the great man.

48 Plotho, I, 84. Brief notes by Admiral Shishkov, 100-103 and 118-119.

49 Plotho, I, 86-88.

50 Kutuzov, used the term 'Ney's force' to mean the French corps gathering near Erfurt.

51 Prince Kutuzov's orders for Count Wittgenstein, dated 6 [18] April (Log of Outgoing Documents, No. 704).

Appendix VIII

General Dovre's letter to Prince Volkonsky, dated 3 (15) April, from Dessau

A copy of this letter, in French, is in the Log of Incoming Documents, No. 625:

> I share your opinion on the reasons proposed for strategic operations by our army fully and find the application of these reasons in the present circumstances quite sound. Count Wittgenstein is also convinced of the justice of your conclusions and has never shied away from this. The disagreement with your concept, as you noted, was due to the influence of factors that, due to the considerable distance from your headquarters, were impossible to inform the Field Marshal of in a timely manner, while remaining in anticipation of his orders.
>
> The objective of his orders was that Count Wittgenstein should link up with General Blücher in a timely manner and operate in unison with him, offensively or defensively.
>
> In order to achieve this objective, the count invited General Scharnhorst to his location and, according to him, made plans that were sent to the Field Marshal on 23 April [*sic*].
>
> Blücher's corps was a significant distance from the Elbe; time was needed by him in order to repair the bridges over this river; the concentration of a 30,000 man enemy army near Magdeburg (50,000 according to other sources) and the Viceroy's intent on Berlin: all these factors prevented Count Wittgenstein from moving off from Belzig until such time as the corps preparing to set out from Magdeburg could be driven back; we were also obliged to wait until Blücher's army had closed up to the Elbe and until it became clear from enemy movements on which side of this river it was more advantageous for us to concentrate our forces.
>
> Had Count Wittgenstein left Berlin, on 16 [28] March, marching towards Dresden, then the Viceroy, having occupied Berlin, would certainly have plundered this city, and in this event, in addition to losing one of the most important logistic hubs, we would have shaken the confidence of our allies in us. Having captured Berlin, the enemy could have gone on to Güstebiese, where our bridge on the Oder was located, and cut off Count Wittgenstein's communications with Königsberg. Spandau, Stettin and Küstrin would have had their blockades lifted.

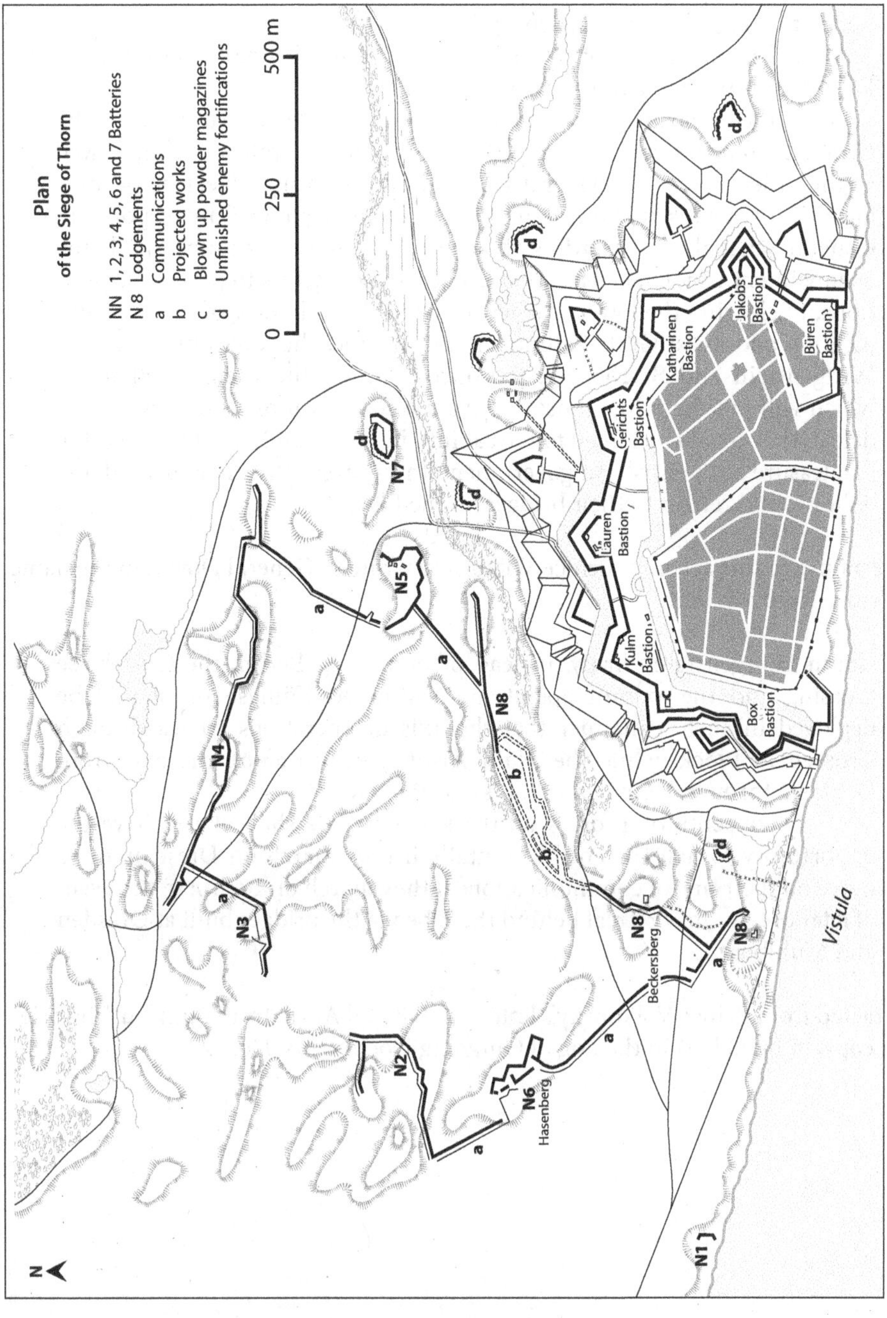

Plan of the Siege of Thorn.

> The action of 24 March (5 April) proved the infallibility of the measures taken by Count Wittgenstein. This battle, which had such important consequences, dispelled our concerns. The Viceroy, having been defeated, was forced to take refuge in Magdeburg.
>
> After this battle, Count Wittgenstein marched to Roßlau, crossed the Elbe and immediately linked up with Blücher.
>
> From the attached documents you can see the measures taken by *Generalleutnant* Bülow to invest Magdeburg and to protect Berlin; as well as the orders issued to General L'Estocq on the same subject, in accordance with your instructions. I am also enclosing a copy of my response to General Scharnhorst regarding the concentration of our army. While the enemy intent is not yet clear, we must confine ourselves to partisan operations, to clearing the lower reaches of the Saale, to harass enemy communication and assist Graf Wallmoden; meanwhile, the forces under Count Wittgenstein and Blücher are to concentrate on the enemy's left flank, which will put them in a most disadvantageous position: in the event of a defeat, they would be forced to retreat into Bohemia and thereby arouse the displeasure of the Austrian government; in the event that they succeed, the Allies would retreat to their bridges on the Elbe.

In response to this account, Prince Volkonsky wrote to General Dovre, in the name of Prince Kutuzov, that:

> Count Wittgenstein's army, instead of protecting Berlin, the Güstebiese crossing and the axis of operations leading to Königsberg, should be deployed in such a manner that the axis of operations passes through Crossen to Płock, while the Main Army operates along the axis from Dresden, through Steinau and Kalisz, to Warsaw.
>
> ... By concentrating forces on the left flank, we shall always have the opportunity to halt the enemy frontally if they march on Dresden, or to move on their line of communications if they march on Berlin; in the event of a failure, we may retreat behind the Elbe via the bridges built at Dresden and Mühlberg...

Extracted from Prince Volkonsky's letter dated 8 [20] April, from Bunzlau. The original copy, in French, is in the Log of Outgoing Documents, No. 722.

5

The sieges of Thorn and Spandau

The Fortress of Thorn. – The composition and strength of the garrison. – The investment of Thorn. – The construction of a bridge by Russian troops downstream of the fortress. – A strong sortie.

The importance of the siege of Thorn. – Barclay de Tolly's orders. – The opening of the trenches. – Siege works. – The surrender of the fortress. – Trophies. – The losses on both sides during the siege. – Barclay's departure for Poznań.

The citadel of Spandau. – The composition and strength of the garrison. – The investment of Spandau. – Troop composition of General Thümen's detachment. – The construction of siege batteries and the opening bombardment. – The convention with the commandant of the citadel. – The bombardment of the citadel. – The attempt to seize the citadel by storm. – The surrender of Spandau. – Trophies. – Thümen's departure for the Elbe.

Two more fortresses still held by enemy forces would surrender in April, besides Częstochowa: Thorn and Spandau.

The fortifications of Thorn, being refurbished but not completed by the French, formed an irregular polygon, with seven bastions and two cavaliers adjoining the Vistula on the flanks of the main rampart and connected by a wall with towers that stretched along the river side of the fortress. Small lunettes had been built in front of the curtain wall. On the left bank and on the island of Pacz, the bridgehead consisted of weak field fortifications. There were no casemated constructions. The fortress is encircled on the right bank of the river by high ground dominating the city within cannon range. The garrison consisted of 4,000 Bavarians and 1,500 French, under the overall command of *général de brigade* Poitevin de Maureilhan [Jean Étienne Casimir Poitevin de Maureilhan].

Back in January, the vanguard of Chichagov's army, under the command of Lieutenant General Chaplits [Yefim Ignatievich Chaplits], deployed facing the fortress on the high ground on the left bank of the Vistula.[1] Following that, by the end of January (early February), the fortress was encircled on the right bank of the Vistula by the corps under Langéron [Alexander Fëdorovich Lanzheron or Louis Alexandre Andrault de Langéron], and on the left by Voinov's corps [Alexander Lvovich Voinov], in each of which there were around 4,000 men. These troops, having repulsed a sortie by the garrison, set up several batteries and opened fire, but after that they moved on to Bromberg, leaving only a line of observation posts around the fortress, under the command of Generals Chaplits and Prince Shcherbatov [Alexei Grigorievich Shcherbatov]. In early [mid] February, Thorn was again blockaded by the troops of the Western Army (formerly Chichagov's), under the command of General Barclay de Tolly. The enemy, anticipating a blockade, quickly burned all the villages within 1½ *verstas* of the city as well as the town of Podgórz, on the left bank of the Vistula, leaving only the Divov castle as well as a few buildings near the bridge intact. This castle with very thick walls and strong vaults, armed with five guns, protected by earthworks and lying within range of the fortress guns and under the protection of a battery built on the island of Pacz, was most suited to a stubborn defence, while the buildings occupied by the enemy on the left bank of the river gave them the opportunity to constantly harass our Cossack outposts. General Barclay intended to force the French out of these buildings and burn the bridge. But, meanwhile, the river ice had demolished the bridge and the enemy troops took refuge in the castle.

On 12 (24) February, the Commander-in-Chief of Western Army, having received reports that the siege artillery, which was intended to join him from the Prussian fortress of Graudenz, had already been loaded onto ships and was preparing to sail, immediately ordered the construction of a bridge on the Vistula downstream of Thorn to proceed, in order to have reliable communications between the elements of the siege corps separated by the river. To cover this work, Commander Dott, who was with the Western Army, with the 75th Ship's Company, was ordered to arm six large boats with artillery in Bromberg. This small flotilla, which managed to complete its preparations by 15 (27) March, was intended to sever communications between the fortress and the castle and cover the right flank of our approach trenches from enemy gunboats. On that same day, the garrison made a strong sortie with several guns and opened a cannonade on our boats, but having been engaged by Major General Rudzevich [Alexander Yakovlevich Rudzevich], with 10th Jägers and 22nd Jägers and by six guns, were driven back with heavy casualties.

According to the plan for the siege works drawn up by engineer Lieutenant Colonel Michaud [Ludwig Michaud],[2] it was intended to build a battery on the Hasenberg on the very first night, immediately after the opening of the trenches, but on 26 March

1 Chaplits' vanguard consisted of: 7th Jägers, 10th Jägers, 27th Jägers, 28th Jägers, 32nd Jägers, 38th Jägers, Kinburn Dragoons, Tver Dragoons, Pavlograd Hussars, Volhynia Ulans, six Cossack regiments and two artillery companies, numbering some 3,000 men.

2 Brother of comte Alexandre Michaud de Beauretour, companion to Emperor Alexander I in 1813 and 1814.

(7 April), on the very day when they were preparing to execute this disposition, the engineer Lieutenant General Oppermann [Karl Ivanovich Opperman or Karl Ludwig Wilhelm Oppermann] arrived from Emperor Alexander's headquarters, who, having approved Michaud's general concept and his choice of front for the attack, thought that the proposed work could not be completed within one night, and that, with this course of action, the enemy, having identified the location on which we intended to build a battery, could, the next night, concentrate fire on our workers and inflict heavy casualties on them. Based on this view, it was decided to open the trenches on the night of 26 to 27 March (7 to 8 April), postponing the construction of the Hasenberg battery for the time being.

Overall, the siege was directed by Barclay de Tolly himself; the siege corps was commanded by General-of-Infantry Langéron; the Chief of Engineers was Colonel Michaud; while General Oppermann limited himself to supervising the siege works; when Michaud was seriously wounded during the siege, Oppermann took over the management of the entire engineering department; the Chief of Artillery was Colonel Veselitsky [Gavriil Petrovich Veselitsky]; while the crews of the 38 siege guns that arrived from Graudenz consisted of Prussian gunners, under the command of *Leutnant* Rohn. The troop strength of the blockading corps in early [mid] March reached some 18,000 men.[3]

The siege of Thorn was the first test for our engineers since the war of 1799; in particular, this siege was of benefit to the troops from Western Army who had arrived from Turkey, where the fortresses were not distinguished by state-of-the-art protection. The Commander-in-Chief considered himself obliged to exploit this opportunity to give a practical demonstration to his troops of siege warfare waged against a skilled opponent, and therefore, being present almost constantly at the mustering of troops assigned to the trenches, he gave them instructions, corrected oversights and prevented errors. Despite the inevitable hardships under such circumstances, the siege was facilitated by the weakening of the garrison through hard labour, incessant sorties and contagious disease. By mid [late] March, the number of defenders in the fortress did not exceed 2,000 men.

As soon as a suitable number of entrenching tools had been collected and a significant amount of hurdles, gabions and other materials had been prepared under the care of the officers of the engineering department, it became necessary to proceed with the opening of the trenches.

On 27 March (8 April), at five o'clock in the afternoon, the labourers and combat units assigned to cover them assembled at the main engineering depot, where they received entrenching tools and, as twilight fell, they went to small depots, arranged in the vicinity of those points from where the work was to begin. Hurdles and gabions were distributed to the labourers there, and after that the troops went to the places assigned for work, observing complete silence and order. The dim light of the moon, screened with light clouds, contributed to the hidden movement of the columns. The direction of each column had been marked in advance by pegs with bunches of straw tied to them. The work was very effective and successful. By dawn,

3 General Barclay de Tolly's report to Prince Kutuzov-Smolensky, dated 25 March [6 April], No. 378. For details of the troop strengths, see Appendix IX at the end of this chapter.

the labourers were already completely underground, all four batteries were almost complete and weapons had been installed in the mortar batteries.[4] The following batteries were built: No. 1, on the right flank, on the bank of the Vistula, with four mortars; No. 2, with eight 12-pounder siege cannon and eight half-*Pud* licornes [18-pounder gun-howitzers]; No. 3, with six mortars, and No. 4, on the left flank, with eight 12-pounder siege cannon and four quarter-*Pud* licornes [nine-pounder gun-howitzers]. On the morning of 28 March (9 April), the enemy, noticing the digging of the first parallel, opened a bombardment along it, to which both mortar batteries responded. During the day, the trenches and lodgements were widened and banks of gabions were erected.[5]

The following night, the construction of the laid out batteries was completely finished, and in the morning all the batteries were armed. After that, the Russian artillery operated with great success on the fortress and on the blockhouse on the Beckersberg, located opposite the right wing of the first parallel. A reconnaissance undertaken that day by our engineers on the left wing, ahead of the first parallel, convinced them of the possibility of driving the enemy out of the unfinished lunette and placing a mortar battery there, 250 *Sazhen* from the main ramparts, extending from one of the curtain walls. In order to fire on this curtain wall, which was shielded from ricochet fire by the high cavalier in Kulm Bastion, it was decided to build a battery for eight mortars at this point, while in order to enfilade some parts of the target frontage and to breach others with direct fire, a battery was to be built in front of the right wing of the first parallel on the Hasenberg.[6]

But in order to secure the construction of these new batteries, it was necessary to drive the enemy off the Beckersberg on the right flank and from the unfinished lunette on the left, so in the early hours of 30 March (11 April) two groups were assembled: one, consisting of 13 sappers and 100 volunteers, under the command of Langéron's aide de camp, Lieutenant Schultz, supported by a detachment under Lieutenant Colonel Zhokhov, was assigned to seize the blockhouse on the Beckersberg, the other, of 100 volunteers under Langéron's other aide de camp, Lieutenant Rühl, supported by Major Blanov's detachment, was to seize the lunette. Lieutenant colonels Michaud and Klimenko [Mikhail Nikitich Klimenko] were to accompany the right-flank detachment with several engineering officers and labourers in order to construct the battery on the Hasenberg; while engineer Captain Gulkovius and Prussian *Hauptmann* Guyette, with their officers and labourers, were to proceed under the protection of the left flank detachment.

On the right wing, upon reaching the Hasenberg, Michaud and Klimenko traced out the battery and set about building it using mantlet saps, while Lieutenant Schultz

4 See Map No. 4, Plan of the Siege of Thorn.

5 On 28 March (9 April) Major General Shcherbatov commanded the following troops in the trenches: 1,500 fighting men escorting the labourers; 165 sappers and pioneers; 2,150 infantry as labourers. The artillery expended: 20 50-pound shells; 50 ten-pound bombs; from the Siege Diary for Thorn, signed by engineer Lieutenant General Oppermann.

6 On 29 March (10 April), Major General Inzov commanded the following troops in the trenches: 1,500 fighting men protecting the labourers; 63 sappers and pioneers; 1,150 infantry as labourers. The artillery expended: 29 50-pound shells, 299 ten-pound bombs, 330 12-pound solid shot and 240 common shell.

drove the enemy out of the blockhouse, demolished this building and destroyed the abatis. The enemy made a sortie and opened heavy fire on the labourers from the main rampart; yet, in spite of this, they succeeded in bringing the construction of the battery almost to the full size for eight 12-pounder cannon and two licorns, while the covering force held out on the Beckersberg until dawn. The casualties to the besiegers were significant, and, unfortunately, the right arm of the brave and skilful engineer Colonel Michaud was severed by round shot. On the left wing, as soon as Lieutenant Rühl, having pushed the enemy back, took up the post assigned to him, Captain Gulkovius detached Lieutenant Braun, with 50 volunteers, instructing him to drive an enemy picket from a hill on which it was intended to lay out assault trenches. Once this picket had been driven off and a screen force placed in front of the high ground, Captain Gulkovius laid out the lodgement using mantlet saps and linked it to the communication trench extended from the first parallel by *Hauptmann* Guyette.

Once full day had broken on 30 March [11 April], the cannonade, which had paused for a short time at dawn, resumed with even greater force. The mortars in Battery No. 1 were transferred to Battery No. 5, built on the site of the unfinished enemy lunette. On this day, an enemy powder magazine was blown up on the target frontage, near the Kulm Bastion. Lieutenant Colonel Magdenko's battery [Ivan Semënovich Magdenko], consisting of two mortars and two licorns, set up near Podgórz, on the left bank of the Vistula, also successfully bombarded the city and the armed barges.[7]

In the early hours of 31 March [12 April], the batteries laid out on the flanks were completely finished and the left, No. 5, was armed with six 50-pounder mortars and two ten-pounder mortars; a powder magazine had been built within it and its internal space had been provided with traverses. In Battery No. 2, set up in the first parallel, four embrasures directed towards the Beckersberg were closed, while four others were cut in their place, for action against the Kulm Bastion. *Hauptmann* Guyette raised and thickened the parapet of the communications trench with the newly constructed Battery No. 5, and also completed the construction of this battery on the site of an unfinished lunette under heavy musket fire from another lunette still occupied by the enemy 80 *Sazhen* away.

During the next day [12 April], work was limited to improving and completing the existing constructions. The bombardment continued throughout the day. Firing from mortar battery No. 5 began at dawn.[8]

In the early hours of 1 (13) April, the communication trench was extended from Battery No. 2 to Battery No. 6; the breastwork of the left mortar Battery No. 5 was raised and another powder magazine was built next to it.

7 On 30 March (11 April), Major General Meshcherinov commanded the following troops in the trenches: 1,500 fighting men protecting the labour force; 130 sappers and pioneers; 1,250 infantry as labourers. The artillery expended: 180 shells; 240 bombs and 400 solid shot.

8 On 31 March (12 April), Major General Kornilov commanded in the trenches: 1,500 men in the covering force; 125 sappers and pioneers; 1,010 infantry as labourers. The artillery expended: 72 50-pound bombs, 269 ten-pound bombs; 390 shells and 360 solid shot.

On 1 (13) April, heavy fire continued from both sides throughout the day. At Battery No. 2, eight 12-pounder siege guns and two half-*Pud* licorns were transferred to Hasenberg, and ten field guns were put in their place.[9]

In the early hours of 2 (14) April, the existing constructions were repaired, materials for the upcoming work were brought up to the trenches from the main depot, two embrasures were cut on the left mortar battery (No. 5) and two quarter-*Pud* licorns and two ten-pounder mortars were emplaced.

On 2 (14) April, in the morning, General Oppermann, with captains Gulkovius and Guyette, surveyed the area in front of the left wing, with the aim of choosing a place for a lodgement and connecting it with a trench to the large mortar battery, forming the left wing of the second parallel. During this survey it was noted that the frontage chosen for the attack was protected by a water-filled moat, and therefore immediately directed fire onto the sluices on two channels which carried water from the swamps and springs to the city.[10]

In the early hours of 3 (15) April, the occupation of the high ground in front of the left mortar battery no more than 100 *Sazhen* from the ditch of the nearest lunette, and the crucial Beckersberg hill, on the right flank of siege works, facing the target frontage of the fortress, was started, as follows:

Detachments, under the command of Colonel Seliverstov and Lieutenant Colonel Kondratiev, after a bitter struggle, captured the Beckersberg and the abatis to the right of this hill down to the bank of the Vistula. The sapper teams and labourers who followed them, having reached the Hasenberg, found pre-prepared hurdles there and dug a parallel, 500 paces long, and two assault trenches, one on the Beckersberg, and the other on the high ground lying to the right of this point. With the beginning of these works, the enemy opened musket fire and heavy salvoes of canister and shell; after that they launched a sortie, but were driven off by the covering force; despite all their efforts and the salvoes of canister and shells from the main ramparts, which continued all night, our lodgements and the communication trenches that served them were finished. The other sapper group proceeded behind their covering force on the left wing to the mortar battery, while the detachment under Major Blanov drove the enemy pickets off the high ground in front and occupied this sector with a screen of their own outposts. Taking advantage of this, the sappers dug the communication trench up to the latter high ground, at a range of 425 paces from the glacis, and dug an assault trench 350 paces long across it by way of mantlet saps. Throughout the night, the enemy fired on the labourers with canister, shells and musketry: but, in spite of this, all this construction was finished just before dawn. Inside the mortar battery, engineer Captain Butkovsky built a log bunker, protected with gabions and earth, and completely impervious to bombs, as a powder magazine.

9 On 1 (13) April, Major General Rudzevich commanded in the trenches: 1,500 men in the covering force; 85 sappers and pioneers; 800 infantry as labourers. The artillery expended: 240 50-pound bombs, 180 ten-pound bombs; 130 shells and 920 solid shot.

10 On 2 (14) April, Major General Benardos commanded in the trenches: 1,500 men in the covering force; 36 sappers and pioneers; 500 infantry as labourers. The artillery expended: 250 50-pound bombs, 74 ten-pound bombs; 129 shells and 1,064 solid shot.

These important works were carried out in the presence of the Commander-in-Chief himself and comte Langéron on the Beckersberg, and General Oppermann, who, as on previous nights, had supervised the progress of all engineering work in general.[11]

On 3 (15) April, the strongest fire was opened from all the siege batteries, moreover, the Beckersberg and left flank not only enfiladed the lines of the target frontage, but acted on the rear of several works. This forced the defenders to hoist a white flag and open negotiations on the surrender of the fortress. But as the governor would not agree to some of the proposed terms, then, the next day, 4 (16) April, a most severe fire was resumed on the fortress, which in the course of an hour caused great damage to the enemy and forced them to agree to all the demands of the Russian Commander-in-Chief.

According to the terms of the capitulation concluded on 4 (16) April: on 6 (18) April, the fortress must be surrendered to the Russian force; having handed their weapons in to the Thorn arsenal, with the exception of generals and officers who retained their swords, the garrison received permission to return to Bavaria, upon accepting the obligation not to serve against the Russians or their allies for the entire duration of the campaign of 1813. This garrison consisted of: two generals, 135 officers and 1,973 lower ranks; in addition, there remained in Thorn: 45 officers and 1,532 lower ranks, sick. More than 10,000 muskets, 52 guns, more than 1,000,000 cartridges, 600 *Pud* of gunpowder, and a significant supply of rations were found in the city. On the part of the Coalition, during the siege, the casualties were as follows:

> Russian forces: 28 lower ranks killed; two field officers, five subalterns and 156 lower ranks wounded.
> Prussian forces: two killed and four subalterns wounded.[12]

As a reward for the conquest of Thorn, Barclay de Tolly was awarded the Order of St Alexander Nevsky with diamonds and 50,000 roubles.

Upon the capture of Thorn, Barclay left Major General Padeisky [Fëdor Fëdorovich Padeisky] as commandant there, with the Apsheron Infantry and 7th Jägers, some 900 men in total, with 25th Light Artillery Company and Skarzhinsky's squadron; while he moved on to Poznań himself, with the rest of the force, numbering 11,700 men. The artillery brought up from Graudenz was sent back there, while the gunpowder was also sent there to replenish the Prussian gunpowder expended during the siege.

11 Major General Inzov commanded in the trenches: 1,600 men in the covering force; 175 sappers and pioneers; 1,650 infantry as labourers.

12 Siege Diary for Thorn, signed by engineer Lieutenant General Oppermann (archive of the Engineering Department). General Barclay de Tolly's reports to Prince Kutuzov-Smolensky, dated 30 March [11 April], and dated 5 [17] April (Log of Incoming Documents, No. 600 and No. 635), the latter with a copy of the capitulation for the surrender of Thorn attached, signed by the Chief-of-Staff, Western Army, Lieutenant General Sabaneev, and *Chef d'État-Major* of the garrison, Colonel La Roche. Vaudoncourt, *Histoire de la guerre soutenue par les Français en Allemagne*, 64.

In total, Supreme Orders were issued to release 41,000 *Pud* of gunpowder from the Riga stores to the Prussian government.[13]

The Spandau citadel lies two *Meilen* (about 15 *verstas*) west of Berlin, at the confluence of the rivers Spree and Havel. The town of Spandau is no further than 100 paces from the citadel. The citadel is surrounded by a double moat, forming a location surrounded on all sides by the waters of the river Havel. It has a square outline, with four low profile bastions, very strong casemates and separate outworks. At the conclusion of the Treaty of Tilsit, the citadel was returned to the Prussian government by the French and its fortifications were significantly strengthened, but in 1812, at the outbreak of war with Russia, the King was forced to accept a French garrison in Spandau, while in 1813, as the Russian army was advancing from the Vistula to the Oder, he had to withdraw his troops from the citadel and place it fully at the disposal of the French. On 20 February (4 March) the commandant General Bruny [Jean-Baptiste Bruny] burned down some of the suburbs. The garrison consisted of 3,140 men for the most part Polish troops and was abundantly supplied with rations and military supplies.[14] Following the occupation of Berlin by Russian troops, on 3 (15) March, a small detachment under Major General Helffreich was sent to invest Spandau; while on 20 March (1 April) the blockade was handed over to *Generalmajor* Thümen, with 1,800 men,[15] who, having relieved Helffreich, kept just 400 Russians with his detachment; cavalrymen with one light battery, under the command of Major General Zagryazhsky [Pëtr Petrovich Zagryazhsky],[16] while General Helffreich immediately set off to join the main force under Count Wittgenstein.

The mission given to General Thümen was extremely daunting: he was to direct the siege of a fortress surrounded by water and swamps and defended by superior numbers. In particular, it was difficult for him to maintain communications between elements of the force isolated by the rivers Havel and Spree and extensive swamps. To that end, two bridges were built across the Havel, one upstream and one downstream of the citadel, and a ferry across the river Spree was set up. But just as the bridges had to be built no closer than 4,000 or 5,000 paces from the citadel in order to protect them against enemy sorties, the outposts of the siege detachment occupied a sector of about 20 *verstas*, and in order to support any part of the force, the nearest units to it had to make a move of at least half a *Meile* (some four *verstas*).

General Thümen, having sent the cavalry under Major General Zagryazhsky onto the right bank of the Spree, in order to invest the citadel from this side, and

13 General Barclay de Tolly's report to Prince Kutuzov-Smolensky, dated 5 [17] April. Prince Kutuzov's dispatches to Scharnhorst, dated 4 [16] April (Log of Outgoing Documents, No. 688) and orders for Count Arakcheev, of the same date (Log of Outgoing Documents, No. 689).

14 The garrison of the Spandau citadel comprised: one French battalion of 530 men; a battalion of *129e ligne* (Dutch and Spanish), 500 men; 1,800 Polish troops; three artillery companies, 260 men; 50 train personnel.

15 General Thümen's force comprised: three battalions of *4. Ostpreußisches Infanterie*; two jäger companies; a volunteer detachment from *1. Ostpreußisches Infanterie*; *Hauptmann* Ludwig's six-pounder foot artillery battery.

16 The Russian troops present at the blockade of Spandau were: 120 Nezhin Mounted Jägers; 200 Poland Ulans, 80 Cossacks; Lieutenant Colonel Salzmann's light artillery company.

having assigned two companies located in the village of Pichelsdorf [2½ miles south of the citadel] to support them if need be, held his *Hauptquartier* and reserves in Charlottenburg; while the rest of the infantry were placed on both banks of the Spree and on the left bank of the Havel.[17]

The commander of the siege force, wishing to avoid a set-piece assault, inevitably fraught with danger to the population of the city, on 22 March (3 April), demanded the surrender in capitulation from the commandant, which was refused. On the following day [4 April], the volunteers from *1. Ostpreußisches Infanterie*, who formed part of the detachment, were sent to the army under Count Wittgenstein, while eight 12-pounder cannon joined the detachment. In anticipation of the arrival of howitzers and mortars, until 27 March (8 April) work was limited to the preparation of hurdles, gabions and other materials, and the construction of a battery to protect the bridges that served as lines of communication between elements of the detachment. At the same time, engineer *Leutnant* Hülsen, selected locations for batteries and calculated the ranges from them to the citadel's works.

On 27 March (8 April), in the evening, four ten-pounder howitzers arrived. That night, a battery was constructed 400 *Sazhen* from the Spree-schanze [south of the citadel], in order to make it hazardous for the enemy to build external fortifications; while on 28 March [9 April], a battery armed with three one-pounder cannon and one howitzer opened fire on enemy labourers.

On 30 March (11 April), six 50-pounder mortars cast in Berlin arrived from there. But it was impossible to make use of them due to a shortage of projectiles, which were also lacking for the licorns.

On 1 (13) April, a convention was concluded with the commandant of the citadel, who undertook: firstly, to evacuate the town on 1 May (new style) and withdraw his troops into the citadel; secondly, to recognise the town as neutral. Based on these terms, the besiegers were not to assault on the side of the citadel facing the town, nor were the besieged to make sorties. It was left to the commandant to send an officer to the Viceroy with news of the terms he had concluded. This convention gave the Coalition the opportunity to spare the town of Spandau from the devastation that might befall it in the event of a blockade by Coalition forces. Moreover, having withdrawn into the citadel where no more than 1,000 men, or just one third of the force, could be accommodated in the casemates, the enemy were exposed to greater danger than occupying the town, in particular from the detonation of bombs in the cramped confines of the citadel. The recognition of the town as neutral was very advantageous for the weak siege corps, because the garrison could only make sorties from the horn-work facing the Jungfernheide [east side], while the besiegers, taking advantage of this, concentrated their strength there.

On 4 (16) April, the officer sent to Count Wittgenstein with a report on the conclusion of the convention returned with orders to begin bombarding the citadel

17 Thümen's force were deployed as follows: headquarters, one battalion, two jäger companies, artillery and Cossacks in Charlottenburg; three companies in Pichelsdorf; one company each in Ruhleben and Jungfernheide; two companies in Meierei farm; one company in Schülerberg. General Zagryazhskiy's cavalry were in Falkenhagener Feld, Seegefeld and Staaken. Subsequently, he was given six guns from Salzmann's company.

immediately. In the meantime, as a park with shells for plunging fire had arrived, then on the night of 4 to 5 (16 to 17) April three batteries were laid out, each for two 50-pounder mortars, on the Oranienburger Vorstadt [north] side, behind the low crest of the Schülerberg, at a distance of 1,000 paces from the citadel. At seven o'clock in the morning of 5 (17) April, the bombardment commenced and 380 bombs were lobbed into the citadel in the course of 24 hours. That night, another battery was built, for four ten-pounder mortars, on the Ruhleben side, between the König and Königin bastions [south-eastern and south-western bastions], in order to enfilade the curtain wall; then on the morning of 6 (18) April, an howitzer battery was built on the road leading to the Försterei gate [south of the citadel] along with a trench laid along the Herzogenwald. On that same morning salvoes were fired from every battery, as a result of which several fires broke out in the citadel; at noon a powder magazine detonated after being struck by round shot and partially destroyed the Königin bastion; a large breach had been made and the garrison, in anticipation of the detonation of a larger powder magazine, under the burning Juliusturm [behind the König bastion], was thrown into confusion and terror. Had the besiegers launched an immediate assault, then, without any doubt, they would have captured the citadel. But they missed their favourable moment, not noticing the breach that had been made.

In the early hours of 7 (19) April, another battery for three licorns was built on the Ruhleben side, connected by trench to the howitzer battery; in addition, two howitzers were emplaced on the Schüllerberg side. At seven o'clock in the morning fire was opened from every battery; whereupon the breach was noticed, as a result of which General Thümen demanded surrender from the commandant, but received no answer. The next day [20 April], a reconnaissance of the breach convinced the besiegers that a significant part of the rampart had collapsed into the ditch, and the booms on the Havel near the Brandenburg bridge had been torn away. The enemy still occupied the outer fortifications at that time, and therefore the breach accidentally formed by the explosion did not present the besieger with such an advantage as would a breach made after the capture of the outer fortifications and upon reaching the glacis. Yet, in spite of this, General Thümen, hoping to take advantage of the confusion in the garrison, decided to storm the citadel.

To that end, the following orders were issued:

> The artillery was ordered to bombard the citadel from morning to night to force the garrison to abandon the fortifications they held, and at seven o'clock in the evening fire was to be directed from several mortars on the only bridge connecting the citadel to the town. Whereupon, the troops assigned to the assault and equipped with ladders, crowbars and planks, headed in four columns from various directions towards the citadel, the horn-work, the Stresow suburb and towards the gate, on which a diversionary attack was to be launched. But the first and third columns, which were supposed to cross in boats, did not arrived at their forming up places until two o'clock in the morning; meanwhile, the marksmen proceeding at the head of the second column, went astray from their intended direction and stumbled into a swamp; when at last these troops arrived at the location

> assigned to them, having had time to prepare for a stubborn defence, the enemy repulsed the column: thus, despite the soundness of the disposition and the courage of the troops, the attempt by Thümen was unsuccessful. The Prussian force suffered some 50 casualties that night. Notwithstanding the Coalition desire to spare the town, it was struck by several bombs, as a result of which 60 houses burned down.

Despite the failure of the attack, the commandant, desperate to leave the citadel still standing, surrendered in capitulation the next day, 9 (21) April. The garrison, numbering 244 officers and 2,986 lower ranks, received permission to withdraw behind the Elbe. In the town, in addition to a significant amount of supplies, 115 guns, 550 hundredweight (about 1,400 *Pud*) of gunpowder, 5,400 muskets, and so on were found.

On 17 (29) April, Thümen's detachment set off for the Elbe in order to join Bülow's corps.[18]

18 Plotho, *Der Krieg in Deutschland und Frankreich*, I, *appendices*, 84-91.

Appendix IX

In the Returns submitted to the Tsar by Barclay de Tolly, dated 7 [19] March, the following strengths are given

	Officers	Fighting Men	Service Support	Total
Regular Cavalry	165	3,071	118	**3,354**
Cossacks	81	1,917	2	**2,000**
Infantry	485	10,243	512	**11,240**
Artillery	62	1,581	94	**1,737**
Pioneers	2	123	4	**129**
75th Ship's Company	8	238	9	**255**
Totals:	**803**	**17,173**	**739**	**18,715**

Yet at the beginning of the siege of Thorn, this total was much smaller, such that the infantry, according to Barclay de Tolly's report, showed 7,462 men.

6

The logistics of both sides

Emperor Alexander's logistics: Establishment of the Reserve Army. – The units included in its composition. – The division of the Reserve Army into corps. – Administrative arrangements: rations and weapons supply, and movement to the borders by Reserve Army units. – The numbers of troops sent from the Reserve Army to the operational armies during the first campaign of 1813. – Resupplying the cavalry with horses, saddlery, etc. – Administration of the artillery: ammunition resupply. – Clothing the troops. – Orders concerning the *Opolchenie*. – Issues to the troops not being credited to semi-annual pay and rations. – The establishment of magazines and delivery of supplies to the theatre of war. – Methods for provisioning the troops abroad. – Determining exchange rates for Russian money. – Reform of the Russian army. – The concerns of the Tsar regarding the improvement of hospitals. – Supplying the army with rations and ammunition.

Napoleon's logistics: His return following the expedition to Russia. – The decree to call up for service 350,000 men and subsequently another 180,000 men. – The training cadres. – Strengthening the army with troops from Spain and Italy. – Supplying the army with horses. – Donations from the cities. – The condition of the cavalry, artillery and trains. – The speed with which the army was generated. – The initial deployment and composition of French forces. – Napoleon's departure to the army.

Having described military events from the movement of Russian forces beyond the Empire to the Coalition invasion of Saxony, where they were intending to engage Napoleon's newly assembled army, I consider it necessary to set out the administrative orders by both parties related to the generation of forces and to providing them with combat supplies and subsistence.

It has already been mentioned that the forces with which Emperor Alexander I had decided to fight for the liberation of Germany were incompatible with the immensity of this enterprise. It was essential to reconstitute the operational armies and to prepare resources for the eventual further continuation of the war. The supply of every necessity to forces outside the Empire presented extreme difficulties, especially since the Russian finances were most disordered, and the resources of the state in general had been exhausted by the sustained struggle alone.

In order to reconstitute the armies in the field, the Reserve Army was established, under the command of Prince D.I. Lobanov-Rostovsky [Dmitry Ivanovich Lobanov-Rostovsky], which was appointed to include all reserves, both infantry and cavalry, as well as all the artillery companies that were in the western governorates at the time. Thus, the Reserve Army received 77 battalions formed by Prince Lobanov-Rostovsky, who were in the vicinity of Belitsa; Lieutenant General Essen 3rd's 48 battalions [Pëtr Kirillovich Essen] in Bobruisk and Chernigov; Major General Bashutsky's 24 battalions [Pavel Yakovlevich Bashutsky] in St Petersburg; Lieutenant General Kleinmikhel's 24 battalions [Andrei Andreevich Kleinmikhel] in Yaroslavl (later in Vitebsk); General-of-Cavalry Kologrivov's 92 squadrons [Andrei Semënovich Kologrivov] in Belorussia, and the Lifeguard reserve in St Petersburg; finally, 37 artillery companies and artillery parks. The Reserve Army was divided into four infantry and two cavalry corps.[1] The area between Grodno, Lida, Minsk, Igumen, Slutsk, Pinsk, Kovel, Lublin, Węgrów, Ostrołęka and Szczuczyn was assigned for the quartering of this army; while the headquarters of the commander of the army was located in Bialystok.[2] The preservation of the men in good condition had been set as the primary objective throughout the march to the borders and beyond to the Army in the field by these formations, and to that end, the provision of meat and wine rations three times a week for all troops was ordered, both in the field army and in the Reserve Army, observing that the lower ranks were to receive meat and wine directly and not cash in lieu.[3] Prince Lobanov-Rostovsky was given the powers of Commander-in-Chief of a Large Operational Army, with the exception of awards and authority over civilian matters, because the governorates in which his troops were stationed were under martial law and were subordinate to Prince Kutuzov.[4]

The provisioning of the troops and care of the sick in the Reserve Army presented extraordinary difficulties at the very beginning of its establishment. The change in lifestyle, during the transition from peasant life to constant military activity, and never-ending marches from place to place led to the spread of contagious diseases among the recruits, and especially typhus. Mobile infirmaries were established for each division, and hospitals for the seriously ill, of which the main ones were in Łomża, Bialystok and Grodno. Equally challenging obstacles were encountered in supplying the troops with clothing and weapons: of a requirement for 117,000 muskets, only 64,000 were received by the army (13,000 collected after the departure of the enemy, while the remainder were imported from Britain). The lack of reliable administrators and the small number of officers greatly delayed the formation of units.

1 Returns attached to Supreme Orders directed to Prince Lobanov-Rostovsky, dated 5 [17] February. For the composition of the Reserve Army, see Appendix X at the end of this chapter.
2 Supreme Orders directed to Prince Lobanov, dated 5 [17] February. Orders from the Head of the War Ministry, Prince Gorchakov, to the Department of Inspections, dated 24 February [8 March], No. 161.
3 Supreme Orders, dated 5 [17] February; for Prince Lobanov, No. 69, and for Prince Kutuzov-Smolensky, No. 70.
4 Decree to the Governing Senate dated 20 March [1 April].

However, despite all these difficulties, just a little over two weeks after receiving the Imperial Decree on the dispatch of the troops of the Reserve Army abroad, Prince Lobanov had sent 38½ battalions from Chechersk, Belitsa and Dobryanka to the armies in the field, numbering around 36,000 men.[5] These units moved slowly, arrived late against the schedules issued to them and lost more than a third died, deserted or left in hospital, such that only 21,853 men joined the field armies. The reasons for these extraordinary losses were:

1. The marches were along very bad roads, and, due to the small number of carts, it was impossible to unburden the soldiers.
2. Negligence in the care of recruits, due to a shortage of officers.

The battalions formed in St Petersburg by Bashutsky and in Yaroslavl by Kleinmikhel, as well as the reserve squadrons formed in St Petersburg by Colonel Gendre, had been sent straight to the border, while the remaining units following the departure of these battalions and squadrons were to come under the jurisdiction of Prince Lobanov-Rostovsky.[6]

In the course of the five months from early March to the end of July [mid March to mid August] 1813, overall, the following were sent from the Reserve Army to the armies in the field: 67,707 infantrymen; 14,014 cavalrymen; five artillery companies (seven, according to other sources), with four pontoon companies and 9½ artillery parks.[7]

The Reserve Army, even after the units had been sent to the active armies, was to contain one battalion for each infantry regiment, and two squadrons for each cavalry regiment, and therefore was to consist of 151 battalions, 125 squadrons and all the artillery companies belonging to the reserve artillery brigades.[8] In order to replenish these units, the remaining half of the recruits of the latest conscription were ordered to be sent to the Reserve Army, eight men per 500 souls, according to the manifesto of 30 November [12 December], 1812.[9]

The supply of remounts for the cavalry was very difficult, and therefore Supreme Orders were issued on the supply by the inhabitants of the Volhynia Governorate and Podolia Governorate for a calculated number of horses instead of recruits.[10] In order to speed up the delivery of saddlery, the Commander-in-Chief in St Petersburg was

5 Prince Lobanov-Rostovsky's report to the Tsar, dated 6 [18] March, No. 24, with an attached return on the number of men despatched in the columns, showing: first column, under Major General Bestuzhev-Ryumin, of eight battalions and two companies, numbering 7,087 men; second column, under Major General Adamovich, of 20 battalions, numbering 19,730 men; third column, under Colonel Alexeev, of ten battalions, numbering 9,838 men; for a total of 36,646 men.

6 Memorandum from the Head of the War Ministry, Prince Gorchakov, to Prince Lobanov-Rostovsky, dated 31 March [12 April], No. 1957.

7 Notes on the composition of the Reserve Army (archive of the M.T.D. No. 47,353, folio 1).

8 According to the establishment statutes, 1,017 men per battalion and 201 men per squadron: it follows that the Reserve Army, fully manned, consisted of: 153,567 infantrymen and 25,738 cavalrymen, for a total of 180,000 men.

9 Instructions for Prince Gorchakov, dated 26 March [7 April], No. 143.

10 Instructions for Adjutant General Komarovsky, dated 31 January [12 February], No. 56.

directed to prepare some 6,000 saddles over and above commissariat contracts.[11] Whereupon, it was also ordered to send officers immediately to every governorate that had been occupied by the enemy in order to inspect the saddles recovered from the enemy or abandoned by our regiments, and to send those that were fit for purpose to the cavalry reserves straight away. Similar orders was issued with regard to pistols.[12] The task of returning the artillery companies to service left in Belarus and Lithuania by Prince Kutuzov, and by Count Wittgenstein in Pskov, as well as replenishing the parks with ammunition and cartridges captured from the enemy, were assigned to Inspector of Artillery, Baron Meller-Zakomelsky [Pëtr Ivanovich Meller-Zakomelsky], who set off from St Petersburg for Vilna in order to accomplish this. But, due to the considerable distance of the active armies from our borders, difficulties were anticipated in the timely delivery of ammunition to them, Emperor Alexander ordered the Russian ambassador to London to enter into correspondence with the British government for the preparation of ammunition and cartridges in Britain for our troops and for the purchase of 20,000 *Pud* of quality gunpowder.[13]

The clothing of the troops, after the winter campaign, required particular attention from the government. Emperor Alexander I, while still in Vilna, had ordered the delivery of 54,000 uniforms and a similar number of greatcoats from St Petersburg. But as this amount could not satisfy the needs of the army, the Tsar gave orders to fix a contract with Prussian merchants, for them to supply the required quantities of cloth to Königsberg, Elbing and Marienwerder and for the making up of uniforms, trousers (breeches for the cavalry), greatcoats and neckcloths, for all units abroad, except for the hussars, for whom clothing was to be delivered from Russia. Overall, orders were placed for the purchase or 740,000 *arshin* of cloth of various colours, at a cost to the treasury of between three paper roubles, 50 kopeks and three paper roubles, 75 kopeks per *arshin*. After the uniforms had been made up, they were to be distributed equally among the regiments,[14] while in addition 3,200 officers' frock-coats and greatcoats were to be made up, without any deductions from the officers' pay.[15] The *opolchenie*, called up during the Patriotic War, were also provided with clothing and footwear; it was commanded to provide emoluments to them from the treasury, from the date of the expiry of subsistence due to them from the nobility. The sums spent on uniforms and pay for the *opolchenie* were recovered from the nobility of the governorates from which they had been called up, in accordance with a formula for each registered soul.[16] The Moscow and Smolensk *opolchenie*, as 'the first to attend in defence of the fatherland' were discharged to their homes, while the remainder were deployed as follows: St Petersburg and Novgorod, to the blockade of

11 Instructions for General-of-Cavalry Kologrivov, dated 13 [25] February, No. 83.
12 Instructions to *Kriegskommisar* General Tatishchev, dated 31 January [12 February], No. 58.
13 Munitions were required in the following quantities: 2,400 24-pounder shells; 6,000 12-pounder shells; 4,800 12-pounder solid shot; 9,450 six-pounder solid shot; 5,000,000 cartridges with ball; 20,000 *Pud* cannon grade gunpowder.
14 Namely: 200 per Lifeguard cavalry regiment; 175 per line cavalry regiment; 700 per Lifeguard infantry regiment; 514 per line infantry regiment; 139 per artillery company; 500 for the pioneers overall.
15 Supreme Instructions for Prince Kutuzov-Smolensky, dated 1 [13] February, No. 66.
16 Rescript to Prince Saltykov.

Danzig and with Count Wittgenstein's force; Vladimir, Kaluga, Tver and Yaroslavl, were on the march from Moscow to the Neman (the latter three would take part in the foreign campaigns); Ryazan and Tula came under the 3rd District, except for the Tula Cossacks, who took part in the foreign campaigns. The *opolchenie* of 3rd District were deployed to Volhynia; The Chernigov and Poltava Cossacks were stationed at Zamość.

Emperor Alexander I, paying particular attention to the hardships suffered by the troops throughout the rapid pursuit of the enemy army, 'through devastated country, where essential supplies were incomparably more expensive than in the interior governorates' ordered that all troops who crossed the border receive an advance of six-month pay,[17] and after that, at the suggestion of Prince Kutuzov, allowed the release of an allotment of cash, from 1 [13] January, 1813 until returning to Russia.[18]

Although the troops abroad mainly procured essentials in-country, nevertheless, three lines of magazines were ordered to be established in the governorates closest to the theatre of operations and the Vilna, Grodno, and Bialystok *Oblasts*, moreover, by Directed Decree, it was strictly forbidden to use supplies from these for troops stationed within the Empire. Returns were ordered to be submitted to headquarters on the available quantities of stores every two weeks, and it was permitted to release stores only in accordance with demands from the Intendant General of the army in the field.[19] Following that, at the suggestion of Prince Kutuzov, Supreme Orders were issued for the immediate delivery to Königsberg of 70,000 *chetvert* of flour, 6,700 *chetvert* of cereals and 70,000 *chetvert* of oats from stocks prepared for the Army in the field, navigation permitting. In the meantime, it was ordered to engage in every possible effort to transfer supplies prepared in Novgorod and Bely by ship to St Petersburg and Riga. While, in order to prevent chartered vessels from remaining idle in St Petersburg awaiting the arrival of stores from Novgorod, it was ordered to take the required quantities of grain and fodder from St Petersburg stores on loan, and having sent these stores to Königsberg, to replenish them with those that were to arrive from Novgorod. It was necessary to send the required amount of grain with the first ships from Riga to Königsberg using similar methods, drawing them on loan from the magazines of the maritime department and replenishing these provisions upon the arrival of barges from the docks at Bely.[20] Upon entering the Duchy of Warsaw and Saxony, Russian troops were to procure rations exclusively by requisitioning. On Prussian territory, the local government undertook to deliver rations for the Russians, but the fulfilment of this promise was impossible, because there were insufficient magazines even in their own Prussian fortresses. Under such circumstances, the only means of saving the army from starvation, due to the

17 Supreme Instructions, dated 18 [30] January, No. 34.

18 Supreme Instructions, dated 20 [31] January, No. 37.

19 Supreme Instructions for Prince Gorchakov, dated 16 [28] January, No. 25, and for General-of-Infantry Rimsky-Korsakov, also dated 16 [28] January, No. 26. By Field Marshal Prince Kutuzov's assignment, the magazines were located in: Vilna Governorate – Schaulen, Wiłkomierz, Vilna, Kovno, Merecz and Tauroggen; Grodno Governorate – Grodno, Slonim and Belitsa; Bialystok *Oblast* – Bialystok, Bielsk and Drohiczyn.

20 Supreme Instructions for Prince Gorchakov, dated 31 January [12 February], No. 63.

scarcity of cash, which prevented the acquisition of provisions by purchase, were mobile magazines and contracting the delivery of grain by ship to Königsberg and other ports, from where it would be transported by land to the troop locations.

Once the Russian army had entered Prussia, Emperor Alexander ordered Prince Kutuzov to publish an announcement in which the value of Russian currency was explained in comparison with Prussian. Based on the table attached to this announcement, the value of the Russian silver rouble and banknotes in five, ten and 25 rouble denominations, in Prussian thaler, and vice versa, the value of thaler and its subdivisions in Russian silver coin, or in banknotes, was set, given that the silver rouble was worth four paper roubles.[21]

By the end of 1812 and the beginning of 1813, there were many reforms in progress in the Russian army. All cavalry regiments were reorganised into a seven squadron establishment, of which six were active and one was replacements; each squadron was established for 208 men and 179 horses.[22] Many dragoon regiments were renamed as cuirassiers, ulans or mounted-jägers.[23] His Majesty's Leib Cuirassier Regiment was enrolled into the Lifeguard for distinguished service in the Patriotic War of 1812, with the title Lifeguard Cuirassiers, moreover, their officers were awarded seniority one rank above their line equivalents.[24] The Leib Grenadiers and Pavlovsk Grenadiers were also enrolled into the Lifeguard, with the promotion of officers to one rank higher than their line equivalents; while the Kexholm Infantry and Pernov Infantry joined 1st Grenadier Division to replace these regiments, being retitled as grenadiers,[25] while the Yekaterinburg Infantry and Rylsk Infantry transferred from 23rd Division to 11th Division in their place. The remaining regiments of 23rd Division, Selenginsk Infantry and 18th Jägers, were supposed to be transferred to the (Finland) corps under Count Steinheil [Faddey Fëdorovich Steingel or Fabian Gotthard von Steinheil], while 23rd Division would be reconstituted with two regiments from Count Steinheil's corps, the Uglich Infantry and 35th Jägers, located in Arkhangelsk, and two new regiments formed from the Moscow Garrison Regiment, renamed Borodino Infantry and Tarutino Infantry. VIII Corps was intended to consist of 11th Division and 17th Division (in IV Corps at the time). General Dokhturov's corps which had remained at Modlin and at Zamość under the overall commander of forces in Warsaw, were assigned to join the vanguard under Miloradovich.[26]

---

21 Supreme Instructions for Prince Kutuzov-Smolensky, dated 13 [25] January, No. 16.

22 Supreme Instructions for Prince Gorchakov, dated 27 December 1812 [8 January 1813], No. 455.

23 Namely: Pskov Dragoons and Starodub Dragoons became cuirassiers; Yamburg Dragoons, Orenburg Dragoons, Siberia Dragoons, Zhitomir Dragoons, Vladimir Dragoons, Taganrog Dragoons and Serpukhov Dragoons became ulans; Nezhin Dragoons, Chernigov Dragoons, Arzamas Dragoons, Lifland Dragoons, Seversk Dragoons, Pereyaslavl Dragoons, Tiraspol Dragoons and Dorpat Dragoons became mounted-jägers. For the subordination of regiments to cavalry divisions, see Appendix XI at the end of this chapter.

24 Supreme Orders dated 13 [25] April 1813.

25 Supreme Orders dated 13 [25] April 1813.

26 Handwritten note by Emperor Alexander I. Some of the plans contained within it were subsequently cancelled.

The hospitals were a particular concern of the benevolent Monarch. During his stay in Poland, having learned about the unsatisfactory state of St Petersburg hospitals from reports by the Commander-in-Chief of St Petersburg, General-of-Infantry Vyazmitinov [Sergei Kuzmich (Kozmich) Vyazmitinov], Emperor Alexander sent the following orders to the Head of the War Ministry, Prince Gorchakov [Alexei Ivanovich Gorchakov]:

> It is My opinion that the increasing numbers of patients in the hospitals of St Petersburg, and especially the rates at which the former are dying, has its reasons, and this was confirmed by the documents recently delivered from the Commander-in-Chief in St Petersburg.[27]
>
> The examination of the hospitals made in accordance with My instructions, has shown that indeed all this stems from various omissions in the absence of My subordinates, and that attention has not been paid to them until such time as I have been told of the necessity of taking care of the state of the hospitals in the capital, from the banks of the Vistula. With all My desire to respect your reasons explained in the note, I cannot, however, fail to express to you My comments thereon.
>
> As you were aware of the assembly of a significant number of recruits in St Petersburg as early as the month of August, there would have been no discomfort in the summerhouses had they been inspected in a timely manner and prepared for the winter, while the advantages of placing the sick in summerhouses was proven by the fact that they have previously been placed in them and have not suffered from the cold.
>
> I am also surprised at the difficulties in transportation because this is nothing new. A sick man, decently dressed and covered with a sheepskin coat, should not suffer covering 30 *verstas*; at least, the men would be less exhausted by this method than by placing them, as by your orders, in the damp Petrovsk barracks, where, moreover, no cleanliness is observed, and where the adviser to the medical department, Rusconi, had not taken it into his head to provide ventilation, until such time as upon the arrival of General Staff Doctor Crichton [Vasily Petrovich Kreyton or Archibald William Crichton].
>
> In explaining the overcrowding, you conclude that it is impossible to better accommodate the sick, but, according to the testimony of the Commander-in-Chief in St. Petersburg, there is space in the Preobrazhensky hospital.
>
> Contrary to the certificate of good provisioning, I have information that it only became so after your stay in the Petrovsk barracks.
>
> The shortage of doctors could also have been averted by insisting that the head of the Ministry of Police detach all those who are in government appointments as well as private practitioners in St Petersburg, as well as seconding them from your department in Finland.

27 These documents contained a presentation of the state of the St Petersburg military hospitals, based on their inspection, by Supreme Command, by the physician Crichton.

I also find evidence of complete disorder in the fact that the garrison does not know to which hospital to take the sick. By such shifting and shunting from one hospital to another, it will very naturally bring the men to a state of exhaustion, such that they are dying that same day. You must always know how many empty spaces there are in the hospitals, and if there is a shortage of bed space, prepare the establishment of special hospitals in advance in St. Petersburg, or even in Tsarskoye Selo or Strelna.

You will find confirmation of these omissions in the documents attached herewith. They will also show you that there is not even the slightest concern for the men in this department.

Finally, even the comparison of death rates you made is incorrect, as you can see from the calculations attached herewith, which clearly show the excessive number of deaths compared to previous years.

I find that the main omission on your part is that you did not foresee in good time the need to provide the recruits arriving in St Petersburg with nutritious food, and failed to tell me about the production of meat and wine rations for them, which could have spared a large number of men from disease.

Considering it superfluous to repeat the methods for correcting all that has been omitted, I remain confident that you will pay the best attention to the hospitals and will not force Me once more to take care of reducing sickness in the St Petersburg garrison from here.[28]

Emperor Alexander I, noting that although many omissions were recounted in the report from the Commander-in-Chief in St Petersburg, on the hospital department, the main point had not been addressed, namely: whether any orders had been issued to eliminate the observed shortcomings, and ordered the following measures to be taken:

1. To make use of all private practitioners and medically qualified employees from state-owned institutions in the hospitals (because, as the Tsar put it: 'one's own private profits and designs should not take precedence over the needs of the state or public matters').
2. To plaçe the patients in the most appropriate accommodation.
3. Finally, to punish the garrison for any neglect of the men.

Observe that the soldiers are not exhausted by their training and receive meat and wine rations in kind. Those who are ill must not be kept for a single day in barracks, through which illness will spread to the point that no medical skill can be of much further use, and do not be in a hurry to discharge convalescents from hospital without a second opinion; upon accepting those who have completely recovered back into their units, do not immediately engage them in training and give them good food and a ration of wine for the speedy recovery of their strength.[29]

28 Supreme Instructions for Prince Gorchakov, dated 8 [20] February, No. 76.
29 Extracted from Supreme Instructions to the Commander-in-Chief in St Petersburg, General-of-Infantry Vyazmitinov, dated 8 [20] February, No. 77.

The foreign campaign, remote from the well-spring of Imperial resources, was fraught with extreme difficulties. The Prussian local authorities did everything they could; but Prussia was exhausted, and therefore the Russian troops, in fulfilling the will of their Monarch, were obliged to get used to the ways of the country, such as paying cash for everything they received from the population.

When the Russian army entered Prussia, Prince Kutuzov consulted Stein, wanting to know whether meat and vodka could be obtained for the troops through requisition or by purchase.[30] In response to this query, Stein wrote that:

> hitherto, Russian forces have received food from the countryside serving as the theatre of operations, thanks to the abundance of supplies, the spread of the army over a vast area and the enthusiasm of the Prussian population; but with the onset of spring, the granaries will be empty and the troops will assume a more concentrated deployment. Therefore, it is necessary to attend in good time to the establishment of magazines on the coast of the Baltic Sea, in accordance with the direction of the army and the navigable inland waterways of the country.
>
> In general, unpaid requisitions of resources from the population deprive them of the opportunity to contribute taxes to the treasury, and therefore this method should be resorted to with absolute moderation. It is much more appropriate to establish the provision of supplies to the troops for cash, at predetermined prices, which, without depleting the regions, also prevents the troops from defrauding the contractors. In any case, it is necessary that the intendants general have the most accurate information about the resources of the country and make their demands in accordance with them.

Whereupon, taking into account the dearth of distilleries and of cattle in the Prussian regions from which Wittgenstein's army were extracting supplies and their abundance in the Duchy of Warsaw, Stein proposed:

1. 'The provision by requisition of the required volume of spirits from the Duchy.
2. That cattle supplied by the population of the Prussian regions, should be paid for in cash, at predetermined prices, and requisitions should be taken exclusively from enemy lands.
3. In order to enable the Coalition governments to maintain the troops, it will be necessary to arrange magazines by the spring and to compensate the population for goods supplied by paying their value, or at least in part.'[31]

In response to Stein's letter, the Field Marshal informed him that Emperor Alexander I wished that for all goods received by the troops from the population, these should be

30 Kutuzov's letter to Stein, dated 21 January (2 February).

31 Extracted from Stein's letter, dated 25 January (6 February).

paid one-fifth in cash, at a predetermined price, and receipts issued for the outstanding sums, which were to be repaid at a later date by the commissariat department.[32]

At the same time, the Prussian government, assisting the Russian in preparing resources for provisioning of the forces, took measures to establish magazines for the armies under Chichagov and Wittgenstein, for a total of 75,000 men, in Königsberg, Insterburg [Chernyakovsk, Kaliningrad *Oblast*] and Angerburg [Węgorzewo] for ten days in each of these locations, and in Elbing, Marienburg [Malbork], Marienwerder, Braunsberg [Braniewo] and Mohrungen [Morąg] for five days each.[33]

For the provisioning of Russian troops in the sector between the Oder and the Elbe, in February 1813, magazines were established in Landsberg, which were supposed to be filled with rations along navigable inland waterways via the Vistula and the Bromberger Kanal [Kanał Bydgoski]. In anticipation of the delivery of these supplies, it was proposed to collect grain immediately by means of requisitioning from the adjacent part of Poland for the Landsberg magazines. Supplies were transported from Landsberg to Crossen, and onwards to Lübben and Spremberg by horse transport from Poland; and in order to supply the troops with provisions, on the march through Silesia, small magazines were set up in Breslau, Liegnitz and Bunzlau, filled partly with resources from the surrounding country, partly from stores collected in Kalisz.[34]

Once the advance to the Elbe had begun, the Coalition armies received subsistence partly through quartering on the population, partly from the magazines. Some enemy ration storehouses that the Coalition overran, such as in Fraustadt [Wschowa] and so on, were of great use to them; but the incessant troop movements made it extremely difficult to provide them with supplies. The Prussian government repeatedly appealed to the commanders of Russian formations, asking them to be more thrifty with fodder, which, for the numerous cavalry, was consumed in huge quantities, to mind that the troops did not demand too many carts from the population and did not drive them too far away, and also that all self-authorisation and threats of violence, which might cool the sympathy of the population for the common cause, were to be strictly prohibited.[35] The Field Marshal, for his part, having received a report from Herzog Alexander von Württemberg about the constant discord with the governments of Pomerania and West Prussia, which had a very unfavourable attitude towards the provisioning of the force investing Danzig, wrote that these troops received rations in a very inefficient manner, and had even gone without bread for three successive days, that the horses in the cavalry were in poor condition from lack of fodder, and finally, that the Herzog, after repeated unsuccessful representations to put an end to such disorder, had been compelled to resort to obtaining supplies from the surrounding country by means of requisition.[36]

32 Letter dated 1 [13] February, from Płock (Log of Outgoing Documents, No. 226).
33 Returns for magazines (Log of Incoming Documents, No. 197).
34 Notes from General Scharnhorst's memo to Prince Volkonsky, dated 9 (21) March (Log of Incoming Documents, No. 437).
35 Baron Stein's letter to Prince Kutuzov, dated 20 April new style, from Dresden (Log of Incoming Documents, No. 647).
36 Adjutant General Prince Volkonsky's letter to Graf von Lottum, dated 24 April [6 May](Log of Outgoing Documents, No. 844).

As the Coalition retreated from Lützen, the stockpiling of ten days of rations for the army was ordered on the right bank of the Oder, from Lebus, not on the left bank of the Oder (as had been intended during the attack on Saxony); during the retreat from Bautzen, some of the stores were ordered to be transferred from Lebus to meet the army in Liegnitz, while some more went to Schweidnitz [Świdnica], where magazines had been re-established. Wintzingerode's corps, sent to the right bank of the Oder, was provisioned from stores in Poznań; in Kalisz, stocks were left for the sick only, while all other provisions were transported to Widawa (in the Duchy of Warsaw) for the new operational route.[37]

In general, during the retreat of the Coalition Army from Saxony to Silesia, much disorder occurred and some magazines were even looted.

The reserve artillery parks, during the advance of Russian forces from the Vistula to the Oder, were established as follows: a first line of parks along the Vistula; a second line along the Neman and the Bug, namely: two divisions [pairs of companies] in Memel; five divisions each in Grodno, Bialystok and Brest-Litvosk, and for the *opolchenie* under the command of Lieutenant General Count Tolstoy [Pëtr Aleksandrovich Tolstoy], three divisions in Polonne: for a total of 20 divisions; the parks of a third line were; two divisions in Riga, five divisions each in Minsk, Nesvizh and Pinsk and three divisions in Kiev [Kyiv], for a total of 20 divisions. In order to reduce costs and save time, the re-stocking of parks was instructed, wherever possible, also with captured enemy charges, as well as cartridges, of calibres similar to the Russians.[38]

Subsequently, Supreme Instructions were issued to transfer some parks from the second line abroad, namely: two divisions from Memel to Marienwerder and one division each from Grodno, Bialystok and Brest-Litovsk to Płock.[39] Of the parks of the first line, 3½ (namely: 1st, 5th, half of 11th and 12th) were sent to Dresden, while the remainder were reconstituted by order of the Inspector of All Artillery. In general, the parks did not manage to move to the locations assigned to them, and even those that were assigned to go abroad, for the most part, were reconstituted in Kopys.

Let us turn to the orders of the brilliant commander, who was to create a new army, halt the Russians and assert his predominance in Germany through new victories.

On 6 (18) December 1812, Napoleon returned to the Palais des Tuileries from his long campaign in Russia. His arrival was completely unexpected; the fatal 29e Bulletin de la Grande Armée, revealing the huge losses of the French army for the first time, had barely reached Paris. Many remained completely unaware of the fate of the Grande Armée; others, and even Napoleon himself, considered their losses to be incomparably fewer than they actually were. The French, trusting in the word

37 Instructions for Intendant General Kankrin, dated 12 [24] May (Log of Outgoing Documents, No. 958).

38 Supreme Directed Instructions for the War Ministry, Lieutenant General Prince Gorchakov, dated 31 December 1812 [12 January 1813], No. 104 (Log of Incoming Documents, No. 198).

39 Count Arakcheev's report to Prince Kutuzov-Smolensky, dated 17 [29] March, No. 205, from Kalisz (Log of Incoming Documents, No. 498).

of their master, hoped that there were sufficient reserves for reinforcement through standard conscription in order to continue the war against Russia and on the Iberian Peninsula. The failure suffered by Napoleon in Russia had shaken confidence in his invincibility, but the memories of the former glory acquired under his banner still aroused admiration in the stunned French. Speeches were made on all sides with expressions of devotion to the government and willingness for significant sacrifice: among those who delivered these speeches were not only Paris, Lyon and other cities of ancient France, but also many newly annexed to the Empire, such as Rome, Milan, Venice, Brussels, Antwerp, Amsterdam, Mainz, Cologne, and even the *Hansestädte*, at that time not yet roused to revolt against the oppressor of Germany. Yet, in the meantime, events were occurring that increased the significance of the losses suffered by the French in Russia: the defection of Yorck from Macdonald, the departure of Murat and the hasty retreat of the remnants of the French army. On 9 January, new style, news was received of these events in Paris; and three days later, on 12 January, the French Senate decided to call up 350,000 men to reconstitute the army, in addition to the conscription of 1812, including: 100,000 from the cohorts of the first draft of *gardes nationaux*; 100,000 from the conscription drafts of 1809, 1810, 1811 and 1812, 150,000 from the conscription draft of 1814,[40] which, together with the draft of 1813, would strengthen the army with 500,000 soldiers. Once the Prussian government had declared war on Napoleon, another decree by the Senate followed, for the strengthening of the army by another 180,000 men,[41] among whom were: 80,000 men from the first draft of *gardes nationaux*; 90,000 conscripts from the 1814 draft and 10,000 mounted *gardes d'honneur*, recruited, willingly or otherwise, from the young men of the French aristocracy.[42]

As at this time the war in Spain had taken a rather favourable turn for the French, who had at least 270,000 men on the Iberian Peninsula at the time, Napoleon demanded cadres of officers and non-commissioned officers for 150 battalions and 50 squadrons, from there, and, moreover, four *Garde* regiments, a gendarme detachment and Polish lancers at full strength. 3,000 gendarmes (officers and non-commissioned officers), scattered across various regions of the Empire, were to serve as cadres for the cavalry regiments.[43] 48 companies of naval artillery and naval crews, overall, some 30,000 men, were used to reconstitute the infantry and artillery. General Bertrand [Henri-Gatien Bertrand] was on the march from Italy to Germany with 30,000 men.[44] In order to remount the cavalry and artillery, General Bourcier [François Antoine Louis Bourcier] was ordered to purchase 10,000 draft

40 *Le Moniteur*, 12 January 1813.

41 *Le Moniteur*, 5 April 1813.

42 The French nobility, for the most part loyal to the Bourbon dynasty, shied away from military service and escaped conscription through substitution. Napoleon wanted to force them to play a personal part in recruitment duty, and to that end he ordered the formation of a special detachment from the nobility, smartly outfitted and with *Garde* status, hoping to instil a desire for service in these young men. Their call up, which did not allow any substitutions, was entrusted to each *Préfet de département*. Thiers, *Histoire du Consulat et de l'Empire, Edit. de Brux*. XV, 393-395.

43 Norvins, *Portefeuille de 1813*, I, 93.

44 Thiers, XV, 291. Richter, *Geschichte de deutschen Freiheitskrieges*, I, 118.

and 20,000 riding horses in Germany, which, given the general dislike of the population there for the French, was very difficult; in addition, a significant number of horses were collected in France itself by purchase or requisition.[45] Napoleon, not content with these methods, urged the cities and districts to send horsemen, equipped with horses and harness, in order to reconstitute the cavalry. He only had to say the word to one of the *Préfets* for the *Conseil municipal* of the regional capital to make the desired sacrifice, and for all the others to follow their example. Paris expressed its readiness to field 500 cavalry, Lyon 120, Strasbourg 100, and so on. The cities attached to the Empire through the right of might also constantly strove to out-do each other in displays of enthusiasm for the French government: Rome offered 240 horsemen, Amsterdam and Hamburg a hundred each, and so on. Yet it later emerged that it was very difficult to find volunteers for service, and therefore it was announced that the government had a need mainly for horses and harness. The only recourse was to purchase them, which was done. In a short time, the population of France and the countries subjugated to her fielded 22,000 horses complete with harness and 16,000 riders.[46]

After his failure in Russia, Napoleon felt the need to win over public opinion and convince his subjects that the means at his disposal were quite sufficient to counter the enemies of France. To that end, the *ministre de l'Intérieur*, Montalivet [Jean-Pierre Bachasson de Montalivet], was ordered to draw up a detailed account of the current situation in the state and read it out in a meeting of the *Corps législatif* on 13 (25) February. This was a remarkable document in which, on the basis of many reliable facts, it gave evidence that, despite the permanent state of war that demanded a huge army, the population of the ancient regions of France had increased from 25,000,000 to 28,000,000 people, that industry in France had developed with extraordinary rapidity, and that never before had the economy of the state been at such a high level. Furthermore, statistical evidence was given that, in the course of the past twelve years, in spite of incessant wars, the government had spent no less than a 1,000,000,000 francs (about 280,000,000 roubles) for the general construction of harbours, canals, roads, buildings and monuments.[47]

From the same report, it emerged that the annual revenue of France was limited to 900,000,000 francs (about 250,000,000 roubles), of which, after deducting 350,000,000 necessary for the payment of interest on the public debt and for the costs of the ministries of internal affairs, of justice and of finance, there remained 550,000,000 francs for the maintenance of the army and fleet. With the strength

45 Thiers, XV, 292-293.

46 Thiers, XV, 279.

47 Spending from 1804 to 1813 was shown as: 30,605,000 francs on bridge construction; 54,700,000 francs on canal construction; 14,200,000 francs on swamp drainage; 277,484,000 francs on roads; 117,328,000 francs on harbour construction; 102,421,000 francs on construction in Paris; 62,054,000 francs on construction of palaces; 149,108,000 francs on construction in the various *départements*; 157,100,000 francs on construction in the annexed *départements*; for a total of 965,000,000 francs. When calculating these amounts, the expenditure was not shown for: construction in Venice; for the highway from Paris to Hamburg; for the fortifications at Danzig, and so on, together with which some 1,000,000,000 francs were spent overall. *Le Moniteur*, 26 February 1813.

of the army at that time, 300,000,000 was required over and above the amount shown for its maintenance. Yet the Emperor gave orders to announce that he could cover the deficit without resorting to new taxes. The method for this was the sale of *domaines communaux* [public estates] and the replacement of the income generated from them with state bonds that brought a constant income, which brought 370,000,000 francs (more than 100,000,000 roubles) into the treasury.

Based on the data contained in the report, the French army, in 1813, consisted of: 1,000 battalions and 400 squadrons, numbering 800,000 infantrymen, 100,000 cavalrymen and 100,000 men in the other arms of service (artillery, engineers, gendarmes, trains, invalids), reaching 1,000,000 men overall.[48]

It must be confessed that this report had been compiled with great skill and that much of the data contained in it was aligned with the truth. Indeed, Napoleon waged all his wars at the expense of the enemies of France and by ruining his neighbours with enormous requisitions, did not exhaust the resources of his state. If one can criticise the minister for anything regarding this report, it is only for the servile crediting to one man that which had been the fruits of the time and efforts of the entire nation. Nevertheless, however, Napoleon's rewards were beyond doubt. Educated people understood very well that although there had been no good reason for him to go to war with Russia, nevertheless, only he could defend the state after the blow suffered in 1812; no one doubted the need to raise a new army for their own defence. But the mass of the people, stupefied by recent events and having lost confidence in Napoleon, desired peace. Stories of the disasters experienced during the winter campaign instilled horror and disgust for the war industry in civilians. The inhabitants of southern France and the western regions of the Empire in particular, evaded conscription. The conscripts directed to the Rhine, mostly young men who had not yet had time to develop, lost their strength on the march, arrived at the assembly areas in a state of exhaustion and filled the hospitals in crowds; others endured the hunger and fatigue, dreaming of the glory they were destined to acquire in the coming war.

No matter how great the losses were from the men sent to the army, the horses, selected indiscriminately out of necessity, unaccustomed to the saddlery placed on them and sent to the assembly areas by forced marches, suffered even more. In addition, those French who had never handled horses at all, had no idea about the care of the animals on which their own fate in battle depended. The training of the cavalrymen was quite poor, due to an insufficient number of experienced, veteran officers; these youths were incapable of making good cavalry, and this became apparent as soon as the newly formed army appeared in the theatre of war.

In the first campaign of 1813 (before the truce), the artillery of the French Army in the field was not numerous and consisted, aside from the Viceroy's force, of only 250 guns, and 350 guns overall; the artillery of the *Jeune Garde* in particular was renowned, numbering 56 guns, forming part of the reserve and was used very successfully.

48 *Le Moniteur,* 26 February 1813.

Significant sums were used to build wagons to replace those lost in Russia. Napoleon, convinced of the limited usefulness of large, heavy wagons, replaced them with light wagons of various designs in 1813 (*chars à la comtoise* etc). Because the Cossacks had captured every straggling wagon in the campaign of 1812, orders were issued to observe the strictest convoy discipline when moving wagons: as soon as any cart opened a gap, the driver teams were immediately to force it, and a hundred others behind it, to move at a trot and make up the lost ground. Such pedantic precision was extremely tiring for the horses, and was almost as harmful as the previous indiscipline.

The organisation of the troops assembled on the Rhine, from Strasbourg to Wesel, was entrusted to the senior duc de Valmy (Kellermann [François Étienne Christophe Kellermann]). Marshal Kellermann, already in his twilight years, but very active and experienced in organising troops, made inspections of the units that came to the assembly areas, chiefly in Mainz, and supplied the troops with everything they needed: clothing, footwear, weapons, replacement officers, and, if necessary, referred directly to Napoleon, who, for his part, found the resources and sent everything needed to the Rhine. Not a single day was lost. At a time when there was still no artillery or cavalry, when they were still casting guns, buying horses and equipping horsemen who still did not know how to ride, the infantry were being sent in small units to the Rhine. Such hasty formation of forces was unsatisfactory, and Napoleon was aware of its shortcomings, but wanted to resolve the matter as quickly as possible so that Europe would not have chance to lose faith in his infallibility.[49]

By 1 February, new style, the first regiments of an observation corps, under the command of *Général de division* comte Souham [Joseph Souham], had already set off towards Frankfurt am Main, while two weeks later this corps, having been designated *3e Corps d'Observation*, marched up the course of the Main; at Frankfurt, the *Garde*, under Marshal Bessières' command [Jean-Baptiste Bessières], and Marshal Marmont's *6e Corps* [Auguste Frédéric Louis Viesse de Marmont] assembled. Following that, *3e Corps* under Marshal Ney, which had been joined by the Baden and Hessen contingents, and Marshal Oudinot's *12e Corps* [Nicolas Charles Marie Oudinot] settled down near Würzburg. The Bavarian forces were forming up in Bamberg, while the Westphalians were in Wesel. Another observation corps – *4e Corps d'Observation*, assembled in Verona at the beginning of the year, under the command of General Bertrand, had crossed Tyrol in March and was approaching the upper Main.[50] All these corps, with the exception of the *Vieille Garde* and the corps under Marmont, consisted almost exclusively of novice recruits.[51]

The French army assembled on the Main consisted of:

Garde impériale – 12,000 infantrymen and 4,000 cavalrymen.
3e Corps under Marshal Ney, numbering 40,000 men:
Souham's division.
Girard's division.

49 Odeleben, *Relation circonstanciée de la campagne de 1813*, I, 17-23 & 27. Thiers, XV, 291-300.
50 *Vossische Zeitung*, 1813.
51 Odeleben, I, 25.

Brenier's division [Antoine-François Brenier de Montmorand].
Ricard's division [Étienne Pierre Sylvestre Ricard].
Marchand's division [Jean Gabriel Marchand](Baden and Hessen contingents).

4e Corps under General Bertrand, numbering 22,000 men.
Morand's division [Charles Antoine Louis Alexis Morand].
Peyri's division [Louis Gaspard Balthazar Pierre Léon Marie Peyri] (Italians).
Franquemont's division [Friedrich Graf von Franquemont](Württemberg contingent).

6e Corps under Marshal Marmont, numbering 25,000 men.
Compans division [Jean Dominique Compans].
Bonet's division [Jean Pierre François Bonet].

12e Corps under Marshal Oudinot, numbering 25,000 men.
Pacthod's division [Michel-Marie Pacthod].
Lorencez division [Guillaume Latrille de Lorencez].
Raglovich's division [Clemens von Raglovich] (Bavarians).

For a total of some 128,000 men, including no more than 8,000 cavalry, namely: 4,000 *Garde* cavalry, 2,500 in Bertrand's corps, and 500 each in the other infantry corps (in addition, Latour-Maubourg was forming hussar and cuirassier regiments in Hanover, numbering overall between 4,000 and 5,000 men). The best infantry units, outside of the *Vieille Garde*, were soldiers from the marine infantry and artillery regiments who had joined Marmont's corps. The cavalry, insufficient in numbers, had poor horses and did not have time to receive proper training; the artillery horses, maimed through the inexperience of their riders, were completely incapable of long marches or swift evolutions. But, despite all these shortcomings, this army, under the leadership of the great commander, could win victories, because the generals and officers, who had grown grey-headed under Napoleon's colours, were able to convey to their subordinates the emotions that would animate them. Yet in the soldiers' circles, and in frank conversations between officers, they condemned Napoleon and cursed his insatiable ambition; but one word from him could make anyone sacrifice themself.

Thus, in the space of three months, Napoleon had managed to create an army of almost 130,000 men, with 250 guns. Moreover, there were some 40,000 concentrated on the Elbe with the Viceroy, while together with Davout's force, there were more than 60,000 men with 100 guns. Consequently, from his first steps into Germany, Napoleon could face the Coalition with about 200,000 men with 350 guns. Strong reserves were forming behind them, and once Saxony had been occupied, the French could hope for the assistance of the garrisons left in the fortresses on the Elbe, Oder and Vistula, which, by diverting elements of the Coalition force, had weakened the Russo-Prussian army. The number of troops in the fortresses on the Elbe reached some 18,000 overall; those on the Oder, some 16,000 (namely: 8,500 in Stettin, 3,000 in Küstrin and 5,000 in Glogau); some 30,000 on the Vistula in Danzig and Modlin, and in Zamość; in addition, 8,000 men were in Kraków with Prince Poniatowski, all in all there were no fewer than 70,000 men in the rear of the Coalition.[52]

It is impossible not to be astonished at the energy, activity and skill with which Napoleon, after the destruction of his army in Russia, was able to create another in the shortest possible time. It was vital to merge the miserable remnants from the slaughter of those who had been lost in the north with novices who had no concept of military life, and animate this amalgam with moral strength. And all this had to be done with extraordinary speed in order to prevent the concentration of the enemy armies; conscription, training, movement to assembly areas: everything was happening simultaneously. Most of the infantry had moved into Germany before they had time to collect their muskets, which were sent on wagons in the wake of the men.[53] The troops were trained in the most necessary techniques and evolutions on the march; the rest would have to be completed through the skill of the commanders, the sharpness of the officers, the diligence of the soldiers. The artillery was insufficient for the size of the force; the cavalry was very weak, but, despite all this, Napoleon intended to act without delay. The Coalition would be struck by their unexpected appearance at a time when they still doubted the existence of this French army. Departing from Saint-Cloud, on 3 (15) April, at one o'clock in the morning, Napoleon arrived in Mainz on 4 (16) April, at around midnight, where he remained until 12 (24) April, expediting through his presence the equipping and forming up of the force. The following day [25 April], he was already in Erfurt, and in Weimar on 16 (28) April. 'I shall execute this campaign as General Bonaparte, and not as the Emperor.' he stated.[54]

52 All figures relating to the numerical strength of the various parts of the French army were taken from a comparison of the statements in Vaudoncourt, Thiers and Sporschill. For the detailed comparison, see Appendix XII at the end of this chapter.

53 Fain *Manuscrit de 1813*, I, 325.

54 '*Je ferai cette campagne comme le général Bonaparte, et non pas en empereur.*' Odeleben, I, 38.

Appendix X

Composition of the Reserve Army In February 1813

General Officer Commanding; General-of-Infantry Prince Lobanov-Rostovsky.
Chief of Cavalry; General-of-Cavalry Kologrivov.
Quartermaster General; Major General Vistitsky.
Duty General; Major General Stavitsky.

I Reserve Infantry Corps: commanded by Major General Bashutsky, assisted by major generals Adamovich and Ushakov.
6th Reserve Division; 21st Reserve Division; 25th Reserve Division; 5th Reserve Division; 14th Reserve Division; 3rd Reserve Division; 4th Reserve Division.

II Reserve Infantry Corps: commanded by Lieutenant General Kleinmikhel, assisted by major generals Miller, Gladkov and Avdulin.
11th Reserve Division; 23rd Reserve Division; 7th Reserve Division; 24th Reserve Division; 1st Reserve Division; 2nd Reserve Division; Lifeguard Reserve Division.

III Reserve Infantry Corps: commanded by Lieutenant General Brozin, assisted by major generals Prince Urusov and Titov.
17th Reserve Division; 27th Reserve Division; 12th Reserve Division; 26th Reserve Division; 9th Reserve Division; 15th Reserve Division.

IV Reserve Infantry Corps: commanded by Lieutenant General Essen 3rd, assisted by Lieutenant General Pushchin and major generals Levitsky and Bestuzhev-Ryumin.
18th Reserve Division; 8th Reserve Division; 10th Reserve Division; 13th Reserve Division; 16th Reserve Division; 22nd Reserve Division.

I Reserve Cavalry Corps: commanded by Colonel Zhandre [or Gendre].
Lifeguard Reserve Cavalry Division; 1st Reserve Cuirassier Division; 2nd Reserve Cuirassier Division; 3rd Reserve Cuirassier Division;

II Reserve Cavalry Corps: commanded by Major General Belsky.
1st Reserve Dragoon Division; 2nd Reserve Dragoon Division; 3rd Reserve Dragoon Division; 4th Reserve Dragoon Division; 1st Reserve Mounted Jäger Division; 2nd Reserve Mounted Jäger Division.

III Reserve Cavalry Corps: commanded by Major General Prince Gorchakov.
1st Reserve Ulan Divison; 2nd Reserve Ulan Divison; 3rd Reserve Ulan Divison; 1st Reserve Hussar Division; 2nd Reserve Hussar Division; 3rd Reserve Hussar Division.

Reserve Artillery: commanded by Major General Ilin.
37 companies with 438 guns; 40 companies without guns;
Reserve Artillery Parks: in 20 divisions.

Appendix XI

The cavalry were reorganised into the following cavalry divisions

---

1st Cuirassier Division: Chevalier Garde, Lifeguard Horse, His Majesty's Leib Cuirassiers, Her Majesty's Leib Cuirassiers.

2nd Cuirassier Division: Yekaterinoslav Cuirassiers, Pskov Cuirassiers, Glukhov Cuirassiers, Astrakhan Cuirassiers.

3rd Cuirassier Division: Military Order Cuirassiers, Malorussia Cuirassiers, Novgorod Cuirassiers, Starodub Cuirassiers.

Lifeguard Cavalry Division: Lifeguard Dragoons, Lifeguard Hussars, Lifeguard Ulans, Lifeguard Cossacks.

1st Dragoon Division: Riga Dragoons, Kargopol Dragoons, Finland Dragoons, Mitau Dragoons.

2nd Dragoon Division: Kurland Dragoons, Moscow Dragoons, Novorossia Dragoons, Kazan Dragoons.

3rd Dragoon Division: Kharkov Dragoons, Ingermanland Dragoons, Tver Dragoons, Kiev Dragoons.

4th Dragoon Division: St Petersburg Dragoons, Kinburn Dragoons, Smolensk Dragoons, Narva Dragoons.

1st Mounted-Jäger Division: Nezhin Mounted-Jägers, Chernigov Mounted-Jägers, Arzamas Mounted-Jägers, Seversk Mounted-Jägers.

2nd Mounted-Jäger Division: Lifland Mounted-Jägers, Pereyaslavl Mounted-Jägers, Tiraspol Mounted-Jägers, Dorpat Mounted-Jägers.

1st Hussar Division: Grodno Hussars, Yelisavetgrad Hussars, Izyum Hussars, Sumy Hussars.

2nd Hussar Division: Mariupol Hussars, Akhtyrka Hussars, Alexandria Hussars, Irkutsk Hussars.

3rd Hussar Division: Pavlograd Hussars, Belorussia Hussars, Olviopol Hussars, Lubny Hussars.

1st Ulan Division: Lithuania Ulans, Yamburg Ulans, Orenburg Ulans, Siberia Ulans.

2nd Ulan Division: Poland Ulans, Zhitomir Ulans, Tatar Ulans, Vladimir Ulans.

3rd Ulan Division: Volhynia Ulans, Chuguev Ulans, Taganrog Ulans, Serpukhov Ulans.

The Nizhegorod Dragoons and Borisoglebsk Dragoons were part of the Georgia Corps and were not assigned to a cavalry division.

Appendix XII

Comparison of numerical strengths of the French army

Under the personal command of Napoleon	**Vaudoncourt**	**Thiers**	**Sporschill**
Infanterie de la Garde impériale	15,000	12,000	10,000
Cavalerie de la Garde impériale	4,000	3,000	5,000
3e Corps – Ney	30,000	48,000	40,000
4e Corps – Bertrand	22,000	45,000	20,000
12e Corps – Oudinot	18,000		25,000
6e Corps – Marmont	12,000	27,000	25,000
TOTAL:	**101,000**	**135,000**	**125,000**
Under the Viceroy's command			
2e Corps – Victor	5,000	4,000	7,400
5e Corps – Lauriston	18,000	24,000	15,000
11e Corps – Macdonald	18,000	24,000	15,000
Garde and cavalry		10,000	16,210
TOTAL:	**41,000**	**62,000**	**53,610**
On the lower Elbe			
Davout's and Vandamme's forces	24,000	18,000	10,000
Grand total for the operational armies:	**166,000**	**215,000**	**188,610**

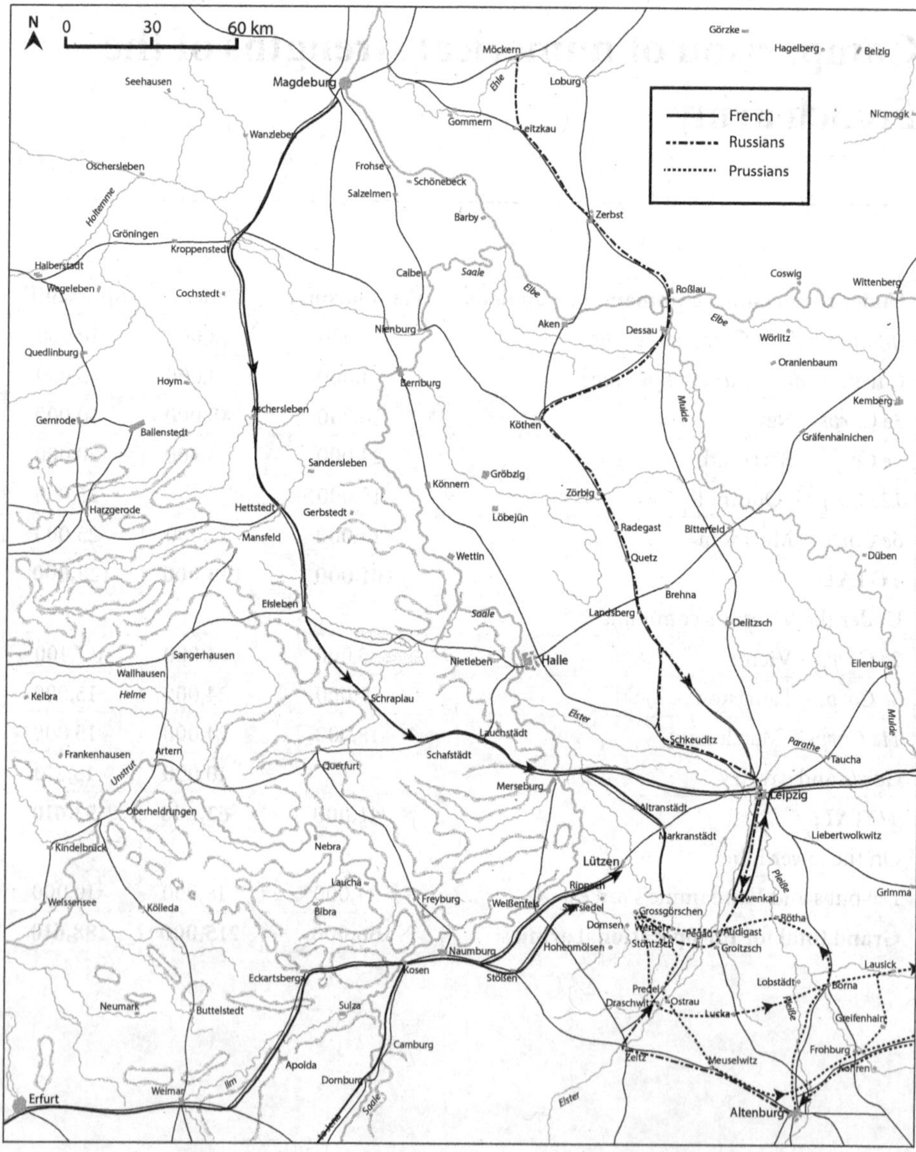

The movements of both sides preceding the Battle of Lützen.

7

The Battle of Lützen

The slowness of the Coalition advance into Saxony. – Appointment of Count Wittgenstein as Commander-in-Chief of the Coalition Army. – Strength and dispositions of the Coalition forces. – Comparison of forces between both sides. – The factors that prompted the Coalition to seek a decisive battle. – Count Wittgenstein's position. – His initial draft of a plan for the concentration of forces. The location of the Russo-Prussian army before the battle of Lützen, 18 (30) April.

The advances of the armies under Napoleon and the Viceroy. – The locations of French forces on the evening of 18 (30) April. – Napoleon's operational plan. – Action at Rippach. – The locations of French and Coalition forces during the night of 19 to 20 April (1 to 2 May). – Operational dispositions of the Russo-Prussian army, for 20 April (2 May). – Strength of the Coalition force. – The Coalition advance towards Lützen. – Forming up into battle order. – The lay of the battlefield. – Napoleon's advance towards Leipzig. – The situation of both sides.

The battle of Lützen. – The advance by Blücher's force. – The struggle for the villages in front of Lützen. – The inactivity of the Coalition cavalry. – The arrival of Marmont's corps in Starsiedel. – Yorck's movement to assist Blücher. – The arrival of Macdonald's corps and part of Bertrand's corps to assist Ney. – Napoleon's preparations to reinforce Ney with the *Garde*. Prince Golitsyn's advance on the Coalition army's left flank, and of II Corps in support of Blücher. – The Prinz von Württemberg's advance on the right wing towards Eisdorf. – Konovnitsyn's advance towards the same location with the Grenadier Corps. – Napoleon's assault on the centre. – The subsequent deployment of forces. – The night attack by Dolffs' Prussian cavalry.

The council of war. – The Coalition decision to retreat. – Losses on both sides. – Awards. – Comments on the actions by both sides during the battle of Lützen.

While Napoleon was creating a new army with astonishing energy, the Coalition were concentrating their forces in Saxony very slowly. Miloradovich's corps arrived in Dresden 14 days after Blücher had crossed the Elbe there, having been blockading the fortress of Glogau until relieved by a Prussian detachment under General Schuler von Senden. The force under Miloradovich, numbering about 12,000 men, having crossed the Elbe over four days, from 4 to 7 (16 to 19) April, joined the army under Blücher, numbering about 25,000 men located in the vicinity of Altenburg. Eventually, on 12 (24) April, the Main Army arrived in Dresden, numbering 18,000 men, with which the headquarters of Emperor Alexander and the King of Prussia was co-located.[1] If the Russo-Prussian forces had pursued the remnants of the French army without pause, they could have cleared the whole of Germany of enemy troops, which would have prevented Napoleon from assimilating the *Confédération du Rhin* contingents into the army he was forming.[2] The loss of more than a month for the Coalition was not used to significantly strengthen their forces at all, rather, in contrast, made it possible for Napoleon to quadruple his army operating in Germany.

The Coalition forces, although they were greeted by the population in Saxony with expressions of enthusiasm and loyalty, nevertheless suffered from a lack for provisions due to the indifference of local government to the common cause of Germany. Blücher's demands were very moderate overall, but the Saxon government commission found them extraordinary and, instead of satisfying the Prussian forces, evaded them with irritable comments, at which the fiery Blücher more than once lost his patience. Having said that, the Coalition generals, observing the will of Emperor Alexander and Friedrich Wilhelm precisely, spared the inhabitants and maintained the strictest discipline among their troops. In contrast, the French, despite the loyalty of the Saxon king to their master, looted without mercy. Only in the vicinity of their *quartier général* was some kind of order observed. The Italian troops in particular devastated the country.[3]

Just at the time that Napoleon had reached the borders of Saxony, news was received at the headquarters of the Coalition Monarchs of the death of Field Marshal Prince Kutuzov, on 16 (28) April, in Bunzlau. Without announcing this to the troops at the decisive moment of their imminent bloody engagement with the French, the Coalition Monarchs appointed Count Wittgenstein as Commander-in-Chief. The successes he had achieved in 1812 swayed general opinion in his favour and contributed to his selection, despite the seniority of Barclay de Tolly, Tormasov, Miloradovich and Blücher.

1 Beitzke, *Geschichte der deutschen Freiheitskriege*, I, 352-353.

2 *'Dass die grosse Armee nicht gefolgt, ist ein grosser Fehler: so schrieb Scharnhorst shon am 6 April. Ihr langes Ausbleiben durchaus gegen die Kalischer Verabredungen hemmte die Operationen Blüchers und Wittgensteins, zwang sie an der unteren Saale und an der Elster Wochen lang still zu liegen, während Napoleons staunenswürdige Thätigkeit seine Heersmassen in Franken und Thüringen sammelte und schon daran war mit überlegener Macht durch die Pässe der Saale hervorzubrechen.*
Im demselben Masse schwanden die grossen moralischen Eindrücke, mit dene man begonnen hatte...' Droysen, *Das Leben des Feldmarschalls Grafen Yorck*, II, 194.

3 Odeleben, *Relation circonstanciée de la campagne de 1813 en Saxe*, I, 45.

The army entrusted to Count Wittgenstein occupied the following locations on 18 (30) April:

From the force previously under his command, the corps under Berg with 7,450 men and Yorck with about 10,000 men were marching from Leipzig and Schkeuditz towards Zwenkau to join the force under Blücher, while Kleist's detachment, numbering 6,000 men (3,200 Prussians and 2,800 Russians), had been entrusted with the defence of Leipzig and the crossings over the Saale.

Included in Blücher's force were: Wintzingerode's cavalry vanguard, around 5,000 strong, stationed at Lützen; his infantry (from II Corps), numbering 8,700 men were between the Floßgraben and the Elster; Blücher's corps, numbering around 25,000 men, were in the vicinity of Borna; Miloradovich's corps, of around 12,000 men, was at Penig [13 miles north-west of Chemnitz]; the Main Army, numbering some 18,000 men, was at Frohburg and Kohren. The headquarters was in Frohburg.[4]

In total, under Count Wittgenstein's command there were about 54,000 Russians with 440 guns and 38,000 Prussians with 216 guns: therefore a total of 92,000 men with 656 guns.[5]

Thus, as he was advancing into Saxony, Napoleon had some 130,000 men under direct command, or some 170,000 taken together with the force under the Viceroy, and had a decisive advantage in numerical strength; but, in relation to the quality of the troops, his army was inferior to that of the Coalition, both in that it consisted mostly of recruits and in the low numbers of cavalry, of which Napoleon had no more than 8,000, while, in contrast, the Coalition had some 20,000 cavalrymen: this latter factor prevented the French from exploiting their victories. There were 350 guns in Napoleon's artillery, while the Coalition had almost double that number. And so the Russo-Prussian army, inferior to the enemy in infantry strength, had an advantage in cavalry and artillery, which partially balanced both sides. This prompted the Coalition to seek a decisive battle: a victory might give them supremacy in Germany; in the event of a reverse, they expected to be able to retreat without being exposed to grave danger. In any case, it was more advantageous for them to fight rather than to retreat to the right bank of the Elbe without a fight, because they would lose influence over the German princes by evading an engagement with the enemy and would have degraded themselves in public opinion.

Count Wittgenstein's situation was most awkward. No sooner had he taken command of the army, than he had to give battle immediately against the greatest commander, who, in the minds of his contemporaries, had acquired the aura of invincibility. Until this point, our commander had not had an encounter with Napoleon. He had defeated the French while commanding Russian troops alone; now he had to command two armies, in one of which he knew neither the troops nor the commanders. In 1812 he had held totally independent command; in contrast, in 1813 he was working in the presence of his Tsar and the King of Prussia, had to report on his intentions to the Monarchs, and had to ask for their consent to execute

4 For details of Berg's, Yorck's, Kleist's, Wintzingerode's, Blücher's and Miloradovich's forces and the Main Army, see Appendix XIII at the end of this chapter.

5 These numbers are derived from those given in Plotho, Beitzke and Prinz Eugen von Württemberg (his diary in the archive of the M.T.D. No. 47,344) and official strength returns.

his plans. All this was bound to lead to sluggish operations, all the more dangerous because Wittgenstein would be fighting a determined adversary.

From the very first day, upon the appointment of Count Wittgenstein as Commander-in-Chief, it emerged that his authority was extremely constrained due to extraneous orders. As soon as he learned of his imminent responsibilities, he instructed his chief of staff to draw up a general disposition for operations by the Russo-Prussian army, in which, in the name of the Commander-in-Chief, it was announced that a general battle would be fought in the vicinity of Leipzig and that the course of the upper Elbe was taken as the base of operations for the army. Furthermore, it was stated that based on the movements of the enemy, a concentration of their forces at Naumburg had been observed, and that, in all probability, they intended to move through Leipzig towards Torgau in order to sever our communications. In order to counter this, according to Count Wittgenstein, it was necessary to concentrate the Coalition Army between Leipzig and Wurzen [3½ miles north of Mühlbach].[6] To that end, on 17 (29) April, Blücher's corps was directed from Altenburg towards Borna, from where it was intended to march via Grimma in order to link up with other forces at Wurzen. General Toll, having learned of this, reported on Blücher's march to Borna and the Main Army's from Geringswalde [6½ miles east of Rochlitz] to Frohburg, to General Miloradovich, who was stationed at Penig, and at the same time noted that, in his opinion, it was necessary for Miloradovich's corps to move to Altenburg, which was done.[7] Meanwhile, Emperor Alexander, having returned to headquarters from Dresden, did not approve of the concentration of the army at Wurzen, and, as a result, at a Council of War convened in Gohlis [two miles north of Leipzig], it was decided to concentrate the Coalition forces between Leipzig and Borna.[8]

Indeed, the plan for the concentration of forces proposed by Count Wittgenstein exposed the Coalition to the danger of being driven back from the upper Elbe and losing communications, both with Silesia as our main supply route, and with Austria. Maintaining communications with this Power was all the more important because, before leaving Dresden, Emperor Alexander had received assurances from the Viennese Court once more of their unchanging loyalty to the common cause of the Coalition. Although such promises could not be completely relied upon, nevertheless, it was necessary to be prepared for the eventuality of an alliance with Austria. Kaiser Franz had already announced to the French government on 14 (26) April that the terms of the treaty concluded with Napoleon in March 1812 for assistance during the war with Russia were 'incompatible with the present situation.'[9]

Napoleon, upon reaching Naumburg, could move across undulating, broken terrain, towards Zeitz and Altenburg, and on to Dresden, or across the plains

6 This disposition may be found in Plotho's *Der Krieg in Deutschland und Frankreich in den Jahren 1813 und 1814*, I, 89-91.

7 Major General Toll's report to General-of-Infantry Miloradovich, dated 18 [30] April.

8 Bernhardi *Denkwürdigkeiten des Grafen v. Toll*, II, 443-444.

9 '*Le 26, (avril) le cabinet de Vienne déclara que les stipulations du traité du 14 mars 1812 n'étaient plus applicables à la situation présente*.' Vaudoncourt, *Histoire de la guerre soutenue par les Français en Allemagne, en 1813*, 124-125.

towards Leipzig. The first of these directions was of great advantage for operations by his numerous infantry without the aid of cavalry, which (as has already been said) was inferior to that of the Coalition, both in numbers and quality. The Coalition, not knowing for certain where Napoleon intended to march, had been obliged to extend their forces. Bülow's corps was monitoring the course of the lower Saale; Kleist's detachment was holding Leipzig and the crossings at Merseburg and Halle. Miloradovich's corps was stationed at Altenburg in order to protect the left flank of the army. The rest of the Coalition forces, numbering 74,000 men, on 18 (30) April, were located as follows: Wintzingerode's vanguard was at Lützen, having pushed a forward detachment out towards Weißenfels under Lanskoy's command; Berg's and Yorck's corps were at Zwenkau on the Elster, while Blücher's corps was at Borna; the reserve (Main Army) was at Frohburg and Kohren.

At the same time as Napoleon's advance, the Viceroy was moving towards Leipzig, which had been nominated as the assembly area for the entire French army. Having left Victor's corps to defend Magdeburg, the Viceroy reached Mansfeld and Alsleben [on the Saale, five miles downstream of Könnern] on 13 (25) April with the corps under Lauriston and Macdonald and with Latour-Maubourg's cavalry, some 40,000 men in total, on the same day that Napoleon arrived in Erfurt.[10] On 14 (26) April, the force under the Viceroy halted for the day, while Napoleon moved to Weimar with his *quartier-général* and *Garde*, from where Ney moved towards Naumburg and, after a small skirmish with one of General Lanskoy's outposts, occupied this town. On 15 (27) April, The Viceroy attempted to seize the crossing over the Saale at Wettin; troops from Maison's division [Nicolas-Joseph Maison] (*5e Corps*) attacked the detachment holding this location, but the Coalition force succeeded in burning the bridge. On the following day, 16 (28) April, Lauriston led an attack on the bridgehead at Halle and captured it, but here, too, the Prussian troops burned the bridge, which forced the Viceroy to turn towards Merseburg. On 17 (29) April, at four o'clock in the afternoon, Macdonald attacked the town, defended by 2,000 Prussian troops, with *11e Corps*, forcing them to retreat towards Leipzig, with the loss of 200 men taken prisoner, and took possession of the bridge. On the same day, General Souham, who was marching at the head of Ney's corps with his division, engaged General Lanskoy's vanguard in front of Weißenfels, pushing him back across the Poserna stream [Rippach] and occupied the town; *6e Corps* arrived in Kösen; *4e Corps* in Dornburg; *12e Corps* was deployed at Saalfeld; while the *quartier-général* and *Garde* passed through Naumburg.

On 18 (30) April, the *quartier-général* and *Garde* moved up to Weißenfels; Ney's corps was deployed forwards of this town; the remaining corps were in echelon between Naumburg and Jena (namely; *6e Corps* at Naumburg, *4e Corps* at Stößen, *12e Corps* at Jena). The Viceroy concentrated his force at Merseburg, at a distance of about 20 *verstas* from Weißenfels, and detached General Roguet, with the *Garde* units which were with his force, to Napoleon's *quartier-général*. Thus the French armies had linked up,[11] but their extended deployment, over a distance of 60 *verstas*

10 At this point, some 1,500 cavalrymen, formed up in Hanover by Latour-Maubourg, had already joined the Viceroy's force.

11 Vaudoncourt, 66-68.

from Merseburg to Jena, not properly screened by outposts due to the low numbers of cavalry, exposed the French to an unexpected encounter with the Coalition.

Napoleon, having learned from several reconnaissances that the main Coalition force was on the upper Elster, between Leipzig and the Bohemian mountains, decided to join his army with the force under the Viceroy at Leipzig, and by crossing the Elster there, envelope the Coalition army from the right flank and push them back into the mountains. To that end, he sent Ney's corps along the Lützen highway, followed by the *Garde* and the corps under Marmont, he sent the corps under Bertrand and Oudinot to the right of them, to Stößen, while the force under the Viceroy was to go to the left towards Markranstädt.[12]

On 19 April (1 May), at nine o'clock in the morning, Napoleon quickly mounted a horse and galloped to the outposts with his entire retinue. It is believed that he had intended to make a routine reconnaissance, but as soon as they had left the town and crested the high ground lying in front, long lines of Russian cavalry drawn up in battle formation came into view behind the Rippach stream. It was Major General Lanskoy's forward detachment, supported by all the cavalry from Wintzingerode's corps. The main road ran in a meandering way through the village of Rippach, located in a valley and then led up the gentle slope of the opposing high ground. This was an advantageous defensive position, in particular because the banks of the stream are quite steep in the direction of the village. Napoleon, surveying our cavalry positions, ordered Souham to attack. The French division formed up in four squares, each of four battalions, at intervals of several hundred paces from one another. Four guns were attached to these squares. Skirmishers were scattered forwards of the squares and in the intervals between them, while to their rear, Laboissière's cavalry brigade [François Garnier de Laboissière] was lined up, under the command of the duc de Valmy (the younger Kellermann [François Étienne Kellermann]). Behind them marched the divisions under Girard and Marchand, also in squares, while to the right of Souham was the entire *cavalerie de la Garde*, under the command of Marshal Bessières.

The French attacked our position at 11 o'clock. The square closest to the road, despite coming under fire from six guns, crossed the valley; behind them proceeded Souham's other three squares. The enemy, having crossed the stream, began to climb the opposite slope; at that very moment, Marshal Bessières, who should not have been involved in the attack on the defile, dashed up to the screen of skirmishers in order to get a closer look at the positions of the Russian force, and was mortally wounded by round shot. Wintzingerode's cavalry, yielding to the superior enemy numbers, withdrew in perfect order, and the fighting thereafter was limited to a cannonade that continued until nightfall. The French, pushing our cavalry back, occupied Lützen, where in the early hours of 20 April (2 May) Napoleon's *quartier-général* and the *Garde* were installed. Ney's corps occupied the villages of Kaja, Rahna, Großgörschen and Kleingörschen; Morand's corps was located at Poserna, Bertrand's was between Stößen and Poserna; Oudinot was on the march from Jena towards Naumburg; Macdonald's corps was at Markranstädt, while Lauriston's was

12 See Map No. 5, to explain the movements of both sides preceding the Battle of Lützen.

at Günthersdorf [2½ miles north of Altranstädt], between Merseburg and Leipzig. On the Coalition side, Wintzingerode's vanguard had moved to Werben in order to cover the army and crossings over the Elster, having left Lanskoy's detachment at Thesau; Berg's and Yorck's corps were deployed at Zwenkau; Blücher's corps and the reserve (Main Army) were on the Pleiße at Rötha and Lobstädt.[13]

In the action at Rippach, the French suffered heavier casualties than the Russians. Odeleben [Otto von Odeleben], an eyewitness to this combat, stated: 'on this day, the lack of coordination in the actions of the newly formed units was clearly exposed. The French generals complained themselves that there was no inter-communication in their operations; assaults in particular were hampered and delayed due to the limited number of cavalry. The infantry, tired from marching, were forced to withstand the onslaught of enemy cavalry because there was little of their own, and since this consisted, for the most part, of *Garde* regiments, they were invariably held in reserve.'[14]

It has already been mentioned that political considerations for the Coalition demanded a decisive battle on the left bank of the Elbe, and that the numerical combat strength of enemy forces was offset by the superior quality of the Coalition forces. This prompted their commanders to attack Napoleon without delay, and, in all probability, they would have executed their intention as early as 19 April (1 May), if their army had been concentrated on the Elster at the time. But since the reserves were moving from Frohburg and Kohren towards Lobstädt at that point, they could not link up with the other forces or take part in any actions before 20 April (2 May).

Orders were drafted that day for the attack on the enemy army, contained in a Disposition, the main concept of which has been attributed by many to Scharnhorst; but in all probability belongs to Diebitsch. This main concept was to flank the enemy army and disperse the nearest French corps before others could come to their aid.

The coordinating instructions were as follows:

> Dispositions dated 19 April [1 May].
> Tomorrow, at five o'clock in the morning, the corps under *General der Kavallerie* Blücher should stand in two columns ordered from the right: the right at Storkwitz [Großstorkwitz, two miles north of Pegau], while the left is at Carsdorf [one mile north of Pegau]. By six o'clock, both columns are to have crossed the Floßgraben and proceed with the right towards Werben, while the left, directly towards Sittel, or towards Weißenfels, while the movement of the left column across the Floßgraben is to be completed half an hour before the right.
>
> The corps under lieutenant generals Berg and Yorck, also at five o'clock in the morning, are to follow both columns under General Blücher, that is, the corps under General Berg on the road to Storkwitz, and General Yorck's on the road from Audigast to Pegau. The heavy artillery assigned to Blücher's corps is to be at the head of its columns, and General Blücher is to issue further orders for it.

13 Plotho, I, 97.
14 Odeleben, I, 47.

Lieutenant General Wintzingerode is to leave three battalions and one light artillery company to cover the Zwenkau defile. The two Cossack regiments are to remain in their present locations, and if they are pressed, then they are to slowly withdraw in the direction of Zwenkau. Lieutenant General Wintzingerode is to instruct the foremost of these battalions to completely demolish all the crossings over the watercourses located between Zwenkau and Leipzig, for which they are to liaise with Lieutenant General Kleist. The remainder of Lieutenant General Winzingerode's corps is to assemble in accordance with the issued order-of-battle, at six o'clock in the morning, at

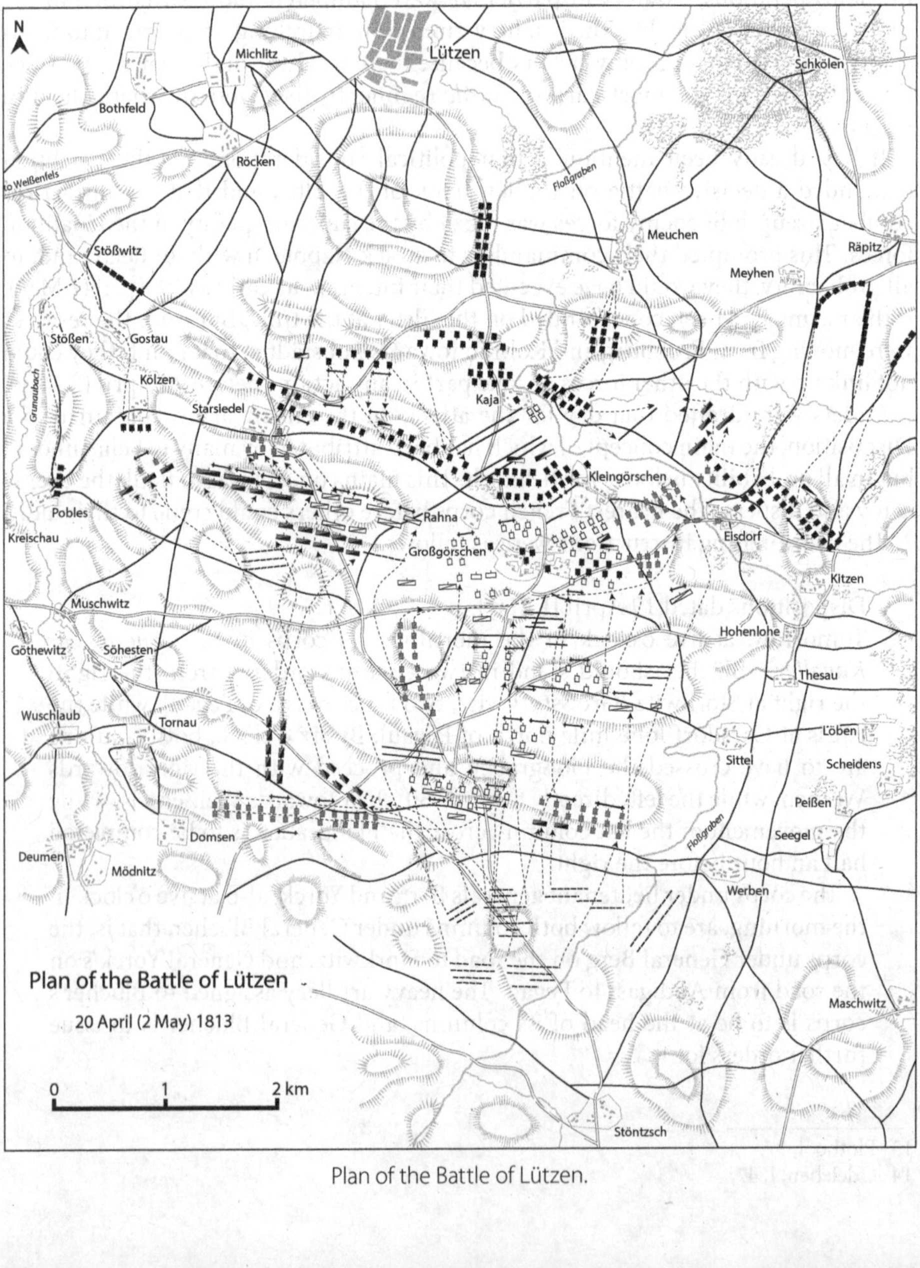

Plan of the Battle of Lützen.

Werben, from where they are to march as protection, level with the corps under General Blücher. On this same wing, Colonel Orlov is to extend his screen-force to the Floßgraben and monitor the road to Weißenfels. Lieutenant General Wintzingerode is in command of the entire Prussian reserve cavalry and is to order his heavy artillery companies to join both columns under General Blücher at Werben.

The Main Army should already be at Pegau and Storkwitz by seven o'clock in the morning, and having occupied the defiles at Stöntzsch, Carsdorf, Werben and Storkwitz with infantry and light cavalry, is to form the reserve of the Coalition Army.

Upon notification from the Commander-in-Chief, *General der Kavallerie* Blücher is to advance with his first line, and extending to the left, is to attempt to join his left flank as quickly as possible to the stream [Grunaubach] flowing from Grossgrimma [just east of Hohenmölsen] to Dehlitz [on the Saale, near Rippach].

The second line and the reserve are immediately to follow all the movements of the first line, in a direction parallel to it, in order to support it, but are to stay out of the enemy line of fire.

General Blücher is immediately to dispatch part of his cavalry and horse artillery to his left flank in order to occupy the opposite bank of the stream and the high ground; the right flank should be drawn back as far as possible and adjoin the Floßgraben. We shall advance in this direction between the rivers, namely between the Rippach and the Floßgraben. If the enemy looks to envelope our right flank, then the artillery is to open fire; the infantry are to proceed directly behind them in battalion columns; the cavalry are to be in support. If the enemy appears in considerable strength, then the reserve cavalry and horse artillery are quickly to move forward. The artillery are to disrupt them with canister fire, whereupon the cavalry are to drive them back.

The corps under General Kleist is not to go into action until they hear heavy fire from us, or if the enemy facing them leaves and begins to move towards us. In the event that overwhelming enemy forces begin to press them, they are to withdraw to Wurzen, protecting the road to Dresden as much as possible, on which they are to destroy all the bridges and are to do the same on the road to Eilenburg, maintaining communications with us via the Cossacks.

The corps under General-of-Infantry Miloradovich is to move towards Zeitz, and if the enemy should advance in significant strength from Weißenfels towards our extended left flank, then the Main Army is to advance to engage them, extending from Stöntzsch to the left in order to envelope their right flank. The cuirassier divisions and horse artillery, taking advantage of the open terrain, may operate to advantage.

The main objective of all manoeuvres is to envelope the enemy right flank, and therefore the formations are to keep to the left side, taking the village of Stöntzsch as the pivot point until further notice. When crossing open ground, skirmishers are to engage in firefights as little as possible, and their supporting columns are to advance with drums beating. The cavalry are to exploit every disorder in the enemy lines.

One officer from each brigade of the Coalition Forcer is to be appointed as an orderly to the Commander-in-Chief, who will be with the reserve of the first line.

In the event of a retreat, against all expectation, it is to be directed towards Altenburg and Frohburg, which is why it is proposed to the gentlemen corps commanders to take care to make themselves familiar with the roads leading there. The entire trains are to leave for Borna and proceed from there, in the event of a retreat, via Rochlitz, to Dresden. The wounded and prisoners are to be directed to Frohburg.

General-of-Cavalry Count Wittgenstein.[15]

This disposition, which is rather lengthy and shows a desire to direct formation commanders for all eventualities (which is impossible), in spite of all this, is vague and gave rise to misunderstandings. In addition, as far as can be judged from statements by eyewitnesses, the disposition was not sent to the corps in a timely manner, and therefore could not be executed at the indicated times. According to Gneisenau: 'the concept of operations was good; the execution bad. They lingered too long on formalities and troop deployments instead of attacking the surprised enemy in column.'[16]

The number of troops in the Coalition Army, on 20 April (2 May), on the day of the battle of Lützen, reached some 73,000 men, including about 50,000 infantry, 17,000 regular and irregular cavalry and 6,000 artillerymen, with 400 guns. There were some 40,000 Russian troops, while the Prussians had some 33,000 men.[17] In addition, the following had been detached:

1. Miloradovich's corps, 11,500 men towards Zeitz.
2. Kleist's detachment, 6,000 men towards Leipzig.
3. Three battalions and one light artillery battery with one Cossack regiment, numbering 1,000 men, in order to secure the crossings at Zwenkau.
4. Major General Prince Gorchakov's detachment [Mikhail Alekseevich Gorchakov], numbering around 2,000 men sent to the crossings over the Floßgraben at Stöntzsch and Werben.

15 The Disposition, signed by Count Wittgenstein, is in the Log of Incoming Documents, 1813, No. 728 (archive of the M.T.D. No. 29,182).

16 '*die Idee zur Schlacht war gut; die Anlage schlecht. Man hielt sich mit Förmlichkeiten und Truppen-entwickelungen zu lange auf, statt mit Colonnen auf den überraschten Feind loszugehen.*' Gneisenau's letter to Graf Münster, dated 29 May 1813, new style.

17 Almost all military historians repeat the calculation of troops participating in the battle of Lützen given by Plotho. Although this is an approximate estimate, it is nevertheless quite consistent with the combat reports on the state of the troops in April 1813 and can be accepted almost without change, with the exception of the number of infantry under Wintzingerode (Prinz Eugen von Württemberg's II Corps), which Plotho shows as 5,700 men, while in the Prince's own diary it states that his corps, before the battle of Lützen, was strengthened to 10,800 men, of whom 8,700 men were committed to action. For the composition of the Russo-Prussian army at the battle of Lützen, see Appendix XIV at the end of this chapter.

The disposition for 20 April (2 May) was only issued from Count Wittgenstein's headquarters at around midnight. Blücher's force, assigned to open the battle in the front line, were near Rötha, and having received the disposition at about one o'clock in the morning, they could not have moved out before two o'clock in the morning. Thus, the 24,000 strong corps, moving at night, from Rötha to Pegau and Storkwitz, over a distance of more than 15 *verstas*, was supposed to arrive at these locations by five o'clock in the morning and, in all likelihood, would have been late if Blücher, who knew in advance about the imminent move, had not set off before receiving the disposition.[18]

Yorck's force moved along the road from Zwenkau to Audigast in order to reach Pegau and cross the Elster there behind Blücher's force; but before reaching Audigast, they bumped into Blücher's right hand column, marching towards Döhlen ([two miles] east of Storkwitz), to cross at this location, while the left hand column was heading for Pegau. *Oberst* Dolffs [Florenz Ludwig von Bockum genannt Dolffs], immediately turned to the left towards Pegau with a reserve cavalry brigade; Yorck's corps followed them there; while Blücher's entire force moved behind Yorck, except for the *Niederschlesischen Brigade*, which crossed the Elster at Storkwitz, where Berg's corps also crossed behind them.

Emperor Alexander and the King of Prussia left Borna at two o'clock in the morning and arrived at Pegau at half past five, where they were waiting for the leading elements of the Coalition columns to arrive; yet as time passed, none arrived. Eventually, at about seven o'clock, Dolffs' brigade and Yorck's corps emerged, followed by other troops (*Oberschlesischen Brigade* and *Brandenburgischen Brigade*). The columns took until ten o'clock in the morning to pass by the Sovereigns. The Prussian volunteers, attached to regular units, were distinguished by their extraordinary enthusiasm. After that, having crossed the Floßgraben, at Stöntzsch and Werben, the Coalition forces advanced their left flank, leaving the right in place, and formed up in battle order between the Floßgraben and Rennbach (Grunaubach), behind the high ground separating them from the enemy.[19] Blücher's force formed the front line; Berg's corps were on the right wing of the second line, while Yorck's were on the left. Dollfs' reserve cavalry had been pushed forwards, to the left of Blücher, towards Starsiedel; Wintzingerode's corps were further back, to the right of the village of Domsen. The Russian reserves, grenadiers, Lifeguard and cuirassiers, were behind the second line. The infantry were formed up in attack column; strong batteries had been placed ahead of the front line. The deployment of the force into battle order was completed by 11 o'clock in the morning, therefore, four hours later than intended according to the disposition. The troops were given about an hour's pause, while, in the meantime, a survey was made of the area between Weißenfels and Lützen, and from Lützen to Leipzig.[20]

The ground on which the Coalition intended to fight Napoleon was already a place of legend from the final victory and heroic death of Gustavus Adolphus [in 1632]. It is an undulating plain, bounded on the north-east by the Floßgraben channel,

18 Droysen, *Yorck's Leben*, II, 204.
19 See Map No. 6, Plan of the Battle of Lützen, 20 April (2 May).
20 Plotho, I, 109 & 111-112. Beitzke, I, 366.

which proceeds from the Elster above Pegau and connects this river with the Saale. The Floßgraben, which was used for rafting timber, is rather narrow, but due to the steepness of its tree-lined banks, it is an obstacle to the free movement of cavalry and artillery as well as obstructing line of sight. The villages lying in the vicinity of Lützen may provide defensive advantages, but in general the area is quite open and suitable for cavalry operations.

During the survey, thick clouds of dust were seen rising along the road from Lützen to Leipzig, from which the movement of the French towards this city was revealed, and from where a cannonade thundered from nine o'clock. Around the village of Großgörschen, close to the positions of the Coalition Army, a large bivouac was visible. This circumstance astonished the Coalition commanders, who had not expected to find the enemy there. Instead of an immediate attack at full strength, Count Wittgenstein, assuming the force stationed at Großgörschen was the strong vanguard of the French army, located, in his opinion, at Lützen, decided firstly to eject the supposed vanguard from the villages they occupied, and then to lead a general attack.[21]

While the Coalition was preparing to attack the French army, Napoleon, unaware of this and not having accurate intelligence on their locations, continued to advance towards Leipzig. General Lauriston, approaching Lindenau, at ten o'clock in the morning, began a powerful artillery exchange with Kleist's force; Macdonald's corps had also set out towards Leipzig from Markranstädt; Napoleon himself, having heard the thunder of guns from Lauriston's corps, proceeded at some distance behind Macdonald's force, together with the *Garde* and the *quartier-général*; Ney's corps had been left at the villages occupied by them overnight, in order to act as the right flank-guard for the corps under Marmont, Bertrand and Oudinot, of which the first had already passed Poserna, the second was moving from Stößen towards Poserna, while the third was on the march from Naumburg towards Weißenfels.[22] Overall, Napoleon's forces were stretched out over 40 *verstas*, and had the Coalition Army, concentrated and completely battle-ready, assaulted Ney with all their infantry, detaching their numerous cavalry to delay the other enemy corps, then the French army, divided into two isolated elements, would have been placed in a very dangerous situation.

It was already around 11 o'clock. Napoleon was passing the monument to Gustavus Adolphus [one mile north-east of Lützen]. Ney was with his retinue, wanting to familiarise himself with the Leipzig area.[23] The cannonade and skirmishing at Lindenau was intensifying. Napoleon watched the course of the battle himself through a large telescope and could see crowds of residents watching from the rooftops. All his attention was turned to the fighting that was in full flow around Leipzig. Suddenly, the thunder of guns was heard from the direction of Ney's force. Napoleon quickly turned towards the marshal, but seeing that he was already galloping back to his troops, he began to monitor the cannonade at the Görschens. A few minutes

21 Plotho, I, 113. Beitzke, I, 367.

22 Fain, *Manuscrit de 1813*, I, 346-347.

23 As reported by Fain (I, 348) and Norvins (*Portefeuille de 1813*, I, 271), but according to Odeleben, Ney remained in the village of Kaja (I, 50).

were enough to assess the situation on both sides and take measures to repulse the unexpected attack: the Viceroy received orders to turn back with Macdonald's corps and march to the sound of the guns in order to support Ney on his left flank; the corps under Marmont were ordered to speed up their march towards Starsiedel and form the right wing of the general deployment; General Bertrand was to move to the right and outflank the Coalition force; the *Garde* immediately turned back towards Lützen, in order to form the reserve behind Ney's corps, which was in the centre of the fighting position, defending the villages of Kaja, Rahna, Großgörschen and Kleingörschen, which constituted the vital ground at Lützen. The commander of the *Artillerie de la Garde* was instructed to combine 80 guns into a massed battery. 'It is a battle as in Egypt' said Napoleon. 'We have no cavalry, but the French infantry and artillery will have to suffice.'[24] He quickly went to the place of battle himself with the *Cavalerie de la Garde*. On the way, he encountered crowds of wounded men leaving or being carried away from the battlefield. These victims, mostly conscripts, being under fire for the first time had not yet even had time to get acquainted with the dangerous trade to which they had been compelled to commit themselves, yet, in spite of this, almost none of them passed Napoleon without the customary greeting: *Vive l'empereur*! Even those who had lost limbs, half-dead from pain and loss of blood, having gathered their last strength, greeted their emperor with formal cheers. Some of them were already doomed to death, but even those, along with their comrades, expressed admiration and loyalty to Napoleon.[25] This state of mind of the young soldiers alone could pull the French army out of the dangerous situation in which it had been placed by the unexpected attack from the Russo-Prussian force.

The Coalition might yet exploit the advantages on their side. The French corps under Marmont, Bertrand and Macdonald would not arrive on the battlefield and be formed up for combat before two or three o'clock in the afternoon, and prior to their arrival Napoleon had no more than 50,000 men (35,000 in Ney's corps and 15,000 in the *Garde*). Instead of crushing the enemy with superior numbers, Count Wittgenstein ordered the *Niederschlesischen Brigade* under *Oberst* von Klüx [Joseph Friedrich Karl von Klüx] to capture the village of Großgörschen, while the reserve cavalry under *Oberst* Dolffs, was to move left towards Rahna, with the mission of disordering the enemy as they withdrew from Großgörschen and Kleingörshen towards Kaja through horse artillery fire, and to complete their defeat with cavalry charges.

At around noon, Emperor Alexander and the King of Prussia joined the troops, who had already had time to rest and recover. Blücher, riding up to Count Wittgenstein, saluted with his sabre and asked permission to begin the action. '*Mit Gottes Hülfe*!' (With the aid of God!) replied the count. Klüx's force, consisting of six battalions, six squadrons and four batteries, including one Russian heavy artillery company, moved towards Großgörschen, while Dolffs moved towards Rahna with 23 squadrons and three horse artillery batteries. Klüx's artillery, numbering 36 guns, having approached the enemy

24 '*C'est une bataille d'Egypte; nous n'avons pas de cavalerie, mais une infanterie française avec de l'artillerie doit savoir se suffire*.' Norvins, I, 274. In Fain, Napoleon's words are phrased somewhat differently (I, 349).

25 Odeleben, I, 50-51.

to a range of 800 paces, opened fire on the village of Großgörschen and on bivouacs set up in the area. The enemy, not expecting an attack, were thrown into chaos; but quickly recovered. General Souham, who was in command of *3e Corps* at the beginning of the battle, in Ney's absence, advanced two batteries to his left (east) of the village and opened a cannonade on the advancing troops, but the Coalition artillery knocked out three French guns and silenced the rest. Thereafter, Klüx's infantry attacked the village and drove the French from it; but as *Oberst* Dolffs dashed towards the retreating troops with the reserve cavalry brigade, he was engaged by enemy guns firing canister and was forced to fall back. Having reinforced his division with fresh troops from the divisions under Brenier and Ricard, Souham attempted to recapture Großgörschen. A bitter struggle ensued, which forced Blücher to commit Zieten's *Oberschlesischen Brigade* [Hans Ernst Karl von Zieten] to action, consisting of seven battalions, six squadrons and six batteries, including two Russian heavy artillery companies. Zieten's force moved to the right of Klüx's brigade, bypassing Großgörschen, towards Kleingörschen, and broke into this village at the same time as Klüx was assaulting Rahna. Bitter fighting ensued in these villages and between them, on terrain intersected by ditches. Every arm of service took part: the infantry resorted to bayonets several times; the cavalry, charging by squadron, crashed into disordered units; artillery was dragged up as much as the limited space between the villages allowed. French conscripts and Prussian volunteers, the flower of nations renowned for their military exploits, covered themselves with glory in the combat between themselves. In the heat of the fierce contest, the villages caught fire: first Großgörschen, then Kleingörschen and Rahna, and finally Kaja. Ney brought up new reinforcements himself, which gave his troops the opportunity to re-take the greater part of the villages of Kleingörschen and Rahna; but the French triumph was short-lived. Blücher brought up Röder's *Brandenburgischen Brigade* [Friedrich Erhard Leopold von Röder] in support of the advancing Prussian columns, which, engaging the French at Kleingörschen and Eisdorf, ejected them and drove them back towards Kaja in complete disarray.[26] Blücher, Scharnhorst and other Prussian generals, drawing their sabres, personally participated in close-quarter combat.[27] While the battle at Kleingörschen and Rahna was in full swing, the reserve brigade under Dolffs had approached the village of Starsiedel, occupied by part of Girard's French division; in order to drive away the Prussian cavalry, three battalions and several squadrons had been sent from there to engage them. Noticing the enemy movement, Prinz Wilhelm von Preußen charged at the nearest battalion with the *Brandenburgisches Kürassier-Regiment*, overran them and drove the French back into Starsiedel. The success of the cuirassiers clearly indicated the important outcome an attack by the numerous Russo-Prussian cavalry in the sector between Rahna and Starsiedel could have had at that moment. But the Coalition commanders did not

26 Vaudoncourt, 76.

27 According to Clausewitz: In the main, Scharnhorst directed the fighting on the right wing, against the three villages. He had dashed into the enemy several times at the head of the cavalry and infantry with sabre drawn, cheering on the men and shouting: Long live the king! (*Scharnhorst führte hauptsächlich das Gefecht auf dem rechten Flügel, gegen die drei Dörfer. Er war mehrere Male mit gezogenem Säbel and der Spitze der Kavallerie un Infanterie in den Feind gedrungen, er feuerte die Leute an und rief: es lebe der König!*). *Beitrage zu einer künftigen Biographie Friedrich Wilhelms III vom Gen. Lieut. v. Minutoli*, 136.

exploit their advantages at the beginning of the battle, and, in the meantime, the enemy were gradually being strengthened with reinforcements; the superiority in numbers had shifted to their side. Count Wittgenstein could have been blamed for such an irresponsible loss of time, had he commanded his forces independently. But this was not the case, indeed, on the contrary, the Coalition Monarchs sometimes issued orders that contradicted the Commander-in-Chief's own. They were not infrequently exposed to obvious danger together with their entire, numerous retinues, which, worrying for the Coalition generals, distracted their attention and even prevented them from following the course of the battle:[28]

At two o'clock in the afternoon, the lead units of Marmont's *6e Corps* appeared on the battlefield near Starsiedel.[29] Napoleon arrived at Kaja almost at the same time: the Prussian troops were just breaking into this village. An eyewitness claimed, 'Never before had I noticed such obvious consternation on Napoleon's face.'[30] It was vital for him to hold on to this location at all costs. General Mouton dashed forwards with Ricard's division to engage Röder's elite force, drove them out of Kaja and led an attack on Rahna and Kleingörschen. The bitter fighting continued here for several hours. The villages continued to change hands. General Girard, although seriously wounded, did not leave the battlefield. 'The time has come' he said, 'when every Frenchman must triumph or perish.'[31]

For our part, as soon as news had been received of the appearance of the enemy from the direction of Weißenfels, Count Wittgenstein ordered Wintzingerode's cavalry to move forward, to the left of Dolffs' brigade, facing Starsiedel. Emperor Alexander, approaching Major General Nikitin, ordered him to advance more than 40 horse artillery pieces, which were in Wintzingerode's and Berg's corps, and open fire.[32] 'I shall be watching the actions of your artillery myself,' said the Tsar. As soon as our cavalry had formed up on the left wing of the Prussian troops, General Nikitin engaged the enemy with fire from his guns. The successful operations by his artillery disordered the French: taking advantage of this, Major General Panchulidzev 1st [Ivan Davydovich Panchulidzev] attacked them with the Novorussia Dragoons and Chernigov Mounted Jägers and captured two guns.[33]

28 Wolzogen, 170. 'Emperor Alexander repeatedly exposed himself to cannon fire, and when riding to the left wing he was in serious danger' (*Kaiser Alexander setzte sich mehrmals dem Kanonenfeuer aus und bei einem Ritt nach dem linken Flügel zu kam er in ernstliche Gefahr*), Beitzke, I, 382.

29 Vaudoncourt, 77.

30 Odeleben, I, 53.

31 Vaudoncourt, 77.

32 Major General Nikitin's 7th Horse Artillery Company; Colonel Shusherin's 8th Horse Artillery Company; Colonel Kozen's Lifeguard Horse Artillery; several guns from Lieutenant General Prince Iashvili's 1st Horse Artillery Company and Colonel Härbel's 3rd Horse Artillery Company (extracted from General Nikitin's notes, archive of the M.T.D. No. 47,353, notebook 37).

33 This attack is shown on the battle plan for Lützen, 20 April [2 May], 1813, signed by Major General Harting (archive of the M.T.D. No. 16,737). In the Schedule of Forces, dated 13 [25] April, signed by Adjutant General Prince Volkonsky, Panchulidzev's brigade is shown in Wintzingerode's corps. In Plotho, they are erroneously placed in Miloradovich's corps, Plotho, I, *Beilagen*, 98. In General Wintzingerode's dispatches, it states that one gun was captured by the Chernigov Mounted Jägers, while the other was taken by the *Brandenburgisches Kürassier-Regiment*.

Count Wittgenstein ordered Yorck to reinforce our left wing artillery with six Prussian heavy guns, and shortly thereafter detached Berg's corps to the left, but then, having received news of the repulse of the enemy at this location, cancelled his orders. Thus, instead of the anticipated decisive offensive, we limited ourselves to holding back the French forces who were enveloping our position on our left flank. At about four o'clock in the afternoon, Count Wittgenstein, wishing to drive the enemy out of the villages for good, sent Yorck's entire corps to assist Blücher. The valiant Horn [Heinrich Wilhelm von Horn], at the head of his adoring soldiers, took possession of Rahna and Kaja in combat. Soon afterwards, Berg's force was also sent into action, but their arrival on the right flank of Yorck's corps had been delayed by the futile march in the opposite direction.[34]

At about five o'clock in the afternoon, Bertrand came to the aid of the French from one direction with Morand's division, while the Viceroy arrived from another with Macdonald's corps: the former crossed the Grunaubach and began to envelope Wintzingerode's cavalry from their left, while the latter moved into the village of Eisdorf. At this decisive moment, Napoleon, seeing the urgent need to shore up his centre, which was in danger of being pierced by Yorck's and Berg's forces, committed all his reserves: 16 battalions of the *Jeune Garde* moved up to storm Kaja; in order to prepare for success, General Drouot [Antoine Drouot] was ordered to push 80 guns of the *Garde* forward (60 guns, according to other sources), under escort from six battalions of the *Vieille Garde*; they were followed by cavalry.[35]

On our part, measures were taken to hold the enemy troops enveloping the flanks of the Coalition Army: to that end, Prince Golitsyn [Dmitry Vladimirovich Golitsyn], with the Lifeguard light cavalry and two cuirassier divisions, moved to the left towards the Grunaubach, while Prinz Eugen von Württemberg went to assist Blücher.[36] At five o'clock, Macdonald's corps, under the personal command of the Viceroy, deployed on the high ground, with their right flank facing Eisdorf, and their left facing Kitzen; the thunder of 60 guns formed up in front of his lines announced the arrival of the French. Meanwhile, the Prinz von Württemberg supported the Prussian troops at Rahna with the 4th Jägers and with three regiments, under the command of Prince Shakhovskoy, at Kleingörschen.[37] The enemy was driven back towards Kaja once more, but the Coalition had suffered a huge loss; Blücher himself and his chief of staff, Scharnhorst, had been wounded. General Yorck took command of both Prussian corps, which continued to fight stubbornly, but being attacked by Ney's force, supported by Bonet's division from *6e Corps*, could barely hold on in the villages they occupied and in the houses on the edge of Kaja. Their attempts to take Starsiedel were unsuccessful: Compans' division from *6e Corps* blocked them frontally, while Morand's division from *4e Corps*, moved around their left flank and struck the Coalition forces with enfilading fire from their artillery. Meanwhile, on the right

34 Droysen, *Yorck's Leben*, II, 208.
35 Vaudoncourt, 77. According to this work, Napoleon formed his *Garde* up to attack the village of Kaja at about four o'clock in the afternoon.
36 Dispatches on the battle of Lützen. Prinz Eugen von Württemberg's diary, archive of the M.T.D. No. 47,344.
37 Chernigov Infantry, Murom Infantry and Reval Infantry regiments.

wing of our army, Prinz Eugen von Württemberg, with the 4th Division, turned towards Eisdorf in order to outflank the enemy, but upon becoming convinced of the superior numbers of French troops advancing towards this location, he occupied the village with the 20th Jägers and placed the Kremenchug Infantry and Volhynia Infantry behind them, under the command of comte Saint-Priest [Ehmmanuil Frantsevich Sen-Pri or Guillaume-Emmanuel Guignard de Saint-Priest]. The enemy attacked Eisdorf and ejected our jägers from there; but the generals comte Saint-Priest and Pyshnitsky [Dmitry Ilyich Pyshnitsky], bypassing the village to the right and left with the Volhynia Infantry and Kremenchug Infantry, forced the French to abandon it; Pyshnitsky was wounded here. The Prinz von Württemberg placed a light artillery company under Lieutenant Colonel Baikov, who arrived with them on the banks of the Floßgraben, to the right of the village in order to support the infantry. The action of these guns on the dense enemy masses was highly effective; but most of our gunners were quickly put out of action by bullets from French marksmen and the battery was forced to retreat. The enemy took possession of the village once more and drove the 20th Jägers back, who had been sent to assist the force under comte Saint-Priest.[38]

Count Wittgenstein, aware of the concentration of enemy masses at Eisdorf, ordered General Konovnitsyn [Pëtr Petrovich Konovnitsyn] to go there with the Grenadier Corps, supported by 50 guns from the reserve. But no sooner had the hero of Smolensk and Borodino managed to join the battle, than he was seriously wounded and forced to surrender command of the grenadiers to Major General Tsvilenev [Alexander Ivanovich Tsvilenev]. The Prinz von Württemberg was in the greatest danger; Colonel Saint-Priest [Lyudvig Frantsevich Sen-Pri or Emmanuel Louis Marie Guignard de Saint-Priest], who was with him (brother of the adjutant general) and four officers were wounded. Enemy batteries placed on the right bank of the Floßgraben, upstream of Eisdorf, struck our columns with enfilade fire. Under the thunder of these guns, the French seized Eisdorf and occupied Kitzen; but were held at the exits from the villages. Fressinet's division, having crossed the Floßgraben, positioned itself in front of Eisdorf, held by the men of Charpentier's division; while Gérard's division was forwards of Kitzen.[39]

At about seven o'clock in the afternoon, the Coalition, having completely abandoned the offensive (having been enveloped by the enemy army), were in a defensive position, facing Starsiedel on one side, and Eisdorf on the other, restricted to a cannonade, which, without resolving the matter, was unfavourable for our numerous cavalry, which remained inactive for several hours under enemy fire. According to Wintzingerode, the reason for this was the nature of the ground, covered with scrub and preventing the cavalry from being brought into action; eventually, just after half past seven, at his request, the Lifeguard Finland Regiment were sent to assist him: from this we can conclude that the Coalition had neither coordination nor liaison in the operations by the various

38 Prinz Eugen von Württemberg's diary.

39 Prinz Eugen von Württemberg's diary. Vaudoncourt wrote that the Prinz von Württemberg had occupied Kitzen, and that the Coalition fought very stubbornly at Eisdorf, and at Kitzen in particular (78-79).

branches of the army. In the centre, the Russo-Prussian force, weakened from lengthy combat, were defending their hold on the villages with difficulty. Almost all of our reserves had already been committed to battle, and even the Lifeguard infantry were under fire from enemy artillery.[40] On the other hand, the French army, having increased to some 100,000 men over the course of the battle, had a significant number of fresh troops in their ranks.[41] Napoleon had taken note of the exhaustion of the Coalition forces and took advantage of it, in his usual way, using his reserves to deliver the deciding blows. At seven o'clock, the Coalition, who had penetrated as far as Kaja, were brought under savage fire from 80 guns of the *Garde* and an attack was made on Kaja by 16 battalions of the *Jeune Garde*, supported by the *Vieille Garde* and cavalry.[42] Some of the enemy artillery were turned against the cavalry under Wintzingerode and Prince Golitsyn; others were assigned to enfilade the Coalition infantry occupying the villages. Caught in a crossfire, the Russo-Prussian troops were forced to retreat from the conflagrations in Kaja, Rahna and Kleingörshen initiated by the French, and littered with countless corpses and wounded. But all the enemy efforts to retake Großgörschen were crushed by the iron steadfastness of the Russo-Prussian soldiers.[43] The Coalition army clung on to the positions taken at the beginning of the battle: the right wing stood on the left bank of the Floßgraben, opposite Thesau and Hohenlohe, the centre, at Großgörschen; the left wing was close to Muschwitz.[44] The cannonade continued until it was completely dark. On the French side, the left wing was stationed between the Floßgraben and Mühlgraben, forwards of Kitzen; the centre extended from Eisdorf, through Kleingörschen, towards Rahna; the right wing from Rahna to Pobles.[45] Consequently, instead of outflanking the surprised French army, the Coalition were themselves enveloped on both flanks.

Night had fallen, illuminated by flames from the burning villages of Eisdorf, the Görschens, Rahna, Kaja and Starsiedel. In place of the thunder of guns, there was a deep silence, broken only by the groans of the wounded. One of the French columns near Rahna stumbled upon Steinmetz's Prussian brigade [Karl Friedrich Franciscus von Steinmetz] in the darkness: the infantry, having piled their muskets, were resting; the cavalry were already preparing fodder for their

40 Plotho, I, 117.

41 Namely: 15,000 in the *Garde*; 35,000 in Ney's *3e Corps*; 25,000 in Marmont's *6e Corps*; 8,000 in Morand's division from *4e Corps*; 20,000 in Macdonald's *5e Corps*; for a total of 103,000 men.

42 '*La garde au feu!*' Such was the laconic order given by Napoleon.

43 Vaudoncourt, 79. Thiers, *Histoire du Consulat et de l'Empire*, XV, *Edit. de Brux*. 543-545. Beitzke, I, 375-376.

44 Final locations of the Coalition at the Battle of Lützen: the cavalry of Yorck's corps on the right flank at the Floßgraben, in the direction of Sittel, facing Hohenlohe; the Prinz von Württemberg's corps and 2nd Grenadier Division opposite Eisdorf; Berg's corps to the right of Großgörschen; 1st Grenadier Division at Großgörschen; Yorck's corps to the left of Großgörschen; Blücher's corps facing Rahna, the Prussian reserve cavalry to the left of Rahna; the two cuirassier divisions to the left and a little behind the Prussian reserve cavalry; Wintzingerode's cavalry facing Starsiedel; Knorring's cavalry brigade and the Lifeguard Finland Regiment facing Kölzen; the Lifeguard light cavalry division at [Hohen]mölsen (Plan of the battle of Lützen, archive of the M.T.D. No. 16,737).

45 Vaudoncourt, 79.

horses. The unexpected attack by the enemy threw the troops into chaos; nevertheless, they soon recovered and repulsed the attack. Blücher, losing his patience at the boldness of the French, decided to retaliate with a night attack, and asking Count Wittgenstein for consent, instructed *Oberst* Dolffs to attack the enemy with 11 squadrons (nine, according to other sources). Heading to the left of Rahna, he had to cross the road from Sössen to Großgörschen in perfect darkness, which runs through deep cuttings in places, and many of his riders were very badly injured. In spite of this, however, the Prussian cavalry galloped between battalions of the *Vieille Garde*, who barely had time to form square. Napoleon was no more than 200 paces from these squares at the time; his entire retinue scattered; no one could find him, and for several minutes many men were asking each other: where is the emperor? Orders were given to bring up guns and to fire canister; eventually, the French recovered. The Prussian cavalry were forced to retreat in haste and were dispersed to the point that some elements only rejoined their regiments beyond the Elbe. The attack achieved no decisive results, and even, on the contrary, disordered the participating Prussian regiments. But having said that, its moral influence was extraordinary: the French army withdrew somewhat; the infantry spent the whole night in square and some of the troops remained under arms, in constant expectation of a new attack.[46] Napoleon himself left for Lützen at 11 o'clock.[47] The Coalition Monarchs also left the battlefield. In the dark of night, escorted by a *Feldjäger* [Crown Courier] who showed them the way with the help of a lantern, they set off through Stöntzsch and Pegau to the town of Groitzsch, where they settled down for the night, in anticipation of a renewed battle.[48]

Meanwhile, Count Wittgenstein had called a meeting of his senior formation commanders before nine o'clock in the evening. The commanders gathered on the high ground in front of the village of Werben, to decide the question – was it better to resume the battle, or withdraw? Count Wittgenstein, as far as can be judged from his opening words, wanted to fight on. Yet many factors made him doubt the success of a battle. It was known that Bülow had driven the enemy out of Halle, but, having said that, Kleist, having been forced to abandon Lindenau and Leipzig, had retreated to Wurzen, while Lauriston had occupied Leipzig as early as three o'clock in the afternoon, which exposed the Coalition to being enveloped on their right flank and losing their line of communications to the Elbe. Moreover, the Russo-Prussian army was already being gripped from both flanks by enemy forces on the battlefield itself. Napoleon, as was known, hoped to add about 40,000 men to his army and maintained a strong reserve, while the Coalition, in contrast, could bring into action no more than 25,000 fresh troops, namely: Miloradovich's 11,500 men; 5,600 Lifeguard infantry; around 2,000 grenadiers and 6,000 cavalrymen. It was also asserted that the Russian artillery had insufficient ammunition for another battle, due to the considerable distance that the parks were lagging behind the army, but

46 Odeleben, I, 58-59. Beitzke, I, 380-381. Thiers wrote that the *37e Ligne* were scattered, and that the soldiers were firing at each other in the darkness. *Histoire du Consulat et de l'Empire*, XV, 546-547.

47 Odeleben, I, 59.

48 Beitzke, I, 382.

this statement was later refuted.[49] Count Wittgenstein, unwilling to be held accountable for any course of action he proposed, immediately went to the headquarters of the Coalition Monarchs, which was in Groitzsch. After explaining all the factors to Emperor Alexander in outline, Wittgenstein asked the Tsar's permission to withdraw towards the Elbe. But it was still necessary to secure the agreement of the Prussian King, which was not easy. Having undertaken a war that, if successful, would restore Prussia to greatness, yet if unsuccessful, risked the complete extinction of the state's independence, Friedrich Wilhelm would have been most fearful for the occupation of Prussian provinces by Napoleon's forces. Emperor Alexander went to the King personally, and having given orders for him to be roused, explained the situation. In persuading His ally and friend of the need to withdraw behind the Elbe, the gentlemanly Alexander could not hide the emotional struggle that tormented him. The King, visibly distressed, responded with some vehemence: 'I already know that if we start to retreat, we will not stop at the Elbe, but will go beyond the Vistula, and I shall have to return to Memel once more.' Emperor Alexander vainly exhausted the argument for the advantage of a retreat; the King did not change his mind, and after the departure of the Tsar, jumping out of bed, he went to the window and remarked sadly: 'Just like at Auerstedt!' The next morning, he was most upset and did not calm down until after meeting the wounded Scharnhorst in Altenburg. Apparently, Scharnhorst dispelled the King's doubts and convinced him of the need for unshakeable unity with Emperor Alexander.[50]

Overall, the battle of Lützen cost the French some 15,000 men killed or wounded. Among those killed were the *Chef d'État-major* [chief-of-staff] of *3e Corps, Général de brigade* Gouré [Louis Anne Marie Gouré de Villemontée], and *Général de brigade* Grillot [Remy Grillot]; among the wounded were *généreaux de division* Girard and Brenier, and *généreaux de brigade* Chemineau [Jean Chemineau] and Guillo [*sic*]. The Coalition captured some 800 men and took five guns in combat. The casualties on our side were also significant. According to official sources, the Prussian force lost some 8,000 men overall, while the Russians lost some 2,000 men; yet taking into account that II Corps, according to statements from the Prinz von Württemberg himself, lost 87 officers and 1,637 other ranks out of the 8,700 men who were in action, we estimate that the losses of the Coalition forces were only slightly fewer than those of the enemy. There were many Prussian volunteers among the dead and wounded who had covered themselves in glory in this battle, as well as officers of all military branches: in Röder's brigade 74 officers were lost from a total of 159; three officers were killed in Carnal's *Füsilier* battalion and all the others were wounded. Prinz Leopold von Hessen-Homburg [Leopold Victor Friedrich von Hessen-Homburg]

49 *Lebensbilder aus dem Befreiungskriege*, second edition, II, 321. Gneisenau wrote that the Chief of Artillery, Prince Iashvili, had announced a shortage of artillery ammunition. But neither he (who did not hold this appointment at that time), nor General Yermolov, who was the Chief of Artillery for the Russian contingent at that time, made any such announcement. Neither was information on an insufficient quantity of ammunition remaining with the troops officially presented to the Tsar.

50 Fascinating details about this meeting between the Coalition Monarchs are contained in the work: *Erinnerungen aus meinem Leben, von Grafen Henckel v. Donnersmark*, Zerbst, 1846, 185-187.

was killed during the assault on Großgörschen, where a monument was later erected to him. Blücher was wounded, rather lightly in the arm, Scharnhorst died upon reaching Prague on the way to Vienna, where he had been sent after the battle of Lützen, on behalf of King Friedrich Wilhelm, Lieutenant General Konovnitsyn, Major General Pyshnitsky and Prussian *Generalmajor* Hünerbein. Very few of our men were taken prisoner, because in no other battle had there been so many wagons for evacuating the wounded as at Lützen.[51]

Awards for the battle of Lutzen were: Count Wittgenstein received the Order of St Andrew the First-Named, Blücher the Order of St George, 2nd class. Tormasov left the army due to ill health and was appointed a Member of the Council of State. General Yorck received the Order of the *Eisernes Kreuz* 1st class.

As the report of the battle of Lützen was being drafted, Emperor Alexander ordered Count Wittgenstein to place the following paragraph in His name, hand written by the Tsar, at the end of the report:

> Overall, I cannot give enough praise to the troops who fought on this memorable day in full view of their Sovereigns, both for their courage and the discipline with which every movement was performed under the fiercest fire. Presently, I shall not fail to nominate those who have distinguished themselves.

One cannot but agree with Gneisenau's opinion that the basic concept of the battle of Lützen was as good as its execution was bad. And indeed, how could it have been more advantageous for the Coalition? The enemy army had been taken by surprise and was attacked by troops superior in numbers and quality. The Coalition had the means on their side not only to win, but also to exploit the victory: their cavalry was incomparably more numerous and better than that of the enemy. Yet, instead, although the Russo-Prussian army was not defeated, although it retained the positions it had occupied at the beginning of the battle, and the enemy had no trophies to boast of, nevertheless, the Coalition were forced to retreat and, and seemingly to give up the role they had taken upon themselves for the time being – that of the liberators of Germany. The main, and one might even say the only, reason for such unexpected results was the slow tempo of operations.

This became apparent from the first steps by the Coalition on the decisive day of battle: the disposition was sent out so late that there was no way to complete it by the indicated time, and, moreover, out of a desire to give Blücher's corps the place of honour, the columns of the Allied Army were dispatched such that they crossed each other's routes; this circumstance, together with the untimely promulgation of the disposition, delayed the crossings of the Elster and Floßgraben and the forming up of the forces for battle by at least four hours. Fortunately for the Coalition, the French, for lack of good cavalry, remained unaware of the gathering storm; nevertheless, had it been delivered at eight o'clock in the morning, then the corps under

51 Vaudoncourt, 80-81. Droysen, *Yorck's Leben*, II, 214. Plotho, I, 118-119. Beitzke, I 382-383. Richter, *Geschichte des deutschen Freiheitskrieges*, I, 158-169. Vaudoncourt, as in other actions, shows bias in the losses of both sides.

Marmont and Bertrand, still a considerable distance from Lützen at the time, would not have had chance to take part in the battle, and Napoleon could have assembled only a part of the Viceroy's force on the battlefield, besides Ney's corps and the *Garde* – hence no more than 70,000 or 80,000 men all told.

At noon, once the Coalition were at full readiness for battle close to Ney's corps, it was vital to attack the enemy who occupied the four villages in front of Lützen with all the infantry under Blücher, Berg, Yorck and Prinz Eugen von Württemberg, numbering more than 40,000 men, and to send the entire cavalry, numbering around 10,000 sabres, to outflank their fighting line via Starsiedel. This cavalry, in enveloping Ney's corps, would have made it difficult to defend the villages he occupied and would have delayed the arrival of reinforcements, which, all things considered, could not have come to the rescue of the French before two or three o'clock in the afternoon; and by this time the outcome of the battle would already have been decided by the defeat of Ney. Yet, instead, the Coalition limited themselves to a piecemeal attack on the villages and used insufficient strength for this, committing each brigade in succession; the cavalry were deployed as if for a review, and got bogged down in an unnecessary cannonade, which would only lead to a waste of ammunition. Even after Napoleon had managed to gather significant forces at Lützen, the Coalition cavalry, taking advantage of the weak enemy cavalry, could have delayed and harassed operations by the French infantry with incessant attacks; yet, instead, they remained in a defensive position, which is inconsistent with the elan of the cavalry.

Our allies criticised the Russian forces for their half-hearted efforts at providing assistance. Indeed, Count Wittgenstein was convinced – and many of our generals shared his opinion – that the Russians, having defended their independence without any outside help, had the right, in the matter of the war for the independence of Germany, to place the bulk of the load upon the Prussian forces. Nevertheless, that said, our II Corps was in very heated combat and lost a fifth of their available manpower in the course of three hours; while Berg's corps also did not contribute enough to the forces under Blücher and Yorck, solely because, being sent first to the left and then to the right flank, they lost a lot of time in pointless counter-marching; the Grenadier Corps were committed to the battle too late, due to the excessive caution of Count Wittgenstein, who believed that in dealing with Napoleon it was necessary to conserve the reserves to the bitter end.

Wittgenstein was criticised for sending Miloradovich's corps to Zeitz, which deprived the army of the assistance of 12,000 men. Some have attributed this circumstance to the rivalry that allegedly existed between Count Wittgenstein and General Miloradovich,[52] but it is much more likely that the memory of the manoeuvre made by Napoleon before the battle of Jena made the Coalition obsessed with guarding the army from having their left flank turned. According to Wittgenstein himself, he did not bring Miloradovich's corps up from Zeitz to join his main force, leaving him there as a reserve, and intending to place them in the front line in the fighting anticipated for the following day. Be that as it may, Miloradovich remained 20 *verstas*

52 *Lebensbilder aus dem Befreiungskriege*, II, 321.

from the field of battle, waiting for orders to go to Lützen. It is claimed that his force remained at instant readiness to move. Intending to speed up the movement of at least a small part of his corps as much as possible, he assembled the majority of his transport in the nearby villages. But evening came, and he had not been summoned. 'For the first time in my life I heard gunfire when I was not in action myself!' Miloradovich said. 'If I am not to be trusted with an army, let them give me a battalion or a company. Count Wittgenstein has always been junior to me in rank, but I am willing to serve under anyone's command.' Although there can be no doubt about Miloradovich's readiness to fight the enemy, it should be noted that his troops only arrived at Zeitz at four o'clock in the afternoon, and therefore could not take part in the battle, even if they had received orders to go to Lützen.[53]

Delving into Napoleon's character and modus operandi in the battle of Lützen, one cannot help but be astonished at the resourcefulness, clarity of his military vision and speed of thought of this brilliant commander. In Napoleon's own words, 'it was a battle offered and won by the Commander-in-Chief of the armies of Italy and of Egypt.' (*une bataille donnée et gagnée par le général en chef d'Italie et d'Egypte*). Napoleon had not anticipated it. It was essential to instantly unravel the enemy intentions, draw up a plan to counter them and find the resources to execute this plan. Within a few minutes, orders had been issued: to the Viceroy to march to the sound of the guns at Lützen with Macdonald's corps and take command of the left wing; to Marmont's corps – form the right wing; Bertrand – move even further to the right and envelope the enemy from the flank; the troops en route from Lützen towards Leipzig were to march at a forced pace in order to rescue Ney. Napoleon himself raced to the battlefield. Success hung in the balance, and the great commander, sensing the importance of this moment of struggle, was exposed to obvious danger along with his conscripts. In the heat of bloody combat, among the deaths of thousands in every manner, they came to him for orders. Marmont, stunned at the sight of the countless Coalition cavalry, asked for the support of reinforcements. 'The marshal is worried over nothing' Napoleon responded. 'This battle will be decided at Kaja.' French columns flocked to the battlefield from various directions. The advantage swung to Napoleon's side. His reserves were fed into action. The Coalition were forced to give up hope of victory.

Such were the actions of Napoleon at Lützen.

53 Miloradovich's letter to Toll, dated 20 April [2 May].

Appendix XIII

Composition of the Coalition Army in late April 1813

Berg's corps:

Mitau Dragoons (three squadrons).

5th Division: Perm Infantry (two battalions); Mogilev Infantry (two battalions); Kaluga Infantry (two battalions); Sevsk Infantry (one battalion); combined grenadiers from 5th Division (two battalions); Her Imperial Highness, Grand Duchess Yekaterina Pavlovich's Battalion.

11th Division: Tenginsk Infantry (two battalions); Estland Infantry (two battalions); combined grenadiers from 14th Division (two Battalions);

Grenadier Division (five battalions): Count Arakcheev's Grenadiers; Pavlovsk Grenadiers; Yekaterinoslav Grenadiers; Tauride Grenadiers; St Petersburg Grenadiers

Opolchenie (two Groups).

The Ataman's Cossack Regiment.

5th Battery Artillery Company; 27th Light Artillery Company; Don Cossack Artillery Company.

Total for Berg's corps: 22 battalions, three squadrons, one Cossack regiment and three artillery companies, numbering 7,450 men, with 36 guns (strength return dated 13 (25) April).

Yorck's corps:

Litthauisches Dragoner (four squadrons); *2. Leib-Husaren* (four squadrons); *2. Westpreußisches Dragoner* (two squadrons); *Brandenburgisches Dragoner* (two squadrons); *2. Bataillon, 1. Ostpreußisches Infanterie*; *Füsilierbataillon, 1. Ostpreußisches Infanterie*; *1. Bataillon, 2. Ostpreußisches Infanterie*; *Füsilierbataillon, Garde-Regiment zu Fuss*; *2. Bataillon, 2. Westpreußisches Infanterie*; *Füsilierbataillon, 2. Westpreußisches Infanterie*; *2. Bataillon, 1. Schlesisches Infanterie*; *2. Bataillon, 2. Schlesisches Infanterie*; *Füsilierbataillon, 2. Schlesisches Infanterie*; *Colbergsches Infanterie* (three battalions); *Ostpreußisches Jäger Bataillon* (two companies); six-pounders (four batteries); 12-pounders (a half-battery); horse artillery (one battery); three-pounders (one battery).

Total for Yorck's corps: 12½ battalions, 12 squadrons and 6½ batteries, numbering 10,000 men (Plotho, *Der Krieg in Deutschland und Frankreich, in den Jahren 1813 und 1814*, I, *Beilagen*, 110).

Kleist's detachment:

Russian Major General Rüdiger: Grodno Hussars; Ilovaisky 4th's Cossacks; Rodionov 2nd's Cossacks; Selivanov 2nd's Cossacks; 23rd Horse Artillery Company.

Russian Major General Vlastov: 23rd Jägers; 24th Jägers; 25th Jägers; 26th Jägers; 23rd Battery Artillery Company.

Prussian Major Thümen: *Brandenburgisches Husaren* (four squadrons); horse artillery (one battery); *Garde-Regiment zu Fuss* (two battalions); *Ostpreußisches Jäger Bataillon* (two companies); *Füsilierbataillon, 2. Ostpreußisches Infanterie*; *1. Bataillon, 1. Westpreußisches Infanterie.*

Total for Kleist's detachment: 2,800 Russians and 3,200 Prussians (Plotho, I, *Beilagen*, 96-97 & 101).

Wintzingerode's corps:

Major General Lanskoy's cavalry brigade: Alexandria Hussars; Belorussia Hussars; Sumy Hussars (two squadrons); Livonia Mounted Jägers.

Major General Panchulidzev's cavalry brigade: Chernigov Mounted Jägers; Novorussia Dragoons; Combined Dragoons.

Major General Knorring's cavalry brigade: Tatar Ulans; Lithuania Ulans (two squadrons).

Total regular cavalry: 25 squadrons.

Major General Ilovaisky 12th's Cossacks: Kuteynikov 4th's Don Cossacks; Semenchikov's Don Cossacks; Grekov 21st's Don Cossacks; Ilovaisky 12th's Don Cossacks; 3rd Ural Cossacks; 1st Ukraine Cossacks; 3rd Ukraine Cossacks.

II Corps under Prinz Eugen von Württemburg:[1]

3rd Division under Major General Prince Shakhovskoy:

Colonel Kapustin's brigade: Reval Infantry; 20th Jägers; 21st Jägers.

Lieutenant Colonel Wolf's brigade: Murom Infantry; Chernigov Infantry; combined infantry (from freed prisoners-of-war).

4th Division under Major General comte Saint-Priest:

Major General Talyzin's brigade (detached from 9th Division): Tobolsk Infantry; Ryazhsk Infantry.

Major General Pyshnitsky's brigade: Volhynia Infantry; Kremenchug Infantry; 4th Jägers; 34th Jägers.

Horse artillery (four companies); light artillery (two companies).

Total for Wintzingerode's corps: 18 battalions, 25 squadrons, seven Cossack regiments and six artillery companies, numbering 13,700 men with 68 guns (strength return, dated 13 (25) April).[2]

1 II Corps was reconstituted before the battle of Lützen to 10,800 men, while 8,700 men remained in it after the detachment of the Tobolsk Infantry and Ryazhsk Infantry to the river Elster (Prinz Eugen von Württemburg's diary, archive of the M.T.D. No. 47,344).

2 In the Order of Battle of troops present at the battle of Lützen, signed by Major General Harting (archive of the M.T.D. No. 20,029), the Kremenchug Infantry and 34th Jägers are not shown.

***General der Kavallerie* Blücher's corps:**

1. Schlesisches Ulanen (two squadrons); *1. Schlesisches Husaren* (two squadrons); *2. Schlesisches Husaren* (two squadrons); *Neumarkisches Dragoner* (four squadrons); *1. Westpreußisches Dragoner* (two squadrons); *1. Westpreußisches Ulanen* (four squadrons); *Brandenburgisches Husaren* (two squadrons); *Brandenburgisches Ulanen* (two squadrons); *Ostpreußisches Kürassiere* (four squadrons); *Schlesisches Kürassiere* (four squadrons); *Brandenburgisches Kürassiere* (four squadrons); *Garde du Corps* (five squadrons); *Leib Leichtes Kavallerie* (six squadrons).

Schlesisches Grenadier Bataillon; 1. Schlesisches Infanterie (three battalions); *2. Schlesisches Infanterie* (two battalions); *Schlesisches Schützen* (one battalion); *Westpreußisches Grenadier Bataillon; 1. Westpreußisches Infanterie* (three battalions); *2. Westpreußisches Infanterie* (two battalions); *Garde Regiment zu Fuss* (three battalions); *Normal-Infanterie-Bataillon; Garde-Jäger-Bataillon; Freiwilligen-Jäger-Bataillon; Leib-Grenadier-Bataillon; 1. Ostpreußisches Grenadier Bataillon; 3. Bataillon, Garde Regiment zu Fuss.*

Prussian artillery: seven horse artillery batteries; three six-pounder foot batteries; a half-battery of 12-pounders.

Russian artillery: three battery companies under lieutenant colonels Glukhov, Velyaminov and Staden.

Total for Blücher's corps: 22 battalions, 43 squadrons and 13½ batteries, numbering 23,350 men (Plotho, I, *Beilagen*, 108-111).

General-of-Infantry Miloradovich's corps:

Kiev Dragoons; Khakov Dragoons; Chuguev Ulans; Lithuania Ulans; Melentiev 3rd's Don Cossacks; Rebrikov's Don Cossacks; Yagodin's Don Cossacks; Stavropol Kalmyk Regiment.

Olonets Infantry; Vyatka Infantry; 11th Jägers; 37th Jägers;

Artillery: one battery company; one light company; one horse company (18 guns in total); Lieutenant Colonel Gebener 2nd's pioneer company.

II Cavalry Corps, under Adjutant General Korff's command:

Pskov Cuirassiers; Moscow Dragoons; Kargopol Dragoons; Akhtyrka Hussars; Lubny Hussars; Karpov's Don Cossacks; 1st Tula Mounted Cossacks; 6th Horse Artillery Company; 10th Horse Artillery Company (18 guns in total).

IV Corps, under Lieutenant General Markov:

11th Division: Kexholm Infantry; Pernov Infantry; Yelets Infantry; 1st Jägers; 33rd Jägers.

22nd Division: Staroskol Infantry.

23rd Division: Koporsk Infantry.

Three artillery companies, with 30 guns.

Lieutenant General Prince Volkonsky's corps:

8th Division: Arkhangelogorod Infantry; Schlüsselburg Infantry; Staro Ingermanland Infantry.

Three artillery companies, with 30 guns.

Total for Miloradovich's corps: around 11,500 men with 96 guns (Strength Returns dated 10 (22) April).

Composition of the Main Army (Russian reserve):

Major General Shevich's Lifeguard Light Cavalry Division: Lifeguard Dragoons; Lifeguard Hussars; Lifeguard Ulans; Lifeguard Cossacks.

Lieutenant General Prince Golityns' corps:

1st Cuirassier Division under Major General Depreradovich: Chevalier Garde; Lifeguard Horse; His Majesty's Cuirassiers; Her Majesty's Cuirassiers; Astrakhan Cuirassiers.

2nd Cuirassier Division under Major General Duka: Yekaterinoslav Cuirassiers; Military Order Cuirassiers; Glukhov Cuirassiers; Malorussia Cuirassiers; Novgorod Cuirassiers.

Lieutenant General Konovnitsyn's Grenadier Corps:[3]

Count Arakcheev's Grenadiers; Yekaterinoslav Grenadiers; Tauride Grenadiers; St Petersburg Grenadiers; Kiev Grenadiers; Moscow Grenadiers; Astrakhan Grenadiers; Fanagoria Grenadiers; Malorussia Grenadiers; Siberia Grenadiers.

1st Lifeguard Division under Major General Rosen:

Preobrazhensky (two battalions); Izmailovsky (two battalions); Semenovsky (two battalions); Lifeguard Jägers (two battalions).

2nd Lifeguard Division under Major General Udom 2nd:

Lithuania Lifeguard (two battalions); Finland Lifeguard (two battalions); Leib Grenadiers (one battalion); Pavlovsk Grenadiers (one battalion).

Lifeguard Horse Artillery (two companies); Lifeguard Battery Artillery (two companies); Lifeguard Light Artillery (two companies); Reserve Battery Artillery (four companies); Reserve Light Artillery (five companies).

Total for the Main Army: 24 battalions, (ten of grenadiers and 14 Lifeguard), 55 squadrons (17 light cavalry and 38 cuirassier) and 15 artillery companies, numbering 17,350 men with 176 guns (troop strength returns).

3 In the Order of Battle of troops present at the Battle of Lützen, signed by Major General Harting (archive of the M.T.D. No. 20,029), the Kexholm Grenadiers and Pernov Grenadiers are also shown.

Appendix XIV

Composition of the Russo-Prussian army at the Battle of Lützen

Lieutenant General Berg's corps: 22 battalions, three squadrons, three batteries, one Cossack regiment, 7,450 men with 36 guns.
Lieutenant General Wintzingerode's corps: 18 battalions, 25 squadrons, six batteries, seven Cossack regiments, 13,700 men with 72 guns.
Reserve: 24 battalions, 55 squadrons, 15 batteries, 17,350 men with 170 guns.
Detached to Blücher: three batteries, 450 men with 36 guns.
Total of Russian troops: 39,000 men with 314 guns.
Prussian forces:
General der Kavallerie Blücher's corps: 22 battalions, 43 squadrons, 10½ batteries, 23,350 men with 84 guns.
Generalleutnant Yorck's corps: 12½ battalions, 12 squadrons, 6½ batteries, 10,000 men with 52 guns.
Total of Prussian troops: 33,350 men with 136 guns.

	Composition			**Manpower**		
Unit/Troop Types	**Russian**	**Prussian**	**Total**	**Russian**	**Prussian**	**Total**
Infantry Battalions	64	34½	**98½**	24,900	24,000	**48,900**
Cavalry Squadrons	83	55	**138**	8,300	7,350	**15,650**
Artillery Batteries	27	17	**44**	4,000	2,000	**6,000**
Cossack Regiments	8		**8**	1,800		**1,800**
						72,350

8

The Coalition retreat to the Elbe following the Battle of Lützen

---

The Coalition operational plan following the battle of Lützen. – The significance of the battle of Lützen in political terms. – General Thielmann in Torgau.

The directions given to the troops of the Coalition Army during the retreat to the Elbe. – Emperor Alexander's orders. – Negotiations between Napoleon and the King of Saxony.

The Coalition retreat and the pursuit by the French. – Rearguard actions: at Gersdorf (or Hartha), Etzdorf and Deutschenbora. – The Coalition crossing onto the right bank of the Elbe. – The Viceroy's seizure of the Neustadt. – Napoleon's arrival in Dresden. – The French crossing onto the right bank of the Elbe. – Further operational plans of the Russo-Prussian army. – The return of the King of Saxony to Dresden. – The occupation of Torgau by French troops. – Thielmann at the headquarters of the Coalition army. – Negotiations. – An armistice proposal.

The Coalition, holding that part of the battlefield at Lützen occupied by them at the start of the fighting, but having been enveloped on the right flank and unable to resume the fight against Napoleon's superior troop strength, were forced to retreat. It was proposed: in anticipation of Austria joining the Coalition Powers, to retreat as slowly as possible, maintaining order in the force, holding the enemy at every step and inflicting losses on them. The Coalition, not losing sight of their objective – to initiate a general uprising against Napoleon – did not intend to refuse battle, but, on the contrary, to seek it wherever there was any probability of success. They were even ready to accept a general battle again, while constantly maintaining the ability to protect their main lines of communication, both along their own main supply routes and with Austria. A retreat towards Silesia, parallel to the Bohemian frontier, satisfied these conditions. In order to weaken the enemy and to divert their attention, it was considered useful to direct several partisan detachments against the enemy lines of communication, which, by destroying the resources of the French forces, could, at the same time, serve to rouse the population against Napoleon.

Such were the measures taken to avert the negative consequences which threatened the Coalition as a result of the loss of the first great battle in Germany. The lack of cavalry prevented Napoleon from exploiting his success, yet nevertheless, the significance of the battle of Lützen was very important politically. Napoleon, wishing to spread the magic of his victory throughout Europe, even in the midst of the battle, sent out couriers with the news: to Paris, to Vienna, and even to Constantinople [Istanbul].[1] The Coalition also sent news of their success to Berlin and Dresden at the beginning of the battle. In all probability, these dispatches were sent from the headquarters of the Coalition Monarchs on the evening of the battle, when it was still intended to resume the struggle the following morning. As soon as the eagerly anticipated news arrive in Berlin, orders were given to fire cannon salutes there and to perform services of thanksgiving across the entire country; everyone celebrated and rejoiced. Shortly thereafter, they learned of the retreat by the army. The unexpected nature of the fatal news struck the population of Prussia hard. But the morale and self-confidence of the Prussian people did not waver in the slightest.

In contrast, in other German lands, the impact of the battle of Lützen was very disadvantageous to the Coalition. The popular uprising was delayed for a considerable time; Napoleon's dominance over the princes of the *Confédération du Rhin* was confirmed by the battle of Lützen, where their troops fought very bravely for a foreign ruler against Prussian soldiers of their own ethnicity. Very comforting news had come to the headquarters of the Coalition Monarchs about the willingness of the German peoples and governments to accept their compatriots: for example, from the Bavarian border they wrote that: 'the entire Bavarian nation and the Kronprinz himself do not want to fight for Napoleon' and so on. But these were merely empty words, and meanwhile the land on the left bank of the Elbe was completely in the grip of Napoleon.[2] Negotiations with Austria had not advanced their accession to the Russo-Prussian Coalition in the least. On 12 May new style, the Austrian diplomat Graf Stadion [Johann Philipp Karl Joseph von Stadion] arrived at Emperor Alexander's headquarters with instructions 'to repeat the emphatic assurances from the Viennese Court to join the Russo-Prussian Coalition at the end of the current month' but at the same time, General Bubna [Ferdinand Bubna von Littitz] had been sent to Napoleon in Dresden with a hand-written letter from Kaiser Franz, in which, offering the mediation of Austria, he wrote; 'I am sending Graf Bubna to Your Imperial Majesty at this crucial moment offered to our empires. Namely – at a time that demands absolute trust.

I thought it necessary to warn you, my sovereign brother, by letter dated 26 April, that I shall address both Powers as soon as possible with a demand for final clarification with regard to a general reconciliation. I have recently sent Graf Stadion to the headquarters of the Russo-Prussian army. I have waited until this time, which I have long foreseen – precisely the time when the first action would have dampened

1 Norvins, *Portefeuille de 1813*, I, 282. According to Odeleben, Napoleon only sent one of the Polish generals who were with him to Kraków with news of the victory. *Relation circonstanciée de la campagne de 1813 en Saxe*, I, 57-58.

2 Droysen, *Yorck's Leben*, II, 217-218. Beitzke, *Geschichte der deutschen Freiheitkriege in dem Jahren 1813 und 1814*, I, 386-387.

passions and dispelled unrealisable dreams. That time has now come, and Your Majesty will have a most enviable destiny – to grant peace to the world after a brilliant feat...'[3]

Saxony's position with regard to the common cause of Germany was even more precarious: King Friedrich August, who was indebted to Napoleon for the significant expansion of his territories, considered it his duty to fulfil the treaty obligations concluded as a member of the *Confédération du Rhin*. On the other hand, in the event of a Coalition success, he had to fear Prussian demands, which had lost large areas annexed to Saxony as a result of the Treaty of Tilsit. Only Austria, due to its centuries-old rivalry with Prussia, offered a realistic defence of Saxony's interests. Such was the reasoning that prompted the King to plump for the fickle policies of the Viennese Cabinet. Having decided to follow their example and remain neutral in the general struggle, the King, as already mentioned, left his capital and sought refuge first in Plauen, then in Regensburg, and finally in Prague. Some of the Saxon forces accompanied the King on his wanderings; the remainder, numbering from 8,000 to 9,000 men, under the command of *Generalleutnant* Thielmann (appointed commandant of Torgau on 14 (26) February) were in Torgau, the most important of the Saxon fortresses. King Friedrich August, in every order to General Thielmann, instructed him to observe the strictest neutrality and not to let any troops into the fortress without orders from the King, and the agreement of the Austrian Kaiser.[4] Thielmann, who had become an admirer of Napoleon in 1806, served in the war of 1809 as a volunteer in the ranks of his forces against Austria; but the winter campaign of 1812 cooled his enthusiasm for the *Empereur des Français*; upon returning to Dresden, he often commented about casting off the foreign yoke and the independence of Germany. But Thielmann had neither the steadfast resolve nor the strength of character of Yorck. According to Stein, 'did he not did behave like a true son of Germany, or as a Saxon blindly devoted to his sovereign, but was vain and prone to verbosity; nonetheless, he was a good officer.'[5] Initially, he wanted to persuade King Friedrich-August to break with Napoleon, informing him, in all his reports, of the general animosity towards the French. But as Friedrich-August remained unshakable in his intention to maintain neutrality, Thielmann, wary of violating his orders, yet swept along by his own sympathy for the Coalition, could not decide on any course of action and became the plaything of important events, the control of which exceeded his mental strength. Thus, he hosted in turn the Coalition generals Wintzingerode, Dovre [Fëdor Filippovich Dovre or Friedrich August Philipp Anton Dovre] and Kleist, and even took the latter, as an old comrade, on a tour of the fortifications, thereafter he entertained General Maison, with all the officers of his division, and Marshal Davout; he once denied Kleist the large-calibre guns needed for the siege of Wittenberg, and then provided the Coalition with the plans to this fortress and loaded mortars onto ships for their speedy dispatch to Wittenberg, just

3 *Dans le moment le plus important qui puisse s'offir pour nos empires... J'ai cru devoir attendre pour effectuer cet envoi le moment que depuis longtems j'ai prévu, celui où une première affaire aurait amorti bien des passions et dissipé beaucoup de chimères.* Letter dated 11 May 1813, new style.

4 King Friedrich August's letters to General Thielmann, dated 19 and 30 April and 5 May new style.

5 Förster, *Geschichte der Befreiungskriege, 1813, 1814, 1815*, I, 259.

in case King Friedrich-August were to join the Russo-Prussian Coalition; he also refused to surrender Torgau to the Coalition, saying that he 'was not Yorck' yet then he went to Dresden to report to the Coalition Monarchs. Emperor Alexander captivated him with His usual charm. Yet he was no longer able to do anything in favour of the Coalition. His prevarication instilled distrust towards him in his men. In addition, he faced opposition from his closest associates, generals Steindel [Friedrich Gottlob von Steindel] and Sahr.

On 27 April new style, the Saxon officers, wishing to celebrate General Thielmann's birthday, arranged a dinner for him. General Sahr, a straightforward and courageous soldier, suspected his superior of intending to take advantage of this opportunity to rouse the officers against the French, and therefore, setting out to congratulate him early in the morning, asked him: 'not to behave towards his subordinates in a spirit contrary to the orders of the King.' Offended by such a request, Thielmann, raising his voice, said: 'General sir! How dare you say that to me, your commander? I can do without your advice.' After that, matters came to the point where Thielmann threatened to shackle Sahr. Such an encounter did not bode well for a joyful time at the impending feast. And indeed, at the start of the dinner everyone was silent and morose. Yet once the company had drained a few glasses, Thielmann stood up and loudly announced that he was proposing three toasts. 'To the health of King Friedrich-August!' he called, raising high a rich goblet, towards a bust of the King, received by him as a gift that morning. After that, raising his voice, he reminded those present of Hermann [Arminius, hero of the battle of Teutoburgerwald] and the sacred cause of independence for the fatherland, announced that his hand would never again be raised in defence of France, and admonishing his subordinates to present the walls of Torgau as another Thermopylae to the enemy, proposed the second toast: 'to the success of the Coalition, in whose ranks the Saxons would soon have the good fortune to fight against the common enemy!' Many of the young officers vociferously expressed their sympathy for Thielmann's words, but almost all the older officers showed their displeasure in sullen silence, and General Sahr responded bluntly: 'Yes, General Sir! We shall fight with all possible courage, with the French against the Russians and Prussians, or with the Russians and Prussians against the French – however our King pleases. We have no need of politics! Our response must only be – long live the King!'

The next day, General Sahr formally requested from Thielmann:

1. Not to operate offensively against any force until orders were received from the King.
2. To defend the fortress against each and everyone to the bitter end.
3. To wait calmly for whatever the King might decide.
4. Not to enter into any untimely negotiations, to declare, if necessary, that Saxon troops themselves will not open hostilities, but also will not tolerate the appearance of foreign troops within cannon range of the fortress.

Not content with this, generals Steindel and Sahr announced, on Garrison Daily Orders, that the King, on the basis of a treaty concluded by him with the Austrian government, had ordered that no one be allowed into the fortress without his permission in conjunction with that of the Austrian Kaiser.

Thus, General Thielmann, having allowed his subordinates to dispose of the fortress entrusted to him with impunity, completely lost influence over the troops of the Torgau garrison.[6]

Let us turn to the Coalition retreat after the battle of Lützen.

The detachment under General Bülow, having the mission to protect Berlin, on 21 April (3 May) received orders to withdraw behind the Elbe, towards Roßlau. This detachment had its own independent sphere of operations, separate from other forces, and therefore all events related to it will be described separately.

The detachment under General Kleist was also ordered, on 21 April (3 May), to withdraw from Wurzen to Mühlberg on the Elbe [between Belgern and Strehla].

The main body of the Coalition Army left the battlefield on that same day [3 May], at dawn. In avoiding having their right flank turned, the Coalition crossed the Elster upstream of Pegau, at Ostrau and Draschwitz, and proceeded by a roundabout route to the roads leading from Pegau to Dresden and Meissen by evening. The entire Russian contingent, as well as Yorck's corps and two brigades from Blücher's corps (*Brandenburgischen Brigade* and *Niederschlesischen Brigade*), settled down for the night at Frohburg, while Blücher was at Borna with the *Oberschlesischen Brigade*, reserve cavalry and wagon trains. Miloradovich, who had been instructed to cover the retreat of the army with his corps and the Prinz von Württemberg's infantry, numbering 18,000 men, moved to the right from Zeitz to the village of Predel on 21 April (3 May), and took up a position on the right bank of the Elster, leaving a detachment under Major General Yuzefovich [Dmitry Mikhailovich Yuzefovich] on the left bank.[7] Miloradovich's rearguard remained in this position, until the Coalition Army had passed the defiles at Draschwitz and Ostrau. When the enemy began crossing at Pegau, then Miloradovich's rearguard withdrew to a position behind the town of Luka, where Korff's light cavalry had been left.[8]

From the first steps, the awkwardness of dual control for the Coalition Army became apparent. The main Chief-of-Staff, Prince Volkonsky, informed the Chief-of-Staff of Count Wittgenstein's army, General Dovre, of the axis of the retreat, while General Dovre, probably believing that orders had already been issued regarding the composition and march-order of the columns, did not, for his part, issue any orders for the army.[9] To avoid such misunderstandings in the future, Emperor Alexander, having departed for Dresden on 22 April (4 May), ordered Prince Volkonsky to write to the Commander-in-Chief that he should operate completely independently. 'The Sovereign Emperor' wrote Volkonsky 'trusting completely in your prudent orders

6 Holtzendorf, *Beiträge zu der Biographie des Generals Freiherrn von Thielmann und zur Geschichte der jüngst vergangenen Zeit*, 1830, 89-125.

7 Major General Yuzefovich's detachment consisted of the Kharkov Dragoons, Kargopol Dragoons, Panteleev 2nd's Cossacks, 11th Jägers and two guns from 4th Horse Artillery Company. Plotho, I, appendices, 98.

8 War Diary of Miloradovich's rearguard, compiled by its Chief-of-Staff, Colonel Sipyagin. Plotho, I, 125-126.

9 Chief-of-Staff, Adjutant General Volkonsky's orders to Major General Diebitsch, dated 23 April [5 May], No. 837 (archive of the M.T.D. No. 29,181).

in every case, is convinced that you will not neglect to use every means to harm the enemy, and to that end he permits you to operate entirely in accordance with the circumstances.'[10] Orders were issued to send several partisan detachments across the enemy lines of communication towards Leipzig in order to disrupt their rear areas, and moreover, having formed a raiding corps under the command of Major General Lanskoy, directed it through Penig and Altenburg towards Zeitz.[11] Emperor Alexander, informing Barclay de Tolly of the retreat of the Coalition Army to the Elbe after the battle of Lützen, ordered him to march via Crossen and Spremberg in order to join the main army with all the troops under his command.[12]

These were the priority orders of Emperor Alexander, and in the meantime his opponent was preparing a persistent pursuit of the Coalition. Proud of the victory won by his conscripts, almost without cavalry and with little artillery, Napoleon said: 'Europe would finally be at peace if sovereigns and ministers had been on this battlefield. They would abandon the dream of dimming the glory of France; they would see that their counsellors, by wishing to divide France and humiliate the Emperor, are preparing the demise of their sovereigns.'[13]

Saxony was supposed to serve as a base for the French army in the war of 1813, and therefore Napoleon valued the alliance with Friedrich-August. Despite the loyalty of the King of Saxony to the French government, being under pressure from Austria, he refused to subordinate his forces to Napoleon's army or to admit the French into the fortresses of Torgau and Königstein. While still in Mainz, Napoleon had sent his aide de camp, General Flahaut [Auguste Charles Joseph de Flahaut de La Billarderie], to the King in Prague, seeking his compliance with his demands; after that, having arrived in Weimar, he instructed the Sovereign Herzog [Carl August von Sachsen-Weimar-Eisenach] to write about the same, threatening the King with loss of territory, in the event of non-compliance. Friedrich-August, having received this dispatch on 21 April (3 May), hesitated to answer, in anticipation of the outcome of the battle (which could not be known to him), confirmed the orders issued by him to General Thielmann, instructing him not to let the French into Torgau, even in the event that the good fortune of their army should bring Napoleon to the Elbe.[14] After that, after several contradictory reports about the battle of Lützen, eventually, on 24 April (6 May), reliable information arrived in Prague about the victory won by the French and Colonel comte Montesquiou [Raymond Aymeric Philippe Joseph de Montesquiou-Fezensac] and Graf Einsiedel [Detlef von Einsiedel] visited the king, demanding in the name of Napoleon that Friedrich-August return to Dresden immediately, to give orders allowing French troops to enter Torgau and to subordinate his troops to Reynier's corps. The King was given only six hours to

10 Supreme Orders for Count Wittgenstein, announced by Adjutant General Prince Volkonsky, dated 23 April [5 May], No. 838.
11 Supreme Orders for Count Wittgenstein, announced by Adjutant General Prince Volkonsky, dated 24 April [6 May], No. 846.
12 Supreme Orders for General-of-Infantry Barclay de Tolly, announced by Prince Volkonsky, dated 25 April [7 May], No. 863 and 26 April [8 May], No. 868.
13 *Le Moniteur* for 9 May 1813.
14 '*…die Festung in dem Falle, wenn das Glück die Waffen der französischen Armee wieder an die Elbe Führen sollte, auch nicht für Frankreich zu öffnen…*' Orders dated 5 May 1813 new style.

accept all these demands, after which, in the event of non-compliance, orders had been issued to declare him deprived of the throne for treachery, as a member of the *Confédération du Rhin*. Friedrich-August, having received this terrifying message, immediately returned to Dresden and became an agent of Napoleon once more;[15] but the orders previously issued by the King to Thielmann hindered French operations and facilitated the Coalition retreat as will be explained in due course.

Upon reaching Frohburg and Borna, the Russo-Prussian army continued its retreat in two columns: the right hand column, consisting of the Prussian corps under Blücher and Yorck, was directed towards Colditz and Meissen, while the left, of the entire Russian contingent, was directed towards Rochlitz and Dresden. The trains and parks moved via Chemnitz and Freiberg also towards Dresden. Miloradovich's rearguard initially headed for Frohburg, and then, from 22 April (4 May) towards Rochlitz. Napoleon, having received intelligence on the division of the Coalition forces, and believing that the Prussians would retreat to Berlin, while the Russians would march via Lusatia to the Oder, decided to pursue the Coalition in both directions: Lauriston's corps, which had advanced on Zwenkau, was to proceed in the wake of Kleist's detachment, towards Wurzen, and on to Mühlberg; Ney's corps, reinforced by Durutte's newly reconstituted division, was ordered to go via Leipzig to Torgau to occupy this fortress and assimilate the Saxons, after which Marshal Ney was to head towards Berlin with the following formations: his own corps, Victor's *2e Corps*, on the march from Magdeburg, Reynier's *7e Corps*, reinforced with the Torgau garrison, Durutte's division and General Sébastiani's *2e corps de cavalerie*, moving from the lower Elbe (subsequently, Lauriston's *5e Corps* was sent there as well). Napoleon himself headed for Dresden with: Macdonald's *11e Corps* forming the vanguard, Marmont's *6e Corps*, Bertrand's *4e Corps*, Oudinot's *12e Corps* and the *Garde*.[16] On the morning of 21 April (3 May), the French army crossed the Elster at several points, in the stretch from Pegau to Zeitz, and moved towards the crossings on the Mulde at Colditz and Rochlitz:[17] the Viceroy went towards the former of these locations with Macdonald's corps, while Marmont and the *Garde* followed him at some distance; while Bertrand's corps headed for the latter location; Oudinot's corps moved towards Altenburg. At the same time as Lauriston's corps were just setting out from Leipzig, the Cossacks from Kleist's detachment, who were stationed as outposts near the village of Paunsdorf [between Taucha and Leipzig], unexpectedly broke into the city, chased the French along the roads to Lindenau and Zwenkau and captured many prisoners.[18]

On the morning of 23 April (5 May), *Oberstleutnant* Steinmetz, whose brigade formed the rearguard of the Prussian column, crossed the Mulde at Colditz and destroyed the bridge behind them; but just at that moment, news arrived that

15 Norvins, *Portefeuille de 1813*, I, 314-316 & 321.

16 Norvins, I, 306-307. Beitzke, I, 393-394.

17 The French corps crossed the Elster as follows: Macdonald's *11e Corps* and the *Garde* at Pegau, Marmont's *6e Corps* at Lützkewitz [one mile north of Predel], Bertrand's *4e Corps* at Predel, Oudinot's *12e Corps* at Zeitz. Ney's *3e Corps*, which had suffered the most at the battle of Lützen, remained in place until the following day.

18 Vaudoncourt, *Histoire de la guerre soutenue par les Français en Allemagne, en 1813*, 84-85. Plotho, *Der Krieg in Deutschland und Frankreich in den Jahren 1813 und 1814*, I, 127.

the Russians had not yet managed to cross at Rochlitz, Steinmetz's brigade were ordered to take up positions at Colditz, on the right bank of the Mulde, and hold out as long as possible in order to give Miloradovich's Russian rearguard time to cross the river and destroy the bridge at Rochlitz. To that end, the Prussian force deployed on the right bank of the Mulde. At nine o'clock in the morning, having closed up to Colditz, the Viceroy opened a cannonade and deployed Charpentier's division facing the town. Meanwhile, a ford was discovered a little downstream [1½ miles north, at Sermuth], using which, the Viceroy crossed the river with Gérard's division and artillery, outflanking Steinmetz's position and settled down on the high ground dominating the main route along which the Prussian force would have to retreat. Part of Steinmetz's brigade managed to retreat to Leisnig [seven miles east of Colditz]; the other was driven back to Gersdorf [ten miles north-east of Rochlitz], near Hartha, and was in danger of being overwhelmed by the superior numbers of enemy troops. The Viceroy hoped to cut the line of retreat of the Russian rearguard by way of a swift march to Waldheim [between Rochlitz and Nossen]. Meanwhile, Miloradovich had received news from the Quartermaster General of the Army, Baron Diebitsch, about the deployment of Adjutant General comte Saint-Priest's 2nd Grenadier Division at Gersdorf, where they had been ordered to remain until the rearguard arrived at Waldheim. General Miloradovich, having already completed the crossing at Rochlitz, and hearing that the enemy had bypassed Steinmetz from the direction of the sound of gunfire and was moving towards Waldheim, sent part of his force to support comte Saint-Priest, under the command of the Chief of Staff of the rearguard, Colonel Sipyagin [Nikolai Martemyanovich Sipyagin], whom he himself followed with the rest of the regiments.

In anticipation of these reinforcements, comte Saint-Priest, as soon he had been joined by elements of Steinmetz's brigade retreating to Gersdorf, deployed his force as follows: the village of Gersdorf was held by the Malorussia Grenadiers and Siberia Grenadiers, supported by the Fanagoria Grenadiers; the remaining three grenadier regiments, the Prussian infantry and the Lifeguard Ulans were held in reserve.[19] Skirmishers were scattered through the scrub forwards of their frontage and in the forest on the left side of the village; the Prussian cavalry were stationed to the right of the village and to the left of the forest. At half-past-three in the afternoon, the enemy opened fire from 20 guns and directed an attack on the village of Gersdorf with six columns. The actions of the Russian artillery were very effective; the grenadiers twice charged with bayonets fixed, but could not hold out against the incomparably superior numbers; at the same time, the French, having pushed the Prussian cavalry stationed on the left flank of the detachment back, occupied the forest, which forced Saint-Priest to retreat [three miles east] behind the village of Hartha, under the protection of Major General Lisanevich's detachment [Grigory Ivanovich Lisanevich], sent by Miloradovich in order to threaten the enemy with envelopment on their right

19 The Lifeguard Ulan regiment, under Major General Chalikov's command, had joined the 2nd Grenadier Division during the retreat after the battle of Lützen. War Diary of Miloradovich's rearguard.

flank.[20] Here the troops under Saint-Priest settled down to block the enemy once more. The heavy artillery company under Colonel Nilus and the 6th Horse Artillery Company under Colonel Zakharzhevsky [Yakov Vasilyevich Zakharzhevsky] silenced the French artillery, while the 11th Jägers, sent into the forest, drove out the enemy skirmishers and covered Lisanevich's withdrawal. But after that the Viceroy resumed his attack with fresh forces from Charpentier's and Gérard's divisions on comte Saint-Priest's left wing: the 11th Jägers were ejected from the forest, while the French skirmishers manoeuvring from there, forced Nilus' battery to pull back. This decisive moment saw Miloradovich's timely arrival with the rest of the rear-guard troops; Major General Karpenko [Moses Ivanovich Karpenko] reinforcing the 11th Jägers with his brigade, recaptured the forest,[21] while the main body of the rearguard advanced in four strong columns and halted the enemy in Hartha. Saint-Priest withdrew to Etzdorf [five miles west of Nossen] and rejoined the army, Miloradovich withdrew to Reichenbach with the rearguard,[22] leaving a detachment at Waldheim, while Steinmetz's brigade withdrew to Döbeln [10½ miles north-west of Nossen]. The Viceroy halted at Hartha, Bertrand's *4e Corps*, at Rochlitz, while the rest of Napoleon's main force was at Colditz or Altenburg. The Russian force's casualties in the action at Hartha consisted of 107 killed and 230 wounded. The French, according to their own statements, lost 600 men.[23]

On the following day, 24 April (6 May), the viceroy, turning to the right, towards Waldheim, against Miloradovich forcing him to retreat to Etzdorf (near Roßwein). Prinz Eugen von Württemberg, joining Miloradovich's force at dawn with his II Corps, took command of the rearguard, composed of II Corps, 22nd Division under Major General Turchaninov [Pavel Petrovich Turchaninov], Major General Karpenko's jäger brigade and Korff's II Cavalry Corps, which was commanded by Major General Melissino [Alexey Petrovich Melissino] due to Korff's illness.[24] Following an insignificant clash at Etzdorf, the Prinz von Württemberg retreated to Nossen, while Miloradovich's main body went to Deutschenbora [three miles east of Nossen]. Total casualties to the Russian forces on this day reached 85 men. On 25 April (7 May), Miloradovich, having in mind to hold the enemy step by step, in order to give the army time to cross to the right bank of the Elbe at Dresden, divided his entire force into several waves, placing them one after the other, along the road from Nossen to Limbach [eight miles east of Nossen], at half-stage

20 Major General Lisanevich's detachment consisted of: the Chuguev Ulans, two Cossack regiments and four guns from 4th Horse Artillery Company. War Diary of Miloradovich's rearguard.

21 Major General Karpenko's jäger brigade consisted of the 1st Jägers, 33rd Jägers and 37th Jägers. Prinz von Württemberg's diary.

22 Reichenbach is midway between Waldheim and Roßwein [Reichenbach is ten miles west of Nossen].

23 War Diary of Miloradovich's rearguard. General Miloradovich's letter to Count Wittgenstein, dated 23 April [5 May], from Waldheim. Vaudoncourt, 85. He gives the Coalition casualties as 2,000 men, which is very probably an exaggeration.

24 Prinz von Württemberg's rearguard consisted of II Corps, II Cavalry Corps, 22nd Division under Major General Turchaninov (Vyatka Infantry, Olonets Infantry, Staroskol Infantry and 43rd Jägers), Major General Karpenko's brigade from 11th Division (1st Jägers, 33rd Jägers and 37th Jägers).

intervals. At half-past-eight in the morning the Viceroy sent Macdonald's corps to attack Lieutenant Colonel Wolf [Ivan Pavlovich Volf or Peter Johann Paul Wilhelm Wolf], who was holding Nossen with the leading wave. The valiant Wolf defended his post until ten o'clock and, upon receiving orders to withdraw, retreated to Niedereula [one mile east of Nossen]. Whereupon the Viceroy, having crossed the river [Freiberger Mulde] upstream of the position occupied by Miloradovich's second wave, swiftly attacked Karpenko in Niedereula as well as Melissino, who was stationed to the right of the jägers with elements of II Cavalry Corps. And here the Russian troops were withdrawn from the battle only when Miloradovich himself, having placed powerful batteries at Deutschenbora, ordered generals Karpenko and Melissino to pull back. At this point, a strong cannonade began. Miloradovich, dodging a thousand deaths with his usual composure, taking care of the preservation of his troops, left only the 4th Jägers and 20th Jägers to protect the artillery, and sent all the rest to Limbach. The brave jägers, fated to die in defence of the retreating army, continued to hold on for several hours in the forest behind Deutschenbora. By evening, Miloradovich had withdrawn his force to Wilsdruff, while the Viceroy halted at Limbach, having managed to advance only 12 *verstas* all day. Our casualties on this day did not exceed 100 men, while the enemy lost 136 men taken prisoner alone.[25]

As these rearguard actions were taking place, the main Coalition forces retreated to the Elbe: on 23 April (5 May) the Russian contingent had departed for Nossen, while the Prussians set off for Döbeln; on 24 April [6 May], the Russians were marching to Wilsdruff, while the Prussians headed for Meissen; on 25 April [7 May], the Coalition forces crossed the Elbe and in the meantime, Miloradovich, retreating towards Dresden with the troops of the rearguard, occupied the suburbs and fortifications covering two bridges built by Russian engineers – a bridge of boats upstream and another of rafts downstream of the city. Here, General Emmanuel's raiding detachment [Georgy (Yegor) Arsenyevich Emmanuel (Manuilovich)] and Lieutenant General Gorchakov's detachment, which had arrived independently of the army from the Elster river, joined the rearguard.[26]

Upon the withdrawal of Miloradovich's force onto the right bank of the Elbe, the bridges were set alight, upstream and downstream of the city, as was the temporary wooden span on the masonry bridge in the city itself. The bridge of boats on the left side of the city was set alight in error, before a battalion of Schlüsselburg Infantry, which was in the bridgehead, could cross. The commander of this unit, Lieutenant Colonel Rehren [Ivan Bogdanovich Reren or Johann Friedrich von Rehren], aware of the incomparably superior enemy forces approaching the bridgehead fortifications he was holding, and having also received orders earlier to retreat to the right bank of the river, raced to the flaming bridge; but by then the ropes had already been cut and the burning boats were floating down the river, whereupon Rehren threw

25 Prinz Eugen von Württemberg's diary.

26 Major General Emmanuel's raiding detachment consisted of the Kiev Dragoons, Moscow Dragoons, two Cossack regiments and four horse artillery pieces. The composition of Lieutenant General Gorchakov's detachment is not recorded. *Die grosse Chronik*, I, 147 states only that it consisted of 2,000 men.

himself into the water with all his men and managed to reach the right bank and rejoin the rearguard, where it was already being reported that he had perished.[27]

The rearguard formations, upon crossing to the right bank of the Elbe, were located as follows: comte Saint-Priest was in the Neustadt with his small detachment, having positioned marksmen in the buildings lining the bank of the Elbe and on the near-side of the masonry bridge; IV Corps were to the right of the city, under Lieutenant General Markov [Yevgeny Ivanovich Markov], and II Cavalry Corps, under the temporary command of General Melissino, due to Korff's illness; Prince Gorchakov 2nd was on the left with his detachment and 8th Division from Prince Volkonsky's corps, as well as Major General Emmanuel with some of the cavalry. A screen of Cossacks was stretched to the left to Wehlen [16 miles upstream of Dresden], and to the right to Meissen, in order to liaise with the outposts of Blücher's force, who, having also destroyed the bridge at Meissen, occupied the right bank of the Elbe.[28]

The French army was hot on the heels of the Coalition. On 25 April (7 May), in the evening, the Viceroy moved up to Dresden with Macdonald's corps. Napoleon's *quartier général* with the *Garde* and the corps under Bertrand and Oudinot were moving along the Chemnitz to Dresden road; Lauriston's corps had arrived at Meissen on the Wurzen road: thus Napoleon's main body, except for one corps, were concentrated against the Russians.[29]

On the following day, 26 April (8 May), at around noon, having stationed *11e Corps* in the Altstadt, the Viceroy set off with a cavalry patrol through the Pillnitz gate, up the Elbe in order to reconnoitre the bridge, which at that time had already been set alight by the Cossacks. Napoleon had intended to spend the night in Wilsdruff; but having received reports of the arrival of the French vanguard in Dresden that morning, he summoned one of the officers of his retinue and sent him to the city with orders for them to send a deputation. 'I have appointed General Durosnel [Antoine Jean Auguste Durosnel] as Commandant of Dresden. Go at the gallop' he commanded.

The population of Dresden, in the depths of despondency, awaited a decision on their fate in trepidation. The main body of the Russian army was retreating along the Bautzen road. Emperor Alexander had left the city at dawn, while the King of Prussia left later that morning; but Miloradovich's troops were stationed in the Neustadt and on the right bank of the Elbe, while on the high ground on the left bank, French forces hovered like menacingly forming clouds. The bridges built by the Coalition, and the wooden span, replacing the arch of the stone bridge destroyed by Marshal Davout, were burning, blanketing the entire area with thick smoke. Silence reigned in the city, occasionally interrupted by cannon fire from the right bank. The Dresden delegation met Napoleon two *verstas* from the Freiberg gate. 'Who you are?' he asked.

'Members of the Municipal Administration' the deputies replied.

27 War Diary of Miloradovich's rearguard.

28 War Diary of Miloradovich's rearguard. War Diary signed by Prince Volkonsky. Plotho, I, 13-135.

29 Vaudoncourt, 86.

'Do you have bread?' And without giving them a moment to give any kind of answer, Napoleon said: 'You must give bread, meat and wine to the troops.' Then, raising his voice, he continued:

> I ought to treat you as a conquered country. I know everything you did during the Coalition occupation of your city: I have statements about the volunteers, whom you dressed and armed against me with a willingness that astounded my enemies. I know how you criticised me, and how many vile libels you now need to burn or hide. You did not hide the delight and the hostility towards me that you indulged in at the entrance of Emperor Alexander and the King of Prussia to your city. The remnants of the garlands you hung out are still visible on your houses, the flowers scattered by your young maidens under the feet of the Coalition monarchs have not yet disappeared. Despite all this, I forgive everything. Bless your sovereign; he has saved you! Send a deputation to him and ask him to return to you. I forgive you solely out of friendship for him. You have had sufficient punishment already! You were governed by Baron Stein, in the name of Kutuzov, and now you know whether you can trust the well-intentioned views of the Coalition. I demand for my troops from you only that which you did not refuse to the Russians and Prussians. I shall even see to it that you suffer as little as possible from the war, and as a pledge of my indulgence I appoint General Durosnel, my aide de camp, as your governor. The King himself would have selected him for you. Go!

After that, having circled the Altstadt, Napoleon arrived on the Pillnitz road, dismounted from his horse and, accompanied by the Viceroy, went down to the river and examined the place where the bridge of boats built by the Coalition had previously been. From there, he went on horseback across the Altstadt to the village of Briesnitz [3½ miles downstream of Dresden], where a floating bridge had previously been built by the Russians. This location was most advantageous for a French crossing to the right bank of the Elbe: at Briesnitz, the left bank dominates the right and the course of the river forms a convenient loop. In addition, although the Russians had set fire to the floating bridge, they succeeded in only partially destroying it; the remaining rafts smouldered weakly. Miloradovich himself, exhausted by the onerous duties of rearguard service, relinquished his command of the corps, and Major General Urusov, who had stationed one of the brigades of IV Corps opposite Briesnitz, had positioned his force between Kaditz and Pieschen, from where they could not properly observe the bend of the river.[30]

Napoleon took advantage of this favourable circumstance. One of the rafts from the former floating bridge, which had fortuitously drifted to the left bank, was used to pass several soldiers across to the far side of the river, who seized and took back two rafts and a large barge moored on the right bank. These rafts and the barge were

30 War Diary of Miloradovich's rearguard. A.A. Scherbinin's notes. Aster, *Schilderung der Kriegsereignisse in und vor Dresden vom 7 März bis 28 August*, Dresden, 1844, 50-52. Fain, *Manuscrit de 1813*, I, 373-377.

used to quickly cross 100 volunteers, who subsequently occupied Schloss Übigau. In the course of the night, two battalions managed to cross, which, having sent forward a skirmishing screen, settled down in the loop of the river. At dawn on 27 April (9 May), other troops began to rebuild the bridge under the guidance of the Chief Pontonier, Colonel Lasalle. The Viceroy having arrived at Briesnitz with Fressinet's division, placed some of his artillery on the high ground, supported by batteries from the *Garde*: in order to defend the area laying to their front with cross-fire, 18 guns were deployed to the left of the village, while 16 more were on the right. At the same time, wanting to force the Russians to evacuate the Neustadt, Napoleon ordered several guns to be brought to the Brühlsche Terrasse and fire was opened on the battery stationed on the opposite bank. A fairly fierce cannonade and firefight broke out here. A number of Dresden residents were killed or wounded; eventually both sides gradually ceased firing, sparing the city. The action at Briesnitz was much more decisive. Hearing the thunder of artillery, Miloradovich hurried from the Neustadt to Markov's force, led them to Übigau himself and brought up four batteries to the enemy crossing point (colonels Nilus' and Maleev's heavy companies, Lieutenant Colonel Bashmakov's light company [Flegont Mironovich Bashmakov] and Lieutenant Colonel Zakharzhevsky's horse artillery company). The Russian force approached the enemy battalion covering the construction of the bridge to the thunder of canister fire and opened heavy fire on them. The Arkhangelogorod Infantry Regiment, under the command of Colonel Shenshin [Vasily Nikanorovich Shenshin], twice broke into the enemy held village of Pieschen.[31] Napoleon, frustrated at the gradual strengthening of Russian artillery, turning to General Drouot, exclaimed: '100 guns!' One of the French batteries, placed at the exit of the Ostra-Allee, enfiladed the Russian troops from the left flank, but was forced into silence. Eventually, once 80 guns had been brought into action by the French, Miloradovich's men, having suffered significant losses, were ordered to retreat, and to evacuate the Neustadt as well, which was completed by dusk. The Russian casualties for this day were nine officers and 119 other ranks killed, 14 officers and 274 other ranks wounded; overall, 416 men were *hors de combat.* On the French side, around 600 men were killed or wounded.[32]

The strength of the Elbe current at Briesnitz and the difficulty in finding sufficient rope, anchors and other materials forced Napoleon to abandon the crossing at this point and begin to repair the wooden span on the permanent masonry bridge in the city. Even before this work was completed, Charpentier's division (Macdonald's corps) crossed over the destroyed part of the bridge by means of long fire-fighting ladders and occupied the Neustadt. Napoleon took part in this escalade himself, with all his staff. At the same time, on 28 April (10 May), several guns were transported across on old rafts; while on the following morning, the city bridge, repaired after 20 hours of work under the direction of Colonel Bernard [Simon Bernard], was used to cross the rest of Macdonald's force, and following in their wake, the corps under Bertrand and Marmont. Napoleon, completely satisfied with the fast work of his pontoniers, sat almost all day on a stone bench near the bridge, while

31 Aster, 53-54. War Diary of Miloradovich's rearguard. Shcherbinin's notes.
32 War Diary of Miloradovich's rearguard. Vaudoncourt, 87. Aster, 55.

his troops passed by, announcing his presence to the neighbourhood with loud cheers of: *Vive l'empereur*! According to Aster [Karl Heinrich Aster], 109 battalions (58 French and 51 foreign), 28 squadrons (16 French and 12 foreign) and 18 batteries (12 French and six foreign) then crossed the bridge, numbering 60,000 to 70,000 men with 140 guns.[33]

Upon the enemy occupation of the Neustadt, on 28 April (10 May) Miloradovich's rearguard retreated to Weißer Hirsch [3½ miles south-east of the Neustadt]. The main body of the Russian army had retreated the day before, 27 April (9 May), to Radeberg, while the Prussian corps under Blücher and Yorck went to Grossenhain. This arrangement of the Coalition forces indicated an intention to retreat in different directions, and gave the impression that the Prussian army was truly headed for Berlin in order to protect their capital directly, while the Russians would withdraw along their line of operations to the Oder, whereupon Napoleon intended to exploit this mistake to operate with the same success with which he had managed in the Italian campaign of 1796. Fortunately, the Coalition managed to assess in time that of all the courses of action, having voluntarily divided their armies, there was nothing worse than to take the fight to a stronger enemy and for this reason it was decided to concentrate forces, even if this resulted in the sacrifice of the capital of Prussia. To that end, on 28 April (10 May), the corps under Blücher and Yorck, having made a march of thirty *verstas*, settled down in the evening at Königsbrück; Kleist's detachment, after burning the bridge at Mühlberg, withdrew to Grossenhain; Wittgenstein's force went to Bischofswerda; Miloradovich's rearguard to Weißig [Schönfeld-Weißig, 6½ miles east of the Neustadt].[34]

Napoleon's primary concern with the occupation of Dresden was to bring King Friedrich-August back there. It was apparent that the friendly goodwill of the King of Saxony was of no importance to the conqueror, whose broad vision was for the subjugation of all Europe to his will; but the King's expulsion by France might prove to be a catalyst for revolt by other princes of the *Confédération du Rhin*. Accordingly, upon moving towards Dresden after the battle of Lützen, Napoleon invited the King to return to his capital most insistently. The king had departed Prague; but his progress was slow: he seemed to have a presentiment of the consequences of this act, so disadvantageous – both for himself and for his realm. He eventually arrived on 30 April (12 May). Napoleon, who never missed an opportunity to perform brilliant spectacles for the benefit of public opinion, wished to appear as the restorer of the Saxon's beloved sovereign, in their eyes, and to that end prepared a most festive reception for him. Troops in full dress uniform were deployed from the palace to the Pirnaisches Tor and from there to Gruna. Napoleon, having met the King in person near the Großer Garten, rode into the city with him on horseback, to the thunder of cannon salutes, cheering troops and the ringing of bells. They were met by a deputation from the city at the gates. The King turned to Napoleon, who said to the deputies: 'Listen, I wish to speak to you. You owe your salvation to the King. I know that there were bad men among you who took the side of the Russians and

33 Aster, 57-60.
34 War Diary, signed by Prince Volkonsky. Prinz Eugen von Württemberg's diary (archive of the M.T.D. No. 47,344). War Diary of Miloradovich's rearguard.

Prussians; but to please the King I forgive you. My troops will pass through Saxony, and you will soon have your responsibilities eased. I shall protect you from all your enemies.'[35] Following the King were two Saxon cavalry regiments arrived from Prague, which joined the corps under Latour Maubourg, which, due to the small numbers of French cavalry, was most important.[36]

The French encountered far greater difficulties assimilating the Saxon infantry stationed in Torgau.

Napoleon, in pursuing the main body of the Coalition Army through Dresden, had sent Ney to Torgau and on towards Berlin – as already mentioned – with his and Victor's corps, to which the Saxon troops occupying Torgau and – depending on the circumstances – Lauriston's corps were to join. On 24 April (6 May), General Thielmann received a dispatch from Eilenburg, in which General Reynier, anticipating his arrival at Torgau with Durutte's division the following day, demanded that measures be taken to provide rations for his troops from Torgau and the vicinity of this fortress. But Thielmann, in his response to this dispatch, as well as during his meeting with General Reynier, announced to him that having received the King's orders not to let any troops into the fortress without his permission, he could not allow anyone to approach Torgau. Thielmann's refusal to hand over the fortress forced Reynier to bivouac at Süptitz [three miles west of Torgau] with Durutte's division and with Ricard's division from Ney's corps. On 27 April (9 May), Reynier repeated his demands, acknowledging that the advance of French forces through Torgau would make it very easy for them to pursue the Coalition army, but Thielmann again refused to give way, while informing the headquarters of the Russian army, writing that he could also not allow Coalition troops into the fortress. On that same day, an official from the Dresden *Regierungs Kommission*, *Oberkammerherr* Baron Friesen [Johann Georg Friedrich von Friesen] was sent by Napoleon to Thielmann, to demand that Torgau be handed over to French troops. General Thielmann showed him the King's orders dated 23 April (5 May), which expressly stated: 'to keep the French out even if the Coalition are forced to pull back behind the Elbe.' Baron Friesen was forced to admit to the impossibility of surrendering Torgau; however, his arrival had finally shaken the confidence of Thielmann's subordinates in him. Being in such a precarious position, he turned to General Kleist, suggesting that he occupy the fortress with Prussian troops; but it was already too late. By this time, Kleist's force had withdrawn from Mühlberg to Grossenhain; other Coalition troops were even further away; while Reynier was stationed quite close to the fortress. Meanwhile, on 28 April (10 May), at around noon, Thielmann received the King's orders dated 8 May: 'to surrender the fortress of Torgau to General Reynier and to attach the garrison to the French army.' Such a sharp turn in Friedrich-August's policy made Thielmann fear the consequences of his actions, which, in the eyes of Napoleon, could not be justified and therefore, having handed over command of his force to General Steindel, he left for the headquarters of Emperor Alexander and was accepted into Russian service as a lieutenant

35 This speech was published, with some amendments in *Darstellung des Ereignisse in Dresden im Jahre 1813, V. einem Augenzeugen*.

36 Norvins, I, 324. Vaudoncourt, 89.

general.[37] The following day, 29 April (11 May), Reynier took command of the Saxon forces. Durutte's division and Ney's corps passed through Torgau onto the right bank of the Elbe. But the four days during which Thielmann had kept the French under the walls of Torgau were irretrievably lost, and Napoleon, having learned of the concentration of the Coalition armies, was forced to abandon the attempt on Berlin and reattach Ney's force to his main body. If the French had succeeded in occupying Berlin as quickly as Napoleon intended, then this would in all probability have led to the splitting of the Coalition armies, and, in any case, the capture of the capital of Prussia on the heels of the victory at Lützen would have had a huge impact on the whole of Germany.

Napoleon, having occupied Dresden, remained there for several days until 6 (18) May. Just as in Paris, he busied himself tirelessly with the affairs of war and politics. King Friedrich-August did not conceal all the twists and turns of the Viennese Cabinet from his powerful ally, or the intercepted letters from the Russian resident in Vienna, Count Stackelberg [Gustav Ottonovich fon Shtakelberg or Gustav Ernst von Stackelberg], to Count Nesselrode, which convinced Napoleon of Austria's rapprochement with Russia and Prussia. Wishing to secure himself from the direction of Italy, he sent the Viceroy there, to take command of the troops, to whom he had given unlimited authority, from the time of his command of the army assembled on the Elbe.

Meanwhile, news of the victory won by French troops at Lützen had arrived in Vienna. The Austrian government, fearing that the Coalition might enter into an agreement with Napoleon, which would completely eliminate the influence of the Viennese Cabinet on European matters, hastened, as already mentioned, to send Graf Bubna to Napoleon and Graf Stadion to the headquarters of the Coalition Monarchs: the former of these diplomats enjoyed the special favour of the *Empereur des Français*, while the latter was known for his loathing of him and of France.

On the evening of 4 (16) May, Graf Bubna arrived in Dresden and was immediately received by Napoleon, while on the following day he had a meeting with the duc de Vicence [Armand Augustin Louis de Caulaincourt]. After repeating his court's usual assurances of unwavering loyalty to Napoleon and peaceful views, he announced that he had not been given any instructions on the negotiation of a continuation of the alliance between France and Austria, but he made it clear that the Austrian government wanted: Illyria from Italy, the expansion of their borders into Poland and Bavaria, and in Germany – the dissolution of the *Confédération du Rhin*. The duc de Vicence gave a non-committal response to these proposals, limiting himself to the remark that: 'Austria may refuse to ally with France; but what is most harmful of all is resorting to half-measures – the usual refuge of indecision and impotence.' After that, Graf Bubna began talking about a congress that could be convened in Prague or elsewhere. The duc de Vicence, having agreed to convene a congress, proposed, for his part, to conclude a truce. Graf Bubna volunteered to write about this to Graf Stadion directly, and Napoleon not only agreed to this, but amended the draft dispatch himself. This letter was sent to the Coalition

37 For Thielmann's correspondence with the French and Russians, see Appendix XV at the end of this chapter.

headquarters on 6 (18) May, on the day of Napoleon's departure from Dresden with the *Garde* along the Bautzen road.[38]

It appeared that the thunder of war was destined to be silenced. The conqueror, having been victorious, expressed readiness for peace, while the Monarchs, who had raised their swords in order to defend Germany, could not wish for war. But in order to achieve a lasting peace, it was necessary to continue the struggle. The Coalition, inferior in strength to Napoleon, but confident in the justness of their cause and of the sympathy of Germany, did not give any response to the offer of an armistice.

38 Fain, 384-395.

Appendix XV

Thielmann's Correspondence with the French and the Russians in May 1813

French Commander *7e Corps*, Comte Reynier's letter to *Generalleutnant* Thielmann:

> General, Sir,
> I warn you that I have arrived in Eilenburg and will march towards Torgau tomorrow. It will be necessary for arrangements to be made in Torgau and the surrounding area for the provisioning of the army. It would please me for you to send an officer to me in good time and give him any intelligence you have on enemy dispositions on the right bank of the Elbe.
>
> You will have learned of the results of the Battle of Lützen; the corps under Blücher and Yorck have suffered significantly as has that under Wittgenstein and particularly the Emperor's Lifeguard and the King of Prussia's guards.
>
> Yesterday, at Waldheim, the Viceroy defeated the corps under Miloradovich who had arrived after the battle and had taken command of the rearguard.
>
> Tomorrow we will have 300,000 men on the banks of the Elbe.
>
> At the battle of Lützen we did not engage a quarter of our army and our young soldiers fought like the best troops.
>
> Accept, *Monsieur le Général*, the assurances of my most distinguished consideration.
>
> Eilenburg, 6 May, 1813.
>
> *Monsieur le Général,*
> *Je Vous previens que je suis arrivé à Eilenburg et marcherai demain vers Torgau. Il sera nécessaire qu'on prenne à Torgau et dans les environs les dispositions nécessaires pour la nourriture de l'armée. Vous me ferez plaisir d'envoyer un officier au devant de moi et de lui donner les renseignements que Vous aurez sur les dispositions de l'ennemi sur la rive droite d l'Elbe.*
>
> *Vous aurez appris les resultats de la bataille de Lutzen; les corps de Blücher et de Iork ont infiniment souffert ainsi que celui de Wittgenstein et particulièrement les gardes de l'Empereur et du Roi de Prusse.*
>
> *Le Viceroi a battu hier à Waldheim les corps de Miloradowitz qui était arrivé après la bataille et avait pris le commandement de l'arriergarde.*

Nous aurons demain 300,000 hommes sur les bords de l'Elbe.

A la bataille de Lutzen on n'a pas engagé le quart de notre armée et nos jeunes soldats ont combattu comme les meilleures troupes.

Agréez, Monsieur le Général, l'assurance de la consideration la plus distinguée.

Eilenburg, le 6 Mai, 1813.

General Thielmann's response:

General, Sir,
I have the honour to acknowledge receipt of the letter you sent me from Eilenburg and its duplicate.

Having received from His Majesty the King, my master, strict orders to open the location of Torgau to no one except by orders signed by His hand and only then if they have been issued with the consent of His Majesty the Kaiser of Austria, I must declare to you, General, Sir, that I shall not allow anyone to approach my fortress.

Please accept the assurances of my highest consideration.

Monsieur le Général,

J'ai l'honneur d'accuser réception de la lettre que Vous m'avez adressé d'Eilenburg et du duplicatum.

Ayant reçu de S.M. le Roi mon maître l'ordre le plus strict de n'ouvrir la place de Torgau pour personne que par un ordre signé de Sa main et qui ne pourrait être donné qu'avec consentement de S.M. l'Empereur d'Autriche, il me faut Vous declarer, Monsieur le Général, que je ne laisserai approcher personne de ma forteresse.

Veuillez agréer les assurances de ma haute considération.

Copies of these letters are attached to Thielmann's memo in the archive of the M.T.D. No. 29,182, Log of Incoming Documents, No. 785.

Comte Reynier's letter to General Thielmann:

9 May, 1813. General, Sir,
You probably have not heard from Dresden, I shall let you know. The Emperor entered the city yesterday morning. The bridge was burning but was extinguished and was repaired, and yesterday we had two divisions in the Neustadt already. The King of Prussia yesterday withdrew from Grossenhain with 35,000 men after burning the bridge at Meissen. You must have news whether he has taken the road to Berlin or the road to Silesia. If you were to do your duty in accordance with the old commitments of Saxony, we could pursue them much better via the bridge at Torgau or any that you might have built close to this place rather than by the one which we are going to lay at Belgern or at Wittenberg, and Saxony might acquire that part of Silesia which separates it from the Grand Duchy

of Warsaw. Your conduct does your Sovereign great harm. We captured the Mühlberg bridgehead last night.

Accept, *Monsieur le Général*, the assurances of my most distinguished consideration.

Le 9 Mai 1813. Monsieur le Général,
Vous n'avez probablement pas des nouvelles de Dresden, je Vous en donnerai. L'Empereur y est entré hier matin. Le pont brulait, on éteint le feu, il a été reparé et hier sour nous avions déjà deux divisions à la Neustadt. Le roi Prusse s'est retiré hier de Grossenhain avec 35,000 hommes après avoir brulé le pont de Meissen. Vous dovrez avoir des nouvelles s'il prend la route de Berlin ou celle de la Silesie. Si Vous faisiez Votre devoir suivant les anciens engagements de la Saxe, nous le poursuivrions bien mieux par le pont de Torgau ou celui que Vous feriez etablir à coté de cette place que par celui qu'on va faire à Belgern et par Wittenberg, et la Saxe pourrait avoir la partie de la Silesie qui la sépare du grand duché de Varsovie. Votre conduite fait bien de tort à votre Souverain. On s'est emparé cette nuit de la tête de pont de Mühlberg.

Agréez, Monsieur le Général, l'assurance de la considération la plus distinguée.

Thielmann's response:

Torgau, 9 May, 1813. General, Sir,
I have the honour to thank you for the news you have just sent me, especially since it is very difficult to get any in my situation. This is also the reason why I cannot satisfy your request regarding the route the King of Prussia took. You give me a glimpse of a bright future of partitioning Silesia in our favour, but I am only a soldier and I leave it to my Sovereign to arrange His future by the commitments he has recently entered into with Austria.

Accept the assurances of my highest consideration.

Torgau le 9 Mai 1813. Monsieur le Général,
J'ai l'honneur de Vous remercier des nouvelles que Vous venez de me donner, d'autant plus qu'il est bien difficile d'en avoir dans ma situation. Voila aussi la raison pourquoi je ne puis pas satisfaire à Votre demande relativement à la route que le roi de Prusse ait pris. Vous me faites entrevoir un bel avenir en partageant la Silesie en notre faveur, mais je ne suis que militaire et je laisse à mon Souverain d'arranger Son avenir dans les engagements qu'il a nouvellement pris avec l'Autriche.

Agréez les assurances de ma considération la plus distinguée.

Copies of these letters are attached to General Thielmann's memo, Log of Incoming Documents, No. 811.

Thielmann's letter to Russian Adjutant General Prince Volkonsky:

Torgau, 10 May, 1813. My Prince,
I must repeat to Your Excellency, that I cannot allow passage through Torgau until Austria has declared itself, for such are my King's orders, and since there has been no response from our Cabinet, why do you want me to disobey my Master for a matter of little importance and at a time when everything depends on Austria, who would only be dishonoured by my conduct? There is nothing to fear for my location regarding disease. I have had camps set up and things are going better.

I have the honour to request Your Excellency to inform His Majesty the Emperor that Torgau is provisioned for 11,500 men and 800 horses for 115 days including today.

I have the honour to remain with the highest consideration, etcetera.

Torgau, le 10 Mai 1813. Mon Prince,
Il me faut répeter à Votre Excellence, que je ne puis pas permettre un passage par Torgau jusqu'au moment que l'Autriche se soit déclarée, car tel est l'ordre de mon Roi, et comme il n'y a plus de retour pour notre Cabinet, pour quoi voulez Vous que je désobeisse à mon Maître pour un objet de petite importance et dans un moment où tout dépend de l'Autriche, qui ne saurait être que désobligée par ma conduite? Il n'y a rien à craindre pour ma place à cause des maladies. J'ai fait dresser des camps et cela va mieux.

J'ai l'honneur de prier Votre Excellence de bien vouloir mettre à la connaisance de S.M. l'Empereur que Torgau est approvisionnée pour 11,500 hommes et 800 chevaux pour 115 jours en comptant d'aujourd'hui.

J'ai l'honneur d'être avec la plus haute consideration, etc.

A copy of this letter is attached to the Log of Incoming Documents, No. 812.

Upon leaving Torgau, General Thielmann sent the following letter to Emperor Alexander I:

Elsterwerda, 11 May, 1813. Sire!
The King of Saxony is in Dresden! He made peace with France upon the arrival of Mr de Serra in Prague.[1]

I have been dismissed from command of the location of Torgau under the pretext of having to command the forces which must immediately join the French armies. The arrival of the King on His territory has suddenly affected the opinion of my commanders;[2] the withdrawal of all Coalition troops, not bringing them into Torgau at night, the presence of the enemy in front of this location, particularly as it was General Reynier, robbed me of all hope. All that remained was for me to resign my commission with the King and leave to save my life and my honour.

I already suspected something of this kind the day before yesterday, when Emperor Napoleon sent *Oberkammerherr* Baron Friesen to me from

1 The French Resident at the Saxon Court.
2 Thielmann is referring here to generals Steindel and Sahr.

Dresden. My response was precise, as I had only to show the King's orders dated the 5th of this month, according to which I should not open the gates to the French even if the fortunes of war had obliged the Coalition to withdraw behind the Elbe. Following the departure of Herr von Friesen, I no longer had a garrison or rather commanders; I had only my friends left, so I first addressed myself to General von Kleist to bring troops, but it was too late; he was no longer in Mühlberg.

Now, wretched as I am, I throw myself at Your Majesty's feet, asking Him for a place in His armies, reminding Him of His gracious promises. My fault is to have served my King too well!

I bring with me Lieutenant-Colonel Aster [Ernst Ludwig Aster], my Chief of Staff, a man of rare talent and certainly one of the most skilful engineers in all of Germany. It was he who conceived the works at Torgau and who carried them out for the most part, not to mention the hydro-technical works which were his specialisation throughout Saxony. He has given up, as have I, homeland, wife, children, so as not to dishonour himself and to serve the greatest and most gracious of Sovereigns.

Elsterwerda, le 11 Mai, 1813. Sire!

Le Roi de Saxe est à Dresde! Il a fait paix avec la France sur l'arrivée de M-r de Serra a Prague.

Je suis destitué du commandement de la place de Torgau sous pretexte de devoir commander les troupes qui doivent de suite joindre les armées françaises. L'arrivée du Roi dans Ses états avait tout d'un coup attéré l'opinion de mes chefs; l'éloignement de toute troupe alliée, pour la faire entrer la nuit dans Torgau, la présence de l'ennemi devant la place, surtout comme c'était le général Reynier, m'otaient tout espoir. Il ne me restait que de donner ma démission au Roi et de m'en aller pour sauver ma vie et mon honneur.

Je m'en doutais déjà avant-hier de quelque chose, lorsque l'Empereur Napoléon m'envoya de Dresde le grand-chambellan le baron Friesen. Ma reponse était précise, car je n'avais qu'à montrer les ordres du Roi du 5 de ce mois, selon les quels je ne devais même pas ouvrir les portes aux Français si le hasard de la guerre aurait obligé les Allies de repasser l'Elbe. Dès le départ de M-r de Friesen je n'avais plus de garnison ou plutôt de chefs; il ne me restèrent que les amis, aussi m'adressai-je d'abord au général de Kleist pour avoir des troupes, mais c'était trop tard; il n'était plus à Mühlberg.

Aprésent, malheureux comme je suis, je me jette aux pieds de Votre Majesté, pour Lui demander une place dans Ses armées, en Lui rappelent Ses gracieuses promesses. Ma faute est d'avoir trop bien servi mon Roi!

J'ammène avec moi le lieutenant-colonel Aster, mon chef d'état-major, une homme d'un mérite rare et certes l'un des plus habiles ingénieurs de toute l'Allemagne. C'est lui qui a conçu le plan de Torgau et qui l'a exécuté en plus grande partie, sans compter les travaux hydrotechniques qui étaient de sa dépendance dans toute la Saxe. Il a abandonné tout comme moi, patrie, femme, enfants, pour ne pas se déshonorer et pour servir le meilleur et le plus magnanime des Souverains.

Sire, de Votre Majesté, le trèshumble, très obeissant et très soumis,
le baron de Thielmann, général de division.

Held in the Log of Incoming Documents, No. 820.

9

The actions at Königswartha and Weißig

The retreat of the Russo-Prussian army from the Elbe. – The advance by Napoleon's army. – The action at Bischofswerda. – The retreat of the Coalition army to the Bautzen position. – Miloradovich's achievements. – The action at Göda. – The retreat of the Russian rearguard towards Bautzen. – Napoleon's arrival in the Bautzen area. – The reasons for Napoleon's slow progress after the Elbe crossing. – Ney's advance in the direction of Berlin. – His march towards Bautzen.

The numerical strength of the Coalition army at Bautzen. – The reasons for Coalition inaction. – The detachment of Barclay de Tolly to face the enemy advancing from the direction of Hoyerswerda. – The advance of his force. – The action at Königswartha. – The action at Weißig. The return of Barclay's force to the Bautzen position. – The casualties on both sides. – Yorck at the action at Weißig. – The significance of both actions.

The superior enemy troop numbers and their occupation of all the fortresses on the Elbe, facilitating their crossing of the river at any point, forced the Coalition to abandon the defence of the Dresden area. On 28 April (10 May), the main body of the Russian army withdrew from Radeberg to Bischofswerda, five *Meilen* (35 *verstas*) from Dresden; the Prussian army marched from Grossenhain to Königsbrück; Miloradovich's rearguard, having left outposts within sight of the Neustadt and a forward detachment at Weißer Hirsch, settled down at Weißig; the rearguard of the Prussian army was shielding the routes leading from Meissen and Dresden towards Königsbrück; the Cossack detachment under Platov and General Lanskoy's detachment were stationed at Moritzburg [five miles south-west of Radeburg]; Kleist's detachment withdrew from Mühlberg to Grossenhain. The headquarters of the Coalition Monarchs was relocated to Bautzen. The next day [11 May], the Prussian army marched to Kamenz, while Kleist's detachment went to Königsbrück; the Russian army, however, remained in its previous locations at Bischofswerda. At the same time, the engineer, Major General Count Sievers [Yegor Karlovich Sivers or Johann Joachim Georg Alexander von Sievers], was instructed to fortify a position near the town of

Bautzen across the river Spree, and to that end several thousand labourers were assigned to him.[1]

On that same day, 29 April (11 May), the French army moved forwards from the river Elbe; the corps under Macdonald and Latour-Maubourg towards Weißer Hirsch, followed by Marmont's corps; Bertrand's corps went in the direction of Königsbrück. Napoleon's *quartier-général* remained in Dresden with the *Garde* and Oudinot's corps; Ney's and Reynier's corps arrived in Torgau; Lauriston's corps also arrived there from Meissen; Victor's corps and Sébastiani's marched towards Wittenberg.[2]

At two o'clock in the afternoon, the French appeared at Weißer Hirsch and pushed the Russian detachment stationed there back to Weißig, where Miloradovich halted the enemy through the actions of a battery and his skirmishers, while General Melissino charged one of the French infantry columns with the Lubny Hussars and captured 76 men; in addition, the Russian cavalry captured around 100 more prisoners that day. Thereafter, Miloradovich, having been deceived about the superior enemy numbers, left a forward detachment at Weißig, while he withdrew himself to Schmiedefeld [three miles north of Stolpen] with his rearguard. The losses to the Russian force reached some 200 men that day; the enemy, forced to advance across rough terrain infested by Miloradovich's skirmishers, lost considerably more.[3]

On 30 April (12 May), both Coalition armies withdrew to Bautzen. Kleist's corps marched to Kamenz; General Lanskoy's detachment deployed to face Bertrand's corps at Königsbrück; Platov's Cossack detachment was still at Moritzburg. Meanwhile, having received word from Count Wittgenstein that in order to deploy the main body into the positions assigned to them, it was vital that the rearguard remain at Bischofswerda until noon, General Miloradovich replied that he hoped to hold the enemy by exploiting the wooded terrain, until five o'clock in the afternoon.

At eight o'clock in the morning, Marshal Macdonald attacked Miloradovich's forward troops at Weißig and pursued them to Schmiedefeld. General Miloradovich, in preparing to halt the enemy, had placed a strong battery behind Schmiedefeld, on Kapellenberg hill, under the protection of a detachment under comte Saint-Priest,[4] with the Prinz von Württemberg's II Corps as their reserve, which, due to the latter's illness, was under Prince Shakhovskoy's command. The remaining rearguard troops were stationed at Großharthau [five miles west of Bischofswerda]. At 11 o'clock in the morning Macdonald's corps occupied the village of Schmiedefeld whereupon he directed an attack on the battery. The Tobolsk Infantry Regiment was sent to halt the enemy by threatening their flank, and recaptured Schmiedefeld. Whereupon Macdonald sent the bulk of his force through the Fischbach forest, enveloping the

1 War Diary signed by Adjutant General Prince Volkonsky. War Diary of Miloradovich's rearguard. War Diary of Prinz Eugen von Württemberg's corps. Plotho, *Der Krieg in Deutschland und Frankreich in den Jahren 1813 und 1814*, I, 138-140.

2 Vaudoncourt, *Histoire de la guerre soutenue par les Français en Allemagne, en 1813*, 88.

3 War Diary of Miloradovich's rearguard. Miloradovich's letter to Prince Volkonsky, dated 29 April [11 May], No. 457. In this letter the enemy losses are given as: 'not less than 1,000 men.'

4 Comte Saint-Priest's detachment consisted of: the Vyatka Infantry, Olonets Infantry, 11th Jägers and 37th Jägers; Adjutant General Korff's II Cavalry Corps, due to the latter's illness, was commanded by Major General Melissino.

right flank of Saint-Priest's position, while then trying to envelope it from the left flank; but General Emmanuel delayed the enemy with the Kiev Dragoons and one Cossack regiment until 4th Horse Artillery Battery halted them from the front. Taking advantage of the stubborn resistance of the force under comte Saint-Priest, Miloradovich withdrew the main body of the rearguard to a position behind the town of Bischofswerda; Saint-Priest also fell back there, under the protection of skirmishers from the Arkhangelogorod Infantry, Schlüsselburg Infantry, 6th Jägers and 11th Jägers. These regiments, under the command of Major General Karpenko, held the enemy with extraordinary resolve every step of the way to Bischofswerda; one of the jäger regiments was ordered to occupy the town in order to secure their retreat. But once the Chuguev Ulans, instead of bypassing Bischofswerda, found themselves entering the town, in error, then enemy skirmishers burst in behind him, whereupon the jägers were forced to abandon the buildings they had occupied and to retreat to the position. The enemy, who were quickly pursuing them, were delayed by skirmishers hastily assembled by Lieutenant Bergenstrahl of the Quartermaster's Department (General Staff), while in the meantime Miloradovich had ordered Major General Nikitin to open fire at the French advancing through the town from every battery. Several shells set fire to a building, producing a raging inferno, which spread very quickly and stopped the enemy. Meanwhile, French troops crossing a stream to the left of Bischofswerda, were driven off by the Kharkov Dragoons, under the command of Major General Yuzefovich, and lost some 100 men taken prisoner alone. By evening, Miloradovich had led his rearguard back to Rothnaußlitz (seven *verstas* east of Bischofswerda), and on to Göda [4½ miles west of Bautzen], leaving a detachment in the village of Wölkau [3½ miles east of Bischofswerda], while the enemy halted in Bischofswerda, where they remained for the next two days. In the actions around Bischofswerda, Russian casualties were: seven officers and 227 lower ranks killed, nine officers and 350 lower ranks wounded. There are no records of enemy casualties, except in Miloradovich's report, in which he wrote that, according to prisoner interrogations, the French lost some 4,000 men.[5]

The position on the river Spree, on which it had been intended to hold the enemy with the main body of the Coalition Army, turned out to be unsuitable, and for that reason another position was selected four *verstas* beyond the Spree. The troops moved to this position on the morning of 1 (13) May, while the Coalition Monarchs had moved their headquarters to the village of Wurschen the day before [12 May].[6]

During the retreat of the Coalition Army from Lützen to Bautzen, General Miloradovich had rendered never-to-be-forgotten service. Thanks to his energy, fearlessness and composure, the main body was able to move unhurriedly along their march-routes, as if in peacetime. The retreat of the rearguard itself was distinguished by its good order. Contrary to false announcements in the *Le Moniteur*, no guns or vehicles were lost. The troops did not suffer for want of anything: every day, having repelled the enemy, the soldiers prepared hot food for themselves; a wine ration was distributed twice daily. This care for the troops had beneficial

5 War Diary of Miloradovich's rearguard. War Diary of Prinz Eugen von Württemberg's corps. Vaudoncourt, 89-90.

6 Plotho, I, 141-142.

consequences: out of the 18,000 men who were in the rearguard, excluding those wounded in action, only 93 men were sent to hospital. There were sufficient carts with each division for the transportation of the sick and wounded. Not a single sick man and almost none of the wounded fell into the hands of the enemy.

Emperor Alexander I, paying tribute to Miloradovich, a protege of Suvorov's, hero of the Patriotic War, on 1 (13) May, granted him the dignity of a count.[7]

Throughout 2 (14) May, the forces of both sides remained quietly in the locations they occupied. Only Major General Ilovaisky 12th [Vasily Dmitrievich Ilovaisky] executed a surprise raid on part of Bertrand's corps near Königsbrück and captured eight officers and 114 lower ranks.[8]

On 3 (15) May, Macdonald's corps advanced on Wölkau and forced the detachment under comte Saint-Priest to retreat to Rothnaußlitz, while Miloradovich's rearguard took up positions at the village of Göda. At one o'clock in the afternoon, Macdonald approached Rothnaußlitz, from where Saint-Priest retreated initially to Semmichau [six miles west of Bautzen], and then to the right flank of the rearguard, located as follows: Lieutenant Colonel Wolf held the village of Birkau with the Murom Infantry; to their right the village of Göda was held by 4th Jägers and 20th Jägers; while further left, the 21st Jägers and 34th Jägers were stationed in the forest, with the following as their reserves, at the village of Preske: Major General Yuzefovich with the Kharkov Dragoons and Kargopol Dragoons, and Major General Pyshnitsky with the Volhynia Infantry and Kremenchug Infantry; the remaining regiments from II Corps under Prince Shakovskoy,[9] and comte Saint-Priest's detachment[10] were stationed in reserve behind the centre and right wing. Some of the cavalry, commanded of Prince Trubetskoy, had been sent to the high ground in front of Göda with several batteries; Adjutant General Uvarov [Fëdor Petrovich Uvarov], with another part of the cavalry, was behind the force under comte Saint-Priest, in support of the right wing. Count Miloradovich, entrusting the defence of the position at Göda to Prinz Eugen von Württemberg, withdrew across the Spree with the corps under Prince Gorchakov and Markov to Bautzen.

The enemy, approaching the position at around noon, attacked Prince Trubetskoy with their cavalry, who, having made several successful counter-attacks, withdrew

7 On this occasion, a Supreme Rescript was sent: 'General-of-Infantry Miloradovich, Sir, The important service rendered by you on the field of honour has long been acknowledged by a grateful Fatherland; while the renowned participation that you have taken in every campaign that has marked Our reign, has directed Our particular gratitude to you at all times. You and victory were inseparable, from the depths of the Fatherland to those countries most distant from it. The current war has crowned your achievements, especially with the leadership of the rearguard of the army, where you have forced the enemy to atone for the blood of many thousands every step of the way. As the reward for all such exploits of yours, We raise you and your future offspring to the status and dignity of a Count of the Russian Empire. May the Fatherland see further evidence of Our gratitude in this and a new pledge imposed upon you for the greater glory of Russia. Nevertheless, we are grateful to you. Alexander. No. 903. 1 [13] May 1813. Wurschen.'

8 War Diary, signed by Prince Volkonsky.

9 Tobolsk Infantry, Ryazhsk Infantry, Chernigov Infantry and Reval Infantry.

10 Vyatka Infantry, Olonets Infantry, 11th Jägers, 37th Jägers, Adjutant General Korff's cavalry under Major General Melissino's command.

behind the right wing via Göda and joined Uvarov's cavalry. After that, the French infantry headed against the left wing of the position in several columns, where the defending regiments (21st Jägers and 34th Jägers) suffered significant casualties. At one o'clock in the afternoon, the front line fell back behind the support line, which, having opened a strong cannonade, halted the enemy. Here, the main efforts of the advancing columns were also directed at the left wing of the Russian force. General Yuzefovich, taking advantage of the rough terrain, covertly placed a Cossack regiment in a ravine, and as soon as the enemy had passed the ambush, he attacked him frontally with the Kharkov Dragoons and Kargopol Dragoons, and from the rear with the Cossacks, and put them to flight, capturing two officers and 176 lower ranks. The cavalry under Adjutant General Uvarov also captured more than 100 men. But the appearance of strong columns from Bertrand's corps on the road from Kamenz, forced the Prinz von Württemberg to follow the move by Miloradovich towards Bautzen. This retreat was conducted in exemplary order, under the protection of Uvarov's cavalry. Losses on our side reached some 600 men; Major General Pyshnitsky was among those wounded. Enemy casualties were in excess of 1,000 men.[11]

Upon retreating through Bautzen beyond the river Spree, Miloradovich's rearguard was located in the forward position as follows:[12] Prinz Eugen von Württemberg's II Corps to the right of the town, which was held by his brigade under Lieutenant Colonel Wolf; to the left of the town were Markov's IV Corps, then Count Osterman's [Alexander Ivanovich Osterman-Tolstoy], together with comte Saint-Priest's detachment. Kleist's corps was located at Burk with Roth's Russian detachment. The forward outposts had been left on the left bank of the Spree and, in order to protect the rearguard more securely against being outflanked, light cavalry detachments remained ahead: on the right flank, Major General Lanskoy's were at Wittichenau [4½ miles south of Hoyerswerda], while Major General Emmanuel's were on the left at Boblitz. The town of Bautzen was being put into a defensible state.[13]

Throughout the retreat by Coalition forces, Napoleon gradually moved the main body of his army towards Bautzen, namely the corps under: Macdonald, Bertrand, Marmont, Oudinot and Latour-Maubourg. The *Garde* departed Dresden on 3 (15) May, while Napoleon departed there himself, with a large retinue on 6 (18) May, spent the night in Großharthau and arrived at the Kleinförstchen manor, four *verstas* from Bautzen on 7 (19) May. Passing through burned-out Bischofswerda, where only three buildings had survived, he was moved at the catastrophe that had befallen the local population, who were wandering about in the ruins of their homes. Having learned from Caulaincourt that the place had been burned down by French troops, Napoleon gave his word to have it rebuilt and issued orders for the most honourable of the citizens to come to him with an estimate of the losses they had suffered. Subsequent events prevented him from receiving this deputation; yet on his way back from Silesia, while passing through Bischofswerda, although he

11 War Diary, signed by Prince Volkonsky. War Diary of Miloradovich's rearguard. War Diary of Prinz Eugen von Württemberg's corps. Vaudoncourt, 90. According to his account, French losses in this action were 300 men while the Russians lost 800.

12 See Map No. 8: Plan of the Battle of Bautzen, 8 to 9 (20 to 21) May 1813.

13 Prinz Eugen von Württemberg's diary. Plotho, I, 143-144.

remembered the promise he had made, he limited himself to issuing 100,000 francs to the townspeople. Upon his arrival in Kleinförstchen, where the *quartier-général* of the French army was being set up, Napoleon immediately went to reconnoitre the Coalition positions and returned to the manor at seven o'clock in the evening; meanwhile, the sound of a cannonade could be heard gradually intensifying from the direction of Königswartha [ten miles north of Bautzen]; at eight o'clock, having suddenly called for his horse, Napoleon rode four *verstas* north towards the village of Kleinwelka and returned at around midnight.[14]

Thus, Napoleon, having taken five days to move the army, numbering about 100,000 men, about 60 *verstas* from Dresden towards Bautzen, left his force inactive for more than three days, from 3 to 7 (15 to 19) May. The reasons for Napoleon's uncharacteristic slowness were: firstly, uncertainty about the direction taken by the Prussian army,[15] and then, once he had finally become convinced of the Coalition concentration on the route to Silesia, the desire to await the outcome of Ney's operations and bring at least part of the force detached towards Berlin closer to him.[16] In addition, Napoleon had to wait a few days for elements of the *Garde* and *Réserve de cavalerie* to join his army.[17]

At the same time as the main body of the French army was advancing from Dresden towards Bautzen, on 1 (13) May, Marshal Ney set off from Torgau towards Berlin with three corps: Reynier went towards Annaburg [14 miles north of Torgau]; Ney went towards Luckau with his own corps, Lauriston towards Doberlug; Victor's corps and Sébastiani, whose reconstitution was still not complete, remained in Wittenberg. The detachment of one of the most renowned French marshals towards Berlin with an entire third of the army, at a considerable distance from the main body, was based on the erroneous assumption that the Coalition, having learned about this division of forces, would abandon their line of retreat to the Oder and race to defend the Prussian capital. But on 3 (15) May, as soon as Macdonald had sent Napoleon confirmed intelligence on the concentration of both Coalition armies at Bautzen, Ney was initially ordered to send Lauriston's corps to Hoyerswerda, and later, to move to Brösa with his entire force, enveloping the Coalition right flank. Since the

14 Odeleben, *Relation circonstanciée de la campagne de 1813 en Saxe*, I, 83-87.

15 Orders dated 13 May for the duc de Raguse (Marmont) to mount a reconnaissance in the direction of Grossenhain, in order to confirm what has become of the Prussian army, which it is said has withdrawn either towards Berlin, or towards Breslau. (*Ordre du 13 mai au duc de Raguse d'envoyer une reconnaissance dans la direction de Grossenhain, à fin de savoir positivement ce qu'est devenue l'armée prussienne, que les uns disent s'être retirée sur Berlin, et les autres sur Breslau*).

16 Orders dated 16 May… Attach a new letter for the prince de la Moscowa (Ney), in which you are to inform him, that we are definitely in contact with the enemy at Bautzen, where the enemy is in force, that I therefore think that he must come with *5e Corps* and to base himself at Hoyerswerda. (*Ordre du 16 mai… Ajoutez-y une nouvelle lettre pour le prince de la Moscowa, dans la quelle vous lui ferez connaître, que décidément nous sommes en présence de l'ennemi à Bautzen, où l'ennemi est en force, que je pense donc qu'il doit venir avec le cinquième corps se placer sur Hoyerswerda*).

17 One division of the *Jeune Garde* (under General Barrois) had only arrived at Dresden on 1 (13) May; another, of the *Vieille Garde* (under General Decouz) and the majority of the cavalry were still on the march to Dresden. Vaudoncourt, 90.

latest orders sent from Dresden on 6 (18) May, could not have been received by Ney before 7 (19) May, besides which he would already have been close to Berlin, it could not be expected that he would have chance to arrive in the vicinity of Bautzen before 11 (23) May. The Coalition, meanwhile, might receive reliable intelligence about the dislocation of the French forces and attack the main body under Napoleon. But, fortunately for him, Ney had turned from the direction towards Berlin assigned to him even before receiving orders from the *quartier-général* in this regard. General Jomini [Antoine Henri de Jomini] as Chief of Staff of his corps, suggested to him that the offensive towards Berlin was a less important objective, and that, on the contrary, the march towards Bautzen with 60,000 men could deliver the most decisive results. Even a modest victory at Bautzen would result in a Coalition retreat beyond the Oder and the exposure of Berlin. In the event of a successful envelopment of the right flank of the Russo-Prussian army, it would be thrown back onto the Austrian border in disarray, which would force the Viennese Cabinet to remain allied to France. Marshal Ney was aware of the soundness of this point of view, but did not dare to violate the direct orders he had received from the *quartier-général.* At that very moment, he came across an issue of a Breslau newspaper, in which the news was announced of the march of Barclay de Tolly's 20,000 strong corps across Silesia. This circumstance gave Ney a reason to ignore the orders issued to him to go to Berlin. Instead, he would go to the aid of Napoleon, who was at risk of engaging the entire concentrated forces of the Coalition army. Having decided to march on Bautzen, the marshal turned towards Calau and on 5 (17) May received orders there to move Lauriston's corps to Hoyerswerda, and on the following day [18 May], to advance towards Bautzen with his entire army.[18]

Napoleon, concerned about maintaining communications with Ney's force, was hampered by the presence of Platov's Cossack detachment near Moritzburg, and ordered Marshal Mortier [Adolphe Édouard Casimir Joseph Mortier] to drive the Cossacks away using Dumoustier's *Jeune Garde* division [Pierre Dumoustier] and Latour-Maubourg's cavalry. On 4 (16) May, Major Löwenstern's detachment, consisting of two Cossack regiments and a Prussian hussar regiment under Major Blücher [Franz Ferdinand Joachim von Blücher], attacked by superior numbers, was forced to retreat to Grossenhain, from where the Coalition force withdrew in diverging directions to Elsterwerda and Ortrand.[19] Following this, having received orders to establish communications with Ney, General Bertrand detached Peyri's division towards Königswartha.[20]

The Coalition army, having retreated to positions at Bautzen, on 4 (16) May, was reinforced by Barclay de Tolly's corps, which had arrived from Thorn, numbering 13,500 men,[21] which, together with 5,000 under Kleist, 3,000 Prussian reserves[22] and

18 Vaudoncourt, 90-91. Norvins, *Portefeuille de 1813*, I, 383-385. Beitzke, *Geschichte der deutschen Freiheitskriege in den Jahren 1813 und 1814*, I, 412-413.
19 Vaudoncourt, 90-91. *Denkwürdigkeiten eines Livländers, II*, 31-33.
20 Orders for General Bertrand, dated 18 May, new style. Vaudoncourt, 90-91.
21 For the report submitted to the Tsar by General Barclay de Tolly, dated 4 [16] May, on the number of troops with the Western Army, see Appendix XVI at the end of this chapter.
22 On the march from Lützen to Bautzen, the Prussian army was reinforced by three reserve battalions and two march-battalions, under the command of Major Graf Dohna. Plotho, I,

3,000 to 4,000 Russian replacements sent after the battle of Lützen, added some 25,000 men to the Russo-Prussian army.[23] The losses to the Coalition in this battle and in the subsequent rearguard actions did not exceed 16,000 or 17,000 men, hence the army assembled at Bautzen, numbered some 100,000 men in its ranks.[24] As the Coalition were determined to fight Napoleon once again, it was better for them, taking advantage of the dislocation of enemy forces, to attack them before Ney arrived, rather than accept battle in a position whose advantages could by no means outweigh an increase to the French army by half as much again. But the Coalition did not have a commander who would dare to take responsibility for such an important decision: Wittgenstein, after losing the battle of Lützen, had lost the confidence inspired by his earlier successes; Barclay de Tolly was considered by many to have too little capability for decisive operations; while Blücher, although a brave warrior, and courageous partisan, was by no means a commander who could compete with an equivalent army led by Napoleon. In addition, it would mean attacking the enemy with the river Spree to their rear and descending into the forests of Bischofswerda, where the Coalition superiority in cavalry would have counted for nothing, while on the French side they had a significant superiority in infantry. Thus, it is not difficult to explain the inaction of the Russo-Prussian army, which allowed Napoleon to concentrate his forces; it is utterly incomprehensible that the Coalition, having a huge number of light cavalry and Cossacks, did not properly reconnoitre the enemy locations stationed within their sight, and undertook a reconnaissance in force on 6 (18) May, which did not achieve its objective at all.[25] Meanwhile, the partisans under Löwenstern and those in Prussian service under Major Hellwig [Karl Ludwig Friedrich Hellwig], who were in the vicinity of Hoyerswerda, had reported on the departure of Lauriston's corps from Senftenberg.[26] The Coalition, not knowing that there were two more corps following them and hoping to catch them in isolation, on the night of 7 (19) May, sent the corps that had arrived from Thorn, Raevsky's Grenadier Corps [Nikolai Nikolaevich Raevsky] and Yorck's corps, with a total of 23,700 men, against them under Barclay de Tolly's command.[27] It had been intended to attack Lauriston's corps with Barclay's force from the right flank, simultaneously with the main body of the Coalition Army attacking the enemy stationed facing the Bautzen position.[28]

The force under Barclay de Tolly set out from their bivouacs at midnight, in two columns: the left, consisting of Russian troops, Lieutenant General Chaplits

136.

23 Clausewitz, VII, 284-295.

24 Before the battle of Lützen there were about 92,000 men in total under Count Wittgenstein's command, 25,000 men had arrived, bringing the total to 117,000 men, 17,000 men had been lost, therefore, about 100,000 men remained prior to the battle of Bautzen.

25 Plotho, I, 146-147.

26 War Diary, signed by Prince Volkonsky. *Denkwürdigkeiten eines Livländers*, II, 34-35. Plotho, I, 148.

27 Those detached against Ney were: Barclay de Tolly's corps of 13,000 men, 5,000 men of the Grenadier Corps and 5,700 men from Yorck's Prussian corps, for a total of 23,700 men.

28 For Count Wittgenstein's letter to General Barclay de Tolly, dated 7 [19] May, No. 941, see Appendix XVII at the end of this chapter.

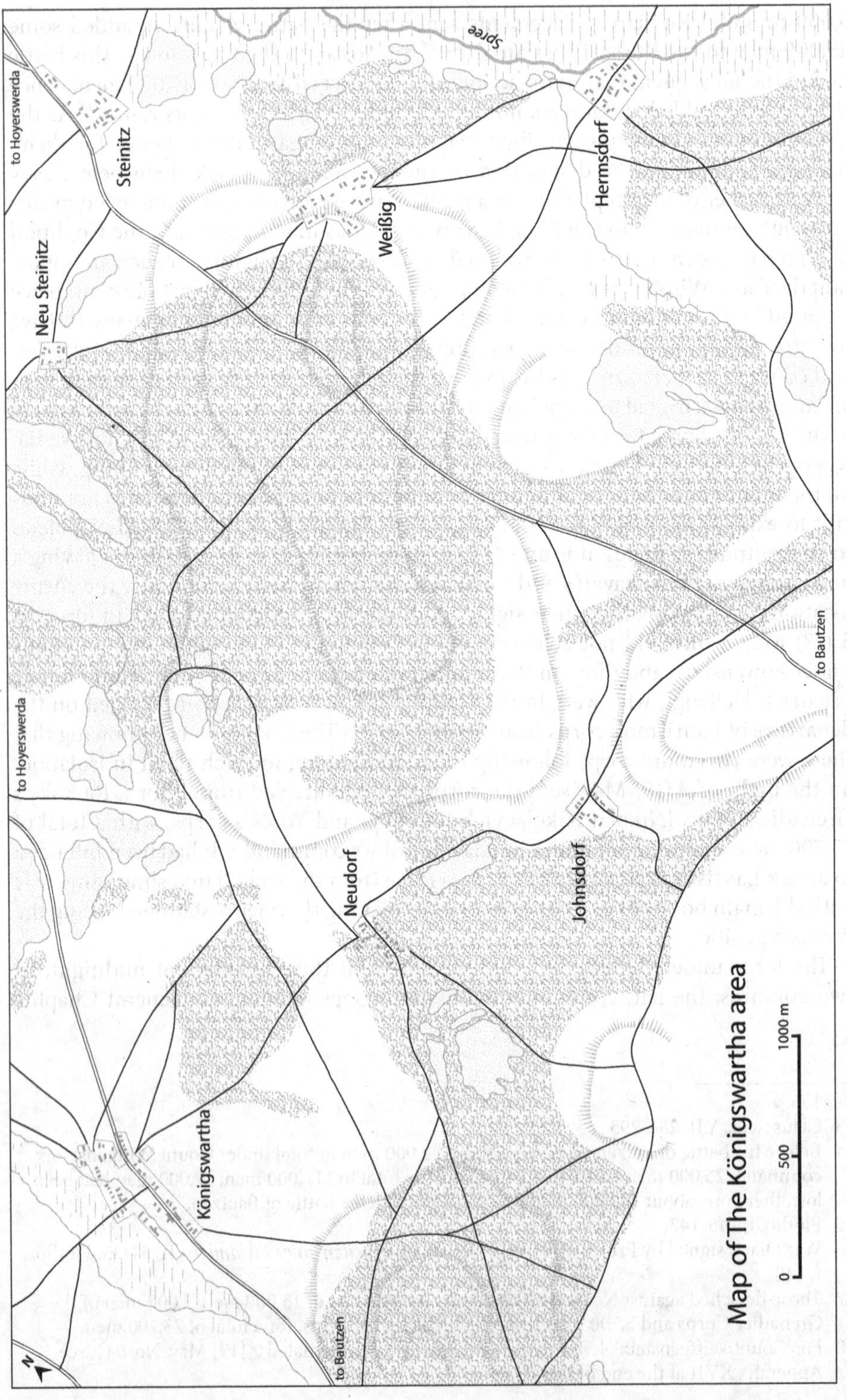

Map of Königswartha area.

advanced with the vanguard of 3,000 men, proceeding from Niedergurig [4½ miles north-east of Bautzen], on the left bank of the Spree, directly towards Johnsdorf; while the right-hand column, with Yorck's Prussian force, moved down the right bank of the Spree, via Gleina, Guttau, Lömischau and Lieske [12 miles north-east of Bautzen] and onwards towards Hermsdorf.[29] Chaplits' vanguard, having completed a difficult night march, appeared in Johnsdorf at one o'clock in the afternoon on 7 (19) May. Intelligence was received there regarding the location of Peyri's Italian division at the town of Königswartha. Barclay immediately decided to attack the enemy with the leading troops and sent Major General Rudzevich along the shortest route towards Königswartha, with the 22nd Jäger Regiment, two guns and a *Sotnia* of Cossacks, followed by the remaining vanguard troops. The enemy, having been positioned very negligently, were taken by surprise and retreated to the town in disarray. But as the dense forest and swampy terrain made it difficult for the jägers to advance from Johnsdorf, Barclay de Tolly, having ordered Chaplits to continue in the same direction, sent Langéron's corps to the left,[30] via the most suitable path emerging onto the Bautzen highway, in order to attack the enemy from the direction of Bautzen and to cut them off from the main body of the French army. At about three o'clock in the afternoon, 18th Division under Major General Shcherbatov encountered the enemy in the forest in front of the town. The 32nd Jägers and Kostroma Infantry, which were in the lead, drove the skirmishers out of the forest, attacked a large square in a clearing, broke it and captured two guns; as Inzov's 9th Division [Ivan Nikitich Inzov] came up, Prince Shcherbatov led an attack on Königswartha, where the enemy defended desperately in the houses and streets for more than an hour, but were finally driven out of the town and dispersed into the surrounding forests. Some of the fleeing soldiers ended up in Bohemia. The victors captured seven guns (of which two dismounted guns were left in place), several ammunition caissons and their entire train, and took *Général de division* Peyri, three *généraux de brigade*, 14 officers and 740 lower ranks prisoner. The pursuit of the enemy was entrusted to the vanguard under Chaplits and Figner's partisan detachment [Alexander Samoilovich Figner]; Langéron's corps and Zass' reserve [Andrey Pavlovich Zass or Andreas Burchard Friedrich von Saß], which had arrived at Königswartha at the end of the action, halted there upon hearing a powerful cannonade from the direction of Weißig; the Grenadier Corps was located between Johnsdorf and Königswartha.[31]

Meanwhile, General Yorck, having completed a strenuous 15-hour march, arrived at Hermsdorf at three o'clock in the afternoon, where he granted a short rest to his weary force. Barclay de Tolly's orders, sent during the advance towards Königswartha by the Russian force, caught up with him here: 'to move to Wartha [three miles north

29 See Map No. 7: Map of the Königswartha area.

30 For the details of Chaplits' and Langéron's forces, see Appendix XVI at the end of this chapter.

31 General-of-Infantry Barclay de Tolly's report to the Tsar regarding the action at Königswartha, dated 8 [20] May, No. 192. Droysen, *Yorck's Leben*, II; 227-228. Vaudoncourt, 91-92. According to Vaudoncourt's account, all-in-all Peyri's division lost two guns and three ammunition caissons, managed to rally once more, and being supported by cavalry under the duc de Valmy (Kellermann the Younger), recaptured the town of Königswartha.

of Königswartha] and attack the enemy should they appear along the road leading through this place from Hoyerswerda.' Having received these orders, Yorck immediately set out in the indicated direction. In the lead were *3. Schlesisches Husaren*; they were followed by: Steinmetz's brigade, Corswant's reserve cavalry [Karl Friedrich von Corswant] and Horn's brigade; the corps, numbering 4,100 infantrymen, 1,200 cavalrymen and 400 artillerymen, included 36 guns. Yorck rode ahead of Steinmetz's brigade himself, with his staff. Upon approaching Weißig, the hussars encountered French skirmishers in the forest, who opened fire. The force was ordered to halt, while Yorck deployed a *Füsilier* battalion from the leading brigade, ordering them to clear the forest of infantry and to hold it, while he rode up Eichberg hill himself, near Weißig, from where it was possible to observe the road leading from Hoyerswerda. Having observed the enemy hurrying from Steinitz towards Weißig, he ordered that this village be occupied by infantry while *Leutnant* Borowski's horse artillery battery be placed on the Eichberg in order to delay the French, who would have to move along a narrow causeway under fire from the Prussian artillery. Steinmetz's infantry occupied the village of Weißig and the forest to the left of the battery, two squadrons of *Westpreußisches Dragoner* were placed to the right behind the high ground in order to support them. A heated battle was developing along the entire line when suddenly, at four o'clock, Barclay de Tolly's aide de camp galloped up with orders to move immediately to Johnsdorf and join the reserve of the Russian force fighting at Königswartha. Although Barclay, having issued these orders, had not yet learned of the Prussian corps' engagement with Lauriston, nevertheless, Yorck answered that he: 'would immediately fulfil the orders received, but consider it my duty to mention that the enemy, who have deployed significant numbers against me, would follow me and be led towards the flank of the Russian force; that, by fighting in this advantageous position, I might be of more use than being at Johnsdorf, especially if I were also supported by Russian troops.' *Oberstleutnant* Steinmetz was instructed to cover the retreat of the remaining troops with two infantry regiments, one of dragoons and one horse artillery battery,[32] and follow them as the rearguard. In executing these orders, Steinmetz first evacuated Weißig, then the forest, and brought the guns down from the Eichberg; as he retreated the enemy gradually increased pressure on the tail of his column.

At about five o'clock in the afternoon, just as Horn's brigade was approaching Johnsdorf, Barclay's orders arrived: Yorck's corps was to return to Weißig and hold there until nightfall; the 1st Grenadier Division, under Major General Sulima [Nikolai Semënovich Sulima], was sent to reinforce him, (eight battalions, numbering 1,600 men); while 9th Division under Major General Inzov headed along a country road through the forest, towards Lauriston's right flank, who, after Steinmetz's retreat, having occupied Weißig and the Eichberg, was moving part of his corps towards Königswartha. Steinmetz's force turned back and drove the French out of the forest; a bitter action flared up on the high ground of the Eichberg, which constituted the key to the position; the enemy gradually fed 14 battalions into battle, some 8,000 men, against Steinmetz's 1,300 men. At six o'clock the first

32 *1. Ostpreußisches Infanterie, Garde-Regiment zu Fuss, 1. Westpreußisches Dragoner, Leutnant* Borowski's *2. Reitende Artillerie Batterie.*

support arrived: *2. Reitende Artillerie Batterie*, reinforced with a half-battery of 12-pounders; whereupon the *Westpreußisches Dragoner* and other regiments of the reserve cavalry deployed in a clearing south of the Eichberg, on the right, as far as the little forest through which the road to Hermsdorf ran; the artillery located in the clearing started a cannonade with the enemy batteries placed in the alder forest beyond Weißig. The 6th Combined Regiment, which arrived soon after, reinforced the *Füsiliers* in the forest to the left of the main road; while Yorck advanced along the main road himself, with both musketeer battalions of the *Garde-Regiment*, screened by a skirmish line moving through the forest. The cannonade thundered along the entire line and small-arms fire could be heard; entire battalions were deployed as skirmishers, fighting at very close quarters; but the most stubborn fighting was taking place around the Eichberg. This hill changed hands several times. The brave *Garde-Regiment*, having lost its regimental commander, Major Zepelin [Konstantin Gottlieb Leberecht von Zepelin], both battalion commanders and many officers killed or wounded, was instrumental in the capture of the corpse-littered hill for a third time. But the strength of the Prussian troops was now spent by the long battle and the losses suffered. Taking advantage of this, the enemy directed the decisive assault: six recently repulsed battalions, supported by six fresh and three more who had arrived from Weißig, moved forward at the *pas de charge*, with loud cries of: *Vive l'empereur*! The Prussian troops were forced to cede the Eichberg once more, but all attempts by the enemy to penetrate further were frustrated by the actions of the battery which had been stationed south of the hill, and attacks by the *Westpreußisches Dragoner* under the command of *Oberst* Wuthenau [Karl Ludwig von Wuthenau].

During these actions, General Inzov was moving along a very poor lane through the forest with the 9th Division, consisting of four weak regiments numbering 2,000 men, when they encountered a strong French column moving towards Königswartha and held the enemy up until evening.[33]

Darkness was falling. Yorck, unable to remain in a position where he could be outflanked and cut off by superior French forces, sent some of his artillery back towards Johnsdorf. Just two batteries remained in the clearing, whose fire was directed at the Eichberg in order to hold off enemy attacks on the road to Hermsdorf. The reserve cavalry stood to the right of the battery, except for the *Litthauisches Dragoner*, who were posted behind them, facing the Hermsdorf forest. Suddenly, a strong enemy column, charging along the Hoyerswerda road through the large forest, threatened to break through the centre, which would have resulted in the loss of the guns sent towards Johnsdorf. At this critical moment, Yorck rushed the Russian grenadiers up to engage the enemy, in a dense column, preceded by a screen

33 Inzov's column was being guided by Sub-Lieutenant Rennenkampff [Karl Pavlovich Rennenkampf or Karl Friedrich Edler von Rennenkampff] of the Quartermaster's Department (later Lieutenant General and Deputy-Director of the Military Academy). General Inzov, disconcerted at encountering superior enemy forces on very rough and swampy ground, wrote in his report that Sub-Lieutenant Rennenkampff had erroneously guided the division onto impassable terrain. This report did not disadvantage Rennenkampff, who was promoted one rank for his work at Königswartha (interview with K.P. Rennenkampff in person).

of skirmishers from the *Garde-Regiment*, and placed four guns right at the exit of the forest. But nothing could hold the French back; canister thundered, lashed by musket fire, they continue to advance, with drums beating, the area resounding to their shouts of *en avant*! Approaching to 250 paces from the Prussian force, the column halted; the lead platoons opened fire. At that very moment, on Yorck's own command, the reserve cavalry, under the command of *Generalmajor* Corswant, charged at the enemy.[34] Platen's *Litthauisches Dragoner*, hacked into the column with loud cries of Hurrah! while the *Westpreußisches Dragoner* completed their rout and drove them back into the forest. The French rallied once more; but the fearless Yorck was ready to engage them: *Leutnant* Stern's half-battery raced up at a fast trot to take up positions on the main road facing the exits from the forest; the dragoons deployed to the right; the Russian grenadiers plunged into the forest to the left of the artillery. The enemy attempted to debouch from there several times, but being engaged with canister, they were forced to return having taken casualties and even give way beyond the edge of the forest. The darkness of the night put a stop to the fighting. General Yorck sent his guns back behind the defile, leaving only Stern's half-battery in position. The Prussian infantry were positioned perpendicular to the main road to Bautzen in battalion columns: on the right flank, three battalions from Horn's brigade were stationed in a little forest; on the left flank were the Russian grenadiers with the cavalry behind the infantry. Large fires were ordered to be lit to make the enemy pull back a little; meanwhile, preparations were made for a covert withdrawal. The French, however, suspected this ruse of war and attacked the troops closest to the large forest at night. York, concerned at staying in front of the defile any longer and having learned that the Russian troops that were with his detachment had withdrawn, he sent some of the cavalry and Stern's guns beyond the causeway at 11 o'clock; the infantry followed them; while Steinmetz's brigade formed the rearguard with the rest of the cavalry.[35]

At six o'clock in the morning of 8 (20) May, Barclay de Tolly's Russian force returned to the Bautzen position, leaving Chaplits' detachment on the Spree river, near Klix. At about five o'clock in the afternoon on that same day, at the time of the battle of Bautzen, Yorck's corps withdrew into the position. The losses to the Prussian force reached 1,883 men, while the Russians lost some 1,000 (the majority in the fighting at Königswartha).[36] The French losses are not known precisely. The troops under Yorck covered themselves in glory, fighting stubbornly for six hours against an enemy three times their strength and losing a third of their available manpower. General Yorck, together with the Russian grenadiers who came to his aid, had less than 8,000 men, but these troops fought so tenaciously that Lauriston reported that there were 32,000 men facing him at Weißig. Barclay de Tolly, informing the King

34 *Litthauisches Dragoner, 1. Westpreußisches Dragoner* and two squadrons of *3. Schlesisches Husaren*.

35 Barclay de Tolly's report to the Tsar, dated 8 [20] May. Droysen, *Yorck's Leben*, II, 227-244. Plotho, I, 148-152.

36 According to Plotho (I, 152), at the action at Weißig, the Prussian force lost 13 officers and 246 lower ranks killed, 62 officers and 1,411 lower ranks wounded, two officers and 149 lower ranks missing, for a total of 77 officers and 1,806 lower ranks. There are no precise figures for Russian losses in both actions.

of Prussia about the actions at Königswartha and Weißig, wrote: 'General Yorck's performance was beyond praise.'[37]

Indeed, these feats brought great honour to Barclay,[38] and even more to Yorck, but did not have the slightest influence on the course of the war overall. Had the Coalition been able to defeat the isolated Ney and then turn against Napoleon, then the consequences of such a success could have been very important. Napoleon, in all probability, would have retreated beyond the Elbe, and Austria, emboldened by the Coalition victory, would have taken their side.

37 Report dated 8 (20) May.

38 Barclay de Tolly was awarded the Order of St Andrew the First Called for the action at Königswartha.

Appendix XVI

Report submitted to the Tsar by General Barclay de Tolly, dated 4 [16] May, on the number of troops with the Western Army

Vanguard: commanded by Lieutenant General Chaplits:
Zhitomir Ulans – two squadrons: ten officers, 142 lower ranks.
Olviopol Hussars – two squadrons: 17 officers, 364 lower ranks.
Total regular cavalry: 27 officers, 506 lower ranks.
Grekov 8th's Cossacks: 13 officers, 350 lower ranks.
Kuteynikov 8th's Cossacks: 13 officers, 313 lower ranks.
Isaev 2nd's Cossacks: nine officers, 240 lower ranks.
Total Cossacks: 35 officers, 903 lower ranks.
12th Jägers, from 13th Division: 28 officers, 772 lower ranks.
22nd Jägers, from 13th Division: 24 officers, 538 lower ranks.
Total infantry: 52 officers, 1,310 lower ranks.
4th Light Artillery Company, from 18th Artillery Brigade: five officers, 164 lower ranks, 12 guns.
Total for Chaplits' vanguard: 119 officers, 2,883 lower ranks; grand total: 3,002 men.

General-of-Infantry comte Langéron's corps:
Right flank under Major General Prince Shcherbatov:
Kinburn Dragoons – two squadrons: 18 officers, 239 lower ranks.
Seversk Mounted Jägers – two squadrons: 11 officers, 274 lower ranks.
Total regular cavalry: 29 officers, 513 lower ranks.

18th Division:
Vladimir Infantry: 21 officers, 502 lower ranks.
Kostroma Infantry: 28 officers, 482 lower ranks.
Tambov Infantry: 22 officers, 520 lower ranks.
Dnieper Infantry: 23 officers, 488 lower ranks.
28th Jägers: 12 officers, 527 lower ranks.
32nd Jägers: 24 officers, 532 lower ranks.
Total infantry: 130 officers, 3,051 lower ranks.
35th Light Artillery Company from 18th Artillery Brigade: six officers, 135 lower ranks, 12 guns.

Total for Prince Shcherbatov's command: 165 officers, 3,699 lower ranks.
Left flank under Major General Inzov:
Tver Dragoons – two squadrons: 12 officers, 312 lower ranks.
Dorpat Mounted Jägers – two squadrons: nine officers, 252 lower ranks.
Total regular cavalry: 21 officers, 564 lower ranks.

9th Division:
Yakutsk Infantry: 20 officers, 514 lower ranks.
Nasheburg Infantry: 22 officers, 613 lower ranks.
10th Jägers: 15 officers, 374 lower ranks.
38th Jägers: 18 officers, 401 lower ranks.
7th Jägers, from 8th Division: 34 officers, 690 lower ranks.
Total infantry: 109 officers, 2,592 lower ranks.
28th Light Artillery Company, 15th Artillery Brigade: seven officers, 134 lower ranks, 12 guns.
Total under Inzov's command: 137 officers, 3,290 lower ranks.
Total for Langéron's corps: 302 officers, 6,989 lower ranks for a grand total of 7,291 men.

Reserve, commanded by Lieutenant General Zass:
15th Division:
Vitebsk Infantry: 13 officers, 552 lower ranks.
Kozlov Infantry: 16 officers, 476 lower ranks.
Kolyvan Infantry: 20 officers, 475 lower ranks.
Kura Infantry, one battalion: 14 officers, 343 lower ranks.
Total infantry: 63 officers, 1,846 lower ranks.
15th Battery Artillery Company, 15th Artillery Brigade: eight officers, 203 lower ranks.
18th Battery Artillery Company, 18th Artillery Brigade: eight officers, 236 lower ranks.
34th Battery Artillery Company, 4th Reserve Artillery Brigade: eight officers, 241 lower ranks.
29th Light Artillery Company, 15th Artillery Brigade: seven officers, 138 lower ranks.
Total artillery: 31 officers, 818 lower ranks.
Captain Kanatchikov's pioneer company: two officers, 119 lower ranks.
Total for General Zass' reserve: 96 officers, 2,783 lower ranks, for a grand total of 2,879 men.

Escort for Headquarters Western Army:
Arzamass Mounted Jägers: five officers, 134 lower ranks.
Kireev's Cossacks: seven officers, 279 lower ranks.
Total escort: 12 officers, 413 lower ranks.
Totals for Western Army:
Regular cavalry: 82 officers, 1,717 lower ranks.
Cossacks: 42 officers, 1,182 lower ranks.
Infantry: 354 officers, 8,799 lower ranks.
Artillery: 49 officers, 1,251 lower ranks.
Pioneers: two officers, 119 lower ranks.
Total: 529 officers, 13,068 lower ranks.

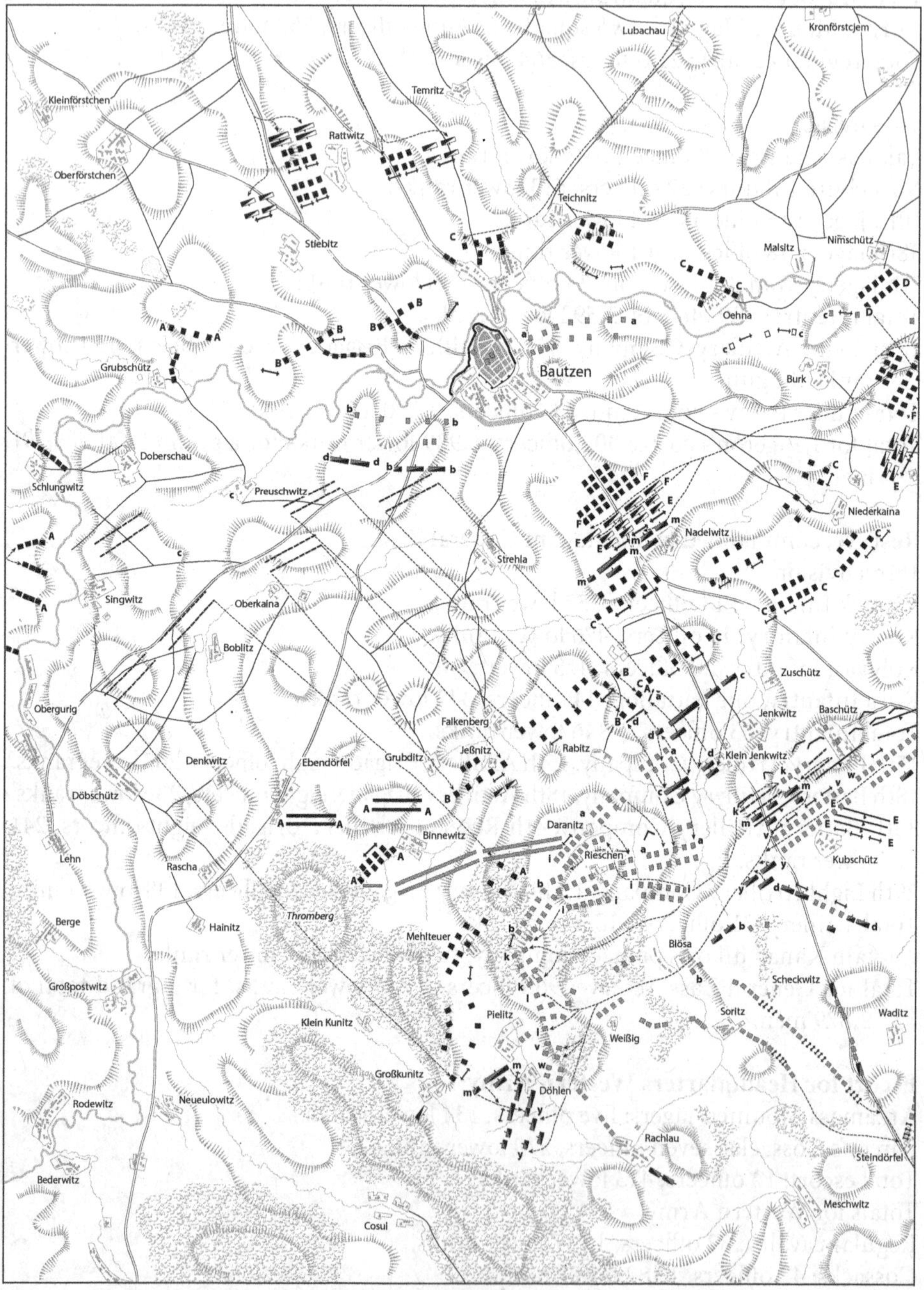

Plan of the Battle of Bautzen.

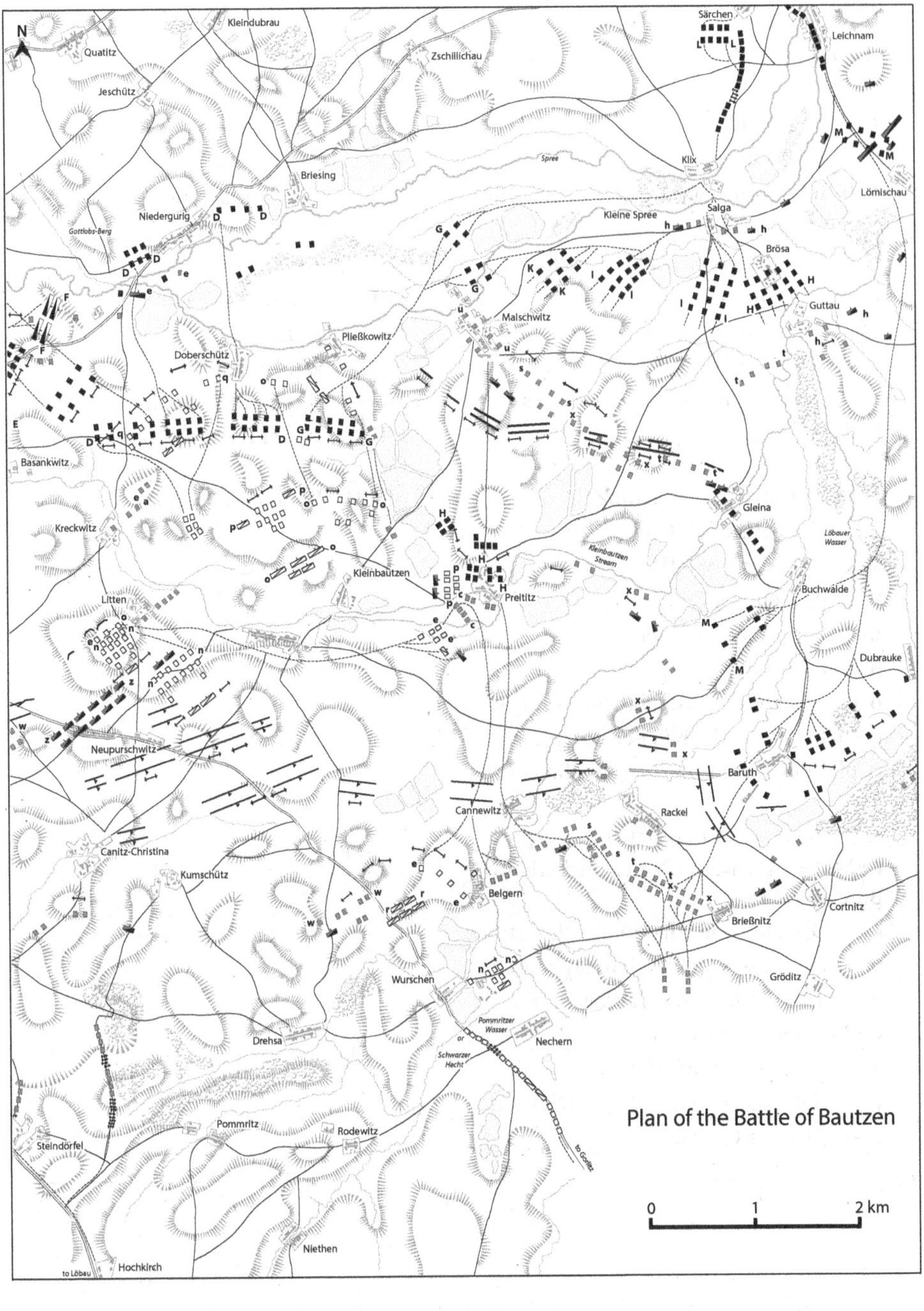

Plan of the Battle of Bautzen

Legend to Map No. 8, Plan of the Battle of Bautzen, 8 to 9 (20 to 21) May 1813:

Coalition Forces:	French Forces:
a, a', a", II Corps.	**A, A', A"** – Oudinot's corps.
b, b', b" – comte Saint-Priest's detachment.	**B, B'** – Macdonald's corps.
c, c' – Knorring's detachment.	**C, C', C"** – Marmont's corps.
d, d' – Prince Obolensky's detachment.	**D, D'** – Bertrand's corps.
c" d" – Knorring's & Obolensky's charge.	**E, E', E"** – *Réserve de cavalerie.*
f, – Panchulidzev's detachment.	**F, F'** – *Garde.*
e, e', e", e'" – Kleist's detachment.	**G, G'** – Maison's division.
g' a – 23rd, 24th, 25th & 26th Jägers.	**H, H'** – Souham's division.
h, h' – Chaplits' vanguard.	**I, K, L** – remaining divisions of *3e Corps.*
i, i' – Engelhardt's detachment.	**M, M'** – Lauriston's corps.
j, j' – elements of IV Corps.	
k, k' – elements of VIII Corps.	
l, l' – elements of Berg's corps.	
m, m' – light cavalry detachments.	
n, n', n" – Yorck's corps.	
o, o' – Zieten's brigade, Blücher's corps.	
q – Klüx's brigade, Blücher's corps.	
p, p' – Röder's reserve brigade, Blücher's corps.	
r, r' – reserve cavalry, Blücher's corps.	
t, t' – 18th Division (Prince Shcherbatov), Barclay's force.	
s, s' – 9th Division (Inzov), Barclay's force.	
x, x', x" – Zass' reserves, Barclay's force.	
u – 10th & 38th Jägers, Barclay's force.	
v, v' – Grenadier Corps.	
w, w' – Lifeguard infantry.	
y, y' – Lifeguard Light Cavalry Division.	
z – Cuirassier Corps.	

10

The Battle of Bautzen

A description of the Bautzen position. – The deployment of Coalition forces. – Their numbers. – Battle Orders for the formations of the Coalition Army. – The deployment of Napoleon's forces on the eve of the battle of Bautzen. – Their numbers. – Comparison of the strength of both sides. – Napoleon's plan of action.

The fighting on 8 (20) May. The assault by French forces on the front line positions near the town of Bautzen. – Miloradovich's retreat and the movement of some of the reserves to assist him. – Kleist's actions and his withdrawal into the main position. – Chaplits' operations. – Losses. – Deployment of both sides during the night of 8 to 9 (20 to 21) May.

The fighting on 9 (21) May. The attacks by Oudinot's and Macdonald's corps on the left wing of the Coalition Army. – The detachment of some of the reserves to this location. – The success of Russian forces on the left wing. – Ney's advance against Barclay de Tolly. – Barclay's withdrawal to Preititz and on towards Baruth. – The action at Preititz. – The advance by Napoleon's centre and reserves against Blücher. – Capture of the high ground at Kreckwitz. – The eventual fall of Preititz to Ney's troops. – The Coalition decision to retreat. – The order of the withdrawal. – The deployment of both armies on the evening of the battle. – Losses. – Comparison of the strength of post sides after the battle of Bautzen.

The Coalition forces, upon retreating to Bautzen, took up two fighting positions, the forward, along the Spree river, and the main, on the high ground, east of Bautzen.[1] The forward position was formed along the rather steep slopes of the right bank of the Spree, near the town of Bautzen and the village of Burk. The town itself, surrounded by a medieval stone wall, was brought into a defensible state. But this position can easily be outflanked on the right, downstream of Niedergurig, where the slopes of the banks of the Spree are gentler than in the vicinity of Bautzen. There is a masonry bridge in the town and wooden ones in the villages of Malsitz, Niedergurig and Klix.

1 See Map No. 8: Plan of the Battle of Bautzen, 8 to 9 (20 to 21) May 1813.

The Blösauer Wasser (Albrechtsbach) flows to the east of the Spree, having its source on the high ground on which the village of Hochkirch lies,[2] and meanders along a marshy valley, past the villages of Blösa, Jenkwitz, Nadelwitz, Kreckwitz, Purschwitz, Kleinbautzen, Preititz, Gleina and Guttau; near the latter, the Blösauer Wasser merges with another river, the Löbauer Wasser. The winding course of the Blösauer Wasser forced the Coalition to take up positions in such a way that their left wing was on the left bank of the river, from the Lusatian mountains [Lausitzer Bergland] to the village of Jenkwitz; onwards, from Jenkwitz to Litten, the position lay along high ground, at a distance of about two *verstas* from where the course of the river forms a convex arc; a series of pointed hills called the Spitzberge [Kreckwitzer Höhen] stretches from Kreckwitz to Plieskowitz, again on the left bank of the river; finally, the right wing of the position, almost at right angles to the centre and left wing, is formed by a series of lakes between the Spitzberge and the village of Gleina. The high ground at Gleina (Windmühlenberg) strengthens the defences of the right wing of the position. To the east of the Blösauer Wasser, the terrain rises in terraces to the village of Hochkirch, which lies 12 *verstas* from Bautzen.

This area, bounded on the north by the vast Lusatian plain [Lausitzer Seenland], and on the south by the wooded Lusatian mountains, is divided into three sectors by the winding course of the Blösauer Wasser, of which the southern is dominated by the slopes of the spurs of the main ridge separating Lusatia from Bohemia, the central sector is undulating, the northern is lowland. The many hills, ravines, woods and villages in this area, advantageous for defence, made an offensive problematic. Moreover, the position had been strengthened with earthworks.

The length of the position for almost two *Meilen* (about 12 *verstas*) did not allow it to be occupied in sufficient strength as well as retaining a significant reserve; while the rugged terrain made it difficult, not only for the observation of its various locations, but also for the movement and mutual liaison between army formations. In addition, the position was vulnerable to being turned on the right flank, all the more dangerous for the Coaliton, since if they were driven back at this point, they would be pushed up into the mountains on the border of neutral Austria.

On the morning of 8 (20) May, the first day of the battle of Bautzen, the Coalition forces were deployed as follows:[3]

In the forward position, at Bautzen, along the right bank of the Spree, under the overall command of Miloradovich, were stationed: comte Saint-Priest's detachment to the left of the town as far as the village of Preuschwitz; General Emmanuel's detachment was at Doberschau; to the left were the detachments under *flügel-adjutants* Orlov and Kaisarov [Paisy Sergeevich Kaisarov]; the rearguard cavalry were some distance behind the force under comte Saint-Priest. The town itself was held by five battalions from Prince Shakhovskoy's 3rd Division, with four guns, under the command of Lieutenant Colonel Wolf. The town walls were modified for defence, the gates were barricaded and the approaches were blocked with palisades. The

2 The village of Hochkirch is famous in military history for the defeat of Frederick the Great by Graf von Daun, on 14 October 1758.

3 For details of the composition of the Coalition army at Bautzen, see Appendix XVIII at the end of this chapter.

remainder of Prinz Eugen von Württemberg's II Corps was located to the right of the town as far as the village of Oehna; Cossacks maintained communications between the forces under Count Miloradovich and under Kleist. Kleist's detachment were stationed at the village of Burk, watching over the crossings at Malsitz, Nimschütz and Niedergurig. The forward element of Barclay de Tolly's corps was located at Klix under Major General Chaplits' command. Finally, the raiding detachments under Major General Lanskoy and Colonel Figner were at Milkel [ten miles north of Bautzen]. The number of men in the forward positions, together with observation detachments, did not exceed 25,000.[4]

In the main position, Coalition forces were deployed as follows:

The left wing, under Lieutenant General Prince Gorchakov 2nd's command, was holding the high ground from Großkunitz to the Blösauer Wasser and along its right bank as far as the village of Klein Jenkwitz and Baschütz; the centre, composed of Prussian troops under Blücher's command, were stationed in the sector between Litten and Purschwitz (Yorck's corps) and onwards along the left bank of the Blösauer Wasser, from Kreckwitz to Pließkowitz (Blücher's corps). His force was deployed in such a way that the front line was stationed on the high ground of the Spitsberge, while the second line was on the reverse slopes. The right wing of the Coalition Army, which consisted of troops from the former Western Army, under the command of General Barclay de Tolly, was deployed from Malschwitz to Gleina. In reserve, under His Highness Tsarevich Grand Duke Konstantin Pavlovich, were the Grenadier Corps and Lifeguard Corps, two cuirassier divisions, Lifeguard light cavalry and reserve artillery, behind the village of Bashütz, covering the intervals between Gorchakov's and Yorck's corps. Overall, on 8 (20) May, there were about 65,000 men in the main position.[5] It is extraordinary to note that at the battle of Bautzen, there were three generals senior in rank to Count Wittgenstein under his command: Count Miloradovich, who commanded the vanguard on the first day of fighting, and the left wing on the second; Blücher in the centre, and Barclay de Tolly on the right wing of the Coalition Army. The corps located in the main position were

4 The number of men in the forward positions at Bautzen. On the extreme left wing in Emmanuel's, Kaisarov's and Count Orlov's detachments was 3,200. In comte Saint-Priest's, around 3,500. In the cavalry behind Saint-Priest, 2,800. In Prinz Eugen von Württemberg's II Corps, around 5,000. In Kleist's detachment, 3,000 Russians and 2,000 Prussians. In Chaplits' detachment, 2,500. In Lanskoy's, Prendel's and Figner's detachments, 3,000. For a total of 25,000 men. Extracted from Returns submitted in early [mid] May 1813.

5 Listing of Coalition troops in the main Bautzen position, 8 (20) May: 12,000 men on the left wing under Prince Gorchakov; 26,000 men in the centre under Blücher; 9,000 men on the right wing under Barclay de Tolly; 18,300 men in reserve; for a grand total of 65,300 men. 13 Cossack regiments with various formations, numbering about 3,000 men.
Subsequently, the strength of the Coalition Army assembled in the vicinity of Bautzen reached some 93,000 men, which is the number given by Plotho, not including the losses suffered by the Coalition in the actions at Königswartha and Weißig. It is impossible to determine the precise number of battalions and squadrons, because some of the Russian infantry regiments consisted of two battalions, while others had just one; similarly, the cavalry regiments were of differing compositions, about which there is no accurate information. There were 474 Russian guns (of which 24 were detached to Blücher's force) and 136 Prussian, for a total of 610. Extracted from Returns submitted in early [mid] May 1813.

isolated from one another: Gorchakov and Yorck by a significant sector unoccupied by troops; Yorck from Blücher by a river and a wide swampy plain; while Blücher was separated from Barclay by lakes. This situation made mutual support between formations and the movement of reserves very difficult. The Coalition hoped to redress these positional disadvantages through field works. Many fortifications were constructed throughout the army's encampment at Bautzen; a large entrenchment was built at the tip of the left wing; there were several batteries to the right and left of Baschütz; there were three more batteries to the left of Litten, and so on.

The number of Coalition troops concentrated at Bautzen reached some 93,000 men in total (65,000 Russians and 28,000 Prussians), with 610 guns. The Coalition Army included:

Russian forces:
118 battalions, numbering 40,000 men.
164 squadrons, numbering 12,000 men.
35 Cossack regiments, numbering 7,000 men.
42 artillery companies, numbering 6,000 men.
For a total of 65,000 men.

Prussian forces:
47½ battalions, numbering 21,000 men.
68 squadrons, numbering 5,200 men.
17½ batteries, numbering 1,800 men.
For a total of 28,000 men.

Overall: 61,000 infantrymen, 17,000 regular cavalrymen, 7,000 Cossacks and around 8,000 artillerymen (the Cossack regiments were used both for reconnaissance on the flanks of the position, and for evacuating the wounded and other security duties in the rear of the army).[6]

In the disposition for the impending battle, issued by Count Wittgenstein, it was prescribed: in the event of a crossing by significant enemy forces over the river Spree, General Miloradovich was to fall back to the high ground between the villages of Auritz and Klein Jenkwitz and hold there for as long as possible; should the enemy force them further back, the cavalry was to withdraw with the horse artillery behind the fighting line and settle down in reserve to the left of the Lifeguard; the infantry and the light guns, however, were to withdraw to the high ground near the village of Rieschen under the command of Lieutenant General Prinz von Württemberg. Upon the re-deployment of the vanguard into the main position, Count Miloradovich was to command all Russian corps on the left wing. In the event of further enemy assaults, it was prescribed: should an attack be made on the force under *Generalleutnant* Kleist, then both cuirassier divisions, and thereafter the remaining corps of the army, were to move in support of him with a flanking march to the right; in the

6 Returns on troop strengths dated 2 and 4 (14 and 16) May. Plotho, I, *Beilagen*, 117-127. As far as can be judged from the figures shown in this work, the author did not take into account the losses suffered by the force under Barclay de Tolly in the actions at Königswartha and Weißig.

event of a full frontal assault on the centre of the Coalition Army, the corps under General Kleist was to attack the enemy on the flank together with the cuirassiers, while the reserves and the left wing, having made a flanking march to the right, were to support Blücher. Should the enemy direct an attack on our left wing with their main force, then Kleist's corps was to move into his rear together with both cuirassier divisions, while Blücher's corps was to change front with the right flank advanced in order to push the enemy army into the mountains; finally, should attacks be launched on both flanks of the Coalition Army simultaneously, then a large part of the reserve was to support the right wing under Blücher, who, supported by these reinforcements, was to throw the enemy back into the mountains. In the event of an offensive by significant elements of the French army towards Klix, in order to cut Barclay de Tolly off from the other Coalition formations, both cuirassier divisions were immediately to cross the Spree and advance to engage the enemy; they were to be followed up by Kleist's corps, then Blücher's corps, the Lifeguard and finally the front line of the left wing, under the command of Prince Gorchakov 2nd, while the second line were to remain in their original positions together with the reserve artillery. General Miloradovich was to take up positions at Jenkwitz and Baschütz and, in the event of a retreat, was to march towards Löbau and Reichenbach. If, however, it were necessary to retreat directly from the position currently occupied, then the troops of the right wing were to withdraw towards Weißenberg, that is, the corps under Kleist and Blücher and both cuirassier divisions, while the Russian forces on the left wing were to march towards Löbau and rendezvous at Reichenbach. At the beginning of the battle, the trains were directed on Reichenbach, where the wounded and prisoners were also to be sent.[7]

Thus, on the basis of this disposition, we were essentially confining ourselves to repulsing enemy attacks, or an almost passive defence. The Coalition forces were over extended, and the Commander-in-Chief, recognising this disadvantage of the army's position, was reliant on its mitigation by supporting each of the threatened locations either with cuirassiers, or through flanking movements by neighbouring corps. The situation was therefore complicated by the intersected terrain, besides which, the Coalition forces, being attacked by superior forces, would be forced to concentrate on self-defence rather than mutual support.[8] It is highly remarkable that Count Wittgenstein, in this disposition, avoided issuing orders with regard to Barclay de Tolly's corps, naming Kleist's corps as the right wing of the army.

On Napoleon's part, on 7 (19) May, on the eve of the battle of Bautzen, his forces were located as follows: Oudinot's corps were on the right flank at the village of Techritz [one mile west of Grubschütz]; Macdonald's corps were forwards of Kleinförstchen were Napoleon had his *quartier général*; Marmont's and Bertrand's corps were facing Bautzen; the latter anchoring his left flank on the road leading to Hoyerswerda; the *Garde* and Latour-Maubourg's cavalry were on the Dresden road behind Göda. Ney's corps had not yet been able to rendezvous with Napoleon's army: Lauriston remained at Weißig, two and a half *Meilen* (18 *verstas*) from Bautzen;

7 Extracted from the Disposition, signed by Count Wittgenstein, dated 6 (18) May (War Diary of Miloradovich's rearguard, Archive of the M.T.D. No. 44,585, folio 55).

8 Plotho, I, 159.

General Souham was at Maukendorf, three and a half *Meilen* (25 *verstas*) away, with *3e Corps* and General Reynier was at Hoyerswerda, four *Meilen* (around 30 *verstas*) from Bautzen with *7e Corps*. The number of troops concentrated against the Bautzen position, under the personal command of Napoleon, reached some 100,000, while a further 50,000 men were advancing from Hoyerswerda, under Ney's command.[9]

In comparing the strengths of both sides, we find that there was an advantage in numbers on the Coalition side, not only of cavalry (24,000 men against 12,000 French cavalry) but also artillery (600 guns against 350 French artillery pieces). On Napoleon's side, there was a significant advantage in numbers overall (143,000 men against 93,000 allies), and an even more decisive advantage in infantry (125,000 men against 60,000), which was especially important when fighting on intersected terrain. The main advantage for Napoleon was in the unity of command in his army, while Wittgenstein was Commander in Chief in name only.

Napoleon's course of action, as much as can be judged from his operations during the battle of Bautzen, was to launch persistent diversionary attacks on the Coalition left wing, thus drawing their reserves there, while then unleashing the main body against the right wing, to outflank it with the assistance of Ney's force, and to drive the Coalition Army into the Bohemian mountains and cut off their line of retreat.

Just as dawn was breaking on 8 (20) May, unusual movements among the enemy force were reported by the forward outposts of the Russo-Prussian army. Napoleon was once again reconnoitring the Bautzen position himself. At around ten o'clock in the morning, the French set off to attack. Marshal Oudinot had received orders to cross the Spree upstream of the town and attack the high ground on which the left wing of the Coalition was stationed; Marshal Macdonald was initially directed on Bautzen; Marmont was to lay a bridge upstream [*sic*] of the town, cross the river and, together with Bertrand's corps, capture the high ground at Burk: command over the latter two corps was entrusted to Marshal Soult. At the same time, orders were sent to Ney to march to Klix with his force, cross the Spree there and march on Wurschen, enveloping the Coalition position. The *Garde* and *Réserve de cavalerie* were left behind Macdonald's corps.[10]

At around noon, a fairly strong cannonade began. At the same time, the Coalition Monarchs, having passed the troops stationed in the centre of the main position, stopped on the high ground at Niederkaina, to the right of Bautzen.

Marshal Oudinot, having built two trestle bridges near the villages of Grubschütz and Singwitz, engaged in a firefight with the troops under comte Saint-Priest, and having forced them back, crossed the river at about four o'clock in the afternoon. Macdonald took advantage of the masonry bridge at Bautzen being left intact, and with the assistance of Compans' division (Marmont's corps) took possession of the town, evicting Prince Shakhovsky's division from there.[11] At the same time as these corps were advancing, the French had placed a battery of 40 guns in line with the

9 For details of the French forces, see Appendix XIX at the end of this chapter.

10 Vaudoncourt, 93-94.

11 According to Vaudoncourt, the commander of the Russian battery stationed forwards of Bautzen was killed and the guns were captured by the French. This statement is unfounded: the Coalition forces did not lose a single gun in combat at Bautzen.

right wing of Prinz Eugen von Württemberg and opened enfilade fire on his force. Prinz Eugen could only counter the powerful enemy artillery with a few light guns, due to the fact that all the others, by order of Miloradovich, had previously been sent to the main position. Marmont's force, taking advantage of their decisive numerical superiority, having laid trestle bridges downstream of Bautzen, crossed the river at three o'clock in the afternoon and shielded themselves with a dense screen of skirmishers. Colonel Kurnosov [Nikolai Andreevich Kurnosov], only recently recovered from a wound received at the battle of Smolensk, dashed forwards to engage the enemy with the Volhynia Infantry Regiment and fell [wounded], shot through by a musket ball. At about six o'clock in the afternoon, the Prinz von Württemberg, unable to hold the advance of incomparably superior numbers any longer, withdrew step by step to the high ground between Auritz and Jenkwitz, where the detachment under comte Saint-Priest joined him. Colonel Rehren, left in the village of Preuschwitz with the Schlüsselburg Infantry, lost many men but rejoined the other units by nightfall. General Emmanuel fell back on Binnewitz with his detachment.

At six o'clock in the afternoon, having completely secured Bautzen, the enemy directed an attack on Miloradovich's left wing, pushed him back and captured the villages of Kunitz and Mehlteuer. The French success at this location worried the Coalition. Almost every Russian and Prussian commander was convinced that Napoleon intended to make his main effort against the left wing of the Russo-Prussian army, where the terrain was conducive to operations by his numerous infantry; Count Wittgenstein, on the contrary, believed that the main attack would be directed at our right wing. In spite of all this, however, Miloradovich's force were moved to the left and some of the reserves (a grenadier brigade of the Leib Grenadiers and Pavlovsk Grenadiers, and the Lifeguard light cavalry) were sent to assist the left wing.[12] These brave troops drove the enemy back behind Binnewitz and reoccupied the high ground near the villages of Kunitz, Mehlteuer and Auritz.

During this period, as operations were unfolding as described on the left wing, General Kleist was staunchly defending the high ground at Burk with the forward troops of the centre. At five o'clock in the afternoon, they were attacked by Marmont, sending Bonet's division from the direction of Oehna, while Bertrand's corps advanced from the direction of Niedergurig: thus, about 20,000 men had been directed against the 5,000 strong detachment under Kleist. After bitter fighting, the French were just gaining the upper hand over the Coalition at Niedergurig, when five battalions of the *Oberschlesischen Brigade* under Zieten, numbering 4,000 men, arrived at this location, having been sent by Blücher, at Kleist's request, together with two Russian battery artillery companies under colonels Staden [Gustav Gustavovich Shtaden or Reinhold Gustav Staden] and Velyaminov [Alexey Alexandrovich Velyaminov 3rd]. These reinforcements enabled the Coalition to repel Bertrand's frontal attack; but in the meantime, at seven o'clock in the evening, Marmont had crossed the Spree downstream of Bautzen with Bonet's division, and enveloped Kleist's force on their left flank. At eight o'clock in the evening, not seeing any

12 Plan of the battle of Bautzen, signed by Quartermaster General Harting. In Prinz Eugen von Württemberg's diary it states that the Lifeguard Jägers and Lifeguard Finland Regiment were detached from the reserves to assist the left wing.

possibility of defending himself further on the ground he held, the valiant Kleist fell back to the main position, behind the village of Litten.

Throughout the day, Barclay's corps was not attacked, and only in the evening did Ney's leading elements engage in combat with the vanguard under Chaplits as they approached Klix, and upon the latter being ejected from the village, he greeted the enemy with canister and small-arms fire as they exited, delaying the French for more than four hours, while the 12th Jägers and 22nd Jägers, under Major General Rudzevich's command, especially distinguished themselves.[13]

The cannonade and firefight on the left wing continued until ten o'clock in the evening. The bivouac fires of both armies flared up and, together with the flames from several burning villages, illuminated the entire area around Bautzen. The Coalition Monarchs, who found themselves on the left wing of the position in the evening, in the large entrenchment, went to rest: Emperor Alexander in Neupurschwitz, where quarters had been prepared for him in an inn, while the King of Prussia was in Wurschen.[14]

The fighting at Bautzen on 8 (20) May, in which 20,000 to 25,000 Coalition troops fought for several hours against 70,000 Frenchmen, cost the Russo-Prussian force some 2,600 men overall; while Napoleon's force suffered many more, but exactly how many is not known.[15]

During the night of 8 to 9 (20 to 21) May, the French army occupied the following locations: Oudinot's corps at the village of Binnewitz facing Kunitz; Macdonald's corps on the high ground forwards of the village of Strehla facing Auritz; Marmont's corps on the high ground forwards of the village of Burk; Bertrand remained on the left bank of the Spree, at Niedergurig: the *Garde* and Latour-Maubourg's cavalry were located, some in Bautzen, some forwards, between the villages Nadelwitz and the Taucherfriedhof cemetery; Napoleon's *quartier général* was in Bautzen. Souham's *3e Corps* and that of Lauriston, were in Särchen facing Klix; Reynier's corps was on the march from Hoyerswerda towards Klix. Consequently, the deployment of the French army consisted of two isolated elements separated from each other by the forces under Blücher, who stood on the Kreckwitzer Höhen, and Barclay at Gleina and Klix.[16]

The Coalition Army, upon the withdrawal of the forward corps to the main position, was deployed in the following manner: the detachments under Kaisarov, Emmanuel and Orlov, the corps under Prinz Eugen von Württemberg, Prince Gorchakov 2nd and Berg, and some of the reserves, numbering about 26,000 men, under the command of Count Miloradovich, were stationed from Kunitz to Baschütz, forming the left wing of the general disposition of the army. Three

13 Lieutenant General Chaplits' report to Barclay de Tolly, dated 10 [22] May, No. 235.
14 War Diary of Count Miloradovich's rearguard. Prinz Eugen von Württemberg's diary. Plotho, I, 160-163. Vaudoncourt, 93-95.
15 On the first day of the battle of Bautzen, Count Miloradovich's force lost 14 officers and 670 lower ranks killed and some 800 men wounded. War Diary of Count Miloradovich's rearguard. Kleist's force lost some 1,100 men, of whom 600 were Russian and 500 Prussian. French losses overall were given as 3,000 killed and 7,000 wounded in Plotho, I, 163. In all likelihood, Plotho's statement is an exaggeration.
16 Vaudoncourt, 95. War Diary of Prinz Eugen von Württemberg's corps.

flèches at Baschütz were held by the guns of the 1st and 2nd Lifeguard light artillery companies.[17] In the centre under Blücher's command were: Kleist's corps behind Litten, Yorck's corps between Litten and Purschwitz and on the Kreckwitzer Höhen was Blücher's corps, all-in-all a total of around 28,000 men. The two flanking flèches in front of the village of Litten were held by the guns of the Lifeguard Battery Artillery Company under Count Arakcheev [Andrey Andreevich Arakcheev]; while the flèche in the centre was held by a Prussian battery. His Majesty's Lifeguard Battery Artillery Company was in Blücher's corps, at Kreckwitz.[18] The right wing consisted of the former Western Army and Major General Lanskoy's detachment, numbering 15,000 men in all, under the command of Barclay de Tolly, and held the sector from Malschwitz to Gleina; the vanguard of this force, under Chaplits' command, was stationed at Klix. Finally, the Lifeguard, grenadiers, cuirassiers and reserve artillery, numbering 18,000 men,[19] under the command of Tsarevich Grand Duke Konstantin Pavlovich, were deployed in reserve: the infantry behind Baschütz, between the roads leading to Hochkirch and Wurschen, while the cavalry were behind Neupurschwitz.[20] Consequently, the strength of the Coalition Army, on the morning of 9 (21) May, concentrated on the main position, reached some 62,000 Russians and 25,500 Prussians, in total some 87,500 men, not counting 3,000 Cossacks who were on various missions, thus overall some 90,000 men.[21]

The outcome of the fighting on 8 (20) May would have been advantageous to the Coalition only if, at that moment during the fighting once the right wing of the enemy army had crossed the Spree, they had counter-attacked these troops (the corps under Oudinot and part of the corps under Macdonald and Marmont: some 40,000 men in total) with the corps of their left wing and centre, supported by some of the reserves. The Coalition could have used at least 60,000 men for this blow. But because the Russo-Prussian army had allowed most of the enemy forces to cross the river and to deploy into battle formation, while in the meantime Ney was preparing to envelope the Coalition position from the right flank with three corps, then they had no choice but to retreat, or to give battle under very disadvantageous circumstances. Barclay de Tolly proposed a retreat to Görlitz, taking up a position there

17 From Major General V.F. Ratch's History of the Lifeguard Artillery. The troop strength of the left wing of the Coalition Army is given minus the loss of 1,500 men in the fighting during 8 (20) May and with the inclusion of some of the reserves, numbering 3,500 men, sent to assist the left wing.

18 From General Ratch's History of the Lifeguard Artillery. The troop strength for the centre of the Coalition Army is shown minus the loss of 1,100 men during the fighting on 8 (20) May and with the inclusion of the detachments under Roth and Rüdiger, who were with Kleist's force on both days of the battle.

19 Minus the troops detached to the left wing.

20 Plan of the battle of Bautzen, signed by General Harting. Plotho, I, 164.

21 Returns showing force composition, dated 2 and 4 [14 and 16] May 1813. Plotho, I, *Beilagen*, 125-127. In all likelihood, when calculating the strengths, he did not take into account the losses suffered by the forces in the actions at Königswartha and Weißig. But as Prussian regiments included squads of volunteers, the strength of Blücher's force on the second day of fighting may have reached some 28,000 men or even a little more; the number of Russian troops was no higher than 60,000 or 62,000.

and, having deceived the enemy with a feigned readiness to give battle once more, to retreat further. Thus, it would have been possible to steal two marches, sparing several thousand brave soldiers who were to fall on the second day of fighting at Bautzen. Many of the Russian generals believed that they should not decide on a general battle; in contrast, the Prussians, and in particular General Knesebeck, who enjoyed the particular trust of Emperor Alexander, desired a fight; in his opinion, a retreat would not only weaken the morale of the troops and the enthusiasm of the Prussian people, but would cause Austria to lose confidence in the Coalition and take the side of Napoleon. Some even suggested going over to the offensive, swayed by exaggerated concerns for Berlin; but Emperor Alexander would not agree to that. The only choice was to accept a defensive battle, and trust in the strength of the fortified position, the courage of the troops, the numerical superiority of the artillery and the plentiful cavalry, which would paralyse the efforts of a pursuing enemy, should the Coalition fail.[22]

On Napoleon's part, the plan of action was to resume intensive assaults on the Coalition left wing by Oudinot and Macdonald, to draw Coalition reserves to this point and, after waiting for Ney's attack on the right wing, to attack the weakened centre of the Russo-Prussian army with the corps under Marmont and Bertrand, and the *Garde*.[23]

At three o'clock in the morning [21 May], the Coalition Monarchs joined the troops from their headquarters and throughout the duration of the battle were mostly at the top of the escarpment behind the village of Baschütz, between the centre and the left wing. Just as dawn broke, from the sparsely wooded high ground between the Blösauer Wasser and Rieschen, Napoleon could be seen in a square, forwards of Bautzen. Thereafter, the entire French *Garde* formed up in several regimental squares. The cavalry corps under Latour-Maubourg was in front of the right wing of their line, while further back, on the left flank towards the town, were the *cavalerie de la Garde*. The corps under Oudinot and Macdonald, as before, were stationed at Binnewitz and facing Gross Jenkwitz; Marmont was on the high ground at Burk; most of Bertrand's corps remained on the left bank of the Spree, and just a single brigade had been pushed forwards to the so-called pine hill (Kiefern Berg).[24]

At dawn on 9 (21) May, the troops under Prinz Eugen von Württemberg were ordered to retreat from Auritz towards Rieschen, while comte Saint-Priest was left for the time being at Falkenberg and Jeßnitz. Prinz Eugen von Württemberg positioned his corps to the right of Rieschen; 24 guns were placed in front of his right wing, under the command of Lieutenant Colonel Sievers.[25]

At five o'clock in the morning, the battle began with a cannonade, which continuously grew in intensity. At about six o'clock, Marshal Oudinot shook out a cloud of skirmishers in front of his columns, began a firefight with Miloradovich's troops and attacked the left wing of the Coalition Army. Comte Saint-Priest was ordered

22 Comments on the events of the war of 1813 (probably compiled in Barclay de Tolly's headquarters), archive of the M.T.D. No. 47,353, notebook 27. Beitzke, I, 433.

23 Beitzke, I, 433-434.

24 Beitzke, I, 434-435.

25 War Diary of Prinz Eugen von Württemberg's corps.

to withdraw towards Rieschen and stationed his troops at Mehlteuer, together with Engelhardt's detachment [Grigory Grigorievich Ehngelgardt or Gotthard Gerhard von Engelhardt]; Markov's IV Corps were to their right, at Daranitz, while VIII Corps were to their left, under Prince Gorchakov; some of Berg's I Corps, the grenadiers, Lifeguard brigade and Lifeguard light cavalry extended further left at Pielitz. The light detachments were monitoring the enemy at the tip of the left wing, at Großkunitz.

At eight o'clock, the divisions under Lorencez and Pacthod (Oudinot's corps), having captured Mehlteuer, Kunitz and Pielitz, charged towards Rachlau. To the left of this force, Gérard's division, with elements of Fressinet's division (Macdonald's corps), were directed towards Daranitz and Rieschen. The Russian troops defended themselves very stubbornly; Major General Engelhardt was wounded; eventually, the commander of the Schlüsselburg regiment, Colonel Rehren, yielding to the superior enemy numbers, abandoned Daranitz, but continued to hold out in Rieschen with the assistance of the Chernigov Infantry Regiment which had been sent to help him. All this notwithstanding, however, the Prinz von Württemberg, enveloped from the left flank by the force under Oudinot, was in a difficult position. The enemy, having pushed comte Saint-Priest back, placed a battery level with the line of II Corps, which, firing across the village of Rieschen, showered the troops under the Prinz von Württemberg with canister. But at that very moment, General Melissino, stationed on the left flank of II Corps with his cavalry detachment, advanced several horse artillery pieces against the enemy battery. At the same time, with his customary courage, Prince Shakhovskoy was fighting at Rieschen with 3rd Division, supported by elements of Saint-Priest's force, the village changing hands several times. Major General Knorring's cavalry, located to the right of II Corps, being struck by heavy fire from enemy batteries, was forced to withdraw behind Klein Jenkwitz. But thereafter, two battalions from Charpentier's division (Macdonald's corps), advancing towards Rabitz, having inadvertently become separated from the other units, were attacked near this village by the Tatar Ulans and two Ukrainian Cossack regiments, under the command of Knorring, and were almost completely wiped out; a gun was captured during this attack. On the left wing of the Coalition Army, the enemy continued to move forward. The success of the French offensive confirmed Emperor Alexander and almost every Russian general in their conviction that Napoleon's main effort was directed at this point; with the objective of cutting the Coalition off from the Austrian border. Count Wittgenstein expressed the opposite opinion: 'I would wager my life' he said to the Tsar, 'that this attack is a diversion. Napoleon wants to envelope us on the right flank and push us back into Bohemia.' But only his Chief of Staff, General Dovre, shared this conviction, and therefore the Coalition not only left Miloradovich with the reinforcements sent to him the day before, but also supported him with the remainder of the grenadier regiments, except the Pernov Grenadiers and Kexholm Grenadiers. The arrival of these reserves enabled the left wing of the Coalition Army to switch to the offensive. The French, greeted with fierce fire from the Russian batteries and counter-attacked by fresh troops as they arrived, were forced not only to abandon the villages of Pielitz, Mehlteuer and Kunitz, but also around noon, to move from the hills onto the plain, where the superior numbers of

Russian cavalry exposed the enemy to great danger.[26] Marshal Oudinot sent word to Napoleon twice that he was unable to hold on to the area he had seized, and asked for reinforcement with fresh troops. Initially, Napoleon did not give him any response, but later, at about two o'clock in the afternoon, he ordered the marshal to be instructed 'to act as best he could, and that by three o'clock the battle would be won.' Oudinot, left to fend for himself, rallied his disordered force under the protection of the less damaged Bavarian division under Raglovich, and Fressinet's division (from Macdonald's corps). His losses were very significant, but the chain of events at other points on the battlefield did not allow Miloradovich to complete the rout of the defeated enemy.[27]

At six o'clock in the morning, almost simultaneously with the opening of the cannonade on the left wing of the Coalition Army, thick smoke was noticed on the high ground at Burk, which served as the signal for Ney to attack. The corps under Souham and Lauriston converged on Klix under cover of the lingering darkness; only Reynier's corps remained behind. Ney's leading troops, having captured the village of Klix the previous evening, began to cross the Spree.[28] Maison's division crossed at Klix, under heavy fire from a battery placed near the village of Salga by Chaplits, while the other two divisions of Lauriston' corps moved through Leichnam, about two *verstas* downstream. Ney's corps, under the immediate command of General Souham, followed Maison's force across several hastily built bridges. General Chaplits, attacked frontally by Souham's superior numbers and outflanked on the right by Lauriston's march towards Brösa, retreated to Guttau, to cover the flank of the position occupied by Barclay between the Malschwitz ponds and the high ground near the village of Gleina (Windmühlenberg [Windmill Hill]), upon which a battery of twelve guns had been placed at dawn. The enemy, having made the crossing, moved forwards in two directions: Lauriston, enveloping the right flank of the Coalition position with the divisions under Lagrange and Rochambeau [Donatien-Marie-Joseph de Vimeur de Rochambeau] (some 10,000 men in total), was heading towards Baruth, while Ney took on Barclay frontally himself with his corps and Maison's division (some 24,000 men in total), in the hope of completely driving him away from Blücher. Barclay had only 12,000 men with which to counter these forces subsequently reinforced by Reynier's corps. Most of them were stationed on the high ground at Gleina, which significantly dominated the surrounding area. Yet on the one hand, he was supposed to maintain communications with Blücher, while on the other, he was to protect the army from being enveloped from their right flank, he was thus forced to occupy the village of Malschwitz and the woods near Guttau with troops from his corps, leaving him no more than 7,000 men in the main position at Gleina.

Meanwhile, Emperor Alexander, believing that Napoleon's main force was directed against the left wing of the Coalition Army, but being concerned about a report from the Prussian army's *Generalquartiermeister* Müffling [Philipp Friedrich

26 War Diary of Prinz Eugen von Württemberg's corps. War Diary of Count Miloradovich's rearguard. Beitzke, I, 435-436.

27 Beitzke, I, 436; Richter, *Geschichte des deutschen Freiheitskrieges*, I, 205.

28 Vaudoncourt, 96; Beitzke, I, 437.

Carl Ferdinand von Müffling genannt Weiß], regarding the possibility of an enemy envelopment from the right flank, asked Count Wittgenstein: 'how many troops does Barclay have?' And having learned from the commander-in-chief that there were 15,000 men in the Western Army, he turned to Müffling, who knew the battlefield in detail, with the question: 'are there enough of them?' Having received an affirmative reply, the Tsar ordered Müffling to go to Barclay de Tolly and assist him in holding the most advantageous defensive position. General Müffling, finding Barclay on the high ground at Gleina, at the very moment when Ney was preparing to attack him, announced the will of the Tsar to him, to hold the French with the 15,000 men under his command. Barclay did not say a word, but once Ney had deployed his forces, which appeared to reach some 40,000 men, the Russian commander invited Müffling to enter the miller's house with him and, carefully closing the door while enemy round shot punched through the fragile walls of the building, said: 'you believe that I have 15,000 men, and the Tsar thinks so too. At such a decisive moment, I can remain silent no longer. I have just 5,000; judge for yourself: can I hold out against 40,000 men? I ask you to go to Blücher as quickly as possible and ask him to assist me.'[29] In anticipation of reinforcements, Barclay, attacked by an enemy five times his strength, sent General Zass through Buchwalde to Baruth with the corps reserves, and ordered Chaplits to retreat thence from Guttau; he retreated himself, with the rest of the force, numbering 3,000 men, step by step towards Preititz, and arriving there at nine o'clock in the morning, reported to the Tsar regarding his retreat, continuing meanwhile to move back towards Baruth.[30]

Emperor Alexander, having received the report from Barclay de Tolly, and being dissatisfied that his troops had abandoned the advantageous ground at Gleina so quickly, sent him orders to defend his newly occupied position to the bitter end.

At the same time as Ney's offensive against Barclay de Tolly's position at Gleina, Maison moved towards Malschwitz and, having ejected the Russian jägers from there (10th Jägers and 38th Jägers), forced them to retreat towards Preititz, where they remained along with four squadrons from the Tver Dragoons and Dorpat Mounted-Jägers, under Major General Berdyaev [Alexander Nikolaevich Berdyaev]. The remainder of Barclay de Tolly's force had retreated to Baruth by 11 o'clock. Meanwhile, Maison, continuing to advance, attacked the Prussian *Garde-Füsilier-Bataillon* in the village of Pließkowitz and drove them back to the high ground near Kreckwitz. The formations of Ney's corps, after capturing the position at Gleina, were redeployed as follows: Souham's division was directed towards Preititz; Delmas' division proceeded at some distance behind them; two divisions, Albert's and Ricard's, were positioned on the high ground at Gleina, awaiting the arrival of Reynier's corps; finally, Marchand's division was left at Klix as a reaction force. In the meantime, having received Napoleon's orders 'to direct forces towards the Hochkirch belfry'[31] the marshal continued to advance towards Preititz with two divisions, numbering just 8,000 to 9,000 men. At 11 o'clock, Souham drove the small Russian detachment from Preititz and occupied this village: thus Blücher was not

29 Müffling, *Aus meinem Leben*, I, 437.
30 Barclay de Tolly's report to the Tsar regarding the battle of Bautzen, dated 6 [18] June.
31 Jomini, *Vie politique et militaire de Napoléon*.

only cut off from Barclay, but was also in danger of losing his line of retreat. It was vital to drive the enemy out of Preititz at any cost: to that end, Blücher directed the *Brandenburgischen Brigade* under General Röder and Kleist's detachment thence; at the same time, elements of the Prussian cavalry reserve were advanced to the Spree, observing the enemy and threatening their right flank.[32] For his part, Barclay had left the 10th Jägers and 38th Jägers and Berdyaev's cavalry brigade near Preititz in order to maintain communications with Blücher, while he took up positions at Rackel, facing Baruth with the remaining troops, having crossed the Löbauer Wasser and linked up with Chaplits' vanguard.[33]

At half past 11 o'clock, Major Alvensleben [Johann Friedrich Karl II. Gebhard von Alvensleben], moving at the head of the other elements of Röder's brigade with three battalions, two squadrons and four horse artillery pieces, having crossed the Blösauer Wasser downstream of Kleinbautzen, formed his detachment up 800 paces from Preititz, where the Russian jägers and dragoons were still in combat. Several shells, fired on Alvensleben's orders, had set the village on fire; three French battalions that emerged from there were driven back by Prussian infantry and pursued by Coalition cavalry. Following this, General Kleist, arriving on the left bank of the river near Preititz from Litten via Kleinbautzen with his detachment, positioned three battalions of *Colbergsches Infanterie* with two companies of *Ostpreußisches Jäger* in the first line facing the village, while the Russian force, coming under his command, moved across the river. Thereafter an attack was launched from the left bank. The *Colbergsches Infanterie*, which had fought well the day before, quickly rushed into Preititz, and although they were twice driven out of there with great losses, eventually established themselves in the village. The arrival at Preititz of the rest of the troops from Röder's brigade gave a decisive advantage to the Coalition over the French: Souham's division was eventually driven back to the high ground at Gleina at noon. Having achieved this success, Röder's force returned to the Kreckwitz high ground held by the main force under Blücher.[34]

At the same time as Kleist's advance from Litten towards Preititz, Yorck's corps moved forwards towards Litten, and positioned themselves there behind three fortified batteries, of which (as already said), the two outer ones were occupied by Count Arakcheev's Lifeguard Battery Company, and the centre one by Prussian artillery. Behind them, in order to protect the guns, were stationed the combined *Schlesisches Husaren*, the village of Litten was occupied by *Füsiliers* from *2. Ostpreußisches Infanterie*; Yorck's other troops were placed in reserve.[35]

Noon had already passed, and the troops stationed in the centre of the French army were still inactive. From the high ground on which the Coalition Monarchs were located near Baschütz, one could see Napoleon surrounded by a large retinue on a hill forwards of Bautzen. He was constantly addressing one of his confidants in a yellow coat: it was the chief of staff of the French army, Berthier, who that day was wearing the uniform of the *bataillon du prince de Neuchâtel*. It is claimed that

32 Plotho, I, 166.
33 Barclay de Tolly's report to the Tsar regarding the battle of Bautzen, dated 6 [18] June.
34 Plotho, I, 166; Beitzke, I, 441-442.
35 Droysen, II, 250.

Napoleon, who had not slept the entire previous night, fell asleep so soundly on the bank of a ravine that it became necessary to rouse him.[36] Having received news of Ney's repulse from Preititz, Napoleon decided to support the envelopment with an attack in the centre. This began with an intensified cannonade against Baschütz, to which the Russian batteries responded with equally rapid fire; but Emperor Alexander, noticing that the enemy was not moving forward, remaining out of range, ordered this general action by the artillery to be stopped in order to avoid squandering ammunition.[37]

Indeed, Napoleon had no intention of attacking the strong fortifications at Jenkwitz and Baschütz, rather, he intended to attack the high ground at Kreckwitz. To that end, at one o'clock in the afternoon, the *Garde*, formed up in several squares, and the cavalry corps under Latour-Maubourg were directed towards Basankwitz, opposite Yorck's corps, while the corps under Marmont and Bertrand, under Soult's overall command, were ordered to advance against Blücher. Bertrand's force, under covering fire from a powerful battery located on the high ground on the left bank of the Spree, crossed the river, drove Zieten's infantry out of the villages of Doberschütz and Pließkowitz and advanced large batteries facing the high ground at Kreckwitz. Marshal Ney also directed his artillery from Malschwitz towards this location. His Highness' Russian Lifeguard Battery Company and Lieutenant Colonel Dietrichs' 7th Battery Company, sent to assist the Prussian troops, halted the enemy.[38] Blücher, taking note of French preparations to attack the position he was holding, ordered the *Brandenburgischen Brigade* to withdraw from Preititz towards Purschwitz, where they would serve as a reserve for the corps under Blücher and Kleist; shortly thereafter, this brigade was directed towards the high ground at Kreckwitz (Spitzberge) in order to assist in their defence; but even before they could arrive there, the Württemberg contingent under General Franquemont, supported by Morand's division and the Württemberg cavalry, attacked Blücher's position. Klüx's brigade repelled two assaults from the Württembergers; but eventually, the Prussian troops, overwhelmed by superior enemy numbers, were forced to cede the high ground and the village of Kreckwitz and retreat back towards Purschwitz. On the march there they were joined by the *Brandenburgischen Brigade*, which had arrived from Purschwitz. Meanwhile, one of Blücher's battalions, with the assistance of elements of Yorck's force (namely: the *Füsilier* battalion of *2. Ostpreußisches Infanterie* and Borowski's horse artillery battery), had managed to retake Kreckwitz. Blücher, hoping to revive this action successfully, wanted Yorck to support him with his entire force. But this could not be done without completely compromising the centre, against which significant elements of the enemy army were stationed. General Yorck sent an aide-de-camp to the Coalition Monarchs, asking that his corps be relieved at Litten by other troops.

36 Fain, *Manuscrit de 1813*, I, 409; Beitzke, I, 442.

37 Plotho, I, 167.

38 According to Clausewitz (VII, 297), these batteries were forced to cease fire due to lack of ammunition. But this statement is completely without foundation (extracted from information regarding the Lifeguard Artillery reported by Major General Ratch).

Emperor Alexander, being on the high ground near Neupurschwitz, monitored the enemy efforts against the centre of the Coalition Army closely. Just as the Tsar was speaking with Yermolov [Alexey Petrovich Yermolov], a French column emerged from Niederkaina, evaded the frontal fire from Count Arakcheev's artillery company in both extreme *flèches* at Litten, moving around to attack the fortifications from the left flank. The Tsar summoned Colonel Kozen [Pëtr Andreevich Kozen], who was stationed in reserve with a Lifeguard Horse Artillery battery under 1st Cuirassier Division, and ordered him to halt the advancing column. The battery raced into the low ground lying to the left of Litten, and, having passed the *flèches* held by Count Arakcheev's company, unlimbered and opened fire at a range of no more than 100 *sazhen* from the enemy, who were engaged at the same time by fire from a battery at Baschütz manned by 1st Lifeguard Light Artillery Company, which forced the French column to fall back to Niederkaina. Following this, 20 enemy guns emplaced on a hill near Kreckwitz directed their fire at the Lifeguard Horse Artillery battery. Avoiding the unequal battle, Kozen quickly moved this battery into dead ground in front of the *flèches* held by Count Arakcheev's company: thus, 20 Russian guns (12 foot pieces from Arakcheev's company and eight horse artillery pieces under Colonel Kozen) opened fire from two elevations against a similar number of guns located at Kreckwitz. The hollow in which the horse artillery battery was stationed provided the Russian guns with favourable cover, such that after being under fire for more than two hours, they had not lost any of their active numbers; the men minding the war horses placed behind the left *flèche* were also safe; while the only losses of riding and artillery horses had been suffered earlier, as they were moving to their right into this position, when two ammunition caissons were blown up by enemy fire.

Emperor Alexander, observing the departure of the Lifeguard Horse Artillery battery towards the front line and successful action from their first position, forcing the retreat of the battered column, saw how the battery had then raced to the right, under a hail of enemy shells which caused two caissons to detonate, and once they disappeared from view behind the *flèches*, the Tsar sought to find out: 'had the Lifeguard Horse Artillery survived?'

After two o'clock in the afternoon, Emperor Alexander, having been informed by the aide de camp sent by General Yorck about the strengthening of enemy forces facing him, personally ordered Yermolov to relieve the Prussian corps with the Lifeguard Jägers, Kexholm Grenadiers, Pernov Grenadiers, Lifeguard Équipage [Ship's Company of the Imperial Yacht] and Glukhov Cuirassiers. As soon as Yorck became aware of Yermolov's approach, leaving two battalions to protect the batteries, he marched with the rest of the force through Litten, and moving to the left of Kreckwitz, crossed the river via a ford. But the Kreckwitz heights had already been strongly occupied by French troops. General Devaux [Pierre Devaux] had placed 50 guns on them and opened fire on Blücher's columns as they attempted to reoccupy their previous positions. At this decisive moment (at about two o'clock in the afternoon), Napoleon committed his reserves into action, sending the *Garde* and Latour-Maubourg's cavalry towards the flank of Yorck's corps. Moving ahead of these reserves, 60 guns commanded by generals Drouot and Dulauloy [Charles

François Dulauloy de Randon], devastated the ranks of the Prussian force and forced them to retreat.[39]

At the same time as the assault on the Kreckwitz heights, Napoleon sent orders to Ney to resume the attack on the right wing of the Coalition Army. Maison's division, from the force commanded by the marshal, having occupied Pließkowitz, was lurking on the flank of Blucher's corps. Having thus secured himself on his right flank and awaiting the arrival of Reynier's corps on the high ground at Gleina, Ney had sent almost the entire *3e Corps* towards Preititz at one o'clock and had ordered Lauriston to detach one of his divisions to Buchwalde. General Kleist, unable to withstand such overwhelming pressure, retreated via Kleinbautzen, to Purschwitz. After occupying Preititz already to the rear of Blücher's force, in accordance with the instructions he had received from Napoleon, the marshal was to go to the Hochkirch belfry and take up positions across the line of retreat of the Coalition forces, between the Löbauer Wasser and the mountains. But Napoleon's orders were evidently vague, that or Ney did not fully appreciate the importance of the mission given to him. After occupying Preititz, instead of moving towards Wurschen, as he should have, he turned right towards the high ground at Kleinbautzen. Some consider the presence at Purschwitz of a significant line of Russian cuirassiers to be the direct cause of this misunderstanding, against whom Ney had only 600 horsemen; others attribute his diversion from the assigned objective to the action of several guns on his flank, placed on the high ground at Kleinbautzen by Blücher.[40]

Meanwhile, Barclay de Tolly was successfully holding his own against Lauriston at Rackel.

The Coalition, taking advantage of the misdirection of Ney's force, escaped the danger that had threatened them. Nevertheless, the significant superiority of enemy strength did not permit us the hope of stealing victory from them. At three o'clock in the afternoon, as Ney's second capture of Preititz had revealed the aim of Napoleon's operations, General Knesebeck proposed a retreat to the Coalition Monarchs, or, as was stated in contemporary dispatches, to discontinue the battle. This proposal was accepted, albeit most reluctantly.[41] Emperor Alexander was unhappy with Blücher's retreat from the Kreckwitz heights. The Russian generals criticised him all the more so since Miloradovich's force not only still held their positions, but had even moved forward somewhat. According to German historians, matters had come to a point where General Yermolov and the Prussian General Horn were ready to resolve the differences that had arisen between them with a simultaneous offensive by the forces entrusted to them against the enemy occupying the Kreckwitz heights; but at the very moment that they were preparing to strive together, Horn received emphatic orders from Yorck to retreat.[42]

The retreat of the Coalition Army, which began before four o'clock in the afternoon, was carried out in three columns:

39 Vaudoncourt, 97-98; Droysen, II, 250-251; Plotho, I, 167-168; Notes on the Lifeguard Artillery by General Ratch.
40 Jomini; Beitzke, I, 444.
41 Droysen, II, 252.
42 Droysen, II, 252-253.

The first column, General Barclay de Tolly's, received orders to hold the enemy advancing from Baruth at Gröditz until the Prussian troops from the centre column had passed through Wurschen. To that end, Barclay retreated beyond the village of Brießnitz, towards the high ground at Gröditz. The French troops advancing against him were reinforced by Reynier's *7e Corps*, which at five o'clock, was directed via Preititz, towards Belgern into the interval between *3e Corps* and *5e Corps*; at the same time, one of Lauriston's divisions moved into Cannewitz, while the other, emerging from Baruth, changed front to face Barclay's position, who, together with Kleist's force, were covering the retreat of the centre column. Having fulfilled this mission, Barclay retreated to Weißenberg, where, together with Blücher, he took up positions behind the Löbauer Wasser.

The centre column, consisting entirely of Prussian troops, under the overall command of General Blücher, crossed the Blösauer Wasser, over bridges laid between Kreckwitz and Purschwitz, and moved towards Wurschen. Blücher's force were in the lead, namely: *Brandenburgischen Brigade, Oberschlesischen Brigade, Niederschlesischen Brigade*. In order to shield the move from Preititz, four Prussian battalions were sent to this village to hold the enemy until all the artillery had been evacuated, and were then to retreat behind the rest of Blücher's force. The Prussian *Garde-Jäger-Bataillon* were initially to hold the village of Kleinbautzen, and thereafter Purschwitz. Yorck's corps rejoined Blücher's column on the march. The line of retreat of the Prussian force was secured from the enemy advancing from Kreckwitz through a powerful bombardment by three batteries located to the left of Litten, protected by the remaining detachment under General Yermolov. The village of Litten itself, by order of General Yorck, was held by one battalion of the 5th Combined Regiment, which was supposed to hold out until the retreat by Yermolov's force and the artillery stationed in the batteries had been completed, and were then to set fire to the village. All these orders were carried out precisely: the artillery did not move from its position until the troops under Blücher and Yorck had managed to reach the high ground beyond Purschwitz, on the Weißenberg road; Yermolov's detachment retreated behind the guns, and behind them came the battalion occupying Litten. An enemy column, which was enveloping Yermolov from the right flank, from the village of Baschütz, was halted by the fire of 6th Horse Artillery Company under Lieutenant Colonel Zakharzhevsky. Whereupon Yermolov's force retreated to Wurschen, under the cover of General Leontiev's brigade (Military Order Cuirassiers and Pskov Cuirassiers).

Kleist's corps and the reserve cavalry of Blücher's corps, commanded by *Oberst* Dolffs, having joined the rearguard of the centre column, covered the retreat of the Prussian forces along the Wurschen road, and upon reaching Belgern, took up very advantageous positions on the high ground to the left of this village, where they were also joined by Yermolov's force, while Barclay de Tolly positioned himself to the right, on the far side of the Löbauer Wasser. Marshal Ney, having withdrawn his leading troops from Klein-Bautzen and Purschwitz, began a fierce cannonade and firefight with the Coalition rearguards. Emperor Alexander ordered the deployment of several Russian horse batteries in order to support Kleist, which delayed the French advance through their successful actions. Taking advantage of this, Kleist remained in position at Belgern while the troops under Blücher and the corps of Barclay de Tolly behind him, having passed Weißenberg, deployed beyond the Löbauer Wasser. Kleist's corps also fell back to there under cover of Horn's brigade, which occupied Wurschen, while Yermolov's detachment, engaging the enemy with fire from Nilus' and Zakharzhevsky's batteries, upon leaving this village, then departed for Kotitz [2⅓ miles south-west of Weißenberg] with the rearguard. The retreat of the Coalition forces, despite the significant losses they had suffered, was carried out in exemplary order. Their abundant cavalry, delaying the advance of the pursuing force and obliging the French infantry to constantly remain in square, prevented the enemy from capturing any trophies. Not a single gun was lost, and furthermore, almost all the wounded were evacuated. A fierce storm with heavy rain hampered the activities of the troops and contributed to the Coalition retreat.

Upon the retreat of the right wing and centre of the Coalition army, Napoleon sent Latour-Maubourg's cavalry towards Kubschütz in order to cut off the left wing, which had moved forward to Denkwitz. To that end, Marmont's *6e Corps*, advancing along the Görlitz road, was ordered to change front with the left flank forward. Macdonald's *11e Corps* moved directly towards Gross Jenkwitz. Oudinot went on the offensive with *12e Corps*.[43] The flanking movement by Latour-Maubourg exposed Miloradovich's force to great danger, who, having received orders to retreat somewhat later than the centre and right wing, managed to withdraw from their position no earlier than half past five o'clock. But the French cavalry were driven back by Colonel Prince Obolensky, with the 1st Ukraine Regiment, supported by the Sumy Hussars and Lubny Hussars, several battalions from II Corps and two horse artillery companies. The Russian reserves located behind the centre, and the force under Miloradovich, stationed on the left bank of the Blösauer Wasser took advantage of this and crossed to the right bank at Blösa and Soritz, and having reached the road leading to the town of Löbau, continued to retreat under the protection of a rearguard under comte Saint-Priest,[44] who held a very advantageous position on the high ground at Waditz. By nightfall, Miloradovich's reserves had retreated beyond the Löbauer Wasser, leaving Saint-Priest's detachment as the rearguard at Steindörfel. The retreat by these troops was also distinguished by good order and coordination. The smoke and flames of burning villages, along with the smoke from gunfire, and the roar of cannonade in the hills gave a menacing grandeur to the close of the two-day battle at Bautzen.

At about five o'clock in the afternoon, the Coalition monarchs left the battlefield and went through Lauske towards Reichenbach. They rode side by side for a long time, separate from their retinue, remaining quiet. Eventually, the King broke silence with the words: 'I did not expect this! We had hoped to go west, but we are heading east!' Emperor Alexander replied that not a single one of the Coalition battalions had been destroyed and that although retreat had become unavoidable, all was not yet lost and with God's help things would get better. 'Should God bless our common efforts' said the King, 'we must confess before the whole world that the glory of success belongs to Him alone.' The Tsar, shaking hands with his faithful ally, told him that he shared these sentiments completely. Upon arrival in Reichenbach,

43 Vaudoncourt, p. 98.
44 Comte Saint-Priest's detachment consisted of six battalions with 12 guns.

the King occupied quarters within the town, while Emperor Alexander stayed in the nearby Nemmersdorf manor.

Napoleon moved his *quartier général* to Klein-Purschwitz in the evening. His *Garde* were located in bivouacs around this village. Ney's corps (Souham) and Lauriston were at Wurschen. Bertrand's, Marmont's and Macdonald's corps were around Hochkirch. Oudinot's corps remained on the battlefield. Reynier's corps and the *réserve de cavalerie*, having passed through Wurschen, formed the vanguard for the remainder of the force around the village of Nechern.[45]

The Coalition losses in the fighting on 9 (21) May, according to the most conservative estimates, reached some 8,000 men but, in all likelihood, were somewhat higher, in that, together with the casualties from the fighting on 8 (20) May, these may almost certainly be taken as 12,000 men, including 6,400 Russians and 5,600 Prussians, not counting those lightly wounded.[46] Seriously wounded were Count Osterman-Tolstoy, who participated in the actions on the left wing, and Major General Prince Sibirsky [Alexander Vasilievich Sibirsky]. Generals Yermolov and Choglokov [Pavel Nikolaevich Choglokov] were slightly wounded. On the French side, the losses from both days of the battle of Bautzen were at least 18,000 men.[47] Two guns were taken from them and some 600 men were taken prisoner.[48] Among the wounded were *général de division* Lorencez (Oudinot's corps), *Generalleutnant* Franquemont and *Generalmajor* Neuffer; the latter two from the Württemberg division.[49]

Following the battle of Bautzen, the Coalition had some 80,000 men, Napoleon between 120,000 and 130,000 men: therefore, the ratio between the respective strengths of both sides had not changed: as before, Napoleon had much more infantry and fewer cavalry and artillery, which did not allow him to exploit the victories he had won. The Coalition were concerned that the second battle they had lost would have an unfavourable effect on the morale of the Prussian people, and therefore the news of the outcome of the battle of Bautzen was made known publicly together with an appeal by King Friederich Wilhelm to his subjects (*Aufruf an die Preussen*), in which, praising the courage of the Coalition troops, he announced that they had avoided a further continuation of the battle, having fallen back on the locations of their resources and having been reinforced, solely in order to resume the fight with a greater likelihood of success. Recalling the fortitude of Frederick

45 Plan of the Battle of Bautzen, signed by General Harting; Vaudoncourt, 97-98; Plotho, I, 169-172; Beitzke, I, 446-448; Yermolov's report to the Commander-in-Chief, Count Wittgenstein, dated 14 [26] May.

46 Coalition losses for both days of the Battle of Bautzen are shown as: 8,000 men on official Russian dispatches; 12,000 to 15,000 men in Clausewitz (VII, 300); 12,000 to 13,000 men in Wollzogen (*Memoiren*, 181); 5,000 Russians and 3,000 Prussians in Plotho (I, 171); 18,000 killed and wounded and several thousand taken prisoner (*sic*) in Vaudoncourt (98).

47 French losses for both days of the Battle of Bautzen were given as: 12,000 men in Vaudoncourt (98); from 5,000 to 6,000 killed and more than 20,000 wounded in Odeleben (I, 96); some 30,000 casualties overall in the actions at Königswartha and Weißig and in the battle of Bautzen in Wollzogen (181-182) and Richter (I, 212); 18,000 wounded alone in Clausewitz (VII, 300); from 6,000 to 8,000 killed and some 18,000 wounded in Plotho (I, 171).

48 One gun was captured by the detachment under General Knorring, and the other by the detachment under Adjutant General Orlov, at the tip of the left wing of the Coalition army.

49 Vaudoncourt, 98.

the Great, the King concluded his proclamation with the words: 'Let everyone do with a will that which the law and duty demand of them. Let nobody abandon their faith in God, in the bravery of the army or in their own strength.' (*Jeder thue willig, was Gesetz und Pflicht ihm gebieten. Keinen verlasse das Vertrauen auf Gott, auf das tapfere Heer und auf die eigene Kraft*).

The trust of the Prussian people in their Sovereign, trust in the courage of the Coalition forces, the expectation of imminent assistance from Austria, and finally, a lack of awareness of the danger that threatened the state, all this weakened the force of the blow inflicted on the Russo-Prussian army in the Battle of Bautzen.

Appendix XVII

Count Wittgenstein's letter to General Barclay de Tolly, dated 7 [19] May

Your Excellency, Sir, Mikhail Bogdanovich.

The Sovereign Emperor has commanded me to inform Your Excellency of the following:

At the first shot from your direction, all the troops stationed here are to set off, and I am to attempt to envelope the left flank of the enemy located at Bautzen with all my strength and thereby secure your left flank and completely divide the enemy into two parts; to that end it would be advantageous that you, on your part, operate on the right flank against the enemy who are in your direction.

If the enemy wishes to launch some kind of offensive movement against me even before your attack, then I shall immediately operate as indicated above, and in this respect, General Kleist has been ordered to mount constant patrols between your army and the enemy, in order at least to be notified in advance of enemy intentions for operations by their left flank.

Although operations by our forces will be hastening to different locations, yet, according to the general advance, it is all based on one axis, and I most humbly request that Your Excellency position the grenadier corps in such a way that, depending on the circumstances, it may serve as support both for you and for me.

Archive of the M.T.D. No. 44,585, folio 30.

Appendix XVIII

Composition of the Coalition army at Bautzen

Forward Detachments

Lieutenant General comte de Saint-Priest's detachment:
Vyatka Infantry; Olonets Infantry; 11th Jägers; 37th Jägers (six battalions with 12 guns).[1]

Major General Emmanuel's and *Flügel-Adjutant* Orlov's detachments:[2]
Kharkov Dragoons (four squadrons); Kiev Dragoons (three squadrons); Chuguev Ulans (two squadrons); Rebrikov's Don Cossacks; Shlyusarev's Don Cossacks; Melentiev's Don Cossacks; Stavropol Kalmyks; two horse artillery pieces.

Major General Kaisarov's detachment:
Neumärkisches Dragoner (one squadron); Ilovaisky 10th's Don Cossacks.
According to the Order of Battle of the Coalition Army at the Battle of Bautzen, 8 to 9 [20 to 21] May 1813 (Archive of the M.T.D. No. 20,028).

Rearguard Cavalry detachment

Major General Knorring: Tatar Ulans (ten squadrons); Combined Dragoons (four squadrons); Sumy Hussars (two squadrons); 7th Horse Artillery Company (six guns).

1 In Prinz Eugen von Württemberg II Corps War Diary, the 43rd Jägers are included in error, having previously been in General Rath's detachment at the Zamość fortress. In this Diary, instead of 11th Jägers, Saint-Priest's detachment included the Staro-Oskol Infantry, 1st Jägers and 33rd Jägers, then part of Markov's corps.

2 The available sources disagree on the composition of the detachments operating at the tip of the Coalition left wing. According to Plotho, I, appendices, 118-119: Major General Emmanuel's detachment; Kharkov Dragoons, Kiev Dragoons, Major General Merlin's 4th Horse Artillery Company, Rebrikov 3rd's Cossacks, Stavropol Kalmyks, *Flügel-Adjutant* Orlov's raiding detachment. Major General Kaisarov's detachment: Panteleev 2nd's Don Cossacks, Barabanshchikov 2nd's Don Cossacks, 1st Teptyarsk Cossacks, 3rd Ural Cossacks, Colonel Yakhontov's Volunteer Cossacks, 1st Bashkirs.

Major General Panchulidzev 1st: Novorussia Dragoons (five squadrons); Chernigov Mounted Jägers (five squadrons); Lithuania Ulans (two squadrons); 7th Horse Artillery Company (six guns).
Colonel Prince Obolensky: 1st Ukraine Cossacks (five squadrons); 3rd Ukraine Cossacks (five squadrons).
(Order of Battle of the Coalition Army at the Battle of Bautzen, Archive of the M.T.D. No. 20,028).

Lieutenant Colonel Wolf's detachment:
Chernigov Infantry; Murom Infantry; 21st Jägers (one battalion); 33rd Light Artillery Company (four guns).
(War Diary of Prinz Eugen von Württemberg's II Corps).

Prinz Eugen von Württemberg's II Corps (elements):
Major General Prince Shakhovskoy's 3rd Division: Reval Infantry; 20th Jägers; 21st Jägers (one battalion).
Major General Pyshnitsky's 4th Division: Kremenchug Infantry; Tobolsk Infantry; Volhynia Infantry; Ryazhsk Infantry; 4th Jägers; 1st Battery Artillery Company (12 guns); 33rd Light Artillery Company (eight guns).
(Order of Battle etc. Schedule of Forces signed by Adjutant General Prince Volkonsky).

Chaplits' detachment:
Major General Rudzevich: 12th Jägers; 22nd Jägers; Olviopol Hussars (two squadrons); Zhitomir Ulans (two squadrons); Colonel Nesterovsky's 34th Light Artillery Company; Grekov 8th's Don Cossacks; Kuteinikov 8th's Don Cossacks; Isaev 2nd's Don Cossacks.
Total for Chaplits' detachment: four battalions, four squadrons, three Cossack regiments, with 12 guns.

Major General Lanskoy's and Colonel Prendel's detachments:
Alexandria Hussars (four squadrons); Belorussia Hussars (four squadrons); Livonia Mounted Jägers (two squadrons); 2nd Horse Artillery Company.
Major General Paradovsky: Kuteinikov 4th's Don Cossacks; Ilovaisky 12th's Don Cossacks; 3rd Ural Cossacks.
Major General Ilovaisky 12th: Popov 13th's Don Cossacks; 1st Bug Cossacks; Akhryrka Hussars (elements) and various Cossacks.
Total for Lanskoy's and Prendel's detachments: ten squadrons, more than seven Cossack regiments, with 12 guns.

Colonel Figner's detachment: Sumy Hussars (one squadron); Colonel Yakhontov's Volunteer Cossacks; Figner's Volunteer Cossacks; two guns.

Kleist's detachment:
Colbergsches Infanterie (three battalions); *2. Ostpreußisches Infanterie* (one battalion); *Ostpreußisches Jäger-Bataillon* (two companies); *1. Schlesisches Husaren* (two squadrons); *2. Schlesisches Husaren* (two squadrons); *3. Reitende Batterie.*

Russian troops:

Major General Vlastov: 23rd Jägers; 24th Jägers.

Major General Roth: 25th Jägers; 26th Jägers.

Major General Rüdiger: Grodno Hussars (six squadrons); 21st Battery Artillery Company; Colonel Markov's 23rd Horse Artillery Company (six guns).

Total for Kleist's detachment: 12½ battalions, ten squadrons and 26 guns (Order of Battle etc. Plotho, I, *Beilagen*, 118. Droysen, I, 223-224).

Main Body

Prince Gorchakov 2nd's left wing:

Lieutenant General Berg's I Corps:

Major General Prince Sibirsky: Perm Infantry; Mogilev Infantry; 11th Jägers.

Major General Lukov: Sevsk Infantry (one battalion); Her Highness, Grand Duchess Yekaterin Pavlovna's Battalion; Kaluga Infantry.

Major General Helffreich: Tenginsk Infantry; Estland Infantry.

Corps artillery: 5th Battery Company; 14th Battery Company; 13th Light Artillery Company.

Major General Engelhardt's Combined Corps: Arkhangelogorod Infantry; Schlüsselburg Infantry; Staro Ingermanland Infantry; 27th Light Artillery Company.

Lieutenant General Markov's IV Corps: Yelets Infantry; Staro-Oskol Infantry; Kaporsk Infantry; 1st Jägers; 33rd Jägers.

Lieutenant General Prince Gorchakov's III Corps: Brest Infantry; Ryazan Infantry; Belozersk Infantry; 48th Jägers.

Adjutant General Uvarov's cavalry (27 squadrons with 12 guns):

Major General Melissino: Moscow Dragoons; Mitau Dragoons; Lubny Hussars; 3rd Horse Artillery Company (six guns).

Major General Lisanevich: Akhtyrka Hussars; Kargopol Dragoons; Chuguev Ulans (two squadrons); 3rd Horse Artillery Company (six guns).

The overall total for the left wing of the main position on 8 (20) May was around 12,000 men.

General Blücher's corps:

Right wing, *Oberschlesischen Brigade* under *Generalmajor* Zieten:

Major La Roche-Starkenfels: *1. Schlesisches Husaren* (four squadrons); *2. Schlesisches Husaren*; *1. Schlesisches Ulanen* (two squadrons); *9. Reitende Batterie*.

Oberstleutnant Pirch 1: *Oberstleutnant* Carnal – *Schlesisches Grenadier Bataillon*; *1. Schlesisches Infanterie* (three battalions). *Oberst* Losthin – six-pounder *8. Fuß-Artillerie-Batterie*; *2. Schlesisches Infanterie* (two battalions); *Schlesisches Schützen Bataillon*. *Garde-Regiment zu Fuss* (third and fourth reserve battalions); six-pounder *13. Fuß-Artillerie-Batterie*.

Left wing, *Niederschlesischen Brigade* under *Oberst* Klüx:

Major Jagow – *Westpreußisches Grenadier Bataillon*; *1. Westpreußisches Infanterie* (four battalions); *2. Westpreußisches Infanterie* (two battalions); *Garde-Regiment zu Fuss* (second reserve battalion); six-pounder *9. Fuß-Artillerie-Batterie.*

Oberst Mutius – *7. Reitende Batterie*; *Neumärkisches Dragoner* (four squadrons); *2. Westpreußisches Dragoner* (two squadrons).

Brandenburgischen Brigade under *Generalmajor* Röder:

Oberstleutnant Katzler – *Westpreußisches Ulanen* (four squadrons); *Brandenburgisches Ulanen* (two squadrons); *Hauptmann* Graevenitz's *reitende Batterie.*

Major Alvensleben – *Garde-Jäger Bataillon*; *Garde-Regiment zu Fuss* (three battalions); model *Leib Bataillon*; *Leib Fuß-Artillerie-Batterie.*

Major Natzmer – *Leib-Grenadier Bataillon*; *Westpreußisches Grenadier Bataillon*; *Garde* regiments (two battalions); *Freiwilligen Jäger Bataillon.*

Major Hobe – *Brandenburgisches Husaren* (two squadrons); *2. Leib Husaren* (four squadrons).

Prussian reserve cavalry brigade under *Oberst* Dolffs:

Oberstleutnant Werder – *Leib Reitende Batterie*; *Garde du Corps* (five squadrons); *Leib Leichtes Kavallerie* (six squadrons).

Oberst Jürgaß – *Ostpreußisches Kürassier* (four squadrons); *Schlesisches Kürassier* (four squadrons); *Brandenburgisches Kürassier* (four squadrons); *10. Reitende Batterie.*

Total for Blücher's corps: 16,700 men.

General Yorck's corps:

Oberstleutnant Wuthenau – *2. Leib Husaren* (two squadrons); six-pounder *2. Reitende Batterie.*

Oberstleutnant Steinmetz – six-pounder *1. Reitende Batterie*; *2. Ostpreußisches Infanterie* (*Füsilier* battalion); *1. Ostpreußisches Infanterie* (first battalion); *2. Ostpreußisches Infanterie* (second battalion); *Garde* regiments (two battalions); *1. Ostpreußisches Infanterie* and *Garde* regiments (combined *Füsilier* battalion); six-pounder *2. Fuß-Artillerie-Batterie.*

Oberst Horn – six-pounder *3. Fuß-Artillerie-Batterie*; *1. Westpreußisches Infanterie* (first battalion); *2. Westpreußisches Infanterie* (second battalion); *1. Schlesisches Infanterie* (second battalion); *2. Schlesisches Infanterie* (second battalion); *Westpreußisches* and *Schlesisches* regiments (combined *Füsilier* battalion); three-pounder *1. Fuß-Artillerie-Batterie.*

Schlesisches Husaren (four combined squadrons).

Generalmajor Corswant's reserve cavalry:

Litthauisches Dragoner (four squadrons); *1. Westpreußisches Dragoner* (four squadrons); *Reitende Batterie.*

Total for Yorck's corps, excluding losses from the action at Weißig, remained some 4,000 men. Moreover, five reserve battalions had arrived as reinforcements, numbering 3,700 men. Consequently, on May 8 (20), there were some 26,000 men under Blücher's command in the main position.

Barclay de Tolly's force: The numerical strength of this corps in the main position on 8 (20) May, excluding losses from the action at Königswartha, remained some 9,000 men, excluding Chaplits detachment (see Forward Detachments above). For further details, see Appendix XVI.

Reserves under Tsarevich Grand Duke Konstantin Pavlovich's command

Front line under Lieutenant General Raevsky's command:
Major General Shevich's Lifeguard Light Cavalry Division: Lifeguard Dragoons; Lifeguard Ulans; Lifeguard Hussars.
Total for the Lifeguard light cavalry division: 1,200 men.

General Raevsky's Grenadier Corps:
1st Grenadier Division: Colonel Knyazhnin – Count Arakcheev's Grenadiers; Yekaterinoslav Grenadiers. Colonel Agte – Tauride Grenadiers; St Petersburg Grenadiers. Colonel Breshinsky – Pernov Infantry; Kexholm Infantry; two combined grenadier battalions from 5th Division; two combined grenadier battalions from 14th Division. Divisional Artillery: 3rd Battery Artillery Company; 36th Light Artillery Company; 14th Light Artillery Company.
2nd Grenadier Division: Colonel Pisarev – Kiev Grenadiers; Moscow Grenadiers. Colonel Golovin – Astrakhan Grenadiers; Fanagoria Grenadiers. Colonel Hesse – Siberia Grenadiers; Malorussia Grenadiers. Divisional Artillery: 32nd Battery Artillery Company; 4th Horse Artillery Company.
Total for the Grenadier Corps: 5,000 men.

Lieutenant General Prince Golitsyn's Cuirassier Corps:
Major General Depreradovich's 1st Cuirassier Division: Chevalier Garde; Lifeguard Horse; His Majesty's Cuirassiers; Her Majesty's Cuirassiers; Astrakhan Cuirassiers.
Major General Duka's 2nd Cuirassier Division: Yekaterinoslav Cuirassiers; Military Order Cuirassiers; Glukhov Cuirassiers; Malorussia Cuirassiers; Novgorod Cuirassiers; Pskov Cuirassiers.
Total for the Cuirassier Corps: 3,800 men.

Lieutenant General Lavrov's Lifeguard Infantry Corps:
Major General Baron Rosen's 1st Lifeguard Division: Major General Potëmkin – Lifeguard Preobrazhensky; Lifeguard Semenovsky. Major General Khrapovitsky – Lifeguard Izmailovsky; Lifeguard Jägers.
Lieutenant General Yermolov's 2nd Lifeguard Division: Major General Udom – Lifeguard Lithuania; Lifeguard Finland; Lifeguard Équipage. Major General Zheltukhin – Leib Grenadiers; Pavlovsk Grenadiers.
Corps Artillery: His Majesty's Battery Artillery Company; Count Arakcheev's Battery Artillery Company; 1st Lifeguard Light Artillery Company; 2nd Lifeguard Light Artillery Company; Lifeguard *Équipage* (two guns); 1st

Lifeguard Horse Artillery Battery (eight guns); 2nd Lifeguard Horse Artillery Battery (eight guns).

Total for the Lifeguard Infantry Corps: 6,500 men.

Major General Euler's Artillery Reserve:

2nd Battery Artillery Company; 7th Battery Artillery Company; 30th Battery Artillery Company; 31st Battery Artillery Company; 33rd Battery Artillery Company; 5th Light Artillery Company; 7th Light Artillery Company; 32nd Light Artillery Company; 42nd Light Artillery Company; 6th Horse Artillery Company; 8th Horse Artillery Company; 10th Horse Artillery Company (six guns); 23rd Horse Artillery Company (six guns); 1st Horse Artillery Company (two guns).

Total for the artillery reserve: 146 guns with 1,800 crewmen.

Total for the reserve: 18,300 men.

Appendix XIX

Composition of the French army at Bautzen

Garde impériale, 20,000 men, under Marshal Mortier's command:
Vieille Garde division – eight battalions commanded by *Général de division* Curial [Philibert Jean-Baptiste Curial].
Jeune Garde (two divisions) – 16 battalions commanded *Généraux de division* Dumoustier and Barrois [Pierre Barrois].
Cavalerie de la Garde – 24 squadrons commanded by *Général de division* comte Walther.

3e Corps, 20,000 men, under Marshal Ney's command:
Souham's division – 16 battalions.
Albert's division [Joseph Jean-Baptiste Albert] – 14 battalions.
Delmas' division [Antoine Guillaume Muralhac Delmas] – 15 battalions.
Ricard's division – 14 battalions.
Marchand's division – 11 battalions of the Baden and Hessen contingents.
Light cavalry brigade – eight squadrons.

4e Corps, 15,000 men, under General Bertrand's command:
Morand's division – 12 battalions.
Peyri's division – 12 (weak) battalions (Italian).
Franquemont's division – eight battalions (Württemberg contingent).
Light cavalry brigade – 12 squadrons.

5e Corps, 12,000 men, under General Lauriston's command:
Maison's division – eight battalions.
Lagrange's division – 12 battalions.
Rochambeau's division – 12 battalions.
Light cavalry brigade – eight squadrons.

6e Corps, 20,000 men, under Marshal Marmont's command:
Compans' division – ten battalions.
Bonet's division – eight battalions.
Friedrich's division [Jean-Parfait Friederichs] – eight battalions.

7e Corps, 14,000 men, under Reynier's command:
Durutte's division – ten battalions.
Sahr's division – eight battalions (Saxon).
Light cavalry – six squadrons.

11e Corps, 12,000 men, under Marshal Macdonald's command:
Charpentier's division – eight battalions.
Gérard's division – eight battalions.
Fressinet's division – eight battalions.
Light cavalry – six squadrons.

12e Corps, 25,000 men, under Marshal Oudinot's command:
Pacthod's division – ten battalions.
Lorencez's division – 14 battalions.
Raglovich's division – ten battalions (Bavarian).
Light cavalry brigade – 14 squadrons.
Cavalry corps, 5,000 men, under General Latour-Maubourg's command:
Six French cuirassier regiments.
Two Saxon cuirassier regiments.
32 squadrons in all.

For a grand total of 143,000 men, including 12,000 cavalrymen and 6,000 artillerymen and the troops of the engineering department.

11

The actions at Reichenbach and Haynau

Dispositions for the withdrawal from the Bautzen battlefield. – The offensive by Napoleon's forces. – Yermolov's rearguard actions: at Kotitz; on the Löbauer Wasser; at Rotkretscham; at Schöps. – The retreat to Reichenbach. – Prinz Eugen von Württemberg's rearguard action at Reichenbach. – Count Miloradovich's rearguard action at Markersdorf. – Duroc's death. – Napoleon in Görlitz.

Napoleon's intention to make peace with Emperor Alexander. – Negotiations for an armistice.

The Coalition withdrawal behind the Bober and the pursuit by Napoleon's forces. – The appointment of Barclay de Tolly as Commander-in-Chief. – His departure for Emperor Alexander's headquarters. – The ambush at Haynau. – The composition of the Coalition forces. – Misunderstandings between the allies. – The flanking movement towards Schweidnitz. – The advance by Napoleon's forces in pursuit of the Coalition and towards Breslau. – The deployment of the Coalition army in positions at Pilzen [bei Schweidnitz]. – Barclay de Tolly's intention to withdraw into Poland. – The composition of the French army. – The factors pushing Napoleon towards peace. – The continuing negotiations for an armistice.

Ney's movement towards Breslau. – General von Senden's operations and his retreat to Ohlau. – The French occupation of Breslau. – The armistice. – Napoleon's residence at Neumarkt and his departure to Dresden. – The effect of the armistice on Prussian public opinion. – The King's manifesto.

As the Coalition forces withdrew from the Bautzen position, a disposition was issued, the essence of which was as follows:

1. The Prussian corps under Blücher, Kleist and Yorck, and Barclay de Tolly's force, were to retreat from Wurschen towards Reichenbach, protected by a rearguard under General Yermolov, consisting of

his detachment, reinforced by the 2nd Cuirassier Division and the Lifeguard horse artillery batteries.

2. The Russian Lifeguard (excluding those troops assigned to Yermolov's detachment), with the artillery reserve and Lifeguard light cavalry, were to retreat from Hochkirch towards Reichenbach.
3. General Miloradovich's force, with all the co-located artillery and cavalry and the trains of the entire army, were to proceed from Löbau towards Reichenbach via the most convenient route, dispatching only some of the cavalry along the road leading from Hochkirch to Kittlitz [2½ miles north of Löbau].[1]

It was not difficult to foresee that Napoleon would tenaciously pursue the retreating army, notwithstanding that they had to cross many rivers: Löbauer Wasser, Lausitzer Neisse, Queis [Kwisa], Bober [Bóbr], Deichsa [Skorą] and Katzbach [Kaczawa]. But, fortunately for the Coalition, their superiority in cavalry and horse artillery gave them great advantages over their incomparably more numerous enemy.

On 10 (22) May, at half past three o'clock in the morning, General Yermolov's force, reinforced by a Prussian light cavalry brigade under *Oberstleutnant* Katzler [Andreas Georg Friedrich von Katzler], were attacked in their positions forwards of the village of Kotitz by two cavalry brigades from Latour-Maubourg's corps and General Reynier's *7e Corps*. These troops were followed by all the other corps from the French army, with the exception of Oudinot's, which had been left at Bautzen in order to operate towards Berlin, facing von Bülow's Prussian corps. Napoleon himself, joining up with the fighting troops at five o'clock, deployed his cavalry on the plain, including the Dutch red lancers [*2e chevau-légers lanciers de la Garde*] and two regiments of Saxon cuirassiers, and advanced Reynier's entire corps. But the Russian artillery greeted the enemy with heavy fire. The French were forced to send some of their force on a detour, while in the meantime the Coalition army, with their entire trains, had managed to pass the choke-point at Reichenbach. Whereupon the rearguard slowly withdrew from their positions and retreated, step by step, beyond the Löbauer Wasser, skilfully using every local obstacle lying on the line of retreat in order to delay the enemy. The crossing of the Löbauer Wasser and the attack on the high ground at Weißenberg were costly for the French. The defence of the position at Rotkretscham [2½ miles south-east of Weißenberg], behind one of the tributaries of the Löbauer Wasser, was even more stubborn. Napoleon countered the Russian artillery with powerful batteries and supported Reynier with a significant part of Ney's corps. But he rushed his numerous columns into battle in vain; every French attack was repulsed with heavy losses. Eventually, under attack by huge forces and enveloped on the left flank, Yermolov retreated [3½ miles south-east] to a new position near the village of Schöps. Here, he blocked the enemy for a fourth time. The deadly cannonade thundered again, Napoleon, driven beyond patience by the stubborn resistance of the Russian rearguard, did not spare his cavalry: General Latour-Maubourg's corps was ordered to trot to the right of the high ground at Schöps and

1 Note signed by Major General Diebitsch, dated 9 [21] May (operational diary of Count Miloradovich's rearguard).

ford the stream in order to envelope the left flank of the Russian position. At the same time, General Lauriston, having been sent along the right bank of the Löbauer Wasser at the Battle of Bautzen to Gröditz with two divisions from his corps, moved to the left of Weißenberg, enveloping the right flank of the Russian position. Threatened with the complete severing of his line of retreat, General Yermolov withdrew his force towards Reichenbach,[2] where Count Miloradovich relieved him with a rearguard consisting of the Grenadier Corps commanded by General Raevsky, the corps under Prinz Eugen von Württemberg, Prince Gorchakov, Markov, and the detachment under comte Saint-Priest.[3]

The town of Reichenbach lies in the fairly deep valley of one of the tributaries of the river Schöps.[4] To the east of the town, on the right bank [*sic*, actually the left bank] of this tributary, there rises a plateau with relatively steep slopes (from eight to ten degrees). The road to Görlitz runs past this plateau. The Töpferberg hill rises on the southern side of the plateau, while it is dominated on the northern side by the Windmühlenberg. Here, at Reichenbach, Prinz Eugen von Württemberg's II Corps had been left to cover the retreat of Miloradovich's rearguard.[5] As the artillery that was attached to Miloradovich's force at the time actually belonged to the Grenadier Corps, while all the other guns had been sent to the rear, without the knowledge of the commander-in-chief or the corps commanders, there was no artillery at all with II Corps at this point.[6] Prinz Eugen, having unexpectedly become the commander of the rearguard, sent an officer to Miloradovich with a request to support him with units, and particularly artillery, while in anticipation of this, he placed his corps in positions behind Reichenbach. The 21st Jägers and 34th Jägers occupied parts of the town, all the remaining infantry were formed up on the plateau in two lines, in attack columns.

The enemy, approaching Reichenbach at about ten o'clock in the morning, deployed their troops on the far side of the stream, advanced a battery and opened fire on the Russian troops, who, lacking artillery, could not respond to this bombardment. Fortunately, the shots fired over the town into Prinz Eugen's position did not cause the slightest harm to his force. Subsequently, the enemy flooded the Reichenbach valley with skirmishers. The jägers holding the town, having received orders to retreat, began to fall back to the position, whereupon part of the 21st Jägers were caught by enemy cavalry and cut down. Several French cavalry regiments, having crossed the river by fording, emerged opposite the left wing of the position.

---

2 Odeleben, *Relation circonstanciée de la campagne de 1813 en Saxe*, I, 97-98; Beitzke, *Geshchichte der deutschen Freiheitskriege in den Jahren 1813 und 1814*, I, 457-459.

3 Count Miloradovich's letter No. 499 to Prince Volkonsky, dated 10 [22] May.

4 See Map No. 9, Plan of the action at Reichenbach, 10 (22) May.

5 The composition of Prinz Eugen von Württemberg's rearguard was: one battalion each of Ryazhsk Infantry, 21st Jägers and 34th Jägers; two battalions each of Tobolsk Infantry, Volhynia Infantry, Kremenchüg Infantry, Chernigov Infantry, Murom Infantry, Reval Infantry, 4th Jägers and 20th Jägers, for a total of 19 battalions, numbering around 5,000 men (Atlas attached to the Operational Diary of Prinz Eugen von Württemberg's II Corps, Archive of the M. T.D. No. 47,344.

6 Miloradovich's letter to Prince Volkonsky, dated 10 [22] May; Operational Diary of Prinz Eugen von Württemberg's II Corps

Lieutenant Colonel Zakharzhevsky's 6th Horse Artillery Company arrived to aid the Russian force at this very moment, and a little later six more horse artillery pieces arrived. At the same time, Count Miloradovich let the prince know about the withdrawal of his force, past Reichenbach, onto the Görlitz road, and put all the cavalry at his disposal as they passed by the Reichenbach position. In addition, 5th Division of I Corps was to remain between Reichenbach and Markersdorf [four miles east of Reichenbach], in support of Prinz Eugen.

As soon as the artillery arrived, the prince positioned it on the left wing of the position in order to engage the cavalry that was gathering against him. The 4th

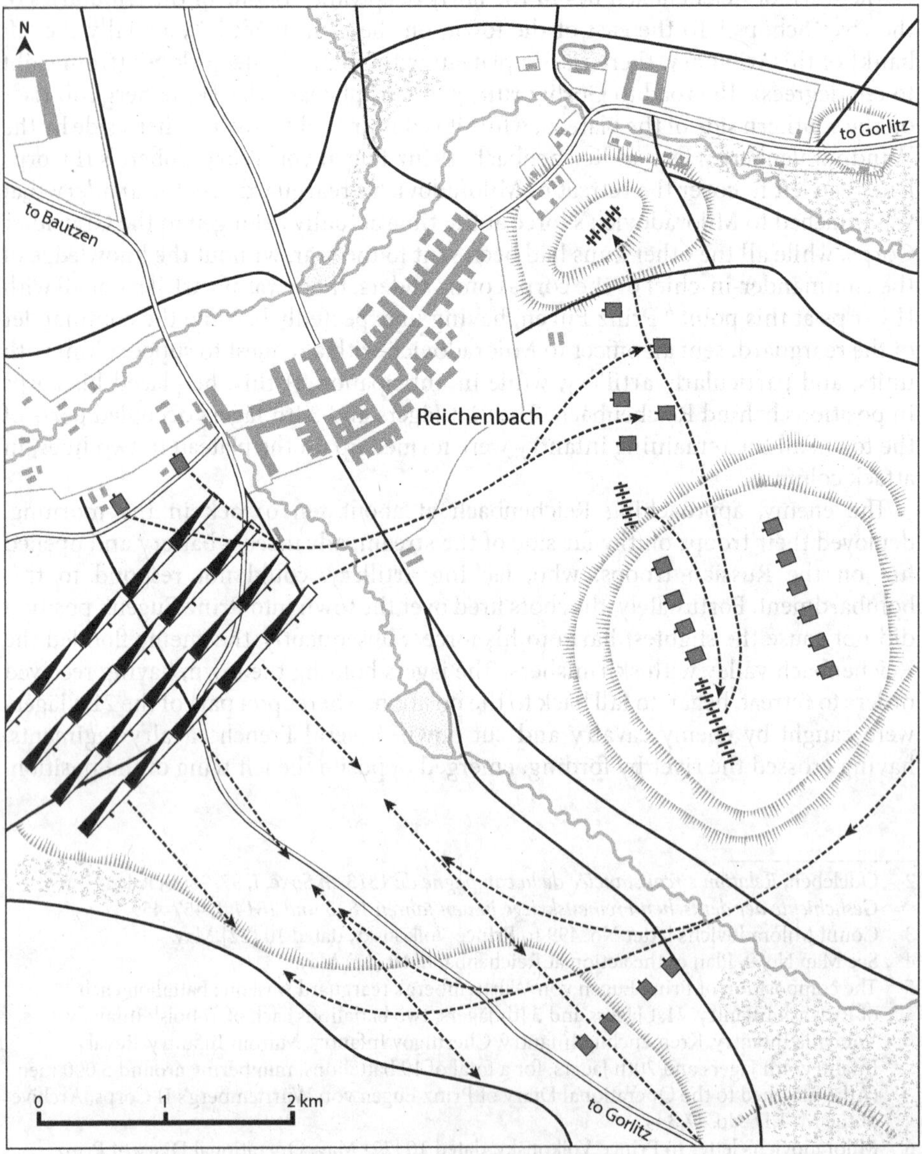

Plan of the action at Reichenbach.

Jägers and 20th Jägers were stationed even further to the left in a forest. The Tobolsk Infantry and Ryazhsk Infantry, on the right wing of the position, moved forward in order to support those jägers still continuing to hold out in the town, exchanging fire with the enemy screen. Meanwhile, on the far side of the river, the movements of strong infantry columns were noticeably advancing towards Reichenbach, while the cavalry facing the left wing were gradually being reinforced. Prinz Eugen, anticipating a decisive attack on this location, requested the assistance of Miloradovich's cavalry. But even before they could arrive, the entire front line of French cavalry went on the attack and, being engaged by the fire of 18 guns, extended their right in order to strike the battery in the flank. During this time, the Russian cavalry gradually began to approach. Their attacks, under the command of generals Korff, Knorring and Melissino, distracted the enemy from the battery. Napoleon was obliged to bring into action the *cavalerie de la Garde*, under the command of General Walther [Frédéric Henri Walther], in addition to Latour-Maubourg's corps. By order of the chief-of-staff of II Corps, Colonel Hofmann, the Russian battery moved its right flank forwards in order to enfilade the enemy column. Almost none of the Russian projectiles were wasted. The casualties suffered by Napoleon's cavalry were grievous. The Dutch lancers, disordered by the cannonade devastating its ranks, was attacked by the cavalry under Adjutant General Korff and lost five officers and 176 lower ranks taken prisoner alone. One of the leading French cavalrymen, *général de division* Bruyère [Jean Pierre Joseph Bruguière, dit Bruyère], had both legs severed by round shot. The arrival of Prince Trubetskoy and General von der Pahlen 1st, with the remainder of Miloradovich's cavalry, equalised the forces on each side. But in the meantime, the enemy had moved huge batteries opposite the town and opened heavy fire on the Russian force. Under the covering fire of this artillery, the Saxon infantry drove the 21st Jägers and 34th Jägers out of the town. At the same time, Lauriston's corps threatened to envelope the right flank of the position. All these factors forced Prinz Eugen to retreat along the road to Görlitz.[7]

Having captured the position at Reichenbach, Napoleon suspended the offensive for half an hour in order to reorganise the corps under Reynier, Ney, Lauriston and the cavalry assembled at this point, numbering some 50,000 men. It was already four o'clock in the afternoon. The troops had been on the move constantly and under fire since five o'clock in the morning. The losses of the French force were significant, and the outcome was limited to the retreat of the Russians from one position to the next. Napoleon, wanting to achieve a more decisive victory, ordered his corps to advance further. General Reynier drew his attention to the extreme fatigue of the soldiers but, in response, received orders to attack the retreating force. Meanwhile, Miloradovich's rearguard had occupied the high ground and forest near the village of Markersdorf. Napoleon directed the attack on this position in person. The artillery thundered and a lively firefight ensued. The *Empereur des Français* was exposed to danger along with his warriors. Shells and round shot fell all around him, but he did not notice them, caring only about the defeat of the enemy. Eventually, the Russian rearguard was forced to withdraw from its position, but Miloradovich's

7 Operational Diary of Prinz Eugen von Württemberg's II Corps.

force retreated in exemplary order once more to the high ground at Görlitz. The cannonade fell silent. It was the quiet before a new storm. The French force advanced onwards in three strong columns accompanied by several huge batteries. Having passed the village of Markersdorf, Napoleon turned slightly to the left along the Görlitz highway. His troops forded the river on either side of the village and formed up for battle. At that very moment, the cannonade was heard again. One of the round shot fired from the new Russian position, passing very close to Napoleon, hit a tree and ricocheted, hitting the engineer General Kirgener [François Joseph Kirgener] and *grand maréchal du palais* Duroc [Géraud Christophe Michel du Roc dit Duroc]: the former was killed instantly; the latter was mortally wounded. The *Empereur des Français* was deeply upset by the loss of Duroc, one of his most devoted people, honoured by his friendship. Having ridden to the left of the road, he got off his horse, staring unseeing at the battery that had struck his favourite for several minutes, and returned to his *Garde* formed in square behind Markersdorf. Meanwhile, the cannonade and firefight did not die down until nightfall.

Thus, the victory in this second general battle and the 14-hour pursuit did not bring Napoleon any decisive results. Neither the significant numerical superiority of forces, nor the genius and perseverance of the great commander, nor his dedication in the heat of battle could make good the lack of cavalry. Napoleon's losses were very great. What struck him in particular was the loss of Duroc.[8]

The *grand maréchal du palais*, duc de Frioul (Duroc), was Napoleon's aide-de-camp as early as the Italian campaigns of 1796 and 1797, had proceeded to Egypt and was constantly with him during the campaign of 1800 and in all the wars waged by the *Empereur des Français*. Neither Berthier nor Caulaincourt dared to express their opinions before him as freely as did Duroc. He alone could speak the truth to his master, and perhaps the loss of such a friend had an impact on Napoleon's subsequent fate.

In the evening, Napoleon visited his favourite accompanied by Berthier, Soult and Caulaincourt. The unfortunate Duroc, wounded in the lower abdomen, suffered in agony for 14 hours, calling for death every minute. Napoleon tried to console him with the hope of a reunion in the afterlife. Duroc commended his daughter to him and asked him to leave. Returning to his *quartier général*, Napoleon paced back and forth for a long time, deep in impenetrable thought. No one dared to break the silence. Eventually, General Drouot gave orders to request from him where the guard batteries should be located. "*A demain tout*" (it can all wait until tomorrow), Napoleon replied.[9]

The next day, in the morning, news was received from the outposts that the Coalition were withdrawing from the positions they had occupied at Görlitz. Napoleon immediately moved his *quartier général* into this city and remained there for about two days, entrusting his marshals with the further pursuit of the Coalition army and dealing with diplomatic correspondence with the *ministre des Affaires étrangères*, duc de Bassano (Maret), who had recently arrived from Paris.

8 Odeleben, I, 99-101; Fain, *Manuscrit de 1813*, I, 422-424; Norvins, *Portefeuille de 1813*, I, 435 & 440-441; Beitzke, I, 461-463.

9 Fain, I, 425; Norvins, I, 436-437; *Vossische Zeitung von 17 Juni 1813*.

Even before the battle of Bautzen, irritated by the duplicitous policies of the Viennese Cabinet, Napoleon had decided to get closer to Emperor Alexander in the hope of concluding a separate peace with Russia. This intention was expressed in Napoleon's dispatches to the French ambassador to the Austrian Court, the comte de Narbonne [Louis-Marie-Jacques-Amalric de Narbonne-Lara], sent while the *Empereur des Français* was in Dresden. 'The Viennese intrigues could perhaps be upset by a rapprochement between Alexander and Napoleon' he wrote. The first step towards this was a proposal to permit the duc de Vicence (Caulaincourt) to visit the headquarters of the Russo-Prussian army for negotiations on an armistice. The choice of this *parlementaire*, who had been awarded the special favour of the Russian Monarch during his residence as ambassador to St. Petersburg, revealed Napoleon's intentions. 'If I must make any concessions' he told Caulaincourt, 'I shall make them in favour of Emperor Alexander, who is openly waging war with me, or to the King of Prussia, taking part in this with Russia, rather than to please Austria, which has broken the alliance with me and arrogated to themselves the right to manage the affairs of Europe, under the pretext of mediation… Emperor Alexander should willingly take advantage of this opportunity to exact glorious vengeance for the foolish Austrian diversion into Russia.'[10] On 6 (18) May, on the day of Napoleon's departure from Dresden for Bautzen, Berthier sent a note to the Russian outposts in which he asked whether the duc de Vicence could be brought into the headquarters of the Russo-Prussian army.

Napoleon very clearly believed that only at this point could he enter into direct relations with Emperor Alexander, and that after a battle, whatever the outcome, it would be impossible to avoid Austrian mediation, which he dreaded almost as much as a clear breach with this power. On the evening of 6 (18) May, he sent for Berthier several times, asking if an answer had been received from the forward outposts. His impatience was very much in evidence. But there was no response. Even the losses from the battle of Bautzen could not change the intentions of the Russian Monarch. Count Nesselrode, by order of the Tsar, let Caulaincourt know that the orders issued to him by Emperor Napoleon could only be executed via the Austrian Cabinet.[11] The battle of Bautzen and the Coalition retreat into Silesia had a completely different impact on Austrian policy. Influenced by the concern inspired by Napoleon's previous successes, Graf Stadion, an avowed adversary of the French government (and located with the headquarters of the Coalition army at the time), wrote to Berthier, the *chef d'état-major*, that Emperor Alexander and the King of Prussia, having discussed Emperor Napoleon's proposal regarding a cessation of hostilities, which would facilitate the opening of negotiations for peace, expressed their consent to all orders on this subject and their readiness to send officers authorised to conclude a truce to the forward outposts.[12]

The Coalition forces set off from Görlitz towards the Neisse river, in two columns on 11 (23) May: the right, consisting of the corps under Barclay de Tolly and the Prussian corps under Blücher, Yorck and Kleist, under Barclay's overall

10 Norvins, I, 400 & 408.

11 Count Nesselrode's letter to duc de Vicence, dated 8 (20) May, sent on 9 (21) May.

12 Graf Stadion's letter to the prince de Neuchâtel, dated 22 May, new style.

command, was directed towards Bunzlau, while the left, consisting of the force under Miloradovich and the Russian reserves, under the immediate command of Count Wittgenstein, was directed towards Löwenberg [Lwówek Śląski]. The rearguard of the former column was commanded by Chaplits and Kleist, while the latter came under Lieutenant General Count von der Pahlen 1st.[13] The headquarters of the Coalition monarchs was transferred to Lauban [Lubań] on 11 (23) May and to Löwenberg on 12 (24) May, from where the King of Prussia left for Breslau the next day [25 May new style].

On 11 (23) May, Napoleon's troops departed from Görlitz in pursuit of the Coalition in three columns: *4e Corps* and *11e Corps* in the direction of Lauban; *7e Corps*, *5e Corps* and Latour-Maubourg's cavalry along the road to Bunzlau; Victor's *2e Corps*, consisting of a single division numbering some 5,000 men, having joined the army from Magdeburg, while Sébastiani's cavalry moved in the left column from Rothenburg [15 miles north of Görlitz] towards Glogau; *3e Corps*, *6e Corps* and the *Garde*, following a rest day in Görlitz, proceeded to the right of the centre column towards Löwenberg and Bunzlau. Oudinot's *12e Corps* remained in Bautzen until 14 (26) May, whereupon it departed for Hoyerswerda.[14]

Count Wittgenstein's situation, in the appointment of commander-in-chief of the Coalition army, was most difficult. Under his command were generals senior in rank to him, Barclay de Tolly, Miloradovich and Blücher. Count Wittgenstein was obliged to convey his orders to them in the form of proposals. In addition, the presence of the monarchs in the army headquarters deprived Wittgenstein of his independence and often forced him to be an unwilling executor of operations that went against his own assessments. The Prussian generals were reluctant to obey him: in a letter from General Gneisenau to the Anglo-Hanoverian minister Graf Münster [Ernst Friedrich Herbert zu Münster], we find: 'The main direction of the army comes from the Russian headquarters. We have no part in it. We cannot even be heard. We are merely the tools of its execution.'[15] Count Wittgenstein's situation had become particularly difficult following the arrival of Barclay de Tolly in the army, as he enjoyed the absolute trust of Emperor Alexander. The day after the battle of Bautzen, Count Wittgenstein requested his discharge from the post of commander-in-chief and this was granted.[16] Barclay de Tolly was appointed commander-in-chief of the Coalition armies, being incomparably more resourceful than his predecessor, surpassing him in military and administrative knowledge and experience. But Barclay is criticised, and not without reason, for removing Toll, who had been a personal friend and protege of Prince Kutuzov. He chose Lieutenant General Sabaneev [Ivan Vasilievich

13 Reports: by Count Wittgenstein, dated 12 [24] May, log of outgoing documents, No. 944; dated 13 [25] May, No. 960, No. 969 and No. 970; by Barclay de Tolly, dated 11 [23] May, No. 949; by Lieutenant General Sabaneev, dated 12 [24] May, No. 955.

14 Vaudoncourt, *Histoire de la guerre soutenue par les Français en Allemagne en 1813*, 105 & 110-111; Norvins, I, 446-447.

15 '*Die Oberleitung der Armee kommt aus dem russischen Hauptquartier. Wir haben keinen Antheil daran. Man hört uns sogar nicht. Wir sind bloss ausführende Werkzeuge*.' From General Gneisenau's letter dated 29 May, new style; *Lebensbilder aus dem Befreiungskriege*, II, 322.

16 General-of-Cavalry Count Wittgenstein's report to His Imperial Majesty, dated 10 [22] May (log of outgoing documents, No. 932).

Sabaneev] as his chief-of-staff, a man not distinguished with high levels of military ability, while Diebitsch became his Quartermaster General.[17] Blücher, who constantly disagreed with Count Wittgenstein's views and orders, was very pleased with this change. In general at this time, as always happens when there are failures, the Coalition could not get along with each other. The Prussians, waging war on their own territory and therefore having to take responsibility for provisioning both armies in the Coalition, complained about the negligence of the Russian commissariat in supplying the troops with vital supplies, which, in their words, prompted our soldiers to plunder and devastate the country.[18] Such complaints, by sowing discord between the troops of two nations which had taken up arms against the common enemy, did not improve matters at all. The looting and disorder continued as before, and military operations had to be temporarily suspended in order to put a stop to it.

Meanwhile, in Emperor Alexander's headquarters, the question of the onward direction of the retreating armies was being discussed. Barclay de Tolly was summoned to the town of Jauer [Jawor] on 13 [25] May for a meeting on this matter. Thus, Blücher unexpectedly became the independent commander of the right column of the Coalition force. The Prussian generals were dissatisfied with the constant retreating, attributing it to Russian indifference for the German cause, and believed that, after losing two pitched battles, it was necessary to pause and restore the self-confidence of the troops through a successful battle. The cavalry, of which the Coalition had a decisive superiority over the enemy in numbers and quality, had hitherto been limited to covering the retreat of other troops. The French were advancing boldly, without observing the usual precautions. It was vital to exploit their recklessness. It had already been decided by this point that the Coalition army, having reached Haynau, would deviate from the direct route to the Oder and move south-east towards Schweidnitz. It seemed most appropriate to attack and push the enemy back in order to conceal this movement from them. The area surrounding Haynau contributed to the surprise of this attack. The road from Bunzlau to Liegnitz runs along the steep mountain slopes bordering the wide plain of Lower Silesia [Niederschlesien]. The ground in this area is covered with isolated wooded hills and intersected by many rivers, along the banks of which small groves are constantly encountered, obstructing visibility for a considerable distance. The advance along this plain posed great risks for the French, because, being short of cavalry, they could not properly reconnoitre the ground across which they had to move. Major Rühle von Lilienstern [Johann Jakob Otto August Rühle von Lilienstern] of the Prussian General Staff, sent to the rear of the Coalition army on 13 (25) May in order to identify lines of retreat, found that the terrain in the vicinity of Haynau was particularly suitable for a cavalry ambush. General Gneisenau, approved Major Rühle's proposal, drew up an ambush plan and secretly drafted all the preliminary orders for a surprise attack on the enemy on 14 (26) May. Blücher's consent was never in doubt. Their only concern was that the cautious Barclay might interfere with the planned enterprise. But no sooner had he left for Jauer, where Emperor Alexander's

17 Bernhardi, *Denkwürdigkeiten des Grafen von Toll*, II, 453.
18 *Lebensbilder*, II, 323; Beitzke, I, 467-468.

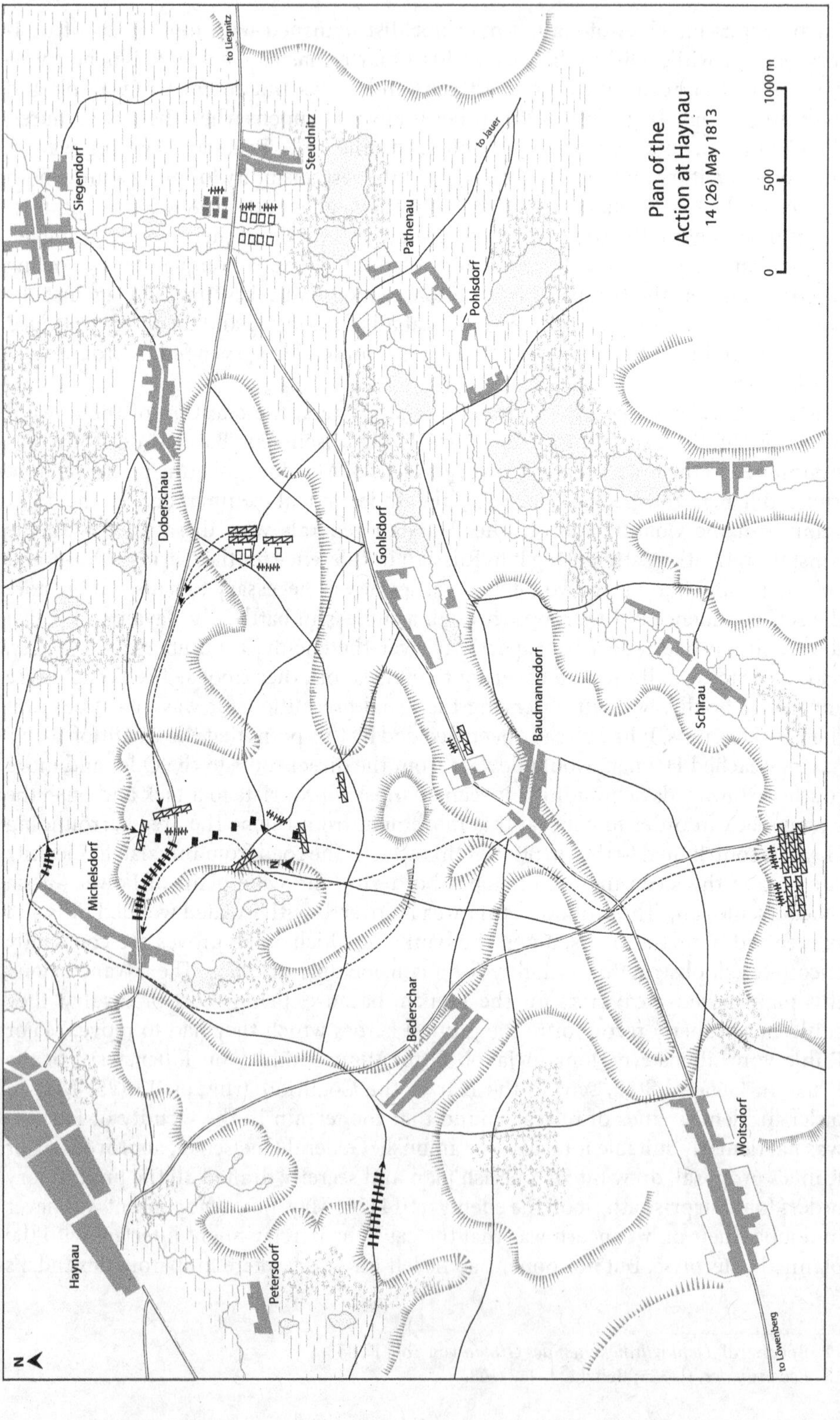

Plan of the action at Haynau.

headquarters were located, than Gneisenau immediately briefed Blücher on his plans, who gladly agreed to this action, as it satisfied his thirst to test himself against the French. The force assigned to the attack consisted of the rearguard under *Oberst* Mutius [Johann Karl Jakob von Mutius], the *Oberschlesischen Brigade* under General Zieten and the reserve cavalry under *Oberst* Dolffs, numbering about 6,000 infantry and 4,000 cavalry, with eight foot and 48 horse artillery pieces.[19] The deployment of the troops into ambush and control of the course of the battle were entrusted to General Zieten. The commander of the rearguard of Barclay's force, retreating to the right of the Prussian column, was General Chaplits, who, having been notified of all measures taken such that he could participate in the proposed attack, expressed his complete readiness.[20]

The orders for operations by the Coalition forces on 14 (26) May were as follows: the enemy will be moving on this day from Haynau towards Liegnitz through fairly open terrain. As has happened previously, in all probability, they will not send patrols any significant distance from the road. *Oberst* Mutius' rearguard are to remain facing Haynau until such time as the enemy leaves the town, whereupon they are to begin to retreat, seeking to lure the French onto the plain. But in order not to expose this detachment to defeat in detail, the rearguard under Chaplits is to be to the right of the road at Doberschau [Dobroszów], while Zieten's brigade are to be on the left, at Pohlsdorf [Pawlikowice], being left in the role of reaction forces. The cavalry assigned to the ambush are to be positioned on the enemy's right in two locations, namely: Dolffs' reserve cavalry in dead ground at Schellendorf [Dzwonów Dolny], about ¾ of a *Meile* (five *verstas*) south of Haynau, while the cavalry from Zieten's brigade, together with a horse artillery battery, are to be about half a *Meile* (3½ *verstas*) from Haynau at Baudmannsdorf [Budziwojów] behind the windmill. The signal for a general attack will be this mill being set on fire. But it should not be lit until Dolffs' cavalry has reached the village of Baudmannsdorf.[21]

On this day, the vanguard of the French column moving along the Liegnitz road was Lauriston's *5e Corps*, at the head of which was Maison's division. Somewhat behind them, to the right of the highway, was Reynier's corps which was marching towards Modelsdorf [Modlikowice, 6⅓ miles south-west of Haynau] in order to cross the river Deichsa there. The French, who usually set out from their overnight camp at around nine or ten o'clock in the morning, had only left Haynau by three o'clock in the afternoon. General Maison had just eight battalions with 18 guns and 50 *éclaireurs* [scouts].

Having almost no cavalry with him, Maison did not dare to move out onto the plain and wanted to wait until the vanguard of Reynier's corps had drawn level

19 Mutius' rearguard consisted of three battalions, nine squadrons and 16 horse artillery pieces; *Generalmajor* Zieten's *Oberschlesischen Brigade* consisted of 8½ battalions, three squadrons of *Schlesisches Husaren*, eight foot artillery pieces and 16 of horse artillery; *Oberst* Dolffs' reserve cavalry consisted of: five squadrons of *Garde de Corps*; six squadrons of *Leib Leichtes Kavallerie*; four squadrons each of *Ostpreußisches Kürassiere, Schlesisches Kürassiere, Brandenburgisches Kürassiere*; *Garde-Batterie Berittene Artillerie*; *10. Batterie Berittene Artillerie*, for a total of 23 squadrons and 16 horse artillery pieces (Beitzke, I, 470).

20 See Map No. 10, Plan of the action at Haynau, 14 (26) May 1813.

21 For Blücher's dispositions, see Appendix XX at the end of this chapter.

with him. But Marshal Ney, who was with Maison's force at the time, did not share his concerns and finding the precautions he was taking to be completely unnecessary, ordered the troops to move on. Having been forced to execute the will of his superior, Maison moved so slowly, however, that he did not manage to pass through Michelsdorf [Michów], a village two *verstas* from Haynau, until six o'clock in the afternoon. Whereupon, having marched about a *versta* from the village, he again waited until Reynier's lead troops had caught up with him. Two battalions were left to occupy Michelsdorf, in an over-watch role. The other six came forward along with the artillery, which opened a cannonade on Mutius' rearguard, which was deployed across the highway between the villages of Doberschau and Gohlsdorf. Meanwhile, Maison's and Mutius' flankers exchanged fire at the foot of the high ground upon which the windmill stood. Several French horsemen approached to within about 200 paces of the mill, but none of them considered riding up the high ground to get a view of the ground beyond. If this had happened, they would have seen a hussar regiment with a horse battery in front of them and Zieten himself with his retinue, and Blücher's ambush would have been discovered.

General Zieten intended to wait until the enemy had moved further from Michelsdorf, but once patrols had reported that another French column was approaching the left flank of the Prussian brigade (Reynier's corps), it was no longer possible to delay. *Oberst* Dolffs received the order to attack. Having formed the *Leib Leichtes Kavallerie*, the *Ostpreußisches Kürassiere* and *Schlesisches Kürassiere* into squadron columns, in two waves, Dolffs moved with them at a canter towards Michelsdorf. The two remaining regiments, the *Garde de Corps* and *Brandenburgisches Kürassiere*, proceeded some distance behind with the horse artillery batteries and received orders to halt between Baudmannsdorf and Iberschaar [Gołaczów, marked on the plan as Bederschar], in order to delay Reynier's leading troops in the event of them emerging onto the left flank of the ambush.

As soon as Dolffs' front line had reached the village of Baudmannsdorf, Zieten moved the horse artillery battery attached to the *Schlesisches Husaren* forward and ordered the mill (filled with straw and brushwood) to be set on fire. On this signal, Dolffs' leading regiments, Mutius' detachment and the *Schlesisches Husaren* stationed behind the mill hill charged at the French, while the three horse artillery batteries, ahead of the cavalry, managed to fire a number of rounds of canister into the enemy.

As soon as Maison noticed the thick dust raised by the rapid movement of the Prussian cavalry, the sudden appearance of several horse artillery batteries and flames from the blazing mill, anticipating an attack, he had ordered his troops to reform in battalion squares. But the French conscripts were not sufficiently trained in evolutions. Only the right-flank battalion managed to form up properly. The remainder crowded into disorderly masses. The guns were positioned in such a rush that only two or three of them managed to open fire on the enemy. Maison's troops had not yet recovered from the turmoil when *Oberst* Dolffs flew at the right-flank square with the *Leib Leichtes Kavallerie* and cut into it. To their left, the *Schlesisches Kürassiere* had set off at full gallop and ended up in a small swamp, but got out of there and assisted the *Garde* in attacking the other battalions, while the *Ostpreußisches Kürassiere*, moving even further to the left, galloped around the village of Michelsdorf into the rear of the enemy. Mutius' cavalry attacked the French on their left flank. Several battalions were cut down. Others, having been scattered, sought salvation in flight and tried to take refuge in the village. The artillerymen wanted to evacuate the guns, but not having enough time to do so, they cut the traces and left with the horses. The Prussian cavalry pursued those fleeing, cut them down, and took crowds of prisoners. Many horsemen burst into Michelsdorf, despite the French firing from every open window and door. Dolffs, at the head of the *Schlesisches Kürassiere*, attempted several times himself to cut through the village, which the cuirassiers finally managed, but with the loss of their worthy leader. They were joined by some other units of the force. All this cavalry was extremely intermixed. One of the French battalions, which had arrived at the scene of the massacre from Haynau, formed square near Michelsdorf and repelled every subsequent attack by the cuirassiers. Overall, the whole affair had lasted just a few minutes. Only 15 squadrons of the reserve cavalry and four squadrons from Mutius' detachment, with three horse artillery batteries, had managed to actually take part in the battle. The *Schlesisches Husaren* were late, and even Blücher himself, with his retinue, who were waiting for the agreed signal in the tree line behind Baudmannsdorf, galloped up only when it was all over. French troops quickly moved from Haynau in order to assist Maison and engaged Blücher with a fierce cannonade. General Zieten, wanting to reorganise his scattered regiments, ordered the '*appel*' to be sounded on the high ground between Michelsdorf and Gohlsdorf: upon this signal, the Prussian cavalrymen reassembled, many of whom, carried away by success, had pursued the enemy to the outskirts of Haynau.[22]

This glorious action cost the French around 400 prisoners, including two field officers and many subalterns. The victors captured 18 guns (of which only 11 were dragged away, due to a lack of harness), and many ammunition and cartridge caissons. Several hundred men had been killed. On the part of the Prussian forces, six officers were killed and 15 wounded; 229 lower ranks were killed, wounded or missing.[23] The action at Haynau forced the enemy to stop their hasty pursuit and continue the further offensive more slowly, with extreme caution. At the same time, the self-confidence and morale of the Prussian troops was increased. Blücher, to whom the success of the ambush at Haynau was solely attributed by general opinion, acquired the unconditional confidence of the Prussian army. But Barclay de Tolly was not pleased with this operation. Praising the bravery of the troops in an Order Of The Day, he nevertheless insisted that: '...in future, it would be better to avoid such undertakings in which strength that must be conserved for greater purposes is expended piecemeal...'[24] In general, the views of Barclay and most

22 Plotho, *Der Krieg in Deutschland und Frankreich, in den Jahren 1813 und 1814*, I, 187-188; Clausewitz, VII, 303-304; Beitzke, I, 470-475; Förster, *Geschichte der Befreiungskriege 1813-1815*, I, 356-357; Vaudoncourt, 106.

23 The sources regarding French troop losses in the action at Haynau are very divergent. The number of prisoners ranges from 300 to 400 men and dead from 400 to 1,000 men. The number of guns dragged away by the Prussians was perhaps 11, Odeleben says six, Vaudoncourt, who described this action most unsatisfactorily, stated that the French lost only two guns, three ammunition caissons and 100 men taken prisoner.

24 '*...dass solche Unternehmungen, in welchen die für grössere Zwecke zusammenzuhaltende Kraft sich einzeln unnütz verschwende, künftig bester unterblieben.*'

of the Russian generals did not match the opinions of Blücher and his staff. The Prussians, fearing Napoleon's vengeance, threatening their lands if the Coalition retreated beyond the Oder, wanted and hoped to give battle once more.[25] In contrast, Barclay de Tolly, in discussing the situation more calmly, with his characteristic thoroughness, believed quite rightly that there was only the slightest of chances that the Coalition could gain a victory from a general battle. Napoleon's strength, far exceeding that which the Coalition could muster, had been increased after the Battle of Bautzen by the addition of Victor's corps and General Sébastiani's cavalry. The several thousand Prussian volunteers who had joined Blücher's army could not counter-balance these reinforcements. According to a statement by one of Barclay's associates, the state of Russian forces at the time prevented them from continuing operations with any hope of success. 'The period in which Barclay de Tolly took command of the army was one of the most critical moments of the war. The battles of Lützen and Bautzen, fought solely to delay the enemy and gain time, were costly in troops and disrupted their organisation. The rapid pursuit from the borders of the Empire to the Elbe distanced the Russian army from its sources of supply and reinforcements. The troops suffered serious shortages of military supplies, and even of rations. There were no magazines across the entire sector between the Elbe and the Oder, as well as between the Oder and the Vistula, and there was also a lack of transport resources, because the mobile convoys either lagged behind the army, or had not been properly organised.'[26]

According to eyewitnesses, most of the infantry regiments in the Russian army were single-battalion units. In some regiments the number of effectives did not exceed 150 or 200 men. Similarly, brigades were commanded by staff captains. In the cavalry regiments, instead of eight squadrons, there were two or three, and only a few had four squadrons. The artillery, after two general battles and many rearguard actions in which they had taken an active part, needed to replenish their ammunition. While the reserve parks had deviated from the directions given to them due to the constant movements of the army, and were so scattered that the chief of artillery himself did not have accurate information about their locations. Likewise, it was a common occurrence that detachment commanders did not know precisely which regiments were under their command, while the troops did not know who commanded them. The soldiers were poorly dressed. The usual discipline and good order of Russian troops had been disrupted.[27] The Prussian generals complained that their territory was suffering as much from their allies as from their enemies, and that the Russians were taking ration convoys from the Prussians.[28]

25 'In a few days we will have to fight another battle, should our allies remain loyal and confident. The fate of the continent depends upon it...' '*In wenig Tagen haben wir wieder eine neue Schlacht zu liefern, wenn anders unsere Verbündeten noch treu und zuversichtlich sind. Von ihr hängt das Schicksal des Continents ab...*' General Gneisenau's letter to Graf Münster, dated 29 May, new style.

26 Friedrich von Kosen, *Journal der Kriegsoperationen der Kaiserlich-Russischen und Verbündeten Armeen von Eroberung Thorns bis zur Einnahme von Paris*, Riga, 1815, 17.

27 Bernhardi, II, 455; A note on various events of the war of 1813 and 1814 (Archive of the M.T.D. No. 47,353, book No. 27); Shcherbinin's Notes.

28 General Gneisenau's letter to Graf Münster, dated 29 May, new style.

The Prussian forces were in a similarly poor condition. Their losses had been very significant, and the *Landwehr*, who were supposed to support the army, had not yet had time to be raised to full strength. The 20,000 muskets purchased from Austria in order to arm the Silesian *Landwehr* had been manufactured in such haste that the touch-holes had not been drilled, and it took at least four weeks to do so. Other muskets were not ready at all and the *Landwehr* battalions assigned to Yorck's corps were armed with pikes.[29] Not a single magazine had been set up in the whole of Silesia. There were no stocks of uniforms or footwear and, due to a lack of cash, it was also impossible to purchase them. When the French invaded Prussian territory, it had been intended to call up the *Landsturm* [militia], but nothing had been prepared for this. Scharnhorst's foresight, energy and administrative ability were lacking and there was no one to replace him. All of *Staatskanzler* Hardenberg's attention was focused on diplomatic relations with foreign states. While he took part in internal affairs, as it were, most reluctantly.[30]

Consequently, Gneisenau, and others after him, pointlessly criticised Barclay de Tolly for lack of energy and determination, because he would not agree to accept a third general battle (just to satisfy them) which in all likelihood would have had an incomparably worse outcome for the Coalition than the first two. The far-sighted Barclay, by preserving Prussian strength, rendered Prussia the same service that Russia owed him from the Patriotic War of 1812. Without any doubt, when he proposed the withdrawal of Russian troops to Poland to Emperor Alexander in order to reconstitute them from the reserves, he had Russia's interests exclusively in mind. Although he offered the hope of returning to Silesia within six weeks, it was hardly possible for him to reorganise the army in such a short time. Meanwhile, Napoleon would have neutralised the Prussian forces remaining on the left bank of the Oder, scattered the national militia and devastated Silesia. Yet one cannot help but admit that the Coalition, if it had accepted a pitched battle, would have completely exhausted their resources and could not have held out in Silesia.

Emperor Alexander, yielding to the wishes of the King of Prussia, agreed to divert the Coalition army from heading towards Breslau and move it to the right towards Schweidnitz in order to occupy a flanking position in the vicinity of this fortress. This course of action made it possible for the Coalition to remain in Silesia for longer without exposing the army to the fickleness of fate on the outcome of a general battle and without moving away from the borders of Austria, which was completely bending in the direction of the Coalition powers and actively continued to prepare for war against Napoleon.

On 15 (27) May, the day after the action at Haynau, the Russo-Prussian army moved from the Katzbach river towards Schweidnitz: the right wing, under Blücher's

29 Müffling, *Aus meinem Leben*, second edition, 43.

30 Beitzke, I, 477-478; The following appraisal by Stein was extracted from the work *Lebensbilder aus dem Befreiungskriege*, II, 268: '... *Scharnhorsts tod ist ein grosses Unglück. Sein richtiger Verstand, seine Ruhe, seine gründliche Wissenschaft, sein aufopfernde, sich selbst verläugnende Hingebung für das Gute, waren die herrlichen Eigenschaften, die seinen vortrefflichen Character bildeten, die ihm eine wohlthätige weit um sich greifende Wirksamkeit verschafften.*
Des Staatskanzlers von Hardenberg Bonehmen ist sehr brav in Beziehung auf die auswärtigen Verhältnisse. Desto schwächer und verworrener ist seine Leitung der Innern Angelegenheiten.'

command, consisting of all the Prussian troops and the former Russian Western Army, which came under the command of Count Langéron, headed from Liegnitz to Mertschütz [Mierczyce, 12 miles south-east of Liegnitz] in two columns, while the left, commanded by Count Wittgenstein, went from Goldberg [Złotoryja] to Jauer. The rearguards of the right columns, commanded by Chaplits and Zieten respectively, retreated to the Wahlstatt monastery [Legnickie Pole, seven miles south-east of Liegnitz], while Count Pahlen went to Hennersdorf [Chroślice, nine miles south-east of Goldberg] with the rearguard of the left column. The enemy pursued the Coalition rather weakly. Napoleon directed the operations of Lauriston's *5e Corps* himself, advancing as the vanguard along the Liegnitz road with the greatest caution. Marmont's *6e Corps* was advancing along the road from Goldberg to Jauer. Emperor Alexander's and Barclay de Tolly's headquarters relocated to Striegau [Strzegom], while Napoleon's *quartier général* was located in the city of Liegnitz, in the vicinity of which the entire French army had concentrated,[31] with the exception of Victor's *2e Corps* and General Sébastiani's *2e Corps de Cavalerie*, which were moving to the left along the axis from Rothenburg to Glogau, in order to raise the blockade of this fortress. Sébastiani's cavalry, having reached Sprottau [Szprotawa], surprised two Russian batteries that were on the march to the army, and captured most of the guns together with their accompanying crews.[32]

On 16 (28) May, not having precise intelligence on the direction taken by the Coalition army, Napoleon set off from Liegnitz on the road to Jauer, along which Marmont's corps was located. It was here that he became convinced that the Coalition were indeed located on the right flank of the French army's axis of operations. The movement of the Russo-Prussian force towards Schweidnitz greatly worried Napoleon. It was evident that the Coalition had decided to hold out in Silesia, hoping for assistance from Austria. Wanting to seize Breslau, Napoleon sent Ney towards this city, with *3e Corps*, Lauriston's *5e Corps* and Reynier's *7e Corps*, while the corps under Marmont, Macdonald, Bertrand and the reserve were on the road to Jauer.[33] On this day, some of the Coalition army retreated beyond the Striegauer Wasser [Strzegomka], while the remainder deployed on the left bank of this river. The headquarters relocated to Schweidnitz.[34] As the movement of significant enemy forces towards Glogau had already been detected, the commander of the blockade corps, the Prussian *Generalmajor* Schuler von Senden, had received timely orders to raise the blockade of the fortress and redeploy onto the right bank of the Oder in the vicinity of Breslau. On the night of 14 to 15 (26 to 27) May, General Senden, leaving pickets around the fortress, transferred his detachment onto the right bank of the Oder and moved towards Breslau, while the Russian contingent from his command headed towards Polnisch-Lissa [Leszno].[35]

31 Plotho, I, 189-191; Vaudoncourt, 107.
32 According to official French sources, 22 guns, 80 carts and 500 prisoners were taken (*Moniteur, 4 Juin 1813*); or 13 guns and 200 prisoners, according to Russian sources.
33 Vaudoncourt, 107.
34 Plotho, I, 192-193.
35 Plotho, I, 193.

The Coalition, having the intention of holding back the superior numbers of enemy troops, planned to occupy the Bunzelwitz camp [Bolesławice, four miles north of Schweidnitz], famous for the protection of Schweidnitz during the Seven Years' War. This fortress had been destroyed by the French in 1807 when they left Silesia. At the end of 1812, as soon as intelligence on the destruction of Napoleon's army had been received, the King ordered the governor of Silesia to restore the Schweidnitz fortifications. But this order was not executed due to lack of time. Although Frederick the Great had held out in the Bunzelwitz camp for six whole weeks against the indecisive Daun and Soltykov, who was openly hostile to him, an inspection of the camp by experienced military men convinced them that it was impossible to hope for a similar favourable outcome when dealing with Napoleon. A position beyond Schweidnitz, on the high ground at Pilzen [Boleścin (Świdnica), 3½ miles south-east of Schweidnitz], turned out to be much more advantageous.[36]

But this position required 150,000 men for a proper defence, while the Coalition did not have half that number of troops. Based on this, Barclay planned to retreat to Poland without indulging in a third pitched battle. In contrast, the Prussian generals urgently wanted to fight. A similar difference of opinion was noticeable in the Prussian *Verwaltungsrath* [State Council]. Schön and Niebuhr criticised Stein for being partial to the Russians (*er moskowitisire*), while Stein objected to them that they were both just too irrationally Prussian (*dass sie beide doch gar zu unvernünftig preußisch wären*). At a council of war convened in Gräditz [Grodziszcze, 5½ miles south-east of Schweidnitz] on 21 May (2 June), two days before the armistice, Barclay de Tolly expressed the opinion that Napoleon, taking advantage of the negotiations, might concentrate his army at Breslau, and heading up the Oder, cut off the Coalition line of retreat to the right bank of this river. As both Monarchs acknowledged that Barclay's assessment was fair, the next day [3 June new style] the Russian military commander ordered every corps to move towards Strehlen [Strzelin] and position themselves north of Nimptsch [Niemcza], with the exception of the vanguards under comte Saint-Priest, Chaplits and Zieten, and the corps under Count Wittgenstein, which he left in support. At the same time, several pontoon bridges were ordered to built on the Oder upstream of Ohlau [Oława]. The Prussian generals, Blücher, Gneisenau, Müffling and Yorck, were extremely dissatisfied with the commander-in-chief's intention to retreat into Poland. In a note presented to the King by Blücher, and General Yorck, in a letter to Knesebeck, sought to detach themselves from the Russians, should they move into Poland, and retreat along the foot of the mountains bordering the Glatz *Grafschaft* [Hrabstwo Kłodzkie], from one position to another, while the *Landwehr* would assemble under the protection of the Glatz [Kłodzko] and Neiße [Nysa] fortresses.[37]

Fortunately for the Coalition, Napoleon was unaware of their dangerous, almost hopeless situation. Meanwhile, his own army was also in dire straits. He had managed to win two major battles with forces hastily raised from conscripts, recaptured

36 Müffling, *Aus meinem Leben*, 42-43; Wollzogen, *Memoiren*, 182-184; A reconnaissance of the positions at Bunzelwitz and Pilzen was entrusted to colonels Michaud and Wollzogen by Emperor Alexander.

37 Plotho, I, 205-208; Droysen, *Yorcks Leben*, II, 255-259; Förster, I, 362-363.

Saxony and Lusatia and invaded Silesia, but this marked the limits of his success. His soldiers had little chance to become physically stronger or mentally tougher and could not endure the prolonged labour and hardships. The haste in the raising of his army did not allow him to properly organise either the *état-major* [general staff] or the *intendance militaire* [logistics departments]. This often resulted in the crowding of several columns onto one road. The supply of provisions to the troops was very negligent: the officials of the French provisioning department, mostly young men, had insufficient experience. Many of them concerned themselves only with their own interests. A consequence of this was the replacement of the requisition system with marauding: the soldier, left to his own devices, would take food by force. The French troops, moving through Saxony and Lusatia where the Coalition army had already passed twice, suffered extreme poverty, which led to great indiscipline. The cavalry, assembled from every French depot and mounted on untrained horses exhausted by forced marches, was in particular disarray. The French, rather mediocre horsemen in general, were incapable of caring for their mounts. In addition, there was a shortage of experienced officers and non-commissioned officers, which resulted in gross errors and negligence in the performance of military duties. Almost all the horses had sores from poor saddling. The weakness of the French cavalry was so evident that Napoleon was almost always reluctant to commit them to action in this campaign. Only once were they in fierce combat, namely at Reichenbach. Napoleon's artillery, in comparison with his opponents, was very lacking. All of this was compounded by the successful operations by Coalition partisans, against whom the French cavalry were powerless.[38]

With his characteristic insight, Napoleon assessed the significance of every factor disadvantageous to him. Despite his victories, the Coalition forces offered stubborn resistance at every step, while their disorder remained largely unknown to him. He foresaw a long struggle and knew how impatiently France longed for peace. There were early signs of general national and government rebellion against the burdens imposed by Napoleon's dominance. Sweden had already joined his foes. The Austrians were sharpening their weapons for his destruction. Louis XVIII reminded France and Europe of their neglected rights with an appeal from Hartwell [in Buckinghamshire]. Finally, the flanking retreat by the Coalition to Schweidnitz demonstrated Emperor Alexander's strong resolve to continue the struggle. All this prompted Napoleon to seek a truce, in the hope of concluding peace, which, after two battles won, he might offer, without reducing his status in Europe.[39]

As early as the eve of the action at Haynau, on 13 (25) May, on the orders of Napoleon, the duc de Vicence wrote to Count Nesselrode in response to a letter dated 8 (20) May, that the sole purpose of the audience he had requested with the Russian Emperor was to propose a truce, and that he had been instructed to conduct negotiations on this subject. At the same time, the duc repeated his request for permission to appear before Emperor Alexander.[40] The next day, 14 (26) May, Count Nesselrode

38 The most important of these partisan operations, up to the conclusion of the armistice, will be presented in a dedicated chapter.

39 Beitzke, I, 484-485.

40 Caulaincourt's letter to Count Nesselrode, dated 25 May, new style.

replied to Caulaincourt that 'following the report of your letter to the Emperor, His Majesty believes that it would be simpler to send a trusted officer from our side to the French outpost screen. In this way, matters will proceed faster and it will be possible to avoid unnecessary diversions from purely military business. Based on the above provisions, Lieutenant General Count Shuvalov [Pavel Andreevich Shuvalov], who has the honour to present you with this letter, and a general appointed by the King of Prussia have been sent as those authorised to conclude a truce.'[41]

Two days later, on 16 (28) May, Count Shuvalov, having notified Caulaincourt of his arrival at the Russian outpost screen together with the Prussian *Generalleutnant* Kleist, handed him a copy of the authority signed by the Commander-in-Chief of the Coalition armies, Barclay de Tolly.[42]

On 17 (29) May, Caulaincourt arrived in Neudorf [Nowa Wieś Legnicka, 4½ miles south of Liegnitz], and the next day the representatives of both sides met in the Wahlstatt monastery, but did not begin negotiations, because Shuvalov and Kleist wanted military operations to cease until a truce was concluded, or at least for 24 hours, and for French troops to evacuate Silesia. Hoping to persuade each other to comply, the representatives exaggerated the advantages of their respective positions: Caulaincourt gave assurances that Berlin and Hamburg had already been seized by Napoleon's troops, while the Coalition claimed that Bülow's corps, numbering 60,000 men, was in Hoyerswerda, and that the Russo-Prussian army was awaiting significant reinforcements. The negotiations were almost broken off, but since both equally desired a truce, the meetings continued, first in the village of Gäbersdorf [Udanin, 7⅔ miles north-east of Striegau], and then, from 20 May (1 June), in the accepted neutral village of Pläswitz [Pielaszkowice, ten miles north-east of Striegau], while Napoleon, having arrived in Neumarkt [Środa Śląska] on 18 (30) May, monitored the progress of the diplomatic wrangling.[43]

During the course of these negotiations, Marshal Ney had advanced towards Breslau with *3e Corps*, *5e Corps* and *7e Corps*.[44]

The detachment under General Schuler von Senden, following the lifting of the blockade of Glogau, was in the vicinity of Breslau on the right bank of the Oder, with 4,400 men and 12 guns (after the departure of the Russian contingent of 1,500 men to Polnisch-Lissa, and the *Landwehr* to the Schweidnitz fortress).[45] On the night of 17 to 18 (29 to 30) May, this detachment recrossed to the left bank of the Oder, near

41 Count Nesselrode's letter to the duc de Vicence, dated 26 May, new style.

42 Norvins, I, 452-454; Plotho, I, 205.

43 Norvins, II, 1-23.

44 Vaudoncourt, 107.

45 General Senden's detachment comprised: two reserve battalions each of *1. Westpreußisches Infanterie* and *2. Schlesisches Infanterie*; one reserve battalion each of *2. Westpreußisches Infanterie* and *1. Schlesisches Infanterie*; *Thuringisches Bataillon*; a detachment of *Schlesisches Schützen*; two squadrons each of *Brandenburgisches Ulanen* and *Brandenburgisches Husaren*; one reserve squadron from the *1. Schlesisches Husaren*; and 12 guns. The Russian contingent of General Senden's detachment at the blockade of Glogau consisted of: 530 men from the Libau Infantry and Moscow Infantry; 500 men of the 1st Mounted Regiment of the Tula *Opolchenie* under Major General Prince Shcherbatov; 420 men from three Don Cossack regiments; four light artillery pieces, for a total of 1,500 men.

Auras, and deployed along the Schweidnitzer-Wasser [Bystrzyca] in order to delay the enemy advance towards Breslau, where they were joined by seven squadrons from Blücher's army, under *Oberst* Mutius. On 19 (31) May, Senden's detachment, having been attacked by Ney's overwhelmingly superior strength, retreated beyond the river Lohe [Ślęza] and held out there until nightfall, whereupon they retreated to Ohlau after dark and established communications with the Coalition army, which, on the evening of 19 [31] May, had occupied a fortified position on the high ground at Pilzen behind the river Peile [Piława]. On 20 May (1 June), Lauriston's *5e Corps* arrived at Bresalu.[46]

Since military operations were constantly changing the relative positions of both sides, it made it difficult to conclude a truce. An agreement was reached to halt the troops, initially for 36 hours, and then for three days, so that, in the event of a resumption of hostilities, this could be delayed for a further 12 hours, in order to give prior notification to the force commanders.[47] During the meetings regarding the terms of the truce, the representatives took a long time to agree among themselves on the following:

1. Napoleon wanted to extend it for two months, and the Coalition for just a month.
2. Napoleon did not want to evacuate Breslau.
3. The Coalition did not want to give up Hamburg, while Napoleon, in contrast, wanted to occupy the entire course of the lower Elbe.

Eventually, on 23 May (4 June), an armistice was agreed until 8 (20) July, not counting the six days' notice which both parties had to give each other with regard to a resumption of hostilities. The demarcation line was defined as follows: in Silesia, the line of the French army, starting from the Bohemian border, ran through Seifershau [Kopaniec, 8½ miles west of Hirschberg] and Berthelsdorf [Barcinek, 6½ miles west of Hirschberg], then along the river Bober to Lähn [Wleń], on to Neukirch an der Katzbach [Nowy Kościół, five miles south-west of Goldberg] and along this river to its confluence with the Oder. While the line for the Coalition army also started at the Bohemian border at Dittersbach [Dzietrzychów, 3½ miles south of Waldenburg], leading to Landeshut [Kamienna Góra], onwards along the river Bober to Rudelstadt [Ciechanowice, eight miles north of Landeshut], thereafter across Bolkenhain [Bolków] to Striegau, along the Striegau river to Kanth [Kąty Wrocławskie, ten miles south of Deutsch-Lissa] and via Bettlern [Bielany Wrocławskie, six miles south-west of Breslau] and Oltaschin [Ołtaszyn, four miles south of Breslau] to the Oder (thus, a neutral sector had been left between the belligerent armies, three to five *Meilen* wide [15 to 25 statute miles], into which neither the Coalition nor the French could enter. Breslau, located inside this demilitarised zone, was evacuated of French forces). From the confluence of the Katzbach with the Oder, the demarcation line ran along the course of the latter river to the Saxon border, thence along this border to the Elbe and downstream of this river. On the lower Elbe, the dividing line was defined

46 Plotho, I, 197 & 201-202; Vaudoncourt, 109.
47 Norvins, II, 38.

as the line of outposts that the belligerent armies were occupying at midnight on 27 May (8 June). If by this time Hamburg was only under siege and was not yet occupied by French forces, then it was agreed to deal with this city in the same manner as with the fortresses of Danzig, Modlin, Zamość, Stettin and Küstrin, which were intended to be resupplied with provisions every five days. A strip half a *Meile* wide (around four *verstas*) around each of the surrounded fortresses was acknowledged as demilitarised. All armies, both Coalition and French, were each to withdraw beyond the agreed demarcation lines by 31 May (12 June). Detachments and patrols from the Coalition army located beyond the Elbe, or in Saxony, had to withdraw onto Prussian territory, and so on.[48]

Throughout the negotiations, Napoleon remained in Neumarkt spending the working days in his office, while riding on horseback in the evenings, getting acquainted with the surrounding country and talking with any inhabitants he came across about their occupations and about issues related to their situation. All this time, he was in a most cheerful mood and sometimes even sang French and Italian songs.[49] And indeed he had reason to rejoice at the truce, in the hope of peace, which would free him from the grave haranguing by the Viennese Cabinet, and besides, he had not lost confidence, sooner or later, of regaining by force of arms everything he had lost. It was confirmed, however, that upon leaving Neumarkt, as if having forebodings of the future, he said: 'if the Coalition are not pursuing peace in good faith, this armistice could prove most fatal to us.'[50] Having received a report from Caulaincourt regarding the conclusion of the negotiations, Napoleon went to Dresden, where he intended to spend the entire period of the truce. He undertook this journey slowly: he spent the night of 5 June (new style) in Liegnitz, 6 June in Haynau, 7 June in Bunzlau, 8 June in Görlitz, 9 June in Bautzen, where he spent the entire day surveying the battlefield, arriving in Dresden on 10 June, where he immediately signed orders for the erection of a majestic monument on Mont Cenis, which was intended to perpetuate the glory of the peoples of France and Italy, who had raised a powerful army within three months. The sum of 15,000,000 francs (around 4,000,000 silver roubles) was allocated for the construction of this monument. Deceived by his perceptions regarding the Coalition, Napoleon considered the war already over![51]

Later, once he was on the island of St. Helena, he realised his mistake. 'Following the victory at Bautzen' he stated, 'I should not have agreed to an armistice. I was already in Breslau, and if I had continued to advance without stopping, the Russians and Prussians would have gone beyond the Vistula, the Poles would have rearmed themselves and my father-in-law would never have dared to openly rebel against me.'[52] Indeed, a third general battle would, in all likelihood, have had a very favour-

48 The Armistice Treaty was signed at Pläswitz on 23 May (4 June), by the Duc de Vicence, Count Shuvalov and General Kleist, and was ratified on 24 May (5 June) by the Commander-in-Chief of the Coalition Armies, General Barclay de Tolly.

49 Odeleben, I, 118-119.

50 '*si les alliés ne veulent pas de bonne foi la paix, cet armistice peut nous devenir bien fatal.*'

51 Odeleben, I, 122; Beitzke, I, 493-494.

52 Las Cases, *Mémorial de St. Hélène.*

able outcome for Napoleon: the Russians would have retreated to Poland; Prussia would have been crushed; Austria would have remained neutral. But upon the conclusion of the truce, the situation could not have been properly assessed, either by Napoleon, despite his foresight, or by the Coalition. The population of Prussia, saved from the vengeance of the embittered conqueror by the armistice, were indignant at the interruption of hostilities. The truce was perceived by them as the first step towards a disadvantageous peace, shameful for all of Germany. In Berlin, the news of the truce left everyone thunderstruck. The Prussian forces, and the volunteers in particular, were extremely dissatisfied with the cessation of hostilities. A number of passionate young men swore oaths to each other that, in the event of a shameful peace being concluded, they would take revenge on all those who had signed it.[53]

The King, wanting to dispel the doubts of his subjects, ordered a manifesto to be printed in the Berlin Gazette [*Königlich Privilegirte Berlinische Zeitung von Staats- und gelehrten Sachen* or *Vossische Zeitung*] with the following content:

> The enemy proposed a truce, and I, together with my allies, agreed to observe it until 20 July. This was done so that the strength of the nation, demonstrated with such glory by my subjects, might fully develop. Tireless activity and constant effort are vital in order to achieve this aim. The enemy hitherto outnumbered us in troop strength and we could only restore the glory of our armed forces. Now, in this short time, we must strengthen ourselves to such an extent that we might re-establish our independence. Stand firm, place your trust in your sovereign, do not slacken in zeal, and we shall achieve our sacred goal.

This manifesto had a positive effect on public opinion and convinced Prussia of the firm resolve of the Coalition monarchs to defend the independence of Germany.[54]

53 Förster, I, 381-382.
54 Beitzke, I, 494-495; Förster, I, 382.

Appendix XX

Blücher's Dispositions for 14 (26) May 1813 at Haynau

The main aim of this operation is to lure the enemy onto the plain between the villages of Iberschaar and Pohlsdorf, ambush them with a significant number of cavalry and artillery, surround them and sever their line of retreat to Haynau.

Oberst Dolfs' 22 squadrons of reserve cavalry, with three horse artillery batteries,[1] are to be in concealed positions between Baudmannsdorf and Iberschaar.

Oberst Mutius' rearguard is to move from Steinsdorf [Osetnica, three miles west of Haynau] directly to Pohlsdorf, behind *Oberst* Pirch 1's infantry. In the event of a reverse, Pohlsdorf is a location that must be held. As soon as the enemy moves forward, General Zieten is to advance to contact with his horse artillery, is to open fire on their advancing columns, and as soon as they are disordered, he is to give the signal by setting fire to the mill at Baudmannsdorf, following which the cavalry are to envelope the enemy and swiftly attack them.

Should this attack fail, and if it is necessary to retreat, then *Oberst* Mutius is to retreat beyond Pohlsdorf with the cavalry of his rearguard, and is to redeploy on the flanks of the position held by *Oberst* Pirch, nevertheless, leaving his artillery and several squadrons on the far side of the defile in order to delay the enemy. *Oberst* Pirch is to form a new rearguard, from a battalion of *1. Schlesisches Infanterie*, two companies of Streit's *Schlesisches Schützen Bataillon* and Sacken's and Offenay's rifle [*Stutzen*] battalions. Major Lange is to take up positions at Pohlsdorf with the troops of this rearguard as follows: the *Schlesisches Schützen* are to cover the entrances to the village; Sacken's and Offenay's riflemen are to deploy into the scrub – the former to the right of Pohlsdorf and the latter to the left, with Lange's battalion between them in reserve.

The following battalions are to be in the front line, commanded by *Oberst* Pirch 1: Major Offenay's, Major Koszitzki's, Major Reichenbach's, Major Sacken's, Major Bülow's. In the support line are to be the *Schlesisches Grenadier Bataillon* and Major Bentheim's battalion.

The batteries are to occupy firing positions from which they can most conveniently shoot into the Pohlsdorf defile, but they are only to open fire once they are already assured of success.

1 From this it is clear that Dolffs' reserve brigade, in addition to its organic horse artillery, had been reinforced by another horse artillery battery.

Should the operation, against expectation, prove unsuccessful, then the cavalry located between Iberschaar and Baudmannsdorf are to retreat in two columns, one retreating through Baudmannsdorf, Schirau and Blumen [Kwiatów, 3⅓ miles south-east of Baudmannsdorf], while the other is to retreat past the Gohlsdorf mill, towards Lobedau [Lubiatów, three miles south-east of Pohlsdorf] beyond the defile, where the troops are to rendezvous and, depending on the situation, they are to take up positions or retreat even further.

Further movements will be directed towards Rothkirch [Czerwony Kościół, five miles west of Liegnitz], Pohlwitz [Pawłowice, five miles south-west of Liegnitz], thereafter, between the Tauergasse and Barzdorf [Bartoszów, 3½ miles east of Liegnitz] beyond the river Katzbach.

12

Operations by Bülow's Corps before the conclusion of the Armistice

The deployment along the Elbe of forces under Bülow and Borstell. – Their mission. – Bülow's crossing of the Elbe. – The seizure of Halle. – News of the results of the battle of Lützen. – Precautions taken for the defence of Berlin.

The crossing by French forces onto the right bank of the Elbe and Bülow's retreat towards Trebbin. – The composition and troop strength of his corps. – Bülow's difficult situation. – Ney's movement towards Hoyerswerda. – Bülow's redeployment to Baruth and thereafter at Calau.

The advance of Oudinot's corps to Hoyerswerda. – Borstell's expedition to oppose him. – The action at Hoyerswerda. – Bülow's march towards Cottbus, while Oudinot marched on Kirchhain and on towards Calau. – Bülow's move towards Luckau. – A description of the ground at the town of Luckau. – The deployment of Coalition troops. – The action at Luckau. – Oudinot's retreat beyond the Schwarze Elster. – News of the conclusion of the armistice. – The redeployment of Bülow's corps in the vicinity of Berlin.

At the same time that Count Wittgenstein, intending to link up with Blücher in Saxony, had crossed to the left bank of the Elbe at Roßlau with Berg's Russian corps and Yorck's Prussians, the forces under Bülow and Borstell, numbering 12,000 men,[1] had been left on the right bank of this river. Borstell's brigade invested Magdeburg until relieved upon the arrival of Count Vorontsov's Russian detachment numbering some 5,400 men,[2] while Bülow's corps had received orders to blockade Wittenberg

1 For the composition of *Generalleutnant* Bülow's corps at the time of the battle of Lützen, see Appendix XXI at the end of this chapter.

2 Lieutenant General Count Vorontsov's detachment comprised: 13th Jägers under Colonel Maevsky and 14th Jägers under Colonel Krasovsky, both from 15th Division; six combined grenadier battalions from 9th Division, 15th Division and 18th Division; the Pavlograd Hussars and Volhynia Ulans under Major General O'Rourke; Melnikov 5th's Cossacks,

and guard the bridgehead at Roßlau and communications with Berlin. To that end, Bülow's force was strengthened by a Russian detachment under General Harpe, who had arrived from Pillau, numbering some 3,000 men with 24 guns.[3] In executing these orders, on 13 (25) April, Bülow moved his *Hauptquartier* to Dessau, with part of his corps, numbering about 5,000 men, and placed the troops in closed quarters between Dessau and Köthen. His vanguard, commanded by *Generalmajor* Oppen, was stationed at Köthen and Aken. Cossack outposts were sent to the lower Saale. A single battalion occupied the bridgehead at Roßlau. Following this, the arrival of Thümen's brigade in Coswig on 19 April (1 May) from Spandau from where they had been directed to move to the Elbe, ensured the protection of the crossing at Roßlau and made it possible for Bülow to expand the operational range of his corps. Just at this moment, because Kleist had been forced to cede the city of Halle to the enemy and retreat to Leipzig, Bülow decided to launch an attack on Halle and, having driven the French from there, reopen direct communications with Kleist. The force assigned for this, numbering 4,500 men with 24 guns,[4] assembled at Oppin, halfway between Zörbig and Halle at three o'clock in the morning on 20 April (2 May), and arrived at Halle two hours later. This city, lying on the right bank of the Saale, was surrounded by an ancient masonry wall with five gates. Vast suburbs surrounded the city outside this enclosure. The French garrison consisted of four battalions from Rochambeau's division (Lauriston's *5e Corps*) and several march battalions, with six guns. The French had barricaded all the gates except the Galgen Tor on the Merseburg turnpike, where four guns were stationed.

General Bülow, having given his force an hours rest, moved them towards the city at six o'clock in the morning. It was planned to conduct two attacks: one on the right wing, along the Saale River, with two *Füsilier* companies, another of jägers and three squadrons of hussars, with four foot artillery pieces, while the other was directed on the Galgen Tor, with the third battalion of *3. Ostpreußisches Infanterie*, two squadrons of *Westpreußisches Dragoner* and four foot artillery pieces, with two more battalions from *3. Ostpreußisches Infanterie* in support. The *Ostpreußisches Grenadiere Bataillon*, four squadrons of *Königin Dragoner* and the other batteries remained in reserve.

Bülow's troops occupied the northern suburbs and reached the three nearest gates of the city but the enemy engaged them here with fire from a dense screen of skirmishers. The fighting continued for two whole hours without any result, and Bülow

Dyachkin's Cossacks, Grekov 9th's Cossacks; 11th Horse Artillery Company, 13th Horse Artillery Company; giving a total of 2,830 infantry, 1,200 regular cavalry, 960 Cossacks and 440 gunners; 5,430 men overall with 24 guns. Extracted from reports on troops strengths, dated 1 [13] June, signed by Barclay de Tolly, based on Count Vorontsov's reports dated 21 May [2 June]. Archive of the M.T.D. No. 46,692, reports on troop strengths.

3 Major General Harpe's detachment consisted of: the Navaginsk Infantry, Tula Infantry, Poland Ulans, Nezhin Mounted Jägers, 12 heavy guns, 12 light guns and three Cossack regiments. Extracted from returns signed by Barclay de Tolly.

4 The detachment assigned to attack Halle consisted of: three battalions and two *Füsilier* companies of *3. Ostpreußisches Infanterie, 2. Ostpreußisches Grenadiere Bataillon*, a company of *Ostpreußisches Jäger*, four squadrons of *Königin Dragoner*, two squadrons of *2. Westpreußisches Dragoner*, three squadrons of *1. Leib-Husaren*, and three artillery batteries.

ordered a retreat. But before this order could be issued to the troops operating on the left wing, Major Uttenhoven [Karl Friedrich Ludwig Georg von Uttenhoven], with the third battalion of *3. Ostpreußisches Infanterie*, and *Sekondleutnant* Tresckow [Karl Wilhelm Ferdinand von Tresckow], with two squadrons of *Westpreußisches Dragoner*, attacked the enemy on the Merseburg turnpike and forced the guns stationed there to withdraw from their positions and retreat into the city. At that very moment, as the Prussian dragoons were racing after the enemy, an officer galloped up through the gatehouse with Bülow's order to retreat. "Fall back! Fall back!" he yelled loudly. *Hauptmann* Weyrauch rushed up to him, telling him to pay attention to the progress of the action. "The enemy are overwhelmed by our troops" he said. "Retreating is out of the question. Go to the general and tell him what you have seen." Indeed, by this time, Prussian skirmishers and dragoons, intermixed with the departing French, had captured the gatehouse and taken three guns. Bülow brought the second battalion of *3. Ostpreußisches Infanterie* into the city himself. Meanwhile, the skirmishers from both battalions, with the assistance of the population, seized the stone gatehouse on the Berlin turnpike. The enemy continued to defend stubbornly in the streets of the city, but were pushed back by the skirmishers followed up by the *Ostpreußisches Grenadiere Bataillon*, and having been completely driven out into the open, at ten o'clock in the morning they began to retreat along the Merseburg road. The cavalry pursued them and did them great harm. The French lost three guns, three ammunition caissons, 400 prisoners and a similar number killed or wounded. The Prussian casualties reached 150 men overall. The battalion under Major Uttenhoven distinguished itself most of all. Raised only in January, poorly dressed, armed with muskets that were almost impossible to fire, this brave battalion used captured muskets, shakos and knapsacks from this battle. Twenty officers and lower ranks were awarded the *Eisernes Kreuz*. Moreover, as a reward for the three captured guns, 150 *chervonets* [gold coins] were given to the soldiers by order of the King.[5]

General Bülow intended to clear the enemy from the lower Saale: General Thümen, having arrived in Köthen with his detachment, was assigned to occupy Bernburg; meanwhile, on the night of 20 to 21 April (2 to 3 May), the *1. Leib Husaren* were sent towards Leipzig to scout out the enemy. News arrived that same night of Kleist's retreat from Leipzig to Wurzen. The next day, some 200 *Confédération du Rhin* deserters arrived in Halle, who spoke of a battle on the plains of Lützen, but could not say anything conclusive regarding its outcome. From the appearance of significant enemy forces in Leipzig and Merseburg, Bülow could conclude however that the Coalition had lost the battle. At seven o'clock on the evening of 22 April (4 May), he received verbal confirmation from a *Feldjäger* from Count Wittgenstein's headquarters that 'the battle had been won, but that the Coalition were retreating beyond the Elbe.' A note from the headquarters on the same subject, was received by General Bülow on 23 April (5 May) on the march to Dessau, where he was moving in order to secure the Roßlau crossing. A few hours later, he was finally brought a letter from the King, dated 21 April (3 May), which ordered him to cross the Elbe at

5 Plotho, I, 211-212; Beitzke, *Geschichte der deutschen Freiheitskriege in den Jahren 1813 und 1814*, I, 497-500; Förster, *Geschichte der Befreiungskriege, 1813, 1814, 1815*, I, 302-306.

Roßlau and in the event of a significant enemy offensive towards Berlin, to mobilise the *Landwehr* and *Landsturm*. Bülow's corps, with Borstell's detachment also placed at his disposal, were intended to assist with the raising of these national militias and support them in waging guerilla warfare.

General Bülow immediately entered into correspondence with the Berlin administration and with all the territorial commanders of the Mark regarding the assembly of the *Landwehr*, the raising of the *Landsturm*, the destruction of bridges, and so on. Thümen's brigade occupied the bridgehead at Roßlau. A battalion from *4. Ostpreußisches Infanterie* and two squadrons of Nezhin Mounted Jägers were detached in order to monitor the fortress of Wittenberg. Just as Bülow was preparing to transfer his entire force across the Elbe, on the night of 23 to 24 April (5 to 6 May) he received orders from Count Wittgenstein to remain on the left bank of this river, because it was intended to hold on the Mulde with the main body of the army, and to send Kleist back towards Leipzig.[6] These orders were delivered to Bülow from Kleist's *Hauptquartier*, who, being dissatisfied with the orders from the commander-in-chief, added to the dispatch in his own hand: 'May heaven help us, we appear to have been abandoned by the generals and humanity.'[7] At seven o'clock on the evening of 24 April (6 May), news came from Kleist of the crossing of the Coalition army onto the right bank of the Elbe and about his own move towards Mühlberg. Following this, intelligence was received: regarding decisive sorties by the Wittenberg garrison, the arrival of Victor's and Sébastiani's forces on the lower Saale and the advance of the corps under Ney and Lauriston from Leipzig towards Torgau. This news, together with the King's emphatic orders dated 26 April (8 May), by which Bülow, as the main commander of the forces in the Mark, was entrusted with the defence of this territory, prompted him to pay exclusive attention to blocking the enemy route threatening the Prussian capital. Bülow informed Wallmoden, who commanded the Coalition forces on the lower Elbe, about the advance of the French army, having it in mind to secure his assistance, while asking General Tauentzien, who was blockading Stettin, to use every means in his power to take this important fortress. In order to provide the most reliable protection for Berlin, Bülow intended to occupy a defensive line along the swampy rivers Nuthe and Notte, of which the former flows into the Havel near Potsdam, while the latter flows into the Spree at Königs Wusterhausen [five miles east of Mittenwalde].[8]

Throughout the sector between the Elbe and the Oder, just as in East Prussia, national mobilisation was actively being pursued. *General der Kavallerie* L'Estocq was diligently assembling the *Landwehr*, preparing the *Landsturm* and putting both Berlin and the outskirts of this capital into a defensive state. But the two months that had elapsed since the French had abandoned the country were insufficient to assemble, arm and train these newly recruited regiments. In the Mark, 28 battalions and 16 squadrons of regular troops had been formed, numbering 20,000 men, while only four battalions of *Landwehr* were stationed in Potsdam, most of whom

6 Plotho, I, 212-215; Beitzke, I, 500-502.

7 '*Der Himmel wolle sich unserer annehmen, von Feldherren und Menschen scheinen wir verlassen zu sein.*' Droysen, *Yorcks Leben*, II, 215.

8 Beitzke, I, 502-503.

were poorly armed with pikes, while others had muskets that were unserviceable as firearms. The soldiers had no uniforms, no footwear, no backpacks, no kettles for cooking their rations. In one of these battalions, only one officer was available to train these warriors for front-line service. Thus, the *Landwehr* could not yet operate in the field. Nevertheless, the local administrations diligently began to raise the *Landsturm*. The territory was divided into districts (*Landsturmbezirke* and *Unterbezirke*) in which battalions and companies were raised, officers and company commanders were elected, cavalry was organised, assembly areas were allocated, signals were agreed upon, and locations for armouries were selected. The population were told the areas that they should evacuate in the event of enemy troops approaching. The orders calling up the *Landsturm* were promulgated through printed announcements in German and French, and so that the enemy would not treat captured militia as rebels, a threat was added that captured Frenchmen would be held hostage to their safety. The King entrusted the monitoring of the implementation of all measures taken to protect the country to *Oberst* Boyen, sent to Berlin on 26 April (8 May). He had suggested to Bülow, a month earlier, the use of the aforementioned defensive line, from Potsdam, through Saarmund, Trebbin and Mittenwalde, to Königs Wusterhausen. Thereafter, having surveyed this area, together with the Russian engineering officer Markov, Boyen found it appropriate for the intended purpose, and with the assistance of the engineer Major Müller and the *Oberbaudirektor* (director of the construction department) Eytelwein [Johann Albert Eytelwein], he drew up a project for fortifying the defensive line with deliberate inundations, entrenchments and abatis. The wooded and rugged area from Potsdam to Jühnsdorf [six miles south-east of Großbeeren] was earmarked for the deployment of the *Landsturm*, while the more open area near Mittenwalde and Königs Wusterhausen was for the *Landwehr*. Several pioneer companies and thousands of labourers were sent to implement this project. Moreover, it was necessary to adapt the immediate surroundings of Berlin for defence by establishing two fortified positions, one from the village of Rixdorf [Neukölln, six miles south of Berlin] through Hasenheide [2½ miles south-east of Berlin] to Kreuzberg [two miles south of Berlin], and the other near the city itself. An innovative concept for fortifying Berlin was submitted by the dramatist [and science-fiction pioneer] Julius von Voß, who had once served in the army.[9]

Despite the activity and diligence of all involved, the equipping of the *Landwehr* proceeded rather slowly. By 8 (20) May, they had managed to clothe the men, but the entire front rank were armed with pikes, while the rest had poor quality muskets. 2,300 muskets were found in Spandau; 2,000 had been manufactured at the Potsdam arms factory; several thousand had been delivered from Austria via Silesia by 13 (25) May. By the end of May (new style), there were just 400 sabres for all the cavalry recruited in the Mark and even fewer pistols. Meanwhile, following the thunderous gunfire with which the population of Prussia had celebrated the news of the victory won by the Coalition at Lützen, rumours began to spread about the defeat they had suffered. These ominous rumours were confirmed by the measures

9 Plotho, I, 216; Beitzke, I, 503-506; Förster, I, 311.

being taken to defend the country. Having been struck by this unexpected blow, the population of Prussia, and Berliners in particular, did not lose heart, but decided to defend themselves to the bitter end. The *Landsturm* mustered on every main street and square. Gray-haired citizens and officials, university professors, pastors, armed themselves with pikes and joined the ranks by company and battalion, led by retired veteran officers. The departure of public capital and other state property from Berlin, however, aroused the fears of some residents and compelled them to leave the capital. On 2 (14) May, General L'Estocq, wanting to reassure the public, ordered the announcement that the removal of the treasury and other items from Berlin should in no way cast doubt on the viability of the means adopted for defence.

> That the courage of each of the citizens of the Mark, faithful to the Sovereign, devoted to their Fatherland, ready to defend their families, their homes, may be most terrifying and most destructive to the enemy. Place your faith in your courage; your foes shall fear it. All your worries are misplaced... Let the faint-hearted, who sneak away unlawfully, leave whenever they want. Their cowardice at this time might be harmful. We pity them.[10]

Meanwhile, the enemy had already crossed to the right bank of the Elbe: the corps under Ney, Lauriston and Reynier at Torgau; Victor and Sébastiani at Wittenberg. As Bülow's principle objective was to protect Berlin and the Mark, he crossed the Elbe at Roßlau on 29 April (11 May) and destroyed the bridge there. The enemy, moving towards Luckau, threatened the Prussian corps with envelopment from the left flank and cutting them off from the capital, which forced Bülow to retreat gradually to Trebbin in order to provide the required protection, where he deployed on 5 (17) May, holding the main roads leading to Berlin with advanced detachments stationed at Treuenbrietzen, Luckenwalde and Baruth. Excluding the *Landwehr* under General Hirschfeld [Karl Friedrich von Hirschfeld], his corps consisted of six brigades (five Prussian and one Russian), numbering 25,000 men with 76 guns.[11]

Having been reinforced with 5,000 men from various march and reserve battalions assembled in Berlin, 25,000 *Landwehr* and *Landsturm* troops, and the detachment under Count Vorontsov, which had arrived outside Magdeburg on 18 (30) April, General Bülow hoped to concentrate some 60,000 men in the fortified positions and deliver a decisive rebuff to the enemy. In contrast, based on intelligence received from informants from Saxony, the Berlin *Militärgouverneur*, L'Estocq, considered the enemy too weak to attack the Prussian capital, and therefore believed that Bülow should have left the occupation of the fortified positions and the direct defence of Berlin to the *Landwehr* and *Landsturm*, while keeping the enemy under observation himself, with his corps, not letting them out of their sight. This disagreement between the Prussian generals led to some rather heated correspondence. Meanwhile, as the French had not appeared and while Count Vorontsov remained undisturbed outside Magdeburg with his small detachment, it was not only L'Estocq and every other government official, but also the citizens of Berlin that considered

10 Beitzke, I, 507-508; Förster, I, 311-312.
11 For the composition of Bülow's corps, see Appendix XXII at the end of this chapter.

Bülow's retreat premature, criticising him for needlessly raising the alarm in the capital and in the surrounding countryside. His position was particularly difficult in relation to L'Estocq, who was senior to him in rank and who had acquired incomparably greater renown. Wanting to publicly express his displeasure at the measures taken by Bülow and encourage him to attack, L'Estocq ordered an article to be published in the newspapers on 18 May (new style), reassuring the public about the security of the capital, to which he added: 'General Bülow is immediately advancing and occupying a defensive line all the way to Magdeburg in order to protect Berlin.' This news aroused even more unfavourable rumours against Bülow and shook the confidence of Berlin citizens in him. To crown all these troubles, he was concerned about the resupply of provisions for the troops. He waited in vain for bread, meat and spirits to be sent from Berlin. The surrounding country could deliver hardly any vital supplies. There was no transport. Under such circumstances, Ney's decisive offensive with a powerful army could have had very unfavourable consequences for the Prussian capital.[12]

Fortunately for the defenders of Berlin, their resolve was not put to the test, the success of which was subject to considerable doubt.[13] On 5 (17) May, Lauriston's corps was stretched from Luckau to Hoyerswerda. Ney's remaining forces were moving to the right in the same direction, while for the time being, only the corps under Victor and Sébastiani, recently arrived in Dahme from Wittenberg, remained facing Bülow.[14] Having discovered this, on 7 (19) May, Bülow transferred most of his corps, numbering 17,000 men, to Baruth.[15] At the same time, *Oberst* Boyen received orders to monitor the Wittenberg fortress and to shield the right flank of Bülow's corps with his brigade composed of march battalions and squadrons. To that end, Boyen's brigade deployed at Luckenwalde.[16] Despite the suggestions of many of his generals, and of Borstell and *Oberst* Boyen in particular, who proposed closely pursuing Ney, General Bülow still did not dare to move away from Berlin. Only the brigades under Borstell and Thümen were sent to Luckau and Dahme, while partisan detachments were sent even further. The main reason for Bülow's inaction was a lack of provisions. Having satisfied himself in this regard, on 11 (23) May, he set out for Dahme from Baruth, and received several conflicting reports on the march regarding the outcome of the battle of Bautzen before arriving in Calau on 13 (25) May. It was here that the Coalition retreat from Bautzen was confirmed and having received orders from his Sovereign to protect the Mark and Berlin, he decided to remain in his positions.[17]

12 Beitzke, I, 511-512; Förster, I, 313.

13 Beitzke, I, 510.

14 Vaudoncourt, *Histoire de la guerre soutenue par les Français en Allemagne, en 1813*, 91-92.

15 The composition of the Coalition force concentrated at Baruth on 7 (19) May consisted of: 14½ battalions, 14 squadrons and 6½ batteries, numbering 14,500 Prussians, with two battalions, four squadrons, two batteries and three Cossack regiments, numbering 2,500 Russians. Beitzke, I, 513, according to whom the Russian force had 10 or 12 guns.

16 General Bülow's report dated 20 May (new style) from Baruth (Log of Incoming Documents, No. 943); Beitzke, I, 512-513.

17 Plotho, I, 217; Beitzke, I, 514-516.

Meanwhile, Oudinot's corps, left to the rear of Napoleon's army following the battle of Bautzen, in order to shield their line of communications and to fix Bülow's corps, set out on 14 (26) May from the outskirts of Bautzen towards Hoyerswerda. On 15 (27) May, a Cossack detachment stationed there was taken by surprise by the leading enemy troops and was completely destroyed. By nightfall on the same day, Oudinot's entire corps, reinforced to 20,000 men, had concentrated at Hoyerswerda. General Bülow, believing that only the vanguard of the French corps was present, ordered Borstell to attack the enemy with his own and Oppen's brigades, numbering 8,000 men with 16 guns.[18] This detachment, having made a night march from 15 to 16 (27 to 28) May in two columns along both banks of the Schwarze Elster river, was supposed to assemble at Laubusch, one *Meile* (around seven *verstas* [west]) from Hoyerswerda. Borstell's brigade, commanded by *Oberst* Krafft, arrived at the rendezvous point at four o'clock in the morning, but Borstell was late himself with Oppen's brigade and only arrived at Laubusch at six o'clock. The troops were extremely tired, and therefore Borstell needed to give them a rest and did not set out again until half past seven o'clock. As it was planned to attack the French along both banks of the Elster, the Prussian columns, separated from each other by the swampy river valley, could not support one another. Moreover, neither the location of the enemy nor their strength were known. This disjointed attack was unsuccessful. Borstell's brigade retreated along the right bank of the Elster towards Cottbus, while Oppen's brigade retreated along the left bank to Senftenberg, and on to Altdöbern. The casualties in the Prussian force reached ten officers and 400 lower ranks overall, while those of the enemy were 600 men.[19]

Following this, intelligence was received in Bülow's *Hauptquartier* about the ongoing advance of Napoleon's army into Silesia, which forced him to pay attention to delaying the enemy marching towards the Oder. To that end, Bülow moved to Cottbus on 18 (30) May. Oppen's brigade was stationed at Drebkau, while Borstell's brigade was advanced to Guben, in the direction of Crossen. The Oder crossing at this important location was defended by *Oberst* Dobschütz [Leopold Wilhelm von Dobschütz] with 3,000 men, while *Generalmajor* Heinrichs was marching to reinforce him with the *Neumärkisches Landwehr*.[20] Bülow's positions around Cottbus prevented the enemy from lifting the blockade of Küstrin, but exposed the route to Berlin to Oudinot's corps. Bülow was criticised for remaining inactive, and not without reason: in the opinion of many, he should have attacked the enemy corps with all his might, taking advantage of the enthusiasm of the troops and his superiority in cavalry, defeated them and saved the capital from the ongoing threat. It was perceived that Bülow's indecision had made the enemy success in the action at Hoyerswerda possible and exposed the route to Berlin to the French. Indeed, having set out from Hoyerswerda on 19 (31) May, Oudinot marched through Ruhland reaching Kirchhain [just north of Doberlug] on 21 May (2 June). From here he

18 Borstell's detachment comprised: 8½ battalions, 14 squadrons, two batteries and a Cossack regiment. Beitzke, I, 518.

19 General Bülow's report dated 31 May (new style) from Cottbus (Log of Incoming Documents, No. 1,008); Plotho, I, 217-219; Beitzke, I, 517-521.

20 Plotho, I, 219; Beitzke, I, 521.

could race straight towards Berlin and forestall Bülow at the town of Luckau, the occupation of which would present great tactical advantages. But Oudinot did not dare to march on Berlin directly, where the national militia might halt him, while Bülow's force could move into his rear. Therefore, wanting primarily to shunt the Prussian corps to the right and then to advance on Berlin, he marched to Calau on 22 May (3 June). General Bülow, for his part, concerned that Oudinot might forestall him at Luckau, sent his force towards this town on that same day, in five columns.[21] The closest of them had to cover more than six *Meilen* (around 45 *verstas*), while Borstell had to cover 12 *Meilen* (more than 80 *verstas*), and since they did not yet know about Oudinot's march towards Calau, the brigades under Thümen and Oppen, directed towards this location, having encountered superior enemy forces, were forced to divert to their right to Vetschau [six miles north-east of Calau] via a roundabout route.[22]

General Bülow, having set out at five o'clock in the morning of 22 May (3 June) with the troops stationed at Cottbus, arrived in the village of Zinnitz, halfway along the road from Calau to Luckau at about four o'clock in the afternoon. This force, having covered five *Meilen* (35 *verstas*) in 11 hours over sandy terrain, shrouded in clouds of dust, during a very hot spell, were extremely tired and left 3,000 stragglers behind on the march. Under these circumstances, Bülow was forced to give his exhausted soldiers a two-hour break. At six o'clock, having roused themselves from their halt, the troops marched onwards, and covered another ten *verstas* to reach the town of Luckau at 11 o'clock at night. The final stage of this forced march, in the darkness of night along poor country roads, disordered the force to such an extent that the smallest detachment of enemy cavalry could have scattered all of Bülow's infantry. Oppen's brigade arrived in the bivouacs around Lukau in a similar condition. But, despite this, all the stragglers managed to catch up during the following morning. Boyen's brigade, which had set out from Jüterbog on the night of 22 to 23 May (3 to 4 June), were unable to arrive at Lukau before nightfall, while Borstell, who had arrived in Cottbus on the evening of 22 May (3 June), was still on the march at nightfall on 23 May (4 June).

The town of Luckau lies on the left bank of the Berste river which, although no more than 15 paces wide, flows through an impassable swampy floodplain for a distance of several *verstas*, upstream and downstream of the town. The town itself, in the midst of these swamps, is surrounded by a sturdy ancient wall and a moat, across which many bridges had been built. But there were only three gates giving access to the town: on the eastern side, the Calau gatehouse, which served as a link to the extensive Calau suburb, lying on the right bank of the Berste and surrounded by gardens; on the western side, the Sando gatehouse and the suburb of the same name,

21 Bülow's five columns marched towards Luckau as follows: First Column under *Generalmajor* Prinz Hessen-Homburg, marching from Cottbus to Vetschau; Second Column under *Generalmajor* Thümen from Cottbus to Calau; Third Column under *Generalmajor* Oppen from Drebkau to Calau; Fourth Column under *Generalmajor* Borstell from Guben towards Cottbus and on to Luckau the following day; Fifth Column under *Oberst* Boyen having left Marwitz's detachment outside Wittenberg, marched from Jüterbog, to Dahme and onwards to Luckau. Plotho, I, 220.

22 Plotho, I, 220-221.

the exits of which ascend the rather significant high ground of the Windmühlenberg. Finally, the gate on the north-eastern side of the wall leading to extensive gardens surrounding the town.[23]

After the very hot day of 22 May (3 June), a thunderstorm broke towards nightfall with heavy rain cooling the air. General Bülow, having no doubts regarding the enemy intention to attack him, was already on horseback at four o'clock the next morning [4 June, new style] and positioning his troops for an imminent battle. Since the occupation of the dominant high ground near the Sando suburb facilitated holding the enemy back even in the event that they managed to seize the town, Bülow transferred the brigades under Prinz Hessen-Homburg, Thümen and Harpe's Russians to the left bank of the Berste, while on the right bank of the river he left only Oppen's brigade, with the third battalion *4. Ostpreußisches Infanterie* and the Tula Infantry. The first three brigades were located on the high ground facing the Berste river. The batteries placed there were assigned to bombard the exits from the town, the defence of which was entrusted to the *4. Reserve Bataillon* of the *Leib Infanterie*. Both the *Ostpreußische Jäger Kompanien* and the volunteer detachments (*freiwilligen Jäger*) were sent to defend the Calau suburb and its surrounding gardens, while the vanguard was stationed forwards of the suburb, in the villages of Cahnsdorf and Freesdorf [two miles west and 2½ miles south-west of Luckau, respectively], consisting of two battalions of *3. Ostpreußisches Infanterie*, with four guns, *1. Leib Husaren* and Beshentsov's Cossack Regiment. Overall, the force assembled at Luckau consisted of 16½ battalions, ten squadrons, 6½ batteries and three Cossack regiments, numbering around 16,000 men with 60 guns.[24]

The heavy rain that persisted throughout the morning of 23 May (4 June) and the fatigue of the troops after a difficult march reduced the effectiveness of the patrols sent by General Oppen along the Calau road and contributed to the enemy approaching the positions occupied by the forward detachments at Cahnsdorf and Freesdorf unnoticed and in significant strength. At ten o'clock in the morning, the French, opening a fierce cannonade, attacked the Coalition and had forced them to retreat to the suburbs by 11 o'clock. The attack was so swift that the enemy burst into the suburbs and into the Calau gatehouse intermingled with the defeated force. It was only with great difficulty that Oppen managed to push the French back with fixed bayonets across the bridge and into the suburbs. But every Coalition effort to drive the enemy further from there was unsuccessful, and Oppen's force were obliged to limit themselves to defending the town and the left bank of the Berste river. As soon as Bülow saw, from the high ground of the Windmühlenberg, that Oppen's troops were retreating, he sent several battalions to assist them, which, with the aid of Prussian *Füsiliere*, Tula Infantry and Navaginsk Infantry, drove the enemy out of the suburbs and into the open. Whereupon Oudinot, having pushed a powerful battery forwards, opened a devastating cannonade on the suburb, to which the Coalition could not respond from the Windmühlenberg, due both to the

23 Plotho, I, 221; Beitzke, I, 527.
24 The Prussian contingent consisted of 14½ battalions, six squadrons and 4½ batteries. The Russian contingent comprised two battalions, four squadrons, two batteries and three Cossack regiments. Plotho, I, 223.

considerable distance between this high ground and the Calau suburb, and out of concern for harming their own troops. They did not dare to drag guns through the narrow streets of the town and suburbs for fear of losing them during renewed French attacks. Under such circumstances, the Coalition, disordered by the actions of the enemy artillery, were driven back to the Calau gatehouse once more, where very bitter fighting ensued. The enemy, being unable to penetrate beyond the gatehouse, attempted to cross the Berste swamps south of the town, but were intercepted and driven back by infantry sent to counter them.

It was now about three o'clock in the afternoon. The enemy had not only been repulsed from the town, but had also been forced to abandon parts of the suburbs. The French lobbed a large number of shells in the hope of driving the Coalition out. These caused fires in the Calau suburb and in the town itself. The suburb, crammed with the wounded of both sides, was engulfed in flames, and almost all of these unfortunates perished. General Bülow, noticing the enemy's disarray, ordered Major Sandrart [Karl Wilhelm Emanuel von Sandrart] to ride through the burning town with *1. Leib Husaren* and four horse artillery pieces and attack the French, but this proved to be impossible. At five o'clock Boyen's brigade arrived. The only element missing was Borstell's force, which, being separated from the corps by enemy occupied territory, were under threat of defeat in detail. Bülow, hoping to facilitate their arrival, instructed General Oppen to move to Wierigsdorf and Giessmannsdorf [1½ miles north and three miles north of Luckau, respectively] with ten squadrons of Russo-Prussian cavalry and with *Hauptmann* Steinwehr's Prussian horse artillery battery, and having crossed the Berste river, was to attack the enemy on their right flank. A Bavarian *Chevauleger* regiment, stationed on the right wing of Oudinot's force, upon seeing the Coalition cavalry, began to fall back on the infantry deployed in a number of squares. But General Oppen catching up with them, scattered the Bavarians, galloped onto an enemy battery, cut down their crews and captured three guns, of which he only managed to drag away an howitzer. This bold counter-attack hastened the retreat by the French corps. But the darkness of the night and the fatigue of the Coalition troops, who had been constantly on the march or fighting for almost 48 hours, prevented them from pursuing the enemy. The casualties from Oudinot's corps that day, reached 1,000 killed or wounded and some 800 taken prisoner. On the Coalition side, 600 men were killed or wounded, of whom 500 were Prussians and about 100 Russians. Major General Harpe was among the wounded.[25]

The action at Lukau saved the capital of Prussia and covered the Coalition forces in glory, who fought for 11 hours against equal enemy numbers without artillery support. During the course of the battle, only ten cannon rounds were fired on our part. The success in this action gave even greater impetus to the raising of the nation in arms. The King of Prussia awarded Bülow the *Eisernes Kreuz*, 1st class and sent

25 Barclay de Tolly's report to the Tsar, No. 737, dated 27 May [8 June], enclosing Bülow's report on the action at Luckau, dated 24 May (5 June), Log of Incoming Documents, No. 1,156; Major General Harpe's report to Count Wittgenstein, No. 103, dated 2 [14] June; Plotho, I, 221-224; Beitzke, I, 527-531; Förster, I, 315-316; Vaudoncourt, 111-112 (According to him, Oudinot's corps lost some 1,000 men, while the Coalition lost almost as many. *Le Moniteur* did not print so much as a word regarding the action at Luckau).

his associates 95 crosses of the 2nd class, while General Harpe received the *Roter Adlerorden* [Order of the Red Eagle], 2nd class.

The next day [5 June new style], Oudinot retreated through Sonnewalde, across the Schwarzer Elster to Uebigau. General Bülow pursued them with elements of the cavalry and infantry from Oppen's brigade alone, while he remained in position at Lukau himself, with the rest of the force, reinforced by Borstell's brigade that had arrived at dawn, and three reserve battalions, until 26 May (7 June), expecting to set off against the enemy corps on the following day. But just at that moment, both sides received news of the armistice putting a stop to hostilities. The reason for Bülow's slowness after his victory was, as before, the lack of provisions. Sparing the country, he did not want to follow the enemy example of imposing requisitions on the population, but waited for supplies to be delivered from magazines, which encumbered his movements.

A few days later, on 31 May (12 June), Bülow moved his *Hauptquartier* to Berlin and stationed his troops in quarters, leaving Borstell's brigade on the Saxon border as the vanguard.

The news of the armistice struck Bülow's force with shock and regret. The officers expressed their displeasure so unguardedly that the King, having learned of it, could not ignore their comments. Shortly before the resumption of hostilities, having reviewed Bülow's corps, he summoned all the field officers to him and, confronting them with the mistakes noted from their parade drill, said: 'But I shall tell you, *Herren*, why this is. Instead of working on your battalions, you worry too much about politics and criticise me for entering into an armistice. *Meine Herren*! Let everyone stick to their own business. Do your duty and do not worry about me at all; I know what I must to do as well as that for which I am accountable.'[26]

26 *Die Officiere, auch die älteren, hatten ihren Unwillen so rücksichtlos ausgesprochen, dass der König, dem Einiges davon zu Ohren gekommen war, sich veranlasst fand, bei einer Musterung, die er vor der Wiedereröffnung des Krieges über das Bülow'sche Corps in Potsdam hielt, die Herren Stabsofficiere tüchtig zu rüffeln. Nachdem er seine Unzufriedenheit mit dem schlechtausgefühten Parademarsche ausgesprochen, fügte er hinzu: 'Ich will aber den Herren sagen, woran es liegt. Anstalt sich mit ihren Bataillons zu beschäftigen, bekümmern sie sich zu viel um die Politik und haben es getadelt, dass ich den Waffenstilstand eingegangen bin. Meine Herren! Ein jeder bleibe bei seinen Leisten. Thun sie ihre Schuldigkeit und bekümmern sie sich gar nicht um mich; ich werde schon wissen, was ich zu thun und zu verantworten habe.' (Nach der Mittheilung des dabei gegenwärtigen Grafen Henckel von Donnersmark).* Förster, I, 317.

Appendix XXI

Composition Of *Generalleutnant* Bülow's Corps at the time of the Battle of Lützen

Generalmajor Prinz Hessen-Homburg:
3. Ostpreußisches Infanterie; 3½ battalions
2. Ostpreußisches Grenadiere Bataillon
A company from the *Ostpreußisches Jäger-Bataillon*

Generalmajor Oppen:
Königin Dragoner.
2. Westpreußisches Dragoner; two squadrons
1. Leib Husaren; three squadrons

Major Holzendorf:
Hauptmann Glazenapp's six-pounder foot artillery battery
Leutnant Baumgarten's six-pounder foot artillery battery
Hauptmann Steinwehr's horse artillery battery

In addition, at the blockade of Wittenberg:
Oberstleutnant Siegholm 1:
2. Ostpreußisches Infanterie; two battalions
3. Ostpreußisches Infanterie; a half-battalion
A company from the *Ostpreußisches Jäger-Bataillon*
Leutnant Witte's 12-pounder foot artillery half-battery
At the blockade of Magdeburg, under *Generalmajor* Borstell's command:

Oberst Krafft:
Pommersches Grenadiere Bataillon
Pommersches Infanterie; two battalions
Füsilier battalion from *4. Ostpreußisches Infanterie*
Two jäger companies
Pommersches Husaren; six squadrons, including attached volunteers.
Leutnant Magenhoffer's six-pounder foot artillery battery
Leutnant Borkhardt's horse artillery battery
Plotho, *Der Krieg in Deutschland und Frankreich in den Jahren 1813 und 1814*, I, *Beilagen*, 102.

Appendix XXII

Generalleutnant Bülow's Corps, as at 5 (17) May 1813

Generalmajor Oppen's vanguard (three battalions, four squadrons and one Cossack regiment):
Füsilier-Bataillon from *3. Ostpreußisches Infanterie*
1. Litthauischen Reserve-Füsilier-Bataillon
3. Litthauischen Reserve-Füsilier-Bataillon
1. Leib Husaren

Bykhalov's Cossack Regiment
Generalmajor Prinz Hessen-Homburg's brigade (seven battalions, four squadrons and 2½ batteries):
2. Ostpreußisches Grenadiere Bataillon
2. Ostpreußisches Infanterie; three battalions
3. Ostpreußisches Infanterie; two battalions
One reserve battalion
2. Westpreußisches Dragoner
Four guns from Witte's 12-pounder artillery battery
Glazenapp's six-pounder foot artillery battery
Steinwehr's horse artillery battery
Generalmajor Thümen's brigade (six battalions and two batteries):
3. Ostpreußisches Infanterie; third battalion
4. Ostpreußisches Infanterie; three battalions
Two reserve battalions
Hauptmann Ludwig's six-pounder foot artillery battery
Hauptmann Spreit's six-pounder foot artillery battery
Generalmajor Borstell's brigade (four battalions, four squadrons, one Cossack regiment and 1½ batteries):
Pommersches Grenadiere Bataillon
Pommersches Infanterie; two battalions
Füsilier battalion from *4. Ostpreußisches Infanterie*
Königin Dragoner
Four guns from *Leutnant* Borkhardt's horse artillery battery
Leutnant Magenhoffer's six-pounder foot artillery battery
A Cossack regiment

Major General Harpe's Russian brigade (two battalions, four squadrons, two Cossack regiments and two artillery companies):

Navaginsk Infantry; Tula Infantry; Poland Ulans; Nezhin Mounted Jägers; 28th Battery Artillery Company (ten guns); 21st Battery Artillery Company (two guns); 26th Light Artillery Company (12 Guns); two Cossack regiments[1]

Oberst Boyen's brigade (nine battalions, nine squadrons and 1½ batteries):

3. Reserve Bataillon from *Colbergshes Infanterie*

Two battalions of convalescent lower ranks

Pommersches march battalion

Two *Schlesisches* march battalions

A battalion formed from foreigners

Westpreußisches Ulanen; fifth Squadron

Litthauisches Dragoner. Jäger Squadron

Two march squadrons

Four six-pounder guns

For a total of: 31 battalions, 25 squadrons, four Cossack regiments and 8½ batteries.

Two Landwehr battalions and five Landwehr squadrons were detached to Wittenberg, commanded by Major Marwitz.

Plotho, I, *Beilagen*, 135-136.

1 In the troop returns, dated 10 [22] June, signed by Barclay de Tolly, in addition to these troops, 1st Battalion of the Sevsk Infantry is shown in the detachment under General Harpe.

13

The French occupation of Hamburg

The reasons for the fall of Hamburg. – Mobilisation of the *Hansestädte*. – The participation of the Coalition powers. – The occupation of Harburg and the island of Wilhelmsburg by Vandamme's forces. – The arrival of Danish forces. – The Herzog von Braunschweig in Hamburg. – His departure and the return of the Danes to Altona. – The arrival of Boije with four Swedish battalions. – His departure. – Tettenborn's situation; his detachment's exit from Hamburg.

French forces occupy Hamburg. – Marshal Davout. – His initial orders. – Indemnities – Fortification of the city. – Confiscations of property. – Davout's predicament in Hamburg. – Measures taken by him to secure the supply of rations to his troops. – General oppression in the territory by the French.

When conferring on the armistice, the Coalition had the salvation of Hamburg in mind, but since their insistence in this regard might lead to a breach in negotiations and a continuation of hostilities, it was agreed that the demarcation line on the lower Elbe would be bounded by the respective outpost lines, as at midnight on 27 May (8 June). Thus the fate of Hamburg, the premier trading city in Germany, containing untold riches, was left to the fortunes of war. Neither the Coalition nor the French knew that this city would be occupied by Vandamme's troops four days before the armistice.

The reasons for the loss of Hamburg were the indifference of its residents to the greater cause of the liberation of Germany and the paltry levels of external assistance. The inhabitants of the city, detesting Napoleon's rule, were prepared to buy independence at a cost in donations, but, being pampered by wealth and luxury, they did not want to join the ranks of the defenders of the fatherland in person: it was much more convenient for them to leave the labours and deprivations of bivouac life to their poorest citizens, and besides, relying utterly on the assistance of powers hostile to their oppressor and guided exclusively by calculations of profit and loss, they would not sacrifice very generously. The *Hanseatische Legion*, fielded by the population of Hamburg, numbered no more than 2,000 men in its ranks, which, together with the 1,500 Cossacks of Tettenborn's detachment[1] and the *Mecklenburgische Bataillon* of 400 men, were not enough for the defence of Hamburg and the lower Elbe against the corps under Davout and Vandamme. Several thousand *Bürgermilitär* [national guard], hastily recruited in the city and its environs, were distinguished by a complete lack of tactical training and discipline. There were just 28 heavy guns available to defend the most important locations, crewed by two officers, four *Feuerwerker* [non-commissioned officers] and 112 gunners who had no idea of artillery operations.

The hopes of the Hamburg residents for aid from the Coalition powers were unfounded. The Russian and Prussian armies, concentrating in Saxony against Napoleon's newly raised hordes, could not take a direct part in operations on the Lower Elbe. Elements of the corps under the Crown Prince of Sweden, which had landed in Pomerania, and 10,000 Danes stationed in the vicinity of Hamburg might have contributed to its defence, but instead the consequences of their interventions were disastrous for the city that had entrusted its fate to them.[2]

As soon as Vandamme's force, closing up to Hamburg, had occupied Harburg on 15 (27) April, the Hamburg citizens turned to the Danish government with a request for help. Their relations with the Danes had been constantly amicable, besides which at that time, Denmark was inclined to side with the Coalition, who offered them hope of retaining Norway if the Danes armed themselves against Napoleon. The commandant of Altona, *Oberst* Hafner, at the insistent requests of the residents of Hamburg, announced to the French that he had been ordered to defend this city, with the Danish government taking an active interest in its welfare. Meanwhile, Vandamme set out to occupy the island of Wilhelmsburg on the Elbe [3½ miles north of Harburg], which was a prerequisite for the attack on Hamburg. At dawn on 27 April (9 May), the enemy landed troops on the southern part of the island, caught the *Lauenburgische Jäger* by surprise, put the battalion behind them to flight and captured the battery facing Harburg. The *Mecklenburgische Bataillon*, having crossed onto the island, was also driven back and the French consolidated themselves on the southern coast of Wilhelmsburg. Although Tettenborn did not trust the Danes, being in dire need of reliable infantry, he was forced to turn to them with a request for assistance. General Wegener, with a Danish detachment of 2,000 men with 16 guns, arrived in Hamburg on 29 April (11 May) and occupied the island of Veddel [three miles south-east of Hamburg], close to the city. Having received this reinforcement, Tettenborn made an attempt on Wilhelmsburg, but the *Hanseatische Bürgergarde* sent there were repulsed by the brigades under Gengoult [Louis Thomas Gengoult] and Reuß [Heinrich LXI. Reuß zu Köstritz] (from Dufour's division), with the loss of more than 800 men and six guns. Following this, French troops occupied Veddel Island, from where, on 2 (14) May, Vandamme began lobbing shells

1 Major General Tettenborn's detachment consisted of: Kommisarov's Don Cossacks, Grebtsov's Don Cossacks, Sulima 9th's Don Cossacks, Denisov 7th's Don Cossacks, four squadrons of Izyum Hussars and two squadrons of Kazan Dragoons; troop strength return dated 11 [23] February, signed by Major General Diebitsch; Plotho, I, Beilagen, 95-96.

2 Beitzke, *Geschichte der Deutschen Freiheitskriege in den Jahren 1813 und 1814*, I, 534-535; W. Zimmermann, *Die Befreiungskämpfe der Deutschen gegen Napoleon*, 702-703.

into the city. The residents were forced to evacuate the magazines closest to the enemy. On 6 (18) May, Napoleon's sworn enemy, Herzog Wilhelm von Braunschweig-Oels [Friedrich Wilhelm von Braunschweig], arrived in Hamburg. Senator Hess, as leader of the deputation of residents, begged him to take command of the entire Hanseatic armed forces. The Herzog von Braunschweig issued orders for a general attack on the island of Wilhelmsburg, but in the evening he received notification from General Tettenborn that as the Russian forces had no orders regarding coming under the command of the Herzog, they could not participate in the proposed attack.[3] Foreign historians attribute the action of our partisan to misplaced pride, but should he have exposed his detachment to obvious risk by subordinating it to a warrior who was distinguished more by blind courage than combat experience? Irritated by Tettenborn's refusal, Herzog Wilhelm called off the attack and left the next day for the headquarters of the Coalition monarchs.[4]

At the same time, on 7 (19) May, the Danish troops also moved back from Hamburg to Altona. The reason for this was a comment from the British government that 'England would insist on the allocation of Norway to the Swedes.' Emperor Alexander, for his part, had made a similar announcement, which made Denmark decisively take the side of the French. King Frederik VI withdrew the force from Hamburg, ordered his corps to link up with the French army and sent his prime minister, Kaas [Frederik Julius Kaas] to Napoleon's *quartier-général* in order to conclude a treaty of alliance with him.[5] The French, notified of the departure of the Danes, intensified the bombardment of the city and launched a feint assault. There is no doubt that they would have seized Hamburg at this point had they launched a genuine assault: the Hanseatic armed forces endured the labours of military life grudgingly, and many of them were also looking to save themselves by fleeing the city. General Tettenborn, finding himself in a desperate situation, turned to the Swedes for help, who had recently landed in Pomerania and had elements stationed in Mecklenburg territory. General Döbeln [Georg Carl von Döbeln], who commanded the Swedish troops during the absence of the Crown Prince, but without his permission, initially did not dare to cooperate with Tettenborn, although eventually reinforced him with four battalions commanded by General Boije, [Gustaf Reinhold Boije af Gennäs] which, having reached Ratzeburg, were ferried from there to Hamburg on carts overnight on 9 (21) May and the next morning. The population of the city were joyous beyond belief at the arrival of the Swedes, but afterwards, on 11 (23) May, having arrived in Stralsund, the Crown Prince expressed his displeasure at Döbeln, for his unauthorised actions, and appointed General Lagerbjelke, who was then ordered to evacuate Hamburg. At the same time, Döbeln was subjected to court martial. Every effort by Tettenborn to delay the departure of the Swedes for at least a few days were unsuccessful, and on 12 (24) May they set off for Boizenburg. With their departure, despondency and fear took possession of the population. The commanders of the *Bürgergarde* announced to Tettenborn that no more than 1,200

3 Sporschill, *Die grosse Chronik*, I, 279.
4 Beitzke, I, 535-536; Sporschill, I, 278-279; Zimmermann, 704, Vaudoncourt, *Histoire de la guerre soutenue par les Français en Allemagne*, 114-115.
5 Schoel, *Histoire abrégée des traités de paix etc*, III, 272.

civilians were in the assembly areas and that almost all of their officers had left the city. Only 300 reliable infantry remained for the defence of Hamburg. Nothing could be expected of the city *Bürgergarde*.

Upon the departure of the Swedes,Tettenborn remained in this situation for five days, until 17 (29) May, When the French, supported by General Schulenburg's entire Danish division [Georg Ludvig von der Schulenburg], occupied the island of Ochsenwerder [6½ miles west of Bergedorf], separated from the right bank only by a narrow branch of the Elbe, while the Danes were at Schiffbek [six miles east of Hamburg] and Altona in significant strength, threatening to block the Russian force's only line of retreat. Tettenborn, unable to defend the city with the small detachment at his disposal, retreated to Lauenburg during the night of 17 to 18 (29 to 30) May. His force by this time consisted of four Cossack regiments, the *Mecklenburgische Bataillon* and the remainder of the city *Bürgergarde*, escaping French reprisals.[6] Many precautions were neglected during the retreat, which was as hasty as it was unexpected: guns abandoned in the batteries were not spiked; the public bank was left in the city; some of the more remote outposts of the *Bürgergarde* were not notified of the departure of the detachment, which exposed them to the risk of capture with weapons in hand by the enemy, who, in this case, would have treated them as rebels.[7]

The next morning [1 June new style], the city was occupied by 5,000 Danish troops, ostensibly to prevent disorder, but in reality to hand Hamburg over to the French. A few hours later, the Danes left the city, and in their place, at six o'clock in the evening, French troops entered, firstly the customs and border guards, who were hated by the people. Thereafter, several regiments came, numbering 8,000 men, and their principle commanders, Davout and Vandamme. At midnight the entire population were given the order: 'illuminate your homes on the occasion of the return of your liberators.' This order was carried out immediately. Nobody thought of resisting. Despite this, however, the French stayed in their bivouacs and went into quarters only after the population had surrendered all weapons in their possession. Two days after Davout's entry into Hamburg, the French also occupied Lübeck. Their rule had been restored throughout the surrounding countryside.[8]

Napoleon declared the *32e division militaire* to be under a state of siege, by way of a Senate resolution of 10 April (new style), which meant depriving the population of the country of the protection of the law, most especially since the execution of the will of the irritated sovereign had been entrusted to the harsh, severe Davout, who had been hardened by all the horrors of war for 20 years. Constant brilliant successes, having elevated him in public opinion, instilled pride in him. Aware of his own worth, he inspired respect from his subordinates as well as unconditional obedience to his sovereign. It should be noted, however, that this man, who terrified all those whose fate depended upon him, was not at all cruel or bloodthirsty. The

6 General Tettenborn's letters to General Toll, dated 24 and 31 May [5 and 12 June], archive of the M.T.D. No. 29,182, Log of Incoming Documents No. 1,074 and No. 1,153; Beitzke, I, 536-538; Zimmermann, 705-707.

7 Zimmermann, 707.

8 Beitzke, I, 538; Zimmermann, 707-708.

marshal's contemporaries praised his justice, administrative talent and the exemplary order he introduced, which curbed the most notorious thieves of the *intendance militaire*. It was a common occurrence for him to ease the severity of the orders he received. Having said that, the extraordinary situation in which he found himself made him the bogeyman of Hamburg, and for many years memories remained of the disasters suffered by the residents of this city under his governance.

The initial measures he took were relatively tolerable. It is true that he treated the city deputies rudely, referred to them as rebels and ordered the population to hand in their weapons, threatening those who disobeyed with the death penalty. The administration of the country was entrusted to Frenchmen: General comte Hogendorp [Dirk van Hogendorp], who had been governor of Vilna in 1812, took up a similar appointment in Hamburg. Comte Chaban [François Louis René Mouchard de Chaban] was appointed *intendant général* of the *32e division militaire*. Baron Breteuil [Achille Le Tonnelier de Breteuil] was appointed *préfet* of the *département des Bouches-de-l'Elbe*, while a native of Oldenburg, Rüder [Friedrich August Rüder], became *maire*. The prosecution of those responsible for the rebellion against French rule was rather weak. Several people were imprisoned, but the police investigation proceeded so slowly that anyone who wanted to escape had plenty of time to do so.

On 26 May (7 June), the marshal imposed an indemnity on the city of 48,000,000 francs (around 14,000,000 silver roubles), which was to be paid in six instalments, from 12 June 12 to July new style. Because the population insisted that they could not pay the required amount, and had only collected the first 8,000,000 with great difficulty, orders were issued that many of the leading merchants be detained and sent to Harburg as hostages. To each of the citizens' protestations, Davout replied: 'What is this talk of property, rebels that you are. Nothing is your own. Your skin itself belongs to the Emperor!'[9] After much negotiating, the Marshal finally agreed to accept various goods and supplies in lieu of the indemnity. It seemed that the fate that had befallen the population of Hamburg had been so calamitous that they could no longer fear greater disasters; things turned out differently. On 26 May (7 June), en route from Neumarkt to Dresden, Napoleon sent Marshal Davout orders to put Hamburg in a defensible state. He wrote: '... The major general must have made you aware of my system, it is the one that I have adopted for all the major cities. A city like Hamburg might only be defended by a garrison of 25,000 men and immense stores; and to mitigate the risk of losing a garrison of 25,000 men and a large amount of equipment, a place would be needed which could defend itself for at least two months from the opening of the trenches. Now it would take not less than ten years and 30,000,000 to 40,000,000 to give the walls of Hamburg a resistance of two months from the opening of the trenches. However, I wish to preserve Hamburg, not only from the inhabitants and against line troops, but also against a siege train. If 50,000 men were to appear before Hamburg, I want the city not only to be safe from a coup de main, but also to be able to defend itself and force the enemy to spend 15 or 20 days opening the trenches. I want to obtain these results this year with the sole expenditure of 2,000,000 to 3,000,000, with an armament of 100 to 150

9 *'Was sprecht Ihr von Eigenthum, Rebellen, die Ihr seid; nichts ist Euer eigen; Eure Haut selbst gehört dem Kaiser!'*

guns and a simple garrison of 6,000 men. Hypothetically, if the city is taken after a blockade of 15 or 20 days from the opening of the trenches, I intend to lose nothing, neither cannon nor men, as the garrison can take refuge in a citadel and defend themselves for one or two months from the opening of the trenches, depending on the capacity and degree of completion of this citadel. The simple exposition of this system is explained, you must work to execute it without wasting an hour. Within 24 hours of the arrival of my *officier d'ordonnance*, 10,000 labourers must be at work. You must:

1. Have all the houses on the rampart demolished, ruthlessly, except for a reassessment of the indemnity to be paid by the city.
2. You must demolish all the houses on the glacis.
3. All the houses close to the citadel.
4. At the same time, you must raise all the parapets by deepening all the ditches.
5. Have drawbridges constructed for all the gates.
6. Have ravelines constructed in front of all the gates.
7. Add as much water as the ditches can hold.
8. Do whatever is necessary in order to inundate areas susceptible to flooding.
9. Enclose all the most important and largest bastions at the gorge with a crenellated wall, those of lesser importance with a good palisade.
10. Work on the covered way and the glacis; have the covered way palisaded.
11. Have at least four cannon placed on each bastion, two of a calibre of twelve or greater, two of a lesser calibre.
12. Place mortars within the perimeter of the citadel in order to be able to turn them against the city, in the two largest bastions, most particularly in the bastions and that part of the wall which is between the two lakes, and which can easily be isolated and used as a citadel.
13. Restore the entrenchments protecting the main suburb, palisade them well, establish some blockhouses there.
14. Have all the islands protected by a system of redoubts and dykes; also construct bridges on piles on the narrow channels; construct two ferries on each of the main channels, as I have done at Antwerp, one for the ebb tide, and the other for the flood tide, such that 100 horses and 500 infantrymen can cross each time; raise, arm and stockade Harburg.

Assuming all these works are completed, and that they can be finished in a few months, it is evident that four companies of artillery and 5,500 infantrymen could hold Hamburg. To complete the system, mark out a citadel between the river and the city, such that the citadel, the islands and Harburg make a single system; this citadel may initially be made of earth with water filled ditches, sound palisades and timber cladding for the artillery magazines, for the powder magazines and for the garrison. You are to see that if the city is taken after a proper siege, the garrison could take refuge in the citadel, on the islands and in Harburg. All this can be done within the year. In the coming years I shall have the citadel clad in stone and given all possible strength.

This is the defensive system that I have adopted for Hamburg. I am ordering General Haxo [François-Nicolas-Benoît Haxo] to study this, mark it out and execute it, but it is very important that you take advantage of the first opportunity to demolish all the houses that might obstruct the location of the citadel, as I have mentioned above. I know that General Haxo had planned to place the citadel on the Altona side; this is not possible, it would alarm the Danes: moreover my intention is that the citadel should be a bridgehead on the right bank, Harburg a bridgehead on the left bank, the islands a means of inter-communication. You know that I have not seen Hamburg; that we must study the spirit of the orders that I have issued and not the letter, so that on 15 July there shall be no difficulty in leaving 6,000 men isolated in Hamburg, and that their communications with the left bank are free from any concerns.'[10]

Having received these orders, the Marshal immediately began to carry them out: every adult resident, without exception, was put to work. However, it was permitted to hire substitute workers for oneself. The daily wage initially did not exceed ten Schillings (around 30 silver kopecks), but later it became difficult to find people, and many wealthy citizens had to work themselves. From mid [late] June until the end of the year, from 8,000 to 10,000 people were constantly at work, assembling in Hamburg, on the Elbe islands, in the surrounding countryside, or as day labourers from Bremen, Lübeck and Lüneburg. Since the ancient earthen ramparts had long been turned into gardens that served as promenades, while houses and other buildings had been built on the glacis, Davout ordered all these buildings to be demolished, the avenues to be cut down and the ground on which the fortifications were to be built to be levelled.[11]

Napoleon himself wrote to the Marshal that all the costs of bringing Hamburg into a defensible state must be paid for by the residents of the *32e division militaire*. The embittered conqueror added: 'These departments must be made to feel the difference between being under a constitutional [lawful] regime and being outside the constitution [emergency powers].'[12] Thereafter, orders were issued to confiscate the possessions and real estate of:

1. All those who taken part in governing the territory following the departure of French forces, or served in the *Hanseatische Legion*.
2. All those in British, Russian or Prussian service.
3. Participants in the rebellion.
4. Those who had left the territory and had not returned within 15 days of the promulgation of these regulations.[13]

Davout petitioned for a softening of this severe decree, which would leave thousands of residents vulnerable not only to the loss of property, but also to destitution. Indeed,

10 For the text of these orders (in French) see Appendix XXIII at the end of this chapter.
11 Beitzke, I, 542-543.
12 '... *Il faut que ces départamens sentent la différence qu'il y a à être sous le régime constitutionnel ou hors la constitution...*' from Napoleon's letter to the Prince d'Eckmühl, dated 17 June (new style) from Dresden.
13 Resolution dated 18 June (new style).

what need was there for confiscation when, even without it, the French authorities had unlimited access to all the country's resources. Convinced by the Marshal's arguments, Napoleon allowed him to deal with the guilty at his own discretion, and even to grant pardons for those necessary exceptions. He wrote to the Marshal: 'The best way to punish merchants is to make them pay.'[14] Taking advantage of this permission, on 12 (24) July, Davout published an amnesty for all residents of the *32e division militaire*, excluding 28 persons declared enemies of the state, who were exiled from French territories and deprived of their property in perpetuity, on pain of death.[15]

Despite the unlimited powers devolved to him and the enormous resources at his disposal, Davout's situation was unenviable. Of the troops comprising the *32e division militaire*, barely half were French, while the remainder were all German or Dutch. The appeals for liberation from the foreign yoke had struck a chord in their ranks. Constant desertion weakened Davout's corps and instilled mutual distrust between the contingents.[16] Being on territory belonging to Napoleon in name only, but in reality hostile to him, the Marshal was, consequently, surrounded by enemies within a city whose population longed for freedom, and he could not fully rely on his troops, half of whom were foreigners serving under duress. Under such circumstances, he resorted to extreme measures out of necessity. Defaulters faced the firing squad almost every Saturday, sometimes several at a time, for desertion, looting, violations of discipline, and even for expressing sympathy for the liberation of Germany. It should be noted, however, that the Marshal was just as severe towards the French as he was towards the Germans. One of the regimental doctors was shot for stealing several bottles of Madeira prescribed for the sick. A number of officials from the *intendance militaire* languished in gaol for several months merely on suspicion of extortion. The soldiers in permanent outposts were not a burden for the city, because all of them, as a precaution against an uprising, were stationed in dedicated buildings converted into barracks, and only the sick were placed in quarters in order to allow them to recover, while the townspeople could not complain about this order, seeing that four men who had been discharged from hospital were permanently quartered in the house occupied by the Marshal himself, indeed, every French officer and official followed this example.[17]

Anticipating the inevitability of a long defence of Hamburg, Davout collected an uncounted amount of stores of every kind, the collection of which could not be carried out without crushing the inhabitants of the surrounding countryside. Supplies were collected initially from those locations remote from the city which would be soonest to fall to the enemy, while the city itself and the areas closest to it were to be requisitioned later, if necessary, and therefore the resources located there were listed and came under the vigilant supervision of the French gendarmes. Despite the abundance of food supplies collected in Hamburg, because the Marshal

14 '*La meilleure manière de punir des marchands, c'est en effet de les faire payer.*' Letter from Dresden, dated 1 July (new style).

15 Beitzke, I, 543.

16 Vandamme's corps would be transferred to Saxony during the armistice.

17 Beitzke, I, 543-544.

feared that there would be difficulties in feeding the large population of the city in the winter, once late autumn had arrived, more than 20,000 of the poorest citizens were expelled from here.

The inhabitants of Lübeck were forced to pay an indemnity of 9,000,000 francs (around 2,500,000 silver roubles), while the population of Bremen and, in general, the entire area along the lower Elbe were burdened with all kinds of taxes and requisitions. Yet it was the citizens of Hamburg who suffered the most. It may be stated categorically that a tenth of the taxes collected from them by the French would have been enough to protect their city from invasion by the corps under Davout and Vandamme. But in order to do this, it would have been necessary to take advantage of the time before Napoleon managed to form a new army to replace the one that had perished in Russia. Having missed this most favourable of opportunities, the residents of Hamburg were subjected to unprecedented calamities.[18]

18 Beitzke, I, 544-546.

Appendix XXIII

Napoleon's Letter to the Prince d'Eckmühl (Davout), dated 7 June (new Style) from Bunzlau

... Le major-général a du vous faire connaitre mon système, c'est celui que j'ai adopté pour toutes les grandes villes. Une ville comme Hambourg ne pourrait être défendue que par une garnison de vingt-cinq mille hommes et un matériel immense; et pour courir les chances de perdre une garnison de vingt-cinq mille hommes et un grand matériel il faudrait une place qui pût se défendre au moins deux mois de tranchée ouverte. Or pour donner à l'enceinte de Hambourg une résistance de deux mois de tranchée ouverte, il ne faudrait pas moins de dix ans et de trente à quarante millions. Toutefois, je veux conserver Hambourg, non-seulement contre les habitans, contre les troupes de ligne, mais même contre un équipage de siége. Je veux que, si cinquante mille hommes se présentent devant Hambourg, la ville soit non-seulement à l'abri d'un coup de main, mais puisse se défendre, obliger l'ennemi à ouvrir la tranchée et soutenir quinze ou vingt jours de tranchée ouverte. Ces résultats, je veux les obtenir cette année avec la seule dépense de deux à trois millions, avec un matériel de cent à cent cinquante bouches à feu et une simple garnison de six mille hommes. Je veux que, dans cette hypothèse, la ville prise après un blocus de quinze ou vingt jours de tranchée ouverte, je ne perde rien, ni en canons ni en hommes, et que la garnison puisse se réfugier dans une citadelle et se défendre un ou deux mois de tranchée ouverte, selon la capacité et le degré de perfection qu quel sera portée cette citadelle. La simple exposition de ce système l'explique, il faut travailler à l'exécuter sans perdre une heure. Vingt-quatre heures après l'arrivée de mon officier d'ordonnance, dix mille travailleurs devront être à l'ouvrage. Vous devez:

1. *Faire abattre toutes les maisons qui sont sur le rempart, impitoyablement, sauf l'évaluation de l'indemnité qui sera payée par la ville.*
2. *Vous devez faire abattre toutes les maisons qui sont sur le glacis.*
3. *Toutes les maisons qui sont près de la citadelle.*
4. *Vous devez en même temps faire relever tous les parapets en creusant tous les fossés.*
5. *Faire faire des ponts-levis à toutes les portes.*

6. *Faire faire des demi-lunes devant toutes les portes.*
7. *Mettre de l'eau autant que les fossés en pourront contenir.*
8. *Faire ce qui est nécessaire pour pratiquer une inondation dans les parties qui en sont susceptibles.*
9. *Fermer à la gorge tous les bastions les plus importants et les plus grands avec un mur crénelé, les moins importants avec une bonne palissade.*
10. *Faire travailler à un chemin couvert et à un glacis; faire palissader les chemins couverts.*
11. *Faire placer sur chaque bastion au moins quatre pièces de canon, dont deux d'un calibre de douze ou supérieur, deux e'un calibre inférieur.*
12. *Faire placer des mortiers en forme de citadelle pour pouvoir les tourner contre la ville, dans les deux bastions les plus grands, et spécialement dans les bastions et la partie de l'enceinte qui est entre les deux lacs, et qui peut facilement être isolée et considérée, comme citadelle.*
13. *Rétablir les retranchémens qui couvrent le grand faubourg, le bien palissader, y établir quelques blockaus.*
14. *Faire occuper toutes les iles par un système de redoutes et de digues; faire même des ponts sur pilotis, sur les petits bras; faire deux bacs sur chaque gros bras, comme je l'ai pratiqué à Anvers, l'un pour la marée descendante, et l'autre pour la marée montante, de manière que cent chevaux et cinq cents hommes d'infanterie puissent passer à la fois; relever, armer et palissader Haarbourg.*

Supposez tous ces ouvrages fait, et ils peuvent l'être en peu de mois, il est évident que quatre compagnies d'artillerie et cinq mille cinq cents hommes d'infanterie seront maitres de Hambourg. Pour compléter le système, tracer une citadelle entre la rivière et la ville, de sorte que la citadelle, les iles et Haarbourg fassent un seul système; cette citadelle peut d'abord être faite en terre avec des fossés pleins d'eau, des bonnes palissades et des blindages en bois pour les magasins d'artillerie, pour les magasins à poudre et pour la garnison. Vous voyez que la ville, prise après un siège en règle, la garnison se réfugierait dans la citadelle, dans les iles et dans Haarbourg. Tout cela peut se faire dans l'année. Les années prochaines je ferai revêtir la citadelle en pierre et lui donnerai toute la force possible. Voilà le système déffensif que j'ai adopté pour Hambourg. Je donne l'ordre au général Haxo de l'étudier, de la tracer et de l'exécuter, mais il est bien important que vous profitiez du premier moment pour jeter à bas toutes les maisons qui gêneraient l'emplacement de la citadelle, comme je l'ai dit plus haut. Je sais que le général Haxo avait projeté de placer la citadelle du côté d'Altona; cela n'est pas possible, cela efraierait les Danois: d'ailleurs mon intention est que la citadelle soit une tête de pont sur la rive droite, Haarbourg une tête de pont sur la rive gauche, les iles un moyen de communication. Vous savez que je n'ai point vu Hambourg; que l'on doit étudier l'esprit de l'ordre que je donne et non la lettre, de manière qu'au 15 juillet il 'ny ait aucune difficulté à laisser six mille hommes isolés a Hambourg, et que leur communication avec la rive gauche soit à l'abri de toute inquiétude.

14

Partisan operations from the Battle of Lützen to the armistice

---

Rittmeister von Colomb's expedition towards the river Saale: His departure from Meissen. – Crossing the Elbe and movement along the Bohemian border. – Colomb's course of action. -The deployment of his detachment at Neustadt an der Orla. – The raid on the enemy parks at Zwickau. – Cooperation with Lützow's detachment. – The plans of the Prussian partisans. – Colomb's march towards the Bohemian border and return to the right bank of the Elbe.

Major Lützow's expedition on the left bank of the Elbe: The training of the *Schwarze Jäger*. – The type and composition of the force raised by Lützow. – Lützow's crossing of the Elbe and the movement between Halberstadt and the Saale valley. – The sweep to the Bohemian border. – The return march from Plauen, to Zeitz, in the vicinity of Lützen. The defeat of Lützow's detachment and the fate of its survivors.

Lieutenant Colonel Borisov's expedition along the Saale valley: His crossing of the Elbe. – The march towards Bernburg. – The defeat of Poinsot's French detachment.

Adjutant General Chernyshev's raid on the Westphalian parks at Halberstadt: The forced march towards Halberstadt. – The defeat of an enemy detachment. – The seizure of the parks. – The return march to the Elbe.

The expedition by generals Count Vorontsov and Chernyshev towards Leipzig: The advance by the detachments to Dessau and on towards Delitzsch. – The plan for the raid on Leipzig. – The action at Taucha. – Negotiations. – The return march to the Elbe.

Partisan operations on the right bank of the Elbe: General Kaisarov's capture of the enemy parks on the road from Reichenbach to Görlitz. – The storming of Schloss Wilhelmsburg. – Colonel Figner's sweep behind enemy lines from the Bohemian border to the Glogau fortress.

During the period after the Russo-Prussian Coalition army had crossed back over the Elbe following the battle of Lützen, raiding detachments were sent to the left bank of this river, under the command of enterprising officers, in order to operate behind enemy lines, destroy their trains and generally inflict all kinds of harm on them. The detachment of units on similar missions continued over subsequent periods. In order to present an accurate depiction of these partisan operations, the most remarkable of them have been listed in chronological order.

After the Prussian forces had crossed to the right bank of the Elbe, while Blücher's *Hauptquartier* was located in Meissen, the commander of the *Schwadron der freiwilligen Jäger* [volunteer squadron] of the *Brandenburgisches Husaren, Rittmeister* [Captain] Colomb [Friedrich August Peter von Colomb], came to him, volunteering to cross the Elbe with his squadron and get behind enemy lines along the Saale. Blücher dissuaded him from this undertaking, citing the inexperience of the volunteers, and besides, he noted that it would not be possible to rely on the assistance of the population on foreign territory. But once Gneisenau supported the request from this brave hussar, Blücher expressed his consent, saying: 'If he wants to go to the Devil, then let him go!'[1] Colomb's comrades bade him farewell as if they were destined never to see him again. Having received permission to take only 90 men on the expedition, Colomb selected 80 jägers from the volunteer squadron and received ten veteran hussars from his regimental commander. Two officers accompanied him. Setting out from Meissen during the night of 25 to 26 April (7 to 8 May), Colomb moved to Dresden, still occupied by Coalition forces at the time, and on to Wehlen, and at 11 o'clock on the evening of 28 April (10 May), he crossed to the left bank of the Elbe at Rathen [seven miles upstream of Pirna]. Thereafter, having passed between the Königstein fortress and a French camp located near Pirna, he reached Hellendorf [three miles north of Peterswald], the last Saxon village on the road from Dresden to Teplitz [Teplice]. Two squadrons of enemy lancers were stationed there. Their horses were unsaddled, and this detachment had not taken any general precautions. Colomb thought about launching a surprise attack on them, but restrained himself from this, being in close country in the midst of the enemy, who might well be supported by more significant forces, close to the Bohemian mountains forming the border of a neutral state. In the event of a reverse, he would have no way of retreating back beyond the Elbe. Colomb's onward movement, along the Bohemian border and in the vicinity of enemy outposts, was successful. For the most part, the detachment marched at night, laying up to rest during the day in forests and ravines, or in villages located far from the main roads. They did not send forward or flanking patrols out: thus the expedition had the unthreatening appearance of a typical route-march by a small sub-unit of troops. The Prussian jägers and hussars passed themselves off as Westphalians, and thanks to this *ruse de guerre*, they not only obtained provisions and fodder on Saxon territory, but were treated to hot food whenever they appeared in a village at mealtimes. During the night of 4 to 5 (16 to 17) May, having reached the highway between Reichenbach and Plauen and deployed covertly in the forest, Colomb learned from the residents that 36 hours

1 *'Wenn er denn zum Teufel fahren will, so fahre er!'*

earlier, the Viceroy had passed along this road with his entire suite on their way to Italy. Had the Prussian partisans managed to reach the Reichenbach road earlier, they might have captured Napoleon's adopted son.

On 9 (21) May, Colomb's detachment arrived in Neustadt an der Orla. The ground around this town, lying at the intersection of many main roads, near forested high ground, between the Saale and the Orla and Roda rivers, helped Colomb both in the collection of intelligence on the enemy as well as providing options in a variety of directions, moreover, the population of the surrounding countryside provided him with every possible assistance. Having received intelligence about the presence of a squadron from the French *7e Régiment de Cuirassiers* in two villages between Lobeda [3½ miles south of Jena] and Stadtroda [nine miles south-east of Jena], on the night of 10 to 11 (22 to 23) May, Colomb attacked one platoon stationed in the village of Zöllnitz [5½ miles south of Jena] and captured Lieutenant Mercier with 28 cuirassiers and 33 horses. And two days later, having set up an ambush on a forested hill, from where it was possible to easily observe the road from Lobeda to Stadtroda, he captured a Württemberg convoy, consisting of 12 wagons with 56 horses, moving under escort of 54 infantrymen, who surrendered without firing a single shot. These men were released on parole, as were all others who were captured, with all the personal possessions they were carrying, swearing not to serve against the Coalition. The best weapons were distributed among the partisans, while the rest were destroyed. Booty and horses were sold for the benefit of the detachment, except for some which were gifted to the population.

Upon returning to Neustadt on 14 (26) May, Colomb received intelligence on the movements of an enemy artillery park through Bayreuth and Hof. Following this, word came in that the park had arrived in Reichenbach. The detachment quickly made their way there, but could not find the park, which, meanwhile, had passed this location and was intending to spend the night of 16 to 17 (28 to 29) May in Zwickau. According to intelligence received, the park's escort consisted of 300 to 500 men. Colomb had just two officers and 85 lower ranks. A night attack held the advantage of surprise, but it was risky because the infantry, of which the escort of the park was mostly formed, could settle down in the buildings and gardens and repel the partisans. Therefore, Colomb decided to attack the enemy just as they were leaving Zwickau. In order to convincingly conceal his intentions, he let it be known that, having not managed to catch the park in Reichenbach, he had turned back to Neustadt, and actually even withdrew as far as Mehla [12½ miles north-west of Reichenbach, but at dusk he set out from there and, moving along a roundabout road to Ebersbrunn [five miles south of Zwickau], crossed the Mulda at Bockwa [two miles south-east of Zwickau] and arrived on the road from Zwickau to Mülsen [towards Chemnitz], at five o'clock on the morning of 17 (29) May, which at this point ran uphill, initially along a deep ravine, then through fairly open country for about a *versta*, and then formed a sharp turn to the right. Here, at this turn in the forest, *Leutnant* Katte [Gottfried Friedrich Wilhelm von Katte] was placed in ambush with 34 men, while Colomb himself, having gone about 800 paces back down the forward slope with the rest of the men, also positioned themselves covertly on one of the bends of the road, in an alder grove. A number of locals who had seen the detachment's movements were detained.

The dispositions for attacking the park were as follows: if the escorting vanguard were weak, then Colomb would let it pass, and Katte, once the enemy had closed up to him, would attack, signalling with several shots. If the vanguard were strong, Colomb intended to attack them immediately, sounding a similar alarm signal to Katte, who would immediately rush to his aid. Four specially chosen men received orders, as soon as the attack was launched, to break into the column, cut down the drivers, shoot several horses and generally cause as much mayhem as possible. Finally, several of the locals who were with the detachment as couriers, and all the people detained by the detachment and being held in the forest under the supervision of an injured jäger, were supposed to emerge from there during the attack, making it appear as if the forest were occupied by troops. Colomb concealed himself in the scrub, in a location from which it was easy to see the enemy movements along the road.

At seven o'clock in the morning the enemy vanguard appeared, consisting of 47 cavalrymen, who, having drawn level with Colomb's ambush, stopped to rest and give time for the stretched out convoy to close up. Half an hour later the vanguard moved on, followed by the guns and ammunition caissons. On either side were small groups of infantry, while the majority of the cavalry were at the tail end of the column. Just about 70 carts had passed when shots from Katte's cut-off group rang out. Upon hearing this, Colomb also sprang his ambush, dispersed the cavalry marching in the rearguard and rushed at the infantry moving through the rye. Some of them were cut down, others were taken prisoner, the rest voluntarily laid down their weapons. While Colomb was trying to re-assemble his men, a squadron was noticed coming from the direction of Zwickau: it was the enemy rearguard that had managed to rally themselves. The Prussian cavalry attacked an enemy twice as strong and after a fierce fight, having put them to flight, pursued them downhill and onwards over the bridge on the Mulde and through the town, where many prisoners were taken. Colomb returned from the bridge himself back to the captured park, which consisted of 18 cannon, six howitzers, 36 ammunition caissons and 12 other carts, with 400 horses. Overall, those taken prisoner included: six officers, a physician and around 300 lower ranks. Immediately thereafter, on Colomb's orders, the destruction of the park began: the ammunition caissons and carts were blown up; the guns spiked and the foresights knocked off; the muskets were smashed; the best horses were kept for the detachment; others were shot or were distributed to the residents of nearby villages. All the prisoners were released on their word of honour that they would not serve against the Coalition, and all their property was returned to them. At the request of the captain commanding the escort, Colomb gave him the following certificate: 'The captain surrendered only because he had no means to resist, having been attacked by brave Prussian volunteers.'

It later emerged that when the park was captured it had consisted of: six officers, one physician, 116 horse artillerymen, 80 Italian infantrymen, 20 French infantrymen and 150 trains personnel, for a total of 373 men.

The casualties in the Prussian detachment consisted of one killed and six wounded, including *Leutnant* Katte.

Following this feat, Colomb returned to Neustadt and, wanting to move closer to the road from Weimar to Jena, reached the forest between Magdala and Schwabhausen at dawn on 23 May [4 June] and concealed themselves there, protecting themselves from surprise attack with a screen of vedettes placed along the edge of the forest. An hussar from Lützow's Prussian detachment visited them, and let them know that his entire detachment was in the same forest. At that time, there were rumours that Austria would soon join the Coalition against Napoleon, and so Colomb decided to move closer to the Bohemian border and invited Lützow, with the combined strength of both detachments, to attack the Saxon force that had retreated through Moravia to Bohemia after the action at Kalisz and had thereafter been sent from the banks of the Eger [Ohře] to Vogtland. These troops, numbering about 2,000 men, had been disarmed while moving through Austrian territory, and upon entering Saxony, were to have their weapons (sent after them on carts) returned. Colomb, knowing this, intended to move to Adorf and attack the Saxons on the border, at a time when they, having just received their weapons, would not yet be ready to fight back. Lützow had 400 men, and therefore the strength of the Prussian partisans together would be sufficient for the proposed attack. Not content with that, they wanted to go on to Augsburg and destroy the significant artillery parks there. Both detachments, taking different routes, moved in the agreed direction. But, upon reaching the Bohemian border, it turned out that the Saxons, having deviated from the march-route issued to them, had already managed to pass into Saxony via Zittau. Subsequently, on 28 May (9 June), news was received of the conclusion of the armistice. Colomb immediately returned to Neustadt an der Orla, and having arrived there on 30 May (11 June), learned that one of the conditions of the armistice was that all units of the Coalition army located beyond the Elbe or in Saxony must return to Prussia not later than 31 May (12 June). Unable to meet this criteria, Colomb granted his detachment a rest day, and then, with the agreement of the Saxon administration, set out for the Elbe, when on 10 (22) June, just as they reached Köthen, they were suddenly overtaken by a Westphalian detachment under General Bastineller, consisting of three squadrons and one battalion. The Westphalians demanded that Colomb go into captivity with all his men, but the cunning partisans evaded the cavalry pursuing them, and on 11 (23) June, crossed by ferry near Aken, at Breitenhagen [eight miles downstream], and having established communications with the Russian force monitoring Magdeburg, moved to rejoin Blücher's army in Silesia. Throughout the entire expedition, the detachment had lost 14 men.[2]

A completely different fate befell the detachment under another Prussian partisan, Major Lützow. When forming this so-called *schwarze Schaar* (black company) or *Schaar der Rache* (company of vengeance), it was imagined that it would serve as a cadre to which every German who loathed the French could join. It was believed that this detachment could, very quickly, become an entire army. Things turned out differently: Germany did not rebel; the entire *Confédération du Rhin* remained loyal to Napoleon. Only the former Prussian regions and Saxony supplied volunteers to the *schwarze Schaar*, and, moreover, in small numbers. Thus, a military unit had been raised that was too large for partisan operations yet was far from achieving the strength and self-sufficiency of an independent army.

2 *Aus dem Tagebuch des Rittmeisters von Colomb, Streifzüge 1813 und 1814*, 10-75.

Lützow's detachment, having set out from Silesia consisting of 800 infantry and 200 cavalry, was reinforced in Saxony by 600 infantry and 100 hussars who had arrived from Altmark. General Wintzingerode added a half Sotnia of Cossacks to the detachment. Thereafter came the excellent Tyrolean marksmen, under the command of Riedl [Jakob Riedl] and Ennemoser [Joseph Ennemoser] (former Hofer [Andreas Hofer] associates), and several Spaniards roused by a thirst for vengeance against the oppressor of their homeland. The detachment gradually increased to three battalions and four squadrons with nine guns, numbering 2,500 men. Many noble young men, notable for their talents, had joined the ranks of the *schwarze Schaar.* Among them were: the Prinz von Carolath, who joined the *Freikorps* as an ordinary jäger, Heinrich Steffens and folk singer Theodor Körner. The commanders of the detachment had established relationships with many of the inhabitants of the Thuringerwald, Harz, Franconia, Westphalia, and Ost-Friesland. Their accomplices secretly prepared weapons caches at various locations and promised to assist the militia against the French.

At the suggestion of General Wallmoden, most of detachment's infantry were reassigned to his corps. The rest of the infantry were supposed to be sent into the Harz at the end of May (new style), but at the same time an expedition to Leipzig was being planned by Count Vorontsov and General Chernyshev, the commander of this infantry, Major Petersdorff [Christian Friedrich Engel von Petersdorff], joined Vorontsov's force with his 900 men, while Major Lützow decided to head behind enemy lines with 400 cavalry. To that end, on 17 (29) May, he crossed the Elbe and set out from Stendal into the Harz. His detachment consisted of four squadrons: two of hussars, one of lancers and one of mounted jägers. He appointed Körner as his aide de camp. Moving through Calvörde in the direction of Halberstadt, Lützow learned that, following a raid on this city by Chernyshev, it had been strongly garrisoned by enemy troops, and therefore the Prussian partisans headed to the left, along the eastern slopes of the Harz, towards Buttelstedt [seven miles north of Weimar] in Thuringia. At that moment there were some 1,000 infantry in Weimar while there were some 1,500 Polish lancers and French dragoons nearby, which obliged Lützow to abandon an attack on this city. Having passed completely undetected by the enemy, on the morning of 22 May (3 June), he arrived on the road from Weimar to Jena and met Colomb there (as mentioned above). Having agreed to act as one, the partisans moved along a variety of routes towards the the Egerland [Chebsko] on the Bohemian border. After crossing the Saale between Jena and Lobeda, Lützow found 400 infantrymen of the *Confédération du Rhin* in Stadtroda, almost all of whom voluntarily joined the detachment and came under the command of *Leutnant* Reiche, one of the most outstanding officers of the *schwarze Schaar.* On 23 May (4 June), the detachment reached Neustadt an der Orla, having travelled 34 *Meilen* (more than 230 *verstas*) along bad roads over the course of six days. Moving onwards to Schleiz, adding another 100 *Confédération du Rhin* men to his detachment, Lützow arrived in Plauen on 25 May (6 June), where he granted the men a rest day and sent patrols out in order to seek out the enemy and to collect intelligence on the views of the Austrian government.[3]

3 Geschichte des *Lützowschen Freikorps*, 23-30; Beitzke, *Geschichte der deutschen Freiheitskriege*, I, 547-551; Förster, *Geschichte der Befreiungskriege, 1813, 1814, 1815*, I, 395-397.

Two days later [8 June new style], having sent *Leutnant* Kropff and *Leutnant* Reiche to Hof with a squadron of lancers and 300 infantry respectively, Lützow headed to Adorf with the rest of the cavalry and with Colomb, for a joint attack on the disarmed Saxons moving towards the Bohemian border. The brave Kropff took the enemy outposts by surprise and destroyed them, captured the suburbs and intended to break into the city together with the infantry under *Leutnant* Reiche, but having received news about the conclusion of a truce from the commander of the Bavarian forces, he released the prisoners of war and withdrew to Regnitzlosau [6½ miles east of Hof] on the way to Adorf, and let Lützow know about the suspension of hostilities. Having received this information, Lützow immediately notified the commander of Saxon forces in Dresden, General Gersdorff [Karl Friedrich Wilhelm von Gersdorff], of his intention, as a result of the conclusion of the truce, to return to the right bank of the Elbe by the shortest route, moreover, considering it to be completely impossible to reach the right bank of the Elbe by 12 June (new style), he asked for a Saxon officer to be sent to accompany the detachment. Lützow remained in Plauen while waiting for a response where, on 2 (14) June, he received a letter from General Gersdorff expressing consent to his request. At the same time, Gersdorff let him know that he had sent a report to Emperor Napoleon's *quartier-général* regarding all the circumstances of this case.

The following day, 3 (15) June, Lützow's detachment set off from Plauen with the Saxon *Leutnant* Gößnitz as commissar. On 4 (16) June, in Gera, Lützow presented himself to the commander of French forces stationed there, who released a Prussian volunteer who had been captured by the French while travelling on a mission in his service, invited Lützow to dinner and wished to have one of his officers accompany the detachment. But Lützow turned down this offer, personally believing that the Saxon commissar accompanying them was quite sufficient for the march security of the Prussian force. In order to avoid a clash with French or *Confédération du Rhin* units, the detachment constantly camped in the open air and on 5 (17) June, having passed through the town of Zeitz, occupied by Württemberg forces, bivouacked in the evening near Lützen at the village of Kitzen [5½ miles to the south-east]. No sooner had Lützow's cavalrymen unbridled their horses, than patrols reported the approach of a strong unit of enemy cavalry. *Leutnant* Kropff, having been sent as a *parlementaire* to the commander of this detachment, was informed that 'the force commander in Leipzig, the duc de Padoue (Jean-Thomas Arrighi de Casanova), demands that Major Lützow halt in anticipation of a French officer, who would accompany them on their onward march.' Both sides gave their word of honour not to violate the truce and, in the meantime, *Leutnant* Kropff and *Leutnant* Gößnitz went to Leipzig, to the duc, in order to finalise the agreement with him. Leipzig youths, expressing public opinion depressed by the presence of the French, met and escorted the Prussian officer to the duc's residence with loud cheers of hurrah! and *Lebe hoch*! with other expressions of sympathy and delight.

Meanwhile, Lützow's detachment had already been doomed to destruction. Napoleon, embittered by the success of the Coalition partisans and concerned at the potential influence of a national uprising on the morale of the *Confédération du Rhin*, ordered 'the extermination of every bandit waging war according to the example of

Schill [Ferdinand Baptista von Schill].[4] No sooner had Kropff gone to duc Arrighi to explain to him the purpose of his mission, than the duc calmly said to him: 'By order of the *Empereur*, Major Lützow and his band of thieves have been declared outside the protection of the law (*hors de la loi*). You are my prisoner.' With these words, four gendarmes entered, who, having disarmed the Prussian officer, took him into custody. After waiting for his return for some time, Lützow set out on the road to Altranstädt [ten miles west of Leipzig]. Wanting to halt the advance of the enemy columns following them and to gain time for his detachment to get away from them, accompanied by Körner, he jumped over a wide ditch that separated them from the nearest column and, turning to the commander of this force, Württemberg General Normann [Karl Friedrich Lebrecht von Normann-Ehrenfels], questioned him about the purpose of their advance. Normann replied that he had been ordered to occupy a village through which the Prussian detachment had already passed. When Lützow asked whether he could see a superior commander, and whether an attack would be made on his detachment during his absence, Normann gave assurances that he could be completely at peace in this regard, and ordered him to be taken to General Fournier [François Louis Fournier-Sarlovèze]. Meanwhile, the Prussian troops withdrew in four small columns, except for a few officers who remained behind, awaiting the return of their commander. Just as Lützow, having approached Fournier, began to ask him to halt his troops, in order to avoid a clash with the detachment as they were intending to return across the Elbe on the basis of the armistice, the French general shouted back at him: 'The armistice is for everyone but you!'[5] This was enough to convince Lützow of the enemy treachery. Turning his horse sharply about, he jumped back over the ditch, dashed past Normann and stationed himself at the head of his detachment. Whereupon, General Fournier rode up to the Württemberg column, expressing his displeasure with Normann for allowing the Prussian force to withdraw from their bivouac, and gave orders for them to be stopped, saying 'If they do not give themselves up, cut them down; I shall support you.' Having received these orders, Normann set off at a trot with two squadrons, got ahead of the Prussian detachment and blocked their path. It was already nine o'clock in the evening. According to Normann's own testimony, Lützow's jägers were the first to open fire on the Württemberg troops, who, embittered by the loss of several of their comrades, went on the attack and cut their way into the Prussian cavalry initially, and then into the infantry. According to Lützow's colleagues, this attack came as a complete surprise. Within a quarter of an hour, the entire detachment had been scattered. Lützow was himself seriously wounded and fell from his horse, being surrounded by enemy on all sides, he owed his salvation to senior jäger Beczwarzowski with 12 lancers, who dispersed the Württemberg dragoons and rescued their commander. Whereupon one of the Prussian hussars jumped off his horse, put Lützow on its back and, having given him the opportunity to escape, fell into the hands of the enemy himself. Meanwhile, Beczwarzowski, taking advantage of the ensuing darkness, picked his way past the Württemberg cavalry with his lancer squadron, crossed the Luppe that same night and then crossed the Elster at

4 *Le Moniteur*, 20 and 27 June 1813.
5 *'l'armistice pour tout le monde excepté pour vous!'*

Schkeuditz [8½ miles north-west of Leipzig], before crossing the Mulde the next day, 6 (18) June at Raguhn [nine miles upstream of Dessau], and having reached the Elbe at Vockerode ([7½ miles] upstream of Roßlau) in the evening, crossed there, some by swimming, others in small boats.

Major Lützow and *Leutnant* Reiche raced towards the Harz with 20 men, past Sangerhausen, and with the help of the population made their way onwards, past Bernburg, occupied by two Westphalian cuirassier regiments, to the Saalhorn promontory near the confluence of the Saale, where they crossed to the right bank of the Elbe. According to Plotho [Carl Johann Joachim Friedrich von Plotho], the Cossacks in the detachment also travelled with them.

Many of Lützow's dispersed warriors, and even some of those captured and taken to Leipzig, escaped death by disguising themselves as peasants or in women's clothing. Among those who were truly miraculously saved was the seriously wounded Theodor Körner.[6]

Napoleon, having received the reports of the destruction of Lützow's detachment, ordered these captured soldiers to be transported under the closest supervision to the Savoy fortresses. These young men, mostly university educated who had became the pioneering defenders of German independence, were chained in pairs like convicts, and sent on forced marches to Savoy. The residents of Leipzig, sympathetic to the fortunes of the wounded and prisoners from Lützow's detachment, aroused Napoleon's anger to the point that, on his orders, Leipzig was declared to be under a state of siege, a severe indemnity was imposed upon the population and they were forced to hand in every weapon they possessed, colonial goods were confiscated, and provisions for the Wittenberg fortress were supplied at the city's expense.[7]

Every representation by the Coalition generals regarding the treacherous act upon Lützow's detachment was unsuccessful. Berthier initially made excuses about misunderstandings and attributed this outrageous business to misfortune, and then blamed Lützow himself, who, according to his testimony: 'Having received a copy of the armistice agreement from an officer of the general staff sent to him, stated that he did not acknowledge it. When it was pointed out to him that he had to return beyond the Elbe by 12 June, he replied that this condition was not obligatory for his detachment (*dass sein Corps ein Freicorps wäre*). From 7 to 18 June, Major Lützow continued hostile operations, intercepting mail, couriers and isolated soldiers, imposing indemnities and recruiting students and other young men into his detachment.'[8] Contrary to international law, these prisoners would not be exchanged and did not get their freedom until the Coalition had seized Paris.

The only retribution for the destruction of Lützow's detachment was that, at Gneisenau's suggestion, the Coalition violated Article 5 of the armistice agreement, by which they were obliged to resupply the fortresses blockaded by the Coalition, of Danzig, Modlin, Zamość, Stettin and Küstrin, with provisions every five days.

6 *Geschichte des Lützowschen Freikorps*, 30-41; Beitzke, I, 551-554; Förster, I, 397-404; Zimmermann, *Die Befreiungskämpfe der Deutschen gegen Napoleon*, 713-717.

7 Förster, I, 404-405.

8 *Chef d'état-major* Berthier's letter to the Commander-in-Chief of the Coalition armies, Barclay de Tolly, dated 23 June, from Dresden; *Vossische Zeitung*, 22 July 1813.

Evading the fulfilment of this condition accelerated the surrender of the aforementioned fortresses upon the resumption of hostilities.[9]

As Napoleon was concentrating his forces prior to the battle of Bautzen, many locations on the left bank of the Elbe, quite strongly garrisoned by his forces up to this point, were stripped bare or were guarded by small detachments. Count Vorontsov, who had recently arrived at Magdeburg from the Oder, having learned that some elements of Graf Wallmoden's corps were beyond the Elbe, sent Lieutenant Colonel Borisov [Khristofor Sergeevich Borisov] from his detachment with Dyachkov's Cossack Regiment, and one squadron each from the Volhynia Ulans and Pavlograd Hussars, some 460 men in total, ordering them to conduct a sweep down the left bank of the Elbe in the vicinity of Magdeburg, and, if possible, to reconnoitre the roads from this city towards Leipzig.[10] On 10 (22) May, Borisov's detachment, having crossed the Elbe near Aken, arrived in Dessau, from where they then sent patrols out in various directions. One of these, having reached Bernburg, captured enemy billeting officers there, who swore that they had been instructed to select quarters for a cavalry detachment under the command of *général de division* Poinsot [Pierre Poinsot de Chansac], numbering 730 men en route to join the army. Having received this intelligence, on 11 (23) May, Borisov set off for the Bernburg to Leipzig road in order to isolate the enemy, and having learned that Poinsot's detachment had stopped for the night in Könnern, diverted to this location, arrived there at night, secured all the exits with his patrols and at dawn attacked an enemy almost twice his strength. The French, without waiting for the attack, quickly left along the road to Halle, but Borisov caught up with them and, after a bitter struggle, had completely scattered the French cavalry, leaving 250 bodies on the ground and capturing Poinsot himself with more than 20 officers and 300 lower ranks. On the Russian side, the casualties consisted of: one officer and 12 privates seriously wounded; two officers, four non-commissioned officers and 18 privates lightly wounded.[11]

Adjutant General Chernyshev, serving in Graf Wallmoden's corps with his detachment, on the lower Elbe, learned from patrols sent out by him about the movement of a significant enemy park along a route via Halberstadt towards Magdeburg and asked his corps commander for permission to make a sweep towards Hanover. Meanwhile, from dispatches intercepted by the Cossacks, it emerged that this park, consisting of 14 guns and 80 ammunition caissons, and a large convoy of weapons and ammunition, escorted by 2,000 infantry and cavalry, were planning to spend the night in Halberstadt from 17 to 18 (29 to 30) May. In the early hours of 16 (28) May, General Chernyshev quickly crossed the Elbe near Ferchland [ten miles upstream of Tangermünde] with his detachment, numbering 2,350 regular cavalry and Cossacks, with two horse artillery pieces,[12] and having covered more than 100

9 Förster, I, 407.

10 Lieutenant General Count Vorontsov's report No. 366 to Count Wittgenstein dated 30 April [12 May] (Log of Incoming Documents, No. 902); Lieutenant Colonel Borisov's report to Count Vorontsov dated 30 May [11 June] (Log of Incoming Documents, No. 1,078).

11 Lieutenant Colonel Borisov's report to Count Vorontsov dated 13 [25] May; Vaudoncourt, *Histoire de la guerre soutenue par les Français en Allemagne*, 112-113. According to Vaudoncourt, only around 200 men were taken prisoner.

12 General Chernyshev's detachment consisted of: 15 officers and 207 other ranks in the Finland Dragoons; 16 officers and 165 other ranks in the Riga Dragoons; 13 officers and 214 other

verstas in 36 hours, arrived in the vicinity of Halberstadt at dawn on 18 (30) May. Seven *verstas* from the town, a report was intercepted, from which it was learned that there was another park of 16 guns in the village of Hessen [Hasserode?], about 20 *verstas* from Halberstadt, with an escort of 4,500 men, which was intending to link up with the park stationed in Halberstadt that same morning and continue moving together with them towards Magdeburg. Having received this intelligence and paying scant attention to the fatigue of the men, Chernyshev decided to attack the enemy immediately. His hopes of taking the park's escort by surprise were not realised: the day before, Westphalian gendarmes had let them know about the Russian advance, which obliged the commander of the enemy force, *Generalmajor* Ochs [Adam Ludwig von Ochs], to take defensive precautions.[13] The artillery park was laid out in the form of a quadrangle, about a *versta* from the town, between the Holtemme river and the embanked road to Hessen. The infantry were located inside this wagon-laager. The artillery pieces had been placed on its two sides facing the road and the open ground. The cavalry were stationed on the wings. Overall, the enemy position, strengthened by natural obstacles, was very advantageous, but in the meantime, a report had come in from patrols that the large park had already set off from Hessen for Halberstadt, so General Chernyshev could not postpone the proposed attack.

Sysoev's Cossack regiment was sent up the Braunschweig road to delay the approaching enemy. Colonel Grekov 18th received orders to break into the town with his Cossacks and the Riga Dragoons, to capture any Westphalians stationed there in quarters and attack the park from there. Colonel Vlasov 3rd was tasked to attack them in the sector between the river and the road. Chernyshev positioned himself facing the road with the rest of the troops of the detachment. Colonel Grekov burst into the town and captured a number of prisoners, while Vlasov, engaged with canister and fierce musket fire, was forced to pull back. Colonel Sysoev reported that the escort of the larger park, having heard the gunfire, had quickened their pace. At this very moment, the Russian horse artillery pieces, very advantageously positioned opposite the corner of the wagon-laager, under Captain Bogdanovich [Ivan Fëdorovich Bogdanovich] of the general staff, opened fire so successfully that they blew up five ammunition caissons with their first shots. General Chernyshev, taking advantage of the confusion that resulted from the detonations in the wagon-laager, led a determined assault with his entire force. Upon giving the signal, the Cossacks, hussars and dragoons rushed at the batteries, dashing through the canister fire and burst into the wagon-laager, cutting some of the defenders down and taking others

ranks in the Izyum Hussars (630 regular cavalry in total); 15 officers and 355 other ranks in Sysoev's Cossacks; 15 officers and 334 other ranks in Grekov 18th's Cossacks; seven officers and 319 other ranks in Vlasov 3rd's Cossacks; six officers and 338 other ranks in Ilovaisky 11th's Cossacks; nine officers and 298 other ranks in Zhurov's Cossacks (1,696 Cossacks in total); one officer and 24 other ranks in 1st Horse Artillery Company, with two guns. For a total of 2,351 men in the detachment (extracted from returns dated 10 [22] June, signed by Barclay de Tolly).

According to Clausewitz (VIII, 306), Chernyshev's detachment had 1,800 men. Plotho gives 2,000 in *Der Krieg in Deutschland und Frankreich, in den Jahren 1813 und 1814, Beilagen*, 96.

13 See Map No. 11, Plan of the action at Halberstadt, 18 (30) May 1813.

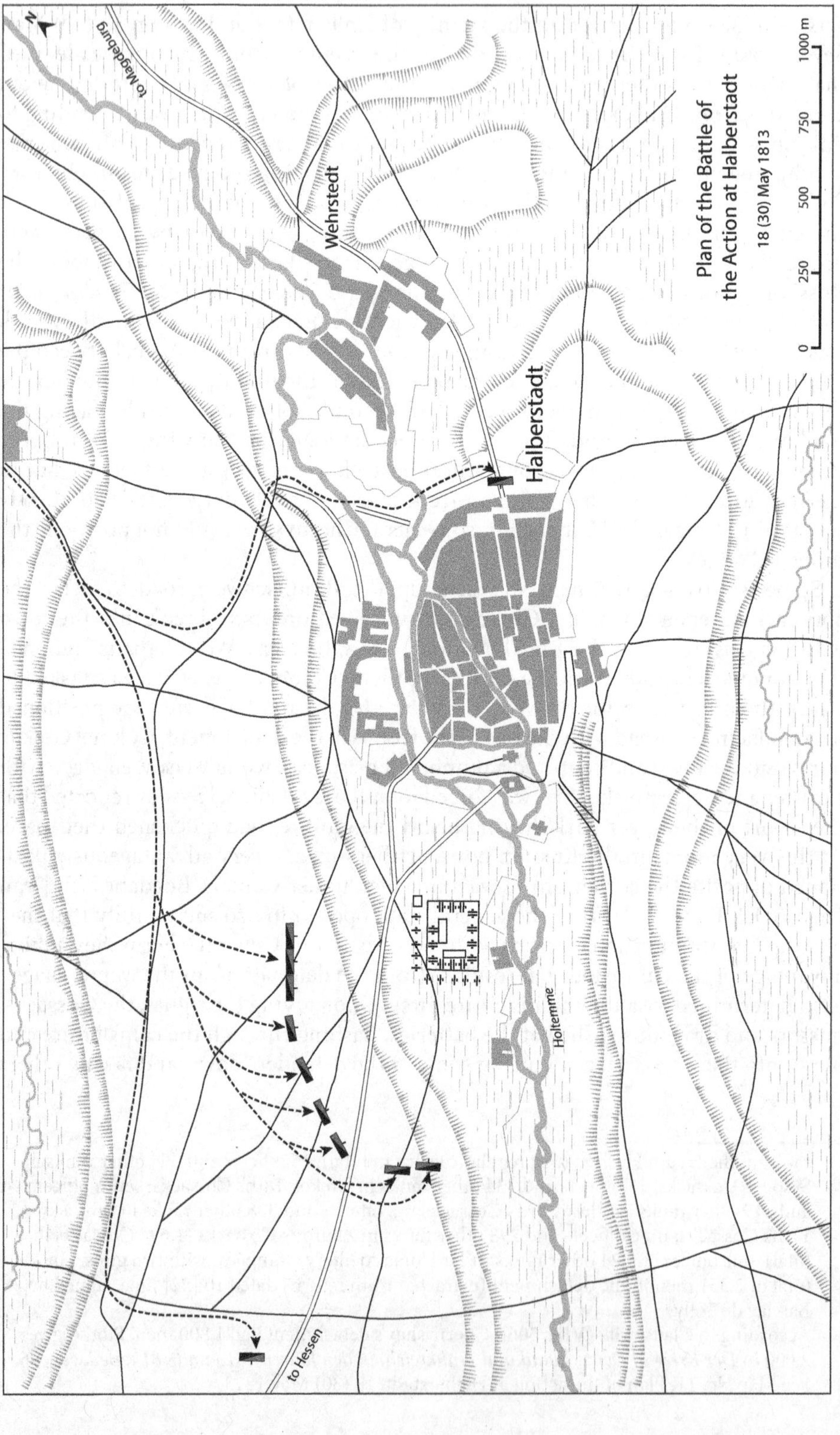

Plan of the action at Halberstadt.

prisoner. The fruits of this victory were all 14 guns, 11 ammunition caissons (the rest having exploded) and more than 1,000 prisoners, including General Ochs himself, one colonel and 15 officers (six, according to other sources). The significant train, with provisions, weapons and munitions, and 800 horses went to the victors as booty. On the Russian side, the casualties did not exceed 40 men overall. Among the wounded was Colonel Drevich [Fëdor Ivanovich Drevich] of the Finland Dragoons.

No sooner was the action over than the large park approached on the road from Hessen. Chernyshev set off to engage them and not only stopped their vanguard, but forced the enemy to pull back somewhat, while, in the mean time, the guns and other booty were being directed along the road to Bernburg. Having secured their march, Chernyshev followed them and transported all the captured guns and vehicles to Roßlau on the right bank of the Elbe.[14]

Meanwhile, Count Vorontsov, located at Magdeburg, sent a strong Cossack patrol up the Saale, with orders to collect all the boats and ferries along the way and float them down to the Elbe, which, together with vessels collected on this river, were intended to be used to construct a bridge a little downstream of the confluence with the Saale. At the same time, all the necessary rope, anchors, planks and other materials were being prepared. Having thus prepared the resources for a crossing over the Elbe, Count Vorontsov agreed with Adjutant General Chernyshev to send Major General O'Rourke [Iosif Kornilovich Orurk of Joseph Cornelius O'Rourke] to the Leipzig – Dresden road with 1,000 infantry and two guns, at the same time as Chernyshev was marching up the Saale. On 24 May (5 June), Count Vorontsov set out from Königsborn [6½ miles east of Magdeburg] for Dessau himself with part of his detachment.[15] At this time, he received intelligence that a cavalry corps was being formed in Leipzig, under the command of the duc de Padoue (Arrighi), including several thousand recruits, yet there were few infantry; and that there were also large arms stores and a significant military treasury. Count Vorontsov decided to march on Leipzig immediately, having agreed with General Chernyshev to attack enemy forces stationed there with the combined strength of both detachments. Having left elements of his corps to blockade Magdeburg, commanded by Colonel Krasovsky [Afanasy Ivanovich Krasovsky],[16] Count Vorontsov moved from Königsborn to Dessau, with a detachment consisting of the 13th Jägers, five combined grenadier battalions, Major Petersdorff's Prussian *Freikorps* battalion with 11th Horse Artillery Company and 13th Horse Artillery Company, together with Count O'Rourke's detachment consisting of the Pavlograd Hussars, Volhynia Ulans and two Cossack regiments, giving a total of around 5,000 men with 24 guns.[17] Count Vorontsov's onward

14 General Chernyshev's report to Prince Volkonsky; War diaries signed by Prince Volkonsky; Clausewitz, VII, 306; Sporschill, *Die grosse Chronik*, I, 268-270.

15 Lieutenant General Count Vorontsov's report to General of Infantry Barclay de Tolly dated 24 May [5 June] (Log of Incoming Documents,No. 1,175).

16 Colonel Krasovsky's detachment consisted of: 14th Jägers; a Prussian battalion; two *Landwehr* battalions; a squadron each of Pavlograd Hussars and Volhynia Ulans; one Cossack regiment, and 26th Light Artillery Company (Count Vorontsov's report to Barclay de Tolly dated 28 May [9 June], Log of Incoming Documents, No. 1,176).

17 On departing for Leipzig, Count Vorontsov's detachment consisted of: 503 men in the 13th Jägers; 1,380 men in five combined grenadier battalions (on returns this is given as 1,670

movement from Dessau, along the road to Delitzsch towards Leipzig, was carried out as a forced march. Upon arrival in the vicinity of this city, on the morning of 26 May (7 June), the force commanders agreed among themselves that Count Vorontsov would advance directly, while General Chernyshev would take the Torgau – Leipzig road. Upon approaching the town of Taucha [6½ miles north-east of Leipzig], Chernyshev blocked all the surrounding roads with strong patrols and then quickly attacked two regiments from General Piré's cavalry division [Hippolyte-Marie-Guillaume de Rosnyvinen de Piré], who were training there. The enemy, taken completely by surprise, were driven off. The other regiments of this division attempted to stop the Russian partisans, but were also dispersed by them, with the loss of 14 officers and 400 lower ranks taken prisoner. General Piré emerged from the town himself with a trumpeter just as Chernyshev, pursuing the defeated enemy cavalry, was coming right up to the gates. Having asked permission to speak with the commander of the Russian force, Piré announced that orders had been received in Leipzig to suspend hostilities on the conclusion of a two-month armistice. Chernyshev, holding General Piré as a hostage, sent to Count Vorontsov to ask for his orders regarding further operations. Meanwhile, the cavalry from Vorontsov's detachment, commanded by Count O'Rourke, drove off several enemy squadrons near the village of Eutritzsch [2½ miles north of Leipzig] and captured four officers and 150 lower ranks. Count Vorontsov, having marched up the Dessau road to the city, formed his infantry in columns of attack and was preparing to storm the city, but at that very moment, riding out to meet him as a *parlementaire* from the duc de Padoue, the chief of staff of *3e corps de cavalerie*, General Lamotte [Auguste Étienne Marie Gourlez de Lamotte], announced the conclusion of an armistice and showed Count Vorontsov a letter from the duc de Bassano (Maret), which contained the official announcement of the cessation of hostilities. Having no reason to doubt the truth of this news, and concerned that the city might catch fire from shots fired at the troops holding it, Count Vorontsov agreed to suspend operations so that the duc could send one of the generals to him as a hostage, as a result of which General Lamotte remained with Count Vorontsov's detachment. The Russian generals then moved back to the Elbe and, upon arrival in Dessau, having received orders to suspend hostilities, released both hostages. Thus the news of the armistice interrupted an expedition which, without any doubt, would have had very important consequences.[18]

At the time of the battle of Bautzen, Major General Kaisarov had been sent to operate behind enemy lines with Ilovaisky 10th's Don Cossack Regiment, joined by 70 men of the Prussian *Neumärkisches Dragoner Regiment*. At dawn on 12 (24) May, Kaisarov's detachment attacked an enemy park moving from Reichenbach to Görlitz,

men in six battalions); 439 men in 11th and 13th horse artillery companies; 900 men in the Pavlograd Hussars and Volhynia Ulans, less the two squadrons left at Magdeburg; 643 Cossacks in Melnikov 5th's and Dyachkin's regiments; for a total of 3,865 men (returns dated 21 May [2 June]). Together with 900 men in Major Petersdorff's Prussian battalion (Plotho, I, 230. According to this work, Count Vorontsov's force were joined by another 300 cavalrymen from Lützow's detachment, in addition to the 900 man battalion).

18 Count Vorontsov's report to General Barclay de Tolly dated 28 May [9 June] (Log of Incoming Documents, No. 1,176); Adjutant General Chernyshev's report to General Barclay de Tolly dated 28 May [9 June] (Log of Incoming Documents, No. 1,177; Vaudoncourt, 113.

drove off their escort and captured eight guns, of which two were dragged away by the Cossacks, while the rest were spiked, in case of a counterattack by an incomparably stronger enemy. Of the personnel who were with the park, the following were killed: one general, one colonel and some 200 lower ranks. 47 men were taken prisoner, while the Russian detachment lost Major Kaisarov [Andrey Sergeevich Kaisarov] of the Moscow *Opolchenie* and one Cossack killed in action. Nine Cossacks were wounded.[19] On 19 (31) May, near the village of Wilhelmsburg, General Kaisarov attacked 150 dismounted cuirassiers sent from Napoleon's *quartier-général* to Dresden. The enemy, surrounded on all sides by Cossacks, dashed into the sturdy *Schloss* [castle] and defended themselves there until skirmishers summoned from the detachment captured the gates, killing some of the cuirassiers and captured two officers and 50 lower ranks, while losing several men wounded. The commander of the enemy detachment, Lieutenant Colonel Cappé, was killed.[20]

During the retreat of the Coalition army to Upper Silesia, Colonel Figner, sent from the vicinity of Greiffenberg [Gryfów Śląski] behind enemy lines, on 17 (29) May, set off from Liebenthal [five miles east of Greiffenberg] towards the road from Lauban to Löwenberg, and reaching it near Seifersdorf [Łukaszów, five miles north of Goldberg], he covertly deployed his detachment.[21] While having discovered in the mean time that there were about 100 men in this village, he attacked them, wiped out the French and, in accordance with their express wishes, added the Italians to his detachment. Thereafter, having passed through Hermannsdorf (west of Bunzlau), he captured many prisoners, taking in the Italians and Spaniards himself, while the French, according to his own report: 'I rendered them harmless.' On 18 (30) May, having crossed the Bunzlau to Haynau road once more, near the village of Krabau, Figner encountered two companies of French artillery marching to Torgau without guns. The artillerymen, having muskets, tried to resist but upon being forced to surrender, they were executed. Only the officers received mercy. The Italians and Spaniards who had joined the detachment were no less inferior in their loathing of the French than Figner himself. Subsequently, on the way from the outskirts of Haynau to the town of Primkenau [Przemków], the Russian partisans attacked an infantry detachment, numbering 400 men, and wiped it out, except for a few Italians and Germans who wished to enter service in the Coalition army. On 19 (31) May, having reached Neustädtel [Nowe Miasteczko], Figner established communications with Bülow's corps and handed over the French officers and German soldiers he had captured to the Prussian forces, while keeping the Italians and Spaniards with him. Thus, over the course of three days, he had marched right across the entire lines of communications of the enemy army, from the Bohemian border to the outskirts of Glogau, and destroyed three detachments, which altogether numbered more than 700 men.[22]

19 Major General Kaisarov's report No. 11 to commander-in-chief Count Wittgenstein dated 13 [25] May.
20 Major General Kaisarov's report No. 18 dated 20 May [1 June].
21 Figner's detachment consisted of: a squadron of Sumy Hussars; Yakhontov's and Figner's volunteer Cossack regiments.
22 Lifeguard Colonel Figner's report to the commander in chief, Count Wittgenstein dated 20 May [1 June] (Log of Incoming Documents, No. 1,122).

15

Sieges of the fortresses behind Coalition lines up to the conclusion of the armistice

The siege of Danzig. A brief description of the fortress. – The garrison. – The encirclement of Danzig: by Platov, by Löwis, by Herzog Alexander von Württemberg. – The Herzog's intention to conduct a siege.

The siege of Modlin. A brief description of the fortress. – The garrison. – The blockade of Modlin by Paskevich and proposal by Oppermann to begin the siege. – Negotiations with General Daendels. – Bombardment of the fortress.

The siege of Zamość. The fortress and its garrison. – The blockade of Zamość by Rath.

The siege of Stettin. The fortress and its garrison. – The encirclement of Stettin by Tauentzien.

The siege of Küstrin. The fortress and its garrison. – The encirclement of Küstrin: by Helffreich, by Vorontsov, by Kaptsevich. – Preparations for the bombardment of the fortress.

The siege of Glogau. The fortress and its garrison. – The initial encirclement of Glogau by Saint-Priest, followed by that of Schuler von Senden. – The action at Zerbau. – The opening of the trenches. – The raising of the siege.

The Siege of Danzig

In accordance with the treaty concluded in Tilsit, Danzig was declared a free city but Napoleon occupied it with his forces under the pretext of enforcing the Continental System. *Gouverneur* Rapp [Jean Rapp], sparing neither labour nor money, eventually turned this city into one of the strongest fortresses in Europe. Danzig, as is well known, lies on the left bank of the Vistula, one *Meile* from the Baltic Sea. Two rivers flow through the city, the Mottlau [Motława] and the Radaune [Radunia], engineered so that they may deliberately inundate the lowlands they water. To the south-west of the city stretch a chain of hills. Danzig consists of five main areas: the Niederstadt, on the right bank of the Mottlau; Speicherinsel [Wyspa Spichrzów], between two branches of this river; the Altstadt [Stare Miasto], Rechtstadt [Główne Miasto] and Vorstadt. There are suburbs outside the fortifications. The island of Holm [Wyspa Ostrów], formed by the main channel of the Vistula and the Lake branch [Łacha] extending from it to the right, was connected to the left bank of the river by a floating bridge and protected by a rampart with a ditch and palisades. Fort Hautpoult had been built on the right bank of the Vistula opposite the Napoleon Redoubt on the northern tip of Holm, guarding communications between Danzig and the fortified harbour of Weichselmünde [Wisłoujście], opposite which, the French erected Fort Montebello [Twierdza Wisłoujście] at Neufahrwasser [Nowy Port]. Fort Desaix had been constructed on the eastern side of the city, forwards of the Niederstadt. On the western side of the city, the Hagelsberg [Góra Gradowa] was fortified with a new stone-clad redoubt, connected to the main ramparts by a strongly vaulted gallery. The high ground at Bischofsberg [Biskupia Górka], south of the Hagelsberg, was also fortified and connected to the main rampart by a gallery. The Judenberg promontory, studded with batteries, was subsequently connected by new entrenchments with a fortified camp built forwards of the Hagelsberg by the time of the armistice. Villages and individual buildings that might be useful to a besieger were demolished.

At the end of 1812 and beginning of 1813, General Rapp gathered in the remnants of the *Grande Armée* at Danzig, numbering some 40,000. Troops from every combat arm and a variety of nationalities flocked there from various directions: French, Germans, Poles, Italians, Dutch, Spanish. Many of them were true invalids. Since there was not enough food or medicine for this multitude of personnel, Rapp sent several thousand unfit men out of the city. Nevertheless, some 35,000 men still remained in Danzig, of whom initially no more than 10,000 were combat capable.[1]

During the advance by Russian forces towards the lower Vistula, Count Platov, moving with a Cossack detachment as an independent column, encircled Danzig in early [mid] January 1813.[2] Two weeks later, Lieutenant General Löwis took command of the blockade corps, numbering about 13,000 men,[3] which were subsequently to be reinforced by another 9,000 men.[4] The enemy made sorties almost daily in order to reconnoitre the blockading force and to collect forage from the surrounding villages, but each time they were repulsed with casualties. Polish soldiers were deserting Danzig and, on Löwis' orders, were released to their homes. On 25 February [9 March], Major General Adadurov [Vasily Vasilievich Adadurov] arrived with 12 Groups of St Petersburg *Opolchenie* and Novgorod *Opolchenie*. At

1 Sporschill, *Die grosse Chronik*, I, 1,142-1,143.
2 Admiral Chichagov's report No. 25 to Prince Kutuzov-Smolensky dated 6 [18] January.
3 For the composition of General Löwis' corps, see Appendix XXIV at the end of this chapter.
4 The reinforcements for Löwis' blockade corps consisted of: 638 men from the Podolia Infantry and a sub-unit of Voronezh Infantry; 5,057 men in 16 Groups of St Petersburg *Opolchenie*; 3,587 men in eight Groups of Novgorod *Opolchenie*; for a total of 9,282 men (returns dated 16 [28] February, signed by Prince Kutuzov-Smolensky).

the same time, the Tula Infantry and Navaginsk Infantry marched off to join Count Wittgenstein's army. On 13 (25) March, the 5th Battery Artillery Company and 3rd Horse Artillery Company were also sent after them, and in addition, some of the artillery from the blockade corps were sent to Dirschau, in order to more easily feed the horses with forage from the left bank of the Nogat. On 14 (26) March, more St Petersburg *Opolchenie* (9th Group) arrived in Dirschau, whereupon, Ilovaisky 9th's Cossacks were sent to Count Wittgenstein's army. On 24 March (5 April), Yakhontov's Volunteer Cossacks and the 11th Light Artillery Company were also sent there.[5]

Upon the arrival at Danzig on 11 (23) April of Herzog Alexander von Württemberg, appointed commander of the blockade corps, he found that the strength of the force entrusted to him did not exceed 13,000 men, while excluding field officers, subalterns and support personnel, there were 11,800 combatants in the corps with 59 guns.[6] According to intelligence received by the Herzog, from Colonel Figner, who had recently left the fortress, the garrison there was more numerous than the force that surrounded it, which, moreover, being divided into several detachments stretched over a considerable area, were constantly being attacked by the enemy in superior strength. Despite the ease of delivering rations by sea or along the Vistula, the Russian force suffered an extreme shortage of provisions, and once went without bread for three full days. The reason for this were the incessant disputes between the local administrations of Pomerania and West Prussia. One of the first commands from the Herzog von Württemberg was the order that all grain and livestock located in the villages a *Meile* or closer to the fortress be moved away, in order to deprive the enemy of the opportunity to exploit these resources. The troops of the blockade corps had very few cartridges,[7] and therefore the chief of artillery of all active armies at that time, General Yermolov, asked the Inspector of All Artillery, Baron Meller-Zakomelsky, to have the required number of cartridges delivered to Danzig from the reserves captured from the enemy in Kovno [Kaunas].[8]

The Herzog von Württemberg wanted to begin the siege of the fortress as quickly as possible, but upon the departure to the active army of 21st Division on 29 April (11 May), with its attached reserve battalions, the blockade corps was greatly weakened. Having received notification from the headquarters of the Coalition army that, due to the prevailing circumstances, the proposed siege had to be postponed for a while, the Herzog nevertheless took measures to prepare the siege artillery. In anticipation of the imminent arrival of guns promised by the Swedish government and also hoping to receive a certain number of them from Britain, He considered it advantageous to have this artillery under his control in case circumstances changed, while intending to place the siege guns in the Pillau fortress in order to protect them

5 Danzig Siege Diary.

6 For the composition of Herzog Alexander's corps, see Appendix XXV at the end of this chapter.

7 General of Cavalry Herzog Alexander von Württemberg's reports to Prince Kutuzov-Smolensky dated 14 and 15 [26 and 27] April, Log of Incoming Documents, No. 743 and No. 744.

8 Chief of Artillery of the active armies, General Yermolov's dispatch No. 435 for Chief of Staff, Adjutant General Prince Volkonsky, dated 24 April [6 May], Log of Incoming Documents, No. 789.

from the enemy. Meanwhile, desertions from the Danzig garrison were increasing. There were plenty of provisions left in the magazines there, but there was no meat. The soldiers had already begun to eat horse meat. This was the state of affairs when the armistice arrived.[9]

The Siege of Modlin

This fortress was surrounded by a strong rampart, with palisades on the covered way and at the base of the counter-scarp. Strongly vaulted casemates had been built for the defence of blind spots. On the steep, high banks of the Vistula and Narew, the works had a lower profile, but were reinforced with a double palisade barricade. Ravelins and lunettes also provided the means for a stubborn defence. Blockhouses had been constructed inside the lunettes, as well as in the *place d'armes* of the covered way. There were many buildings hardened against plunging fire inside the fortress. The garrison consisted of 4,500 Polish infantry and three artillery companies, two French and one Saxon, under the command of *général de division* Daendels [Herman Willem Daendels]. There was plenty of gunpowder. Flour, hard-tack, salted meat and livestock were also present in significant quantities. General Paskevich, who had been entrusted with the blockade of Modlin, hoped to encourage desertions from the fortress through relations with the population and the garrison.[10]

Lieutenant General Paskevich's corps, consisting of 7,000 men with 48 guns,[11] encircled Modlin in February. Following the capture of Thorn, the engineer Lieutenant General Oppermann proposed to begin the siege of Modlin immediately, using all the suitable artillery available from Thorn for this purpose, but it turned out that these guns were insufficient, while in addition, at least 12,000 infantry were required in order to conduct the siege. Therefore, having received orders from Prince Kutuzov to send the fortress artillery, gunpowder and projectiles from Thorn to Modlin, Barclay de Tolly expressed the opinion that it would be necessary to abandon the proposed siege for the time being, limiting ourselves to a close blockade of the fortress.[12] Meanwhile, Daendels, via an aide de camp he sent to Zakroczym for negotiations, expressed a desire to surrender the fortress on the following conditions:

9 Herzog Alexander von Württemberg's dispatch No. 161 for Adjutant General Prince Volkonsky dated 2 [14] May, Log of Incoming Documents, No. 961; the Herzog's dispatch No. 1,035 for Barclay de Tolly dated 11 [23] May; the Herzog's dispatch No. 324 to Prince Volkonsky dated 21 May [2 June], Log of Incoming Documents, No. 1,037.

10 Description of the state of the Modlin fortress submitted to Prince Kutuzov-Smolensky by Lieutenant General Oppermann in Kalisz on 16 [28] February, Log of Incoming Documents, No. 289.

11 For the composition of Lieutenant General Paskevich's corps, see Appendix XXVI at the end of this chapter.

12 General Barclay de Tolly's report No. 25 to Prince Kutuzov dated 15 [27] April from Bromberg, with General Oppermann's report No. 59 dated 14 [26] April attached, Log of Incoming Documents, No. 764.

1. The Poles in the garrison were to be declared pardoned by the Russian government.
2. That the troops of other nationalities could join the German Legion, being raised in Königsberg at the time.
3. Daendels himself, along with some officers, wished to enter Russian service until such time as a Dutch uprising against Napoleon had begun, transferring thereafter to the forces of their homeland.
4. He demanded that, for the sake of decency, a token siege of the fortress be made.[13]

Dokhturov's report on the conditions proposed by Daendels arrived at the headquarters of the Coalition army at a time when armistice negotiations were already close to completion, and therefore Emperor Alexander directed a letter to Dokhturov that all proposed conditions should be fulfilled, and that he should try to conclude this matter, if possible, within 24 hours. As these negotiations continued, General Oppermann, setting off from Thorn to Modlin, persuaded the Prussian commandant in Graudenz to send the heavy artillery and gunpowder from there up the Vistula. The fortress guns and military stores were also sent from Thorn. Hoping for the compliance of the Modlin commandant, General Oppermann intended, immediately upon the arrival of artillery from Graudenz, to open a heavy bombardment of the fortress and thereby induce the enemy to surrender.[14] But, in all probability, Daendels had faced resistance to his views in the garrison, or had received news of an advance by the French army towards the Oder: the aide de camp he had sent (the same one that had come to Zakroczym previously) let it be known, on behalf of his commander, that 'he had some cause to conclude that the military situation had changed in favour of French forces and would not keep his word.'[15] Following such a clear breach of promise, the negotiations were suspended and General Paskevich had already begun to bombard the fortress by late May [early June], when news of the armistice forced him to suspend hostilities.

The Siege of Zamość

The Zamość fortress, 80 *verstas* from Lublin, lies on a plateau washed on both sides by marshy rivers. Between 1809 and 1813, many works were carried out that greatly strengthened this fortress.[16] The garrison consisted of 4,500 Polish troops,

13 General of Infantry Dokhturov's report No. 265 to Emperor Alexander I dated 19 [31] May, Log of Incoming Documents, No. 1,106.
14 Engineer Lieutenant General Oppermann's report to Emperor Alexander I dated 18 [30] May, Log of Incoming Documents, No. 1,110.
15 General Oppermann's report to Emperor Alexander I dated 22 May [3 June], Log of Incoming Documents, No. 1,161.
16 Extracted from the brief description of the Zamość fortress, attached to Lieutenant General Rath's report to Emperor Alexander I dated 17 [29] May, Log of Incoming Documents, No. 1,203.

commanded by *général de division* Hauke [Hans Johann Moritz Hauke].[17] Lieutenant General Rath, who was entrusted with the encirclement of Zamość, having received command of the detachment under Lieutenant General Musin-Pushkin [Pëtr Klavdievich Musin-Pushkin] in late January [early February], numbering 4,800 men with 16 guns,[18] arrived in Lublin, left a battalion of Okhotsk Infantry there and, after detaching several small task forces, approached Zamość with no more than 3,000 infantry in early [mid] February.[19] No sooner had he encircled the fortress and severed communications between the garrison and the surrounding countryside, than he received orders from headquarters to raise the blockade and link his force up with Sacken's corps, which was operating in the southwestern part of the Duchy of Warsaw. Although this order was subsequently cancelled, General Hauke took advantage of the suspension of the blockade, not only to collect provisions from the Lublin and Siedlce *Départements*, but also to recruit soldiers. Upon returning to Zamość, Rath controlled all routes leading to the fortress, established outposts along the upper Vistula and the administration of the surrounding countryside. Deserters often emerged from Zamość and the garrison lost some to 20 men daily to disease.[20] General Rath, wanting to encourage the commandant to surrender sooner rather than later, wrote to him that if he persisted, he and all the officers of the Zamość garrison would be exiled to the most remote regions of the Russian Empire.[21] Then, having received several thousand men from the Poltava *Opolchenie* as reinforcements, commanded by Major General Prince Zhevakhov [Filipp Semënovich Zhevakhov], General Rath left only 1,200 of them with the blockade corps, and placed the rest at various locations around the countryside in order to maintain order and to collect provisions and other requisitions. Several forays made by the garrison had been successfully repulsed, but on the night of 15 (27) April, the Poles managed to attack one of the Russian batteries erected at close range

17 General Rath's letter to Chief of Staff Prince Volkonsky dated 2 [14] February, Log of Incoming Documents, No. 281; Plotho, *Der Krieg in Deutschland und Frankreich in den Jahren 1813 und 1814*, I, *Beilagen*, 59.

18 Rath's detachment consisted of: 994 men in the Nyslott Infantry; 229 men in the Mingrela Infantry; 291 men in the Okhotsk Infantry; 1,022 men in the Penza Infantry; 1,051 men in the 43rd Jägers and four men from the Riga Infantry, for a total of 3,591 infantry, all from 16th Division.
136 men in one squadron of Pereyaslavl Dragoons; 148 men in one squadron of Tiraspol Dragoons and 12 men from the Kiev Dragoons and Serpukhov Dragoons, for a total of 296 cavalry.
210 men in Turchaninov 1st's Cossacks; 359 men in Platov 5th's former Cossack regiment and 40 men from various regiments, for a total of 600 irregular cavalry.
177 men with 12 guns in the 22nd Battery Artillery Company; 49 men with four guns in the 31st Light Artillery Company, for a total of 226 artillerymen.
For a grand total at Zamość of 4,713 men with 16 guns (extracted from returns dated 13 [25] March, signed by Prince Kutuzov-Smolensky).

19 Lieutenant General Rath's report No. 437 to Prince Kutuzov-Smolensky dated 14 [26] February, Log of Incoming Documents, No. 326.

20 General Rath's reports dated 5 and 11 [17 and 23] March, Log of Incoming Documents No. 430 and No. 490.

21 Rath's letter to Adjutant General Prince Volkonsky dated 21 March [2 April], Log of Incoming Documents, No. 556.

from the fortress with significant numbers, and captured four guns. General Rath, having restricted himself to a close investment of Zamość, considered it essential to bombard the fortress, and to that end he requested several mortars to be delivered from Kiev. In the meantime, news had arrived of the conclusion of the armistice.

The Siege of Stettin

This fortress had been strengthened by the French; Fort Damm [Dąbie], on the right bank of the Oder, had been rebuilt; the suburbs had been demolished. The garrison, numbering 8,000 men, commanded by *général de division* Grandeau [Louis Joseph Grandeau], was stocked with an abundance of food and military stores.

On 6 (18) March, *Generalleutnant* Graf Tauentzien encircled Stettin with a detachment of 11,000 men on both banks of the Oder.[22] The Prussian force armed two large boats in order to sever enemy communications by water and, in addition, there were four Swedish gunboats on the Dammschen See [Jezioro Dąbie]. The enemy launched strong sorties, consistently and successfully repulsed by the Prussian force, but their situation was made more difficult as they had to spare their city as much as possible.[23]

During the retreat of the Coalition army from the Elbe to Bautzen, the King of Prussia ordered General Tauentzien to detach all but four reserve battalions in order to reinforce Bülow's corps, which was shielding Berlin. After the departure of these troops, Tauentzien limited himself to monitoring the fortress until the arrival of the *Pommersches Landwehr*, but by then the armistice had come into force, following which, having received another assignment, he handed over command of the blockade corps to *Generalmajor* von Ploetz [Christian Friedrich Wilhelm von Ploetz].[24]

The Siege of Küstrin

The Küstrin fortress, on the right bank of the Oder at the confluence of the Warta, which forms a large lake to the south and south-east, is covered on the north-eastern side by a swampy lowland, and was occupied by 4,000 troops of various nations, commanded by *général de brigade* Fornier d'Albe [Gaspard Fornier d'Albe].[25]

On 22 February (6 March), at the same time as Count Wittgenstein's corps arrived on the Oder, General Helffreich was sent to Küstrin with a detachment of 1,700

22 *Generalleutnant* Graf Tauentzien's detachment consisted of: a battalion each of *2. Ostpreußisches Infanterie* and *Colbergsches Infanterie*; two reserve battalions each of *3. Ostpreußisches Infanterie* and *4. Ostpreußisches Infanterie*; three reserve battalions each of *Pommersches Infanterie* and *Colbergsches Infanterie*; one reserve battalion of *1. Ostpreußisches Infanterie*, for a total of 13 battalions numbering 10,400 infantrymen; two squadrons each of *Pommersches Husaren* and *Brandenburgisches Dragoner*, for a total of four squadrons numbering 350 cavalrymen; Ilovaisky 3rd Cossacks numbering 200 men (Plotho, I, *Beilagen*, 102-103).

23 Plotho, I, 240-243.

24 Plotho, I, 243.

25 Sporschill, I, 79.

men in order to monitor this fortress.[26] Approaching the fortress on the night of 24 to 25 February (8 to 9 March), Helffreich opened a strong cannonade from the right bank of the Oder and demanded their surrender. The response to him was an equally powerful salvo from the fortress guns and the razing of the Kietz suburb [west of Küstrin]. A few days later, the French made a sortie and, having driven in the Russian outpost stationed at Bleyen manor [on the left bank of the Oder 2½ miles downstream of Küstrin], foraged in the surrounding villages.

On 5 (17) March, the detachment under General Helffreich, having received orders to join Count Wittgenstein's corps in Berlin, was relieved at Küstrin by the detachment under Count Vorontsov, numbering 2,500 men with 12 guns,[27] which, a few days later, was reinforced by Count O'Rourke's detachment, comprising 1,500 men with 14 guns.[28] Count Vorontsov, having crossed to the left bank of the Oder at Frankfurt, left six combined grenadier battalions with eight guns from 13th Horse Artillery Company in this city, stationed the 13th Jägers and 14th Jägers with four remaining guns from this same company at the town of Lebus, and stationed Barabanshchikov's and Vykhalov's Cossack regiments at the fortress itself on the left bank of the Oder, while Panteleev's Cossacks were on the right bank of the river, supporting them with several squadrons of hussars stationed at Seelow and Balz [Białcz], on the Berlin to Landsberg road. The composition of the garrison from troops of various nations and the constant desertion by soldiers from the fortress prompted some Prussian officers, with Count Vorontsov's, to establish relations with the officers in the fortress, but the commandant would not dream of surrendering. On 2 (14) April, the men of 24th Division, with a manpower strength of less than 2,000,[29] under Lieutenant General Kaptsevich relieved Count Vorontsov, who, having left Barabanshchikov's and Panteleev's Cossacks from his detachment at Küstrin, marched towards Magdeburg.[30] General Kaptsevich, seeing no possibility of forcing the surrender of the fortress, which was abundantly supplied with stores, hoped to speed up its capture through bombardment. At the end of May [early June], eight mortars, two 24-pounder and four 12-pounder cannon were delivered from Berlin: having received this artillery, the Russian troops began constructing

26 Major General Helffreich's detachment consisted of: the Tenginsk Infantry, Estland Infantry, 14th Battery Artillery Company, one Cossack regiment and the Tver Mounted *Opolchenie*.

27 Count Vorontsov's detachment consisted of: six combined grenadier battalions from 9th Division, 15th Division and 18th Division; 13th Jägers; 14th Jägers; 13th Horse Artillery Company; three Cossack regiments (orders from Barclay de Tolly dated 17 [29] March, Log of Incoming Documents, No. 526).

28 Count O'Rourke's detachment consisted of: the Volhynia Ulans; Pavlograd Hussars; 11th Horse Artillery Company; 18th Horse Artillery Company (with 14 guns between them); Dyachkin's Cossacks; Melnikov 5th's Cossacks (orders from Barclay de Tolly dated 17 [29] March, Log of Incoming Documents, No. 526).

29 Lieutenant General Kaptsevich's detachment consisted of: 463 men in the Shirvan Infantry; 512 men in the Butyrsk Infantry; 412 men in the Ufa Infantry; 283 men in the 19th Jägers; 80 in 46th Light Artillery Company, for a total of 1,750 men (extracted from returns on force strengths for 21 March [2 April], signed by Prince Kutuzov-Smolensky).

30 Orders for Barclay de Tolly dated 17 [29] March, log of outgoing documents, No. 326; Lieutenant General Kaptsevich's report to Prince Kutuzov-Smolensky dated 2 [14] April.

batteries,[31] but this work had not yet been completed when the order came to suspend military operations on the occasion of the conclusion of the armistice.

The Siege of Glogau

The fortress of Glogau, the most important of all the strongholds in Silesia, had been painstakingly strengthened by the French. Its garrison consisted of 6,000 men of various arms, commanded by *général de division* Laplane [Jean Grégoire Barthélemy Rouger de Laplane]. This fortress had been surrounded by comte Saint-Priest since 1 (13) March, with elements of Miloradovich's corps, numbering around 5,000 men with 18 guns.[32] Both sides fired on one another from time to time and the garrison made forays to collect supplies from the surrounding countryside. In the meantime, because Miloradovich's corps had received a mission to march on the Elbe, General Schuler von Senden was ordered to relieve the detachment stationed at Glogau with a Prussian detachment assembled in Parchwitz [Prochowice] consisting of 3,000 infantry with two squadrons, one pioneer company and ten guns.[33] Count Miloradovich, having received an assessment from General Senden that his detachment of Prussian troops could not surround the fortress on both banks of the Oder without assistance due to their small numbers, left the Moscow Infantry, Libau Infantry and four Cossack regiments at Glogau, numbering 1,500 men with four light guns.[34] On 21 March (2 April), Miloradovich's corps departed for Bunzlau. In order to invest the fortress, General von Senden's troops were located mostly on the left bank of the Oder, while the two Russian infantry and three Cossack regiments, numbering about 1,000 men with four guns, were on the right bank.[35] The garrison made sorties almost every day from 20 March (1 April), which had no significant effect. Deserters from the fortress admitted that there were sufficient supplies for the fighting men, but that the townspeople were already suffering from food shortages. This intelligence was confirmed upon the expulsion of many residents from Glogau on 30 March (11 April). The arrival in the blockading corps of four Prussian reserve battalions[36] on 7 (19) April allowed General Senden to harass the enemy at night with small patrols that made their way right up to the glacis of the enemy fortifications.[37]

Meanwhile, the garrison had constantly held the village of Zerbau [Serby, three miles north-east of Glogau] on the right bank of the Oder, connected by a bridge

31 Lieutenant General Kaptsevich's dispatch to Adjutant General Prince Volkonsky dated 16 [28] May.

32 For the composition of comte Saint-Priest's detachment, see Appendix XXVII at the end of this chapter.

33 General Schuler von Senden's detachment consisted of: six reserve battalions; two squadrons of *Brandenburgisches Ulanen*; one pioneer company; a six-pounder battery; two howitzers (Plotho, I, 234).

34 Returns dated 28 March [9 April].

35 Plotho, I, 234-235.

36 At the same time, the *2es Reserve Bataillon* of the *Leib Infanterie* was sent to join Blücher's army.

37 Siege Diary for Glogau, signed by General von Senden, Log of Incoming Documents, No. 636.

to the fortress, where there were several windmills. By controlling this village, the French could assemble forces there for sorties and to forage in the surrounding area. In order to deprive them of this advantage, it was decided to blow up the bridge connecting the fortress with Zerbau and to attack this village in three columns, two Prussian and one Russian, each of which consisted of 300 men. A boat loaded with 18 *Pud* of gunpowder was prepared for the demolition, and its detonation was intended to serve as the signal for a general assault. At one o'clock in the morning of 17 [29] April, the force covertly moved towards Zerbau. At the same time, the demolition vessel approached the bridge, but was stopped 30 paces away, because the enemy had obstructed the course of the Alte Oder [Stara Odra] with a boom. Noticing the approaching boat, the French began to fire at it, which forced the crew to light the fuse and hurriedly swim for the shore. As soon as the explosion occurred, all three columns charged towards Zerbau: the Russians attacked in the centre, the Prussians on the flanks. Despite the many barricades erected in the village, the Coalition took possession of it and forced the enemy to retreat across the bridge into the fortress, but when they rushed at the bridge, they were engaged with fierce fire from heavy guns and were forced to stop. Thus, the outcome of this attack was limited to the razing of the village of Zerbau and its windmills.[38]

In May, the blockade corps was reinforced by several battalions of *Schlesisches Landwehr*. At the same time, four Prussian reserve battalions were sent to join the army. Upon the arrival of the siege artillery from Breslau, on the night of 24 to 25 April [6 to 7 May], the first trenches were opened, which led to a rather heated fight the next day, from which there were around 100 casualties on the Coalition side, and some 260 on the French side. News of the results of the battle of Bautzen forced General von Senden to send the siege artillery up the Oder to Breslau.[39] Subsequently, on 14 (26) May, having received orders to raise the blockade of Glogau (as was mentioned in Chapter 11), he detached his Russian contingent to Polnisch-Lissa and sent the *Landwehr* battalions to Schweidnitz, while he positioned himself in front of Breslau with the rest of the force, numbering 4,400 men with 12 guns, having received some reinforcements, and then retreated up the Oder.

38 Siege Diary for Glogau, Log of Incoming Documents, No. 767.
39 Plotho, I, 238-239.

Appendix XXIV

Composition of Lieutenant General Löwis' corps, according to returns dated 16 [28] February, signed by Prince Kutuzov-Smolensky

Unit	Men
Nizov Infantry	168
Azov Infantry	484
Navaginsk Infantry	562
Tula Infantry	401
Bryansk Infantry	844
Neva Infantry	340
Petrovsk Infantry	327
Lithuania Infantry	164
Voronezh Infantry	283
3rd Jägers	304
44th Jägers	1,065
Combined Infantry & Jägers	760
1st Marines and 2nd Marines	2,365
Infantry Total:	**8,067**
Combined Dragoons	207
Kazan Dragoons	299
Yamburg Ulans	320
Poland Ulans, replacement & reserve squadrons	121
Yakhontov's Volunteer Regiment	257
Schmitt's and Nirod's *Freikorps*	111
Cavalry Total:	**1,315**
Ilovaisky 3rd's Cossacks	206
Ilovaisky 5th's Cossacks	236
Kharitonov 7th's Cossacks	205
Grekov 17th's Cossacks	195
Suchilin's Cossacks	150

Unit	Men
Ilovaisky 10th's Cossacks	201
Grekov 1st's Cossacks	197
Grekov 5th's Cossacks	257
Simferopol Tatars	147
Perekop Tatars	138
Cossack Total:	**1,932**
5th Battery Artillery Company – 12 guns	157
6th Battery Artillery Company – 12 guns	204
10th Light Artillery Company – 12 guns	151
11th Light Artillery Company – 12 guns	158
40th Light Artillery Company – 12 guns	160
55th Light Artillery Company – 4 guns	41
3rd Horse Artillery Company – 12 guns	218
19th Horse Artillery Company – 12 guns	166
Artillery Total – 88 guns:	**1,255**
Captain Gerua's Pioneer Company	82
Löwis' Corps Total:	**12,651**

Appendix XXV

Composition of Herzog Alexander von Württemberg's corps, in April 1813

Division	Unit	Men
6th Division	Nizov Infantry	214
	Azov Infantry	358
	Bryansk Infantry	408
	3rd Jägers	248
21st Division	Neva Infantry	214
	Petrovsk Infantry	195
	Lithuania Infantry	276
	Podolia Infantry	282
	44th Jägers	658
25th Division	Voronezh Infantry	236
	1st Marines	229
	2nd Marines	504
	1st Combined Infantry	457
	2nd Combined Infantry	644
	3rd Combined Infantry	461
	4th Combined Infantry	664
St Petersburg *Opolchenie*	Five groups with the Voronezh Infantry	474
	Three groups with the Neva Infantry	323
	One group with the Lithuania Infantry	195
Novgorod *Opolchenie*	Two groups with the Nizov Infantry	239
	Two groups with the 3rd Jägers	131
	Infantry Total:	**7,410**
	Combined Dragoons – four squadrons	209
	Kazan Dragoons – three squadrons	250
	Yamburg Ulans – four squadrons	339
	Cavalry Total:	**798**
	Kharitonov 7th's Cossacks	297
	Chernozubov 8th's Cossacks	245
	Yagodin's Cossacks	37
	Grekov 17th's Cossacks	279

Division	Unit	Men
	Suchilin 2nd's Cossacks	264
	Ilovaisky 10th's Cossacks	372
	Grekov 1st's Cossacks	226
	Grekov 5th's Cossacks	389
	Simferopol Tatars	203
	Perekop Tatars	231
	Schmitt's *Freikorps*	108
	Nirod's *Freikorps*	36
	Cossack Total:	**2,687**
	6th Battery Artillery Company – 12 guns	257
	10th Light Artillery Company – 12 guns	200
	11th Light Artillery Company – 11 guns	55
	40th Light Artillery Company – 12 guns	181
	19th Horse Artillery Company – 12 guns	186
	Artillery Total – 59 guns:	**879**
	Herzog Alexander von Württemberg's Corps Total:	**11,776**

Extracted from a report on the composition of the blockading force at Danzig, signed by Herzog Alexander von Württemberg, Log of Incoming Documents, No. 743.

Appendix XXVI

Composition of Lieutenant General Paskevich's corps, from returns dated 23 February [7 March], signed by Prince Kutuzov-Smolensky

Division	Unit	Men
12th Division	Smolensk Infantry	254
	Narva Infantry	319
	Alexopol Infantry	259
	6th Jägers	431
13th Division	Saratov Infantry	684
	Veliky Luki Infantry	900
	Galits Infantry	545
26th Division	Ladoga Infantry	237
	Poltava Infantry	190
	Orël Infantry	232
	9th Jägers	382
	Infantry Total:	**4,433**
	Siberia Ulans	107
	Orenburg Ulans	129
	Regular Cavalry Total:	**236**
	Vlasov 2nd's Cossacks	259
	Andriyanov 2nd's Cossacks	323
	Andriyanov 3rd's Cossacks	384
	Shamshev 2nd's Cossacks	292
	Danilov 2nd's Cossacks	210
	2nd Kalmyks	265
	Irregular Cavalry Total:	**1,733**
	26th Battery Artillery Company – 12 guns	186
	47th Light Artillery Company – 12 guns	73
	18th Light Artillery Company – 12 guns	159
	19th Light Artillery Company – 12 guns	164
	Artillery Total – 48 guns:	**582**
	Lieutenant General Paskevich's Corps Total:	**6,984**

Appendix XXVII

Composition of comte Saint-Priest's detachment, from Flügel-Adjutant Colonel Sipyagin's report No. 241 to Adjutant General Prince Volkonsky dated 1 [13] March

Unit	**Men**
Vyatka Infantry	873
Olonets Infantry	479
11th Jägers	495
37th Jägers	459
Infantry Total:	**2,306**
Kiev Dragoons	198
Kharkov Dragoons	202
Akhtyrka Hussars	608
Chuguev Ulans	558
Lithuania Ulans	90
Regular Cavalry Total:	**1,656**
2nd Ukrainian Cossacks	502
Chernozubov's Don Cossacks	116
Melentiev's Cossacks	72
Slyusarev's Cossacks	33
Irregular Cavalry Total:	**723**
2nd Battery Artillery Company – four guns	49
44th Light Artillery Company – six guns	63
4th Horse Artillery Company – eight guns	109
Artillery Total – 18 guns:	**221**
Lieutenant Colonel Gebener's Pioneer Company	64
Comte Saint-Priest's Detachment Total:	**4,970**

16

The deployment of the forces of both sides upon the conclusion of the armistice

The locations of Wittgenstein's army, Langéron's corps (formerly the Western Army), Blücher's Prussian army, Sacken's corps and Wintzingerorde's corps, the reserves. – Precautionary measures taken by the Coalition army. – The locations of Bülow's Prussian corps, Vorontsov's detachment and the Crown Prince of Sweden's corps. – The locations of Napoleon's forces.

Based on the armistice agreement, orders were issued by both sides to immediately withdraw their troops from the mutually recognised neutral zone between the demarcation lines. While, an assembly was convened in Neumarkt in order to avoid clashes between forces and to monitor the exact fulfilment of the conditions relating to the delineation of the sectors they occupied, the authorised Russians were: Adjutant General Count Shuvalov and *Flügel-Adjutant* Colonel Orlov. For the Prussians: *Generalleutnant* Kleist and *Oberstleutnant* Valentini [Georg Wilhelm von Valentini] of the *Generalstab*, and for the French: *général de division* Dumoustier and Emperor Napoleon's aide de camp *général de brigade* Flahaut.

The Russo-Prussian Coalition army, under the command of Barclay de Tolly, was located as follows:[1]

General-of-Cavalry Count Wittgenstein's army (excluding the vanguard) numbering 20,000 men with 48 guns were in positions around Pilzen. His vanguard, commanded by comte Saint-Priest, was between Striegau and Schweidnitz with the detachments under Emmanuel, Rüdiger [Fëdor Vasilievich Ridiger or Friedrich Alexander von Rüdiger] and Kaisarov, numbering 12,000 men with 48 guns. Their forward outposts occupied a line starting from the Bohemian border at Dittersbach down the Bober to Rudelstadt, then through Bolkenhain to Striegau and along the Striegau river to the road from Kostenblut [Kostomłoty, 21 miles west of Breslau] to Ebersdorf [Dzikowa, 25 miles south-west of Breslau].

General-of-Infantry comte Langéron's corps (excluding the vanguard), numbering 9,000 men with 84 guns, were around Heidersdorf [Łagiewniki, ten

1 For the composition of Coalition forces, see Appendix XXVIII at the end of this chapter.

miles east of Reichenbach (Dzierżoniów)]. His vanguard, commanded by Major General Rudzevich, numbering 3,000 men with 12 guns, were around Wernersdorf [Wojnarowice, 19 miles south-west of Breslau]. The left flank of their outposts adjoined the outposts of Wittgenstein's army and extended from there along the Striegau river to the town of Kanth, strongly garrisoned by jägers and cavalry.

General der Kavallerie Blücher's Prussian army, with an overall strength of 34,600 men with 146 guns, were in positions around Strehlen. His vanguard, commanded by *Generalmajor* Corswant, was between Wiltschau [Wilczków, 11 miles south of Breslau] and Peltschütz [Pełczyce, 12 miles south of Breslau], his outposts ran from Kanth to Oltaschin.

Lieutenant General Sacken's corps, numbering 9,000 men with 48 guns, and *Generalmajor* Schuler von Senden's Prussian detachment, numbering 6,000 men, were around Ohlau (from 5 (17) June Senden's detachment garrisoned the fortress of Schweidnitz). General Sacken's vanguard, commanded by Major General Yurkovsky [Anastasy Antonovich Yurkovsky], was around Kattern [Święta Katarzyna, seven miles south-east of Breslau]. Their outposts ran from Oltaschin to the river Oder. An independent detachment occupied Hundsfeld [Psie Pole, five miles east of Breslau], stretching a line of outposts along the right bank of the river Weide [Widawa] to its confluence with the Oder [9½ miles downstream of Breslau]. The detachment under Major General Lanskoy was around Wohlau [Wołów]. Their outposts stretched from the mouth of the Weide to Steinau.

Adjutant General Wintzingerode's detachment, numbering 9,000 men with 48 guns, were around Polnisch-Lissa. His forward detachments held Fraustadt, Schlichtingsheim [Szlichtyngowa, eight miles east of Glogau], Herrnstadt [Wąsosz] and Trachenberg [Żmigród]. His outposts ran down the Oder from Steinau to Crossen.

Lieutenant General Raevsky's III Corps (Grenadier), numbering 8,000 men, Lieutenant General Lavrov's V Corps (Lifeguard), numbering 7,300 men, and the Prussian Guard Brigade, numbering 7,000 men, were around Reichenbach [Dzierżoniów]. The three cuirassier divisions, numbering 4,000 men, the Lifeguard Light Cavalry Division, numbering 1,000 men and the Lifeguard Horse Artillery, were on both banks of the Schlesische Neiße [Nysa Kłodzka] between Grottkau [Grodków] and Falkenberg [Niemodlin, 12½ miles south-east of Grottkau]. The reserve artillery, numbering around 5,000 men with 300 guns, were between Frankenstein [Ząbkowice Śląskie] and Münsterberg [Ziębice].[2]

The troops of the Coalition army were ordered to settle in concentrated quarters in the vicinity of the locations assigned to them, with the exception of the vanguards, who lived in bivouacs. The line of outposts was divided into sectors subordinated to formation commanders, who were to supervise the strictest observance of normal military precautions, both to protect against surprise attack by enemy forces, and to intercept all communications between the inhabitants of the territory in which the Coalition was located and those in the demilitarised zone or territory occupied by

2 In general, all the Russian reserves came under the Tsarevich Grand Duke Konstantin Pavlovich's command.

the enemy. All suspect individuals were ordered to be detained or sent away under orders.

In order to relay signals between units on the outpost line and to their parent units, beacons were constructed on dominant features, at which sentry posts were also established. In the event of beacons being lit, the troops were to assemble at pre-designated locations and station themselves in the positions assigned to them. To ensure the uninterrupted transfer of information, dispatch rider posts were established between the main headquarters of the Coalition army and the corps under Blücher and Sacken.[3]

Emperor Alexander's headquarters were in Schloss Peterswaldau [Pałac w Pieszycach], a distance of one *Meile* (about seven *verstas*) [west] of Reichenbach, while that of the King of Prussia was in the village of Neudorf [Nowizna], on the Schweidnitz road, ¾ of a *Meile* [north] of Reichenbach and ¼ of a *Meile* from Peterswaldau. Commander-in-Chief Barclay de Tolly's headquarters were in Reichenbach.[4]

Bülow's Prussian corps was located in the vicinity of Berlin, where the corps *Hauptquartier* was located. The vanguard was around Mittenwalde, the outposts along the Mark border.

Count Vorontsov's detachment, numbering 5,000 men with 24 guns,[5] was on the Havel and in Brandenburg. The Cossack outposts of his detachment ran from Brük to the Elbe.[6]

The corps under the Crown Prince of Sweden, which had arrived in Stralsund on 6 (18) May, numbering around 24,000 men with 62 guns,[7] having linked up with the combined corps under Graf Wallmoden, for the duration of the armistice, was deployed to shield Mecklenburg and Swedish Pomerania, as follows: Wallmoden's force along the right bank of the lower Elbe. His headquarters were in Boizenburg. His vanguard, commanded by Major General Tettenborn, was around Lauenburg. His outposts ran from Dassow [13 miles east of Lübeck] to the Ratzeburger See, and onwards along the course of the river Stecknitz. Having reached a point one *Meile* from Lauenburg, the line of outposts crossed to the right bank of the Stecknitz and described an arc half a *Meile* from Lauenburg to the Elbe. The Swedish 1st Division under *Generallöjtnant* Sandels [Johan August Sandels] were stationed in quarters between Gadebusch, Schwerin and Wismar, together with the *Mecklenburgisches Landwehr.* The Swedish 2nd Division under *Generalmajor* Bosse was based around Rostock. The 3rd Swedish Division under *Generallöjtnant* Skjöldebrand [Anders Fredrik Skjöldebrand], was between Tribsees and Grimmen. The reserve was around Richtenberg and Franzburg [11 to 15 miles south-west of Stralsund]. The

3 Dispositions, signed by Quartermaster General Diebitsch, dated 24 May [5 June], Log of Incoming Documents, No. 1,138.

4 Dispositions, signed by Diebitsch; Plotho, *Der Krieg in Deutschland und Frankreich in den Jahren 1813 und 1814*, I, 252.

5 Count Vorontsov's report dated 21 May [2 June].

6 Plotho, I, *appendices*, 165-167.

7 Plotho, II, *appendices*, 54.

Huvudkontor [headquarters] of the Crown Prince and *Fältmarskalk* [field marshal] Stedingk [Curt von Stedingk] were located in Stralsund.[8]

Napoleon's *quartier général* was moved to Dresden on 29 May (10 June). His forces, upon the conclusion of the armistice, were located as follows:

The *Vieille Garde* division under Laborde [Henri François Delaborde] was forwards of Dresden, on the right bank of the Elbe. The *Jeune Garde*, commanded by Marshal Mortier, were encamped around Polkwitz [Polkowice], near Glogau. Marshal Davout's *1er Corps*, had their *quartier général* at Hamburg. Marshal Victor's *2e Corps* were around Grünberg [Zielona Góra] in Silesia. The *3e Corps*, under Marshal Ney, were around Liegnitz. *Général de division* Bertrand's *4e Corps* were around Sprottau. *Général de division* Lauriston's *5e Corps* were around Goldberg. The *6e Corps*, under Marshal Marmont, were around Thomaswaldau [Tomaszów Bolesławiecki, 5½ miles east of Bunzlau]. The *7e Corps*, commanded by *général de division* Reynier, were around Görlitz. The Poles of *8e Corps*, under *général de division* Poniatowski, were on the march from Austrian territory and were thereafter deployed around Zittau. *Général de division* Rapp's *10e Corps* were in Danzig. Marshal Macdonald's *11e Corps* were around Greiffenberg and Friedeberg [Mirsk, 5½ miles south of Greiffenberg] in Silesia. Marshal Oudinot's *12e Corps* were around Cottbus in Lower Lusatia. The *9e Corps*, *13e Corps* and *14e Corps* had yet to be activated. The *1er Corps de cavalerie*, under *général de division* Latour-Maubourg, were around Sagan [Żagań]. *Général de division* Sébastiani's *2e Corps de cavalerie* were around Nieder Siegersdorf [Podbrzezie Dolne, two miles north of Freystadt] in Silesia. *Général de division* Arrighi's corps were around Leipzig. Marshal Augereau's *Corps d'observation* were forming up on the Main, around Würzburg.[9]

The population of the area under French military occupation endured all kinds of abuse during the armistice. Upper Silesia and the parts of Lower Silesia in which the Russo-Prussian army were located, were devastated by the constant presence of a huge number of troops there, reaching some 300,000 men by the end of the armistice. Those Silesian *Landkreise* [districts] in the accepted neutral zone were in an incomparably better situation, namely: Hirschberg [Jelenia Góra], Jauer, Leignitz, Neumarkt and the majority of Breslau, including the city itself.[10]

8 Disposition by the Swedish Crown Prince, dated 19 June, new style.
9 Plotho, I, 255; Fain, *Manuscrit de 1813*, II, 4.
10 Plotho, I, 252-253.

Appendix XXVIII

Composition of the Coalition forces in early June 1813

Count Wittgenstein's army, extracted from the report on the strength of forces dated 1 [13] June 1813, signed by Commander-in-Chief Barclay de Tolly, Archive of the M.T.D. No. 46,692.

Formation	Combat Arm	Officers	Men
Comte Saint-Priest's Vanguard	Infantry	381	8,634
	Regular Cavalry	14	234
	Irregular Cavalry	88	2,187
	Artillery	24	836
Vanguard Total (with 48 guns):			**12,398**
Lieutenant General Olsufiev's Corps	Infantry	275	6,909
	Artillery	15	371
Lieutenant General Prinz Eugen von Württemberg's Corps	Infantry	308	8,228
	Artillery	12	364
Major General Melissino's Cavalry	Cavalry	164	3,326
Main Body Total (with 48 guns):			**19,972**
Army Total (with 96 guns):			**32,370**

Comte Langéron's corps, extracted from the report on the strength of forces dated 1 [13] June 1813, signed by Commander-in-Chief Barclay de Tolly.

Formation	Combat Arm	Officers	Men
Vanguard	Infantry	29	973
	Regular Cavalry	40	694
	Irregular Cavalry	42	962
	Artillery	5	150
Vanguard Total (with 12 guns):			**2,895**
Main Body	Infantry	234	6,407
	Cavalry	85	1,352
	Artillery	56	1,236
Main Body Total (with 84 guns):			**9,370**
Corps Total (with 96 guns):			**12,265**

Blücher's Army, from the report on the strength of forces dated 1 [13] June 1813, signed by Commander-in-Chief Barclay de Tolly.

Formation	Combat Arm	Officers	Men
Generalleutnant Kleist's Corps[1]	Infantry	329	16,468
	Cavalry	122	2,976
	Artillery	39	1,429
Kleist's Corps Total (with 80 guns):			**21,363**
Generalleutnant Yorck's Corps	Infantry	254	10,544
	Cavalry	73	1,588
	Artillery	20	687
	Pioneers	1	32
Yorck's Corps Total (with 66 guns):			**13,199**
Army Total (with 146 guns):			**34,562**

Sacken's Force, extracted from the report on the strength of forces dated 1 [13] June 1813, signed by Commander-in-Chief Barclay de Tolly.

Formation	Combat Arm	Officers	Men
Sacken's Force	Infantry	178	4,633
	Regular Cavalry	121	2,047
	Irregular Cavalry	36	1,306
	Artillery	26	769
Sacken's Total (with 48 guns):			**9,116**

Wintzingerode's Detachment, extracted from the report on the strength of forces dated 10 [22] June 1813, signed by Commander-in-Chief Barclay de Tolly, Archive of the M.T.D. No. 46,692.

Formation	Unit	Officers	Men
21st Division	Neva Infantry	28	526
	Petrovsk Infantry	30	652
	Lithuania Infantry	30	525
	Podolia Infantry	32	665
	44th Jäger	31	996
24th Division	Shirvan Infantry	35	497
	Butyrsk Infantry	39	505
	Ufa Infantry	28	453
	Tobolsk Infantry (one battalion)	9	378
	19th Jägers (replacement battalion)	11	268
	Infantry Total:	**273**	**5,465**

1 Including the reserve guards brigade.

Formation	Unit	Officers	Men
Regular Cavalry	St Petersburg Dragoons	17	324
	Yelisavetgrad Hussars	46	510
	Regular Cavalry Total:	**63**	**834**
Irregular Cavalry	Ilovaisky 4th's Cossacks	11	401
	Barabanshchikov 2nd's Cossacks	13	186
	Panteleev 2nd's Cossack	14	353
	Formerly Belogorodtsov's Cossacks	6	246
	1st Bug Cossacks	13	318
	3rd Ural Cossacks	13	287
	Yakhontov's Volunteer Cossacks	20	198
	Irregular Cavalry Total:	**90**	**1,989**
Artillery	31st Battery Artillery Company – 12 guns	5	182
	19th Light Artillery Company – 12 guns	5	164
	42nd Light Artillery Company – 12 guns	2	58
	46th Light Artillery Company – 12 guns	10	73
	Artillery Total – 48 guns:	**22**	**477**
Wintzingerode's Detachment Total (with 48 guns):			**9,170**

Tsarevich Grand Duke Konstantin Pavlovich's Reserve, extracted from the report on the strength of forces dated 1 [13] June 1813, signed by Barclay de Tolly.

Formation	Combat Arm	Officers	Men
Raevsky's III Corps (Grenadier)	Infantry	366	6,840
	Artillery – 48 guns	21	534
III Grenadier Corps Total:			**7,761**
Lavrov's V Corps (Lifeguard)	Infantry	359	6,557
	Artillery[2]– 50 guns	13	405
V Guard Corps Total:			**7,334**
Cuirassier Regiments	Cuirassiers[3]	197	3,685
Lifeguard Light Cavalry Division	Light Cavalry	81	1,036
	Artillery – 16 guns		
Cavalry Total:			**5,000**

The reserve artillery, excluding companies belonging to the foot and horse artillery reserves consisted of 159 officers and 4,700 lower ranks with 305 guns (extracted from the report on the strength of forces dated 10 [22] June, signed by Barclay de Tolly.

2 Including two Lifeguard companies and the artillery sub-unit of the Lifeguard Équipage. There were also two line companies whose manpower strength was not recorded.

3 Excluding the Starodub Cuirassiers, which are not shown in the manning return.

17

The armistice

Napoleon's attempts to form an alliance with Austria and Russia. – The agreement on subsidies.

Diplomatic relations between Napoleon and Austria. Austria's rapprochement with Russia and Prussia. – The reasons preventing Austria from overtly taking the side of the Coalition. – Duplicity in Austrian policy. – Schwarzenberg's visit to Paris. – Metternich's relations with the French Resident, Otto, and with the Russian Ambassador Count Stackelberg. – Lebzeltern's visit to Emperor Alexander's headquarters. – Comte Narbonne replaces Otto. – The wavering of the Austrian aristocracy. – Austria openly acknowledges the situation of an armed mediation. – The influence of Austrian policy on the Saxon King Friedrich-August. – Napoleon's cooling towards Austria and his readiness for rapprochement with Russia. – Napoleon's intentions.

Graf Bubna's visit to Napoleon in Dresden with an offer of Austrian mediation. – Napoleon's wishes for the treaty of alliance of 1812 to be respected. – Kaiser Franz arrives in Bohemia. – His meeting with the Coalition monarchs in Josefstadt. – The secret agreement between Austria, Russia and Prussia. – Metternich's visit to Dresden. – Napoleon's exasperation with Austria. – His conversations with Metternich. – The collapse of the treaty of alliance. – Formula for convening the Congress of Prague.

The armistice which temporarily suspended hostilities in 1813 would not lead to the conclusion of peace between the belligerent powers. The reason for this was the impossibility of deconflicting the points of view of the opposing parties. Napoleon, who owed his dominance over France and Europe to military success, could not sacrifice its fruits without losing his moral influence, which would inevitably have led to the demise of his regime. Although his victories had been bought at a high price and forced the desire for peace upon the French, an unfavourable peace would not satisfy the expectations of national pride. On the other hand, it was essential to compensate exhausted Europe for all the loss and abuses suffered over the course of many years – both by the people and their rulers. Up until this point, they only had themselves to blame that their efforts to throw off the foreign yoke that burdened them remained unfulfilled. Every coalition against France lacked unity of purpose: Prussia passively observed the misfortunes of Austria, which, for their part, permitted the complete subjugation of their neighbour – their ethnic kin. Britain, having incited the continental powers to take up arms against the common enemy, refused them subsidies, the only assistance that their allies needed, being richer in men and iron than in gold. But Europe's patience was already reaching its limit: governments were preparing to unite with each other for collective defence, and nations were preparing to support their efforts unanimously. A general coalition had not yet been sealed by agreement, but its necessity was obvious to all.

Napoleon, for all his genius, not appreciating the current state of affairs, believed that the European powers, even in this great era, would be driven by the craven motives that had dissolved the previous coalitions. Under the influence of such an erroneous belief, even prior to the armistice, he twice attempted to disrupt a coalition between the great continental powers. To that end, in April 1813, Napoleon offered to concede Silesia to the Austrian government and yet, as has already been mentioned, shortly before the battle of Bautzen, he wanted to send Caulaincourt to Emperor Alexander I with an offer of peace on terms which, although quite beneficial for Russia, would have sacrificed Germany to the ambitions of the conqueror. Napoleon wanted to extend the *Confédération du Rhin* as far as the Oder, expanding the Kingdom of Westphalia, and to give Prussia the Duchy of Warsaw and Danzig in exchange for the areas lying between the Elbe and the Oder. Thus, Prussia would have a Slav majority, Poland would lose its independence in perpetuity, and finally, dominance over Europe would be divided between Russia and France, separated by significant buffers.[1] We have already seen that Emperor Alexander, not having the personal benefits to His Empire as a priority, rather the restoration of general peace on solid foundations, would not consent to a visit by Caulaincourt to the headquarters of the Coalition army.

Hugely important negotiations were ongoing throughout the armistice. The British Administration, having rejected the proposal made to them – to conclude an alliance with the Viennese Court – due to distrust of its ambiguous relationship with Napoleon, considered it vital to unite with Russia and Prussia against the common enemy. On 2 and 3 (14 and 15) June, the representatives of the British Government, Lord Cathcart [William Schaw Cathcart] and Sir Charles Stewart [Charles William Stewart], signed two treaties on subsidies: under the terms of the former, Britain undertook to pay Prussia 666,666 pounds sterling (4,000,000 silver roubles) for the maintenance of 80,000 men for the remaining six months of 1813. In the specific secret articles of the treaty, the British monarch assumed the obligation, in the event of success for the Coalition armies, to assist with the expansion of Prussia to at least the same extent as it was before 1806, while the King of Prussia pledged to cede Bistum [Diocese] Hildesheim, with a population of 300,000 souls, in favour of Hanover.[2] The next day, the second treaty was signed, on the basis of which it was decided:

1 Norvins, *Portefeuille de 1813*, I, 406.
2 Treaty signed in Reichenbach by Sir Charles Stewart and Baron Hardenberg on 14 June, new style.

1. That on 1 January 1814, Britain would pay the Russian government 1,333,334 pounds sterling (8,000,000 silver roubles) for the maintenance of 160,000 men, and would assume the costs of supplying victuals to the Russian fleet stationed in British harbours, in the amount of some to 500,000 pounds sterling (3,000,000 silver roubles).
2. It was agreed to issue banknotes to the value of 5,000,000 pounds sterling (30,000,000 silver roubles), known as 'federation money' underwritten by Britain, Russia and Prussia. Two-thirds of this sum was placed at the disposal of Russia, and the remaining third to Prussia. Britain undertook to redeem half of this sum by 1 July, 1815, or six months after the conclusion of a general peace – one third to Russia and one sixth to Prussia.[3]

The most important of all the events that occurred during the armistice was the accession of Austria to the Coalition against Napoleon.

Even before the Berezina crossing, marking the end of the existence of the *Grande Armée*, the Austrian government was secretly leaning towards hostility to France. From subsequent diplomatic correspondence it emerged that Kaiser Franz advised the King of Prussia at that time: 'not to stifle the noble passion that has prompted Prussia to gather the resources to cooperate in the efforts of the Russian Emperor to defend the independence of Europe.'[4] The destruction of the *Grande Armée* dealt the final blow to the forced alliance between Austria and Napoleon, and this was revealed at the end of 1812 from the half-hearted operations by Schwarzenberg, which can only be explained by assuming that he had been given secret instructions in the event of the defeat of Napoleon's hordes, or that he was privy to a secret Austrian policy, which had already taken this new direction. Many personalities in the Imperial Household, the entire aristocracy, and the population in general, sympathised with Russia and Prussia, but Kaiser Franz did not dare to take up arms himself against his son-in-law. The reasons for his hesitation were: fear of Napoleon's might and the unsatisfactory state of the armed forces and of Austrian finances. In addition, the treaty of alliance concluded in 1812 and the family connections with Napoleon prevented the Austrian Kaiser from abruptly changing the political direction taken by the Viennese Cabinet. Neither common law nor public opinion allowed him to take advantage of the disaster that had befallen the French army in Russia. All these factors forced him to adopt a wait-and-see attitude, and Austria, in all likelihood, would even have remained on Napoleon's side if he had made some concessions in their favour at this time.

The position of the Viennese Cabinet was very awkward: their joining either of the belligerent factions would achieve a decisive outcome only if Austria had time and resources to raise a powerful army. It was vital to lull Napoleon's vigilance: this was not easy, but Metternich's mental agility and Kaiser Franz's feigned straightforwardness achieved the desired end. Napoleon was right not to trust the Austrian

3 Treaty signed in Reichenbach by Lord Cathcart and Baron Anstett on 15 June, new style.
4 Metternich's letter to Hardenberg, dated 22 October 1814, new style. *Lebensbilder aus dem Befreiungskriege*, III, 444.

Government, yet despite this, he relied utterly on the amity of his father-in-law and did not suspect that the Kaiser's views were in alignment with Metternich's policies.

At the beginning of 1813, the Viennese Cabinet did their best to reassure Napoleon that the treaty of alliance concluded nine months earlier remained binding on both parties. Then, having begun to raise an army, the Austrians began to discuss mediation. Upon their successful mobilisation, there was talk of armed mediation. At the Congress of Prague, Austria took on the role of resolving the dispute between the belligerent powers, and eventually openly rose up against Napoleon.

At the same time that Kaiser Franz was advising King Friedrich Wilhelm 'not to stifle the noble passions of his people' Metternich wrote to Paris: 'nothing could be more disastrous or more contrary to the personal conviction of His Majesty the Kaiser of Austria than the severance of sacred ties between sovereigns and peoples, distancing – as in Prussia – the Monarch from his subjects.' In Kaiser Franz's response to Napoleon's letter from Dresden, we find: 'I shall never renounce the alliance with France and shall always take care of the Napoleonic dynasty as if it were my own.'[5] A little earlier, the Fürst zu Schwarzenberg had been sent to Paris 'in order to receive orders as commander of the Austrian corps attached to the French army.'[6] It was much more difficult to deceive the French envoy in Vienna, comte Otto, yet Metternich also succeeded in this. From Otto's reports to *ministre des Affaires étrangères* Maret, it appeared that, despite the hostility of public opinion towards the French, he was convinced of the unwavering loyalty of the Austrian Government towards Napoleon. Comte Otto wrote in one of his dispatches to the minister: 'Mr. de Metternich spoke for half an hour with a perfect outpouring from the heart regarding Austria's intentions and their entire devotion to our cause.'[7] Having received word from Berlin regarding the defection of Yorck's corps, Metternich invited the French ambassador to his residence. 'This is proof of that which I have so often told you about the Greek loyalty (*Groeca fides*) of the Russians,' he told him. Then, having mentioned his intention to send a reliable diplomatic officer to Vilna to discover Emperor Alexander's intentions, Metternich continued: 'we have an idea of your immense resources; we know what you have done and what you can do. In addition to the 7,000,000 pounds sterling granted to Russia by the British government, they offered us 10,000,000. Yet we rejected this proposal with contempt, despite the extreme disarray of our finances.'[8] Metternich's duplicity and secrecy extended to the point that neither the French Resident nor Count Stackelberg, representative of the Russian Government to Vienna, could unravel his intentions. When

5 *Lebensbilder*, III, 450-451.

6 Schwarzenberg was instructed: 'to inform the *Empereur des Français* regarding the current state of affairs and to demonstrate Austria's position to Europe through your appearance at the French Court as the commander of an auxiliary corps, sent to his commander-in-chief in order to receive orders from him.' Metternich's own words spoken to comte Otto on 14 February, new style. Extracted from Otto's letter to the duc de Bassano (Maret), dated 15 February 1813, new style.

7 '*M. de Metternich a parlé pendant une demiheure avec une effusion de coeur parfaite des intentions de l'Autriche et de son entier dévouement à notre cause.*' Otto's letter to Maret dated 8 January 1813, new style.

8 Comte Otto's letter dated 11 January, new style.

Stackelberg, having recounted the victories achieved by the Russians, stated that 'Emperor Alexander, having repelled the French invasion, intended to assist other powers, and especially Austria, to regain lost territories,' Metternich replied: 'The policy adopted by our Sovereign remains unchanged: he does not seek acquisitions bought at a high price, but has in mind only the preservation of peace and invites you to assist in this. We have had the opportunity to explore the French points of view and found them appropriate to our interests. We do not complain about our losses and believe that other powers have no right to care about them more than ourselves.' Amazed by the moderation of the Austrian diplomat, Count Stackelberg announced to him that the Russian government was completely ready to open peace talks. 'The Russian question has been resolved.' He said: 'It remains to settle the general affairs of Europe.' Metternich, disappointed with this answer and not wanting the belligerent powers to make peace at all without Austria's participation, interrupted Count Stackelberg's speech, noting that the Viennese Cabinet did not intend to negotiate at all, but merely wanted to know whether Russia agreed to the convening of talks.[9]

A consequence of this meeting was Lebzeltern's visit to Emperor Alexander's headquarters. The cunning Metternich knew how to present this mission in the most favourable light to Otto's eyes. In his words, 'Lebzeltern was ordered only to discuss peace and to limit himself to hints that, were the war to continue, the Russians might suffer setbacks and have to make peace on less favourable terms than at present... This has not been Austria's war thus far. If it became one in the future, then we would not put up just 30,000 men against the Russians, but the entire strength of the monarchy.'[10] Austria mobilised its army using the pretext of securing their own borders, which, according to Metternich, had the sole purpose of accelerating the pace towards peace.[11]

The Austrian government had been in constant communication with Napoleon's enemies since the opening months of 1813. No sooner had Russian troops entered East Prussia, than Metternich tried his best to convince Count Wittgenstein to advance quickly to the Oder and Elbe, promising assistance from Austria.[12] Baron Wessenberg [Johann Philipp von Wessenberg-Ampringen] was sent secretly from Vienna, via Denmark, to London to negotiate with the British government, in a completely different spirit than the mission sent to Napoleon, while on 2 (14) March, Lebzeltern went to Kalisz where the headquarters of the Coalition sovereigns was located at the time, with verbal assurances about Austria's readiness to join the Coalition: thus, the Viennese Cabinet, not being inconvenienced with binding obligations, had the opportunity to buy some time. As has already been explained above, following the departure of the Fürst zu Schwarzenberg, the Austrian auxiliary corps moved from the Duchy of Warsaw to Galicia under the command of Baron Frimont, on the basis of a convention concluded by Lebzeltern in Kalisz. After the Austrians had withdrawn into this region, they entered into an agreement with the Russians regarding a truce. All this was reported to the King of Prussia, but was kept secret

9 Comte Otto's letter to Maret dated 26 January, new style.
10 Also from comte Otto's letter to Maret dated 26 January, new style.
11 Comte Otto's letter to Maret dated 17 February, new style.
12 Garden, *Histoire générale des traités de paix*, XIV, 160.

from the French government. The Viennese aristocracy, distancing themselves as far as possible from the former republican comte Otto, hid the truth from him, but Napoleon, with his characteristic insight, realised that much remained unknown to his envoy, and that his personal qualities, a man of humble birth (*homme nouveau*), frank and straightforward, were interfering with the success of the mission assigned to him. A consequence of this was a change of French Resident. The man who took his place, *général de division* comte de Narbonne, a descendant of a family dating back to the 11th century, briefly acquainted with many in the highest circles in Vienna, could rightly be considered a representative of the ancient nobility of France. The Viennese aristocracy greeted him as a champion of the conservative revolution and its creation – the Napoleonic Empire. But this perception turned out to be completely false. Narbonne, loving his homeland more than the fallen Bourbon dynasty, saw Napoleon as the restorer of power and glory to France, and being completely devoted to him, took advantage of the gullibility of the Viennese nobility. The hostile Austrian policy towards France could not be hidden from him.

Meanwhile, very important events were taking place in Prussia: the defection of Yorck's corps, the independent uprising of East Prussia, without any participation by the government or even their knowledge, the call to the population for a general mobilisation, revealing the strength of popular sentiment, more terrifying to Austria than Napoleon's predominance. The appeal by Prince Kutuzov, dated 13 (25) March, from Kalisz, showed the intentions of the Coalition – to involve all of Germany in the struggle they had undertaken and to establish a *Deutscher Bund* [German Federation] with the assistance of the people. The ruling princes who had persisted in their loyalty to the common enemy, stood to lose their lands. All this worried the Austrian aristocrats to such an extent that they were ready to bend towards the French once more. The patriotic efforts of the population of Prussia were turned, under the pen of Metternich and his agents, into Jacobin attempts to dissolve the sacred bond between Sovereigns and their subjects.[13] Stein, Blücher, Yorck, men who had earned the respect of their peers and of posterity, were perceived as Jacobins! At the time that the northern Germans were dying the death of the brave on the battlefields of Lützen and Bautzen their passion was being ridiculed, with the permission of the censors, in every Viennese theatre.[14] But the public did not sympathise with these shameful suggestions, and therefore the Austrian government, concerned about being in complete discord with their subjects and not expecting any concessions from Napoleon, continued their relations with both belligerent parties. Upon Austria's successful mobilisation, the tone of their diplomacy changed.

The Fürst zu Schwarzenberg, arriving in Paris on 1 (13) April, and receiving an audience with Napoleon the next day, on the eve of his departure for the army, was confirmed as commander of the Austrian contingent. Napoleon said 'I am leaving, and a week ago orders were sent to General Frimont to resume operations. In the first days of May, I shall be on the right bank of the Elbe myself with 300,000 men. Austria may bring the strength of the *armée de Cracovie* (army in Galicia) to 150,000 men, raise a corps of 30,000 or 40,000 in Bohemia, and we could mount a general

13 *Lebensbider*, III, 450.
14 Bernhardi, *Denkwürdigkeiten des Grafen von Toll*, III, 10-11.

offensive against the Russians. By operating in this manner, we could secure Europe.' Schwarzenberg replied that, without any doubt, General Frimont would carry out the orders received from the *chef d'état-major* of the French army. Yet a few days later, on 10 (22) April, he sent a note to the French *ministre des Affaires étrangères*, in which he announced that in order to bring about peace, his government had no choice but armed mediation, and that the approaching hostilities at the borders of the Empire did not permit his Sovereign, in the event of a continuation of the war, to limit his participation to that of an auxiliary corps. Therefore, the terms of the treaty of 14 March, 1812 were no longer applicable in the present situation, but Austria's friendly relations with the French government remained unchanged.[15] When the comte de Narbonne sent Metternich a note in which he demanded that the Austrian auxiliary corps remain at the disposal of the *Empereur des Français* in pursuance of the treaty of 1812, Metternich, explaining the untimeliness of Austria's participation in the war as an auxiliary power, noted that the increase in its armed forces was in complete alignment with the plans of the French government, expressed by the comte de Narbonne himself on 7 [19] April.[16]

Thus, the Austrian government put itself in a position of self-determination, independent of France. Not content with this, Metternich tried to display the armed mediation of Austria to the German Courts in the form of a magnanimous deed undertaken in defence of their common fatherland, and managed to achieve this aim in relation to the King of Saxony. The retreat by the French army had forced Friedrich-August (as has been previously mentioned) to seek refuge first in Plauen and then in Regensburg. He approved a convention here, signed in Vienna on 27 March (8 April), on the basis of which it was agreed that the forces under Gablenz and Prince Poniatowski, having left the Duchy of Warsaw, could pass through Galicia, Moravia and Bohemia, and that all officers, non-commissioned officers and officials attached to these forces, could keep their side-arms. Upon their entry into Austrian territory, the firearms of the privates had to be carried on carts behind the forces, until their exit. Napoleon was extremely dissatisfied with these conditions, most particularly because a French battalion attached to Schwarzenberg's corps also had to pass through Austrian territory without weapons.[17] On the basis of another convention, King Friedrich-August undertook not to allow troops of any belligerent power into Torgau or Königstein (the only fortresses garrisoned by the Saxons) without the consent of the Austrian Kaiser. Following this, the King of Saxony went to Prague with the *Leibgrenadiergarde* and the *Kürassiere* brigade accompanying him, which made him completely dependent on Austria. After the battle of Lützen, once Napoleon had occupied Dresden and forced the King to return there, Friedrich-August handed over to him all his correspondence with the Viennese

15 Norvins, I, 177-178; *Le Moniteur*, 1813. From this it is clear that Austria arrived at the position of armed mediation, not as a result of the note submitted on 24 April (new style) by the comte de Narbonne, as Norvin asserts, stating: '*D'après le nouvel état de choses que venait de produire a Vienne l'imprudence du comte de Narbonne, le prince de Schwartzenberg reçut de sa cour de nouvelles instructions, et à la suile de la communication qu il en donna au duc de Bassano, la question de la médiation armée fut posée sans detour.*'

16 From Graf Metternich's note dated 26 April, new style.

17 The convention between Austria and Saxony of 8 April, new style; Norvins, I, 226-227.

Cabinet, which left no doubt about the duplicity of the Austrian government, while the intercepted dispatches of the Russian envoy to Vienna, Count Stackelberg, to Count Nesselrode convinced Napoleon even more that his hopes for the favour of Kaiser Franz were misplaced.[18]

The consequence of this was Napoleon's complete cooling towards Austria: in a dispatch from the duc de Vicence to the comte de Narbonne, dictated by him, we find: 'The Viennese Cabinet is mistaken. Graf Metternich vainly considers intrigue to be politics, yet politics leads to specific objectives, while intrigue involves contradictory acts that do not have a consistent aim. This is how the actions of the Viennese Cabinet appear to His Majesty. He is cunning yet all his machinations turn to his own detriment, while by acting directly and matching his demands to his own strengths and means, he would achieve the fulfilment of his objectives. It is easy to realise, even without particular forethought, that this meddling will bother Emperor Alexander as much as Emperor Napoleon, and might prompt these sovereigns to reach a bilateral agreement between themselves.'[19] In another dispatch to the comte de Narbonne, Napoleon demanded that he seek to reunite Poniatowski's corps and the battalion attached to the Austrian force with the French army. Caulaincourt wrote: 'The French battalion was ordered to march to Zittau. It would be better for the Emperor if they fought against the Austrians and were captured by them rather than to see them adrift.' Thereafter Napoleon calculated the strength of his armed forces, mentioned Metternich's ambiguous relations with the enemies of France once more, and spoke of his desire to maintain friendly relations with the House of Austria, if only this were possible. In the event of a breach, Napoleon threatened a rapprochement with the Russian government. The duc de Vicence wrote to Narbonne: 'A mission to the Russian headquarters would split the world in two.'[20]

The policies of the Viennese Cabinet were influenced by the outcome of the battle of Lützen. On 14 (26) April, while this was still impossible to foresee, Schwarzenberg announced to *ministre* Maret in Paris that his sovereign would soon notify Emperor Napoleon of the decisive measures which he intended to take in order to induce the Coalition powers to give a definitive explanation of their intentions. In a letter to Napoleon, delivered to him on 14 (26) May, by Graf Bubna, Kaiser Franz notified his son-in-law of the departure of Graf Stadion for the headquarters of the Russo-Prussian army. Kaiser Franz wrote: 'I have waited until this time, which I have long foreseen – precisely the time when the first action would have dampened passions and dispelled unrealisable dreams. That time has now come, and Your Majesty will have a most enviable destiny – to grant peace to the world after a brilliant feat… If you consider it best to support my efforts with moderation, which will glorify you and strengthen a fortunate future for Your Imperial Majesty, securing your dynasty, so closely connected with mine, on unshakable foundations, I shall consider myself fortunate to have taken part in such a useful undertaking…'[21] Despite the familial

18 Norvins, I, 326.
19 From the duc de Vicence's (Caulaincourt) letter to comte de Narbonne, dated 12 May new style.
20 '*Une mission au quartier-général russe partagerait le monde en deux.*' From Caulaincourt's letter to the comte de Narbonne, dated 14 May, new style.
21 From Kaiser Franz's letter to Napoleon, dated 11 May, new style.

tone of this letter, Napoleon was dissatisfied with the choice of Graf Stadion, his notorious enemy, for negotiations with Sovereigns hostile to him. Even more so as he had made an insulting reference to himself regarding the need to strengthen the dominance of his dynasty. In his response to Kaiser Franz, while expressing feelings of devotion to his father-in-law, he showed his customary inflexibility. Therefore, rightly doubting the good faith of Austria, he wrote: 'trusting entirely to your Majesty in the matter of my honour, which I value above dominion, more than life itself, I have firmly resolved to die with weapons in hand with all the gracious people of France rather than accept humiliating conditions.'[22] Yet the less he trusted in assistance for his intentions from Kaiser Franz, the more he should have been compliant and satisfied the requests of the Viennese Cabinet, which could not have been onerous in the wake of his victory. On the contrary, Napoleon decided to suddenly change his policy and attempted to enter into direct relations with Emperor Alexander. But the duc de Vicence, who was entrusted with these negotiations, did not even get a chance of permission to appear at the headquarters of the Coalition army. However, the foundations of peace themselves outlined by Napoleon were such that the Russian Monarch, in accepting them, would clearly violate the obligations he had assumed in relation to Prussia, Sweden, Britain and Austria.[23] The demarcation of Europe proposed by Napoleon was far from satisfying Russian and Prussian interests. On 4 (16) May, Graf Stadion received a note from the Coalition courts containing the following terms:

1. The dissolution of the Duchy of Warsaw and its partition between Russia, Austria and Prussia, without French interference.
2. The expansion of Prussia as a result of this partition and the concession of Danzig with its environs. The evacuation of French forces from all fortresses in Prussia and the Duchy of Warsaw.
3. The return of the Illyrian provinces to Austria.
4. The liberation of the *Hansestädte*, or at least Hamburg and Lübeck with their environs, and the cession of all lands annexed in the *32e division militaire* of the Empire of the French.
5. The dissolution of the *Confédération du Rhin*.
6. The restoration of Prussia, where possible, within the borders existing before 1806.[24]

Napoleon wishing, in all probability, to eliminate the unfavourable impression made by his failed attempt at rapprochement with Russia and to show his subjects an inclination towards peace, announced that he proposed convening a congress in Prague, with representation on one side from France, the United States of America, Denmark, Spain and all powers allied to them, while on the other side would be Britain, Russia and the Cortes of Cádiz (Sweden was deliberately omitted). At the

22 Norvins, I, 394-395; Thiers, *Histoire du Consulat et de l'Empire*, XV, *Edit. de Brux.* 618.
23 Instructions for Caulaincourt; Norvins, I, 404-407.
24 A copy of this note was attached to the instructions issued to Anstett for his visit to Prague (Archive of the M.F.A.).

same time, it was made public that an armistice would proceed once negotiations had opened in order to avoid unnecessary bloodshed.[25]

Napoleon's victory at Bautzen strengthened the desire of the Viennese Cabinet to end the conflict with France peacefully. No sooner had Napoleon returned to Dresden, on 29 May (10 June), than Graf Bubna (who had returned once more) submitted a note to the duc de Bassano (Maret), and having announced the Russian and Prussian courts' acceptance of Austrian mediation, he wished to bring to the attention of the *Empereur des Français* the principles of the peace treaty proposed by them. At the same time, the Austrian government also expressed a desire to know the terms that would be offered by France. The Viennese Court, in offering its assistance and, in order to speed matters up, intended to limit themselves to a peace treaty between the continental powers, which was intended to facilitate or prepare for the establishment of a general peace in Europe.[26] Napoleon saw the inevitability of Austria's mediation but his pride could not bear the thought of making himself dependent on the state to which he had dictated peace terms on four occasions. Instead of a direct response to the Austrian note, Napoleon demanded to know whether the treaty of 2 (14) March 1812 remained extant. This led to correspondence between the respective foreign ministers, Maret and Metternich, which did not advance them towards a desirable outcome in the slightest.[27] Metternich's arrival in Dresden on 15 (27) June also did nothing to speed things up, despite a concession by the Austrian government, which permitted Poniatowski's corps to pass through Moravia and Bohemia in order to rejoin the French army. As soon as Napoleon had, to some extent, satisfied Austrian demands they would, in all probability, not have taken part in the struggle that was intended to decide the fate of Germany. But Napoleon, instead of acting on the basis of cool-headed reason, was carried away by his lust for power and missed a favourable opportunity to dissolve the formidable Coalition. For the Austrian government, which had very accurate intelligence regarding everything that was happening in the theatre of war, it could not have been a secret that although Napoleon had won victories at Lützen and Bautzen, he had not managed to exploit his success. The fate of the war, the fate of Germany, still remained unknown. It was up to Austria to resolve the issue by joining one or other of the belligerent parties and they had to do this because they could not take advantage of the benefits of their position by remaining neutral. As no concessions were to be forthcoming from Napoleon, the Austrian government eventually leaned towards the Russian and Prussian side, who had publicly announced their intention to compensate the German rulers hostile to France for their losses.

A few days later, after the conclusion of the armistice, on 31 May (12 June), Kaiser Franz arrived at Schloss Jitschin [Jičín], the ancestral home of the renowned Wallenstein [Albrecht Wenzel Eusebius von Waldstein] in Bohemia, with his entire court and the highest state dignitaries. The purpose of the Austrian Kaiser's trip was to get closer to the theatre of war and the imminent negotiations. Among the main

25 *Le Moniteur*, Monday, 24 May, new style.
26 Graf Bubna's note dated 11 June, new style.
27 Maret's notes dated 15 and 27 June, new style, and Metternich's dated 22 and 28 June, new style; Norvins, II, 99-102.

personalities accompanying him were Graf Metternich and the celebrated publicist Gentz [Friedrich von Gentz]. On 8 (20) June, the Coalition sovereigns had a meeting with Kaiser Franz in Josefstadt [Josefov, 1½ miles south of Jaromir].[28] The consequence of this was a secret agreement with Austria to declare war on France at the end of the armistice if Napoleon had not accepted the following conditions before that time:

1. The placing of the Duchy of Warsaw at the disposal of the Coalition powers.
2. The expansion of Prussia, as a result of the partition of the Duchy of Warsaw and the cession of Danzig with its environs. The evacuation of French forces from all fortresses in Prussian territory and in the Duchy of Warsaw.
3. The restoration of the Illyrian provinces to Austria.
4. Napoleon's renunciation of the *Hansestädte* and the coastal areas of northern Germany in general.[29]

Having thus drawn closer to Russia and Prussia, the Austrian government wanted to know what concessions Napoleon might agree to in order to avoid war. Metternich went to Dresden with this mission. Napoleon was extremely embittered against the Viennese Cabinet at this time. This is apparent from his instructions to Caulaincourt. He wrote:

> Russia has every right to generous peace terms. They have paid for them with two harsh campaigns, the devastation of their provinces, and the loss of their capital. Austria, on the contrary, deserves nothing. Nothing would grieve me more than if Austria received the benefits and glory of restoring peace in Europe as a reward for their treachery.'[30]

The correspondence arising between the foreign ministers of both powers further increased Napoleon's displeasure. In evading the obligations assumed by the Austrian government under the treaty of 1812, Metternich stated that 'mediation can be valid only when the power that has taken on the task is completely independent.'[31] At the same time as this note was submitted to the duc de Bassano, Graf Metternich asked the *Empereur des Français* for an audience in order to present him with a letter from his Kaiser. Napoleon, receiving Metternich on 16 (28) June, greeted him with the words: 'so here you are, Metternich! Punctual, yet why have you arrived so late? We have already lost a whole month... The idleness of your mediation has done me a great deal of harm. You find it disadvantageous to yourselves to vouch for the integrity of French territory. Let it be your way, but

28 *Vossische Zeitung*, 1 July.

29 Secret convention, concluded in Reichenbach on 15 (27) June. A copy of this convention was attached to the instructions issued to Anstett for his visit to Prague (Archive of the M.F.A.).

30 *Lebensbilder*, III, 480.

31 Graf Metternich's note dated 28 June, new style.

why did you not inform me of this earlier? Had you not concluded a treaty of alliance with me, perhaps I would not have gone to Russia; had you explained yourself frankly to me upon my return from there, I would have changed my plans and could have avoided a new war. In all likelihood, you wanted to exhaust me through new exertions... Suddenly you are creeping between the belligerent powers, offering me your mediation, while offering my enemies an alliance with you. Without your disastrous intervention, we would have already concluded peace. I was not seeking your assistance. For me, your neutrality was sufficient. Yet you, under the pretext of mediation, have conducted a large mobilisation, and having completed this, you want to dictate peace terms to me...

What have been the results of the armistice thus far? I know only that two treaties have been concluded in Reichenbach by Britain with Russia and Prussia. There is also talk of a third, but you, having Graf Stadion on site at the negotiations, should know of this better than me.

Admit it yourself: you became my adversaries from the moment you took on the mediation. You hope to recoup your losses by taking advantage of my predicament. What is it you want?

Metternich, with perfect composure, responded to this stormy monologue saying: 'My sovereign desires nothing more than such influence as would instil his own feelings of moderation and respect across the governments of Europe for the rights and inviolability of other states. Austria desires a peace secured by a Coalition of independent states.'

Napoleon interrupted: 'Speak more clearly. I offered you Illyria in order for you to remain neutral. Would you agree to this?'

'*Ach*, Sovereign! Why would you continue to fight alone? Why not double your strength?' Metternich enquired. 'We can no longer restrict ourselves to neutrality. It is unavoidable that we be either for you or against you!' Whereupon, the Austrian diplomat, with his customary dexterity, recounted all the concessions required by the Coalition.

Napoleon, barely giving him time to express these demands, cried out: 'What! Not only Illyria, but also Poland, Lübeck, Hamburg and Bremen, and the dissolution of the *Confédération du Rhin*! You act as the spirit of moderation, you speak of your respect for the rights of independent states. As I understand it... You want to get all of Italy; Russia wants Poland; Sweden wants Norway; Prussia wants Saxony; Britain wants Holland and Belgium. You hope to acquire those fortresses that I conquered through so many victories with one stroke of a pen! You suppose that I would ransom my future to the dubious generosity of those very same whom I have just defeated. And they make such offers to me when my victorious forces are at the gates of Berlin and Breslau, when I am here myself with an army of 300,000! Austria, without going into battle, without even drawing swords, hopes to force me to agree to such terms. Without drawing swords! An unprecedented insult! Yet this is what my father-in-law offers me! In what situation does he want to place me before the people of France? He is terribly mistaken in believing that the humiliated throne of France might be a sanctuary for his daughter and grandson!' Then, having completely lost his temper, Napoleon said: 'Ah! Metternich, how much did Britain pay you for you to become my enemy?

At these offensive words, erupting in the heat of anger, Metternich's expression changed. There was a profound silence. Napoleon, continuing to pace with long strides back and forth, threw his hat from his hands. At any other time, Metternich would have hastened to pick it up… But now, both were passed several times… Napoleon, having come to his senses somewhat, expressed hope for peace if only Austria could understand their true advantage, insisted on convening a congress, suggested that even if hostilities were resumed, negotiations could continue, and finally, in parting with Metternich, hinted that French concessions in favour of Austria would not be limited to Illyria.[32]

After such a demonstration, there would be no more talk of the treaty of alliance of 1812. The next day, 17 (29) June, Maret responded to the note sent to him by Metternich the previous day: 'It is not in anyone's power to make that which exists not exist. However, we could say that the treaty of alliance no longer exists if all the terms were put in abeyance… His Majesty can only consider the wishes of the Viennese Court to be the equivalent of a renunciation of the alliance… His Majesty, who does not want to make His alliance onerous to His friends, has no difficulty in renouncing the one which linked Him to Austria, if such is the wish of Kaiser Franz.'[33]

Metternich, having achieved his objective of breaking the alliance with France, repeated the offer of mediation, and, referring to his previous note of 10 (22) June, asked for the appointment of representatives from the French government to the congress that was about to convene in Bohemia.[34]

Napoleon, having been forced to accept the mediation of Austria, but not wanting to give the Viennese Cabinet the right to resolve contested issues, proposed convening a congress to negotiate the reconciliation of Europe, in which Britain would also participate. The duc de Bassano wrote: 'Europe, in shock from 30 years of war, had to be pacified by universal measures concluded not by Cabinets, but within sight of the whole of Europe, of all nations. Such were the congresses of Münster, Nijmegen, Rijswijk, Utrecht,' and so on.[35] The following draft convention was attached to this note:

32 This remarkable conversation could not be conveyed verbatim, but Fain and Savary are almost completely in agreement on its content. Metternich never publicly denied what they had published, and it was only after 24 years, in 1837, according to an account by the famous English tourist, Mrs. Trollope, that he told her 'everything written about this conversation is fictitious and only the anecdote about the hat is true.' But these words can hardly be taken as undoubted truth, especially since the tourist who conveyed them to the public was not known for truthfulness. Fain, *Manuscrit de 1813*, II, 36-44; Beitzke, *Geschichte der deutschen Freiheitskriege in den Jahren 1813 und 1814*, I, 623; Thiers, XVI, *Edit. de Brux*, 72-81. There is much in the latter work that diverges from the accounts by Fain and Savary.

33 '*… Il n'est au pouvoir de personne de faire que ce qui existe n'existe pas. Or, on ne pourrait dire que le traité d'alliance existe, si toutes les stipulations étaient placées dans les réserves… Sa Majesté ne peut considérer le voeu de la cour de Vienne que comme l'équivalent de la renonciation à l'alliance… Sa Majesté, qui ne veut pas rendre Son alliance onéreuse à Ses amis, ne fait aucune difficulté de renoncer à celle qui La liait avec L'Autriche, si tel est le voeu de l'Empereur François…*' Extracted from the duc de Bassano's note dated 29 June, new style.

34 Graf Metternich's note dated 29 June, new style.

35 The duc de Bassano's (Maret) note dated 29 June, new style.

1. 'His Majesty the Austrian Kaiser offers his mediation for the establishment of a general peace.
2. His Majesty proposes mediation not for a decision on reciprocal claims, but for their accord, as a mediator, guided by complete selflessness and impartiality, and with the goal of facilitating, if possible, the conclusion of a common peace.
3. That mediation is extended to Britain, the United States of America, the King of Spain, the Cortes of Cádiz, and in general to all the powers of each warring side.

His Majesty the Kaiser of Austria proposes to convene the congress in Vienna or Prague.

1. His Majesty the *Empereur des Français* accepts, both for himself and for his allies, the mediation of the Kaiser of Austria, on the basis of the above-mentioned conditions.

His Majesty also agrees to the convening of a congress in Vienna or Prague.

1. The plenipotentiaries of France, Russia and Prussia shall come to the agreed city, in the first five days of July, together with mediators from Austria, in order to open negotiations and to stop the bloodshed, through preliminary terms, or by a specific peace treaty.
2. If by 20 July either of the warring factions announces the end of the armistice, in accordance with the convention of 4 June (concluded in Pläswitz), then the negotiations at the congress shall not be suspended.'

If the Austrian government had agreed to mediate under such terms, then, as a power governed by perfect impartiality, it could not take part in the war and would have renounced the advantages of its position. On the other hand, the participation of King Joseph's representatives at the congress, as an implied recognition of his right to the Spanish throne, would not be acceptable to Britain. Therefore, the Viennese Cabinet, having rejected the proposed convention, insisted on the unconditional acceptance of their mediation. There was also no agreement to continue negotiations beyond the expiration of the armistice, rather, it was proposed to extend the armistice until 10 August, new style. These terms gave Austria complete freedom to take the side of the Coalition in response to a failure of negotiations, who, at the same time, taking advantage of the three-week delay in the resumption of hostilities, could strengthen their forces. Napoleon, nevertheless, approved the newly drafted convention.[36] The consequences of this were: a rise in demands from the Coalition powers,

36 The convention, signed by Graf Metternich and the duc de Bassano, on 30 June, new style, contains the following terms:
'H.M. the Kaiser of Austria offers their mediation for the conclusion of a general or continental peace.
H.M. the *Empereur des Français* accepts the said mediation.

Napoleon's refusal to satisfy them and the accession of Austria to the Coalition. It is quite difficult to understand how Napoleon could have made such a grave mistake, knowing the duplicity of Austria, the intransigence of Britain, Prussia's thirst for war, the willingness of Emperor Alexander I to continue the struggle for the independence of Europe and the hatred of populations for the hegemony of France. Napoleon knew all this, and agreed to the unconditional mediation by Austria and to the continuation of the armistice. Subsequently, once on the island of St. Helena, he told his comrades in captivity that he considered himself essential to a general peace, being the regenerator of the monarchy of France and having put an end to the revolutionary flood that had threatened to engulf everything, and believed that every sovereign shared this opinion. With regard to Austria, he thought that the Viennese Cabinet wanted to benefit from his difficult situation, but it did not occur to him that his father-in-law would bring the matter to the point of dethroning him, especially since in this case the predominance of France might be replaced by the predominance of Russia – even more dangerous to Austria. Napoleon imagined that even Prussia, despite their hatred of him, could not have wished for his downfall, which would upset the political balance of power in Europe. In addition, he wished to display a readiness for peace, which all of France so impatiently desired.[37]

The Austrian government, having achieved recognition of their mediation and the extension of the armistice, leaned towards Russia and Prussia completely. The Coalition agreed to assemble for a conference on the overall plan of military operations in the town of Trachenberg, where Graf Hatzfeld had a Schloss, five *Meilen* (35 *verstas*) north of Breslau.[38] By 27 June (9 July), the following had arrived there: Emperor Alexander I, King Friedrich Wilhelm III, the Crown Prince of Sweden, generals Sukhtelen [Pëtr Kornilovich Sukhtelen, or Johann Pieter van Suchtelen], Volkonsky, Pozzo di Borgo [Karl Osipovich Potstso-di-Borgo, or Carlo Andrea Pozzo di Borgo], Knesebeck, Stedingk and Löwenhielm [Carl Axel Löwenhielm]. There were no representatives from Austria, but the Coalition were so confident of their assistance that this was taken into account when drafting the overall plan of operations, which was immediately communicated to the Austrian government. Kaiser Franz, completely approving of these plans, expressed the desire that the Russo-Prussian army would not enter Bohemia until the expiry of the armistice. Thus, even before the opening of negotiations at the Prague Congress, Austria was on the Coalition side and was preparing to support their argument with armed force.[39]

Representatives from France, Russia and Prussia shall travel to Prague by 5 July [new style]. Due to the short time remaining until 20 July, the expiration date of the armistice concluded in Pläswitz, the *Empereur des Français* undertakes not to terminate the aforementioned armistice until 10 August, and the Austrian Kaiser also permits himself (*se reserve*) to accord with Russia and Prussia.

This convention shall not be made public.

This shall be ratified and ratifications exchanged within four days.

Drafted and signed in Dresden, 30 July, 1813.'

37 Beitzke, I, 624-628.

38 [Bogdanovich is mistaken – the distance from Breslau to Schloss Trachenberg is 39½ statute miles – almost 60 *verstas*].

39 Beitzke, I, 629-630.

Austria's accession to the Coalition changed the nature of the war. The participation of the civilian population in the struggle against France aroused the concerns of the Viennese Court, which, upon joining the Coalition, tried by all means to water this down, while Russia and Prussia, out of necessity, had to take Austrian opinions into account. The national uprisings evolved into battles by regular forces. Therefore, the rulers of the *Confédération du Rhin*, worried by the popular uprisings of northern Germany at the beginning of the war of 1813, were pacified, and, being less in need of Napoleon's patronage, little by little, began to lean towards the side of those who would liberate their fatherland from the foreign yoke.

18

The Prague Congress

The views of both sides. – The instructions issued to the plenipotentiaries. – The arrival of Anstett and Humboldt. – The arrival of the comte de Narbonne. – The Coalition plenipotentiaries' discussions with Graf Metternich. – The delays to the Prague Congress due to negotiations in Neumarkt on extensions to the armistice. The arrival of Caulaincourt. – Metternich's announcements to the French representatives. – The peace terms proposed by the Coalition. – Disagreements between the representatives regarding the methods for conducting negotiations. – The secret talks between Caulaincourt and Metternich. – Proposals from the Viennese Court. – Napoleon's response. – The final days of the armistice. – The Austrian government's declaration of war on Napoleon. – Napoleon's agreement to the proposed peace terms. – The Viennese Court's response. – Napoleon's proposal to continue negotiations at the same time as military operations. – The last words of the Prague Congress. – To whom does Germany owe their good fortune?

The French government had recognised the mediation of Austria based on the convention concluded in Dresden on 18 (30) June. Yet even as they were committing to this act, both sides were concealing their intentions: the Viennese Court saw this as a means to fulfil the obligations it had assumed in relation to Russia and Prussia, while Napoleon, in authorising his ministers to negotiate for peace, deliberately kept silent about the mediation of Austria, which was so painful to his pride. The Coalition granted the mediators the right to resolve disputed points, while Napoleon only allowed impartial settlement of reciprocal demands. The Coalition, having good reason not to trust their power-hungry foe, wanted to bring him to such a state that he could never again become a disturber of the peace of Europe, while Napoleon, whose armies had just suffered a reverse in Spain, did not dare to make any significant concessions in Germany, concerned that the blaze of glory acquired by many years of constant success might have been dimmed. The impossibility of agreement between the respective belligerents is apparent from the instructions received by the representatives of both parties from their Courts upon their departure for Prague.

The instructions to the Russian minister, Privy Councillor Anstett, approved personally by Emperor Alexander, and completely in alignment with those given to the Prussian minister, Baron Humboldt [Friedrich Wilhelm Christian Carl Ferdinand von Humboldt], state:

> ... In delving into the evolution in relations between the Coalition courts and Austria, we see that the Viennese Cabinet, having initially accepted mediation between the belligerent powers, thereafter formally pledged to assist the Coalition in the war against France if they had not accepted the terms proposed, by 10 August.

And therefore it would transpire that negotiations should have been conducted exclusively, or at least predominantly, between the mediating power and France. But since the Austrian government wanted representatives of Russia and Prussia to also participate in the talks, the Coalition courts agreed to this proposal.

> The purpose of these negotiations is to lay the foundations for a general peace, or to convince the Viennese Court that France is preventing their conclusion, and thereby force Austria to take up arms against this power... This is a particular requirement of the relations of Russia and Prussia with their allies, and especially with Britain. It will be necessary to satisfy such divergent demands in order to achieve a common peace that a simultaneous agreement through this general congress would be possible only by continuing the war ad infinitum, or by concluding an armistice for an indefinite period and thereby losing sight of the actual aims of the war. The current negotiations are necessary as much in order to prepare for war, should it becomes necessary to continue it, as for the conclusion of a subsequent definitive peace (*d'une paix définitive*). Russia and Prussia are in a rather delicate position: on the one hand, they do not have the right to open immediate negotiations with the enemy without the consent of their allies; on the other hand, the Viennese Court, whose assistance is so important to us, does not want to take part in a war until all means to achieve peace have been exhausted. Two stumbling blocks must be avoided: a violation of obligations towards the allies, and the obstruction of negotiations through unnecessary intransigence, which would give Austria a reason to criticise Russia and Prussia for groundless demands rendering the conclusion of peace impossible. Indeed, in relation to France, where peace is generally wished for, it would be inappropriate to show intractability, which would serve as a pretext for Napoleon to accuse the Coalition of pointless warmongering...
>
> It should not be forgotten that the peace will only be permanent once it guarantees the interests of every ally of Russia and Prussia... During negotiations, in addition to achieving the principle objective, it will be necessary to convince Europe that the Coalition powers are guided by the magnanimous principles of justice and impartiality, but also that no efforts might shake their determination to uphold these principles and bring them to fruition.

Furthermore, it was ordered that ministers from the Coalition courts must not negotiate directly with the French representatives, but through an Austrian intermediary...

> As Austria has already announced that it does not want to dictate peace terms itself, the Viennese Cabinet will invite the ministers of Russia and Prussia to present their demands, which they will forward in accordance with the note delivered to Graf Stadion on 16 May; but they are to note that since some of these demands relate directly to Britain, the Coalition courts, wanting on this occasion to limit themselves to concluding a preliminary peace that may serve as the basis for a general peace, are content with the terms communicated to Graf Metternich on 7 June, which will be forwarded in their entirety. At the same time, the commissioners must verbally lobby the Viennese Court such that they strongly support the above-mentioned demands.
>
> If Napoleon really wants peace, then the return of Illyria and the cession of the Duchy of Warsaw should not prove to be great problems on his part. But the expansion of Prussia into Germany and the complete independence of the *Hansestädte*, or at least of Hamburg and Lübeck, will no doubt be contentious. It is vital that the ministers of the Coalition courts clearly explain the intent of their governments, proving clearly that they, not being carried away by wishful thinking for the expansion of their territories, simply want Prussia to receive such borders as are necessary for their security. In a similar vein, the Coalition courts would wish for Austria to be secure with regard to their own defence, through the return of the Tyrol and that part of Italy up to the river Mincio with Mantua. As for Prussia, the only border that could protect their German territories from enemy invasion is the river Elbe, with the fortresses located thereon, with the exception of the capital of Saxony. Other Saxon territories that might go to Prussia should be compensated by the cession of other German territory in favour of Saxony. Should it prove impossible to reach an agreement on this subject, then it is essential that Prussia at least receive Magdeburg, the return of which not only contributes to its strengthening in defensive terms, but is also generally important in that this fortress would serve as a great obstacle to French domination of northern Germany. If Napoleon succeeds in building a new fortress at the mouth of the Havel and in fortifying Hamburg, as he anticipates, then the borders of the French Empire would actually extend to the Elbe and the territory of France would be covered by a line of fortresses, just as its former borders were guarded by a triple row of strongholds. The consequences of such a state of affairs would be the total subjugation of Germany and the destruction of free trade therein, because Napoleon would have acquired dominance along the Baltic coast. It is clear from all this that it is vital to break this line along the Elbe by giving Magdeburg to Prussia. Moreover, Prussian territory must be protected from French troops crossing the lower reaches of this river. The independence of Hamburg and Lübeck and the freedom of their interactions with

Britain are vital not only for Prussia, but also for Germany and for Europe in general.

Should negotiations take such a turn that France does agree to the four terms set out in the convention of 27 June, then the ministers from the Coalition courts might easily convince the Viennese Cabinet of the impossibility of limiting ourselves to these demands and must try to ensure that they give themselves greater leeway. Apart from the striking contradiction between these terms and the publicly expressed intentions of the Coalition, the following must be resolved: what use do the provinces returned to Prussia and Austria serve as a guarantee for their preservation, if their defensive resources are only strengthened slightly? Would France resume their aggressive efforts as soon as the German militia are demobilised and the Russian forces return to their homeland? Would they not initially increase their influence and thereafter dominance over Prussia, and even over Austria, as they have previously? To what extent must these attempts reach in order to call forth such immense efforts to counter them once again as are being currently made? And is it possible to hope that it might be feasible to reassemble armies so extensive, so generously supplied with every resource, and still eager to confront the common enemy? Not to mention the instability of such a future state of affairs, this would be unbearable for Prussia at the present time. They would only receive provinces whose inhabitants would never be sincerely loyal to them, provinces devastated by war and with the potential to generate unsustainable expenditure, while the lands that have belonged to them since ancient times have been exhausted in the struggle undertaken for a good cause – the achievement of a better world order. Of all the four terms, the complete dissolution of the Duchy of Warsaw and the expansion of the Austrian Monarchy might be considered satisfactory. But the former of these is not a concession on the part of France as this territory has already been taken from them by force of arms; while the return of the Illyrian provinces to Austria is not yet sufficient to ensure their independence.

From all that has been said, it is clear that it is necessary to dissolve the *Confédération du Rhin*, which is especially harmful because the rulers within it cannot escape their dependence on Napoleon; and besides, the independence and security of Prussia are incompatible with the membership of Mecklenburg and Anhalt territory within this confederation.

Based on these conclusions, the representatives of the Coalition courts may drop hints to the mediators of the vulnerabilities to which Austria is exposed in the event of Russia and Prussia resuming hostilities without their assistance. But they are not to express these before confirming that the Viennese Court does not consider itself obliged to commence hostilities against Napoleon on the basis of the convention of 27 June. In particular, they must try their best to ensure that the French representatives do not notice the slightest disagreement between the Coalition and the Viennese Court regarding peace terms.

> Should France refuses the demands proposed by the mediating power, the convention concluded in the event of war will be replaced by a treaty of alliance. Should France agree to these terms, then the ministers of the Coalition courts are to accept the peace treaty for reference (*ad referendum*) to their Sovereigns subject to final approval (*sub sperati*).
>
> Napoleon, in all probability, will begin to look for excuses to delay matters in order to gain time without making any concessions to the Coalition. The plenipotentiaries may prevent the implementation of such plans by demanding the immediate evacuation of the French occupied fortresses in the theatre of war. Should the French refuse to comply, it will become obviously apparent that no agreement can be reached and that Austria must fulfil the obligations they have taken on.[1]

In the instructions to the French commissioners, the duc de Vicence (Caulaincourt) and the comte de Narbonne, after minute details regarding the method of conducting the negotiations and diplomatic formalities, the French Cabinet outlined its intentions as follows:

> His Majesty, without rejecting the possibility of such factors that might serve to restore his previous relations with Austria (*à rentrer dans un système avec l'Autriche*), intends to conclude a peace with Russia favourable to this power (*une paix qui soit glorieuse pour cette puissance*) and to punish Austria for their treacherous and unfounded violation of the alliance of 1812, through the reduction of their influence in Europe (*par la perte de son influence en Europe*)... French interests require that Austria receive not so much as a village (*pas un village*).

Napoleon wanted everything to return to how it was before the war (*uti possidetis ante bellum*).

> The mediator, who must be guided by impartiality above all, cannot demand anything in their own favour. Negotiations should be conducted only in relation to those territories whose situation has changed since 1812, but not before.

This latter condition excluded every territory that came under the influence of France from the negotiations, except for Prussia which had freed itself from the yoke that burdened it, and also Mecklenburg and the Duchy of Warsaw, occupied by Coalition forces. In the instructions issued to his representatives, Napoleon wrote:

> the situation for both sides remains almost the same as it was before the commencement of the war. Nothing has changed. We have never been defeated, indeed, on the contrary, our operations have constantly been

1 Extracted from the original instructions to Privy Councillor Anstett, dated 26 June [8 July], held in the Archive of the M.F.A.

> accompanied by success. The losses we suffered due to the influence of the weather, as much as to the enemy, have been made good, and since then we have been continuously victorious. The fortresses we hold remain in our hands, and if the enemy holds some of the land belonging to our allies, then we have almost the same advantage on our side.

Napoleon went on to say: 'Overall, the negotiations are to be slow. We shall begin the real business no earlier than in the last ten or 12 days... The plenipotentiaries will receive instructions for the final decision (*pour le parti définitif*) in due course.'[2] Napoleon cared so little about the success of the negotiations that he set off during the night of 12 to 13 (24 to 25) July for Mainz for a visit with the Empress Marie-Louise, without waiting for Caulaincourt's departure for Prague, which was postponed day after day under empty pretexts.[3]

Thus, neither of the belligerent parties displayed moderation, which might have served as an assurance of reciprocal agreement. The Coalition maintained decorum at least by not delaying the arrival of their representatives. According to the convention of 30 June, new style, they were supposed to assemble in Prague together with the representatives of France by 5 July. But Metternich proposed delaying the congress, initially until 8 July, and then until 12 July. The Coalition diplomats, Privy Councillor Anstett and Baron Humboldt, arrived in Prague the day before, while the comte de Narbonne, although he had arrived there as early as 9 July, nevertheless, having not been given authority to negotiate, had to wait for the duc de Vicence (Caulaincourt).

At his first meeting with the representatives of the Coalition courts, in response to Anstett's delegation of unlimited authority to him, Graf Metternich replied:

> I hope that you will soon be convinced of my sincerity... The most important thing is to give the objective of our labours the appearance of a desire for common peace and to demonstrate that everything we might seek from France is as a guarantee of peace in Europe. In a word, we must, through our combined efforts, put Napoleon in such a position that he will be forced to compose a wretched manifesto against Austria.

Anstett remarked:

> That is not enough. We hope also to force him to wage a wretched campaign against Austria.

Whereupon, the Austrian diplomat, having briefed the enormous resources of the Coalition in detail and the advantages of their position, stated:

> I do not think this war will be very difficult; I would only wish to convince one individual of this. I also do not believe that anyone could overcome our

2 Norvins, *Portefeuille de 1813*, II, 205-208.
3 Fain, *Manuscrit de 1813*, II, 82.

> threefold advantage in troop numbers, and, in my opinion, the great man is reeling on the throne (*le grand homme est à coté du trône*).

Baron Humboldt, who knew Metternich well, attributed his passion to the desire to charm the Russian minister, however, despite this, he admitted that Metternich had never spoken in such a spirit in his presence. Indeed, his frankness went so far that he explained to the Coalition ministers not only all the preparations for war by his government, but also the measures he had taken to incite an uprising in Illyria and the Tyrol.[4]

The negotiations held in Neumarkt regarding an extension of the armistice gave Napoleon an excuse to delay the opening of the Prague Conference, which he had begun with great reluctance. The Coalition *parlementaires* at the Neumarkt congress, Count Shuvalov and Baron Krusemarck, not having definitive information regarding the terms of the Dresden Convention, to extend the armistice until 29 July (10 August), not counting the six days after this period, before the expiration of which hostilities were not supposed to resume, and therefore did not consider themselves empowered to extend the truce beyond 23 July (4 August). Moreover, the Coalition *parlementaires* would not agree to permitting French officers to be sent, one to each of the fortresses blockaded by Coalition forces, or to increasing the amount of supplies delivered to the garrisons of these fortresses during the armistice.[5] On 10 (22) July, with the permission of the Commander-in-Chief of the Coalition armies, Barclay de Tolly, they agreed to extend the truce until 29 July (10 August), but refused the other demands of the French *parlementaires*. This gave rise to some rather caustic correspondence. In a letter from the *Chef d'État-major* of the French army, Berthier, to the French commissioners in Neumarkt, Dumoustier and Flahaut, outlining, from his point of view, all the advantages that were currently on Napoleon's side, and noting that his army had no need for the armistice, wrote:

> The Coalition must have the same misconceptions about the situation of the French army as they had before the battle of Lützen. Otherwise, they would not flatter themselves with the hope of success for their operations. They will retreat beyond the Vistula even faster than they left the Elbe behind. They will have to deal with an army that will astound them with its strength in infantry, cavalry and artillery, even more than the one they encountered at Lützen...[6]

Barclay de Tolly, having received Berthier's letter forwarded to him by Count Shuvalov and Baron Krusemarck, sent them a dispatch that was intended to be used to respond to the *Chef d'État-major* of the French army. In this dispatch, having pointed out the Russian Monarch's amenability firstly to accept and later to extend the armistice, Barclay wrote:

4 From Anstett's letter to Emperor Alexander I, dated 1 (13) July (Archive of the M.F.A.).

5 Count Shuvalov's and Baron Krusemarck's memoranda to the French commissioners, generals Dumoustier and Flahaut, dated 5 (17) July.

6 From Berthier's letter dated 19 July, new style (Archive of the M.F.A.).

... One does not know whether the French army needs a truce or not, but one firmly remembers that the armistice was proposed by Caulaincourt, that during its conclusion the detachments under Vorontsov and Chernyshev were at the gates of Leipzig and General Arrighi owes his salvation solely to the suspension of hostilities, and that Bülow, having defeated Marshal Oudinot, was two stages from Dresden and had completely severed the French army's lines of communication. From all this it is apparent, gentlemen, that we have assessed the current situation quite correctly. Without being diverted from this thought by any assumptions regarding the consequences that a resumption of hostilities might entail, I consider myself entitled to state emphatically that His Majesty the Emperor took them into account during the drafting of his assessments, and that His valiant forces would fight against French forces on the banks of the Oder with the same courage with which they defended their homeland, whatever might be the strength of their opponents in infantry, cavalry and artillery, that the most immense army could neither astound nor overawe them. Yet notwithstanding the confidence that His Majesty has in the morale of His troops and in the steadfastness of His allies, the Sovereign Emperor will not abandon an agreement on peace, and in order to achieve this aim He has provided the Viennese Cabinet with every possible assistance and completely entrusted himself to them. Through a similar convergence of views with Kaiser Franz, the Tsar has agreed to extend the armistice. Yet it does not follow from this that the Russian government considers itself obliged to satisfy the new demands from the French commissars, which cannot, under any circumstances, be considered a consequence of the extension of the armistice. And therefore, you are formally refused permission to send French officers to the besieged fortresses, the true reasons for which are obvious to us.

As for the complaints about the insufficiency of provisions supplied to the Danzig garrison, they would be valid if the strength of this garrison actually reached 25,000 men. But since the number of troops in its establishment is much smaller, it is obvious that the Prinz von Württemberg has not in any way violated the terms of the armistice, which determined the amount of supplies to be delivered in accordance with the available strength of the garrison, and not according to what the besieged fortress might request.[7]

Eventually, the Coalition agreed to allow French officers into Küstrin and Stettin. In relation to the other invested fortresses, Danzig, Modlin and Zamość, it was agreed that sealed dispatches from the *Chef d'État-major* of the French army and the convention on the extension of the armistice were to be delivered to the commandants of these fortresses by Russian officers, who were to bring back their responses in sealed

7 *Copie d'une dépêche ostensible du Général en chef Barclay de Tolly à Messieurs le comt de Schouvaloff et le baron de Krusemarck, pour servir de reponse à celle du prince de Noufchatel, en date du 19 de juillet. Reichenbach, le 21 de juillet, n. st. 1813* (Archive of the M.F.A.).

envelopes no more than eight days later. With regard to the supply of rations to the fortresses during the extension of the armistice, it was decided to leave the solution to the disagreements that had arisen on this subject to the representatives of the belligerent powers in Prague, through Austrian mediation, and taking how they had acted previously under similar circumstances as their guide.[8]

It would seem that these disputes regarding the extension and about some of the terms of the armistice should not have delayed the commencement of the incomparably more important negotiations in Prague, but Napoleon postponed Caulaincourt's departure from Dresden until the armistice convention had been signed. The delays to his arrival in Prague almost exhausted the patience not only of Metternich, but also of Kaiser Franz, who was in Brandeis [Brandýs nad Labem] at the time, and who considered such an act a personal insult. The representatives of Russia and Prussia, fearing that Napoleon might take advantage of the uncertainty of the armistice and violate it with a surprise attack on the Russo-Prussian army, wanted to know what the Austrian government intended to do in such an event and whether the Coalition troops would be permitted to enter Austria, should the circumstances so require. Graf Metternich, by order of Kaiser Franz, replied that Napoleon's resumption of operations before the agreed date of 16 August [new style] would be considered an insult to the mediating power and an act of war against them. Consequently, should Napoleon violate the armistice, nothing would prevent the Coalition armies from entering Austria.[9] While waiting for Caulaincourt, the commissioners discussed the format for the impending meetings. Metternich proposed, as had already been previously agreed, to conduct negotiations following the model of the 1779 Congress of Teschen, at which representatives from both sides presented drafts of the terms they required to the mediator and received from him responses to their proposals from the other side. This method of conducting negotiations, to which France, among other powers, agreed at the time, by preventing the heat of a verbal debate and giving the mediator the opportunity to soften the harshness of the respective claims, would serve to save time, which remained very short, and therefore this method was readily accepted by the ministers of the Coalition courts.[10]

Eventually, on 16 (28) July, the duc de Vicence arrived in Prague: thus, 16 days had been lost from the time available to the representatives at the Congress. At his first meeting with Metternich, the duc, in discussing current affairs, admitted that the French had suffered an important setback in Spain. 'What will happen from all this?' asked Metternich.

'I do not know,' Caulaincourt answered. 'It depends on some whim. Yet I was enchanted by everything I was able to observe of your mobilisation. Just tell me, will you have enough to bring us to reason, once and for all?'

8 Barclay de Tolly's letter to Count Shuvalov and Baron Krusemarck, dated 13 (25) July, from Reichenbach.
9 Anstett's letter to the Tsar dated 12 (24) July, with Graf Metternich's note dated 11 (23) July attached (Archive of the M.F.A.).
10 Antett's letter to the Tsar, dated 1 (13) July (Archive of the M.F.A.).

'Do not worry,' Metternich said. 'Your service shall be as you wish it.'[11] Whereupon, turning to the comte de Narbonne, Metternich solemnly announced that it was his responsibility, as the French ambassador to the Viennese Court, to inform Emperor Napoleon that should peace not be concluded by 10 August, then Austria would declare war on him on 11 August. Having relayed the contents of this conversation to the Russian envoy on the same day, Metternich told him: 'finally, on 10 August we shall have a peace more advantageous than we could ever have expected, or on 11 August we shall have war.' He repeated several times: 'On this occasion, Napoleon has already almost fallen once because, by occupying Moscow, he hoped to force Emperor Alexander to accept peace. Now he will fall because he doubts Austria's readiness for war.'[12]

The Coalition representatives, having agreed to negotiate in writing, following the model of the Teschen Congress,[13] briefed the views of their governments to the mediator, demanding from France via him:

1. The restoration of Austria to the degree of power and the area of territory, in accordance with the situation of this power prior to 1805, both in Italy and in Germany.
2. The restoration of Prussia to its same extent prior to 1806.
3. The dissolution of the *Confédération du Rhin*. The independence of Germany and the return of the northern regions of this country, annexed to the French Empire.
4. The partition of the Duchy of Warsaw.
5. The detachment of the Netherlands from France.
6. The restoration of the previous dynasty to the throne of Spain.
7. The independence of Italy from French rule and influence.

11 *'... Je n'en sais rien,' repondit le duc. 'Cela depend d'une lubie. Mais ce que j'ai vu de vos armemens, m'enchante. Dit moi seulement, si vous en avez assez pour nous rendre une bonne fois raisonnables?'*
'Soyez tranquille,' lui dit le comte de Metternich, 'vous serez servis à souhait.' The original conversation as conveyed by Metternich to Anstett.

12 Anstett's letter to the Tsar, dated 16 (28) July (Archive of the M.F.A.).

13 *Formes qui ont été observées dans les négociations de paix au congrès de Teschen, en 1779. L'instruction des plénipotentiaires des puissances belligérantes, connue des ministres médiateurs portait de traiter de la paix sans aucun appareil de congrès, sans aucune formalité ou étiquette quelconque, en se renfermant dans les procédés et les usages ordinaires de la société. Au moment de leur réunion, les envoyés se légitima vis-à-vis d'eux.*
Les plénipotentiaires des puissances belligérantes adressèrent dès lors leurs projets de paix au médiateur, et c'est par son canal qu'ils reçurent les reponses et les contre-projets de la partie adverse.
Les plénipotentiaires n'ont, pendant toute la durée du congrès, tenu aucune conférence générale, ils furent cependant en contact journalier entre eux.
Ce ne fut que le jour de la signature du traité de paix que les plénipotentiaires de puissances belligérantes s'assemblerent pour la première et pour la dernière fois, avec les médiateurs en séance générale pour échanger les pleins-pouvoirs respectifs avec les traités signés. Archive of the M.F.A.

Thus, the Coalition commissioners sought to demand much more than what had been intended on the basis of the Reichenbach Convention of 15 (27) June. The French commissioners, having been invited by Count Metternich to proceed with a written response, following the Congress of Teschen model,[14] replied that they had forwarded the note they had received to their court.[15] Thereafter, once Metternich had informed the duc de Vicence and the comte de Narbonne of the agreement with the Coalition representatives to negotiate in writing, then the French ministers, reminding him that, on the basis of the convention of 30 June (new style) the mediator must be impartial and limited to securing agreement between the opposing parties, accused Russia of opening negotiations not to achieve peace, but to involve Austria in the war, and, on their part, proposed that negotiations be conducted both verbally and in writing.[16] The Coalition ministers, in response to this dispatch, highlighting the lack of decorum in the phrasing of the French note, pointed out to the mediator that the opponents of peace were not those who had hastened to arrive in Prague and begin the task entrusted to them, but the French representatives, who, four days before the final deadline for negotiations, were now raising disputes about formalities, deviating from the priority objective.[17]

The French commissioners were concerned that hostilities might resume, yet they despaired of cooperating for a peaceful resolution of matters, being bound by the instructions issued to them and knowing without doubt that the proposals of their master would not satisfy the demands of the Coalition, who, not trusting Napoleon, did not want to make peace with him, rather to continue the war with Austrian assistance. Time was slipping away… Already the commissioners were calculating not in days, but in hours. Anstett wrote: 'There are now only 52 hours until the armistice expires.' It was obvious that the Prague Conference would no longer lead to peace. In the meantime, Napoleon had returned to Dresden from Mainz on 23 July (4 August). Convinced of the success of his mobilisation from everything he had seen, he decided to make one more attempt to deflect Austria from participating in the Coalition. The duc de Vicence was ordered to find out in the deepest secrecy under what conditions Austria would agree to enter into an alliance with France, or at least to remain neutral. It was not only the Coalition representatives, but also the comte de Narbonne who were not to know of these orders. As a result of Caulaincourt's meeting with Metternich the following conditions were therefore proposed to Napoleon by the Austrian government: the dissolution of the Duchy of Warsaw and the *Confédération du Rhin*; the independence of Hamburg, Lübeck and other *Hansestädte*; the restoration to Prussia of parts of Poland including Danzig, with their border along the Elbe; the return of the Illyrian provinces including Trieste to Austria; reciprocal guarantees of the inviolability of the integrity of states as determined by peace treaty. The issues of the

14 Graf Metternich's note to the French representatives, dated 29 July, new style; Fain, II, 171-173.

15 Copy of a note signed by the duc de Vicence and the comte de Narbonne, dated 30 July, new sytle (Archive of the M.F.A.).

16 Copy of a note signed by the duc de Vicence and the comte de Narbonne, dated 6 August, new sytle (Archive of the M.F.A.).

17 Copy of Anstett's and Humboldt's note to Graf Metternich dated 7 August, new style (Archive of the M.F.A.).

independence of the Netherlands and Spain were to be postponed until the conclusion of a general peace.

Napoleon received the dispatch with these terms on 7 August (new style) and, had he accepted them immediately, the war would have been over. Yet such a peace seemed problematic to him, but more than this, despite Metternich's warnings, he did not believe that Austria would immediately decide to take the side of his enemies after the armistice, on 29 July (10 August). Influenced by his self-destructive arrogance, Napoleon hesitated in responding to the proposals made to him, and finally, on 29 July (10 August), he sent the following dispatch to Prague:

> There shall be no Duchy of Warsaw; agreed. But Danzig is to remain a free city. The Danzig fortifications shall be destroyed and the King of Saxony is to receive the Silesian and Bohemian enclaves inside Saxony (*enclavés de Saxe*) as compensation for Polish territory.
>
> The Illyrian provinces shall be ceded to Austria; one might even abandon the harbour of Fiume [Rijeka]. But Trieste will not be returned.
>
> *La confédération germanique* shall reach as far as the Oder.
>
> Finally, the integrity of Danish territory is to be guaranteed.[18]

It is obvious that the Coalition powers could not have agreed to such terms even if they had been brought to the attention of their plenipotentiaries before the passing of the armistice deadline, 10 August, new style. But Napoleon's dispatch arrived in Prague the very next day, 11 August.[19]

Several more notes were exchanged between the Coalition and French representatives via Graf Metternich during the last days of the truce: their essence was that both sides tried to shift the blame for the failure of the negotiations onto each other, while at midnight on 29 July (10 August), Anstett sent the following note to Metternich:

> The efforts of the mediating Power and its capacity for conciliation in order to achieve peace between the belligerent Powers having not been achieved by the irrevocably fixed deadline for this objective, the success of which one should have expected from negotiations conducted under the mediation of a powerful, impartial and just court, the undersigned is charged by express order of his August Sovereign, to request the execution of the treaty concluded on 15 (27) June of the current year on the part of Austria. I am at the same time responsible for assuring in the most emphatic manner that His Majesty the Emperor of all Russia will, on his part, fulfil all the articles, terms and conditions of said treaty.
>
> The undersigned would be most obliged to His Excellency Graf von Metternich, if he were able to transmit the response to this official *démarche* to my August Sovereign as quickly as possible.[20]

18 Norvins, II, 238-245; Fain, II, 93-94.
19 Fain, II, 96.
20 For details of these exchanges, see Appendix XXIX at the end of this chapter.

At the same time, the representatives of the Coalition courts announced to the mediator, in dedicated notes, that upon the expiration of the final deadline for the Prague negotiations, on 10 August, both their authority and the mission entrusted to them would cease.[21]

Graf Metternich, having forwarded copies of the latter two notes to the French plenipotentiaries, added his own, in which he expressed regret at the failure of his mediation. He wrote:

> I am consoled in this only by the conviction that on my part every means was used to achieve this noble objective.[22]

The duc de Vicence and the comte de Narbonne, in response to this note, criticised the Coalition representatives for the haste with which they terminated the negotiations, giving assurances that nothing had been missed on their part to bring about the peace-loving intent of their sovereign.[23]

On 12 August new style, Metternich sent the declaration of war to the comte de Narbonne, as the French ambassador to the Viennese Court. Having indicated that the autocratic commands from Napoleon in Germany, which had aroused the justified fears of every European power and had caused the war between France and Russia, the Austrian minister attributed the participation to be taken in it by Kaiser Franz to the impossibility of remaining in a neutral position amid the flames of a conflict that had engulfed the surrounding countries, and of the intention to put an end to the unavoidable disaster through their influence. As the declaration of war stated:

> Yet unfortunately, neither the brilliant successes of the 1812 campaign, nor the unprecedented misfortunes that marked its end, could induce the French government to moderation…

According to the statement on factors that forced Austria to mobilise their armed forces:

> thanks to the trust instilled in the Coalition powers by His Majesty, they agreed to extend the armistice, which, in the opinion of the French government, was essential for the impending negotiations: such compliance is evidence of the peace-loving moderation of the Coalition. The Emperor shared their views…

In contrast, the French limited themselves to promises, which were constantly contradicted by the course of the negotiations:

> delaying the arrival of the French representatives, under pretexts inconsistent with the vital purpose of the congress; the inadequacy of the

21 Anstett's and Baron Humboldt's notes of midnight 29 July (10 August); Fain, II, 202-204.
22 Graf Metternich's note dated 11 August, new style.
23 Note from the French representatives, dated 11 August, new style; Fain, II, 204-205.

instructions they received regarding formalities, which caused the irrevocable loss of already limited time: all these circumstances combined revealed that such a peace as Austria and the Coalition sovereigns desired, would not satisfy Napoleon's intentions, and that the French government, having agreed to negotiate, solely for the sake of appearances and to avoid criticism for continuing the war, wanted to render them unworkable, or perhaps to use them to sow discord between Austria with the powers that shared their views, before treaties could seal an alliance concluded for common peace and prosperity. The Austrian government, in terminating the negotiations, the results of which could not satisfy their expectations, are mobilising themselves solely in order to achieve the noble aim they proposed with the assistance of powers guided by the same sentiments' and so on.[24]

The declaration of war was delivered to Napoleon by the comte de Narbonne on 3 (15) August, in Dresden, where great preparations were being made at that time for a celebration of the eagerly awaited peace. Napoleon himself, despite his overconfidence inspired by the rapid increase of his armed forces during the armistice, had been carried away by the general desire for peace that dominated those closest to him, and despite the breach with Austria, he continued to negotiate in secret with his father-in-law. To that end, Caulaincourt remained in Prague even after the departure of the comte de Narbonne. Having received Napoleon's response to the proposals made by the Austrian government, Metternich again demanded Trieste, refused to extend the borders of the *Confédération du Rhin* and demanded the independence of this alliance as well as of Switzerland. Eventually, Napoleon accepted all the terms proposed to him by the Viennese Cabinet, and insisted only on retaining the *Hansestädte* and the Netherlands, as a form of insurance, until the conclusion of a general peace, which, according to the *Empereur des Français*, was the sole purpose of his intent. But it was already too late. Having received Napoleon's proposals on 2 (14) August, Metternich replied that such concessions could still have led to an agreement on 10 August (new style); but now he was no longer a mediator, rather an ally of the powers at war with France, he had no choice but to bring the proposed terms to the attention of Emperor Alexander and the King of Prussia upon their arrival in Prague. No matter how poor the hopes for peace were after such a response, having received emphatic orders from the duc de Bassano (Maret) to continue relations with Metternich until the last opportunity, but not considering it appropriate to remain in Prague, Caulaincourt took up residence for several days in Schloss Königsaal [Zbraslav] (about ten *verstas* outside Prague), allotted to him by order of Kaiser Franz. Napoleon, meanwhile, immediately after receiving the declaration of war via the comte de Narbonne, departed for Königstein on 3 (15) August, ordering the duc de Bassano to write a note to Metternich, in which a continuation of peace negotiations was proposed at the same time that hostilities were being

24 The Austrian government's declaration of war on France, together with comments on it dictated by Napoleon, are found in Fain's work, II, 251-263.

resumed, and to that end to immediately convene a congress in any border city, to be considered neutral.[25] Metternich replied that the proposals by the *Empereur des Français* had been brought to the attention of the Coalition courts by order of the Austrian Kaiser, and that Their Majesties Emperor Alexander and the King of Prussia, sharing the peace-loving views of Their August ally, issued orders to announce to the duc de Bassano that 'being unable to decide matters related to the common cause unilaterally, without prior communication with other allies, they would lose no time in informing them of the French proposals…'[26]

This was the last word on the Prague Conferences. Stein and Pozzo di Borgo contributed greatly to the formation of the formidable Coalition against Napoleon: the former, driven by a spiritual sense of love for the fatherland; the latter, by family vengeance against the Bonapartes. Emperor Alexander I's determination to continue the war after the demise of Napoleon's army in Russia was owed in part to Stein's German patriotism. He is primarily responsible for the brilliance of the East Prussian uprising and the conclusion of the Russo-Prussian alliance. He was the first to suggest the concept of reviving Germany. Count Pozzo di Borgo also rendered important services to the common causes of Germany and Europe, promoting the conclusion of Russian treaties of alliance with Britain and Sweden. Gifted, rich in knowledge, mentally agile, Pozzo di Borgo sought out opportunities to harm Napoleon with the passion of a Corsican and was in communication with all his enemies. He was renowned for having said 'If I do not kill Napoleon, then at least I shall throw a last handful of earth on his grave.' Once Britain had joined the Coalition, a third, very active enemy of France, Sir Charles Stewart, appeared as a British representative. The Russian Minister of Foreign Affairs, Count Nesselrode, and the Anglo-Hanoverian Minister, Graf Münster also had an important part in the diplomatic struggle that paved the way for the fall of Napoleon. All these statesmen distrusted Metternich, believing that, following the Austrian disasters of 1805 and 1809, he should not have hesitated to assist the Coalition. It has been claimed (and is highly likely) that his enemies raised Napoleon's suspicions against Metternich, that he had handed over the secret correspondence between him and the Austrian diplomat to the Coalition courts: this affected Napoleon to such an extent that Metternich completely lost his trust and he had taken the side of the enemies of France out of necessity.[27] Having received word of Austria's accession to the Coalition, Stein wrote to Graf Münster:

> I hope Your Excellency has received my letter from Reichenbach – in the meantime the great matter of Austria's accession has developed. We owe it, along with God, to the clever conduct of Humboldt and Anstett, to Napoleon's follies, to the noble sentiments of the Emperor Alexander, to the

25 Fain, II, 96-101; Norvins, II, 271-276; the duc de Bassano's note to Graf Metternich dated 18 August, new style.

26 Graf Metternich's note to the duc de Bassano dated 21 August, new style.

27 Beitzke, *Geschichte der deutschen Freiheitskriege*, I, 651-654.

> perseverance of the King and the *Staatskanzler* (Hardenberg) – not to the soft, selfish politics of Metternich and that good Kaiser.[28]

During the night of 29 to 30 July (10 to 11 August), beacons blazed across the entire stretch from Prague to the headquarters of the Coalition armies. These were the signal that announced the suspension of negotiations. That same night, Barclay de Tolly sent messages to the enemy outposts announcing the end of the armistice. The next day, more than 100,000 Russo-Prussian troops marched from Silesia into Bohemia.[29]

28 '*... Prag, den 23sten August, 1813. Ich hoffe, Eure Excellenz haben mein Schreiben aus Reichenbach erhalten – unterdessen hat sich die grosse Angelenheit des Beitritt Oesterreich entwickelt. Wir verdanken ihn, nächts Gott, dem klugen Benehmen Humboldts und Anstetts, der Tollheit Napoleons, denen edlen Gesinnungen des Kaisers Alexander, der Beharrlichkeit des Königs und des Staatskanzlers – nicht der weichlichen egoistischen Politik Metternichs und sienes guten Kaisers...*' From Stein's letter to Graf Münster dated 23 August, new style; Pertz, *Das Leben des Ministers Freiherrn vom Stein*, III, 406.

29 Pertz, *Stein's Leben*, III, 403.

Appendix XXIX

The exchange of notes at the Prague Congress from 8 to 10 August

1. Graf Metternich's note to the French representatives dated 8 August, new style, in which he pointed out the fallacy of their conclusions: regarding the promise, according to them given by the Viennese Cabinet, that he would observe impartiality and would not commit himself, throughout the duration of the negotiations, to any kind of convention; the mediating power's assurances of their own impartiality would be inconsistent with their dignity. Metternich denied that he had determined the format of the upcoming negotiations together with the duc de Bassano, or that the Russian government, when embarking on them, had the intent to set Austria and France at odds with each other.
2. The response of the French delegates, dated 9 August, new style, in which they, agreeing to negotiate in writing, proposed, at the same time, verbal conferences, following the model of the congresses of Münster, Nijmegen and Rijswijk.
3. Notes from the Coalition representatives to Count Metternich, dated 10 August, new style. Both of them confirming their conviction of the necessity of the mode of negotiations proposed to them.
4. The response from the French representatives, on that same day, in which they strove to demonstrate the Coalition fear of entering into any agreement with France.

Copies of the notes from the representatives of both sides are held in the Archive of the M.F.A.; Fain, II, 180-200; Norvins, II, 222-238.

Anstett's note to Graf Metternich, dated midnight, 29 July (10 August).

Les soins de la Puissance médiatrice et ses moyens de conciliation pour arriver à une pacification entre les Puissances belligérenates n'ayant point eu au terme irrévocablement fixé pour cet objet, le succès, qu l'on devait se promettre d'une négociation conduite sous la médiation d'une cour puissante, impartiale et juste, le soussigné est chargé d'ordre exprès de son Auguste Maître, de reclamer de la part de l'Autriche l'exécution du traité eventucl du 15 (27) Juin de la présente année. Il est chargé en même tems d'assurer de la manière la plus positive que Sa Majesté l'Empereur de toutes les Russies accomplira de Son coté tous les articles, clauses et conditions du dit traité.

Le soussigné auroit une obligation particulière à S.E. Mr le Comte de Metternich, s'il était mis à même de transmettre dans le plus court délai possible une reponse à Son Auguste Maître, à cette démarche officielle...

Archive of the M.F.A.

19

The preparations by both sides for the resumption of military operations

The advance of the reserves to the Vistula: from St Petersburg and Yaroslavl; from Prince Lobanov-Rostovsky's reserve army. – The onward advance of the reserves to the active armies. – The advance to the army of those troop formations left in the rear. – The number of troops in the active Russian army at the end of the armistice.

The composition and quality of Prussian forces. Their equipment. – *Landwehr* and *Landsturm*. – The number of troops in the active Prussian army. The composition and quality of Austrian forces. – The number of troops in the active Austrian army.

The strength of Coalition forces overall.

The advance of French reserves to the army. – The composition and troop strength of the active French army. – The number of artillery pieces.

A comparison of the strengths of both sides. – The plan of operations of the Coalition armies, drafted at Schloss Trachenberg. – Napoleon's planning: the strongholds on the Elbe. – The fortification of Dresden. – Securing the crossing point at Königstein. – Napoleon's plan of operations. – The deployment of his forces at the end of the armistice.

Orders for the movement of reserves from their assembly areas to the Neman and Vistula were directed by Count Arakcheev. In early [mid] February, in pursuance of Supreme Orders, 22 battalions raised by Major General Bashutsky (subsequently two more battalions were sent), and 22 squadrons raised by Colonel Gendre, were sent from St. Petersburg to Jurburg [Jurbarkas] and Tauroggen. Seven battalions and ten squadrons from this force were assigned to the Lifeguard; two battalions to the Grenadier Corps; four battalions to 6th Division, six more to 21st Division and three battalions to 25th Division; 12 squadrons were assigned to the cavalry of the line. Of these, 13 battalions and two squadrons were to arrive at Danzig from 27 to 29 April (9 to 11 May), while the remaining nine battalions and 20 squadrons were to arrive in Płock between 1 and 18 (13 and 30) May.[1] From Yaroslavl, 24 battalions (12 for the Grenadier Corps and six each for 5th Division and 14th Division), raised by Lieutenant General Kleinmikhel, were directed to Olita [Alytus] and Kovno, from where they began to proceed towards Płock, arriving there between 18 (30) May and 1 (13) June.[2]

A Directed Supreme Decree dated 5 (17) February ordered that at least two companies from each battalion from the Reserve Army, raised and commanded by General-of-Infantry Prince Lobanov-Rostovsky, be sent to Warsaw, for a total of 154 companies. General-of-Cavalry Kologrivov was also tasked to send the reserve squadrons to Warsaw as soon as they were raised. Prince Lobanov-Rostovsky's infantry should have reached Warsaw in several waves between 3 and 11 (15 and 23) April, but arrived later. From 12 to 18 (24 to 30) April, 20 battalions commanded by Major General Adamovich[3] arrived, numbering about 12,000 men, having lost

1 Schedule of forces marching from St. Petersburg to the Neman and onwards to the Vistula:
To Płock via Jurburg: first wave under Colonel Kaptsevo – seven Lifeguard battalions and two of grenadiers; second wave under Colonel Vietinghoff – ten Lifeguard squadrons and two of Poland Ulans.
To Danzig via Tauroggen: first wave under Lieutenant Colonel Stepanov – four battalions for 6th Division and three battalions for 25th Division; second wave under Major Safronov – six battalions for 21st Division and two squadrons of Kazan Dragoons.
To Płock via Tauroggen: third wave under Lieutenant Colonel Lobri – eight squadrons of Finland Dragoons, Mitau Dragoons and Grodno Hussars.
Subsequently, two more battalions were sent to Danzig for the 31st Jägers and 47th Jägers.
Count Arakcheev's report dated 13 [25] January, regarding the imminent departure of 46 battalions and 22 squadrons from St Petersburg and Yaroslavl, Archive of the Military Topographic Depot (M.T.D.), No. 29,182, Log of Incoming Documents, No. 199.

2 Schedule of forces marching from Yaroslavl to the Neman and onwards to the Vistula:
Via Olita under Major General Avdulin: first wave – six battalions for 1st Grenadier Division; second wave – six battalions for 2nd Grenadier Division.
Via Kovno under Major General Gladkov: first wave – six battalions for 5th Division; second wave – six battalions for 14th Division.
All 24 battalions departed for Płock.
Count Arakcheev's report dated 13 [25] January, regarding the imminent departure of 46 battalions and 22 squadrons from St Petersburg and Yaroslavl, Archive of the Military Topographic Depot (M.T.D.), No. 29,182, Log of Incoming Documents, No. 199.

3 Major General Adamovich's force consisted of:
First detachment under Colonel Krechetnikov – one battalion each of Sofia Infantry, 18th Jägers, 30th Jägers, and one combined battalion of Pskov Infantry and Moscow Infantry.
Second detachment under Lieutenant Colonel Cheremisinov – one battalion each of Tomsk Infantry, 34th Jägers, and two combined battalions of Libau Infantry and Ufa Infantry, 11th Jägers and 19th Jägers.
Third detachment under Colonel Rehbinder – one battalion each of Wilmanstrand Infantry and 40th Jägers, and two combined battalions of Shirvan Infantry and Butyrsk Infantry, Brest Infantry and Ryazan Infantry.
Fourth detachment under Lieutenant Colonel Turchaninov – one battalion of Nizhegorod Infantry, and three combined battalions of Belozersk Infantry and Orël Infantry, Ladoga Infantry and Poltava Infantry, 5th Jägers and 47th Jägers.
Fifth detachment under Colonel Kaftyrev – one battalion each of Tarnopol Infantry and 41st Jägers, and two combined battalions of Odessa Infantry and Simbirsk Infantry, Vilna Infantry and 49th Jägers.

1,200 to death or desertion on the march and leaving more than 4,800 men in hospital.[4] The remaining 18½ battalions commanded by Major General Bestuzhev-Ryumin,[5] reached Warsaw on 19, 21 and 25 April (1, 3 and 7 May), numbering some 8,000 men, having lost more than 1,000 dead or deserters on the march, with more than 2,000 men in hospital.[6] The military governor of Riga, Marquis Paulucci [Filip Osipovich Pauluchchi or Filippo Paulucci], had sent the replacement battalions of 5th Division and 14th Division to Königsberg in March, and in April, the replacement battalions of 6th Division, 21st Division and 25th Division to Danzig, while those of 3rd Division, 4th Division and 17th Division had been sent to Płock. The number of men constituting all these battalions reached some 3,000 men.[7]

The troops sent from St. Petersburg to Danzig, comprising I Reserve Corps (13 battalions and two squadrons), arrived there on 29 April (11 May), numbering about 6,000 men.[8] On 8 (20) July, the reserve battalions of 31st Jägers and 47th Jägers also arrived at Danzig from St. Petersburg, numbering around 1,100 men.[9] Ten Lifeguard and grenadier battalions commanded by Colonel Kartsov [Pavel Stepanovich Kartsov] arrived in early [mid] June from Major General Gladkov's II Reserve Corps [Ivan Vasilievich Gladkov] in order to reconstitute the Lifeguard and Grenadier corps as well as Count Wittgenstein's force (5th Division and 14th Division), while another 12 grenadier battalions[10] commanded by Colonel Zaitsev [Alexey Dmitrievich Zaitsev] departed Płock between 19 and 21 May (31 May and 2 June), numbering 5,442 men,[11] and reached the army in July. Count Wittgenstein's corps were thus replenished in July.[12]

Extracted from Major General Adamovich's returns attached to his report No. 269 to Adjutant General Prince Volkonsky, dated 27 April [9 May], Log of Incoming Documents No. 935.

4 Major General Adamovich's report No. 269 to Adjutant General Prince Volkonsky, dated 27 April [9 May], Log of Incoming Documents No. 935.

5 Major General Bestuzhev-Ryumin's force consisted of: one battalion each of 50th Jägers, 36th Jägers, Novoingermanland Infantry, Polotsk Infantry, 21st Jägers, Rylsk Infantry, 42nd Jägers, Selenginsk Infantry and Minsk Infantry; eight combined battalions of Narva Infantry and Smolensk Infantry, Kexholm Infantry and Pernov Infantry, Alexopol Infantry and 6th Jägers, 1st Jägers and 33rd Jägers, Yekaterinburg Infantry and Kaporsk Infantry, Murom Infantry and Reval Infantry, 4th Jägers and 20th Jägers, Kremenchug Infantry and Tobolsk Infantry, Volhynia Infantry and Chernigov Infantry; two companies of Yelets Infantry.

Extracted from returns attached to Lieutenant General Neverovsky's letter No. 106 to Prince Volkonsky, dated 4 [16] May, Log of Incoming Documents, No. 919.

6 The losses to the force under Bestuzhev-Ryumin were derived approximately from the losses shown in the returns for the 8½ battalions from his corps that arrived in Warsaw on 19 April (1 May).

7 Returns attached to the military governor of Riga, Marquis Paulucci's report No. 132 to Emperor Alexander I, dated 26 April [8 May], Log of Incoming Documents, No. 924.

8 Baron Steinheil, Notes On The St. Petersburg *Opolchenie*, II, 65.

9 Herzog Alexander von Württemberg's dispatch No. 784 to the Chief of the General Staff, Adjutant General Prince Volkonsky, dated 20 July, Log of Incoming Documents, No. 1,212.

10 The Leib Grenadiers and Pavlovsk Grenadiers had been incorporated into the Lifeguard.

11 Colonel Zaitsev's report No. 488 to Prince Volkonsky, dated 21 May [2 June] from Płock, Log of Incoming Documents, No. 1,129.

12 Schedule of forces, signed by army commander-in-chief, Barclay de Tolly.

Two detachments, under Colonel Krechetnikov and Lieutenant Colonel Cheremisinov, from Major General Adamovich's III Reserve Corps, crossed the Vistula on 16 (28) April, leaving a half-battalion of 19th Jägers with Count Pahlen's detachment holding Warsaw, and having detached a battalion of 18th Jägers to Danzig. Now consisting of four battalions and five half-battalions, under the command of Colonel Krechetnikov,[13] they advanced via Błonie and Sochaczew to Kłodawa, where they were joined by the Pskov Infantry, left behind in Vilna with other troops from 7th Division (VI Corps) for reconstitution, and which had set out earlier than the other regiments for Kłodawa via Płock. From there, Krechetnikov's detachment continued to march towards Poznań, and upon reaching this town, on 6 (18) May, headed onwards to join the army via Brieg [Brzeg]. The following two detachments, Colonel Rehbinder's and Lieutenant Colonel Turchaninov's [Andrei Petrovich Turchaninov], crossed the Vistula on 18 (30) April. Colonel Kaftyrev's detachment and the battalions of 36th Jägers and 50th Jägers also crossed on 20 April (2 May). Of the troops of these detachments, the Nizhegorod Infantry and 41st Jäger battalions and half-battalions of Orël Infantry, Ladoga Infantry, Poltava Infantry and 5th Jägers marched on Modlin to join 12th Division and 26th Division. Four battalions and ten half-battalions were directed via Błonie and Sochaczew to Poznań in two detachments under Colonel Rehbinder and Major Antonov,[14] and having arrived there between 8 and 12 (20 and 24) May, continued marching towards the Oder. One battalion of 36th Jägers, with some sub-units of reserve troops that had remained in Warsaw commanded by Colonel Kaftyrev, arrived in Poznań on 22 May (3 June) and moved on to rendezvous with the army.[15]

From Major General Bestuzhev-Ryumin's IV Reserve Corps, the Novoingermanland Infantry and 42nd Jäger battalions and half-battalions of Narva Infantry, Smolensk Infantry, Alexopol Infantry and 6th Jägers were sent to Modlin. The remaining five battalions and 15 half-battalions[16] crossed the Vistula from 23 to 26 April (5 to 8 May), passed through Skierniewice and Stryków to Kalisz where they linked up with the

13 Colonel Krechetnikov's first detachment of III Corps consisted of one battalion each of Sofia Infantry, Tomsk Infantry, 30th Jägers and 34th Jägers and half-battalions of Moscow Infantry, Pskov Infantry, Ufa Infantry and 11th Jägers, for a total of 2,689 combatants, with another 490 sick with the battalions.

14 These detachments of III Reserve Corps consisted of:
Colonel Rehbinder's detachment – one battalion each of Wilmanstrand Infantry and 40th Jägers; half-battalions of Brest Infantry, Ryazan Infantry, Butyrsk Infantry and Shirvan Infantry, for a total of 1,437 combatants, with 364 sick with the battalions.
Major Antonov's detachment – one battalion each of Tarnopol Infantry and 50th Jägers; half-battalions of Odessa Infantry, Simbirsk Infantry, Vilna Infantry, 49th Jägers, Belozersk Infantry and 48th Jägres, for a total of 1,762 combatants, with 145 sick with the battalions.

15 Colonel Kaftyrev's force had an overall strength of 1,570 combatants with another 167 sick.

16 Upon their departure for Kalisz, IV Reserve Corps consisted of:
Major Peshchansky's detachment – one battalion each of Polotsk Infantry and 21st Jägers, half-battalions of Kexholm Infantry, Pernov Infantry, Yelets Infantry, 1st Jägers and 33rd Jägers, for a total of 2,180 combatants and 240 sick with the battalions.
Colonel Timofeev's detachment – one battalion each of Rylsk Infantry and Selenginsk Infantry, half-battalions of Yekaterinburg Infantry, Koporsk Infantry, Murom Infantry, Reval Infantry 4th Jägers and 20th Jägers, for a total of 2,102 combatants and 561 sick with the battalions.

Yekaterinburg Infantry (23rd Division, IV Corps), which had been reconstituted in Vilna and arrived in Kalisz from Wyszogród and Płock. They continued on through Poznań and joined the army in Reichenbach in early (mid) June. Overall, 144 men from both corps sent to the army by Prince Lobanov-Rostovsky remained in Warsaw; 447 men had been sent to Danzig and 4,154 to Modlin; 15,236 men had been sent to the active armies: in total some 20,000 men had passed through Warsaw.[17]

Of the cavalry reserves raised by General Kologrivov, eight hussar squadrons and six of dragoons were sent to the active army on 16 and 25 April [28 April and 7 May], commanded by Major General Bezobrazov [Lavrenty Afanasievich Bezobrazov].[18] Upon reaching Warsaw, these troops set out from there, on 16 (28) May, numbering 1,420 fighting men and 595 recruits, passing through Kalisz towards Brieg.[19]

Of the artillery reserves, the Inspector of All Artillery, Baron Meller-Zakomelsky, sent five battery companies to the army (less guns).[20]

Of the troops left behind during the advance by the active army, the following were sent from Warsaw to Kalisz on 17 (29) April: Bialystok Infantry, 19th Jägers and 45th Jägers, commanded by Major General Zheltukhin [Sergei Fëdorovich Zheltukhin]. Following them, also from Warsaw to Kalisz, were the regiments of III Cavalry Corps: Kurland Dragoons, Sumy Hussars, Orenburg Ulans, Siberia Ulans, 29th Battery Artillery Company and 19th Light Artillery Company, commanded by Major General Pahlen 2nd [Pavel Petrovich Palen or Paul Carl Ernst Wilhelm Philipp von der Pahlen]. On 17 (29) May, this force, together with both Jäger regiments, marched to the Oder and were assimilated into the active army at the end of May [early June].[21] The Bialystok Infantry joined the army a little later, along with the troops under General Neverovsky, who had also been joined on the march by Major Lisovsky with 1,092 convalescents from the hospitals; Major Menzhinsky with two reserve squadrons of Lubny Hussars and Popov 3rd's Don Cossack Regiment.[22]

Colonel Barkov's detachment – one battalion of Minsk Infantry, half-battalions of Kremenchug Infantry, Tobolsk Infantry, Volhynia Infantry and Chernigov Infantry, for a total of 1,223 combatants and 402 sick with the battalions.

Note: following the death of Bestuzhev-Ryumin, Major Peshchansky's detachment joined III Reserve Corps, while the other two detachments came under the command of Colonel Alexeev.

17 Lieutenant General Neverovsky's letter No. 106 to the chief of the General Staff, Adjutant General Prince Volkonsky, dated 4 [16] May, with attached schedules of forces for III Reserve Corps and IV Reserve Corps, Log of Incoming Documents, No. 919.

18 Count Arakcheev's note No. 419 to Adjutant General Prince Volkonsky, dated 24 April [6 May], Log of Incoming Documents, No. 771.

19 Major General Bezobrazov's report No. 89 to Prince Volkonsky, dated 16 [28] May, from Warsaw, with attached schedule of forces for the hussars and dragoons, Log of Incoming Documents, No. 1,086.

20 Count Arakcheev's report No. 170 to Prince Kutuzov-Smolensky, dated 11 [23] March, from Kalisz, Log of Incoming Documents, No. 481.

21 Major General Count Pahlen 2nd's detachment consisted of: 1,156 men in four cavalry regiments, 1,116 men in two jäger regiments and 413 men in two artillery companies, for a total of 2,685 men. Extracted from the schedule of forces attached to Count Pahlen 2nd's report No. 80 to Adjutant General Prince Volkonsky, dated 15 [27] May, Log of Incoming Documents, No. 994.

22 Lieutenant General Neverovsky's letter No. 155 to Prince Volkonsky, dated 23 May [4 June], from Olszowa [Kempen], Log of Incoming Documents, No. 1,135.

In addition to all the aforementioned reinforcements, a large number of recovered sick and wounded men, having been discharged from hospital, rejoined the army.

Throughout the duration of the armistice, the active Russian army, having retreated into Silesia, was being significantly strengthened. At the end of May [early June], it had 83,000 men (including Sacken's corps that had arrived from the Duchy of Warsaw), indeed, in addition there were 7,000 in the detachments under generals Count Vorontsov and Harpe, thus, in total there were 90,000 men.[23] At the end of the armistice, the number of troops in the active Russian army had reached 175,000 men with 648 guns.[24] In addition, there were over 30,000 regular troops and *opolchenie* with 59 guns around Danzig; in the Duchy of Warsaw, Bennigsen's so-called Army of Poland was forming up, gradually increasing in strength to 70,000 men with 200 guns, followed by the reserve army under Prince Lobanov-Rostovsky, numbering some 50,000.[25]

The majority of the Russian army consisted of recruits, of which only a few had taken part in the spring campaign of 1813. The incessant wars waged since 1805 had depleted the population of Russia to the point that the recruits, of necessity, were no longer young men merely having the appearance of veteran soldiers. The uniforms and weapons of the troops were very satisfactory. The horse harness, and especially the artillery, were in excellent condition.[26]

Throughout the duration of the armistice, Silesia could not meet the needs of the Coalition forces stationed in concentrated quarters in this region. In the beginning, the situation seemed hopeless: the regimental wagons were empty, and the mobile magazines were far behind the army.

In the first instance, provisions were delivered from store located in the Prussian fortresses, and, at the same time, large requisitions were collected in Poland, throughout the entire area as far as Bromberg, Krakow and Warsaw, from where the provisions were delivered to the Oder. Deliveries from Thorn had also been arranged. In Silesia itself, the troops found plentiful resources, yet quite often foragers obtained cut grass as a substitute for hay. Many supplies were obtained by local purchase, in particular, much was smuggled in from Austrian territory. Quite a significant amount of flour was brought from upper Silesia. The population of Breslau, and in general the neutral demilitarised zone between the belligerent armies provided a lot of grain, mainly to Schweidnitz. Mobile magazines were used to deliver provisions to the troops. One of them, consisting of 3,000 peasant carts, having been assigned, back in 1812, to the former Army of Moldavia, had fallen behind and arrived on the Vistula in very poor condition, but after spending the winter in the Duchy of Warsaw, recovered and moved on to Silesia, with 25,000 *centners* [hundredweight] of hard-tack, which, having a long shelf-life, were used to feed the troops, not only in 1813, but also into the subsequent campaign.[27]

23 Returns dated 1 [13] June 1813, signed by the Commander-in-Chief Barclay de Tolly.

24 For details of the Russian forces, see Appendix XXX at the end of this chapter.

25 Returns dated 21 July [2 August], signed by Barclay de Tolly; Report on the troop state of the Army of Poland, signed by General Bennigsen.

26 Bernhardi, *Denkwürdigkeiten des Grafen von Toll*, III, 79.

27 Graf von Cancrin, *Ueber die Militärökonomie im Frieden und Krieg*, I, 87-88.

The basis of the Prussian armed forces raised throughout the armistice, were the *Landwehr.* Yet in the initial campaign of 1813, they had managed neither to complete their military training, nor even to procure proper weapons: Prussia had many men ready to defend their sacred motherland. Yet these men were not warriors, in any sense of the word. Prior to the armistice, the active Prussian army consisted of line troops, reinforced by detachments of volunteer jägers, both mounted and on foot, with the 52 reserve battalions mostly being used to blockade the French held fortresses. During the armistice, these battalions were reorganized into 17 reserve regiments. As the *Landwehr* battalions became operational, they replaced the reserve battalions around the fortresses, the latter rejoining the army. Most of the *Landwehr* were in four-battalion regiments, which joined the army on an equal basis with line (active) and reserve regiments. Likewise, the army was reinforced with *Landwehr* cavalry, and only a small number of them were allocated to the blockading detachments. The entire *Landwehr* was raised on the country's account. Almost all officers were appointed on election by their comrades. Many of them had previously served as officials in the civil service, or were engaged in commerce or other trades, and some veteran non-commissioned officers were promoted. Battalion and company commanders were appointed from retired officers without exception, but among them there were many who had left the service without having gained experience in their former rank, or had served in invalid sub-units. The lack of non-commissioned officers capable of training recruits was also sorely felt. This forced training to be limited to the most essential skills. Action in loose formation was out of the question; but the *Landwehr* learned the commands: *Bataillon vorwärts!* (battalion will advance!) and *zur Attake Gewehr rechts!* (right shoulder arms, attack!). For the most part, when firepower could not resolve the issue, the warriors fought with rifle butts. In the *Landwehr* cavalry, almost all officers and non-commissioned officers were retired veterans.

Landwehr uniform consisted of a short, blue caftan (*Litewka*), with a collar in the facing colour: red for East Prussia, white for Pomerania, rose madder (*krapprot*) for the Mark, yellow for Silesia. Subsequently, for the Elbe districts it was blue with red piping and green for Thuringia. Tin crosses were worn on the blue caps of *Landwehr* soldiers with the inscription: *mit Gott für König und Vaterland* (with God, for King and fatherland). Not every fighting man was issued with a greatcoat; their short caftans were made from striped, unfinished cloth, which, in the first rain-shower, shrank to the point that the clothing became almost unusable. In Silesia, the *Landwehr* fighters, for the most part, had linen shirts; shod in shoes without gaiters, they lost them in the thick mud at every step, and marched barefoot; there were few backpacks. All *Landwehr* infantry were issued muskets, but there was a shortage of cartridge pouches and hanger-swords. The cavalry were armed with sabres and lances; some of the horsemen, in addition, had single pistols. The broad-shouldered, rosy-cheeked population of Pomerania were the best of the *Landwehr* fighting men, in appearance, athleticism and capability for combat work and hardship. In contrast, many Silesian battalions, recruited from the factories, exhausted by poor diet and sedentary work, presented a rather pitiful sight.

Napoleon spoke of the Prussian *Landwehr* with contempt, calling them *canaille* (mongrels). Indeed, the Prussians themselves did not give due justice to the

Landwehr, who served as the foundation of their army: according to concepts of that period, the status of subject-warrior was a contradiction in terms. Line officers were considered incomparably superior to *Landwehr* officers; volunteers serving as private soldiers (*freiwilliger Jäger*) were reluctant to become *Landwehr* officers. Subsequently, through many exploits on the field of honour, the *Landwehr* were able to earn the respect of both their own and their enemies.

In addition to the raising of the *Landwehr*, the *Landsturm* were activated in Prussia. Veteran, invalid officers were appointed as battalion commanders; company commanders from civil servants, *Burgemeister* (mayors) and even pastors; squadrons were commanded by retired cavalry officers. Since civil servants did not have the slightest idea about military service, the training of newly recruited fighting men was usually carried out on Sundays by long-service non-commissioned officers. Some turned up for training with muskets, while the rest had pikes. Long lines of fighting men were visible in every assembly area, in cities and towns, there was a queue of men from all walks of life in a hurry to take part in military exercises. The farmer, swept along on a wave of enthusiasm for the common cause, led his nag out of the stall, saddled it and, taking a lance with a colourful pennant, like a favour, went to the squadron's rendezvous point. Indeed, at that time generally, no one went anywhere on horseback without a lance.

It is quite difficult to determine the precise number of *Landwehr* raised in the period of the resumption of hostilities. According to almost all contemporary and subsequent sources, the *Landwehr* actually reached 100,000 men, namely: 20 battalions and 19 squadrons in the Prussian provinces; 12 battalions and 12 squadrons in Pomerania; 12 battalions and 8 squadrons in Neumark; 28 battalions and 21 squadrons in Kurmark, and 60 battalions and 40 squadrons in Silesia, for a total of 132 battalions and 100 squadrons, numbering 90,000 infantry and 10,000 cavalry.

The overall number of Prussian line troops and *Landwehr*, reached 235,000 men, and after excluding the blockade detachments, depots, fortress garrisons, and so on, the active Prussian army counted some 170,000 in its ranks with 876 guns.[28]

These troops, mostly consisting of young soldiers, had no time to undergo combat training; in particular, the *Landwehr* were poorly trained, where not only were entire battalions and regiments formed from recruits, but Tauentzien's entire corps also consisted of men who had never been in action before. The troops, although generally distinguished by spirit and diligence, but poorly clothed and shod, could not endure the difficulties of the autumn campaign and were melting away noticeably from illness.[29]

28 According to a strength return dated 10 August, the Prussian army comprised: 78,400 line infantry in 98 battalions; 112,000 *Landwehr* infantry in 140 battalions; 2,400 jägers in 12 companies; 700 pioneers in seven companies; 12,600 line cavalry in 84 squadrons; 21,000 Landwehr cavalry in 140 squadrons; 8,100 artillerymen in 54 batteries, for a total of 235,200 men. Excluded from these totals were: 33,200 men in various depots and fortress garrisons; 32,000 men blockading fortresses, for a total of 65,200 men. Thus, the active army consisted of 170,000 men.
These figures differ only slightly from those shown in Plotho's work *Der Krieg in Deutschland und Frankreich in den Jahren 1813 und 1814*, II, *Beilagen*, 2-23.

29 Bernhardi, III, 79-80.

Although Austria began intensive preparations for war at the end of 1812, nevertheless, due to the disorderly state of their finances, they would not manage to finish their mobilisation in a timely manner. The position of the Austrian Monarchy after the war of 1809 required great frugality in terms of government expenditure, cutting costs mainly on the maintenance of the army: many regiments had been disbanded; the remainder consisted of two grenadier companies and three (six-company) battalions; but in each of the companies there were only about 100 privates enlisted, half of whom were on permanent leave: thus, battalions had 300 men each. Those on furlough assembled quite rarely and for such a short time that their training could not be considered satisfactory. Under such circumstances, given the shortage of cash and various stores essential to equip the newly raised troops, their rapid mobilisation presented difficulties that could only be overcome by extraordinary energy from the government. Yet the failures of previous wars, and especially the war of 1809, in which Austria made a final attempt to defend its independence, instilled distrust in its own forces, both in the government and among the population. The troops, influenced by the failures they had suffered, did not want war, and this factor was the primary cause of both the slowness of the raising of the army and the sluggishness of their operations. The inhabitants of the Alps and Carpathians, the Hungarians, the Bohemians, the Moravians and the population of Galicia, brave peoples, had nothing in common with each other; while the military institutions of Austria at that time could neither raise the morale of their troops nor direct their efforts towards achieving the common goal. Soldiers were obligated to serve their entire lives, were subjected to humiliating punishment for the slightest offence and had no hope of commissioning as officers – granted exclusively to the nobility. The highest appointments in the army were occupied by persons belonging to the aristocracy, and little attention was paid to aptitude. Austrian tactics were also based on old doctrine that had become obsolete and inapplicable to the modern military state-of-the-art.

The raising of the troops was mirrored by the general apathy of the military class. Initially, the third battalions of infantry regiments were disbanded in order to complete the manning of the other two battalions; thereafter, they detached subunits from them in order to form cadres for the third battalions, which were replenished with recruits and did this to maintain the correct number of regiments and grenadier battalions. As for the *Landwehr* battalions that were supposed to join the army as soon as the armistice had been concluded – they barely had time to begin to assemble. Those Hungarian regiments which remained constantly in service were stronger and in better condition than the others. In a similar manner, cavalry, which take a long time to raise, had been constantly kept up to strength and was fairly well combat trained. Once hostilities had resumed after the armistice, Austria claimed its armed forces had been present in greater numbers than they actually were in order to give weight to their participation in the war: a consequence of this was the exaggeration of the Austrian army in official reports and in military-historical works; the number of troops present at the opening of the campaign did not exceed 110,500 men. But it was replenished over time, and after retreating to Bohemia from Dresden, despite the losses suffered, was stronger than previously.[30]

30 Beitzke, *Geschichte der deutschen Freiheitskriege*, I, 692-693; Bernhardi, III, 71-75.

The composition of the Coalition armies was as follows:

	Infantry		Cavalry		Cossacks		Artillery		
	Battalions	Men	Squadrons	Men	Regiments	Men	Companies /Batteries	Guns	Men
Russian	191	106,742	225	28,388	65	25,928	58	630	12,392
Prussian	193	135,188	200	26,061	-	-	47	376	7,496
Austrian	106-112	89,600	112-124	15,500	-	-	45	270	5,400
Swedish[31]	42	22,073	32	4,342	-	-	10	68	1,853
British	-	-	4	400	-	-	1[32]	-	100
Various German	18	10,072	25	2,380	-	-	6½	39	1,020
TOTAL:	**550-556**	**363,675**	**598-610**	**77,071**	**65**	**25,928**	**167½**	**1,383**	**28,261**

Consequently, the number of Coalition troops in the active armies reached 500,000 men with 1,383 guns (together with several Cossack regiments that were on a variety of tasks).[33]

In addition, the following were in the theatre of war: 100,000 Russians at Danzig and in the Duchy of Warsaw; 65,000 Prussians blockading fortresses, as fortress garrisons or being raised; 130,000 Austrians on the Bavarian border, in Italy or in reserve; 3,000 men in five British battalions and one from Anhalt-Dessau, stationed as the garrison of Stralsund,[34] for a total of 300,000 men.

During the armistice, Napoleon more than doubled the number of troops in his active army. This had been achieved by means of depots in which conscripts assembled and quickly received military training. But since necessity itself had forced the French to recruit men into the army who had not yet reached the conscription age mandated by law, many of the soldiers turned out to be very under developed and could not endure labour and hardship in the field.[35] The contingents from the *Confédération du Rhin* were brought up to strength. As soon as 100 conscripts had been assembled, uniformed and armed in whichever of the depots, they formed a march company, which immediately set out and trained on the march. Several march companies belonging to the same division, being directed such that they could link up with each other, constituted march battalions, which were combined into march regiments (*régiments de marche*) or were assigned to provisional regiments (*régiments provisoires*). At border crossings, these troops were combined

31 Including Wallmoden's attached corps.

32 Bogue's Rocket 'Brigade' Royal Horse Artillery.

33 Schedule of troop strengths, dated 21 July [2 August] and 1 [13] August, signed by Barclay de Tolly; Bernhardi, III, 509-519.

34 Bernhardi, III, 519.

35 Saint-Cyr, *Mémoires, Campagne de 1813*, 53.

into march columns and were directed to the army by Marshal Kellermann. Upon leaving the borders of France, the movements were carried out by detachments made up of all combat arms, which contributed to the safe passage of individual echelons and, in the eyes of the inhabitants of Germany, gave them the appearance of new brigades and divisions sent to increase the army. During the march, on rest days, the conscripts received combat training and got used to the discipline. Upon the arrival of the march column in Dresden, the regiments were sent to their corps, and thereafter the battalions to their divisions, and companies were distributed to complete the manning of regiments. In the same way, the [permanently] weak and injured, having been assembled in march detachments under the command of officers, were sent from the army to their depots and from there to France. Parks and convoys with vital supplies moved under the protection of the march forces.[36]

The strength of Napoleon's forces when they resumed operations after the armistice, is shown to be less than their actual strength, both by French writers who wanted to attribute the failures of their fellow countrymen to the enormous numerical superiority of the Coalition, and in German works that repeated the figures given by the French without critical examination. But their statements are contradicted by official returns on the numbers of French troops and statements by Napoleon himself, who, knowing the real strength of his army better than anyone, calculated it to be 400,000 men, excluding Davout's corps.[37]

The French army had the following composition:

Formation	Battalions	Squadrons	Men
Vieille Garde – Marshal Lefebvre & *Jeune Garde* – Marshal Mortier	65	61	58,191
1er Corps – général de division Vandamme	42	4	33,298
2e Corps – Marshal Victor	42	6	25,158
3e Corps – Marshal Ney	63	10	40,006
4e Corps – général de division Bertrand	36	8	21,217
5e Corps – général de division Lauriston	37	7	27,905
6e Corps – Marshal Marmont	42	8	27,754
7e Corps – général de division Reynier	33¼	13	21,283
8e Corps – général de division Prince Poniatowski	10	6	7,573
11e Corps – Marshal Macdonald	38	11	24,418
12e Corps – Marshal Oudinot	34	14	18,986
13e Corps – Marshal Davout	33	5	27,034
Danish Contingent – Lieutenant General Landgraf Friedrich von Hessen	13	10	10,480
14e Corps – Marshal Saint Cyr	53	12	26,149
***Réserve de cavalerie* – Marshal Murat**			

36 Fain, *Manuscrit de 1813*, II, 51-54.

37 *Lettre de l'empereur Napoléon au maréchal Gouvion St. Cyr, de Bautzen, le 17 août 1813*; *Mémoires de St. Cyr*, 365-367.

Formation	Battalions	Squadrons	Men
1er Corps de cavalerie – général de division Latour-Maubourg		78	16,537
2e Corps de cavalerie – général de division Sébastiani		52	10,304
3e Corps de cavalerie – général de division Arrighi (duc de Padoue)		87	10,801
4e Corps de cavalerie – général de division Kellermann		32	4,831
TOTAL:		**249**	**42,473**

Réserve d'artillerie et de génie: 15 batteries of foot artillery; three batteries of horse artillery; five companies and 16 independent platoons; nine pontoon companies; 12 labour companies (sailors); one arsenal company and one armoury company; three sapper companies; two miner companies; one labour company (engineering department); one *train de genie* company, for a total of 8,010 men.

According to these figures (extracted from Bernhardi's *Denkwürdigkeiten des Grafen von Toll*, III, 493-504), the number of troops in the French army reached 370,000 men.

According to the schedule of troop strength, dated 6 August (new style), submitted to Napoleon by *chef d'état-major* Berthier, the troop totals were: 312,306 infantry; 69,707 cavalry; 32,528 artillerymen; 4,087 troops of the engineering department, for a total of 418,628 men.

This schedule does not show: *général de division* Girard's detachment (17 battalions and six squadrons), numbering around 11,000 men; Dąbrowski's Polish division (four battalions and two squadrons), numbering 4,000 men, and the observation detachment under *général de brigade* Margaron [Pierre Margaron], at Leipzig (ten battalions, two cavalry *regiments provisoires*), numbering 7,600 men, for a total of 22,600 men.[38] There is no definitive information anywhere regarding the number of guns that Napoleon's army had at the end of the armistice. But the figure can be deduced from official information, dated 1 October (new style) on the number of remaining guns, and showing the number of guns lost by the French from the resumption of hostilities until the end of September. According to a statement by General Pelet [Jean-Jacques Germain Pelet-Clozeau], based on reports on the state of the French army, on 1 October, after *12e Corps* under Marshal Oudinot had already been disbanded, the number of guns was: 202 in the *Garde*; 47 in *1er Corps*; 55 in *2e Corps*; 61 in *3e Corps*; 32 in *4e Corps*; 55 in *5e Corps*; 82 in *6e Corps*; 48 in *7e Corps*; 44 in *8e Corps*; 68 in *11e Corps*; 33 in *13e Corps*; 59 in *14e Corps*; 27 in *1er Corps de cavalerie*; 12 in *2e Corps de cavalerie*; nine in *3e Corps de cavalerie*; 12 in *4e Corps de cavalerie*, for a total of 846 guns.

38 In addition to the corps shown in the French operational army, there were: Marshal Augereau's *9e Corps* formed on the Rhine and joining the army shortly before the battle of Leipzig, *10e Corps* under *général de division* Rapp in Danzig. The number of troops in both corps may have reached 50,000 men. Vaudoncourt, *Histoire de la guerre soutenue par les Français en Allemagne*, 130 & 246.

Knocked out by the Coalition were: 14 guns at Großbeeren; nine at the fall of Luckau Wobeser; 103 at Katzbach and Macdonald's retreat from the Bober; 80 at Kulm; 80 at Dennewitz; eight at Görde; three at Hollendorf on 5 (17) September; five at Zeitz on 16 (28) September, for a total of 302 guns.

In addition, the detachments under Girard and Margaron, and Dąbrowski's division had from 28 to 36 guns at the end of the armistice.

Consequently, by the time hostilities resumed, Napoleon's army consisted of 440,000 men with 1,180 guns. The garrisons of fortified locations on the Elbe should be added to these forces, as they assisted the French army by forcing the Coalition to detach elements of their forces for their blockade. The Hamburg garrison consisted of at least 12,000 men; Magdeburg 3,250; Wittenberg 2,380; Torgau about 2,000; Dresden some 4,500 men; in total there were 24,000 men in garrisons on the Elbe.[39]

From a comparison of the number of troops on both sides, it emerges that the Coalition, even after Austria joined them, did not have a significant superiority over the French; in particular, bearing in mind that 25,000 Cossacks could not be brought in to advantage in pitched battles, we shall confirm the balance of power when hostilities resume. We have already had occasion to note that both the French and their enemies, the Russians and Prussians, had a great many recruits, and therefore neither side was superior to the other in the training or combat experience of the troops. Only the French cavalry, and especially the light cavalry, were inferior to those of the Coalition; Napoleon's artillery were in good condition.

The Coalition had to operate on the offensive not because they had a decisive superiority of forces on their side, but because of the influence of the situation in which they found themselves. Having assumed the role of liberators of Germany, they could not restrict themselves to defence, besides which, the salient position of Bohemia would help them to outflank the enemy army deployed along the Elbe, without exposing their own lines of communications to great danger. These same factors forced Napoleon to restrict himself to the defence of the Elbe, without moving a significant distance from this river. Had he moved beyond the Oder, having launched a decisive offensive operation, he would have given the allies the opportunity to incite the Rhine principalities against him, to occupy the ground on the left bank of the Elbe and sever his communications with France.

These considerations informed the operational planning of both sides.

Emperor Alexander I, the Prussian King and the Crown Prince of Sweden gathered at Schloss Trachenberg, seven *Meilen* from Breslau, on 28 June (10 July) for a meeting on impending operations by the Coalition armies. Prince Volkonsky, Sukhtelen, Pozzo di Borgo, Toll, Knesebeck and the Swedish generals Stedingk and Graf Löwenhielm accompanied them. The general opinion attributed the drafting of this plan to the Crown Prince of Sweden, as a commander trained in the 'Napoleon school' himself, but it is now known that his concept was completely different from that to which the Coalition proceeded to generally consent. Others believe that the plan of operations approved at Trachenberg was drafted by Knesebeck. In fact, no definitive plan had been drafted or proposed prior to the convening of the

39 Bernhardi, III, 493-508.

Trachenberg conference. The first meeting, on 29 June (11 July), began with a verbal briefing from the Crown Prince. Knesebeck disagreed with him, while Toll presented his ideas with his customary passion. The Coalition Monarchs, noticing the total differences of opinion and wishing to widen the consultation, left the Crown Prince with Löwenhielm, Knesebeck and Toll in order to co-author an operational plan.

'General, you seem to disagree with my opinion.' The Prince remarked to Toll.

'Might I, the most junior, be permitted to express…' began Toll.

The Crown Prince interrupted him, saying: 'speak, speak freely!'

Whereupon General Toll outlined his plan of operations, based on a draft he had submitted to Emperor Alexander at Reichenbach on 28 May (9 June), and forwarded by Toll personally, on the Tsar's orders, to the Fürst zu Schwarzenberg and the *Generalstabschef* [Chief of the General Staff] of the Austrian army, General Radetzky [Johann Josef Wenzel Anton Franz Karl Radetzky von Radetz], in Jitschin, in early [mid] June.

The Crown Prince, listening to Toll's project, expressed his approval with the words: 'Good! – Alright! this is very true!'[40] but then raised several objections. This led to another meeting later that evening. Eventually, on 30 June (12 July), the matter was finally decided in the presence of the Coalition monarchs. Knesebeck, who had previously received a briefing from King Friederich-Wilhelm on Toll's plans, supported them, the Crown Prince, expressing some further doubts, eventually said: 'you have convinced me, general,'[41] and requested that Toll set out the operational plan discussed at the meetings in writing.[42]

The disposition for operations written out by Toll was reviewed by the Crown Prince once more, who, although changing a few words, did not make any significant additions to it. It included the following orders:

> The main basis for the concept of operations is: to direct all Coalition forces to where the main enemy force is located, and therefore:
>
> Corps finding themselves operating on the enemy flanks or rear, are to take the shortest route to his line of operations.
>
> The Coalition main force must be positioned in such a way that they can always forestall the enemy. The salient position of Bohemia lends itself to this, like a bastion.
>
> Based on these principles, the Coalition armies should be located before the expiration of the armistice as follows:
>
> Elements of the army currently located in Silesia, with a strength of from 90,000 to 100,000 men, are to march through Landeshut and Glatz to Jungbunzlau [Mladá Boleslav] and Budin [Budyně nad Ohří] a few days

40 *'bien! – très bien! c'est très vrai!'*

41 *'vous m'avez convaincu, général'*

42 Bernhardi, III, 17-33 & 49-52. [Crediting Toll almost exclusively for the concept of the Trachenberg Plan is Tsarist propaganda; the plan (with subsequent amendments) was an amalgam of input from Russian, Prussian, Swedish and Austrian sources. For a detailed assessment, see Michael V. Leggiere's (2015) Napoleon And The Struggle For Germany, Volume 2].

> before the end of the armistice, in order to join the Austrian force in the shortest possible time, and to form a joint army with them of 200,000 to 220,000 men.
>
> The army under the Crown Prince of Sweden, leaving a corps of 15,000 or 20,000 men facing Lübeck and Hamburg in order to monitor the Danes and French, are to assemble a total of about 70,000 men in the vicinity of Treuenbrietzen in order to cross the Elbe between Torgau and Magdeburg, and proceed towards Leipzig without delay.
>
> The remaining troops from the Coalition army in Silesia, numbering 100,000 men, are to follow the enemy up to the Elbe, avoiding a pitched battle unless all the advantages are on our side, and are to cross the Elbe between Torgau and Dresden in order to link up with the army of the Crown Prince of Sweden, which will increase them to 120,000 men.
>
> Should it become necessary to reinforce the Army of Bohemia before the Army of Silesia has joined the force under the Crown Prince of Sweden, then the Army of Silesia is to immediately go to Bohemia.
>
> Depending on the circumstances, the Army of Bohemia is to move either towards Eger [Cheb] and Hof, towards Saxony or Silesia, or in the direction of the Danube. Should Napoleon forestall the Coalition and invade Bohemia, then the Crown Prince is to move by forced marches into the enemy rear. Should Napoleon move against the Crown Prince, the Army of Bohemia is to dash across enemy lines of communication and give battle.
>
> All Coalition armies are to operate on the offensive; the enemy camp is to be their rendezvous point.
>
> The Russian reserve army, under General Bennigsen, is to march from the Vistula, to Kalisz, and on to the Oder, in the direction of Glogau, and, operating under the same principles, is to march against the enemy should they remain in Silesia, or is to protect Poland from enemy invasion.[43]

Upon approval of this plan of operations by both Coalition monarchs, General Diebitsch went, under Supreme orders, with the original minutes of the meeting, signed by all persons participating, to Kaiser Franz, resident at Brandeis at that time. The operational plan of the Coalition armies was communicated to the Austrian government under the strictest secrecy. It has been claimed, however, that Napoleon received a copy of this document through the Saxon General Gersdorff, who allegedly bribed one of the officials at the headquarters of the Coalition army.[44]

Napoleon, taking the course of Elbe as the base of his operations, was obliged to secure its possession and the ability to quickly move from one bank of this river to the other by way of crossing points arranged at several locations and protected by fortifications. These locations in the operational area were the fortresses of Magdeburg, Wittenberg and Torgau; but it was also vital to reinforce Dresden, the most likely immediate operational objective of the Coalition army, most particularly in the event of Austria joining the Coalition. It was also very useful to have a

43 Minutes of the meetings in Trachenberg, 30 June (12 July).

44 Beitzke, I, 666; Förster, *Geschichte der Befreiungskriege, 1813, 1814, 1815*, I, 506.

fortified crossing where the Elbe flows out of Bohemia into Saxony, which would complicate a Coalition advance from the Ore Mountains towards Dresden and facilitate Napoleon's operations from the right bank of the river on their lines of communication with Bohemia. Tactically, the most advantageous point for this was the area around Pirna, where the Elbe is constrained by the mountains that dominate its course. On the left side of the river, an impregnable fort had been built on the Königstein outcrop; while on the right rises another outcrop, Lilienstein. Napoleon, having undertaken to reinforce Dresden and arrange a fortified crossing in the vicinity of Königstein, ordered the following works to be carried out.

At the beginning of the armistice, when there was still some doubt about whether Austria would join the Coalition, it was intended to limit work to the fortification of Dresden Neustadt, which lies on the right bank of the Elbe. This part of the city was surrounded, at a distance of about two *verstas*, by several lunettes and redoubts, while the intervals between them were obstructed with palisades and abatis. A rampart with bastions of a rather low profile had been built directly around the outer edge of the Neustadt. In addition to this double row of fortifications, a separate large entrenchment had been built in front of the Schwarzen Thor, called Fort Impérial, with a covered way and a blockhouse. A prominent part of the ancient ramparts, near the Weissen Thor, was turned into a cavalier [raised gun platform]. All these works were surrounded by palisades and armed with a number of guns. Behind the double perimeter of the Neustadt, two bridges were built on boats, above and below the permanent masonry bridge, while a trestle boom was built upstream to protect it.

Subsequently, once Austria's intention to take the side of the Coalition had become apparent, then on 2 (14) July, work began on the left bank of the Elbe to bring the Altstadt into a defensible state. Over the course of a month and a half, six field fortifications were constructed, of which one flèche on the banks of the Elbe, upstream of the Pirna suburb, and five lunettes: No. 1 forwards of the Ziegelschlag; No. II at the Pirnaischer Schlag; No. III at the Mosczinski Garten; No. IV at the Falkenschlag, and No. V at the Freiberger Schlag. These temporary fortifications were reinforced by palisades of stakes placed vertically at the bottom of the ditch, two feet from the scarp; and in some lunettes, in addition, there were palisades on the berm. The guns were stationed on platforms; in each of the fortifications there were small wooden bunkers covered with earth for holding artillery ammunition. Important gaps between the lunettes were obstructed by palisades; while the walls surrounding the gardens and of the buildings closest to the outer line were adapted for defence, loopholes were punched through them, openings were made for gun limbers and so on. The suburb of Friedrichstadt was not protected by any fortifications, except for a flèche assigned to bombard the area downstream of the Neustadt and the buildings flanking both this flèche and the nearest fieldworks of the Neustadt.

The fortifications constructed for the defence of the Altstadt were located at such considerable distances from one another that they were completely incapable of mutual support. It was hoped to ease this disadvantage by deploying field guns into the intervals between the fortifications during combat. But the superiority of the Coalition artillery gave them a clear advantage over these batteries in the open. Moreover, many terrain features would allow Coalition troops to get close to the French fortifications without being exposed to their fire; in order to eliminate this important disadvantage, it would be necessary to raze or obstruct the Großer Garten, hold it with troops, or destroy Feldschlößchen and some other buildings in the vicinity of lunette No. IV, and so on.[45]

In order to secure the crossing in the vicinity of Pirna, Napoleon ordered two bridges to be built near Königstein also protected by strong *têtes-de-pont* [bridgeheads] on the right bank of the Elbe. A fortified camp was set up at the foot of the Lilienstein, and for the shortest and most convenient communication with Lusatia, a road was laid through the rocky, forested mountains from Königstein to Stolpen, named Napoleonstraße, at the suggestion of the King of Saxony, in honour of his powerful ally. All the main routes from Bohemia were obstructed with abatis in the forests, while fortifications were built on open ground for the same purpose; Schloss Sonnenstein was refurbished; the gorge at Hellendorf [three miles north of Peterswald] was put into a defensible state. However, many of these constructions were very weak and could have no other purpose than to add importance to the French preparations. Napoleon, moreover, wanting to have strongholds in the event of a retreat from the Elbe to the Rhine, ordered the fortification of Erfurt and the citadel in Würzburg.

All works in the vicinity of Dresden, designed on the basis of a reconnaissance conducted by Napoleon himself, were carried out by the renowned engineers, General Rogniat [Joseph Rogniat] and Colonel Bernard [Simon Bernard]. During the armistice, Napoleon, having chosen the Palais Brühl-Marcolini, on the outskirts of Friedrichstadt [1⅓ miles north-west of Dresden] as his residence, very often left there for days at a time, inspecting the countryside and fortified locations along the Elbe, while also inspecting the garrisons of Torgau, Wittenberg, Magdeburg, Leipzig and Oudinot's force stationed in Calau. As has already been mentioned above, at the end of July (new style) he went to Mainz to visit Empress Marie-Louise, and returned to Dresden from there on 23 July (4 August).[46]

As for Napoleon's appreciation for the impending campaign, it depended for the most part on Austria's participation in the war. Had the Austrians remained neutral, then Napoleon, having an advantage over the united armies of Russia and Prussia in troop numbers, could have launched offensive operations, which if successful, would have reached the Vistula and his allies in the Duchy of Warsaw. In contrast, Austria joining the Coalition against Napoleon not only gave the Coalition superiority in numbers, but also forced the French to detach significant elements of their forces in order to form two armies on the Danube and in Italy. Taking into account, moreover, that the attitude of the *Confédération du Rhin* towards Napoleon was most doubtful, while the Tyrol and Illyria were clearly hostile towards him, it is obvious that he could not think of advancing to the Vistula under such circumstances. Thus, of necessity he was obliged to confine himself to a defence on the Elbe. Having conceded this line, he could not have hung on in Germany, but would

45 Aster, *Schilderung der Kreigsereignisse in und vor Dresden, vom 7 März bis 28 August 1813*, second edition, 1856, 96-104.

46 Fain, II, 21-22; Odeleben, *Relation circonstanciée de la campagne de 1813, en Saxe*, I, 218-221; Förster, I, 483-484.

have been forced to retreat beyond the Rhine. Napoleon, in deciding to defend the course of the Elbe, was in danger of being deeply outflanked from Bohemia. Yet by occupying a central position in Saxony and reliant on a number of fortresses, he had reason to hope not only to counter a Coalition envelopment by operating against their lines of communication through Bohemia, but also to spoil their offensive by invading this country with the bulk of his forces. In order do this, he ought to have left enough of a force on the Elbe between Magdeburg and Dresden to keep the Coalition from operating out of Berlin and Silesia, while he thrust into the Army of Bohemia himself, with all the remaining troops. If successful, he would seize Prague and push the Coalition back into Moravia, which would facilitate him maintaining his army using resources from enemy territory that had not yet experienced the disasters of war, and might lead to Austria withdrawing from the Coalition. Instead, Napoleon undertook to commence operations by advancing part of the army towards Berlin, while his main force, numbering more than 200,000 men, was concentrated in Silesia and Lusatia, in an observation role facing the Coalition armies assembled in Silesia and Bohemia, and in support of the force intending to march on Berlin. Saint-Cyr's corps was assigned to hold the Pirna camp and for the immediate defence of Dresden, while Napoleon, depending on the situation, intended to support the forward elements of his army with 60,000 men of the *Garde*, also in Dresden. Having thus deployed his forces, he was prone to the following disadvantages:

1. The primary offensive was directed towards Berlin, the capture of which would not lead to a decisive outcome, and moreover, this advance would be undertaken by an insufficient force, because Napoleon had under-estimated the true strength of the army under the Crown Prince of Sweden.
2. The concentration of the main force against the Coalition Army of Silesia was completely pointless: it was easy to foresee that this army, by evading an engagement with significant French forces, would retreat beyond the Oder, and that Napoleon could not pursue them without endangering his lines of communication, especially since Dresden was very weakly fortified at this point.
3. Following Napoleon's departure for Lusatia with the *Garde*, only Saint-Cyr remained to defend Dresden on the left bank of the Elbe with 26,000 men, while the greatest danger threatened the French army from this direction.
4. This division of forces deprived Napoleon of the opportunity to redeploy his troops immediately and left the success of his operations under the influence of his marshals, none of whom could equal him in the art of waging war in such large masses.

It has been suggested that the reason for the concentration of a significant part of Napoleon's troops in Silesia and Lusatia was intelligence conveyed to him by the comte de Narbonne regarding an imminent offensive by the Austrian Army of Bohemia, along the right bank of the Elbe, through Zittau. Narbonne, deceived by a false statement from one of the officials of the Austrian general staff, unintentionally misled Napoleon, which was one of the main reasons for his failure.[47] But his own hubris was even more damaging to him. To the suggestions from his entourage about the need to retreat to the Rhine, Napoleon retorted: 'Dresden is my main focus for counter offensives. The enemy are stretched in an arc from Berlin to Prague, in which my forces occupy the centre… Is it possible that the Coalition could maintain unity despite such uncoordinated operations? Yet should I not hope to catch them by surprise and take advantage of their mistakes? The enemy will send partisans into the area between the Elbe and the Rhine. I have foreseen this, I have taken the proper precautions. In addition to strong garrisons in Mainz, Wesel, Würzburg and Erfurt, Augereau has assembled a *corps d'observation* on the Main. And what if the Coalition dares to thrust between the defensive lines of the Elbe and the Rhine? Should they be so brave, I shall enter Bohemia and strike them from behind… I shall tell you again, the position I hold offers such advantages that the enemy, having defeated me in ten battles, could barely push me back to the Rhine, while a single battle won would lead us to the enemy capital, liberate the garrisons of our fortresses on the Oder and Vistula and force the Coalition to sue for peace… Nevertheless, I have taken everything into account… The rest is up to Fate; no matter what the merits of my appreciation, I will be judged by the result. One must submit to destiny in general; that is the strict law of history itself.'[48] Napoleon believed that his enemies would make the same errors that they had in the past, and hoped to take advantage of their mistakes. He was confident that his colleagues would execute his concepts with the same dedication as they had shown in his previous wars. Yes indeed, the Coalition gave Napoleon the opportunity to achieve some success; yet, on the other hand, the failures of the French military commanders had disastrous consequences for him. His troops fought very bravely; but no longer with the passion that boosts the strength of warriors and makes them invincible.

47 Saint-Cyr, 55-62; Hofmann, *Zur Geschichte des Feldzuges von 1813*, second edition, 104-105; Vaudoncourt, 139.

48 Fain, II, 28-30.

Appendix XXX

Schedule of forces for the Russian active army, dated 21 June [3 July], signed by Barclay de Tolly, showing the strength as 171,000 men

Right Wing, commanded by General of Infantry comte Langéron:

Corps	Divisions/Units	Men
VI Corps – Lieutenant General Prince Shcherbatov – 16 battalions	7th Division 18th Division	8,081
IX Corps – Lieutenant General Olsufiev – 14 battalions	9th Division 15th Division	6,529
X Corps – Lieutenant General Kaptsevich – 17 battalions	8th Division 22nd Division	7,739
Cavalry – Adjutant General Baron Korff – 24 squadrons	3rd Dragoon Division 1st Mounted Jäger Division 2nd Mounted Jäger Division 3rd Ulan Division	3,308
Cossacks	Six regiments	1,879
Artillery – 108 guns	15th, 18th & 34th Battery companies 3rd, 19th, 28th, 29th & 34th Light companies 8th Horse Artillery Company	1,807
	TOTAL:	**29,343**

Left Wing, commanded by General-of-Cavalry Count Wittgenstein:

Corps	Divisions/Units	Men
I Corps – Lieutenant General Prince Gorchakov 2nd – 23 battalions	5th Division 14th Division	14,445
II Corps – Lieutenant General Prinz Eugen von Württemberg – 22 battalions	3rd Division 4th Division	11,762
VIII Corps – Lieutenant General comte Saint-Priest – 19 battalions	11th Division 17th Division	8,604

Corps	Divisions/Units	Men
Cavalry – Lieutenant General Count Pahlen – 49 squadrons	1st Dragoon Division 4th Dragoon Division 1st Hussar Division	5,482
Cossacks	Seven regiments	2,629
Artillery – 132 guns	3rd, 5th & 32nd Battery companies 6th, 7th, 13th, 27th, 32nd & 33rd Light companies 6th & 7th Horse Artillery companies	2,352
	TOTAL:	**45,274**

Reserve, commanded by H.I.H. Grand Duke Konstantin Pavlovich:

Corps	Divisions/Units	Men
III Corps (Grenadier) – Lieutenant General Raevsky – 24 battalions	1st Grenadier Division 2nd Grenadier Division	13,962
III Corps Artillery – 22 guns	34th Battery Company 14th Light Company	384
V Corps (Lifeguard) – Lieutenant General Lavrov – 22 battalions	1st Lifeguard Division 2nd Lifeguard Division	12,286
V Corps Artillery – 24 guns	2nd Lifeguard Battery Company 2nd Lifeguard Light Company	444
Cavalry – Lieutenant General Prince Golitsyn 5th	1st, 2nd & 3rd Cuirassier Divisions Lifeguard Light Cavalry Division	8,412
Attached cavalry	Adjutant General Baron Korff	1,766
Cossacks	Four Don Cossack regiments Three Ukraine Cossack regiments One Black Sea Cossack regiment	4,740
Horse Artillery – 16 guns	1st & 2nd Lifeguard Horse Artillery batteries	388
Reserve Artillery – Major General Euler – 92 heavy guns, 26 light guns & 56 horse guns.	1st Lifeguard Battery & 2nd Lifeguard Light companies, seven battery, one light, four horse & two Don companies & Lifeguard Équipage sub-unit.	3,133
	TOTAL:	**45,515**

Independent Corps and Detachments:

Corps/Detachment	Divisions/Units	Men
Lieutenant General Baron Sacken – 48guns	10th Division (five regiments Okhostsk& Kamchatka regiments 27th Division (four regiments & two replacement battalions)	8,383
	3rd Dragoon Division (two regiments) 2nd Hussar Division	3,697

Corps/Detachment	Divisions/Units	Men
	Eight Cossack regiments	3,322
	One battery, two light and one horse companies	801
	TOTAL:	**16,203**

Overall, the Russian forces assembled in Silesia numbered: 91,791 infantry; 22,665 regular cavalry; 12,570 irregular cavalry and 9,309 artillerymen, for a total of 136,335 men.

In addition, the following were with the army assembled in Silesia: 740 sappers and pioneers, commanded by Major General Count Sievers, and 620 men with 4th and 5th pontoon companies, 75th Ship's Company and a temporary labour battalion.

Five Cossack regiments, with 1,199 men, were assigned to escort the headquarters.

Count Wittgenstein's headquarters had an escort of: 326 men from the Ingermanland Dragoons and (a sub-unit) of Irkutsk Hussars; 193 men in three Cossack sub-units and 528 men from the Olonets *Opolchenie* and Vologda *Opolchenie*, for a total of 1,047 men.

Attached to the Crown Prince of Sweden's army:

Corps/Detachment	Divisions/Units	Men
Adjutant General Baron Wintzingerode – 44 guns.	21st Division 24th Division	7,388
	Two dragoon regiments	1,338
	Eight Cossack regiments	2,877
	One battery, two light & one horse companies	750
	TOTAL:	**12,353**
Lieutenant General Graf Wallmoden's corps	Four Don Cossack regiments	1,415

Corps/Detachment	Divisions/Units	Men
Lieutenant General Count Vorontsov's detachment	Elements of 5th, 9th, 14th, 15th, 18th & 21st divisions (Major General Harpe)	5,304
Artillery – 24 field guns.	Two battery & one light companies	426
Cavalry – Adjutant General Chernyshev	Finland Dragoons, Riga Dragoons & Izyum Hussars	1,801
Cossacks	Six Cossack regiments	2,402
Horse Artillery – ten guns	1st & 5th Horse Artillery companies	174
Cavalry – Major General Count O'Rourke	Nezhin Mounted Jägers, Volhynia Ulans, Poland Ulans & Pavlograd Hussars	2,464
Cossacks	Seven Cossack regiments	2,780
Horse Artillery – 24 guns	11th & 13th Horse Artillery companies	425
	TOTAL:	**15,766**

The 7th Battery Company and 21st Battery Company with a total of 22 guns had been sent to the Crown Prince of Sweden's army, together with 453 gunners.

Two Cossack regiments, with 440 men, were attached to General Bülow's corps.

Two Cossack regiments, numbering 534 men, were at the blockade of Stettin.

Overall, Russian forces attached to the Crown Prince of Sweden's army numbered: 12,692 infantry; 5,603 regular cavalry; 10,448 irregular cavalry; 2,228 artillerymen, for a total of 30,971 men.

Between 21 June [3 July] and 1 [13] August, a total of 3,500 men joined the army.

By 1 [13] August the army had a total of 174,412 men.

20

The Coalition armies and their commanders

The transfer of elements of the Russo-Prussian forces assembled in Silesia to join the Austrian army in Bohemia. – The numerical strength of the Coalition armies. – The appointment of commanders-in-chief: Fürst zu Schwarzenberg to the Army of Bohemia; the Crown Prince of Sweden to the Army of the North; Blücher to the Army of Silesia. General Gneisenau. – The arrival of generals Moreau and Jomini in the Coalition headquarters.

Based on the disposition drawn up by Quartermaster General Diebitsch and sent to the troops assembled in Silesia, elements of the Russo-Prussian Coalition army were to close up to the borders of Bohemia by the time the armistice ended, namely by 28 July (9 August), and were to be located in *Kreis* Bolkenhain-Landeshut and in *Grafschaft* Glatz, from Landeshut to Mittelwalde [Międzylesie]. Included in this force, which was to join the Main, or Army of Bohemia, commanded by Barclay de Tolly, were:

1. Count Wittgenstein's army, numbering 32,000 men with 92 guns.
2. *Generalleutnant* Kleist's Prussian corps, some 42,000 men with 112 guns.
3. The Russo-Prussian reserves commanded by the Tsarevich, Grand Duke Konstantin Pavlovich, numbering 50,000 men with 198 guns

Giving a total of some 124,000 men with 402 guns, excluding the troops making up the escort of the headquarters and under the orders of the Intendant General and Provost General of the Russian army.[1] The troops and the parks under Count Wittgenstein and Kleist, having assembled at Landeshut, Neurode [Nowa Ruda], Reinerz [Duszniki-Zdrój, 12 miles east of Nachod] and Mittelwalde, entered Bohemia in four columns on 30 July (11 August), and concentrated in an encampment at Budin, on the river Eger on 7 (19) August. The reserves assembled at Landeshut, Neurode, Reichenbach and Silberberg [Srebrna Góra] on 30 July (11 August), entered Bohemia on 1 (13) August in two columns, towards Trautenau [Trutnov] and Politz [Police nad Metují, 7½ miles south-west of Braunau], arriving at the camp at Budin

1 For details of these forces, see Appendix XXXI at the end of this chapter.

by 10 (22) August,[2] where the troops under Barclay de Tolly linked up with the Austrian army, which calculated its strength at 110,500 men with 270 guns,[3] under the overall command of Field Marshal the Fürst zu Schwarzenberg. According to Count Kankrin [Yegor Frantsevich Kankrin or Georg Ludwig Cancrin], the Russian troops had a whole month's supply of provisions in a mobile convoy, and, in addition, ten days' worth in regimental transport and on the men.

The remaining Russo-Prussian forces assembled in Silesia were deployed as follows: assigned to Blücher's army were:

1. Langéron's force, supplemented with VIII Corps under comte Saint-Priest, 1st Dragoon Division, 4th Dragoon Division under major generals Borozdin [Nikolai Mikhailovich Borozdin 2nd] and Emmanuel, respectively, three Ukrainian regiments, three heavy artillery companies, two light companies and one Don horse artillery company, for a total of 43,500 men with 176 guns.
2. Sacken's force, supplemented with three Cossack regiments and one heavy artillery company, numbering 17,700 men with 60 guns.
3. Yorck's Prussian corps, numbering 38,000 men with 104 guns.

Finally, the Army of the North, commanded by the Crown Prince of Sweden (Bernadotte), numbering around 160,000 men with 276 guns, deployed forwards of Berlin and on the lower Elbe.

Thus, the Coalition forces were divided into three armies, of which two, the Army of Bohemia and Army of the North, were assigned for decisive operations against Napoleon's lines of communications, while the third, the Army of Silesia, in accordance with the general plan, would be limited for the time being to secondary operations: protecting Silesia and diverting enemy forces from those locations where they [the Coalition] were intending to strike. One of these armies was commanded by an Austrian; another by a Prussian; the third by the Crown Prince of Sweden. In spite of the significant numbers of Russian troops, and the dedication with which Russia continued the war following losses suffered in two hard-fought campaigns, Russian generals were subordinate to military commanders from other powers. It is mistaken to believe that Emperor Alexander was unanimously offered supreme command of the armies deployed against Napoleon by all the allies, or that, having declined the overall direction of operations for himself, he subsequently regretted his modesty when matters took a turn for the worst. Such a proposal might have been possible on the part of Prussia and the few small German territories that had joined the Coalition, but it was by no means possible that Austria would ever agree to entrust the main body of their army to a foreign commander who was also the ruler of a powerful neighbour that had always aroused the rivalry and concerns of the Viennese Cabinet. Even more so because Europe was already greeting the Russians as their liberators… Yet it has taken many years to erase the memory of their decisive participation in the liberation of Germany. The Austrian government

2 For details of this movement, see Appendix XXXII at the end of this chapter.
3 For details of the Coalition armies, see Appendix XXXIII at the end of this chapter.

sided with the Coalition out of concern for Napoleon's dominance, yet would never agree to promote the ascendancy of Emperor Alexander. The argument that our Tsar aspired to supreme authority is also mistaken.[4] Had it been offered as a voluntary gift of gratitude and faith in him, then, in all likelihood, he would not have declined such a flattering role, but to seek it would have been be an error in political terms, incompatible either with Emperor Alexander's customary tact or with his previous actions. There had been nothing preventing him from taking command of the Russo-Prussian army at the beginning of the spring campaign, rather, his preference was to entrust it to Count Wittgenstein. In addition, in agreement with King Friedrich Wilhelm, while doing everything possible to attract Austria to the Coalition side, he considered one of the most effective means for this to be the appointment of an Austrian general as Commander-in-Chief of the largest army, and having given his word to facilitate such a choice, he gave no further thought to command of the allied forces.[5]

Many believed that an Austrian Erzherzog [Archduke] should be appointed Commander-in-Chief; in particular, the consensus of public opinion was in favour of Erzherzog Karl [Karl Ludwig Johann Joseph Laurentius von Österreich], who had already fought honourably against Napoleon more than once. But many factors made this a problematic choice and forced the Austrian government to prefer the Fürst zu Schwarzenberg who never managed, either before or after, to acquire great military glory, rather than the renowned warrior. Ever since Suvorov's Italian and Swiss campaigns, Erzherzog Karl suffered the disfavour of the Russians, who considered him (not entirely correctly) to be the main culprit for Rimsky-Korsakov's defeat and the unsatisfactory outcome of the war. In addition, the Erzherzog was in open enmity with Metternich and had aroused the suspicions of Kaiser Franz himself: there had been rumours that, during the 1809 campaign when matters had taken an unfavourable turn for Austria, Erzherzog Karl, having entered into talks with Napoleon, had been ready to join the Confédération du Rhin as King of Bohemia: that was how intriguing courtiers had interpreted attempts by the Erzherzog to halt Napoleon's rapid advances through negotiation after the battles of Landshut and Regensburg. In his posthumous memoirs, Napoleon confirmed this accusation, but his statement is barely credible. Reports by enemies of the Erzherzog, based on their sophisticated understanding of Kaiser Franz's character, instilled doubts and distrust of Erzhertzog Karl in him, who, in 1809, having received no diplomatic commissions, had acted completely unilaterally and thereby aroused the displeasure of his brother against himself. Generally, Kaiser Franz did not like anyone to go beyond the limits of the powers granted to them and could never forgive Erzhertzog Karl for his unauthorised activities.[6]

Since, with the exception of the victor of Aspern, there was not a single general in the Austrian army who had won honours in Europe, all that remained was to elect one of the personalities from the highest aristocracy as Commander-in-Chief. This

4 Lebensbilder aus dem Befreiungskriege, III, 497.
5 Bernhardi, *Denkwürdigkeiten des Grafen von Toll*, III, 87-88; Förster, *Geschichte des Befreiungskriege, 1813, 1814, 1815*, I, 512.
6 Bernhardi, III, 89-90; Förster, I, 512.

condition was satisfied by *Feldmarschal* Fürst zu Schwarzenberg, who was distinguished by his broad education, dexterity in relations with crowned heads, amenability and selflessness. In addition to all this, he combined the qualities of a noble, brave warrior, but not those of a commander. Justice demands the statement that it was not easy to command an army in the circumstances in which he had been placed. Half of the army entrusted to him consisted of foreign troops; his planning was not only encumbered by the presence of Coalition sovereigns in his headquarters, but almost none of them could be executed without first being reported to Emperor Alexander. The *Feldmarschal* was no less shackled by the views of his own government, which often went against the intentions of other Coalition members: all these difficulties are obvious, and therefore, in such a situation, even a military genius could barely maintain their honour. Nevertheless, it is highly doubtful that Schwarzenberg, who did not possess either determination, willpower, or self-confidence (the essential qualities of great commanders), could operate independently, even under the most favourable of circumstances. Everything he did during the war of 1813 and 1814 (and very little was done), as Austrian officers who were his contemporaries and associates testify, was accomplished by virtue of the assessments of the members of the General Staff who were with him. Throughout the war, he needed advisers and directors. It was understood in the Austrian army that the main personality was the chief of staff, *Feldmarschallleutnant* Graf Radetzky, but, in all likelihood, the reason for this assumption resulted from Radetzky's subsequent, equally long and famous military career, in whose nature it was to never seek influence on matters, and to restrict himself to the performance of his primary duties and that he expressed his opinions without insisting on acceptance of the ideas he proposed. In contrast, *Generalquartiermeister* Langenau [Friedrich Karl Gustav August von Langenau] clearly sought pre-eminence in the Austrian headquarters, which was facilitated by Schwarzenberg's customary indulgence and his conviction that Langenau had the most definitive geographic intelligence on the theatre of war in which the Army of Bohemia was to operate. Prior to this time, *Generalmajor* Langenau had served in the Saxon forces, and enjoyed the particular patronage of minister Senfft von Pilsach [Friedrich Christian Ludwig Senfft von Pilsach] and was briefly acquainted with many of the personalities surrounding Emperor Napoleon. He played an important role in Reynier's headquarters during the campaign in Russia and became known to Schwarzenberg. Langenau left Saxony when his patron, the Saxon minister, was being persecuted by Napoleon for the wavering loyalty of King Friedrich August, and was accepted into Austrian service. The basis of all his assessments were one-sided exaggerated ideas on the importance of the influence of the ground, the dominant locations in the theatre of war, and so on. *Feldmarschallleutnant* Duka [Friedrich Peter Duka von Kádár] was another personality with great influence and occupied a prime position in the Austrian headquarters as chief of the secret police, and was endowed with the friendship and special authority of Kaiser Franz.[7]

7 Bernhardi, III, 90-94.

As for Emperor Alexander and King Friedrich Wilhelm, they, having given command of the main army to an Austrian commander, did not consider themselves as having the right to interfere with his choice. None of the generals directly subordinate to Schwarzenberg were offended by his promotion. While the Commanders-in-Chief of the other armies, Blücher and the Crown Prince of Sweden, were convinced that, being in separate theatres of war, they had every opportunity to operate independently.[8]

While the appointment of Prince Schwarzenberg as Commander-in-Chief of the Army of Bohemia might have been justified solely by a combination of circumstances that prevented the appointment of an incomparably more renowned commander to this high status, then, as if in recompense for that, public opinion had already approved the choice of the Swedish Crown Prince as Commander-in-Chief of the Army of the North. Having begun his military career at the age of 17, Bernadotte served in the lower ranks for a long time and was promoted to lieutenant at the age of 28. The hard school he endured familiarised him with the life of a soldier, while the French Revolution subsequently contributed to his rapid promotion: Bernadotte, who was a *Capitaine* at the beginning of 1794, became a *Général de division* in October of the same year. In 1799, as *Ministre de la Guerre*, on 18 *brumaire* [9 November, new style] he opposed the ascendancy of Bonaparte, and, as we know, was unsuccessful. In all likelihood, this factor would have been a serious stumbling block to his future career had he not married the sister of the wife of Napoleon's brother Joseph. The result of these family ties was Bernadotte's promotion to Marshal and his elevation to princely dignity, under the title prince de Ponte-Corvo. Napoleon had no sympathy with him and was almost never satisfied with his operations, but did not oppose his election as heir to the Swedish throne. During his service with the French colours, Bernadotte never commanded an independent army; but Napoleon's military fame was so great in public opinion that its reflection was enough to glorify the associates of the *Empereur des Français* with a radiant crown of ringing renown. No one doubted the ability of the former French Marshal Bernadotte to independently command a 150,000-strong army of very multi-national composition, in which there were no more than 24,000 Swedes directly subordinate to him, and even then he could not communicate with them, not yet having had chance to learn the language of the people who had entrusted their futures to him. His task was to lead into battle a horde from various nations, assembled from the opposite extremities of Europe, against his compatriots, against his fellow soldiers. His entire past belonged to France, his present and entire future belonged to Sweden. The fate of Germany was a matter of little concern to him, and instead of the life-or-death struggle, as was being waged by the Prussians making up the majority of the Army of the North, all his orders were aimed at preserving his small Swedish corps, which he needed in order to secure Norway. It was impossible to expect greater activity from the Crown Prince when his objectives were so insignificant in comparison with those for which the other allies had taken up arms. The consequences of this were doubts regarding his abilities and distrust from his allies,

8 Förster, I, 513.

especially the Prussian soldiers, from general to private. For his part, the prince had no sympathy for them, spoke dismissively about the *Landwehr* and criticised Bülow's operations. All this was very natural: being put in an awkward position, the Crown Prince was unable to demonstrate either his own military abilities or give due justice to his associates. He was also criticised for allegedly revealing his power-hungry ambitions for the throne of France with the intent of rewarding his [political] allies. The French themselves stated at the time: 'The Crown Prince of Sweden, who grew up in our camp and learned the art of war from us, is only putting up a show of fighting against the Great Nation.'[9] It is claimed that, during a meeting with the prince in Åbo [Turku], in 1812, Emperor Alexander hinted at the possibility of him ascending the French throne, but this has never been verified, while Bernadotte himself never referred to any such offer, but only said, in an unguarded moment with Russian minister Alopeus [David Maximovich Alopeus or Frans David Alopaeus], that he might be preferred to the degenerate house of Bourbon.[10]

The Army of Silesia counted more Russians in its ranks than Prussians. Yet, leadership of this army was granted to the Prussian commander, Blücher, as soon as the matter of the independence of Prussia was raised. Blücher had committed himself to the art of war almost from childhood, against the wishes of his parents. At the age of 15, he ran away from school, enlisted in the Swedish armed forces, was captured by Prussian Black Hussars, joined the army of Frederick the Great, participated in the final campaigns of the Seven Years' War and was wounded in the battle of Freiberg. The young man was distinguished by his free-spiritedness and insolence, constantly started quarrels, fighting many duels, but was respected and loved by his comrades for the straightforwardness and nobility of his character. In 1773, having been passed over for promotion to major, Blücher wrote to Frederick the Great: 'Von Jägersfeld [Georg Wilhelm von Jägersfeld], whose only merit is that he is the son of a *Markgraf* [margrave], was promoted ahead of me. I request Your Majesty's permission to resign.' The king responded: '*Rittmeister* von Blücher has been dismissed from service and can go to hell.'[11] Having had his resignation accepted, Blücher returned to his Pomeranian estate, gained the respect and devotion of his fellow citizens and was elected by them to membership of the Council of Nobility (*Ritterschaftsrat*). After the death of Frederick the Great, he re-entered armed service as a major, in 1787, at the age of 45. Blücher, in the ranks of *Oberst* and *Generalmajor* commanding *Husarenregiment von Belling*, acquired such fame throughout the course of the revolutionary wars that he was nicknamed 'the second Zieten' [Hans Joachim von Zieten]. During the campaign of 1806, *Generalleutnant* Blücher was criticised for having detached the cavalry under his command from Hohenlohe's corps [Friedrich Ludwig zu Hohenlohe-Ingelfingen-Öhringen] and

9 Beitzke, *Geschichte der deutschen Freiheitskriege in den Jahren 1813 und 1814*, I, 676-680; Förster, I, 755.

10 Pertz, *Das Leben des Ministers Freiherrn von Stein*, III, 573.

11 ['*Der von Jägersfeld, der kein andres Verdienst hat, als der Sohn des Markgrafen von Schwedt zu sein, ist mir vorgezogen worden. Ich bitte Ew. Majestät um meinen Abschied*.' The King responded: '*Der Rittmeister von Blücher ist seiner Dienste entlassen; er kann sich zum Teufel scheren*'].

fatally weakened them; thereby giving rise to their surrender at Prenzlau, without achieving any beneficial results and being forced to lay down his arms at Lübeck. Thus, in 1813, having already passed 70 years of age, Blücher had not yet had the opportunity to become renowned for truly great military exploits. Barclay de Tolly, Wittgenstein and Langéron had commanded significant formations in previous wars. Even in the Prussian army, General Yorck had managed to garner fresh laurels in the campaign of 1812 and gain great fame through his defection from the French and the raising of a national mobilisation in East Prussia. In contrast, all of Blücher's most glorious operations had been performed by him in an era long since passed, where he commanded formations of a few thousand men.

Despite all this, however, the old warrior enjoyed the unconditional trust and devotion of the Prussian troops. With his combative demeanour, expressive facial features and gray hair, combined with passionate qualities of willpower and spirit, he was resolute either in danger or under the stress of responsibility: everything indicated heroism in him and inspired instinctive respect for him among the population and the troops. It seemed as if time itself could not break the mighty master. Having already reached old age, he was in vigorous health, aggressive, courageous and enterprising. His fearlessness, resolve in adversity and valour, which increased with difficulties, were based on the self-awareness of his physical strength, developed and tested by him many times in individual combat. Convinced that there was no situation so difficult that escape might be impossible, always maintaining his presence of mind, Blücher demanded the same self-confidence from his subordinates, valued courage in them above all, and respected only those whom he considered enterprising. Gifted with quick thinking and insight, he showed extraordinary resourcefulness in the most diverse situations; his friendly manner, jocularity and inexhaustible playfulness were attractive to everyone around him. Having not received any scientific education, despite this, he did not reject scientific methodology, but also did not have exaggerated ideas of its influence on military matters. He often happened to comment on the neglect of his early upbringing, but he knew very well that a great deal could be accomplished even with such deficiencies. The speed of his military observation was amazing, especially in decisive moments in the heat of battle. It was here that his ability to implement his own ideas, or those of others that he had taken on, manifested itself in all its brilliance. Whenever he had the time to analyse operations from a map, he barely bothered to glance at it, and it was only then that it became apparent how alien staff work was to him. But this disadvantage was neutralised by the very knowledgeable military men who accompanied him, *Chef des Generalstabs* Gneisenau and *Generalquartiermeister* Müffling.[12]

General Gneisenau, the foremost of Blücher's associates, combined all the qualities that this Prussian hero lacked in himself: discretion, caution and definitive knowledge of many subjects. Blücher could not have accomplished such great feats without his assistance, and the noble acknowledgement from Blücher himself may

12 Beitzke, I, 681-685; Von C.v.W. (Müffling); *Zur Kriegsgeschichte der Jahre 1813 und 1814, Zw. Auflage, Vorwort*, VI-VII.

serve as a magnanimous testimony to this.[13] Having been forced to endure extreme poverty in his youth, Gneisenau, managed to acquire a higher education with great difficulty, and was already 23 years old in 1782 when, as an ensign, he joined the *Ansbach-Bayreuther Regiment* at the very moment that this regiment, hired by the British government, was sent overseas to operate against the renegade United States of America. Thereafter, having enlisted in the Prussian army, he reached the rank of major at the beginning of 1807, when he was already 47 years old. At this time, he became known to Scharnhorst, who, being able to appreciate his abilities, contributed to his appointment as commandant of Kolberg in place of the incompetent Lucadou [Ludwig Moritz von Lucadou]. The excellent defence of Kolberg, at the time of a general collapse of morale, drew the attention of the population to Gneisenau and brought him status and the order of the *pour le mérite*. Thereafter, under the leadership of Scharnhorst, together with Borstell, Clausewitz, Boyen, Grolman, and others, he was engaged in the reform of the army. In 1809, he retired with the rank of *Oberst*, it is alleged on the insistence of Napoleon himself, but, having accepted a position in the *Außenministerium* [Ministry of Foreign Affairs], he was sent on important assignments to the Stockholm and London Courts. During his stay in England, Gneisenau enjoyed the special favour of the Prince-Regent [later King George IV] and became friends with the Earl of Munster [later King William IV], the soul of relations between the British government and Germany. Upon returning to his fatherland, he constantly stuck by the party ready to resume the desperate struggle with Napoleon. When Prussia entered into an alliance with his sworn enemy in 1812, Gneisenau left for Britain, where he remained until the situation opened up a vast field for his vigorous activism.[14]

Emperor Alexander arrived in Prague on 3 (15) August, where the famous French generals, Moreau [Jean Victor Marie Moreau] and Jomini, soon came to visit him. The former arrived at the request of the Russian Monarch, who, back in 1805, had wanted to have this famous commander at his side: the Tsar had been prompted to do this by an overstated idea of the skill of Moreau's operations on the Rhine. Many believed that his name would exert a strong influence on French soldiers and shake their loyalty to Napoleon. Moreau himself was mistaken in this regard, thinking that the displeasure aroused by Napoleon's incessant wars was dominant in France more than anywhere else, and especially in the French army. During the many years of his exile, having retired to America, living on his small estate on the banks of the Delaware, Moreau, although he followed the course of current affairs, nevertheless, had a completely mistaken concept of them. He believed that the demise of the huge French army in Russia had instilled a hatred of Napoleon in his subjects and that his dominance over France was propped up solely by fear. According to Moreau, it

13 It is claimed that when leaving for the army in 1815, Blücher stated: 'I am leaving today, but my brains (Gneisenau) set off eight days ago.' There was also an occasion when Blücher and Gneisenau were in a house where some youngsters were amusing themselves by posing riddles. Expressing a desire to take part in the game, the old warrior requested that one of them should kiss his brain, and when no one could solve this riddle, he approached Gneisenau and, hugging his companion, kissed him on the head.

14 Beitzke, I, 688-691.

would be enough for him, having taken command of 30,000 or 40,000 French prisoners of war, roused by a thirst for vengeance against Napoleon, to appear on the borders of his fatherland for all of France to rise up against the common oppressor: this was, in his opinion, the sole means for the overthrow of Napoleon. At the beginning of 1813, he wrote to the Russian ambassador to the United States, Dashkov [Andrey Yakovlevich Dashkov]:

> It is most unfortunate for humanity that the craven author of every misfortune has escaped his army's disaster. He may still do much harm, such is the influence gifted to him by the terror of his name over the much weakened and much maligned French people. There is no doubt in my mind that he is fleeing his indignant soldiers as much as the lances of your Cossacks. The prisoners in Russia must be enraged over what has happened to them and must live and breathe on vengeance alone. Should a suitably large number of these wronged men agree to assault the borders of France, I dare to respond that Bonaparte could not escape them. But I remember the Quibéron affair and know the precautions that must be taken…[15]

Moreau set out on a North American ship on 12 (24) June, and two months later, having arrived in Gothenburg [Göteborg] harbour, sent the following letter to Emperor Alexander:

> Sire! Mr. Dashkov has expressed to me Your Majesty's desire that I come to Europe, I have hastened to obey Your orders and I have just taken the time to warn my wife to leave France where the state of her health has forced her to remain.
>
> I shall disembark in Gothenburg tomorrow and will only stop there long enough to prepare for my journey.
>
> Your Majesty can rely on my eagerness to come to Him and of my desire to be of some use to Him.[16]

After a meeting with his former colleague, the Crown Prince of Sweden, Moreau went to Bohemia and arrived in Prague on 4 (16) August. Emperor Alexander,

15 *'Il est bien malheureux pour l'humanité que le lâche auteur de tous les malheurs soit échappé au désastre de son armée. Il peut encore faire bien du mal, tant est grand l'ascendant que lui donne la terreur de son nom sur les trop faibles et trop malheureux Français. Il n'est pas douteux pour moi, qu'il a fui ses soldats indignés autant que les lances de vos cosaques. Les prisonniers en Russie doivent être furieux de ce qui leur est arrivé et ne doivent respirer que vengeance. Si un nombre assez considerable de ces malheureux consentait à être jeté sur la côte de France, j'ose répondre que Bonaparte n'y échapperait pas. Mais je rappelle de l'affaire de Quibéron et connais les precautions qu'il faut prendre.'*

16 *'Sire! Mr Daschkoff m'ayaut exprimé le desir de Votre Majesté, que je me rendisse en Europe, je me suis empressé d'obéir à Ses ordres et je n'ai pris que le tems d'avertir mon epouse de quitter la France où l'état de sa santé l'avait forcé de se rendre. Je debarquerai demain à Gottenbourg et ne m'y arrêterai que le temps pour preparer mon voyage. Votre Majesté peut compter sur mon empressement à me rendre auprès d'Elle et sur mon desir de pouvoir Lui être de quelqu'utilité. Gottenbourg, 26 juillet, 1813.'*

having learned of this, pre-empted Moreau by visiting him and introduced him personally to the Kaiser of Austria and the King of Prussia. Having no intention of entering Russian service, Moreau remained in civilian clothing, a round hat, gray frock coat and boots with spurs. Being a constant part of the Retinue of Emperor Alexander, he was honoured with the favour of the Tsar, but found no sympathy or trust in himself in the principal associates of the Coalition Monarchs.[17]

General Jomini, a Swiss native, had long had the intention of transferring into Russian service, and by 1813, having been passed over for promotion to *Général de division*, due to Berthier's dissatisfaction with him, had left Dresden for the main headquarters of the Coalition army. Emperor Alexander honoured him with benevolent attention and accepted him into his service as a lieutenant general. General Jomini was welcomed very cordially by the Russian officers, who, having studied his writings, had deep respect for him, acknowledged the authority of the renowned author unconditionally and were confident that he could provide important services. But it soon turned out that Jomini's practical abilities did not match the expectations of his admirers: for example, he never knew how to estimate the number of enemy troops located in a position or moving within sight of him. He never managed to assess the influence of terrain swiftly: all this led to the conclusion that 'General Jomini was no tactician' but his importance as 'a great strategist' long remained intact in the Russian army.[18]

17 Bernhardi, III, 117-119.

18 According to Bernhardi, educated officers in the Russian army still recognise the undoubted authority of General Jomini with regard to strategy: '*... auf diesen Gebiete (als Stratege) gilt er wohl bis heute den unterrichteten Offizieren der russischen Armee so ziemlich für die höchste Autorität...' Denkwürdigkeiten des Grafen von Toll*, III, 119. Being quite familiar with the system of study of military science in Russia, I cannot agree with this opinion from Mr. Bernhardi.

Appendix XXXI

Barclay de Tolly's force attached to the Army of Bohemia in August 1813

Schedule of forces commanded by Barclay de Tolly, assigned to join the Austrian army in Bohemia, signed by Major General Diebitsch (Archive of the Military Topographic Depot, No. 29,202).

Count Wittgenstein's army:

Formation	Unit	Battalions	Squadrons	Cossack Regiments	Guns	Men
1st Hussar Division. Lieutenant General Pahlen	Grodno Hussars		6			872
	Sumy Hussars		7			816
	Olviopol Hussars		2			283
	Lubny Hussars		4			659
	TOTAL:		**19**			**2,630**
Irregular Cavalry	Rodionov 2nd's			1		396
	Yagodin 2nd's			1		362
	Gorin 2nd's			1		399
	Ilovaisky 10th's			1		443
	TOTAL:			**4**		**1,600**
Artillery	6th Horse Artillery Company				8	172
	7th Horse Artillery Company				12	266
	TOTAL:				**20**	**438**
I Corps. Lieutenant General Prince Gorchakov						
5th Division. Major General Mezentsov	Perm Infantry	2				1,390
	Mogilev Infantry	2				1,524
	Kaluga Infantry	2				1,343

Formation	Unit	Battalions	Squadrons	Cossack Regiments	Guns	Men
	Sevsk Infantry	2				1,212
	Grand Duchess' Battalion	1				503
	23rd Jägers	2				1,450
	24th Jägers	2				1,370
	TOTAL:	**13**				**8,792**
14th Division. Major General Helffreich	Tenginsk Infantry	2				1,182
	Estland Infantry	2				1,249
	25th Jägers	2				1,362
	26th Jägers	2				1,418
	TOTAL:	**8**				**5,211**
	I CORPS TOTAL:	**21**				**14,003**
Artillery	3rd Battery Company				12	256
	6th Light Company				12	186
	7th Light Company				12	196
	TOTAL:				**36**	**638**
II Corps. Lieutenant General Prinz Eugen von Württemberg						
3rd Division. Major General Prince Shakhovsky	Murom Infantry	2				1,203
	Reval Infantry	2				1,013
	Chernigov Infantry	2				1,250
	Selenginsk Infantry	2				800
	20th Jägers	3				1,762
	21st Jägers	1				570
	TOTAL:	**12**				**6,598**
4th Division. Major General Pyshnitsky	Tobolsk Infantry	2				983
	Volhynia Infantry	2				771
	Kremenchug Infantry	2				1,050
	Minsk Infantry	1				581
	4th Jägers	2				1,501
	34th Jägers	1				484
	TOTAL:	**10**				**5,370**
	II CORPS TOTAL:	**22**				**11,968**
Artillery	5th Battery Company				12	267
	13th Light Company				12	191
	27th Light Company				12	178
	TOTAL:				**36**	**636**

Formation	Unit	Battalions	Squadrons	Cossack Regiments	Guns	Men
	ARMY TOTAL:	**43**	**19**	**4**	**92**	**31,913**

In addition, Count Wittgenstein's army included Kanatchikov's Pioneer Company of 73 men. Forming the headquarters escort were: the Ingermanland Dragoons, 2nd Bug Cossacks, Olonets Infantry and Vologda Infantry – around 1,000 men.

Generalleutnant Kleist's Corps:

Formation	Units	Battalions	Squadrons	Guns	Men
9. Brigade. Generalmajor Klüx	*Schlesisches Jäger*	½			425
	1. Westpreußisches Infanterie	3			2,550
	6. preußisches Reserve Infanterie	3			2,550
	7. Schlesisches Landwehr	4			2,904
	Neumark Dragoner		2.		325
	Landwehr Kavallerie		2		189
	7. Batterie (six-pounders)			8	162
	TOTAL:	**10½**	**4**	**8**	**9,105**
10. Brigade. Generalmajor Pirch	*2. Westpreußisches Infanterie*	3			2,550
	7. preußisches Reserve Infanterie	3			2,550
	9. Schlesisches Landwehr	4			2,904
	Neumark Dragoner		2		325
	Landwehr Kavallerie		2		189
	8. Batterie (six-pounders)			8	162
	TOTAL:	**10**	**4**	**8**	**8,680**
11. Brigade. Generalmajor Zieten	*Schlesisches Jäger*	½			425
	1. Schlesisches Infanterie	3			2,550
	10. Reserve Infanterie	3			2,550
	8. Schlesisches Landwehr	4			2,904
	1. Schlesisches Husaren		2		325
	Landwehr Kavallerie		2		189
	14. Batterie (six-pounders)			8	163
	TOTAL:	**10½**	**4**	**8**	**9,106**
12. Brigade. Oberst Zielinski	*2. Schlesisches Infanterie*	3			2,850
	11. Reserve Infanterie	3			2,550

Formation	Units	Battalions	Squadrons	Guns	Men
	10. Schlesisches Landwehr	4			2,904
	1. Schlesisches Husaren		2		335
	Landwehr Kavallerie		2		189
	13. Batterie (six-pounders)			8	162
	TOTAL:	**10**	**4**	**8**	**8,980**
Reserve Cavalry. *Generalmajor* Roeder	*Ostpreußisches Kürassieren*		4		750
	Brandenburgsches Kürassieren		4		750
	Schlesisches Kürassieren		4		750
	2. Schlesisches Husaren		2		375
	Schlesisches National Kavallerie		2		335
	Schlesisches Ulanen		4		670
	Landwehr Kavallerie		8		756
	10. Reitende Batterie			8	172
	TOTAL:		**28**	**8**	**4,558**
Reserve Artillery. *Oberstleutnant* Braun	*3. Batterie* (12-pounders)			16	416
	6. Batterie (12-pounders)				
	9. Leichter Batterie (six-pounders)			24	486
	11. Leichter Batterie (six-pounders)				
	21. Leichter Batterie (six-pounders)				
	1. Haubitze Batterie (seven-pounders)			8	188
	7. Reitende Batterie			24	516
	8. Reitende Batterie				
	9. Reitende Batterie				
	TOTAL:			**72**	**1,606**
	KLEIST'S CORPS TOTAL:	**41**	**44**	**112**	**42,035**

In addition, Kleist's corps included: four pontoon parks; one labour company and two pioneer companies.

The Reserve, commanded by the Tsarevich, Grand Duke Konstantin Pavlovich: Cavalry component commanded by Lieutenant General Prince Golitysn 5th (including three lancer regiments under Adjutant General Meller-Zakomelsky); V Corps (Lifeguard) commanded by Lieutenant General Yermolov; III Corps (Grenadier) commanded by Lieutenant General Raevsky.

Formation	Unit	Battalions	Squadrons	Cossack Regiments	Guns	Men
1st Cuirassier Division. Major General Depreradovich	Chevalier Garde		6			757
	Lifeguard Horse		6			814
	His Majesty's Cuirassiers		3			409
	Her Majesty's Cuirassiers		4			448
	Two Lifeguard horse artillery batteries commanded by Colonel Kozen				16	389
	TOTAL:		**19**		**16**	**2,817**
2nd Cuirassier Division. Major General Kretov	Yekaterinoslav Cuirassiers		3			355
	Pskov Cuirassiers		3			510
	Glukhov Cuirassiers		5			617
	Astrakhan Cuirassiers		3			378
	TOTAL:		**14**			**1,860**
3rd Cuirassier Division. Major General Duka	Military Order Cuirassiers		4			520
	Starodub Cuirassiers		4			590
	Malorussia Cuirassiers		4			571
	Novgorod Cuirassiers		4			484
	TOTAL:		**16**			**2,165**
Lifeguard Light Cavalry Division. Major General Shevich	Lifeguard Dragoons		6			677
	Lifeguard Ulans		6			680
	Lifeguard Hussars		6			713
	Lifeguard Cossacks		4			275
	TOTAL:		**22**			**2,345**
3rd Ulan Division.	Chuguev Ulans		6			925
	Serpukhov Ulans		4			463
2nd Ulan Division	Tatar Ulans		6			552
	TOTAL:		**16**			**1,940**
Cossacks	Ataman's			1		796
	Ilovaisky 12th's			1		457
	Rebrikov 3rd's			1		382
	TOTAL:			**3**		**1,635**
Horse Artillery	1st Don Company				12	167

Formation	Unit	Battalions	Squadrons	Cossack Regiments	Guns	Men
	CAVALRY TOTAL:		**87**	**3**	**28**	**12,929**
1st Lifeguard Division. Major General Rosen	Lifeguard Preobrazhensky	3				1,793
	Lifeguard Semeovsky	3				1,826
	Lifeguard Izmailovsky	3				1,759
	Lifeguard Jägers	3				1,751
	Lifeguard Équipage	1				596
	TOTAL:	**13**				**7,725**
2nd Lifeguard Division. Lieutenant General Yermolov Later Major General Udom 1st	Lifeguard Lithuania	3				1,865
	Leib-Grenadiers	2				1,349
	Pavlovsk Grenadiers	2				1,222
	Lifeguard Finland	3				1,505
	TOTAL:	**10**				**5,914**
Lifeguard Artillery	2nd Battery Company				12	269
	1st Light Company				12	188
	2nd Light Company				12	175
	TOTAL:				**36**	**632**
	V CORPS TOTAL:	**23**			**36**	**14,298**
1st Grenadier Division. Major General Choglokov	Arakcheev's Grenadiers	2				1,225
	Yekaterinoslav Grenadiers	2				1,209
	Tauride Grenadiers	2				1,179
	St Petersburg Grenadiers	2				1,189
	Kexholm Grenadiers	2				1,171
	Pernov Grenadiers	2				1,234
	TOTAL:	**12**				**7,206**
2nd Grenadier Division. Lieutenant General Prinz von Mecklenburg	Kiev Grenadiers	2				1,132
	Moscow Grenadiers	2				1,096
	Astrakhan Grenadiers	2				1,024
	Fanagoria Grenadiers	2				1,166
	Siberia Grenadiers	2				1,192
	Malorussia Grenadiers	2				1,146
	TOTAL:	**12**				**7,756**

Formation	Unit	Battalions	Squadrons	Cossack Regiments	Guns	Men
Artillery	33rd Battery Company				12	250
	14th Light Company				12	132
	TOTAL:				**24**	**382**
	III CORPS TOTAL:	**24**			**24**	**14,344**
Reserve Artillery	1st Battery Company (Guard)				12	281
	1st Battery Company				12	259
	14th Battery Company				12	266
	29th Battery Company				12	223
	30th Battery Company				12	232
	Guard Équipage Platoon				2	29
	1st Horse Artillery Company				2	57
	3rd Horse Artillery Company				12	235
	10th Horse Artillery Company				6	98
	23rd Horse Artillery Company				12	247
	TOTAL:				**94**	**1,927**
RUSSIAN RESERVE TOTAL:		**47**	**87**	**3**	**182**	**43,498**

The Prussian *Garde*:

Formation	Units	Battalions	Squadrons	Guns	Men
Oberst Werder	*Garde du Corps*		4		703
	Leib Leichtes Kavallerie		4		670
	Garde Reitende Batterie			8	172
	TOTAL:		**8**	**8**	**1,545**
Oberstleutnant Albensleben	*1. Garde zu Fuß*	3			2,250
	2. Garde zu Fuß	3			2,250
	Garde Jäger	½			425
	Garde Batterie (six-pounders)			8	162
	TOTAL:	**6½**		**8**	**5,687**
	PRUSSIAN GUARD TOTAL:	**6½**	**8**	**16**	**7,232**

The grand total for the Russo-Prussian reserves commanded by Grand Duke Konstantin Pavlovich was: 53½ battalions; 95 squadrons; three Cossack regiments; 198 guns; 50,730 men.

The grand total for the Russo-Prussian contingent of the Main Army was: 137½ battalions; 158 squadrons; seven Cossack regiments; 402 guns; 124,675 men.

In addition, forming the escort for various headquarters were: Kireev's Don Cossacks; Platov 4th's Don Cossacks; Tabunchikov's Don Cossacks; Popov 3rd's Don Cossacks; 1st Tula Cossacks; the Malorussia Chernigov Regiment; 2nd Poltava Regiment; for a total of 2,500 men

Appendix XXXII

The composition and order of March of the columns of the Russo-Prussian army on the move from Silesia to Budin

Schedule signed by Quartermaster General Diebitsch (Archive of the M.T.D. No. 29,202).

First Column, departing Landeshut, commanded by Lieutenant General Prince Gorchakov: I Corps; II Corps, less artillery; artillery of I Corps; 7th Horse Artillery Company; Olviopol Hussars; Rodion 2nd's Cossacks; Kanatchikov's Pioneer Company.

Second Column, departing Neurode, commanded by *Generalmajor* Zieten: Prussian *9. Brigade* and *11. Brigade*, less artillery; Prussian reserve cavalry, less artillery; Yagodin 2nd's Cossacks; Prussian pioneer company.

Third Column, departing Reinerz, commanded by *Generalleutnant* Kleist: Prussian *10. Brigade* and *12. Brigade* with artillery; Prussian artillery from units in the Second Column; Prussian pioneer company. Russian contingent: three regiments from 1st Hussar Division; artillery of II Corps; 6th Horse Artillery Company; Gorinov 2nd's Cossacks; Ilovaisky 10th's Cossacks.

Fourth Column, departing Mittelwalde: parks and ration transport of I Corps, II Corps and 1st Hussar Division.

Fifth Column, commanded by Major General Raevsky: Grenadier Corps with artillery; 2nd Cuirassier Division; Chuguev Ulans; Serpukhov Ulans; Ataman's Cossacks; Ilovaisky 12th's Cossacks; Rebrikov 3rd's Cossacks; one pioneer company (departing from Landeshut). 3rd Cuirassier Division; Tatar Ulans (departing from Freiburg).

Sixth Column, commanded by Lieutenant General Prince Golitsyn: Russian Lifeguard infantry with artillery; Prussian *Garde* with artillery; 1st Cuirassier Division; Lifeguard horse artillery; Don artillery company; reserve artillery; two pioneer companies (departing from Neurode). Lifeguard light cavalry division; Lifeguard *Équipage* (departing from Frankenstein).

The troops of the first four columns are to cross the Bohemian border on 30 July (11 August), moving towards Budin in accordance with the following route-plan:

	First Landeshut	**Second Neurode**	**Third Reinerz**	**Fourth Mittelwalde**
30 July (11 August)	Trautenau	Politz	Opotschno [Opočno]	Geiersberg [Letohrad]
31 July (12 August)	Neupaka [Nová Paka]	Gross Skalitz [Česká Skalice]	Königrätz [Hradec Králové]	Hohenmaut [Vysoké Mýto]
1 (13) August	Sobotka	Nedielischt [Neděliště]	Chlumetz [Chlumec]	Chrudim
2 (14) August	Rest Day	Rest Day	Rest Day	Rest Day
3 (15) August	Schloss Stránov [Jizerní Vtelno]	Skohowitz [Skochovice]	Nimburg [Nymburk]	Czaslau [Čáslav]
4 (16) August	Melnik [Mělník]	Lautschin [Loučeň]	Mochov	Plaňany
5 (17) August	to be confirmed by Fürst zu Schwarzenberg	Elbekosteletz [Kostelec nad Labem]	Meschitz [Měšice u Prahy]	Mochov

The troops from the final two columns, having crossed the Bohemian border from 1 (13) August, moved towards Budin along the following routes:

	Fifth Column		**Sixth Column**		
31 July (12) August	Landeshut	Freiburg	Neurode	Neurode (Prussians)	Frankenstein
1 (13) August	Trautenau	Landeshut	Politz	Rest Day	Neurode
2 (14) August	Neupaka	Rest Day	Gross Skalitz	Politz	Rest Day
3 (15) August	Sobotka	Trautenau	Nedielischt	Gross Skalitz	Politz
4 (16) August	Rest Day	Neupaka	Rest Day	Nedielischt	Gross Skalitz
5 (17) August	Stránov	Sobotka	Skohowitz	Rest Day	Nedielischt
6 (18) August	Melnik	Rest Day	Lautschin	Skohowitz	Rest Day
7 (19) August	to be confirmed by Fürst zu Schwarzenberg	Stránov	Elbekosteletz	Lautschin	Skohowitz
8 (20) August		Melnik		Elbekosteletz	Lautschin
9 (21) August					Elbekosteletz

Appendix XXXIII

The Austrian Army, the Army of Silesia and the Army of the North

---

Austrian Army

At the opening of the campaign, the Austrian field army was divided into: three light divisions; right wing; left wing; and Klenau's corps, as follows:

1. leichte Division, Feldmarschallleutnant Fürst von und zu Liechtenstein, [Moritz Joseph Johann Baptist von und zu Liechtenstein]: *1. Jäger Bataillon*; *2. Jäger Bataillon*; *Broder Bataillon*; *7. Jäger Bataillon*; *Kaiser Chevauleger*; *Vincent Chevauleger*; (subsequently joined by *Levenehr Dragoner*); one three-pounder foot battery; one six-pounder horse battery, for a total of four battalions, 12 squadrons and 12 guns.

2. leichte Division, Feldmarschallleutnant Graf Bubna: *5. Jäger Bataillon*; *6. Jäger Bataillon*; *Peterwardeiner Bataillon*; *Kaiser Husaren*; *Liechtenstein Husaren*; *Blankenstein Husaren*; one three-pounder foot battery; one six-pounder horse battery, for a total of three battalions, 18 squadrons and 12 guns

3. leichte Division, Feldmarschallleutnant Mesko [Joseph Mesko de Felsö-Kubiny]: *Wallach-Illyrien Bataillon*; *Wallach Bataillon*; *Beaulieu Infanterie* (two battalions); *Pfalz Husaren*; *Erzherzog Ferdinand Husaren*; one six-pounder horse battery, for a total of four battalions, 12 squadrons and six guns.

Right Wing, commanded by *General der Kavallerie* Erbprinz zu Hessen-Homburg [Friedrich (VI.) Joseph Ludwig zu Hessen-Homburg]:

Feldmarschallleutnant Graf Colloredo-Mansfeld's division [Hieronymus Karl von Colloredo-Mansfeld]: three battalions each of: *Froon Infanterie*; *De Vaux Infanterie*; *Argentau Infanterie*; *Czartoryski Infanterie*; two battalions each of: *Erbach Infanterie*; *de Ligne Infanterie*; three six-pounder batteries, for a total of 16 battalions and 18 guns.

Feldmarschallleutnant Bianchi's division [(Vincenz Ferrer) Friedrich von Bianchi]: *Hiller Infanterie*; *Hieronymus Colloredo Infanterie*; *Simbschen Infanterie*; *Hessen-Homburg Infanterie*; *Esterhazy Infanterie*; *Davidovich Infanterie*; three six-pounder batteries, for a total of 12 battalions and 18 guns.

Feldmarschallleutnant Crenneville's division [Ludwig Karl Folliot de Crenneville(-Poutet)]: *Warasdin-Kreuz Bataillon*; *Warasdin-St. Georg Bataillon*; *Gradiska*

Bataillon; two battalions of *Deutsch-Banat Infanterie*; *Wallach-Illyrien Bataillon*; *Klenau Chevauleger*; *Rosenberg Chevauleger*; two six-pounder batteries, for a total of six battalions, 12 squadrons and 12 guns.

Feldmarschallleutnant Civalart's division [Karl Leopold Civalart d'Happoncourt]: *Albert Gyulai Infanterie*; *Reuss-Plauen Infanterie*; *Strauch Infanterie*; *Bellegarde Infanterie*; *Weidenfeld Infanterie*; *Ignaz Gyulai Infanterie*; three six-pounder batteries, for a total of 12 battalions and 18 guns.

Feldmarschallleutnant Chasteler's division [(Johann) Gabriel Chasteler de Courcelles]: *Czarnotzay Grenadiere*; *Obermayer Grenadiere*; *Berger Grenadiere*; *Oklopsia Grenadiere*; *Habinay Grenadiere*; *Portner Grenadiere*; *Leiningen Grenadiere*; *Rueber Grenadiere*; two six-pounder batteries, for a total of eight battalions and 12 guns.

Feldmarschallleutnant Nostitz's cavalry division [Johann Nepomuk Nostitz-Rieneck]: *Erzherzog Franz Kürassiere*; *Kronprinz Ferdinand Kürassiere*; *Hohenzollern Kürassiere*; *Sommariva Kürassiere*, for a total of 16 squadrons.

Feldmarschallleutnant Schneller's cavalry division [Andreas von Schneller]: *O'Reilly Chevauleger*; *Hohenzollern Chevauleger*; *Hessen-Homburg Husaren*; *Kienmeyer Husaren*, for a total of 24 squadrons.

Left Wing, commanded by *Feldzeugmeister* Graf Gyulai [Ignaz Gyulai von Máros-Németh und Nádaska]:

Feldmarschallleutnant Weissenwolf's division [Nikolaus Joseph Rochus von Weissenwolf]: *Kottulinsky Infanterie*; *Kaiser Infanterie*; *Kollowrat Infanterie*; *Frelich Infanterie*; *Würzburg Infanterie*; *Erzherzog Ludwig Infanterie*; three six-pounder batteries, for a total of 12 battalions and 18 guns.

Feldmarschallleutnant Fürst von und zu Liechtenstein's division [Alois Gonzaga Joseph von und zu Liechtenstein]: *Kaunitz Infanterie*; *Wenzel Colloredo Infanterie*; *Vogelsang Infanterie*; *Reuss-Greitz Infanterie*; *Erzherzog Rainer Infanterie*; *Lusignan Infanterie*; three six-pounder batteries, for a total of 12 battalions and 18 guns.

Feldmarschallleutnant Lederer's cavalry division [Ignaz Ludwig Paul von Lederer]: *Kaiser Kürassiere*; *Erzherzog Johann Dragoner*; *Levenehr Dragoner*; *Riesch Dragoner*, for a total of 22 squadrons.

Feldzeugmeister [*sic, General der Kavallerie*] **Graf Klenau's corps** [Johann Joseph Cajetan von Klenau und Janowitz]:

Feldmarschallleutnant Mayer's division [Anton Mayer von Heldensfeld]: *Coburg Infanterie* (three battalions); two battalions each of: *Erzherzog Karl Infanterie*; *Kerpen Infanterie*; *St. Julien Infanterie*; two six-pounder batteries, for a total of nine battalions and 12 guns.

Feldmarschallleutnant Prinz zu Hohenlohe's division [Ludwig Alois Joachim zu Hohenlohe-Bartenstein]: two battalions of *Josef Colloredo Infanterie*; three battalions each of: *Zach Infanterie*; *Herzog Württemberg Infanterie*; *Lindenau Infanterie*; *Alois Liechtenstein Infanterie*; two six-pounder batteries, for a total of 14 battalions and 12 guns.

Cavalry brigade: *Herzog Albert Kürassiere*; *Lothringen Kürassiere*, for a total of eight squadrons.

In addition, there was an artillery reserve of 17 batteries with 102 guns.

Thus, the Austrian army in Bohemia, at the start of hostilities, consisted of:

Infantry in 112 battalions, each of 800 men, for a total of 89,600 men.

Cavalry in 124 squadrons, each of 125 men, for a total of 15,500 men.

Artillery in 45 batteries, each of six guns with 120 crew, for a total of 5,400 men.

Giving a grand total of 110,500 men with 270 guns.

This order of battle of Austrian forces in Bohemia, at the opening of hostilities, after the armistice in 1813 was extracted from: the Archive of the M.T.D. No. 29,202; Plotho, *Der Krieg in Deutschland und Frankreich in den Jahren 1813 und 1814*, Vol. II, *Beilagen*, 27 (Plotho shows the number of troops somewhat higher); Bernhardi, *Dunkwürdigkeiten des Grafen von Toll*, Vol. III, 509.

Upon the retreat into Bohemia after the battle of Dresden, the Austrian army was reorganised, as will be described later (see also Plotho, II, appendices, 34-37).

Army of Silesia

Right wing, Lieutenant General Sacken's Russian corps:
Regular cavalry component commanded by Lieutenant General Vasilchikov.

Formation	Unit	Battalions	Squadrons	Cossack Regiments	Guns
10th Division Major General Count Lieven 3rd	Yaroslavl Infantry	2			
	Crimea Infantry	1			
	Bialystok Infantry	2			
	8th Jägers	2			
	39th Jägers	1			
16th Division Major General Repninsky	Okhotsk Infantry	2			
	Kamchatka Infantry	2			
27th Division Lieutenant General Neverovsky	Odessa Infantry	1			
	Vilna Infantry	1			
	Tarnopol Infantry	1			
	Simbirsk Infantry	1			
	49th Jägers	2			
	50th Jägers	1			
Major General Panchulidzev 2nd	Smolensk Dragoons		2		
	Kurland Dragoons		5		

Formation	Unit	Battalions	Squadrons	Cossack Regiments	Guns
2nd Hussar Division Major General Lanskoy	Alexandria Hussars		5		
	Belorussia Hussars		6		
	Mariupol Hussars		6		
	Akhtyrka Hussars		6		
Irregular Cavalry Major General Karpov 2nd	4th Ukrainian Cossacks			1	
	Baron von Bode's Cossacks			1	
	Karpov 2nd's Cossacks			1	
	Lukovkin's Cossacks			1	
	Grekov 1st's Cossacks			1	
	Kuteynikov 4th's Cossacks			1	
	Semenchikov's Cossacks			1	
	Ilovaisky 9th's Cossacks			1	
	Chernozubov 5th's Cossacks			1	
	Grekov 8th's Cossacks			1	
	2nd Bashkirs			1	
	2nd Kalmyks			1	
Artillery Major General Nikitin	10th Battery Company				12
	13th Battery Company				12
	24th Light Company				12
	35th Light Company				12
	18th Horse Company				12
	Pioneer company				
	TOTAL:	**19**	**30**	**12**	**60**

Sacken's corps had: 8,383 infantrymen; 3,697 regular cavalry; 4,524 irregular cavalry; 996 artillerymen and 89 pioneers, for a total of 17,689 men.
Centre: *Generalleutnant* Yorck's Prussian corps:

Formation	Units	Battalions	Squadrons	Guns
1. Brigade *Oberst* Steinmetz	*Grenadiere*	4		
	Ostpreußischer Jäger	½		
	5. & 13. Landwehr	8		
	2. Leib Husaren		4	
	2. Batterie zu Fuss (six-pounders)			

Formation	Units	Battalions	Squadrons	Guns
2. Brigade Generalmajor Herzog Karl zu Mecklenburg-Strelitz	*1. Ostpreußisches Infanterie*	3		
	2. Ostpreußisches Infanterie	3		
	6. Schlesisches Landwehr	4		
	Mecklenburg-Strelitz Husaren		4	
	1. Batterie zu Fuss (six-pounders)			
7. Brigade Generalmajor Horn	*Leib Infanterie*	3		
	Thüringisches Infanterie	1		
	Garde Jäger	½		
	4. & 15. Schlesisches Landwehr	8		
	Brandenburgisches Husaren		2	
	3. Schlesisches Landwehr Kavallerie		2	
	3. Batterie zu Fuss (six-pounders)			
8. Brigade Generalmajor Hünerbein	*Brandenburgisches Infanterie*	3		
	12. Reserve Infanterie	3		
	14. Schlesisches Landwehr	4		
	Brandenburgisches Husaren		2	
	3. Schlesisches Landwehr Kavallerie		2	
	15. Batterie zu Fuss (six-pounders)			
Reserve Kavallerie Generalmajor Jürgaß	*1. Westpreußisches Dragoner*		4	
	Litthauisches Dragoner		4	
	Brandenburgisches Ulanen		4	
	Ostpreussiches National Kavallerie		4	
	1. Neumarkisches Landwehr		4	
	5. & 10. Schlesisches Landwehr		8	
	1. & 2. Reitende Batterie			
Reserve Artillerie Oberstleutnant Schmidt	*1. & 2. Batterie* (12-pounders)			
	12. & 24. Batterie (six-pounders)			
	1. Batterie (three-pounders)			
	3. & 12. Reitende Batterie			
	1. 3. 5. & 13. Park			
	1. Pioniere, 1. & 2. Arbeits Kompanie			
	TOTAL:	**45**	**44**	**104**

Yorck's corps had: 30,116 infantrymen; 6,038 cavalrymen; 1,917 artillerymen; 149 pioneers, for a total of 38,220 men.
Left Wing, General-of-Infantry Langéron's Russian corps:
VI Corps, commanded by Lieutenant Genral Shcherbatov:

Formation	Unit	Battalions	Squadrons	Cossack Regiments	Guns
7th Division Major General Talyzin	Pskov Infantry	2			
	Moscow Infantry	2			
	Libau Infantry	1			
	Sofia Infantry	1			
	11th Jägers	2			
	36th Jägers	1			
18th Division Major General Benardos	Vladimir Infantry	1			
	Tambov Infantry	1			
	Dnieper Infantry	1			
	Kostroma Infantry	1			
	28th Jägers	1			
	32nd Jägers	1			

VIII Corps, commanded by Lieutenant General comte Saint-Priest:

Formation	Unit	Battalions	Squadrons	Cossack Regiments	Guns
11th Division Major General Prince Guryalov	Yelets Infantry	1			
	Polotsk Infantry	1			
	Yekaterinburg Infantry	2			
	Rylsk Infantry	1			
	1st Jägers	1			
	33rd Jägers	1			
17th Division Major General Pillar	Ryazan Infantry	1			
	Belozersk Infantry	1			
	Brest Infantry	2			
	Wilmanstrand Infantry	1			
	30th Jägers	1			
	48th Jägers	2			

IX Corps, commanded by Lieutenant General Olsufiev:

Formation	Unit	Battalions	Squadrons	Cossack Regiments	Guns
9th Division Major General Udom 2nd	Nasheburg Infantry	1			
	Ryazhsk Infantry	1			
	Yakutsk Infantry	1			
	10th Jägers	1			
	38th Jägers	1			
15th Division Major General Rudzevich (jägers attached from 13th Division)	Vitebsk Infantry	1			
	Kozlov Infantry	1			
	Kura Infantry	1			
	Kolyvan Infantry	1			
	12th Jägers	1			
	22nd Jägers	1			

X Corps, commanded by Lieutenant General Kaptsevich:

Formation	Unit	Battalions	Squadrons	Cossack Regiments	Guns
8th Division Major General Urusov	Arkhangelogorod Infantry	1			
	Schlüsselburg Infantry	1			
	Staroingermanland Infantry	1			
	7th Jägers	1			
	37th Jägers	1			
22nd Division Major General Turchaninov	Vyatka Infantry	2			
	Staro-Oskol Infantry	2			
	Olonets Infantry	1			
	29th Jägers	1			
	45th Jägers	1			

Adjutant General Baron Korff's cavalry corps:

Formation	Unit	Battalions	Squadrons	Cossack Regiments	Guns
3rd Dragoon Division Major General Berdyaev	Tver Dragoons		2		
	Kinburn Dragoons		2		
1st Dragoon Division Major General Borozdin	Moscow Dragoons		2		
	Kargopol Dragoons		4		
	Mitau Dragoons		4		
	Novorossia Dragoons		4		
4th Dragoon Division Major General Emmanuel	Kharkov Dragoons		4		
	Kiev Dragoons		4		
1st Mounted Jäger Division Major General Panchulidzev 1st	Chernigov Mounted Jägers		3		
	Arzamass Mounted Jägers		2		
	Siberia Mounted Jägers		2		
2nd Mounted Jäger Division Major General Count Pahlen 2nd	Livland Mounted Jägers		2		
	Dorpat Mounted Jägers		2		

Irregular Cavalry, commanded by Major General Grekov 8th:

Formation	Unit	Battalions	Squadrons	Cossack Regiments	Guns
Major General Count Witt	1st Ukrainian Cossacks			1	
	2nd Ukrainian Cossacks			1	
	3rd Ukrainian Cossacks			1	
	Isaev 2nd's Cossacks			1	
	Semenchikov 2nd's Cossacks			1	

Formation	Unit	Battalions	Squadrons	Cossack Regiments	Guns
	Kuteynikov 8th's Cossacks			1	
	Grekov 21st's Cossacks			1	
	Ezhov 2nd's Cossacks			1	
	Stavropol Kalmyks			1	

Artillery, commanded by Major General Veselitsky: 2nd Battery Company; 15th Battery Company; 18th Battery Company; 32nd Battery Company; 34th Battery Company; 39th Battery Company; 3rd Light Company; 19th Light Company; 28th Light Company; 29th Light Company; 32nd Light Company; 33rd Light Company; 34th Light Company; 8th Horse Artillery Company; 2nd Don Cossack Artillery Company; Gresser's Pioneer Company; Helwig's Pioneer Company; Häberer's Pioneer Company; 4th Pontoon Company; 5th Pontoon Company; 75th Ship's Company.

Langéron's corps had: 30,953 infantrymen in 53 battalions; 4,604 cavalrymen in 37 squadrons; 4,276 irregular cavalrymen in nine regiments; 2,975 artillerymen with 176 guns; 723 pioneers, pontoniers, and sailors, for a total of 43,531 men.

In total, Blücher's Army of Silesia consisted of:

Infantry: 72 Russian battalions with 39,336 men; 45 Prussian battalions with 30,116 men, for a total of 117 battalions with 69,452 infantrymen.

Regular cavalry: 67 Russian squadrons with 8,301 men; 44 Prussian squadrons with 6,038 men, for a total of 111 squadrons with 14,339 cavalrymen.

Irregular cavalry: 21 Cossack regiments with 8,800 men.

Artillery: 236 Russian guns with 3,971 crew; 104 Prussian guns with 1,917 crew, for a total of 340 guns with 5,888 artillerymen.

Engineers: 812 Russians; 149 Prussians, for a total of 961 pioneers and pontoniers.

Giving a manpower total of: 61,220 Russians; 38, 220 Prussians; 99,440 men overall.

Extracted from: returns signed by generals Langéron and Sacken; Plotho, II, appendices, 46-48 & 51; Bernhardi, III, 514-516.

Army of the North

First (Swedish) Corps, commanded by *Fältmarskalk* Stedingk:

Formation	Units	Battalions	Squadrons	Guns
1st Division *Generalmajor* Posse	Swedish Lifeguard	1		
	2nd Swedish Grenadiers	1		
	Leib-Regiment Grenadiers	1		
	Leib-Grenadiers	2		
	King's Leib-Regiment	2		
	Uppland Infantry	2		
	Södermanland Infantry	3		
	Jönköping Infantry	2		
	Two six-pounder batteries			
2nd Division *Generalmajor* Sandels	Västgöta Infantry	2		
	Västmanland Infantry	3		
	Närike Infantry	2		
	Skaraborg Infantry	3		
	Elfsborg Infantry	3		
	Varmland Fält Jägare	1		
	Two six-pounder batteries			
3rd Division *Generalmajor* Boyen 5th Brigade[1]	Kronoberg Infantry	3		
	Kalmar Infantry	3		
	Södra Skånska Infantry	1		
	Two six-pounder batteries			
Cavalry Division *Generallöjtnant* Skjöldebrand	Lif Dragoons		5	
	Smaland Dragoons		6	
	Pomerania Mounted Jägers		1	
	Lif Kürassiere		4	
	Skånska Hussars		6	
	Mörner Hussars		6	
Artillery Reserve *Generalmajor* Kardell	One 12-pounder battery			
	Two six-pounder horse batteries			
	TOTAL:	**35**	**28**	**62**

1 6th Brigade of 3rd Division was attached to Graf Wallmoden's combined corps.

Giving a total for the Swedish corps of: 18,573 infantrymen; 3,742 cavalrymen; 1,703 artillerymen, for a total of 24,018 men.

The number of men present in the Swedish corps did not exceed 20,000.

Second (Russian) Corps, commanded by Lieutenant General Wintzingerode:

Formation	Unit	Battalions	Squadrons	Cossack Regiments	Guns
21st Division Major General Laptev	Neva Infantry	1			
	Petrovsk Infantry	1			
	Lithuania Infantry	1			
	Podolsk Infantry	1			
	44th Jägers	2			
24th Division Major General Vuich	Shirvan Infantry	2			
	Butyrsk Infantry	2			
	Ufa Infantry	2			
	Tomsk Infantry	1			
	19th Jägers	2			
	40th Jägers	1			
Major General Graf Manteuffel	St Petersburg Dragoons		4		
	Yelisavetgrad Hussars		6		
	Yakhontov's Volunteers		2		
Cossacks	Don Cossacks			5	
	Bug Cossacks			1	
	Ural Cossacks			1	
Artillery Lieutenant Colonel Winspeare	31st Battery Company				12
	42nd Light Company				12
	46th Light Company				12
	4th Horse Artillery Company				8
Lieutenant General Count Vorontsov's force:					
Infantry component Major General Harpe	Navaginsk Infantry	2			
	Tula Infantry	2			
	13th Jägers	2			

Formation	Unit	Battalions	Squadrons	Cossack Regiments	Guns
	14th Jägers	2			
	Sevsk Infantry	1			
	2nd Jägers	1			
	Combined Grenadiers (9th, 15th & 18th divisions)	3			
Cavalry component Major General O'Rourke	Nezhin Mounted Jägers		5		
	Pavlograd Hussars		6		
	Poland Ulans		7		
	Volhynia Ulans		3		
	Don Cossacks			6	
	Tver-coachmen			1	
	Bashkirs			1	
Adjutant General Chernyshev's force (4,061 men, 4 guns):					
	Finland Dragoons		4		
	Riga Dragoons		5		
	Izyum Hussars		6		
	Don Cossacks			5	
	1st Horse Artillery Company				4
	TOTAL:	**29**	**48**	**20**	**96**

Wintzingerode's corps had: 13,814 infantrymen; 6,087 regular cavalrymen; 8,028 Cossacks; 1,710 artillerymen, for a total of 29,639 men.

Third (Prussian) Corps, under *Generalleutnant* Bülow:

Formation	Units	Battalions	Squadrons	Guns
3. Brigade Generalmajor Prinz Ludwig von Hessen-Homburg	*2. Ostpreußisches Grenadiere*	1		
	3. Ostpreußisches Infanterie	3		
	4. Reserve Infanterie	3		
	3. Ostpreußisches Landwehr	4		
	1. Leib Husaren		5	
	5. Batterie (six-pounders)			8
4. Brigade Generalmajor Thümen	*4. Ostpreußisches Infanterie*	3		

Formation	Units	Battalions	Squadrons	Guns
	5. Reserve Infanterie	4		
	Elbe Infanterie	2		
	Ostpreußisches Jäger	½		
	Pommersches National Kavallerie		3	
	6. Batterie (six-pounders)			8
5. Brigade Generalmajor Borstell	*Pommersches Grenadiere*	1		
	Pommersches Infanterie	3		
	2. Reserve Infanterie	3		
	2. Kurmärkisches Landwehr	4		
	Pommersches Husaren		5	
	10. Batterie (six-pounders)			8
6. Brigade Oberst Krafft	*Colbergsches Infanterie*	3		
	9. Reserve Infanterie	3		
	1. Neumark Landwehr	4		
	1. Pommersches Landwehr Kavallerie		4	
	16. Batterie (six-pounders)			8
Reserve Cavalry *Generalmajor* Oppen	*Brandenburgisches Dragoner*		5	
	Königin Dragoner		5	
	2. Westpreußisches Dragoner		4	
	Westpreußisches Ulanen		4	
	2. Schlesisches Husaren		2	
	2. Pommersches Landwehr Kavallerie		4	
	2. Kurmärkisches Landwehr Kavallerie		4	
	4. Kurmärkisches Landwehr Kavallerie		4	
	5. Reitende Batterie			8
	6. Reitende Batterie			8
Reserve Artillery *Oberstleutnant* Holzendorf	*4. Batterie* (12-pounders)			8
	5. Batterie (12-pounders)			8
	19. Batterie (six-pounders)			8
	11. Reitende Batterie			8
	3. 4. & 6. Park			
	4. & 5. Pionier Kompanie			
	TOTAL:	**41½**	**49**	**80**

Bülow's Corps had a total of 32,000 infantry, 6,350 cavalry, 1,500 artillerymen and 600 pioneers, etcetera. For a total of 40,450 men.

In addition, attached to the corps were: 450 artillerymen of 7th Battery Company, and 14th Battery Company (22 guns); 450 men in two Cossack regiments, for a total of 900 Russians.

This gave a grand total in Bülow's Corps, including the attached Russians, of 41,350 men and 102 guns.

Fourth (Prussian) Corps, under *Generalleutnant* Tauentzien:

Formation	Units	Battalions	Squadrons	Guns
Berlin Reserves: *Generalmajor* Dobschütz & *Generalmajor* Graf Lindenau	*3. Reserve Infanterie Regiment*	4		
	1. Kurmärkisches Landwehr	3		
	2. NeumärkischesLandwehr	4		
	5. Kurmärkisches Landwehr	4		
	2. Schlesiches Landwehr	4		
	1. Schlesiches Landwehr	3		
	2. Neumärkisches Landwehr Kavallerie		2	
	3. Neumärkisches Landwehr Kavallerie		4	
	2. Ostpreußisches Landwehr Kavallerie		4	
	3. Ostpreußisches Landwehr Kavallerie		4	
	1. Kurmärkisches Landwehr Kavallerie		4	
	7. Kurmärkisches Landwehr Kavallerie		4	
	3. Pommersches Landwehr Kavallerie		4	
	Berlin Landwehr Kavallerie		2	
	A foot half-battery of eight-pounders			4
	2½ foot batteries of six-pounders			20
	One horse battery of six-pounders			8
Generalmajor Wobeser's corps on the Oder: *Oberstleutnant* Pletz	*1. Westpreußisches Landwehr*	4		

Formation	Units	Battalions	Squadrons	Guns
	2. Westpreußisches Landwehr	4		
	3. Westpreußisches Landwehr	4		
	1. Schlesisches Landwehr	3		
Oberst Jeanneret	*1. Westpreußisches Landwehr Kavallerie*		4	
	2. Westpreußisches Landwehr Kavallerie		4	
	3. Westpreußisches Landwehr Kavallerie		4	
	22. Batterie (six-pounders)			8
Generalmajor Hirschfeld's corps at Magdeburg: *Oberst* Bismarck	*1. Reserve Infanterie Regiment*	4		
	6. Kurmärkisches Landwehr	4		
	7. Kurmärkisches Landwehr	4		
	5. Kurmärkisches Landwehr Kavallerie		4	
	6. Kurmärkisches Landwehr Kavallerie		4	
	1½ six-pounder batteries			12
Generalmajor Putlitz's corps on the lower Elbe: *Oberst* Boguslawski	*3. Kurmärkisches Landwehr*	4		
	4. Kurmärkisches Landwehr	4		
	3. Kurmärkisches Landwehr Kavallerie		4	
	One foot half-battery of six-pounders			4
	TOTAL:	**57**	**52**	**56**

Tauentzien's Corps had a total of 33,000 infantry, 5,200 cavalry, and 700 artillerymen, for a total of 38,900 men.

In addition, Ilovaisky 3rd's Cossack regiment was attached to the Berlin Reserves, and two more Cossack regiments were at the blockade of Stettin.

Fifth (Russo-German) Corps, under Lieutenant General Count Wallmoden:

Formation	Units	Battalions	Squadrons	Guns
Major General Tettenborn's Detachment (1,415 men):	Four Cossack regiments			
	1st Horse Artillery Company			2
	TOTAL:		**4 Regts**	**2**
Russo-German Legion (4,250 men): Major General Arentschildt	1st Infantry	3		
	2nd Infantry	3		
	1st Hussars		4	
	2nd Hussars		4	
	Six-pounder foot battery			6
	Horse artillery battery			6
	TOTAL:	**6**	**8**	**12**
Oberstleutnant Lützow's *Freikorps* (2,230 men):	Major Helmerstreit's Infantry	3		
	Major Reiche's Volunteer Jägers	1		
	Hauptmann Riedl's Tyrolean Marksmen			
	Major Bernstedt's Cavalry		4	
	Major Schill's Raiding Detachment		1	
	Hauptmann Lucadou's Detachment		1	
	Horse artillery battery			8
	TOTAL:	**4**	**6**	**8**
Mecklenburg-Schwerin Contingent (3,550 men): *Generalmajor* Falloa	Grenadiers	1		
	Infantry	2		
	Volunteer Jägers	1		
	Volunteer *Jäger-zu-Pferd*		4	
	Foot artillery battery			4
	TOTAL:	**4**	**4**	**4**
Swedish-Pomeranian Contingent (4,000 men): *Generalmajor* Engelbrecht	Smaland Infantry	1		
	Norra Skånska Infantry	1		
	Queen's Leib Infantry	1		

Formation	Units	Battalions	Squadrons	Guns
	Engelbrecht Infantry	2		
	Sodra Skånska Infantry	2		
	Skansk Carabiniers		4	
	One foot artillery battery			6
	TOTAL:	**7**	**4**	**6**
Generalmajor Dörnberg's Force (6,372), comprising: Hanseatic Contingent (2,450 men): *Oberstleutnant* Mettlerkamp	Hamburg Infantry	2		
	Lübeck Infantry	1		
	Hamburg Cavalry		6	
	Lübeck Cavalry		2	
	Foot artillery battery			6
	Horse artillery battery			6
	TOTAL:	**3**	**8**	**12**
Hanovarian Contingent (3,922 men):	Ratzeburg Infantry	1		
	Hanover Marksmen	1		
	Lüneburg Jägers	1		
	Bremen-Verden Jägers	1		
	Hanover Jägers	1		
	Lüneburg Hussars		3	
	Bremen-Verden Hussars		2	
	1½ artillery batteries			9
	TOTAL:	**5**	**5**	**9**
British Contingent (500):	3rd Hussars		4	
	Rocket Battery			
	TOTAL:		**4**	
	GRAND TOTAL:	**29**	**39**	**53**

Overall, Wallmoden's Corps numbered 22,567 men.

Thus, the Army of the North consisted of: 189½ battalions, 213 squadrons, 27 Cossack regiments, and 47½ batteries with 369 guns, for a total of 156,474 men.

Note: in addition, there were five British battalions (2,500 men), and one Anhalt battalion (538 men) holding Stralsund.

Index

From Reason to Revolution – Warfare 1721-1815

http://www.helion.co.uk/series/from-reason-to-revolution-1721-1815.php

The 'From Reason to Revolution' series covers the period of military history 1721–1815, an era in which fortress-based strategy and linear battles gave way to the nation-in-arms and the beginnings of total war.

This era saw the evolution and growth of light troops of all arms, and of increasingly flexible command systems to cope with the growing armies fielded by nations able to mobilise far greater proportions of their manpower than ever before. Many of these developments were fired by the great political upheavals of the era, with revolutions in America and France bringing about social change which in turn fed back into the military sphere as whole nations readied themselves for war. Only in the closing years of the period, as the reactionary powers began to regain the upper hand, did a military synthesis of the best of the old and the new become possible.

The series examines the military and naval history of the period in a greater degree of detail than has hitherto been attempted, and has a very wide brief, with the intention of covering all aspects from the battles, campaigns, logistics, and tactics, to the personalities, armies, uniforms, and equipment.

Submissions

The publishers would be pleased to receive submissions for this series. Please email reasontorevolution@helion.co.uk, or write to Helion & Company Limited, Unit 8 Amherst Business Centre, Budbrooke Road, Warwick, CV34 5WE

You may also be interested in:

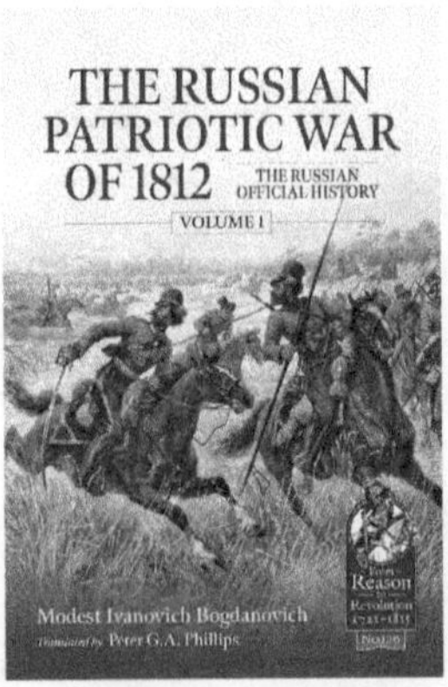

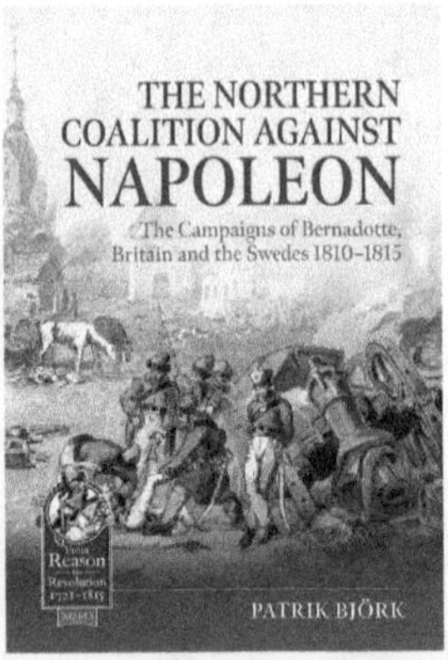

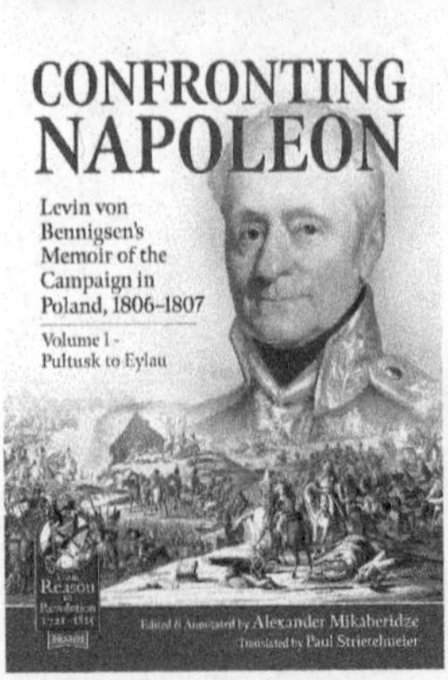

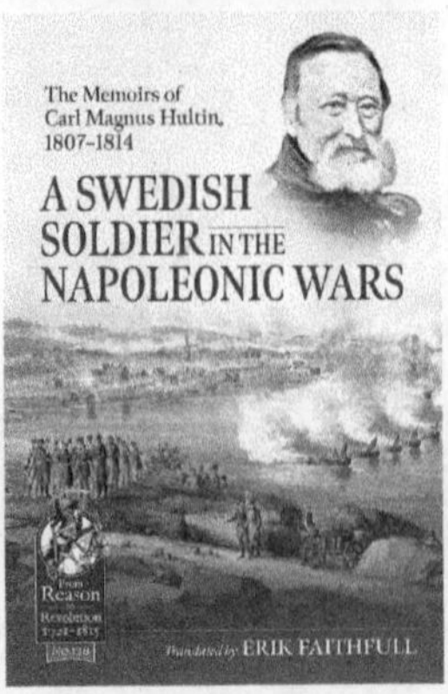